Vessa Awesina
CPSC 211 [502]
vjunh@email.com

D0938371

Data Structures
and
Problem Solving
Using Java™

Data Structures and Problem Solving Using Java™

Mark Allen Weiss

Florida International University

 **ADDISON-WESLEY**

An imprint of Addison Wesley Longman, Inc.

Reading, Massachusetts • Harlow, England • Menlo Park, California • Berkeley, California
Don Mills, Ontario • Sydney • Bonn • Amsterdam • Tokyo • Mexico City

Acquisitions Editor: Susan Hartman
Associate Editor: Katherine Harutunian
Production Editor: Patricia A.O. Unubun
Design Editor: Alywn R. Velásquez
Packager: Sarah Hallet-Corey
Manufacturing Coordinator: Judy Sullivan
Copyeditor: Laura K. Michaels
Cover Designer: Syndi Hirsch

Access the latest information about Addison Wesley titles from our
World Wide Web site: http://www.awl.com/cseng/

Java is a trademark of Sun Microsystems, Inc.

Many of the designations used by manufacturers and sellers to distinguish their products are claimed as trademarks. Where those designations appear in this book, and the publisher was aware of a trademark claim, the designations have been printed in initial caps or in all caps.

The programs and the applications presented in this book have been included for their instructional value. They have been tested with care but are not guaranteed for any particular purpose. Neither the publisher or the author offers any warranties or representations, nor do they accept any liabilities with respect to the programs or applications.

Reprinted with corrections, March 1999.

Library of Congress Cataloging-in-Publication Data

```
Weiss, Mark Allen.
    Data structures and problem solving using Java / Mark A. Weiss.
       p. cm.
    Includes index.
    ISBN 0-201-54991-3
    1. Java (Computer program language)  2. Data structures (Computer
  science)  3. Problem solving -- Data processing.   I. Title
QA76.73.J38W45 1998
005.13'3--dc21                                          97-30970
                                                           CIP
```

ISBN 0-201-54991-3

7 8 9 10 MA 010099

Preface

This book is designed for a two-semester sequence in computer science, beginning with what is typically known as Data Structures (CS-2).

The content of the CS-2 course has been evolving for some time. While there is some general consensus concerning topic coverage, there still exists considerable disagreement over the details. One uniformly accepted topic is principles of software development, most notably the concepts of encapsulation and information hiding. Algorithmically, all CS-2 courses tend to include an introduction to running time analysis, recursion, basic sorting algorithms, and elementary data structures. An advanced course is offered at many universities that covers topics in data structures, algorithms, and running time analysis at a higher level. The material in this text has been designed for use in both levels of courses, thus eliminating the need to purchase a second textbook.

Although the most passionate debates in CS-2 center around the choice of a programming language, there are other fundamental choices that need to be made, including these:

- Whether to introduce object-oriented design or object-based design early
- The level of mathematical rigor
- The appropriate balance between the implementation of data structures and their use
- Programming details related to the language chosen (for instance, should GUIs be used early)

My goal in writing this text is to provide a practical introduction to data structures and algorithms from the viewpoint of abstract thinking and problem solving. I try to cover all of the important details concerning the data structures, their analyses, and their Java implementations, while staying away from data structures that are theoretically interesting but not widely used. It is impossible to cover all of the different data structures, including their uses and the analysis, described in this text in a single course. So, I have designed the textbook to allow instructors flexibility in topic coverage. The instructor will need to decide on an appropriate balance between practice and theory and then choose those topics that best fit the course. As I discuss later in the Preface, the text is organized in a way that tends to minimize dependencies among the various chapters.

A Unique Approach

The text takes a unique approach by separating the data structures into their specification (via a Java `interface`) and subsequent implementation. This approach provides several benefits, including the promotion of abstract thinking. Class interfaces are written and used before the implementation is known, thus forcing the student to think at an early stage about the functionality and potential efficiency of the various data structures. For example, students will see programs using a hash table hundreds of pages before the hash table is implemented. In this textbook, the interfaces for the data structures are discussed in a single chapter in Part II. Part II also describes basic analysis techniques, recursion, and sorting. Part III contains a host of applications that use the data structures. Implementation of the basic data structures is not shown until Part IV, once the data structures have already been used. Since all of the textbook code is available (see *Code Availability*, page xii), students can design large projects early on, using existing software components. Software development tools in all languages come with large libraries, and most data structures will eventually be part of these libraries. I envision an eventual shift in emphasis of data structures courses from implementation to use.

Many instructors will prefer a more traditional approach in which each data structure is defined, implemented, and then used. Because there is no dependency between material in Parts III and IV, a traditional course can easily be taught from this book.

Prerequisites

Students using this book should have knowledge of either an object-oriented or procedural programming language. Knowledge of basic features, including primitive data types, operators, control structures, functions (methods), and input and output (but not necessarily arrays and classes) is assumed.

Students who have taken a first course using Java can begin at Chapter 3 (or perhaps later). Students who have had a first course in another language should begin at Chapter 1. They also should use the Appendix, which, combined with Part I, provides plenty of Java information. If a student would like also to use a Java reference book, some recommendations are given in Chapter 1, page 25.

Knowledge of discrete math is helpful but is not an absolute prerequisite. Although there are several mathematical proofs, many are preceded by a brief math review. Chapters 7 and 18 through 23 require some degree of mathematical sophistication. The instructor may easily elect to skip mathematical aspects of the proofs by presenting only the results. All proofs in the text are clearly marked and are separate from the body of the text.

Java

This textbook presents material using the Java programming language. Java is a relatively new language that is often examined in comparison with C++. Java offers many benefits, and programmers often view Java as a safer, more portable, and easier-to-use language than C++.

The use of Java requires that some decisions be made when writing a textbook. Some of the decisions made are as follows:

1. *Java 1.1 constructs are used exclusively*: Although at the time of this writing there is only one Java 1.1 compiler available, others are sure to follow. Please make sure you are using a compiler that is Java 1.1-compatible. The most noticeable difference in the main text is the use of Java 1.1 classes for I/O instead of deprecated classes from Java 1.0.2, including the `BufferedReader`, `FileReader`, and `InputStreamReader` classes.

2. *GUIs are not emphasized*: GUIs are a nice feature in Java, and their use is described in Appendix D. However, they seem to be an implementation detail rather than a core CS-2 topic. In keeping with the goal of the book, the Appendix is the most appropriate place to discuss GUIs. Also, this is the part of the language that changed the most in Java 1.1. It further is the most unstable part of the language.

3. *Applets are not emphasized*: Applets use GUIs. Further, the focus of the course is on data structures, rather than language features. A discussion of applets is in the Appendix. Instructors can elect to have students design applets as part of the use (or simulation) of data structures.

4. *Newer Java 1.1 features are not used*: These features include inner classes, new rules for final variables, and so on. I have attempted to use core Java and avoid excessively fancy features.

5. *The concept of a pointer is discussed when reference variables are introduced*: Java does not have a pointer type. Instead, it has a reference type. However, pointers have traditionally been an important CS-2 topic that needs to be introduced. I illustrate the concept of pointers in other languages when discussing reference variables.

6. *Threads are mentioned only in the Appendix in the context of animations*: Some members of the CS community argue that multi-threaded computing should become a core CS-1/2 topic. Coverage in the Appendix will allow flexibility if professors want to cover it.

As with every programming language, Java also has some disadvantages. It does not directly support generic programing; a workaround is required that is discussed in Chapter 3. I/O support when using Java is minimal. The examples herein make minimal use of the Java I/O facilities.

Text Organization

This text introduces Java and object-oriented programming (particularly abstraction) in Part I. I discuss primitive types, reference types, and some of the predefined classes and exceptions before proceeding to the design of classes and inheritance.

Part II discusses Big-Oh and algorithmic paradigms, including recursion and randomization. An entire chapter is devoted to the topic of sorting, and a separate chapter contains a description of basic data structures. The interfaces and running times of the data structures are presented *without* the implementations being given. At this point in the text, the instructor may take several approaches to present the remaining material, including these two:

1. Use the corresponding implementations in Part IV as each data structure is described. The instructor can ask students to extend the classes in various ways, as suggested in the exercises.

2. Show how the interface is used and cover implementation at a later point in the course. The case studies in Part III can be used to support this approach. Since complete implementations are available on the Internet, the instructor can provide a library of classes for use in programming projects. Details on using this approach are given shortly.

Part V describes advanced data structures such as splay trees, pairing heaps, and the disjoint set data structure, which can be covered if time permits or, more likely, in a follow-up course.

Chapter-by-Chapter Text Organization

Part I consists of four chapters that describe the basics of Java used throughout the text. Chapter 1 describes primitive types and illustrates how to write basic programs in Java. Chapter 2 discusses reference types and illustrates the general concept of a pointer — even though Java does not have pointers — so that students learn this important CS-2 topic. Several of the basic reference types (strings, arrays, files, and string tokenizers) are illustrated, and the use of exceptions is discussed. Chapter 3 continues this discussion by describing how a class is implemented. Chapter 4 illustrates the use of inheritance in designing hierarchies (including exception classes) and generic components.

Part II focuses on the basic algorithms and building blocks. Chapter 5 provides a complete discussion of time complexity and Big-Oh notation. Binary search is also discussed and analyzed. Chapter 6 is a crucial chapter that discusses the interface to the data structures and argues intuitively what the running time of the supported operations should be for each data structure. (The implementation of these data structures is provided in Part IV.) Chapter 7 describes recursion by first introducing the notion of proof by induction. It also discusses divide-and-conquer, dynamic programming, and backtracking. A section describes several recursive numerical algorithms that are used to implement an important encryption algorithm, the RSA cryptosystem. For many students, the material in the second half of Chapter 7 is more suitable for a follow-up course. Chapter 8 describes, codes, and analyzes several basic sorting algorithms, including the insertion sort, Shellsort, mergesort, and quicksort. It also proves the classic lower bound for sorting and discusses the related problem of selection. Finally, Chapter 9 is a short chapter that discusses random numbers, including their generation and use in randomized algorithms.

Part III provides several case studies, with each chapter organized along a general theme. Chapter 10 illustrates several important techniques by examining games. Chapter 11 discusses the use of stacks in computer languages by examining an algorithm to check for balanced symbols and the classic operator precedence parsing algorithm. Complete implementations with code are provided for both algorithms. Chapter 12 discusses the basic utilities of file compression and cross-reference generation and provides a complete implementation of the cross-reference generator. Chapter 13 broadly examines simulation by looking at one problem that can be viewed as a simulation and then at the more classic event-driven simulation. Finally, Chapter 14 illustrates how data structures are used to implement several shortest-path algorithms efficiently for graphs.

Part IV presents the data structure implementations that correspond to the interfaces in Chapter 6. Some mathematics is used in this part, especially in Chapters 18 to 20, and can be skipped at the discretion of the instructor. Chapter 15 provides implementations for both stacks and queues. These data structures are first implemented using an expanding array. Then they are implemented using linked lists. General linked lists are described in Chapter 16. Extensions such as doubly linked lists, circular linked lists, and cursor implementations are left as exercises. Chapter 17 describes trees and illustrates the basic traversal schemes. Chapter 18 is a detailed chapter that provides several implementations of binary search trees. Initially, the basic binary search tree is shown, and then a binary search tree that supports order statistics is derived. AVL trees are discussed but not implemented; however, the more practical red-black trees and AA-trees are. Finally, the B-tree is examined. Chapter 19 discusses hash tables and implements the quadratic probing scheme, after examination of a simpler alternative. Chapter 20 describes the binary heap and examines heapsort and external sorting.

Part V contains material that is suitable for a more-advanced course or for general reference. The algorithms are accessible even at the first-year level. For completeness, sophisticated mathematical analyses have been included. Chapter 21 describes the splay tree, which is a binary search tree that performs well in practice and is competitive with the binary heap in some applications that require priority queues. Chapter 22 describes priority queues that support merging operations and provides an implementation of the pairing heap. Finally, Chapter 23 examines the classic disjoint set data structure.

The Appendix contains additional Java reference material. Appendix A illustrates how to compile and run Java programs on several platforms. Appendix B lists the operators and their precedence. Appendix C summarizes the Java libraries used in the text. Appendix D describes the AWT and applets. It also discusses threads in the context of animation.

Chapter Dependencies

Generally speaking, most chapters are independent of each other. Here are some of the notable dependencies:

- *Part I*: With the exception of the `Shape` case study in Chapter 4, all material in Part I should be covered, in sequence, prior to continuing to the rest of the text. The `interface` must be introduced, but the details of inheritance can be covered in broad detail if the instructor so chooses.
- *Chapter 5* (*Algorithm Analysis*): This should be covered prior to Chapters 6 and 8. Recursion (Chapter 7) can be covered prior to this chapter, but the instructor will have to gloss over some details about avoiding inefficient recursion.
- *Chapter 6* (*Data Structures*): This can be covered prior to, or in conjunction with, material in Part III or IV.
- *Chapter 7* (*Recursion*): The material in Sections 7.1–7.3 should be covered prior to discussing recursive sorting algorithms, trees, the tic-tac-toe case study, and shortest-path algorithms. Material such as the RSA cryptosystem, dynamic programming, and backtracking (unless tic-tac-toe is discussed) is otherwise optional.
- *Chapter 8* (*Sorting*): This should follow Chapters 5 and 7. However, it is possible to cover Shellsort without Chapters 5 and 7, since Shellsort is not recursive (hence, there is no need for Chapter 7) and a rigorous analysis of its running time is too complex and is not covered in the book (hence, there is little need for Chapter 5).
- *Chapters 15 and 16* (*Stacks/Queues/Lists*): These may be covered in either order. However, I prefer to cover Chapter 15 first, since I believe it has a simpler example of linked lists.
- *Chapters 17 and 18* (*Trees/Search trees*): These can be covered in either order or simultaneously.

Separate Entities

The other chapters have little or no dependencies:

- *Chapter 9* (*Randomization*): The material on random numbers can be covered at any point as needed.
- *Part III* (*Case Studies*): This can be covered at any point in roughly any order. There are a few references to earlier chapters that can easily be followed. These include Section 10.2 (tic-tac-toe), which references a discussion in Section 7.7, and Section 12.2 (cross-reference generation), which

references similar lexical analysis code in Section 11.1 (balanced symbol checking).

- *Chapters 19 and 20* (*Hashing/Priority Queues*): These can be covered at any point.
- *Part V* (*Advanced Data Structures*): This material is self-contained and is typically covered in a follow-up course.
- *Appendices* (*More Java*): The material on GUIs in Appendix D can be covered at any point after Chapter 4, as needed.

Mathematics

I have attempted to provide mathematical rigor for use in CS-2 courses that emphasize theory and for follow-up courses that require more analysis. However, this material stands out from the main text in the form of separate theorems and, in some cases, separate sections (or subsections). Thus it can be skipped in courses that choose to deemphasize theory.

In all cases, the proof of a theorem is not necessary to the understanding of the theorem's meaning. This is another illustration of the separation of an interface (the theorem statement) from its implementation (the proof). Some inherently mathematical material, such as Section 7.4 (*Numerical Applications of Recursion*), can be skipped without affecting comprehension of the rest of the chapter.

Course Organization

A crucial issue in teaching the course is deciding how the materials in Parts II to IV are to be used. The material in Part I should be covered in depth, and the student should write one or two programs that illustrate the design, implementation, and testing of classes and generic classes, and perhaps object-oriented design using inheritance. Chapter 5 discusses Big-Oh notation. An exercise in which the student writes a short program and compares the running time with an analysis can be given to test comprehension.

In the separation approach, the key concept of Chapter 6 is that different data structures support different access schemes with different efficiency. Students can be asked first to write an inefficient data structure. Any case study (except the tic-tac-toe example that uses recursion) can be used to test their programs, and the students can compare their inefficient data structures with an efficient library routine (provided by anonymous ftp, as discussed later in the Preface). In this scheme, all of the case studies (except tic-tac-toe) can be examined to see how each of the particular data structures is used. In this way, the student can see the interface for each data structure and how it is used but not see how it is efficiently implemented. This is truly a separation. Viewing things this way will greatly enhance the ability of students to think abstractly. Students then can be asked to extend the case study, but, once again, they are not required to know any of the details of the data structures.

The implementation of the data structures can be discussed afterward, and recursion can be introduced whenever the instructor feels it is appropriate, provided it is prior to binary search trees. The details of sorting can be discussed at any time after recursion. At this point, the course can continue by using the same case studies and experimenting with modifications to the implementations of the data structures. For instance, the student can experiment with various forms of balanced binary search trees.

Instructors who opt for a more traditional approach can simply discuss a case study in Part III after discussing a data structure implementation in Part IV. The book's chapters are designed to be as independent of each other as possible.

Exercises

Exercises come in various flavors; I have provided four varieties. The basic *In Short* exercise asks a simple question or requires hand-drawn simulations of an algorithm described in the text. The *In Theory* section asks questions that either require mathematical analysis, or perhaps, asks for theoretically interesting solutions to problems. The *In Practice* section contains simple programming questions, including questions about syntax or particularly tricky lines of code. Finally, the *Programming Projects* section contains ideas for extended assignments and suggestions for Java applets.

Pedagogical Features

- Margin notes are used to highlight important topics.
- The *Objects of the Game* section lists important terms along with definitions and page references.
- The *Common Errors* section at the end of each chapter provides a list of common errors.
- References for further reading are provided at the end of most chapters.

Code Availability

The code in the text is fully functional and has been tested on Sun's JDK 1.1. It is available via anonymous ftp at `aw.com` and through the World Wide Web at `http://www.aw.com/cseng/titles/0-201-54991-3/` (follow the links from there). The *On the Internet* section at the end of each chapter lists the filenames for the chapter's code.

Instructor's Resource Guide

An Instructor's Guide is available that illustrates several approaches to the material. It includes samples of test questions, assignments, and syllabi. Answers to select exercises are also provided. Instructors should contact their Addison-Wesley local sales representative for information on the Guide's availability.

Acknowledgments

Many, many people have helped me in the preparation of this book. Many have already been acknowledged in the previous work, *Algorithms, Data Structures, and Problem Solving with C++*, on which this book is based. Others, too numerous to list, have sent e-mail messages and pointed out errors or inconsistencies in explanations that I have tried to fix in this version.

For this book, I would like to thank all of the folks at Addison-Wesley: my Editor, Susan Hartman, and Associate Editor, Katherine Harutunian, helped me make some difficult decisions regarding the organization of the Java material and were very helpful in bringing this book to fruition. My copyeditor and proofreaders suggested numerous rewrites that improved the text. They are Laura K. Michaels, Phyllis Coyne, and Sarah Hallet-Corey. Syndi Hirsch did a lovely cover design. As always, Tom Ziolkowski has done a superb job in the marketing department. I would especially like to thank Pat Unubun, my production editor, for her outstanding effort coordinating the entire project.

I also thank the reviewers, who provided valuable comments, many of which have been incorporated into the text: John Chenoweth, Rob Clark, John Franco, Susanne Hupfer, Steven L. Jenkins, Josephine DeGuzman Mendoza, Viera K. Proulx, and Amr Sabry.

Some of the material in this text is adapted from my textbook *Efficient C Programming: A Practical Approach* (Prentice-Hall, 1995) and is used with permission of the publisher. I have attempted to place end-of-chapter references where appropriate.

My World Wide Web page, `http://www.cs.fiu.edu/~weiss`, will contain updated source code, an errata list, and a link to submit bug reports.

Contents

Part IV: *Implementations*

Part V: *Advanced Data Structures*

APPENDICES

Data Structures
and
Problem Solving
Using Java™

Part I

Tour of Java

1

Primitive Java

THE primary focus of this book is problem solving techniques that allow the construction of sophisticated, time-efficient programs. Nearly all of the material discussed is applicable in any programming language. Some would argue that a broad pseudocode description of these techniques could suffice to demonstrate concepts. However, we believe that working with live code is vitally important.

There is no shortage of programing languages available. At the time of this writing, C++ is the language in widest use both academically and commercially. However, in 1996, Java exploded onto the scene as a viable contender.

Java's massive media hype is due largely to its use as the language in which applets are written. *Applets* are Java programs that are run by a World Wide Web ("Web") browser, such as *Netscape Navigator*. Nowadays, most Web pages contain some animations, many of which are Java applets. Although applets are nice, they are not the reason we use Java. Indeed, this textbook does not discuss applets at all except in a brief appendix.

Java also provides support for concurrent programming, whereby several processes run in parallel, communicating with each other in a primitive way. This is important for more advanced programming, but this feature is not used in this text.

Java's primary appeal is that it is a safe, portable language that supports modern object-oriented constructs. Many C++ constructs that are confusing to novices are not found in Java. Compared to C++, many common programming errors are caught by Java either at compile time or at run time. Java has an exception mechanism that requires the programmer to explicitly deal with errors and a relatively simple model that distinguishes between primitive types (such as `int`) and user-defined types. Java does not have an explicit pointer type.

Java is portable: for example, an integer has the same range of values in every Java implementation, regardless of the underlying computer architecture. Java also provides a graphical user interface (GUI) toolkit that allows input and output to be performed using forms. Although we do not discuss this toolkit in the main text (see rather Appendix D), it is relatively easy to use. Most important, it is also portable to every Java implementation. Java's philosophy is "write once, run everywhere."

In the first four chapters, we discuss the features of Java that are used throughout the book. Unused features and technicalities are not covered. Those looking for deeper Java information will find it in the many Java books that are available.

We begin by discussing the part of the language that mirrors a 1970's programming language such as Pascal or C. This includes primitive types, basic operations, conditional and looping constructs, and the Java equivalent of functions.

In this chapter, we will see:

- Some of the basics of Java, including simple lexical elements
- The Java primitive types, including some of the operations that primitive-typed variables can perform
- How conditional statements and loop constructs are implemented in Java
- The static method — the Java equivalent of the function and procedure

1.1   The General Environment

How are Java application programs entered, compiled, and run? The answer, of course, depends on the particular platform that hosts the Java compiler. Several of the popular development systems are described in Appendix A.

javac compiles
`.java` files and
generates `.class`
files containing
j-code. java
invokes the Java
interpreter.

Java source code resides in files whose names end with the `.java` suffix. The local compiler, *javac*, compiles the program and generates `.class` files, which contain *j-code*. j-code is a portable intermediate language that is interpreted by running the Java interpreter, *java*.

For Java programs, input can come from one of many places:

- The terminal, whose input is denoted as *standard input*
- Additional parameters in the invocation of the executable program — *command-line arguments*
- A GUI component
- A file

Command-line arguments are particularly important for specifying program options. They are discussed in Section 2.4.4. Java provides mechanisms to read and write files. This is discussed in Section 2.6.3. Many operating systems provide an alternative known as *file redirection*, in which the operating system arranges to take input from (or send output to) a file in a manner that is transparent to the running program. On Unix, for instance, the command

```
java Program < inputfile > outputfile
```

automatically arranges things so that any terminal reads are redirected to come from `inputfile` and terminal writes are redirected to go to `outputfile`.

1.2   The First Program

Let us begin by examining the simple Java program shown in Figure 1.1. This program prints a short phrase to the terminal. Note the line numbers shown on the left of the code *are not part of the program*. They are supplied for easy reference.

Place the program in the source file `FirstProgram.java` and then compile and run it. Appendix A describes how to do this on several popular platforms. Note that the name of the source file must match the name of the class (shown on line 4).

1.2.1   Comments

Java has three forms of comments. The first form, which is inherited from C, begins with the token `/*` and ends with `*/`. Here is an example:

```
/* This is a
   two line comment */
```

Comments do not nest.

The second form, which is inherited from C++, begins with the token `//`. There is no ending token. Rather, the comment extends up to the end of the line. This is shown on lines 1 and 2 in Figure 1.1.

The third form begins with `/**` instead of `/*`. This form can be used to provide information to the *javadoc* utility, which will generate documentation from comments. This form is discussed in Section 3.3.

Comments exist to make code easier for humans to read. These humans include other programmers who may have to modify or use your code, as well as yourself. A well-commented program is a sign of a good programmer.

Comments make code easier for humans to read. Java has three forms of comments.

```
 1  // First program
 2  // MW, 9/1/97
 3
 4  public class FirstProgram
 5  {
 6      public static void main( String [ ] args )
 7      {
 8          System.out.println( "Is there anybody out there?" );
 9      }
10  }
```

Figure 1.1   A simple first program

1.2.2 `main`

When the program is run, the special function `main` is invoked.

A Java program consists of a collection of interacting classes, which contain methods. The Java equivalent of the function or procedure is the *static method*, which is described in Section 1.6. When any program is run, the special static method `main` is invoked. Line 6 of Figure 1.1 shows that the static method `main` is invoked, possibly with command-line arguments. The parameter types of `main` and the `void` return type shown are required.

1.2.3 Terminal Output

`println` is used to perform output.

The program in Figure 1.1 consists of a single statement, shown on line 8. `println` is the primary output mechanism in Java. Here, a constant string is placed on the standard output stream `System.out` by applying a `println` method. Input and output is discussed in more detail in Section 2.6. For now we mention only that the same syntax is used to perform output for any entity, whether that entity is an integer, floating point, string, or some other type.

1.3   Primitive Types

Java defines eight *primitive types*. It also allows the programmer great flexibility to define new types of objects, called *classes*. However, primitive types and user-defined types have important differences in Java. In this section, we examine the primitive types and the basic operations that can be performed on them.

1.3.1   The Primitive Types

Java's primitive types are integer, floating-point, Boolean, and character.

The Unicode standard contains over 30,000 distinct coded characters covering the principle written languages.

Java has eight primitive types, shown in Figure 1.2. The most common is the integer, which is specified by the keyword `int`. Unlike with many other languages, the range of integers is not machine-dependent. Rather, it is the same in any Java implementation, regardless of the underlying computer architecture. Java also allows entities of type `byte`, `short`, and `long`. Floating-point numbers are represented by the types `float` and `double`. `double` has more significant digits, so use of it is recommended over use of `float`. The `char` type is used to represent single characters. A `char` occupies 16 bits to represent the Unicode standard. The Unicode standard contains over 30,000 distinct coded characters covering the principle written languages. The low end of Unicode is identical to ASCII. The final primitive type is `boolean`, which is either `true` or `false`.

Primitive Type	What It Stores	Range
byte	8-bit integer	–128 to 127
short	16-bit integer	–32,768 to 32,767
int	32-bit integer	–2,147,483,648 to 2,147,483,647
long	64-bit integer	-2^{63} to $2^{63} - 1$
float	32-bit floating-point	6 significant digits, (10^{-46}, 10^{38})
double	64-bit floating-point	15 significant digits, (10^{-324}, 10^{308})
char	Unicode character	
boolean	Boolean variable	false and true

Figure 1.2   The eight primitive types in Java

1.3.2 Constants

Integer constants can be represented in either decimal, octal, or hexadecimal notation. Octal notation is indicated by a leading 0; hexadecimal is indicated by a leading 0x or 0X. The following are all equivalent ways of representing the integer 37: 37, 045, 0x25. Octal and hexadecimal integers are not used in this text. However, we must be aware of them so that we use leading 0s only when we intend to.

A *character constant* is enclosed with a pair of single quotation marks, as in 'a'. Internally, this character sequence is interpreted as a small number. The output routines later interpret that small number as the corresponding character. A *string constant* consists of a sequence of characters enclosed within double quotation marks, as in "Hello". There are some special sequences, known as *escape sequences*, that are used (for instance, how does one represent a single quotation mark?). In this text we use '\n', '\\', '\'', and '\"', which mean, respectively, the newline character, backslash character, single quotation mark, and double quotation mark.

Integer constants can be represented in either decimal, octal, or hexadecimal notation.

A string constant consists of a sequence of characters enclosed by double quotes.

Escape sequences are used to represent certain character constants.

1.3.3 Declaration and Initialization of Primitive Types

Any variable, including those of a primitive type, is declared by providing its name, its type, and optionally, its initial value. The name must be an *identifier*. An indentifier may consist of any combination of letters, digits, and the under-

A variable is named by using an identifier.

Java is case-
sensitive.

score character; it may not start with a digit, however. Reserved words, such as
`int`, are not allowed. Nor should you reuse identifier names that are already vis-
ibly used (for example, do not use `main` as the name of an entity).

Java is *case-sensitive*, meaning that `Age` and `age` are different identifiers.
This text uses the following convention for naming variables: All identifiers start
with a lowercase letter and new words start with an uppercase letter. An example
is the identifier `minimumWage`.

Here are some examples of declarations:

```
int num3;                      // Default initialization
double minimumWage = 4.50;     // Standard initialization
int x = 0, num1 = 0;           // Two entities are declared
int num2 = num1;
```

A variable should be declared near its first use. As will be shown, the placement of a declaration determines its scope and meaning.

1.3.4 Terminal Input and Output

Basic formatted terminal I/O is accomplished by `readLine` and `println`. The
standard input stream is `System.in`, and the standard output stream is
`System.out`.

The basic mechanism for formatted I/O uses the `String` type, which is discussed in Section 2.3. For output, + combines two `String`s. If the second argument is not a `String`, a temporary `String` is created for it if it is a primitive
type. These conversions to `String` can also be defined for objects (Section
3.4.3). For input, we must associate a `BufferedReader` object with
`System.in`. Then a `String` is read and can be parsed. A more detailed discussion of I/O, including a treatment of formatted files, is in Section 2.6.

1.4   Basic Operators

This section describes some of the operators available in Java. These operators
are used to form *expressions*. A constant or entity by itself is an expression, as are
combinations of constants and variables with operators. An expression followed
by a semicolon is a simple statement. In Section 1.5, we examine other types of
statements, which introduce additional operators.

1.4.1 Assignment Operators

A simple Java program that illustrates a few operators is shown in Figure 1.3. The basic *assignment operator* is the equals sign. For example, on line 16 the variable a is assigned the value of the variable c (which at that point is 6). Subsequent changes to the value of c do not affect a. Assignment operators can be chained, as in z=y=x=0.

Another assignment operator is the +=, whose use is illustrated on line 18 of the figure. The += operator adds the value on the right-hand side (of the += operator) to the variable on the left-hand side. Thus, in the figure, c is incremented from its value of 6 before line 18, to a value of 14.

Java provides various other assignment operators, such as -=, *=, and /=, which alter the variable on the left-hand side of the operator via subtraction, multiplication, and division, respectively.

Java provides a host of *assignment operators*, including =, +=, -=, *=, and /=.

```
 1  public class OperatorTest
 2  {
 3          // Program to illustrate basic operators
 4          // The output is as follows:
 5          // 12 8 6
 6          // 6 8 6
 7          // 6 8 14
 8          // 22 8 14
 9          // 24 10 33
10
11      public static void main( String [ ] args )
12      {
13          int a = 12, b = 8, c = 6;
14
15          System.out.println( a + " " + b + " " + c );
16          a = c;
17          System.out.println( a + " " + b + " " + c );
18          c += b;
19          System.out.println( a + " " + b + " " + c );
20          a = b + c;
21          System.out.println( a + " " + b + " " + c );
22          a++;
23          ++b;
24          c = a++ + ++b;
25          System.out.println( a + " " + b + " " + c );
26      }
27  }
```

Figure 1.3   Program that illustrates operators

1.4.2 Binary Arithmetic Operators

Java provides several *binary arithmetic operators,* including +, −, *, /, and %.

Line 20 in Figure 1.3 illustrates one of the *binary arithmetic operators* that are typical of all programming languages: the addition operator (+). The + operator causes the values of b and c to be added together; b and c remain unchanged. The resulting value is assigned to a. Other arithmetic operators typically used in Java are −, *, /, and %, which are used, respectively, for subtraction, multiplication, division, and remainder. Integer division returns only the integral part and discards any remainder.

As is typical, addition and subtraction have the same precedence, and this precedence is lower than the precedence of the group consisting of the multiplication, division, and mod operators; thus 1+2*3 evaluates to 7. All of these operators associate from left to right (so 3−2−2 evaluates to −1). All operators have precedence and associativity. The complete table of operators is in Appendix B.

1.4.3 Unary Operators

Several *unary operators* are defined, including −.

In addition to binary arithmetic operators, which require two operands, Java provides *unary operators,* which require only one operand. The most familiar of these is the unary minus, which evaluates to the negative of its operand. Thus −x returns the negative of x.

Autoincrement and *autodecrement* add 1 and subtract 1, respectively. The operators for doing this are ++ and −−. There are two forms of incrementing and decrementing: prefix and postfix.

Java also provides the autoincrement operator to add 1 to a variable — denoted by ++ — and the autodecrement operator to subtract 1 from a variable — denoted by −−. The most benign use of this feature is shown on lines 22 and 23 of Figure 1.3. In both lines, the *autoincrement operator* ++ adds 1 to the value of the variable. In Java, however, an operator applied to an expression yields an expression that has a value. Although it is guaranteed that the variable will be incremented before the execution of the next statement, the question arises: What is the value of the autoincrement expression if it is used in a larger expression?

In this case, the placement of the ++ is crucial. The semantics of ++x is that the value of the expression is the new value of x. This is called the *prefix increment.* In contrast, x++ means the value of the expression is the original value of x. This is called the *postfix increment.* This feature is shown in line 24 of Figure 1.3. a and b are both incremented by 1, and c is obtained by adding the *original* value of a to the *incremented* value of b.

1.4.4 Type Conversions

The *type conversion operator* is used to generate a temporary entity of a new type.

The *type conversion operator* is used to generate a temporary entity of a new type. Consider, for instance,

```
double quotient;
int x = 6;
int y = 10;
quotient = x / y;     // Probably wrong!
```

The first operation is the division, and since x and y are both integers, the result is integer division, and we obtain 0. Integer 0 is then implicitly converted to a `double` so that it can be assigned to `quotient`. But we had intended `quotient` to be assigned 0.6. The solution is to generate a temporary variable for either x or y so that the division is performed using the rules for `double`. This would be done as follows:

```
quotient = ( double ) x / y;
```

Note that neither x nor y are changed. An unnamed temporary is created, and its value is used for the division. The type conversion operator has higher precedence than division does, so x is type-converted and then the division is performed (rather than the conversion coming after the division of two `int`s being performed).

1.5 Conditional Statements

This section examines statements that affect the flow of control: conditional statements and loops. As a consequence, new operators are introduced.

1.5.1 Relational and Equality Operators

The basic test that we can perform on primitive types is the comparison. This is done using the equality and inequality operators, as well as the relational operators (less than, greater than, and so on).

In Java, the *equality operators* are == and ! =. For example,

In Java, the equality operators are == and ! =.

```
leftExpr==rightExpr
```

evaluates to `true` if `leftExpr` and `rightExpr` are equal; otherwise, it evaluates to `false`. Similarly,

```
leftExpr!=rightExpr
```

evaluates to `true` if `leftExpr` and `rightExpr` are not equal and to `false` otherwise.

The *relational operators* are <, <=, >, and >=.

The *relational operators* are <, <=, >, and >=. These have natural meanings for the built-in types. The relational operators have higher precedence than the equality operators. Both have lower precedence than the arithmetic operators but higher precedence than the assignment operators, so the use of parentheses is frequently unnecessary. All of these operators associate from left to right, but this fact is useless: In the expression a<b<6, for example, the first < generates a boolean and the second is illegal because < is not defined for booleans. The next section describes the correct way to perform this test.

1.5.2 Logical Operators

Java provides *logical operators* that are used to simulate the Boolean algebra concepts of AND, OR, and NOT. The corresponding operators are &&, ||, and !.

Java provides *logical operators* that are used to simulate the Boolean algebra concepts of AND, OR, and NOT. These are sometimes known as *conjunction*, *disjunction*, and *negation*, respectively, whose corresponding operators are &&, ||, and !. The test in the previous section is properly implemented as a<b && b<6. The precedence of conjunction and disjunction is sufficiently low that parentheses are not needed. && has higher precedence than ||, while ! is grouped with other unary operators. Inputs and outputs for the logical operators are boolean. Figure 1.4 shows the result of applying the logical operators for all possible inputs.

Short-circuit evaluation means that if the result of a logical operator can be determined by examining the first expression, then the second expression is not evaluated.

One important rule is that && and || are short-circuit evaluation operations. *Short-circuit evaluation* means that if the result can be determined by examining the first expression, then the second expression is not evaluated. For instance, in

```
x != 0 && 1/x != 3
```

if x is 0, then the first half is false. Automatically the result of the AND must be false, so the second half is not evaluated. This is a good thing because division-by-zero would give erroneous behavior. Short-circuit evaluation allows us to not have to worry about dividing by zero.[1]

X	Y	X && Y	X || Y	!X
false	false	false	false	true
false	true	false	true	true
true	false	false	true	false
true	true	true	true	false

Figure 1.4 Result of logical operators

---

[1] There are (extremely) rare cases in which it is preferable to not short-circuit. In such cases, the & and | operators with boolean arguments guarantee that both arguments are evaluated, even if the result of the operation can be determined from the first argument.

1.5.3   The `if` Statement

The `if` statement is the fundamental decision maker. Its basic form is

The `if` statement is the fundamental decision maker.

```
if( expression )
    statement
next statement
```

If *expression* evaluates to `true`, then *statement* is executed; otherwise, it is not. When the `if` statement is completed (without an unhandled error), control passes to the next statement.

Optionally, we can use an `if-else` statement, as follows:

```
if( expression )
    statement1
else
    statement2
next statement
```

In this case, if *expression* evaluates to `true`, then *statement1* is executed; otherwise, *statement2* is executed. In either case, control then passes to the next statement, as in

```
System.out.print( "1/x is " );
if( x != 0 )
    System.out.print( 1 / x );
else
    System.out.print( "Undefined" );
System.out.println( );
```

Remember that at most one statement is allowed to be subjected to each of the `if` and `else` clauses, no matter how you indent. Here are two mistakes:

```
if( x == 0 );     // ; is null statement (and counts)
    System.out.println( "x is zero " );
else
    System.out.print( "x is " );
    System.out.println( x ); // Two statements
```

The first mistake is the inclusion of the `;` at the end of the first `if`. This semicolon by itself counts as the *null statement*; consequently, this fragment won't compile (the `else` is no longer associated with an `if`). Once that mistake is fixed, we have a logic error: that is, the last line is not part of the `else`, even though the indentation suggests it is. To fix this problem, we have to use a *block*, in which we enclose a sequence of statements by a pair of braces:

A semicolon by itself is the *null statement*.

A *block* is a sequence of statements within braces.

```
if( x == 0 )
    System.out.println( "x is zero" );
else
{
    System.out.print( "x is " );
    System.out.println( x );
}
```

The `if` statement can itself be the target of an `if` or `else` clause, as can other control statements discussed later in this section. In the case of nested `if`-`else` statements, an `else` matches the innermost dangling `if`. It may be necessary to add braces if that is not the intended meaning.

1.5.4   The `while` Statement

The `while` *statement is one of three basic forms of looping.*

Java provides three basic forms of looping: the `while` statement, `for` statement, and `do` statement. The syntax for the *`while` statement* is

```
while( expression )
    statement
next statement
```

Note that like the `if` statement, there is no semicolon in the syntax. If one is present, it will be taken as the null statement.

While *expression* is true, *statement* is executed; then *expression* is reevaluated. If *expression* is initially `false`, then *statement* will never be executed. Generally, *statement* does something that can potentially alter the value of *expression*; otherwise, the loop could be infinite. When the `while` loop terminates (normally), control resumes at the next statement.

1.5.5   The `for` Statement

The `for` *statement is a looping construct that is used primarily for simple iteration.*

The `while` statement is sufficient to express all repetition. Even so, Java provides two other forms of looping: `for` statement and `do` statement. The *`for` statement* is used primarily for iteration. Its syntax is

```
for( initialization; test; update )
    statement
next statement
```

Here, *initialization*, *test*, and *update* are all expressions, and all three are optional. If *test* is not provided, it defaults to `true`. There is no semicolon after the closing parenthesis.

The `for` statement is executed by first performing the *initialization*. Then, while *test* is `true`, the following two actions occur: *statement* is performed, and then *update* is performed. If *initialization* and *update* are omitted, then the `for` statement behaves exactly like a `while` statement. The advantage of a `for` statement is clarity in that for variables that count (or iterate), the `for` statement makes it much easier to see what the range of the counter is. The following fragment prints the first 100 positive integers:

```
for( int i = 1; i <= 100; i++ )
    System.out.println( i );
```

This fragment illustrates the common technique of declaring a counter in the initialization portion of the loop. This counter's scope extends only inside the loop.

Both *initialization* and *update* may use a comma to allow multiple expressions. The following fragment illustrates this commonly used technique:

```
for( i = 0, sum = 0; i <= n; i++, sum += n )
    System.out.println( i + "\t" + sum );
```

Loops nest in the same way as `if` statements. For instance, we can find all small numbers whose sum equals their product (such as 2 and 2, whose sum and product are both 4):

```
for( int i = 1; i <= 10; i++ )
    for( int j = 1; j <= 10; j++ )
        if( i + j == i * j )
            System.out.println( i + ", " + j );
```

As we will see, however, when we nest loops we can easily create programs whose running times grow quickly.

1.5.6 The do Statement

The `while` statement repeatedly performs a test. If the test is `true`, it then executes an embedded statement. However, if the initial test is `false`, the embedded statement is never executed. In some cases, however, we would like to guarantee that the embedded statement is executed at least once. This is done using the do statement. The *do statement* is identical to the `while` statement, except that the test is performed after the embedded statement. The syntax is

The do statement is a looping construct that guarantees the loop is executed at least once.

```
do
    statement
while( expression );
next statement
```

Notice that the do statement includes a semicolon. A typical use of the do statement is shown in the following pseudocode fragment:

```
do
{
    Prompt user;
    Read value;
} while( value is no good );
```

The do statement is by far the least frequently used of the three looping constructs. However, when we have to do something at least once, and for some reason a for loop is inappropriate, then the do statement is the method of choice.

1.5.7   break and continue

The for and while statements provide for termination before the start of a repeated statement. The do statement allows termination after execution of a repeated statement. Occasionally, we would like to terminate execution in the middle of a repeated (compound) statement. The *break statement*, which is the keyword break followed by a semicolon, can be used to achieve this. Typically, an if statement would precede the break, as in

```
while( ... )
{
    ...
    if( something )
        break;
    ...
}
```

The break statement exits the innermost loop or switch statement. The *labelled* break *statement* exits from a nested loop.

The break statement exits the innermost loop only (it is also used in conjunction with the switch statement, described in the next section). If there are several loops that need exiting, the break will not work, and most likely you have poorly designed code. Even so, Java provides a *labelled* break statement. In the labelled break statement, a loop is labelled, and then a break statement can be applied to the loop, regardless of how many other loops are nested. Here is an example:

```
outer:
    while( ... )
    {
        while( ... )
            if( disaster )
                break outer; // Go to after outer
    }
    // Control passes here after outer loop is exited
```

Occasionally, we want to give up on the current iteration of a repeated statement for the current value and go on to the next iteration. This can be handled by using a *continue statement*. Like the `break` statement, the `continue` statement includes a semicolon and applies to the innermost loop only. The following fragment prints the first 100 integers, with the exception of those divisible by 10:

The continue *statement goes to the next iteration of the innermost loop.*

```
for( int i = 1; i <= 100; i++ )
{
    if( i % 10 == 0 )
        continue;
    System.out.println( i );
}
```

Of course, in this example, there are alternatives to the `continue` statement. However, `continue` is commonly used to avoid complicated `if-else` patterns inside loops.

1.5.8   The `switch` Statement

The *switch statement* is used to select among several small integer values. It consists of an expression and a block. The block contains a sequence of statements and a collection of *labels*, which represent possible values of the expression. All the labels must be distinct. An optional default label, if present, matches any unrepresented label. If there is no applicable case for the `switch` expression, the `switch` statement is over; otherwise, control passes to the appropriate label and all statements from that point on are executed. A `break` statement may be used to force early termination of the `switch` and is almost always used to separate logically distinct cases. An example of the typical structure is shown in Figure 1.5.

The switch statement is used to select among several small integer values.

1.5.9   The Conditional Operator

The *conditional operator* `?:` is used as a shorthand for simple `if-else` statements. The general form is

The conditional operator `?:` *is used as a shorthand for simple* `if-else` *statements.*

```
testExpr ? yesExpr : noExpr
```

testExpr is evaluated first, followed by either *yesExpr* or *noExpr*, producing the result of the entire expression. *yesExpr* is evaluated if *testExpr* is `true`; otherwise, *noExpr* is evaluated. The precedence of the conditional operator is just above that of the assignment operators. This allows us to avoid using parentheses when assigning the result of the conditional operator to a variable. As an example, the minimum of x and y is assigned to `minVal` as follows:

```
minVal = x <= y ? x : y;
```

```
1  switch( someCharacter )
2  {
3    case '(':
4    case '[':
5    case '{':
6      // Code to process opening symbols
7      break;
8
9    case ')':
10   case ']':
11   case '}':
12     // Code to process closing symbols
13     break;
14
15   case '\n':
16     // Code to handle newline character
17     break;
18
19   default:
20     // Code to handle other cases
21     break;
22 }
```

Figure 1.5   Layout of a `switch` statement

1.6   Methods

A *method* is similar to a function in other languages. The *method header* consists of the name, return type, and parameter list. The *method declaration* includes the body. A `public static` method is the equivalent of a C-style global function.
In *call-by-value*, the actual arguments are copied into the formal parameters. Variables are passed using call-by-value.

In Java, what is known as a function or procedure in other languages is called a *method*. A more complete treatment of methods is provided in Chapter 3. This section presents some of the basics for writing C-like functions, such as `main`, so that we can write some simple programs.

A *method header* consists of a name, a (possibly empty) list of parameters, and a return type. The actual code to implement the method, sometimes called the method body, is formally a block. A *method declaration* consists of a header plus the body. An example of a method declaration and a `main` routine that uses it is shown in Figure 1.6.

By prefacing each method with the words `public static`, we can mimic the C-style global function. Although this is a useful technique in some instances, it should not be overused.

The method name is an identifier. The parameter list consists of zero or more *formal parameters*, each with a specified type. When a method is called, the *actual arguments* are sent into the formal parameters using normal assignment. This means primitive types are passed using *call-by-value* parameter passing only. The actual arguments cannot be altered by the function. As with most modern programming languages, method declarations may be arranged in any order.

```
 1  public class MinTest
 2  {
 3      public static void main( String [ ] args )
 4      {
 5          int a = 3;
 6          int b = 7;
 7
 8          System.out.println( min( a, b ) );
 9      }
10
11      // Method declaration
12      public static int min( int x, int y )
13      {
14          return x < y ? x : y;
15      }
16  }
```

Figure 1.6   Illustration of method declaration and calls

The *return statement* is used to return a value to the caller. If the return type is void, then no value is returned, and `return;` should be used.

The return statement is used to return a value to the caller.

1.6.1 Overloading of Method Names

Suppose we need to write a routine that returns the maximum of three ints. A reasonable method header would be

```
int max( int a, int b, int c )
```

In some languages, this may be unacceptable if max is already declared. For instance, we may also have

```
int max( int a, int b )
```

Java allows the *overloading* of method names. This means that several methods may have the same name and be declared in the same class scope as long as their *signatures* (that is, their parameter list types) differ. When a call to max is made, the compiler can deduce which of the intended meanings should be applied based on the actual argument list. Two signatures may have the same number of parameters, as long as at least one of the parameter list types differs.

Overloading of a method name means that several methods may have the same name as long as their parameter list types differ.

Note that the return type is not included in the signature. This means it is illegal to have two methods in the same class scope whose only difference is the return type. Methods in different class scope may have the same names, signatures, and even return types; this is discussed in Chapter 3.

1.6.2 Storage Classes

Entities that are declared inside the body of a method are local variables and can be accessed by name only within the method body. These entities are created when the method body is executed and disappear when the method body terminates.

`static final`
variables are constants.

A variable declared outside the body of a method is global to the class. It is similar to global variables in other languages if the word `static` is used (which is likely to be required so as to make the entity accessible by static methods). If both `static` and `final` are used, they are global symbolic constants. As an example,

```
static final double PI = 3.1415926535897932;
```

Note the use of the common convention of naming symbolic constants entirely in uppercase. If several words form the identifier name, they are separated by the underscore character, as in `MAX_INT_VALUE`.

If the word `static` is omitted, then the variable (or constant) has a different meaning, which is discussed in Section 3.4.5.

Summary

This chapter discussed the primitive features of Java, such as primitive types, operators, conditional and looping statements, and methods that are found in almost any language.

Any nontrivial program will require the use of nonprimitive types, called *reference types*, which are discussed in the next chapter.

 ### Objects of the Game

assignment operators In Java, used to alter the value of a variable. These operators include =, +=, -=, *=, and /=. (9)

autoincrement (++) and autodecrement (--) operators Operators that add and subtract 1, respectively. There are two forms of incrementing and decrementing, prefix and postfix. (10)

binary arithmetic operators Used to perform basic arithmetic. Java provides several, including +, -, *, /, and %. (10)

block A sequence of statements within braces. (13)

break statement A statement that exits the innermost loop or `switch` statement. (16)

call-by-value The Java parameter-passing mechanism whereby the actual argument is copied into the formal parameter. (18)

comments Make code easier for humans to read but has no semantic meaning. Java has three forms of comments. (5)

conditional operator (?:) An operator that is used as a shorthand for simple `if-else` statements. (17)

`continue` statement A statement that goes to the next iteration of the innermost loop. (17)

`do` statement A looping construct that guarantees the loop is executed at least once. (15)

equality operators In Java, `==` and `!=` are used to compare two values; they return either `true` or `false` (as appropriate). (11)

escape sequence Used to represent certain character constants. (7)

`for` statement A looping construct used primarily for simple iteration. (14)

identifier Used to name a variable or method. (7)

`if` statement The fundamental decision maker. (13)

integral types `byte`, `char`, `short`, `int`, and `long`. (6)

j-code Portable intermediate code generated by the Java compiler. (4)

java The java interpreter. (4)

javac The java compiler; generates j-code. (4)

labelled `break` statement A `break` statement used to exit from nested loops. (16)

logical operators `&&`, `||`, and `!`, used to simulate the Boolean algebra concepts of AND, OR, and NOT. (12)

`main` The special function that is invoked when the program is run. (6)

method The Java equivalent of a function. (18)

method declaration Consists of the method header and body. (18)

method header Consists of the name, return type, and parameter list. (18)

null statement A statement that consists of a semicolon by itself. (13)

octal and hexadecimal integer constants Integer constants can be represented in either decimal, octal, or hexadecimal notation. Octal notation is indicated by a leading `0`; hexadecimal is indicated by a leading `0x` or `0X`. (7)

overloading of a method name The action of allowing several methods to have the same name as long as their parameter list types differ. (19)

primitive types In Java, integer, floating-point, Boolean, and character. (6)

relational operators In Java, `<`, `<=`, `>`, and `>=` are used to decide which of two values is smaller or larger; they return `true` or `false`. (12)

`return` statement A statement used to return information to the caller. (19)

short-circuit evaluation The process whereby if the result of a logical operator can be determined by examining the first expression, then the second expression is not evaluated. (12)

signature The combination of the method name and the parameter list types. The return type is not part of the signature. (19)

standard input The terminal, unless redirected. There are also streams for standard output and standard error.

static final entity A global constant. (20)

static method A method that is the equivalent of a global function. (19)

string constant A constant that consists of a sequence of characters enclosed by double quotes. (7)

switch statement A statement used to select among several small integral values. (17)

type conversion operator An operator used to generate an unnamed temporary variable of a new type. (10)

unary operators Require one operand. Several unary operators are defined, including unary minus (−) and the autoincrement and autodecrement operators (++ and −−). (10)

Unicode International character set that contains over 30,000 distinct characters covering the principle written languages. (6)

while statement The most basic form of looping. (14)

 ## Common Errors

1. Adding unnecessary semicolons gives logical errors because the semicolon by itself is the null statement. This means that an unintended semicolon immediately following a for, while, or if statement is very likely to go undetected and will break your program.

2. At compile time, Java detects some instances in which a method that is supposed to return a value fails to do so. But ultimately, it is your responsibility to remember to return a value.

3. A leading 0 makes an integer constant octal when seen as a token in source code. So 037 is equivalent to decimal 31.

4. Use && and || for logical operations; & and | do not short circuit.

5. The else clause matches the closest dangling if. It is common to forget to include the braces needed to match the else to a distant dangling if.

6. When a switch statement is used, it is common to forget the break statement between logical cases. If it is forgotten, control passes through to the next case; generally, this is not the desired behavior.

7. Escape sequences begin with the backslash \, not the forward slash /.

8. Mismatched braces may give misleading answers. Use checkBalance, described in Section 11.1, to check if this is the cause of a compiler error message.

9. The name of the Java source file must match the name of the class being compiled.

On the Internet

Following are the available files for this chapter. Everything is self-contained, and nothing is used later in the text. All programs are in directory **Chapter01**.

FirstProgram.java   The first program, as shown in Figure 1.1
MinTest.java   Illustration of methods, as shown in Figure 1.6.
OperatorTest.java   Demonstration of various operators, as shown in
           Figure 1.3.

Exercises

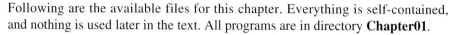

In Short

1.1. What extensions are used for Java source and compiled files?
1.2. Describe the three kinds of comments used in Java programs.
1.3. What are the eight primitive types in Java?
1.4. What is the difference between the `*` and `*=` operators?
1.5. Explain the difference between the prefix and postfix increment operators.
1.6. Describe the three types of loops in Java.
1.7. Describe all the uses of a `break` statement. What is a labelled `break` statement?
1.8. What does the `continue` statement do?
1.9. What is method overloading?
1.10. Describe call-by-value.

In Theory

1.11. Let b have the value of 5 and c have the value of 8. What is the value of a, b, and c after each line of the following program fragment:

```
a = b++ + c++;
a = b++ + ++c;
a = ++b + c++;
a = ++b + ++c;
```

1.12. What is the result of `true && false || true`?
1.13. For the following, give an example in which the `for` loop on the left is not equivalent to the `while` loop on the right:

```
                                  init;
for( init; test; update )         while( test )
{                                 {
    statements                        statements
                                      update;
}                                 }
```

1.14. For the following program, what are the possible outputs:

```
public class WhatIsX
{
    public static void f( int x )
        { /* body unknown */ }

    public static void main( String [ ] args )
    {
        int x = 0;
        f( x );
        System.out.println( x );
    }
}
```

In Practice

1.15. Write a `while` statement that is equivalent to the following `for` fragment. Why would this be useful?

```
for( ; ; )
    statement
```

1.16. Write a program to generate the addition and multiplication tables for single-digit numbers (the table that elementary school students are accustomed to seeing).

1.17. Write two static methods. The first should return the maximum of three integers, and the second should return the maximum of four integers.

1.18. Write a static method that takes a year as a parameter and returns `true` if the year is a leap year, and `false` otherwise.

Programming Projects

1.19. Write a program to determine all pairs of positive integers, (a, b), such that $a < b < 1000$ and $(a^2 + b^2 + 1)/(ab)$ is an integer.

1.20. Write a method that prints the representation of its integer parameter as a Roman numeral. Thus, if the parameter is 1998, the output is MCMXCVIII.

1.21. Suppose you want to print out numbers in brackets, formatted as follows: [1] [2] [3], and so on. Write a method that takes two parameters: howMany and lineLength. The method should print out line numbers from 1 to howMany in the previous format, but it should not output more than lineLength characters on any one line. It should not start a [unless it can fit the corresponding].

1.22. In the following decimal arithmetic puzzle, each of the ten different letters is assigned a digit. Write a program that finds all possible solutions (one of which is shown).

```
     MARK      A=1  W=2  N=3  R=4  E=5        9147
   + ALLEN     L=6  K=7  I=8  M=9  S=0      + 16653
     -----                                   -----
     WEISS                                   25800
```

References

Some of the C-style material in this chapter is taken from [5]. The complete Java language specification may be found in [4]. A handy reference that lists the library packages and provides full examples is [3]. Introductory Java books include [1] and [2].[2]

1. G. Cornell and C. S. Horstmann, *Core Java*, 3d ed., Prentice-Hall, Englewood Cliffs, NJ (1998).

2. J. Lewis and W. Loftus, *Java Software Solutions: Foundations of Program Design*, Addison-Wesley, Reading, Mass. (1997).

3. D. Flanagan, *Java in a Nutshell*, 2d ed., O'Reilly and Associates, Sebastopol, Calif. (1997).

4. J. Gosling, B. Joy, and G. Steele, *The Java Language Specification*, Addison-Wesley, Reading, Mass. (1996).

5. M. A. Weiss, *Efficient C Programming: A Practical Approach*, Prentice-Hall, Englewood Cliffs, NJ (1995).

[2.] Reference [4] describe Java 1.0.2. At the time of this writing, Java 1.1 has been introduced. It incorporates some significant changes. An update to this book in the form of a future edition likely will reflect the new language features. References [1], [2], and [3] use Java 1.1.

2

References

CHAPTER 1 examined the Java primitive types. All types that are not one of the eight primitive types are *reference types*, including important entities such as strings, arrays, and file streams.
In this chapter, we will see:

- What a reference type and value is
- How reference types differ from primitive types
- Examples of reference types, including strings, arrays, and streams
- How exceptions are used to signal erroneous behavior

2.1 What Is a Reference?

Chapter 1 described the eight primitive types, along with some of the operations that these types can perform. All other types in Java are reference types, including strings, arrays, and file streams. So what is a reference? A *reference variable* (often abbreviated as simply *reference*) in Java is a variable that stores the memory address where an object resides.

As an example, in Figure 2.1 are two objects of type `Point`. It happens, by chance, that these objects are stored in memory locations 1000 and 1024, respectively. For these two objects, there are three references: `point1`, `point2`, and `point3`. `point1` and `point3` both reference the object stored at memory location 1000; `point2` references the object stored at memory location 1024. Both `point1` and `point3` store the value 1000, while `point2` stores the value 1024. Note that the actual locations, such as 1000 and 1024, are assigned by the compiler at its discretion (when it finds available memory). Thus these values are not useful externally as numbers. However, the fact that `point1` and `point3` store identical values is useful: It means they are referencing the same object.

A reference will always store the memory address where some object is residing, unless it is not currently referencing any object. In this case, it will store the *null reference*, `null`. Java does not allow references to primitive variables.

There are two broad categories of operations that can be applied to reference variables. One allows us to examine or manipulate the reference value. For instance, if we change the stored value of `point1` (which is 1000), we could have it reference another object. We can also compare `point1` and `point3` and determine if they are referencing the same object. The other category of operations applies to the object being referenced; perhaps we could examine or change the internal state of one of the `Point` objects. For instance, we could examine some of `Point`'s *x* and *y* coordinates.

Before we describe what can be done with references, let us see what is not allowed. Consider the expression `point1*point2`. Since the stored values of `point1` and `point2` are 1000 and 1024, respectively, their product would be 1024000. However, this is a meaningless calculation that could not have any possible use. Reference variables store addresses, and there is no logical meaning that can be associated with multiplying two addresses.

Similarly, `point1++` has no Java meaning; it suggests that `point1` — 1000 — should be increased to 1001, but in that case it would not be referencing a valid `Point` object. Many languages define the *pointer*, which behaves like a reference variable. However, pointers in C++ are much more dangerous because arithmetic on stored addresses is allowed. Thus, in C++, `point1++` has a meaning. Because C++ allows pointers to primitive types, one must be careful to distinguish between arithmetic on addresses and arithmetic on the objects being referenced. This is done by explicitly *dereferencing* the pointer. In practice, C++'s unsafe pointers tend to cause numerous programming errors.

Some operations are performed on references themselves, while others are performed on the objects being referenced. In Java, the only operators that are allowed for reference types (with one exception made for `Strings`) are assignment via = and equality comparison via == or !=.

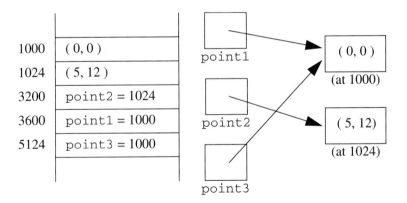

Figure 2.1   An illustration of a reference: The `Point` object stored at memory location 1000 is referenced by both `point1` and `point3`. The `Point` object stored at memory location 1024 is referenced by `point2`. The memory locations where the variables are stored are arbitrary

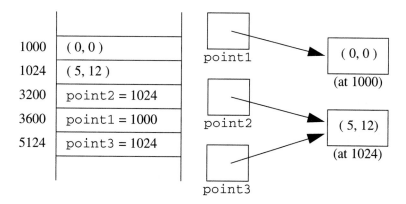

Figure 2.2 The result of `point3=point2`: `point3` now references the same object as `point2`

Figure 2.2 illustrates the assignment operator for reference variables. By assigning `point3` the stored value of `point2`, we have `point3` reference the same object that `point2` was referencing. Now, `point2==point3` is `true` because `point2` and `point3` both store 1024 and thus reference the same object. `point1!=point2` is also `true` because `point1` and `point2` reference different objects.

The other category of operations deals with the object that is being referenced. There are only three basic actions that can be done:

1. Apply a type conversion (Section 1.4.4).
2. Access an internal field or call a method via the dot operator (`.`) (Section 2.2.1).
3. Use the `instanceof` operator to verify that the stored object is of a certain type (Section 3.6.3).

The next section illustrates in more detail the common reference operations.

2.2 Basics of Objects and References

In Java, an *object* is an instance of any of the nonprimitive types. Objects are treated differently from primitive data. Primitive types, as already shown, are handled by *value*, meaning that the values assumed by the primitive variables are stored in those variables and copied from primitive variable to primitive variable during assignments. As shown in Section 2.1, reference variables store references to objects. The actual object is stored somewhere in memory, and the reference variable stores the object's memory address. Thus a reference variable simply represents a name for that part of memory. This means that primitive variables

In Java, an *object* is an instance of any of the nonprimitive types.

and reference variables behave differently. This section examines these differences in more detail and illustrates the operations that are allowed for reference variables.

2.2.1 The Dot Operator (.)

The dot operator (.) is used to select a method that is applied to an object. For instance, suppose we have an object of type `Circle` that defines an `area` method. If `theCircle` references a `Circle`, then we can compute the area of the referenced `Circle` (and save it to a variable of type `double`) by doing this:

```
double theArea = theCircle.area( );
```

It is possible that `theCircle` stores the `null` reference. In this case, applying the dot operator will generate a `NullPointerException` when the program runs. Generally, this will cause abnormal termination.

The dot operator can also be used to access individual components of an object, provided arrangements have been made to allow internal components to be viewable. Chapter 3 discusses how these arrangements are made. It also explains why it is generally preferable to not allow direct access of individual components.

2.2.2 Declaration of Objects

We have already seen the syntax for declaring primitive variables. For objects, there is an important difference. When we declare a reference variable, we are simply providing a name that can be used to reference an object that is stored in memory. However, the declaration by itself does not provide that object. For example, suppose there is an object of type `Button` that we want to add into an existing `Panel` p, using the method `add` (all this is provided in the Java library). Consider the statements

```
Button b;             // b may reference a Button object
b.setLabel( "No" );   // Label the button b refers to "No"
p.add( b );           // and add to Panel p
```

When a reference type is declared, no object is allocated. At that point, the reference is to `null`. *To create the object, use* new.

All seems well with these statements until we remember that b is the name of some `Button` object but no `Button` has been created yet. As a result, after the declaration of b the value stored by the reference variable b is `null`, meaning b is not yet referring to a valid `Button` object. Consequently, the second line is illegal because we are attempting to alter an object that does not exist. In this scenario, the compiler will probably detect the error, stating that "b is uninitialized." In other cases, the compiler will not notice and a run-time error will result in the cryptic `NullPointerException` error message.

The (only common) way to allocate an object is to use the new keyword. new is used to construct an object. One way to do this is as follows:

```
Button b;              // b may reference a Button object
b = new Button( );     // Now b refers to an allocated object
b.setLabel( "No" );    // Label the Button b refers to "No"
p.add( b );            // and add it to Panel p
```

The new keyword is used to construct an object.

Note, parentheses are required after the object name.

It is also possible to combine the declaration and object construction, as in

```
Button b = new Button( );
b.setLabel( "No" );    // Label the Button b refers to "No"
p.add( b );            // and add it to Panel p
```

Parentheses are required when new is used.

Many objects can also be constructed with initial values. For instance, the Button can be constructed with a String that specifies the label:

```
Button b = new Button( "No" );
p.add( b );            // add it to Panel p
```

The construction can specify an initial state of the object.

2.2.3 Garbage Collection

Since all objects must be constructed, we might expect that when they are no longer needed, we must explicitly destroy them. In Java, when a constructed object is no longer referenced by any object variable, the memory it consumes will automatically be reclaimed and therefore be made available. This technique is known as *garbage collection*.

Java uses garbage collection. With garbage collection, unreferenced memory is automatically reclaimed.

2.2.4 The Meaning of =

Suppose we have two primitive variables lhs and rhs where *lhs* and *rhs* stand for *left-hand side* and *right-hand side*, respectively. Then the assignment statement

```
lhs = rhs;
```

lhs and rhs stand for left-hand side and right-hand side, respectively.

has a simple meaning: The value stored in rhs is copied to the primitive variable lhs. Subsequent changes to either lhs or rhs do not affect the other.

For objects, the meaning of = is the same: stored values are copied. If lhs and rhs are references (of compatible types), then after the assignment statement, lhs will refer to the same object that rhs does. Here, what is being copied are addresses. The object that lhs used to refer to is no longer referred to by lhs. If lhs was the only reference to that object, then that object is now unreferenced and subject to garbage collection. Note that the objects are not copied.

For objects, = is a reference assignment, rather than an object copy.

Here are some examples. First, suppose we want two `Button` objects. Then suppose we try to obtain them first by creating `noButton`. Then we attempt to create `yesButton` by modifying `noButton` as follows:

```
Button noButton = new Button( "No" );
Button yesButton = noButton;
yesButton.setLabel( "Yes" );
p.add( noButton );
p.add( yesButton );
```

This does not work because only one `Button` object has been constructed. Thus the second statement simply states that `yesButton` is now another name for the constructed `Button` at line one. That constructed `Button` is now known by two names. On line three, the constructed `Button` has its label changed to `Yes`, but this means that the single `Button` object, known by two names, is now labelled `Yes`. The last two lines add that `Button` object to the `Panel p` twice.

The fact that `yesButton` never referred to its own object is immaterial in this example. The problem is the assignment. Consider

```
Button noButton = new Button( "No" );
Button yesButton = new Button( );
yesButton = noButton;
yesButton.setLabel( "Yes" );
p.add( noButton );
p.add( yesButton );
```

The consequences are the same. Here, there are two `Button` objects that have been constructed. At the end of the sequence, the first object is being referenced by both `noButton` and `yesButton`, while the second object is unreferenced.

At first glance, the fact that objects cannot be copied seems like a severe limitation. Actually, it is not, although this does take a little getting used to. (Some objects do need to be copied. For those, if a `clone` method is available, it should be used. `clone` calls `new` to obtain a duplicate object. However, `clone` is not used in this text.)

2.2.5 Parameter Passing

Call-by-value means that for reference types, the formal parameter references the same object as does the actual argument.

Because of call-by-value, the actual arguments are sent into the formal parameters using normal assignment. If the parameter is a reference type, then we know that normal assignment means that the formal parameter now references the same object as does the actual argument. Any method applied to the formal parameter is thus also being applied to the actual argument. In other languages, this is known as *call-by-reference parameter passing*. Using this terminology for Java would be somewhat misleading because it implies that the parameter passing is different. In reality, the parameter passing has not changed; rather, it is the parameters that have changed, from nonreference types to reference types.

2.2.6 The Meaning of ==

For primitive types, == is true if the stored values are identical. For reference types, its meaning is different but is perfectly consistent with the previous discussion.

Two reference types are equal via == if they refer to the same stored object (or they are both null). Consider, for example, the following:

```
Button a = new Button( "Yes" );
Button b = new Button( "Yes" );
Button c = b;
```

For reference types, == is true only if the two references reference the same object.

Here, we have two objects. The first is known by the name a, and the second is known by two names: b and c. b==c is true. However, even though a and b are referencing objects that seem to have the same value, a==b is false, since they reference different objects. Similar rules apply for !=.

Sometimes it is important to know if the objects being referenced are identical. All objects can be compared by using equals, but for many objects (including Button) equals returns false unless the two references are referencing the same object (in other words, for some objects equals is no more than the == test). We will see an example of where equals is useful when the String object is discussed in Section 2.3.

The equals method can be used to test whether two references reference objects that have identical states.

2.2.7 Operator Overloading for Objects

Except for the single exception described in the next section, operators cannot be defined to work for objects. Thus there is no < operator available for any object. Instead, a named method, such as lessThan, must be defined for this task.

2.3 Strings

Strings in Java are handled with the String object. The language does make it appear that the String is a primitive type because it defines the + and += operator for concatenation. However, this is the only reference type for which any operator overloading is allowed. Otherwise, the String behaves like any other object.

The String object behaves like a reference type.

2.3.1   Basics of String Manipulation

Strings are *immutable*; that is, the String object will not be changed.

There are two fundamental rules about the String object. First, with the exception of the concatenation operators, it behaves like an object. Second, the String is *immutable*. This means that once a String object is constructed, its contents may not be changed.

Because a String is immutable, it is always safe to use the = operator with it. Thus a String may be declared as follows:

```
String empty   = "";
String message = "Hello"
String repeat  = message;
```

After these declarations, there are two String objects. The first is the empty string, which is referenced by empty. The second is the String "Hello" which is referenced by both message and repeat. For most objects being referenced by both message and repeat could be a problem. However, because Strings are immutable, the sharing of String objects is safe, as well as efficient. The only way to change the value that the string repeat refers to is to construct a new String and have repeat reference it. This has no effect on the String that message references.

2.3.2   String Concatenation

Java does not allow operator overloading for reference types. However, a special language exemption is granted for string concatenation.

String concatenation is performed with + (and +=).

The operator +, when at least one operand is a String, performs concatenation. The result is a reference to a newly constructed String object. For example,

```
"this" + " that"    // Generates "this that"
"abc" + 5           // Generates "abc5"
5 + "abc"           // Generates "5abc"
"a" + "b" + "c"     // Generates "abc"
```

Single-character strings should not be replaced with character constants; Exercise 2.5 asks you to show why. Note that operator + is left-associative, and thus

```
"a" + 1 + 2         // Generates "a12"
1 + 2 + "a"         // Generates "3a"
1 + ( 2 + "a" )     // Generates "12a"
```

Also, operator += is provided for the String. The effect of str+=exp is the same as str=str+exp. Specifically, this means that str will reference the newly constructed String generated by str+exp.

2.3.3   Comparing Strings

Since the basic assignment operator works for `String`s, it is tempting to assume that the relational and equality operators also work. This is not true.

In accordance with the ban on operator overloading, relational operators (`<`, `>`, `<=`, and `>=`) are not defined for the `String` object. Further, `==` and `!=` have the typical meaning for reference variables. For two `String` objects `lhs` and `rhs`, for example `lhs==rhs` is `true` only if `lhs` and `rhs` refer to the same `String` object. Thus, if they refer to different objects that have identical contents, `lhs==rhs` is `false`. Similar logic applies for `!=`.

To compare two `String` objects for equality, we use `equals`. `lhs.equals(rhs)` is `true` if `lhs` and `rhs` reference `String`s that store identical values.

A more general test can be performed with the method `compareTo`. `lhs.compareTo(rhs)` compares two `String` objects, `lhs` and `rhs`. It returns a negative number, zero, or a positive number, depending on whether `lhs` is lexicographically less than, equal to, or greater than `rhs`, respectively.

Use *equals* *and* *compareTo* *to perform string comparison.*

2.3.4   Other `String` Methods

The length of a `String` object (an empty string has length zero) can be obtained with the method `length`. Since `length` is a method, parentheses are required.

Two methods are defined to access individual characters in a `String`. The method `charAt` gets a single character by specifying a position (the first position is position 0). The method `substring` returns a reference to a newly constructed `String`. The call is made by specifying the starting point and the first nonincluded position.

Here is an example of these three methods:

Use *length*, *charAt*, *and* *substring* *to compute string length, get a single character, and get a substring, respectively.*

```
String greeting = "hello";
int len     = greeting.length( );        // len is 5
char ch     = greeting.charAt( 1 );      // ch  is 'e'
String sub = greeting.substring( 2, 4 ); // sub is "ll"
```

2.3.5   Converting between Strings and Primitive Types

An appropriate method `toString` can be used to convert any primitive type to a `String`. As an example, `Integer.toString(45)` returns a reference to the newly constructed `String` `"45"`. Many objects also provide an implementation of `toString`. In fact, when operator `+` has only one `String` argument, the non`String` argument is converted to a `String` by automatically applying `toString`. For the integer types, an alternative form of `toString` allows the specification of a radix. Thus

toString *converts primitive types (and objects) to a* *String*.

```
System.out.println( Integer.toString( 55, 2 ) );
```

prints out the binary representation of 55.

The int value that is represented by a String can be obtained by calling the method Integer.parseInt. This method generates an exception if the String does not represent an int. Exceptions are discussed in Section 2.5. More work is required to obtain a double from a String. Here are some examples:

```
int    x = Integer.parseInt( "75" );
double y = Double.valueOf( "3.14" ).doubleValue( );
```

2.4   Arrays

An *array* stores a collection of identically typed entities.

An *aggregate* is a collection of entities stored in one unit. An *array* is the basic mechanism for storing a collection of identically typed entities. In Java the array is not a primitive type. Instead, it behaves very much like an object. Thus many of the rules for objects also apply to arrays.

The *array indexing operator* [] provides access to any object in the array.

Each entity in the array can be accessed via the *array indexing operator* []. We say that the [] operator *indexes* the array, meaning that it specifies which object is to be accessed. Unlike C and C++, bounds checking is performed automatically.

Arrays are indexed starting at zero. The number of items stored in the array is obtained by the *length* field. No parentheses are used.

In Java, arrays are always indexed starting at zero. Thus an array a of three items stores a[0], a[1], and a[2]. The number of items that can be stored in an array a can always be obtained by a.length. Note that there are no parentheses. A typical array loop would use

```
for( int i = 0; i < a.length; i++ )
```

2.4.1   Declaration, Assignment, and Methods

An array is an object, so when the array declaration

```
int [ ] array1;
```

To allocate an array, use new.

is given, no memory is yet allocated to store the array. array1 is simply a name (reference) for an array, and at this point is null. To have 100 ints, for example, we issue a new command:

```
array1 = new int [ 100 ];
```

Now array1 references an array of 100 ints.

There are other ways to declare arrays. For instance, in some contexts

```
int [ ] array2 = new int [ 100 ];
```

is acceptable. Also, initializer lists can be used, as in C or C++, to specify initial values. In the next example, an array of four `ints` is allocated and then referenced by `array3`.

```
int [ ] array3 = { 3, 4, 10, 6 };
```

The brackets can go either before or after the array name. Placing them before makes it easier to see that the name is an array type, so that is the style used here. Declaring an array of objects (rather than primitive types) uses the same syntax. Note, however, that when we allocate an array of objects, each object initially stores a `null` reference. Each also must be set to reference a constructed object. For instance, an array of five buttons is constructed as

```
Button [ ] arrayOfButtons;
arrayOfButtons = new Button [ 5 ];
for( int i = 0; i < arrayOfButtons.length; i++ )
    arrayOfButtons[ i ] = new Button( );
```

Figure 2.3 illustrates the use of arrays in Java. In the Florida lottery, six different numbers between 1 and 49 (inclusive) are selected each week. The program in the figure repeatedly chooses numbers for 1,000 games. The output is the number of times each number has occurred. Line 15 declares an array of integers that keeps count of the occurrences of each number. Because arrays are indexed starting at zero, the + 1 is crucial. Without it, we would have an array whose indexible range was 0 to 48, and thus any access to index 49 would be out-of-bounds. The loop on lines 16 and 17 initializes the array entries to zero. The rest of the program is relatively straightforward. It uses the `Random` object defined in Chapter 9. The `randomInt` method repeatedly gives a (somewhat) random number in the specified range. The results are output at lines 26 and 27.

> Always be sure to declare the correct array size. Off-by-one errors are common.

Since an array is a reference type, = does not copy arrays. Instead, if `lhs` and `rhs` are arrays the effect of

```
int [ ] lhs = new int [ 100 ];
int [ ] rhs = new int [ 100 ];
    ...
lhs = rhs
```

is that the array object that was referenced by `rhs` is now also referenced by `lhs`. Thus changing `rhs[0]` also changes `lhs[0]`. (To make `lhs` an independent copy of `rhs`, one would use the `clone` method.)

Finally, an array can be used as a parameter to a method. The rules follow logically from our understanding that an array name is a reference. Suppose we have a method `methodCall` that accepts one array of `int` as its parameter. The caller/callee views are

```
 1  import Supporting.Random;
 2
 3  public class Lottery
 4  {
 5      // Generate lottery numbers (from 1-49)
 6      // Print number of occurrences of each number
 7
 8      public static final int DIFF_NUMBERS      =   49;
 9      public static final int NUMBERS_PER_GAME =    6;
10      public static final int GAMES            = 1000;
11
12      public static void main( String [ ] args )
13      {
14          // Generate the numbers
15          int [ ] numbers = new int [ DIFF_NUMBERS + 1 ];
16          for( int i = 0; i < numbers.length; i++ )
17              numbers[ i ] = 0;
18
19          Random r = new Random( );
20
21          for( int i = 0; i < GAMES; i++ )
22              for( int j = 0; j < NUMBERS_PER_GAME; j++ )
23                  numbers[ r.randomInt( 1, DIFF_NUMBERS ) ]++;
24
25          // Output the summary
26          for( int k = 1; k <= DIFF_NUMBERS; k++ )
27              System.out.println( k + ": " + numbers[ k ] );
28      }
29  }
```

Figure 2.3   Simple demonstration of arrays

```
methodCall( actualArray );            // method call
methodCall( int [ ] formalArray )  // method declaration
```

The contents of an array are passed by reference.

In accordance with the parameter-passing conventions for Java reference types, formalArray references the same array object as actualArray. Thus formalArray[i] accesses actualArray[i]. This means that the variables represented by the indexed array are modifiable. This will always be the case. Also note that a statement such as

```
formalArray = new int [ 20 ];
```

has no effect on actualArray. Finally, since array names are simply references, they can be returned.

2.4.2   Dynamic Array Expansion

Suppose we want to read a sequence of numbers and store them in an array for processing. The fundamental property of an array requires us to declare a size so that the compiler can allocate the correct amount of memory. Also, we must make this declaration prior to the first access of the array. If we have no idea how many items to expect, then it is difficult to make a reasonable choice for the array size. This section shows how to expand arrays if the initial size is too small. This technique is called *dynamic array expansion* and allows us to allocate arbitrary-sized arrays and make them larger or smaller as the program runs.

Dynamic array expansion allows us to allocate arbitrary-sized arrays and make them larger if needed.

The allocation method for arrays that we have seen thus far is

```
int [ ] a = new int[ 10 ];
```

Suppose that we decide, after the declarations, that we really need 12 `int`s instead of 10. In this case, we can use the following maneuver:

```
int [ ] original = a;      // 1. Save reference to a
a = new int [ 12 ];        // 2. Have a reference more memory
for( int i = 0; i < 10; i++ )   // 3. Copy the old data over
    a[ i ] = original[ i ];
```

A moment's thought will convince you that this is an expensive operation. This is because we copy all of the elements from `original` back to a. If, for instance, this array expansion is in response to reading input, it would be inefficient to reexpand every time we read a few elements. Thus when array expansion is implemented, we always make it some *multiplicative* constant times as large. For instance, we might expand it to be twice as large. In this way, when we expand the array from N items to $2N$ items, the cost of the N copies can be apportioned over the next N items that can be inserted into the array without an expansion.

Always expand the array to a size that is some multiplicative constant times as large. Doubling is a good choice.

To make things more concrete, Figure 2.4 shows a program that reads an unlimited number of integers from the standard input and stores the result in a dynamically expanding array. The routine `resize` performs the array expansion (or shrinking), returning a reference to the new array. Similarly, the method `getInts` returns (a reference to) the array where it will reside.

At the start of `getInts`, `itemsRead` is set to 0 and we start with an initial five-element array. We repeatedly read new items at line 27 and 29. If the array is full, as indicated by a successful test at line 30, then the array is expanded by calling `resize`. Lines 43 to 49 perform the array expansion using the exact strategy outlined previously. At line 32, the actual input item is assigned to the array and the number of items read is incremented. If an error occurs on input, we simply stop processing. Finally, at line 37 we shrink the array to match the number of items read prior to returning.

```
 1  import java.io.*;
 2  public class ReadInts
 3  {
 4      public static void main( String [ ] args )
 5      {
 6          int [ ] array = getInts( );
 7          for( int i = 0; i < array.length; i++ )
 8              System.out.println( array[ i ] );
 9      }
10
11      // Read an unlimited number of ints with no attempts at
12      // error recovery; return an int [ ]
13      public static int [ ] getInts( )
14      {
15              // BufferedReader is discussed in Section 2.6
16          BufferedReader in = new BufferedReader( new
17                              InputStreamReader( System.in ) );
18          int inputVal = 0;
19          int [ ] array = new int[ 5 ];
20          int itemsRead = 0;
21          String oneLine;
22
23          System.out.println( "Enter any number of integers," +
24                              "one per line: " );
25          try
26          {
27              while( ( oneLine = in.readLine( ) ) != null )
28              {
29                  inputVal = Integer.parseInt( oneLine );
30                  if( itemsRead == array.length )
31                      array = resize( array, array.length * 2 );
32                  array[ itemsRead++ ] = inputVal;
33              }
34          }
35          catch( Exception e ) { } // No error handling
36          System.out.println( "Done reading" );
37          return resize( array, itemsRead );
38      }
39
40      // Resize an int[ ] array; return new array
41      public static int [ ] resize( int [ ] array, int newSize )
42      {
43          int [ ] original = array;
44          int numToCopy = Math.min( original.length, newSize );
45
46          array = new int[ newSize ];
47          for( int i = 0; i < numToCopy; i++ )
48              array[ i ] = original[ i ];
49          return array;
50      }
51  }
```

Figure 2.4   Code to read an unlimited number of `int`s and output them

2.4.3   Multidimensional Arrays

Sometimes arrays need to be accessed based on more than one index. A common example of this is a matrix. A *multidimensional array* is an array that is accessed by more than one index. It is allocated by specifying the size of its indices, and each element is accessed by placing each index in its own pair of brackets. As an example, the declaration

A multidimensional array is an array that is accessed by more than one index.

```
int [ ][ ] x = new int[ 2 ][ 3 ];
```

defines the two-dimensional array x, with the first index ranging from 0 to 1 and the second index ranging from 0 to 2 (for a total of six objects). The compiler sets aside six memory locations for these objects.

2.4.4   Command-line Arguments

Command-line arguments are available by examining the parameter to `main`. The array of strings represents the additional command-line arguments. For instance, when the program is invoked,

Command-line arguments are available by examining the parameter to main.

```
java Echo this that
```

`args[0]` references the `String "this"` and `args[1]` references the `String "that"`. Thus the program in Figure 2.5 implements the `echo` command.

```
1  public class Echo
2  {
3        // List the command-line arguments
4        public static void main( String [ ] args )
5        {
6            for( int i = 0; i < args.length - 1; i++ )
7                System.out.print( args[ i ] + " " );
8            if( args.length != 0 )
9                System.out.println( args[ args.length - 1 ] );
10           else
11               System.out.println( "No arguments to echo" );
12       }
13 }
```

Figure 2.5   The echo command

2.5 Exception Handling

Exceptions are
used to handle
exceptional oc-
currences such as
errors.

Exceptions are objects that store information and are transmitted outside the normal return sequence. They are propagated back through the calling sequence until some routine *catches* the exception. Exceptions are used to handle *exceptional occurrences* such as errors.

2.5.1 Processing Exceptions

A *try block* en-
closes code that
might generate
an exception.

The code in Figure 2.6 illustrates the use of exceptions. Code that might result in an exception's being propagated is enclosed in a try block. The try block extends from lines 15 to 19. Immediately following the try block are the exception handlers. This part of the code is jumped to only if an exception is raised; at the point the exception is raised, the try block in which it came from is considered terminated. Each catch block is attempted in order until a matching handler is found. Since Exception matches all exceptions that are of interest for us, it will match whatever exception is generated in the try block. Specifically, these exceptions are IOException, generated by readLine if some unexpected error occurs, and the NumberFormatException, generated by parseInt if oneLine is not convertible to an int.

```
1  import java.io.*;
2
3  public class DivideByTwo
4  {
5      public static void main( String [ ] args )
6      {
7              // BufferedReader is discussed in Section 2.6
8          BufferedReader in = new BufferedReader( new
9                              InputStreamReader( System.in ) );
10         int x;
11         String oneLine;
12
13         System.out.println( "Enter an integer: " );
14         try
15         {
16             oneLine = in.readLine( );
17             x = Integer.parseInt( oneLine );
18             System.out.println( "Half of x is " + ( x / 2 ) );
19         }
20         catch( Exception e )
21           { System.out.println( e ); }
22      }
23  }
```

Figure 2.6   Simple program to illustrate exceptions

The code in the `catch` block — in this case line 21 — is executed. Then the `catch` block and the block containing the `try`/`catch` combination is considered terminated.[1] A meaningful message is printed from the `Exception` object `e`. Alternatively, additional processing and more detailed error messages could be given.

A catch block processes an exception.

2.5.2 The `finally` Clause

Some objects that are created in a `try` block must be cleaned up. For instance, files that are opened in the `try` block may need to be closed prior to leaving the `try` block. One problem with this is that if an exception object is thrown inside the `try` block, the clean up might be omitted because the exception will cause an immediate break from the `try` block. Although we can place the clean up immediately after the last `catch` clause, this works only if the exception is caught by one of the `catch` clauses. And this may be difficult to guarantee.

The finally clause is always executed prior to completion of a block, regardless of exceptions.

The `finally` clause that follows the last `catch` block (or the `try` block if there are no `catch` blocks) is used in this situation. The `finally` clause consists of the keyword `finally` followed by the `finally` block. There are three basic scenarios.

1. If the `try` block executes without exception, transfer passes to the `finally` block. This is true even if the `try` block exits prior to the last statement via a `return`, `break`, or `continue`.
2. If an uncaught exception is encountered inside the `try` block, control passes to the `finally` block. Then, after executing the `finally` block, the exception propagates.
3. If a caught exception is encountered in the `try` block, control passes to the appropriate `catch` block. Then, after executing the `catch` block, the `finally` block is executed.

2.5.3 Common Exceptions

There are several types of standard exceptions in Java. The *standard run-time exceptions* include events such as integer divide-by-zero and illegal array access. Since these events can happen virtually anywhere, it would be overly burdensome to require exception handlers for them. If a `catch` block is provided, these exceptions behave like any other exception. If a `catch` block is not provided for a standard exception, and a standard exception is thrown, then it propagates as usual, possibly past `main`. In this case, it causes an abnormal program termination, with an error message. Some of the common standard run-time exceptions are shown in Figure 2.7.

Run-time exceptions do not have to be handled.

---

[1]. Note that both `try` and `catch` require a block and not simply a single statement. Thus braces are not optional. Some older Java compilers illegally accept code containing missing braces.

Standard Run-time Exception	Meaning
`ArithmeticException`	Overflow or integer division by zero.
`NumberFormatException`	Illegal conversion of `String` to numeric type.
`IndexOutOfBoundsException`	Illegal index into an array or `String`.
`NegativeArraySizeException`	Attempt to create a negative-length array.
`NullPointerException`	Illegal attempt to use a null reference.
`SecurityException`	Run-time security violation.

Figure 2.7   Common standard run-time exceptions

Checked excep-tions must be han-dled or listed in a *throws clause*.

Most exceptions are of the *standard checked exception* variety. If a method is called that might either directly or indirectly throw a standard checked exception, then the programmer must either provide a `catch` block for it, or explicitly indicate that the exception is to be propagated by use of a *throws clause* in the method declaration. Note that eventually it should be handled because `main` should not have a `throws` clause. Chapter 4 shows how we can design new exceptions. Some of the common standard checked exceptions are shown in Figure 2.8.

Errors are unrecov-erable exceptions.

Errors are exceptions, but they are not matched by `Exception`. They are typically unrecoverable. The most common error is `OutOfMemoryError`. To catch every possible exception, catch a `Throwable` object.

2.5.4 The `throw` and `throws` Clauses

The *throw clause* is used to throw an exception.

The programmer can generate an exception by use of the *throw clause*. For instance, we can throw an `Exception` object by

```
throw new Exception( "Bad news" );
```

Standard Checked Exception	Meaning
`java.io.EOFException`	End-of-file before completion of input.
`java.io.FileNotFoundException`	File not found to open.
`java.io.IOException`	Includes most I/O exceptions.
`InterruptedException`	Thrown by the `Thread.sleep` method.

Figure 2.8   Common standard checked exceptions

```
 1  import java.io.*;
 2
 3  public class ThrowDemo
 4  {
 5      public static void processFile( String toFile )
 6                                          throws IOException
 7      {
 8          // Omitted implementation propagates all
 9          // thrown IOException back to the caller
10      }
11
12      public static void main( String [ ] args )
13      {
14          for( int i = 0; i < args.length; i++ )
15          {
16              try
17                { processFile( args[ i ] ); }
18              catch( IOException e )
19                { System.err.println( e ); }
20          }
21      }
22  }
```

Figure 2.9   Illustration of the throws clause

Typically, Exception is not thrown; instead, a user-defined exception object is thrown. Details of this are provided in Chapter 4.

As mentioned earlier, standard checked exceptions must either be caught or explicitly propagated to the calling routine, but they should, as a last resort, eventually be handled in main. To do the latter, the method that is unwilling to catch the exception must indicate, via a *throws clause*, which exceptions it may propagate. The throws clause is attached at the end of the method header. Figure 2.9 illustrates a method that propagates any IOExceptions that it encounters; these must eventually be caught in main (since we will not place a throws clause in main).

The throws clause indicates propagated exceptions.

2.6   Input and Output

Input and output (I/O) in Java is achieved through the use of the java.io package. The statement

```
import java.io.*;
```

should appear in any program that makes more than trivial use of the I/O routines. The Java library is very sophisticated and has a host of options. We examine only the most basic uses, concentrating entirely on formatted I/O.

java.io should be imported for any nontrivial I/O.

2.6.1 Basic Stream Operations

The predefined streams are System.in, System.out, and System.err.

Three streams are predefined for terminal I/O: System.in, the standard input; System.out, the standard output; and System.err, the standard error.

As already mentioned, the print and println methods are used for formatted output. Any type can be converted to a String suitable for printing by calling its toString method; in many cases, this is done automatically. Unlike with C and C++, which have an enormous number of formatting options, output in Java is done almost exclusively by String concatenation, with no built-in formatting.

BufferedReader is used for line-at-a-time input.

A simple method for reading formatted input is to read a single line into a String object using readLine. The readline method reads until it encounters a line terminator or end of file. The characters that are read, minus the line terminator (if read), are returned as a newly constructed String. To use readLine, we must first construct a BufferedReader object from an InputStreamReader object that is itself constructed from System.in. This was illustrated in Figure 2.6 at lines 8 and 9.

If an immediate end of file is encountered, then null is returned. If a read error occurs for some reason other than end of file, then some IOException is generated. Note that the IOException, which is a standard checked exception, must eventually be caught. In many instances, the IOException is allowed to propagate back to a catch block in the main method; this technique was illustrated in Figure 2.9.

2.6.2 The **StringTokenizer** Object

Recall that to read a single primitive type, such as an int, we use readLine to read the line as a String and then apply a method to generate the primitive type from the String. For int, we can use parseInt.

StringTokenizer is used to extract delimited strings from a large array.

Sometimes we have several items on a line. For instance, suppose each line has two ints. Java provides the StringTokenizer object to separate a String into tokens. To use it, provide the import directive

```
import java.util.*;
```

Use of the string tokenizer is illustrated in Figure 2.10. First, at line 19, we construct a StringTokenizer object by providing the String representing the line of input. The countTokens method, shown on line 20, will provide the number of tokens in the String; in this example, this should be two, or else the input is in error. Then, the nextToken method returns the next token as a String. This method throws NoSuchElementException if there is no token, but this is an Error and does not have to be caught. At lines 22 and 23, we use nextToken followed by parseInt to obtain an int. All errors, including the failure to provide exactly two tokens, are handled in the `catch` block. As usual, more effort could go into better error messages.

By default, tokens are separated by whitespace. The `StringTokenizer` can be constructed to recognize other characters as delimiters and to include these delimiters as tokens.

2.6.3 Sequential Files

One of the basic rules of Java is that what works for terminal I/O also works for files. To deal with a file, we do not construct a `BufferedReader` object from an `InputStreamReader`. Instead, we construct it from a `FileReader` object, which itself can be constructed by providing a filename.

FileReader is used for file input.

```
 1  import java.io.*;
 2  import java.util.*;
 3
 4  public class MaxTest
 5  {
 6      public static void main( String [ ] args )
 7      {
 8          BufferedReader in = new BufferedReader( new
 9                          InputStreamReader( System.in ) );
10          String oneLine;
11          StringTokenizer str;
12          int x;
13          int y;
14
15          System.out.println( "Enter 2 ints on one line: " );
16          try
17          {
18              oneLine = in.readLine( );
19              str = new StringTokenizer( oneLine );
20              if( str.countTokens( ) != 2 )
21                  throw new NumberFormatException( );
22              x = Integer.parseInt( str.nextToken( ) );
23              y = Integer.parseInt( str.nextToken( ) );
24              System.out.println( "Max: " + Math.max( x, y ) );
25          }
26          catch( Exception e )
27            { System.err.println( "Error: need two ints" ); }
28      }
29  }
```

Figure 2.10   *Program that demonstrates the string tokenizer*

```
 0  import java.io.*
 1  public class ListFiles
 2  {
 3      public static void main( String [ ] args )
 4      {
 5          if( args.length == 0 )
 6              System.out.println( "No files specified" );
 7          for( int i = 0; i < args.length; i++ )
 8              listFile( args[ i ] );
 9      }
10
11      public static void listFile( String fileName )
12      {
13          FileReader theFile;
14          BufferedReader fileIn = null;
15          String oneLine;
16
17          System.out.println( "FILE: " + fileName );
18          try
19          {
20              theFile = new FileReader( fileName );
21              fileIn  = new BufferedReader( theFile );
22              while( ( oneLine = fileIn.readLine( ) ) != null )
23                  System.out.println( oneLine );
24          }
25          catch( Exception e )
26            { System.out.println( e ); }
27
28          // Close the stream
29          try
30          {
31              if( fileIn != null )
32                  fileIn.close( );
33          }
34          catch( IOException e ) { }
35      }
36  }
```

Figure 2.11   Program to list contents of a file

An example that illustrates these basic ideas is shown in Figure 2.11. Here, we have a program that will list the contents of the text files that are specified as command-line arguments. The main routine simply steps through the command-line arguments, passing each one to listFile. In listFile, we construct the FileReader object at line 20, and then use it to construct a BufferedReader object — fileIn — at line 21. At that point, reading is identical to what we have already seen.

After we are done with the file, we must close it; otherwise, we could eventually run out of streams. Note that this cannot be done at the end of the try block, since an exception could cause a premature exit from the block. Thus we close the file after the `try/catch` sequence. Because all recoverable errors are caught by `Exception`, a `finally` clause is not needed. We are certain to reach the close statement if there is more work to do.

Formatted file output is similar to file input. Since we do not use file output in this text, you should refer to a Java reference for more details on file output.

Summary

This chapter examined reference types. A reference is a variable that stores either the memory address where an object resides or the special reference `null`. Only objects may be referenced; any object can be referenced by several reference variables. When two references are compared via ==, the result is `true` if both references refer to the same object. Similarly, = makes a reference variable reference another object. Only a few other operations are available. The most significant is the dot operator, which allows the selection of an object's method or access of its internal data.

Because there are only eight primitive types, virtually everything of consequence in Java is an object and is accessed by a reference. This includes `Strings`, arrays, `Exception` objects, data and file streams, and the string tokenizer.

The `String` is a special reference type because + and += can be used for concatenation. Otherwise, a `String` is like any other reference; `equals` is required to test if the states of two `Strings` are identical. An array is a collection of identically typed values. The array is indexed starting at 0, and index range checking is guaranteed to be performed. Arrays can be expanded dynamically by using `new` to allocate a larger amount of memory and then copying over individual elements.

Exceptions are used to signal exceptional events. An exception is signaled by the `throw` clause; it is propagated until handled by a `catch` block that is associated with a `try` block. Except for the run-time exceptions and `Errors`, each method must signal the exceptions that it might propagate by using a `throws` list.

The `StringTokenizer` is used to parse a `String` into other `Strings`. Typically, it is used in conjunction with other input routines. Input is handled by `BufferedReader`, `InputStreamReader`, and `FileReader` objects.

The next chapter shows how to design new types by defining a *class*.

Objects of the Game

aggregate A collection of objects stored in one unit. (36)
array Stores a collection of identically typed objects. (36)
array indexing operator [] Provides access to any element in the array. (36)
BufferedReader Used for line-at-a-time input. (46)
call by reference In many programming languages, means that the formal

parameter is a reference to the actual argument. This is the natural effect achieved in Java when call-by-value is used on reference types. (32)

catch block Used to process an exception. (43)

checked exception Must be either caught or explicitly allowed to propagate by a `throws` clause. (44)

command-line argument Accessed by a parameter to `main`. (41)

construction For objects, is performed via the `new` keyword. (30)

dot member operator (.) Allows access to each member of the structure. (30)

dynamic array expansion Allows us to make arrays larger if needed. (39)

equals Used to test if the values stored in two objects are the same. (33)

Error An unrecoverable exception. (44)

exception Used to handle exception occurrences, such as errors. (42)

FileReader Used for file input. (47)

finally clause Always executed prior to exiting a `try/catch` sequence. (43)

garbage collection Automatic reclaiming of unreferenced memory. (31)

immutable Object whose state cannot change. Specifically, the `String` is immutable. (34)

input and output (I/O) Achieved through the use of the `java.io` package. (45)

java.io Package that is imported for nontrivial I/O. (45)

java.util Package that is imported to use `StringTokenizer`. (46)

length field Used to determine the size of an array. (36)

length method Used to determine the length of a string. (35)

lhs and rhs Stands for left-hand side and right-hand side, respectively. (31)

multidimensional array An array that is accessed by more than one index. (41)

new Used to construct an object. (31)

null reference The value of an object reference that does not refer to any object. (27)

NullPointerException Generated when attempting to apply a method to a `null` reference. (30)

object A nonprimitive entity. (29)

reference type Any type that is not a primitive type. (29)

run-time exception Does not have to be handled. Examples include `ArithmeticException` and `NullPointerException`. (43)

String A special object used to store a collection of characters. (33)

string concatenation Performed with + and += operators. (34)

StringTokenizer Used to extract delimited `Strings` from a single `String`. (46)

System.in, **System.out**, and **System.err** The predefined I/O streams. (46)

throw clause Used to throw an exception. (44)

throws clause Indicates that a method might propagate an exception. (45)

toString method Converts a primitive type or object to a `String`. (35)

try block Encloses code that might generate an exception. (42)

Common Errors

1. For reference types and arrays, = does not perform a copy of object values. Instead, it copies addresses.

2. For reference types and strings, `equals` should be used instead of == to test if two objects have identical states.

3. Off-by-one errors are common in all languages.

4. Reference types are initialized to `null` by default. No object is constructed without calling `new`. An "uninitialized reference variable" or `NullPointerException` indicates that you forgot to allocate the object.

5. In Java, arrays are indexed from 0 to `N-1`, where `N` is the array size. However, range checking is performed, so an out-of-bounds array access is detected at run-time.

6. Two-dimensional arrays are indexed as `A[i][j]`, not `A[i,j]`.

7. Checked exceptions must either be caught or explicitly allowed to propagate with a `throws` clause.

8. Use `" "` and not `' '` for outputting a blank.

On the Internet

Following are the available files for this chapter. Everything is self-contained, and nothing is used later in the text. All files are in directory **Chapter02**.

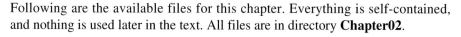

DivideByTwo.java	Contains the code for the example in Figure 2.6
Echo.java	Contains the code for the example in Figure 2.5.
ListFiles.java	Contains the code for the example in Figure 2.11.
Lottery.java	Contains the code for the example in Figure 2.3.
MaxTest.java	Contains the code for the example in Figure 2.10.
ReadInts.java	Contains the code for the example in Figure 2.4.

Exercises

In Short

2.1. List the major differences between reference types and primitive types.
2.2. List five operations that can be applied to a reference type.
2.3. Describe how exceptions work in Java.
2.4. List the basic operations that can be performed on strings.

In Theory

2.5. If x and y have the values of 5 and 7, respectively, what is output by the following:

```
System.out.println( x + ' ' + y );
System.out.println( x + " " + y );
```

In Practice

2.6. A *checksum* is the 32-bit integer that is the sum of the Unicode characters in a file (we allow silent overflow, but silent overflow is unlikely if all the characters are ASCII). Two identical files have the same checksum. Write a program to compute the checksum of a file that is supplied as a command-line argument.

2.7. Modify the program in Figure 2.11 so that if no command-line arguments are given, then the standard input is used.

2.8. Write a method that returns `true` if `String str1` is a prefix of `String str2`. Do not use any of the general string searching routines except `charAt`.

Programming Projects

2.9. Write a program that outputs the number of characters, words, and lines in the files that are supplied as command-line arguments.

2.10. Implement a text file copy program. Include a test to make sure that the source and destination files are different. You will need to read a Java reference to learn how file output is performed.

References

More information can be found in the references at the end of Chapter 1.

3   *Objects and Classes*

T HIS chapter begins the discussion of *object-oriented programming*. A fundamental component of object-oriented programming is the specification, implementation, and use of objects. In Chapter 2, we saw several examples of objects, including strings and files, that are part of the mandatory Java library. We also saw that these objects have an internal state that can be manipulated by applying the dot operator to select a method. In Java, the state and functionality of an object is given by defining a *class*. An object is then an instance of a class.

In this chapter, we will see:

- How Java uses the class to achieve *encapsulation* and *information hiding*
- How classes are implemented and automatically documented
- How classes are grouped into *packages*

3.1   What Is Object-oriented Programming?

Object-oriented programming appears to be emerging as the dominant paradigm of the nineties. In this section we discuss some of the things that Java provides in the way of object-oriented support and mention some of the principles that are seen in object-oriented programming.

At the heart of object-oriented programming is the *object*. An object is a data type that has structure and state. Each object defines operations that may access or manipulate that state. As we have already seen, in Java an object is distinguished from a primitive type, but this is a particular feature of Java rather than the object-oriented paradigm. In addition to performing general operations, we can do the following:

Objects are entities that have structure and state. Each object defines operations that may access or manipulate that state.

- Create new objects, possibly with initialization.
- Copy or test for equality.
- Perform I/O on these objects.

An object is an *atomic unit*. Its parts cannot be dissected by the general users of the object.

Also, we view the object as an *atomic unit* that the user ought not to dissect. Most of us would not even think of fiddling around with the bits that represent a floating-point number, and we would find it completely ridiculous to try to increment some floating-point object by altering its internal representation ourselves.

The atomicity principle is known as *information hiding*. The user does not get direct access to the parts of the object or their implementations; they can be accessed only indirectly by methods supplied with the object. We can view each object as coming with the warning, "Do not open—no user-serviceable parts inside." In real life, most people who try to fix things that have such a warning wind up doing more harm than good. In this respect, programming mimics the real world. The grouping of data and the operations that apply to them to form an aggregate, while hiding implementation details of the aggregate, is known as *encapsulation*.

Information hiding makes implementation details, including components of an object, inaccessible.

An important goal of object-oriented programming is to support code reuse. Just as engineers use components over and over in their designs, programmers should be able to reuse objects rather than repeatedly reimplementing them. When we have an implementation of the exact object that we need to use, reuse is a simple matter. The challenge is to use an existing object when the object that is needed is not an exact match but is merely very similar.

Encapsulation is the grouping of data and the operations that apply to them to form an aggregate, while hiding the implementation of the aggregate.

Object-oriented languages provide several mechanisms to support this goal. One is the use of *generic* code. If the implementation is identical except for the basic type of the object, there is no need to completely rewrite code: Instead, we write the code generically so that it works for any type. For instance, the logic used to sort an array of objects is independent of the types of objects being sorted, so a generic algorithm could be used.

The *inheritance* mechanism allows us to extend the functionality of an object. In other words, we can create new types with restricted (or extended) properties of the original type. Inheritance goes a long way toward our goal of code reuse.

Another important object-oriented principle is *polymorphism*. A polymorphic reference type can reference objects of several different types. When methods are applied to the polymorphic type, the operation that is appropriate to the actual referenced object is automatically selected. In Java, this is implemented as part of inheritance. Polymorphism allows us to implement classes that share common logic. As is discussed in Chapter 4, this is illustrated in the Java libraries. The use of inheritance to create these hierarchies distinguishes object-oriented programming from the simpler *object-based programming*.

In Java, generic algorithms are implemented as part of inheritance. Chapter 4 discusses inheritance and polymorphism. In this chapter, we describe how Java uses classes to achieve encapsulation and information hiding.

A *class* in Java consists of *fields* that store data and *methods* that are applied to instances of the class.

An *object* in Java is an instance of a class. A *class* is similar to a C structure or Pascal/Ada record, except that there are two important enhancements. First, members can be both functions and data, known as *methods* and *fields*, respectively. Second, the visibility of these members can be restricted. Because methods that manipulate the object's state are members of the class, they are accessed by the dot member operator, just like the fields. In object-oriented terminology, when we make a call to a method we are passing a message to the object.

3.2 A Simple Example

Recall that when you are designing the class, it is important to be able to hide internal details from the class user. This is done in two ways. First, the class can define functionality as class members, called *methods*. Some of these methods describe how an instance of the structure is created and initialized, how equality tests are performed, and how output is performed. Other functions would be specific to the particular structure. The idea is that the internal data fields that represent an object's state should not be manipulated directly by the class user but instead should be manipulated only through use of the methods. This idea can be strengthened by hiding members from the user. To do this, we can specify that they be stored in a *private* section. The compiler will enforce the rule that members in the private section are inaccessible to the user of the object. Generally speaking, all data members should be private.

Figure 3.1 illustrates a class declaration for an `IntCell` object.[1] The declaration consists of two parts: public and private. The *public* section represents the portion that is visible to the user of the object. Since we expect to hide data, generally only methods and constants would be placed in the public section. In our example, we have methods that read and write to the `IntCell` object. The private section contains the data: this is invisible to the user of the object. The `storedValue` member must be accessed through the publicly visible routines `read` and `write`; it cannot be accessed directly by `main`. Another way of viewing this is shown in Figure 3.2.

Functionality is supplied as additional members; these methods manipulate the object's state.

Public members are visible to non-class routines; private members are not.

```
1  // IntCell class
2  //   int read( )         -->  Returns the stored value
3  //   void write( int x ) -->  x is stored
4
5  public class IntCell
6  {
7          // Public methods
8      public int read( )         { return storedValue; }
9      public void write( int x ) { storedValue = x; }
10
11          // Private internal data representation
12      private int storedValue;
13  }
```

Figure 3.1   A complete declaration of an `IntCell` class

[1.] Recall that classes must be placed in files of the same name. Thus `IntCell` must be in file *IntCell.java*.

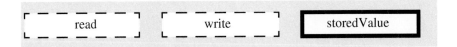

Figure 3.2 `IntCell` members: `read` and `write` are accessible, but `storedValue` is hidden

Members that are declared private are not visible to nonclass routines.

A *field* is a member that stores data; a *method* is a member that performs an action.

Figure 3.3 shows how `IntCell` objects are used. Since `read` and `write` are members of the `IntCell` class, they are accessed by using the dot member operator. The `storedValue` member could also be accessed by using the dot member operator, but since it is private, the access at line 14 would be illegal if it were not commented out.

Here is a summary of the terminology. The class defines *members*, which may be either *fields* (data) or *methods* (functions). The methods can act on the fields and may call other methods. The visibility modifier *public* means that the member is accessible to anyone via the dot operator. The visibility modifier *private* means that the member is accessible only by other methods of this class. With no visibility modifier, we have friendly access, which is discussed in Section 3.5.4. There is also a fourth modifier known as *protected*, which is discussed in Chapter 4.

```
1  // Exercise the IntCell class
2
3  public class TestIntCell
4  {
5      public static void main( String [ ] args )
6      {
7          IntCell m = new IntCell( );
8
9          m.write( 5 );
10         System.out.println( "Cell contents: " + m.read( ) );
11
12         // The next line would be illegal if uncommented
13         // because storedValue is a private member
14     //  m.storedValue = 0;
15     }
16 }
```

Figure 3.3 A simple test routine to show how `IntCell` objects are accessed

3.3 Javadoc

When designing a class, the *class specification* represents the class design and tells us what can be done to an object. The *implementation* represents the internals of how this is accomplished. As far as the class user is concerned, these internal details are not important. In many cases, the implementation represents proprietary information that the class designer may not wish to share. However, the specification must be shared; otherwise, the class is unusable.

The *class specification* describes what can be done to an object. The *implementation* represents the internals of how the specifications are met.

In many languages, the simultaneous sharing of the specification and hiding of the implementation is accomplished by placing the specification and implementation in separate source files. For instance, C++ has the class interface, which is placed in a `.h` file and a class implementation, which is in a `.cpp` file. In the `.h` file, the class interface restates the methods (by providing method headers) that are implemented by the class.

Java takes a different approach. It is easy to see that a list of the methods in a class, with signatures and return types, can be automatically documented from the implementation. Java uses this idea: The program *javadoc*, which comes with all Java systems, can be run to automatically generate documentation for classes. The output of *javadoc* is a set of HTML files that can be viewed or printed with a browser.

The *javadoc* program automatically generates documentation for classes.

The Java implementation file can also add *javadoc* comments that begin with the token starter `/**`. Those comments are automatically added in a uniform and consistent manner to the documentation produced by *javadoc*.

There also are several special tags that can be included in the *javadoc* comments. Some of these are `@author`, `@param`, `@return`, and `@exception`. Figure 3.4 illustrates the use of the *javadoc* commenting features for the `IntCell` class. At line 3, the `@author` tag is used. This tag must precede the class definition. Line 10 illustrates the use of the `@return` tag and line 19, the `@param` tag. These tags must appear prior to a method declaration. The first token that follows the `@param` tag is the parameter name. The `@exception` tag is not shown, but it has the same syntax as `@param`.

javadoc tags include `@author`, `@param`, `@return`, and `@exception`. They are used in *javadoc* comments.

The output that results from running *javadoc* is shown in Figure 3.5 (on page 59). Run *javadoc* by supplying the name (including the `.java` extension) of the source file. To obtain the pictures for the constructors, methods, and so on, you must have an `images` subdirectory in the directory where the HTML files are generated (this subdirectory is part of the JDK distribution and is duplicated in our online code).

The output of *javadoc* is purely commentary, except for the method headers. The compiler does not check that these comments are implemented. Nonetheless, the importance of proper documentation of classes can never be overstated. *javadoc* makes the task of generating well-formatted documentation easier.

```
 1  /**
 2   * A class for simulating an integer memory cell
 3   * @author Mark A. Weiss
 4   */
 5
 6  public class IntCell
 7  {
 8      /**
 9       * Get the stored value.
10       * @return the stored value.
11       */
12      public int read( )
13      {
14          return storedValue;
15      }
16
17      /**
18       * Store a value.
19       * @param x the number to store.
20       */
21      public void write( int x )
22      {
23          storedValue = x;
24      }
25
26      private int storedValue;
27  }
```

Figure 3.4   `IntCell` declaration with *javadoc* comments

3.4 Basic Methods

Some methods are common to all classes. This section discusses *mutators*, *accessors*, and three special methods: the constructors, `toString`, and `equals`. Also discussed is the static method, one of which is `main`.

3.4.1 Constructors

A *constructor* tells how an object is declared and initialized.

As mentioned earlier, a basic property of objects is that they can be defined, possibly with initialization. In Java, the method that controls how an object is created and initialized is the *constructor*. Because of overloading, an object may define multiple constructors.

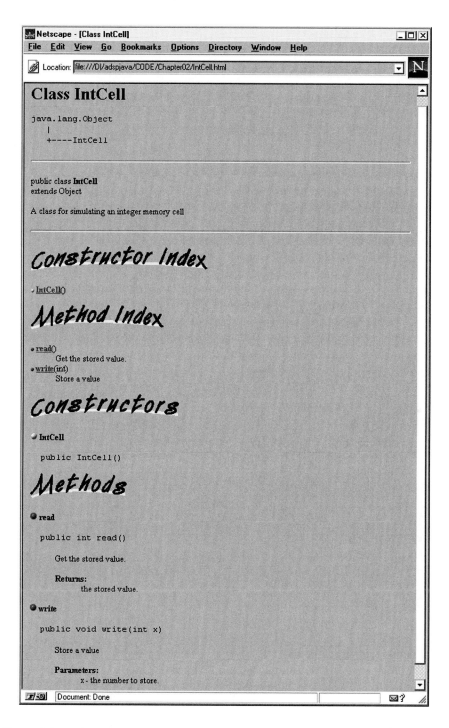

Figure 3.5   *javadoc* output for Figure 3.4

The default con-
structor is a mem-
ber-by-member ap-
plication of a
default initialization.

If no constructor is provided, as in the case for the `IntCell` class in Figure 3.1, a default constructor is generated that initializes each data member using the normal defaults. This means that primitive fields are initialized to zero and reference fields are initialized to the null reference. Thus, in the case of `IntCell`, the `storedValue` component is 0.

To write a constructor, we provide a method that has the same name as the class and no return type. In Figure 3.6, there are two constructors: one begins at line 7 and the other at line 15. Using these constructors, we can construct `Date` objects in either of the following ways:

```
Date d1 = new Date( );
Date d2 = new Date( 4, 15, 1998 );
```

Note that once a constructor is written, a default zero-parameter constructor is no longer generated. If you want one, you have to write it. Thus the constructor at line 7 is required in order to allow construction of the object that `d1` references.

3.4.2 Mutators and Accessors

Class fields are typically declared private. Thus they cannot be directly accessed by nonclass routines. Sometimes, however, we would like to examine the value of a field. We may even want to change it.

A method that ex-
amines but does
not change the
state of an object
is an *accessor*.
A method that
changes the state
is a *mutator*.

One alternative to do this is to declare the fields public. This is typically a poor choice, however, because it violates information-hiding principles. Instead, we can provide methods to examine and change each field. A method that examines but does not change the state of an object is an *accessor*. A method that changes the state is a *mutator* (because it mutates the state of the object).

Special cases of accessors and mutators examine only a single field. These accessors typically have names beginning with `get`, such as `getMonth`, while these mutators typically have names beginning with `set`, such as `setMonth`.

The advantage of using a mutator is that the mutator can ensure that changes in the state of the object are consistent. Thus a mutator that changes the `day` field in a `Date` object can make sure that only legal dates result.

3.4.3 Output and `toString`

The `toString`
method can be
provided. It returns
a `String` based
on the object state.

Typically, we want to output the state of an object using `print`. The way this is done is by writing the class method `toString`. This method returns a `String` suitable for output. As an example, Figure 3.6 shows a bare-bones implementation of the `toString` method for the `Date` class.

```
 1  // Minimal Date class that illustrates some Java features
 2  // No error checks or javadoc comments
 3
 4  public class Date
 5  {
 6          // Zero-parameter constructor
 7      public Date( )
 8      {
 9          month = 1;
10          day = 1;
11          year = 1998;
12      }
13
14          // Three-parameter constructor
15      public Date( int theMonth, int theDay, int theYear )
16      {
17          month = theMonth;
18          day   = theDay;
19          year  = theYear;
20      }
21
22          // Return true if two equal values
23      public boolean equals( Object rhs )
24      {
25          if( ! ( rhs instanceof Date ) )
26              return false;
27          Date rhDate = ( Date ) rhs;
28          return rhDate.month == month && rhDate.day == day &&
29                  rhDate.year == year;
30      }
31
32          // Conversion to String
33      public String toString( )
34      {
35          return month + "/" + day + "/" + year;
36      }
37
38          // Fields
39      private int month;
40      private int day;
41      private int year;
42  }
```

Figure 3.6   A minimal Date class that illustrates constructors and the
equals and toString methods

3.4.4 **equals**

The equals method can be provided to test if two references are referring to the same value.

The `equals` method is used to test if two references are referring to the same value. The signature is always

```
public boolean equals( Object rhs )
```

Notice that the parameter is of reference type `Object`, rather than the class type. Typically, the `equals` method for class `ClassName` is implemented to return `true` only if `rhs` is an instance of `ClassName`, and after the conversion to `ClassName`, all the primitive fields are equal (via `==`) and all the reference fields are equal (via member-by-member application of `equals`).

The parameter to equals is of type Object.

An example of how `equals` is implemented is provided in Figure 3.6 for the `Date` class. The `instanceof` operator is discussed in Section 3.6.3.

3.4.5 static Methods

A *static method* is a method that does not need a controlling object.

A *static method* is a method that does not need a controlling object. The most common static method is `main`. Other static methods are found in the `String`, `Integer`, and `Math` classes. Examples are the methods `String.valueOf`, `Integer.parseInt`, `Math.sin`, and `Math.max`. Access to a static method uses the same visibility rules as do static fields.

Recall from Chapter 1 that some fields of the class use the modifier `static`. Specifically, in conjunction with the keyword `final`, we have constants. Without the word `final`, we have *static fields*, which have another meaning, discussed in Section 3.6.4.

3.4.6 **main**

When the *java* command is issued to start the interpreter, the `main` method in the class file referenced by the *java* command is called. Thus each class can have its own `main` function, without problem. This makes it easy to test the basic functionality of individual classes. However, although functionality can be tested, placing `main` in the class gives `main` more visibility than would be allowed in general. Thus calls from `main` to nonpublic methods will succeed in the test, even though they will be illegal in a more general setting.

3.5   Packages

A *package* is used to organize a collection of classes.

Packages are used to organize similar classes. Each package consists of a set of classes. Two classes in the same package have slightly fewer visibility restrictions among themselves than they would if they were in different packages.

Java provides several predefined packages, including `java.applet`, `java.awt`, `java.io`, `java.lang`, and `java.util`. The `java.lang` package includes the classes `Integer`, `Math`, `String`, and `System`, among others. Some of the classes in the `java.util` package are `Date`, `Random`, and `StringTokenizer`. `java.io` is used for I/O and includes the various stream classes seen in Section 2.6. `java.applet` includes classes that are used for designing applets. `java.awt` includes the classes that form the *abstract window toolkit*, which is used for graphical user interfaces.

Class `C` in package `P` is specified as `P.C`. For instance, we can have a `Date` object constructed with the current time and date as an initial state using

```
java.util.Date today = new java.util.Date( );
```

Note that by including a package name, we avoid conflicts with identically named classes in other packages (such as our own `Date` class).

3.5.1 The `import` Directive

Using a full package and class name can be burdensome. To avoid this, use the *import directive*. There are two forms of the `import` directive:

```
import PackageName.ClassName;
import PackageName.*;
```

> The *import directive* is used to provide a shorthand for a fully qualified class name.

In the first form, `ClassName` may be used as a shorthand for a fully qualified class name. In the second, all classes in a package may be abbreviated with the corresponding class name.

For example, with these `import` directives,

```
import java.util.Date;
import java.io.*;
```

we may use

```
Date today = new Date( );
FileReader theFile = new FileReader( name );
```

Using the `import` directive saves typing. And since the most typing is saved by using the second form, you will see that form used often. There are two disadvantages to `import` directives. First, the shorthand makes it hard to tell, by reading the code, which class is being used when there are a host of `import` directives. Also, the second form may allow shorthands for unintended classes and introduce naming conflicts that will need to be resolved by fully qualified class names.

> Careless use of the `import` directive can introduce naming conflicts.

Suppose we use

```
import java.util.*;   // Library package
import util.*;        // User-defined package
```

with the intention of importing the `java.util.Random` class and a package that we have written ourselves. Then, if we have our own `Date` class, the `import` directive will generate a conflict with `java.util.Date` and will need to be fully qualified. Furthermore, if we are using a class in one of these packages, by reading the code we will not know whether it originated from the library package or our own package. We would have avoided these problems if we had used the first form:

```
import java.util.Random;
```

java.lang.* is automatically imported.

The `import` directives must appear prior to the beginning of a class declaration. We saw an example of this in Figure 2.11. Also, the entire package `java.lang` is automatically imported. This is why we may use shorthands such as `Math.max`, `Integer.parseInt`, `System.out`, and so on.

3.5.2 The **package** Statement

The package statement indicates that a class is part of a package. It must precede the class definition.

To indicate that a class is part of a package, we must do two things. First, we must include the *package statement* as the first line, prior to the class definition. Second, we must place the code in an appropriate subdirectory.

In this text, we use the three packages shown in Figure 3.7. Other programs, including test programs and the application programs in Part III of the text, are stand-alone classes and not part of a package.

An example of how the `package` statement is used is shown in Figure 3.8. Here, we have the static method `longPause` that simply sleeps for a billion milliseconds (approximately two weeks). This method is useful because when some integrated environments run console applications from inside their environments, they close the output console as soon as the program terminates. This can make it hard to see the output. `longPause` keeps the console from closing in this situation.

Package	Use
`DataStructures`	Classes that implement data structures and sorting.
`Exceptions`	Exception classes.
`Supporting`	Various supporting classes and interfaces.

Figure 3.7   Packages defined in this text

```
 1  package Supporting;
 2
 3  public class Exiting
 4  {
 5      // Suspend current program for a long time
 6      public static void longPause( )
 7      {
 8          try
 9              { Thread.sleep( 1000000000 ); }
10          catch( InterruptedException e ) { }
11      }
12  }
```

Figure 3.8   A class `Exiting` with a single static method, which is part of the
package `Supporting`

3.5.3 The CLASSPATH Environment Variable

Packages are searched for in locations that are named in the CLASSPATH variable. What does this mean? Here are possible settings for CLASSPATH, first for a
Windows 95 system and second for a Unix system:

> The CLASSPATH variable specifies files and directories that should be searched to find classes.

```
SET CLASSPATH=.;C:\cafe\java\lib\
setenv CLASSPATH .:$HOME/java:/usr/java/lib
```

In both cases, the CLASSPATH variable lists directories (or zipped files) that
contain the package's class files. For instance, if your CLASSPATH is set incorrectly, you will not be able to compile even the most trivial program because
java.lang will not be found.

A class in package P must be in a directory P that will be found by searching
through the CLASSPATH list. The current directory (directory .) is always in the
CLASSPATH variable, so if you are working from a single main directory, you
can simply create subdirectories in it. Most likely, however, you'll want to create
a separate Java subdirectory and then create package subdirectories in there. You
would then augment the CLASSPATH variable to include the Java subdirectory.
This was done in the previous Unix declaration when we added $HOME/java to
the CLASSPATH. Inside the java directory, you create subdirectories named
Supporting, DataStructures, and Exceptions. In the Supporting
subdirectory, you place the code for the Exiting class.

> A class in package P must be in a directory P that will be found by searching through the CLASSPATH list.

An application can then use the longPause method by issuing

```
Exiting.longPause( );
```

if an appropriate import directive is provided.

3.5.4 Package-friendly Visibility Rules

Fields with no visibility modifiers are package *friendly*, meaning that they are visible only to other classes in the same package.

Packages have several important visibility rules. First, if no visibility modifier is specified for a field, then the field is (package) *friendly*. This means that it is visible only to other classes in the same package. This is more visible than private (which is invisible even to other classes in the same package) but less visible than public (which is visible to nonpackage classes, too).

Friendly classes are visible only to other classes in the same package.

Second, only public classes of a package may be used outside the package. That is why we have always used the `public` qualifier prior to class. Classes may not be declared `private`. Friendly access extends to classes, too. If a class is not declared `public`, then it may be accessed by other classes in the same package only; this is a *friendly class*. In Part IV, we will see that friendly classes can be used without violating information-hiding principles. Thus there are some cases in which friendly classes can be very useful.

All classes that are not part of a package but are reachable through the `CLASSPATH` variable are considered part of the same default package. As a result, friendly access applies between all of them. This is why visibility is not affected if the `public` modifier is omitted from nonpackage classes. However, this is poor use of friendly access. Avoid friendly access except for the cases that are in some of the data structures implementations in Part IV.

3.5.5 Separate Compilation

Java source files may be compiled in any order.

When a program consists of several `.java` files, each file must be compiled separately. Typically, we place each class in its own `.java` source file. As a result, we get a collection of `.class` files. As mentioned earlier, when the *java* command is issued to start the interpreter, the `main` method in the class file referenced by that command is used. Java source files may be compiled in any order, so long as all `.class` files are available when the interpreter runs.

3.6 Additional Constructs

Three additional keywords are `this`, `instanceof`, and `static`. `this` has several uses in Java; two are discussed in this section. `instanceof` also has several general uses; it is used here to ensure that a type-conversion can succeed. Likewise, `static` has several uses. We have already discussed *static methods*. This section covers the *static field* and *static initializer*.

this is a reference to the current object. It can be used to send the current object, as a unit, to some other method.

3.6.1 The `this` Reference

The first use of `this` is as a reference to the current object. Think of the `this` reference as a homing device that, at any instant in time, tells you where you are. An important use of the `this` reference is in handling the special case of self-assignment. An example of this is a program that copies one file to another. A normal algorithm begins by truncating the target file to zero length. If no check is performed to make sure the source and target file are indeed different, then the source file will be truncated — hardly a desirable feature. When dealing with two objects, one of which is written and one of which is read, we first should check for this special case, which is known as *aliasing*.

For a second example, suppose we have a class `Account` that has a method `finalTransfer`. This method moves all the money from one account into another. In principle, this is an easy routine to write:

> *Aliasing* is a special case that occurs when the same object appears in more than one role.

```
// Transfer all money from rhs to current account
public void finalTransfer( Account rhs )
{
    dollars += rhs.dollars;
    rhs.dollars = 0;
}
```

However, consider the result:

```
Account account1;
Account account2;
    . . .
account2 = account1;
account1.finalTransfer( account2 );
```

Since we are transferring money between the same account, there should be no change in the account. However, the last statement in `finalTransfer` assures that the account will be empty. One way to avoid this is to use an alias test:

```
// Transfer all money from rhs to current account
public void finalTransfer( Account rhs )
{
    if( this == rhs )      // Alias test
        return;
    dollars += rhs.dollars;
    rhs.dollars = 0;
}
```

3.6.2 The `this` Shorthand for Constructors

Many classes have multiple constructors that behave similarly. We can use `this` inside a constructor to call one of the other class constructors. An alternative to the zero-parameter `Date` constructor in Figure 3.6 would be

> `this` can be used to make a call to another constructor in the same class.

```
public Date( )
{
    this( 1, 1, 1998 ); // Call the 3-parameter constructor
}
```

More complicated uses are possible, but the call to `this` must be the first statement in the constructor; thereafter more statements may follow.

3.6.3 The `instanceof` Operator

The `instanceof` operator is used to test if an expression is an instance of some class.

The `instanceof` operator performs a run-time test. The result of

```
exp instanceof ClassName
```

is `true` if `exp` is an instance of `ClassName`, and `false` otherwise. If `exp` is `null`, the result is always `false`. The `instanceof` operator is typically used prior to performing a type conversion and is `true` if the type conversion can succeed.

3.6.4 Static Fields

Static fields are essentially global variables with class scope.

Static fields are used when we have a variable that all the members of some class need to share. Typically, this is a symbolic constant, but it need not be. When a class variable is declared `static`, only one instance of the variable is ever created. It is not part of any instance of the class. Instead, it behaves like a single global variable but with the scope of the class. In other words, in the declaration

```
public class Sample
{
    private int x;
    private static int y;
}
```

each `Sample` object stores its own `x`, but there is only one shared `y`.

A common use of a static field is as a constant. For instance, the class `Integer` defines the field `MAX_VALUE` as

```
public final static int MAX_VALUE = 2147483647;
```

If a constant were not a static field, then each instance of an `Integer` would have a data field named `MAX_VALUE`, thus wasting space. Instead, there is only a single variable named `MAX_VALUE`. It can be accessed by any of the `Integer` methods by using the identifier `MAX_VALUE`. It can also be accessed by an `Integer` object `Obj` using `Obj.MAX_VALUE`, as would any field. Note that this is allowed only because `MAX_VALUE` is public. Finally, `MAX_VALUE` can be accessed by using the class name as `Integer.MAX_VALUE` (again allowable because it is public). This would not be allowed for a nonstatic field.

Even without the `final` qualifier, static fields are still useful. Suppose we want to keep track of the number of `IntCell` objects that have been constructed. What we need is a static variable. In the `IntCell` class, we declare

```
private static int activeInstances = 0;
```

We could then increment `activeInstances` in the constructor. Without the `static` modifier, we would have incorrect behavior, since each `IntCell` object would have its own data field `activeInstances` that would be incremented from 0 to 1 in the constructor.

Notice that since a static field has no controlling object, but is instead shared by all instances of the class, it may be accessed and modified by a static class method, if its visibility permits. A nonstatic field, which is part of each instance of the class, can be accessed by a static class method only if a controlling object is provided.

3.6.5 Static Initializers

Static fields are initialized when the class is loaded. Occasionally, we need a complex initialization. For instance, suppose we need a static array that stores the square roots of the first 100 integers. It would be best to have these values computed automatically. One possibility is to provide a static method and require the programmer to call it prior to using the array.

A static initializer is a block of code that is used to initialize static fields.

An alternative is the *static initializer*. An example is shown in Figure 3.9. There, the static initializer extends from lines 5 to 9. The simplest use of the static initializer places initialization code for the static fields in a block that is preceded by the keyword `static`. The static initializer must follow the declaration of the static member.

```
1  public class Squares
2  {
3      private static double squareRoots[ ] = new double[ 100 ];
4
5      static
6      {
7          for( int i = 0; i < squareRoots.length; i++ )
8              squareRoots[ i ] = Math.sqrt( ( double ) i );
9      }
10
11     // Rest of class
12 }
```

Figure 3.9   Example of a static initializer

Summary

This chapter described the Java class and package constructs. The class is the Java mechanism that is used to create new reference types; the package is used to group similar classes. For each class, we can

- define the construction of objects,
- provide for information hiding and atomicity, and
- define methods to manipulate the objects.

The class consists of two parts: the specification and the implementation. The specification tells the user of the class what the class does; the implementation does it. The implementation frequently contains proprietary code and in some cases is distributed only as a .class file. The specification, however, is public knowledge. In Java, a specification that lists the class methods can be generated from the implementation by using *javadoc*.

Information hiding can be enforced by using the `private` directive. Initialization of objects is controlled by the constructor functions, and the components of the object can be examined and changed by accessor and mutator functions, respectively. Other methods, including `toString` and `equals`, can be written.

The features discussed in this chapter implement the fundamental aspects of object-based programming. The next chapter discusses inheritance, which is central to object-oriented programming.

 ## Objects of the Game

accessor A method that examines an object but does not change its state. (60)

aliasing A special case that occurs when the same object appears in more than one role. (67)

atomic unit In reference to an object, its parts cannot be dissected by the general users of the object. (54)

class Consists of fields and methods that are applied to instances of the class. (54)

class specification Describes the functionality, but not the implementation. (57)

CLASSPATH variable Specifies directories and files that should be searched to find classes. (65)

constructor Tells how an object is declared and initialized. The default constructor is a member-by-member default initialization, with primitive fields initialized to zero and reference fields initialized to `null`. (58)

encapsulation The grouping of data and the operations that apply to them to form an aggregate while hiding the implementation of the aggregate. (54)

equals method Can be implemented to test if two references are referring to the same value. The formal parameter is always of type `Object`. (62)

field A class member that stores data. (56)

friendly access Members that have no visibility modifiers are only accessible to methods in classes in the same package. (66)

friendly class A class that is not public and is accessible only to other classes in the same package. (66)

implementation Represents the internals of how the specifications are met. As far as the class user is concerned, the implementation is not important. (57)

import directive Used to provide a shorthand for a fully qualified class name. (63)

information hiding Makes implementation details, including components of an object, inaccessible. (54)

`instanceof` operator Tests if an expression is an instance of a class. (68)

javadoc Automatically generates documentation for classes. (57)

javadoc **tag** Includes `@author`, `@param`, `@return`, and `@exception`. Used inside of *javadoc* comments. (57)

method A function supplied as an additional member that, if not static, operates on an instance of the class. (55)

mutator A method that changes the state of the object. (60)

object An entity that has structure and state and defines operations that may access or manipulate that state. An instance of a class. (53)

object-based programming Uses the encapsulation and information hiding features of objects but does not use inheritance. (54)

object-oriented programming Distinguished from object-based programming by the use of inheritance to form hierarchies of classes. (54)

package Used to organize a collection of classes. (62)

package statement Indicates that a class is a member of a package. Must precede the class definition. (64)

private A member that is not visible to nonclass methods. (56)

public A member that is visible to nonclass methods. (56)

separate compilation Each class is compiled separately, in any order. (66)

static field Essentially a global variable with class scope. (68)

static initializer A block of code that is used to initialize static fields. (69)

static method A method that does not need a controlling object. (62)

`this` constructor call Used to make a call to another constructor in the same class. (67)

`this` reference A reference to the current object. It can be used to send the current object, as a unit, to some other method. (66)

`toString` method Returns a `String` based on the object state. (60)

Common Errors

1. Private members cannot be accessed outside of the class. Remember that, by default, class members are friendly. They are visible only within the package.

2. Use `public class` instead of `class` unless you are writing a throw-away helper class.

3. The formal parameter to `equals` must be of type `Object`. Otherwise, although the program will compile, there are cases in which a default `equals` (that always returns `false`) will be used instead.

4. Static methods cannot access nonstatic members without a controlling object.

5. A common error is forgetting the `.*` in the second form of the import.

6. Classes that are part of a package must be placed in an identically named directory that is reachable by the `CLASSPATH` variable.

7. `this` is a final reference and may not be altered.

On the Internet

Following are the files that are available:

Date.java	Contains the `Date` class, shown in Figure 3.6. Found in directory **Chapter03**.
Exiting.java	Contains the `longPause` method, shown in Figure 3.8. Found in directory **Supporting**.
IntCell.java	Contains the `IntCell` class, shown in Figure 3.4. Found in directory **Chapter03**. The output of *javadoc* can also be found there.
Squares.java	Contains the static initializer sample code in Figure 3.9. Found in directory **Chapter03**.
TestIntCell.java	Contains a `main` that tests `IntCell`, shown in Figure 3.3. Found in directory **Chapter03**.

Exercises

In Short

3.1. What is information hiding? What is encapsulation? How does Java support these concepts?

3.2. Explain the public and private sections of the class.

3.3. Describe the role of the constructor.

3.4. If a class provides no constructor, what is the result?

3.5. What is package friendly access?

3.6. For a class `ClassName`, how is output performed?

3.7. Give the two types of import directive forms that allow `longPause` to be used without providing the `Supporting` package name.

In Theory

3.8. Why can classes not be declared private?

3.9. Suppose that the `main` method in Figure 3.3 was part of the `IntCell` class.
  a. Would the program still work?
  b. Could the commented-out line in `main` be uncommented without generating an error?

In Practice

3.10. A *combination lock* has the following basic properties: the combination (a sequence of three numbers) is hidden; the lock can be opened by providing the combination; and the combination can be changed, but only by someone who knows the current combination. Design a class with public methods `open` and `changeCombo` and private data fields that store the combination. The combination should be set in the constructor. Disable copying of combination locks.

Programming Projects

3.11. Write a class that supports rational numbers. The fields should be two `long` variables, one each that stores the numerator and denominator. Store the rational number in reduced form, with the denominator always nonnegative. Provide a reasonable set of constructors; the methods `add`, `subtract`, `multiply`, and `divide`; as well as `toString`, `equals`, and `compareTo` (that behaves like the one in the `String` class). Make sure that `toString` correctly handles the case in which the denominator is zero.

3.12. Implement a simple `Date` class. You should be able to represent any date from January 1, 1800, to December 31, 2500; subtract two dates; increment a date by a number of days; and compare two dates using both `equals` and `compareTo`. A `Date` is represented internally as the number of days since some starting time, which, here, is the start of 1800. This makes all methods except for construction and `toString` trivial.

The rule for leap years is a year is a leap year if it is divisible by 4 and not divisible by 100 unless it is also divisible by 400. Thus 1800, 1900, and 2100 are not leap years, but 2000 is. The constructor must check the validity of the date, as must `toString`. The `Date` could be bad if an increment or subtraction operator caused it to go out of range.

Once you have decided on the specifications, you can do an implementation. The difficult part is converting between the internal and external representations of a date. What follows is a possible algorithm.

Set up two arrays that are static fields. The first array, `daysTill-FirstOfMonth`, will contain the number of days until the first of each month in a nonleap year. Thus it contains 0, 31, 59, 90, and so on. The second array, `daysTillJan1`, will contain the number of days until the first of each year, starting with `firstYear`. Thus it contains 0, 365, 730, 1095, 1460, 1826, and so on because 1800 is not a leap year, but 1804 is. You should have your program initialize this array once using a static initializer. You can then use the array to convert from the internal representation to the external representation.

3.13. Implement a `Complex` number class. Recall that a complex number consists of a real part and an imaginary part. Support the same operations as the `Rational` class, when meaningful (for instance, `compareTo` is not meaningful). Add accessor methods to extract the real and imaginary parts.

3.14. Implement a complete `IntType` class that supports a reasonable set of constructors, `add`, `subtract`, `multiply`, `divide`, `equals`, `compareTo`, and `toString`. Maintain an `IntType` as a sufficiently large array. For this class, the difficult operation is division, followed closely by multiplication.

References

More information can be found in the references at the end of Chapter 1.

CHAPTER

4

Inheritance

AS mentioned in Chapter 3, an important goal of object-oriented programming is code reuse. Just as engineers use components over and over in their designs, programmers should be able to reuse objects rather than repeatedly reimplement them. In an object-oriented programming language, the fundamental mechanism for code reuse is *inheritance*. Inheritance allows us to extend the functionality of an object. In other words, we can create new types with restricted (or extended) properties of the original type, in effect forming a hierarchy of classes. Also, inheritance is the mechanism that Java uses to implement generic methods and classes.

In this chapter, we will see:

- General principles of inheritance, including *polymorphism*
- How inheritance is implemented in Java
- How a collection of classes can be derived from a single abstract class
- The *interface*, which is a special kind of a class
- How Java implements generic programming using inheritance

4.1   What Is Inheritance?

Inheritance is the fundamental object-oriented principle that is used to reuse code among related classes. Inheritance models the *IS-A relationship*. In an IS-A relationship, we say the derived class *is a* (variation of the) base class. For example, a Circle IS-A Shape and a Car IS-A Vehicle. However, an Ellipse IS-NOT-A Circle. Inheritance relationships form *hierarchies*. For instance, we can extend Car to other classes, since a ForeignCar IS-A Car (and pays tariffs) and a Domestic-Car IS-A Car (and does not pay tariffs), and so on.

Another type of relationship is a *HAS-A* (or IS-COMPOSED-OF) *relationship*. This type of relationship does not possess the properties that would be natural in an inheritance hierarchy. An example of a HAS-A relationship is that a car HAS-A steering wheel. HAS-A relationships should not be modeled by inheritance. Instead, they should use the technique of *composition*, in which the components are simply made private data fields.

In an IS-A relationship, we say the derived class is a (variation of the) base class.

In a HAS-A relationship, we say the derived class has a (instance of the) base class. Composition is used to model HAS-A relationships.

The Java language itself makes extensive use of inheritance in implementing its class libraries. Two examples are *exceptions* and the *components* in the *abstract window toolkit*:

- *Exceptions*. Java defines the class `Exception`. As we have seen, there are several kinds of exceptions, including `NullPointerException` and `ArrayOutOfBoundsException`. Each is a separate class, but for all of them, both the `toString` and `printStackTrace` methods can be used to provide debugging help.
- *Components*. The abstract window toolkit (which is described in more detail in Appendix D) defines an object known as a `Component`. There are many kinds of `Components`, including `Button`, `Canvas`, `Checkbox`, `List`, and `TextField`. Any of these components can be added to a `Frame`, `Panel`, or `Window` (which themselves are `Components`).

In both cases, the inheritance models an IS-A relationship. A `Button` IS-A `Component`. A `NullPointerException` IS-A `Exception`. Because of the IS-A relationship, the fundamental property of inheritance guarantees that any method that can be performed by `Exception` can also be performed by `NullPointerException`, and further, a `NullPointerException` object can always be referenced by an `Exception` reference. (Note that the reverse is not true.) Thus, since `printStackTrace` is a method available in the `Exception` class, we can always write

```
catch( Exception e ) { e.printStackTrace( ); }
```

If `e` references a `NullPointerException` object, `e.printStackTrace` will make sense. Depending on the circumstances of the class hierarchy, the `printStackTrace` method could be invariant or it could be *specialized* for each different class. When a method is invariant over a hierarchy, meaning it always has the same functionality for all classes in the hierarchy, we avoid having to rewrite an implementation of a class method.

A *polymorphic* variable can reference objects of several different types. When operations are applied to the polymorphic variable, the operation appropriate to the referenced object is automatically selected.

The call to `printStackTrace` also illustrates an important object-oriented principle known as *polymorphism*. A reference variable that is polymorphic can reference objects of several different types. When operations are applied to the reference, the operation that is appropriate to the actual referenced object is automatically selected. All reference types are polymorphic in Java. In the case of an `Exception` reference, a run-time decision is made: the `printStackTrace` method for the object that `e` actually references at run-time is the one that is used. This is known as *dynamic binding* or *late binding*.

In *inheritance*, we have a *base class* from which other classes are derived. The base class is the class on which the inheritance is based. A *derived class* inherits all the properties of a base class, meaning that all public methods available to the base class become public methods, with identical implementations for the derived class. It can then add data fields and additional methods and change the meaning of the inherited methods. Each derived class is a completely new class. However, the base class is completely unaffected by any changes that are made in the derived class. Thus, in designing the derived class, it is impossible to break the base class. This greatly simplifies the task of software maintenance.

A derived class is type compatible with its base class, meaning that a reference variable of the base class type may reference an object of the derived class, but not vice versa. Sibling classes (that is, classes derived from a common class) are not type compatible.

As mentioned earlier, the use of inheritance typically generates a hierarchy of classes. Figure 4.1 illustrates a small part of the Exception hierarchy. Notice that NullPointerException is indirectly, rather than directly, derived from Exception. This fact is transparent to the user of the classes because IS-A relationships are transitive. In other words, if *X* IS-A *Y* and *Y* IS-A *Z*, then *X* IS-A *Z*. The Exception hierarchy illustrates the typical design issues of factoring out commonalities into base classes and then specializing in the derived classes. In this hierarchy, we say that the derived class is a *subclass* of the base class and the base class is a *superclass* of the derived class. These relationships are transitive, and furthermore, the instanceof operator works with subclasses. Thus if obj is of type X (and not null), then obj instanceof Z is true.

Inheritance allows us to derive classes from a *base class* without disturbing the implementation of the base class.

Each *derived class* is a completely new class that nonetheless has some compatibility with the class from which it was derived.

If *X* IS-A *Y*, then *X* is a *subclass* of *Y* and *Y* is a *superclass* of *X*. These relationships are transitive.

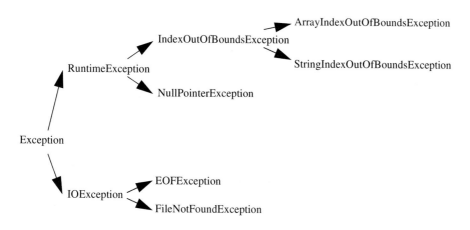

Figure 4.1   Part of the Exception hierarchy

The next few sections examine some of the following issues:

- What is the syntax used to derive a new class from an existing base class?
- How does this affect public or private status?
- How do we specify that a method is invariant over the class hierarchy?
- How do we specialize a method?
- How do we factor out common differences into an abstract class and then create a hierarchy?
- Can we derive a new class from more than one class (*multiple inheritance*)?
- How is inheritance used to implement genericity?

Some of these issues are illustrated by implementing a Shape class (in Section 4.2.5 and Section 4.3) that derives Circle, Square, and Rectangle. In doing so, we will see how Java implements run-time polymorphism as well as how inheritance can be used to implement generic methods.

4.2   Basic Java Syntax

The extends *clause* is used to declare that a class is derived from another class.

Recall that a derived class inherits all the properties of a base class. It can then add data members, override methods, and add new methods. Each derived class is a completely new class. A typical layout for inheritance is shown in Figure 4.2 and uses an *extends clause*. An extends clause declares that a class is derived from another class. A derived class *extends* a base class. Here is a brief description of a derived class:

```
1  public class Derived extends Base
2  {
3      // Any members that are not listed are inherited unchanged
4      // except for constructor
5
6        // public members
7      // Constructor(s) if default is not acceptable
8      // Base methods whose definitions are to change in Derived
9      // Additional public methods
10
11       // private member
12     // Additional data fields (generally private)
13     // Additional private methods
14 }
```

Figure 4.2   General layout of public inheritance

- Generally all data is private, so we add additional data fields in the derived class by specifying them in the private section.

- Any base class methods that are not specified in the derived class are inherited unchanged, with the exception of the constructor. The special case of the constructor is discussed in Section 4.2.2.

- Any base class method that is defined in the derived class' public section is overridden. The new definition will be applied to objects of the derived class.

- Public base class methods may not be redefined in the private section of the derived class.

- Additional methods can be added in the derived class.

A derived class inherits all data members from the base class and may add more data members. The derived class inherits all methods from the base class. It may accept or redefine them. It also can define new methods.

4.2.1 Visibility Rules

We know that any member that is declared with private visibility is accessible only to methods of the class. Thus any private members in the base class are not accessible to the derived class.

Occasionally we want the derived class to have access to the base class members. There are two basic options. The first is to use either public or friendly access. However, public access allows access to other classes in addition to derived classes. Friendly access only works if both classes are in the same package.

If we want to restrict access to only derived classes, we can make members protected. A *protected class member* is private to every class except a derived class (and classes in the same package). Declaring data members as protected or public violates the spirit of encapsulation and information hiding and is generally done only as a matter of programming expediency. Typically, a better alternative is to write accessor and mutator methods or to use friendly access. However, if a protected declaration allows you to avoid convoluted code, then it is not unreasonable to use it. In this text, protected data members are used for precisely this reason. Using protected methods is also done in this text. This allows a derived class to inherit an internal method without making it accessible outside the package hierarchy.

A protected class member is private to every class except a derived class (and classes in the same package).

4.2.2 The Constructor and `super`

Each derived class should define its constructors. If no constructor is written, then a single zero-parameter default constructor is generated. This constructor will call the base class zero-parameter constructor for the inherited portion and then apply the default initialization for any additional data fields (meaning 0 for primitive types, and `null` for reference types).

Constructing a derived class object by first constructing the inherited portion is standard practice. In fact, it is done by default, even if an explicit derived class constructor is given. This is natural because the encapsulation viewpoint tells us that the inherited portion is a single entity, and the base class constructor tells us how to initialize this single entity.

If no constructor is written, then a single zero-parameter default constructor is generated that calls the base class zero-parameter constructor for the inherited portion, and then applies the default initialization for any additional data fields.

```
1  package Exceptions;
2
3  public class Underflow extends Exception
4  {
5      public Underflow( String thrower )
6      {
7          super( thrower );
8      }
9  }
```

Figure 4.3 Constructor for new exception class Underflow; uses super

Base class constructors can be explicitly called by using the method super. Thus the default constructor for a derived class is in reality

```
public Derived( )
{
    super( );
}
```

super is used to call the base class constructor.

The super method can be called with parameters that match a base class constructor. As an example, Figure 4.3 illustrates a class Underflow that is used when implementing data structures. Underflow is thrown when an attempt is made to extract from an empty data structure. An Underflow object is constructed by providing a String. The Underflow object adds no data members, so the construction method is simply to construct the inherited portion using the Exception constructor.

The super method can be used only as the first line of a constructor. If it is not provided, then an automatic call to super with no parameters is generated.

4.2.3 final Methods and Classes

A *final method* is invariant over the inheritance hierarchy and may not be overridden.

As described earlier, the derived class either overrides or accepts the base class methods. In many cases, it is clear that a particular base class method should be invariant over the hierarchy, meaning that a derived class should not override it. In this case, we can declare that the method is *final* and cannot be overridden.

Declaring invariant methods final is not only good programming practice. It also can lead to more efficient code. It is good programming practice because in addition to declaring your intentions to the reader of the program and documentation, you prevent the accidental overriding of a method that should not be overridden.

To see why using final may make for more efficient code, suppose base class Base declares a final method f and suppose Derived extends Base. Consider the routine

```
void doIt( Base obj )
{
    obj.f( );
}
```

Since f is a final method, it does not matter whether obj actually references a Base or Derived object; the definition of f is invariant, so we know what f does. As a result, a compile-time decision, rather than a run-time decision, can be made to resolve the method call. This is known as *static binding*. Because binding is done during compilation rather than at run time, the program should run faster. Whether this is noticeable would depend on how many times we avoid making the run-time decision while executing the program.

Static binding is used when the method is invariant over the inheritance hierarchy.

A corollary to this observation is that if f is a trivial method, such as a single field accessor, and is declared final, the compiler can replace the call to f with its inline definition. Thus the method call will be replaced by a single line that accesses a data field, thereby saving time. If f is not declared final, then this is impossible, since obj could be referencing a derived class object, for which the definition of f could be different. Static methods have no controlling object and thus are resolved at compile time using static binding.

Static methods have no controlling object and thus are resolved at compile time using static binding.

Similar to the final method is the *final class*. The final class cannot be extended. As a result, all of its methods are automatically final methods. As an example, the Integer class is a final class. Notice that the fact that a class has only final methods does not imply that it is a final class. Final classes are also known as *leaf classes* because in the inheritance hierarchy, which resembles a tree, final classes are at the fringes, like leaves.

A final class may not be extended. A leaf class is a final class.

4.2.4   Overriding a Method

Methods in the base class are overridden in the derived class by simply providing a derived class method with the same signature. The derived class method must have the same return type and may not add exceptions to the throws list.

The derived class method must have the same return type and signature and may not add exceptions to the throws list.

Sometimes the derived class method wants to invoke the base class method. Typically, this is known as *partial overriding*. That is, we want to do what the base class does, plus a little more, rather than doing something entirely different. Calls to a base class method can be accomplished by using super. Here is an example:

Partial overriding involves calling a base class method by using super.

```
public class Workaholic extends Worker
{
    public void doWork( )
    {
        super.doWork( );    // Work like a Worker
        drinkCoffee( );     // Take a break
        super.doWork( );    // Work like a Worker some more
    }
}
```

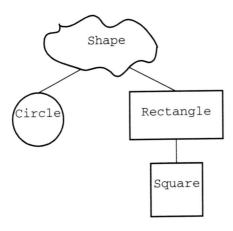

Figure 4.4   The hierarchy of shapes

4.2.5   Abstract Methods and Classes

So far we have seen that some methods are invariant over a hierarchy (these are final methods) and that other methods can have their meaning changed over the hierarchy. A third possibility is that the method is meaningful for the derived classes and an implementation must be provided for the derived classes; however, that implementation is not meaningful for the base class. In this case, we can declare that the base class method is *abstract*.

An *abstract method* is a method that declares functionality that all derived class objects must eventually implement. In other words, it says what these objects can do. However, it does not provide a default implementation. Instead, each object must provide its own implementation.

A class that has at least one abstract method is an *abstract class*. Java requires that all abstract classes be declared as such. When a derived class fails to override an abstract method with an implementation, the method remains abstract in the derived class. As a result, if a class that is not intended to be abstract fails to override an abstract method, the compiler will detect the inconsistency and report an error.

An example is an abstract class Shape, which is used in a larger example later in this chapter. Specific shapes, such as Circle and Rectangle, are derived from Shape. We can then derive a Square as a special Rectangle. Figure 4.4 shows the class hierarchy that results.

The Shape class can have data members that are common to all classes. In a more extensive example, this could include the coordinates of the object's extremities. It declares and provides a definition for methods, such as positionOf, that are independent of the actual type of object; positionOf would be a final method. It also declares methods that apply for each particular type of object. Some of these methods make no sense for the abstract class

> An *abstract method* has no meaningful definition and is thus always defined in the derived class.

Shape. For instance, it is difficult to compute the area of an abstract object; the area method would be declared abstract.

As mentioned earlier, the existence of at least one abstract method makes the base class abstract and disallows creation of it. Thus a Shape object cannot itself be created; only the derived objects can. However, as usual, a Shape can reference any concrete derived object, such as a Circle or Rectangle. Thus

A class with at least one abstract method must be an abstract class.

```
Shape a, b;
a = new Circle( 3.0 );        // Legal
b = new Shape( "circle" );    // Illegal
```

Figure 4.5 shows the abstract class Shape. At line 24, we declare a String that stores the type of shape. This is used only for the derived classes. The member is private, so the derived classes do not have direct access to it. The rest of the class specifies a collection of methods.

The constructor never actually gets called directly because Shape is an abstract class. We need a constructor, however, so that the derived class can call it to initialize the private members. The Shape constructor sets the internal name data field.

An abstract class object can never be constructed. However, we still provide a constructor that can be called by derived classes.

Line 13 declares the abstract method area. A run-time decision will select the appropriate area in a derived class. area is an abstract method because there is no meaningful default that could be specified to apply for an inherited class that chose not to define its own.

The comparison method shown at lines 18 to 19 is not abstract because it can be meaningfully applied for all derived classes. In fact, its definition is invariant throughout the hierarchy of shapes, so we have made it a final method.

The toString method, shown at lines 21 and 22, prints out the name of the shape and its area. Like the comparison method, it is invariant over the entire hierarchy and is thus declared final.

Before continuing, let us summarize the four types of class methods:

1. *Final methods*. Overloading is resolved at compile time. We use a final method only when the method is invariant over the inheritance hierarchy (that is, when the method is never redefined).

2. *Abstract methods*. Overloading is resolved at run time. The base class provides no implementation and is abstract. The absence of a default requires either that the derived classes provide an implementation or that the classes themselves be abstract.

3. *Static methods*. Overloading is resolved at compile time because there is no controlling object.

4. *Other methods*. Overloading is resolved at run time. The base class provides a default implementation that may be either overridden by the derived classes or accepted unchanged by the derived classes.

```
 1  // Abstract base class for shapes
 2  //
 3  // CONSTRUCTION: is not allowed; Shape is abstract
 4  //      one-parameter constructor provided for derived classes
 5  //
 6  // *****************PUBLIC OPERATIONS*********************
 7  // double area( )           --> Return the area (abstract)
 8  // boolean lessThan( rhs ) --> Compare 2 Shape objects by area
 9  // String toString( )       --> Standard toString method
10
11  public abstract class Shape
12  {
13      abstract public double area( );
14
15      public Shape( String shapeName )
16        { name = shapeName; }
17
18      final public boolean lessThan( Shape rhs )
19        { return area( ) < rhs.area( ); }
20
21      final public String toString( )
22        { return name + " of area " + area( ); }
23
24      private String name;
25  }
```

Figure 4.5   Abstract base class Shape

4.3   Example: Expanding the Shape Class

This section implements the derived Shape classes and shows how they are used in a polymorphic manner. The following problem is used:

SORTING SHAPES

Read N shapes (circles, squares, or rectangles) and output them sorted by area.

The implementation of the derived classes, shown in Figure 4.6, is completely straightforward and illustrates almost nothing that we have not already seen. The only new item is that Square is derived from Rectangle, which itself is derived from Shape. This derivation is done exactly like all the others. In implementing these classes, we must do the following:

1. Provide a new constructor.
2. Examine each method that is not final or abstract to decide if we are willing to accept its defaults. For each method whose defaults we do not like, we must write a new definition.

```
 1  // Circle, Square, Rectangle classes;
 2  //      all based on Shape
 3  //
 4  // CONSTRUCTION: with (a) radius (for circle), side length
 5  //      (for square), length and width (for rectangle)
 6  // *****************PUBLIC OPERATIONS********************
 7  // double area( )          --> Implements Shape abstract area
 8
 9  public class Circle extends Shape
10  {
11      public Circle( double rad )
12      {
13          super( "circle" );
14          radius = rad;
15      }
16
17      public double area( )
18      {
19          return Math.PI * radius * radius;
20      }
21
22      private double radius;
23  }
24
25
26  public class Rectangle extends Shape
27  {
28      public Rectangle( double len, double wid )
29      {
30          super( "rectangle" );
31          length = len;
32          width = wid;
33      }
34
35      public double area( )
36      {
37          return length * width;
38      }
39
40      private double length;
41      private double width;
42  }
43
44  public class Square extends Rectangle
45  {
46      public Square( double side )
47      {
48          super( side, side );
49      }
50  }
```

Figure 4.6   Complete Circle, Rectangle, and Square classes that
are placed in separate source files

3. Write a definition for each abstract method.

4. Write additional methods if appropriate.

For each class, we provide a simple constructor that allows initialization with basic dimensions (radius for circles, side lengths for rectangles and squares). We first initialize the inherited portion by calling super. Each class is required to provide an area method because Shape has declared that it is an abstract method. If the area method is not provided for some class then an error will be detected at compile time. This is because if an implementation of area is missing, a derived class will itself be abstract. Note that Square is willing to inherit the area method from the Rectangle, so it does not provide a redefinition.

Now that we have written the classes, we are ready to solve the original problem. We simply use an array of Shapes. Note that this does not allocate any Shape objects (which is illegal); it simply allocates an array of Shape *references*. The references can reference Circle, Square, and Rectangle objects.

Figure 4.7 uses this approach. First, we read the objects. At line 23, the call to readShape consists of reading a character and then the dimensions of some shape and then creating a new Shape object. Figure 4.8 (page 88) shows a bare bones implementation. Note that if there is bad input, a circle of radius zero is created and a reference to it is returned. A better solution in this case would be to define and throw an exception. Doing this is left as Exercise 4.14.

Next, each object created by readShape is referenced by one of the array slots. Then we then call insertionSort to sort the shapes. Finally, we output the resulting array of Shape, thereby implicitly calling the toString method.

4.3.1   Digression: An Introduction to Sorting

Insertion sort is a simple sorting algorithm that is appropriate for small inputs.

Sorting is implemented by an algorithm known as *insertion sort*. Insertion sort is generally considered a good solution if only a few elements need sorting because it is such a short algorithm. However, it also is too time consuming, so if we are dealing with a large amount of data, insertion sort is a poor choice. In this case, better algorithms should be used, as discussed in Chapter 8. The insertion sort algorithm is coded in Figure 4.9 (on page 89).

Insertion sort works as follows. The initial state is that the first element, considered by itself, is sorted. The final state that we need to attain is that all elements, considered as a group, are sorted. Figure 4.10 (on page 89) shows that the basic action of insertion sort is to arrange for elements in positions 0 through p to be sorted (where p ranges from 1 to $N-1$ and N is the number of elements to sort). In each stage, p increases by 1. That is what the outer loop at line 4 in Figure 4.9 is controlling.

When the body of the for loop is entered at line 6, we are guaranteed that the elements in array positions 0 through p−1 are already sorted. We need to extend this to positions 0 to p. Figure 4.11 (on page 89) gives a closer look at what has to be done, detailing only the relevant part of the array. At each step, the element in boldfaced type needs to be added to the previously sorted part of the array. This is easily done by placing it in a temporary variable and sliding all of the elements that are larger than it over one position to the right. After that is done, we can copy the temporary variable into the former position of the left-most relocated element (indicated by lighter shading on the following line). We keep a counter j, which is the position to which the temporary variable should be written back. j decreases by 1 every time an element is slid over. Lines 6 to 11 (in Figure 4.9) implement this.

```
1  import java.io.*;
2
3  class TestShape
4  {
5      private static BufferedReader in;
6
7      private static Shape readShape( )
8        { /* Implementation in Figure 4.8 */ }
9
10     public static void main( String [ ] args )
11     {
12         try
13         {
14                 // Get number of shapes
15             System.out.println( "Enter # of shapes: " );
16             in = new BufferedReader( new
17                             InputStreamReader( System.in ) );
18             int numShapes = Integer.parseInt( in.readLine() );
19
20                 // Read the shapes
21             Shape [ ] array = new Shape[ numShapes ];
22             for( int i = 0; i < numShapes; i++ )
23                 array[ i ] = readShape( );
24
25                 // Sort and output
26             insertionSort( array );
27             System.out.println( "Sorted by area:" );
28             for( int i = 0; i < numShapes; i++ )
29                 System.out.println( array[ i ] );
30         }
31         catch( Exception e )
32           { System.out.println( e ); }
33     }
34 }
```

Figure 4.7   main routine to read shapes and output them in increasing order of area

```
1  // Create an appropriate Shape object based on input.
2  // Part of class TestShape in Figure 4.7.
3  // The user types 'c', 's', or 'r' to indicate the shape
4  // and then provides dimensions when prompted.
5  // A zero-radius circle is returned for any error.
6
7    private static Shape readShape( )
8    {
9        double rad;
10       double len
11       double wid;
12       String oneLine;
13
14       try
15       {
16           System.out.println( "Enter shape type:" );
17           do
18           {
19               oneLine = in.readLine( );
20           } while( oneLine.length( ) == 0 );
21
22           switch( oneLine.charAt( 0 ) )
23           {
24             case 'c':
25               System.out.println( "Enter radius: " );
26               rad = Double.parseDouble( in.readLine( ) );
27               return new Circle( rad );
28
29             case 's':
30               System.out.println( "Enter side: " );
31               len = Double.parseDouble( in.readLine( ) );
32               return new Square( len );
33
34             case 'r':
35               System.out.println( "Enter length and width "
36                                   + "on separate lines: " );
37               len = Double.parseDouble( in.readLine( ) );
38               wid = Double.parseDouble( in.readLine( ) );
39               return new Rectangle( len, wid );
40
41             default:
42               System.err.println( "Need c, r, or s" );
43               return new Circle( 0 );
44           }
45       }
46       catch( Exception e )
47       {
48           System.err.println( e );
49           return new Circle( 0 );
50       }
51   }
```

Figure 4.8   Simple input routine for reading and returning a new Shape

```
1   // InsertionSort: sort array a
2      private static void insertionSort( Shape [ ] a )
3      {
4          for( int p = 1; p < a.length; p++ )
5          {
6              Shape tmp = a[ p ];
7              int j = p;
8
9              for( ; j > 0 && tmp.lessThan( a[ j - 1 ] ); j-- )
10                 a[ j ] = a[ j - 1 ];
11             a[ j ] = tmp;
12         }
13     }
```

Figure 4.9   Insertion sort

Array Position	0	1	2	3	4	5
Initial State:	8	5	9	2	6	3
After a(0..1) is sorted:	5	8	9	2	6	3
After a(0..2) is sorted:	5	8	9	2	6	3
After a(0..3) is sorted:	2	5	8	9	6	3
After a(0..4) is sorted:	2	5	6	8	9	3
After a(0..5) is sorted:	2	3	5	6	8	9

Figure 4.10   Basic action of insertion sort (shaded part is sorted)

Array position	0	1	2	3	4	5
Initial State:	8	5				
After a(0..1) is sorted:	5	8	9			
After a(0..2) is sorted:	5	8	9	2		
After a(0..3) is sorted:	2	5	8	9	6	
After a(0..4) is sorted:	2	5	6	8	9	3
After a(0..5) is sorted:	2	3	5	6	8	9

Figure 4.11   A closer look at the action of insertion sort (dark shading indicates sorted area; light shading is where the new element was placed)

Always check the boundary cases.

It is important to check that this insertion sort works in two boundary cases. First, in Figure 4.11 if the boldfaced element already is the largest in the group, then it is copied out to the temporary variable and then back immediately, and thus is correct. If the boldfaced element is the smallest in the group, then the entire group moves over and the temporary is copied into array position zero. We just need to be careful that we do not run past the end of the array. Thus we can be sure that when the outer `for` loop terminates, the array is sorted.

4.4 Multiple Inheritance

Multiple inheritance is used to derive a class from several base classes. Java does not allow multiple inheritance.

All the inheritance examples seen so far derived one class from a single base class. In *multiple inheritance*, a class may be derived from more than one base class. For instance, we may have a `Student` class and an `Employee` class. A `StudentEmployee` could then be derived from both classes.

Although multiple inheritance sounds attractive, and some languages (including C++) support it, it is wrought with subtleties that make design difficult. For instance, the two base classes may contain two methods that have the same signature but different implementations. Alternately, they may have two identically named fields. Which one should be used?

For example, suppose that in the previous `StudentEmployee` example `Person` is a class with data field `name` and method `toString`. Suppose, too, that `Student` extends `Person` and overrides `toString` to include the year of graduation. Further, suppose that `Employee` extends `Person` but does not override `toString`; instead, it declares that it is `final`.

1. Since `StudentEmployee` inherits the data members from both `Student` and `Employee`, do we get two copies of `name`?
2. If `StudentEmployee` does not override `toString`, which `toString` method should be used?

When many classes are involved, the problems are even larger. It appears however, that the typical multiple inheritance problems can be traced to conflicting implementations or conflicting data fields. As a result, Java does not allow multiple inheritance. Instead, it provides an alternative known as the *interface*.

4.5 The Interface

The interface is an abstract class that contains no implementation details.

The *interface* in Java is the ultimate abstract class. It consists of public abstract methods and public static final fields, only.

A class is said to *implement* the interface if it provides definitions for all of the abstract methods in the interface. A class that implements the interface behaves as if it had extended an abstract class specified by the interface.

```
1  package Supporting;
2
3  public interface Comparable
4  {
5      int compares( Comparable rhs );      // Like compareTo
6      boolean lessThan( Comparable rhs );
7  }
```

Figure 4.12 Comparable interface

In principle, the main difference between an interface and an abstract class is that although both provide a specification of what the subclasses must do, the interface is not allowed to provide any implementation details either in the form of data fields or implemented methods. The practical effect of this is that multiple interfaces do not suffer the same potential problems as multiple inheritance because we cannot have conflicting implementations. Thus, while a class may extend only one other class, it may implement more than one interface.

4.5.1 Specifying an Interface

Syntactically, virtually nothing is easier than specifying an interface. The interface looks like a class declaration, except that it uses the keyword interface. It consists of a listing of the methods that must be implemented. An example is the Comparable interface, shown in Figure 4.12, which is used throughout this text.

The Comparable interface specifies two methods that every subclass must implement: compares and lessThan. compares behaves like the String compareTo method. Note that we do not have to specify that these methods are public and abstract. Since these are required for interface methods, they can and should be omitted.

4.5.2 Implementing an Interface

A class implements an interface by

1. declaring that it implements the interface, and
2. defining implementations for all the interface methods.

An example is shown in Figure 4.13. Here, we define the MyInteger class, which will serve as a standard class throughout the text. The MyInteger class will behave like the Integer standard class, but it will also be usable wherever a Comparable object is required.

Line 3 shows that when implementing an interface, we use *implements* instead of extends. We can provide any methods that we want, but we must

The *implements clause* is used to declare that a class implements an interface. The class must implement all interface methods or it remains abstract.

provide at least those listed in the interface. The interface is implemented at lines 23 to 30. Notice that we must implement the *exact method* specified in the interface. Thus these methods take `Comparable` as a parameter, instead of `MyInteger`.

A class that implements an interface can be extended if it is not final. Thus, if `MyInteger` was not final, it could be extended.

A class that implements an interface may still extend one other class. For instance, we could in principle have written

```
public class MyInteger extends Integer implements Comparable
```

This is illegal only because `Integer` is a final class and cannot be extended.

```
1  package Supporting;
2
3  final public class MyInteger implements Comparable
4  {
5          // Constructor
6      public MyInteger( int x )
7        { value = x; }
8
9          // Some methods
10      public String toString( )
11        { return Integer.toString( value ); }
12
13      public int intValue( )
14        { return value; }
15
16      public boolean equals( Object rhs )
17      {
18          return rhs instanceof MyInteger &&
19                  value == ((MyInteger)rhs).value;
20      }
21
22          // Implement the interface
23      public int compares( Comparable rhs )
24      {
25          return value < ((MyInteger)rhs).value ? -1 :
26                  value == ((MyInteger)rhs).value ? 0 : 1;
27      }
28
29      public boolean lessThan( Comparable rhs )
30        { return value < ((MyInteger)rhs).value; }
31
32          // Data field
33      private int value;
34  }
```

Figure 4.13 The `MyInteger` class (preliminary version), which implements the `Comparable` interface

```
1 package Supporting;
2
3 public interface Hashable
4 {
5     int hash( int tableSize );
6 }
```

Figure 4.14   The Hashable interface

```
1 package Supporting;
2
3 /**
4  * Wrapper class for use with generic data structures.
5  * Mimics Integer.
6  */
7 final public class MyInteger implements Comparable, Hashable
8 {
9     public MyInteger( int x )
10       { /* As before */ }
11    public String toString( )
12       { /* As before */ }
13    public int intValue( )
14       { /* As before */ }
15    public boolean equals( Object rhs )
16       { /* As before */ }
17
18    public int compares( Comparable rhs )
19    {
20        return value < ((MyInteger)rhs).value ? -1 :
21                value == ((MyInteger)rhs).value ? 0 : 1;
22    }
23
24    public boolean lessThan( Comparable rhs )
25    {
26        return value < ((MyInteger)rhs).value;
27    }
28
29    public int hash( int tableSize )
30    {
31        if( value < 0 )
32            return -value % tableSize;
33        else
34            return value % tableSize;
35    }
36
37    private int value;    /* As before */
38 }
```

Figure 4.15   The MyInteger class, which implements two interfaces

4.5.3   Multiple Interfaces

As we mentioned earlier, a class may implement multiple interfaces. The syntax for doing so is simple. A class implements multiple interfaces by

1. listing the interfaces that it implements, and
2. defining implementations for all of the interface methods.

Figure 4.14 (page 93) shows the Hashable interface, which is explored in detail in Section 6.7 and Chapter 19. We can augment our MyInteger class to implement both the Comparable and Hashable interfaces. The result (with noninterface methods removed for brevity) is shown in Figure 4.15 (page 93).

The interface is the ultimate in abstract classes and represents an elegant solution to the multiple inheritance problem.

4.6   Implementing Generic Components

Generic program-
ming allows us to
implement type-
independent logic.

Recall that an important goal of object-oriented programming is the support of code reuse. An important mechanism that supports this goal is the *generic* mechanism: If the implementation is identical except for the basic type of the object, a *generic implementation* can be used to describe the basic functionality. For instance, a method can be written to sort an array of items; the *logic* is independent of the types of objects being sorted, so a generic method could be used.

In Java, genericity is
obtained by using
inheritance.

Unlike many of the newer languages (such as C++, which uses templates to implement generic programming), Java does not support generic implementations directly. This is because generic programming can be implemented using the basic concepts of inheritance. This section describes how generic methods and classes can be implemented in Java using the basic principles of inheritance.[1]

The basic idea in Java is that we can implement a generic class by using an appropriate superclass, such as Object. Java specifies that if a class does not extend another class, then it implicitly extends the class Object (defined in java.lang). As a result, every class is a subclass of Object.

Consider the IntCell class shown in Figure 3.2. Recall that the IntCell supports the read and write methods. We can, in principle, make this a generic MemoryCell class that stores any type of Object by replacing instances of int with Object. The resulting MemoryCell class is shown in Figure 4.16.

[1.] Direct support for generic methods and classes is under strong consideration as a possible language addition, using the keyword generic. Currently, the method described in this section is the one most widely used.

```
 1  // MemoryCell class
 2  //   Object read( )           -->   Returns the stored value
 3  //   void write( Object x ) -->   x is stored
 4
 5  public class MemoryCell
 6  {
 7          // Public methods
 8      public Object read( )          { return storedValue; }
 9      public void write( Object x ) { storedValue = x; }
10
11          // Private internal data representation
12      private Object storedValue;
13  }
```

Figure 4.16   Generic MemoryCell class

There are two details that must be considered when we use this strategy. Both are illustrated in Figure 4.17, which depicts a main that writes a 5 to a MemoryCell object and then reads from the MemoryCell object. First, a primitive type is not an Object. As a result, m.write(0) would be illegal. However, this is not a problem, since Java provides *wrapper classes* for the eight primitive types. Thus the MemoryCell stores an Integer object.

Wrapper classes must be used to have generics apply to primitive types.

The second detail is that the result of m.read() is an Object. We must first use a type conversion to generate the actual stored type, which is an Integer, and then apply the intValue method to obtain an int.[2]

Type conversions are usually needed when using generic return values.

Because the wrapper classes are final classes, the constructor and intValue accessor can be expanded inline by the compiler, thus yielding code that can be as efficient as if an int were being used directly.

```
 1  public class TestMemoryCell
 2  {
 3      public static void main( String [ ] args )
 4      {
 5          MemoryCell m = new MemoryCell( );
 6
 7          m.write( new Integer( 5 ) );
 8          System.out.println( "Contents are: " +
 9                  ( (Integer) m.read( ) ).intValue( ) );
10      }
11  }
```

Figure 4.17   Using the generic MemoryCell class

[2.] Actually, intValue does not need to be applied, since toString is meaningfully defined for the Integer class. It is used here to illustrate how the int value would be obtained in a more general setting.

A second example is the problem of sorting. We have already written an insertionSort method that works for an array of Shape. It would be nice to have it written for a generic array.

Figure 4.18 shows a generic insertion sort routine that is virtually identical to the method in Figure 4.9. It is a method in the Sort class defined in package DataStructures; several other sorting routines will be placed in this class and are discussed in Chapter 8. Notice that we do not use Object. Instead, we can sort an array of Comparable items because we expect to be able to apply the lessThan method. As a result, only classes that implement the Comparable interface can be sorted by this method. Note that this method, as written, cannot sort an array of Shape, because the Shape class in Figure 4.5 does not implement the Comparable interface. Exercise 4.15 asks you to make the necessary modifications to the Shape class.

To see how the generic Sort method is used we will write a program that reads an unlimited number of integers, sorts them, and outputs the result, as shown in Figure 4.19. The getInts method, written in Figure 2.4, is used to read the array of ints at line 11. Next, we generate an array of objects that implement our Comparable interface. The predefined class Integer does not implement Comparable, but the MyInteger class written in this chapter does. At lines 14 to 16, we create the array. Then we construct each MyInteger object that is stored in the array. The sort is performed at line 19 (we did not use the import clause, so a fully qualified method name is needed). Finally, we output the result at lines 22 to 24. Note that the toString method is implicitly called for MyInteger.

```
1  // InsertionSort: sort array a
2  // The is part of class DataStructures.Sort
3  // The package imports Supporting.*
4
5      private static void insertionSort( Comparable [ ] a )
6      {
7          for( int p = 1; p < a.length; p++ )
8          {
9              int j = p;
10             Comparable tmp = a[ p ];
11
12             for( ; j > 0 && tmp.lessThan( a[ j - 1 ] ); j-- )
13                 a[ j ] = a[ j - 1 ];
14             a[ j ] = tmp;
15         }
16     }
```

Figure 4.18   Generic insertion sort

```
1  import Supporting.*;
2
3  // Test program to read ints from the terminal (one per line)
4  // sort them, and then output them
5
6  public class SortInts
7  {
8      public static void main( String [ ] args )
9      {
10             // Read an array of int
11         int [ ] arr = ReadInts.getInts( ); // Figure 2.4
12
13             // Convert to an array of MyInteger
14         MyInteger [ ] theArray = new MyInteger[ arr.length ];
15         for( int i = 0; i < theArray.length; i++ )
16             theArray[ i ] = new MyInteger( arr[ i ] );
17
18             // Apply the sorting method
19         DataStructures.Sort.insertionSort( theArray );
20
21             // Output sorted result
22         System.out.println( "Sorted result: " );
23         for( int i = 0; i < theArray.length; i++ )
24             System.out.println( theArray[ i ] );
25      }
26  }
```

Figure 4.19   Read a bunch of ints, sort them, and output the result

Summary

Inheritance is a powerful feature that is the essential part of object-oriented programming and Java. It allows us to abstract functionality into abstract base classes and have derived classes implement and expand on that functionality. Several types of methods can be specified in the base class, as illustrated in Figure 4.20.

The most abstract class, in which no implementation is allowed, can be specified by using the *interface*. The interface lists methods that must be implemented by a derived class. The derived class must both implement all of these methods (or itself be abstract) and specify, via the *implements* clause, that it is implementing the interface. Multiple interfaces may be implemented by a class, thus providing a simpler alternative to multiple inheritance.

Finally, inheritance allows us to easily write generic methods and classes that work for a wide range of generic types. This will typically involve using type conversion operators.

Method	Overloading	Comments
final	Compile time	Invariant over the inheritance hierarchy (method is never redefined).
abstract	Run time	Base class provides no implementation and is abstract. Derived class must provide an implementation.
static	Compile time	No controlling object.
Other	Run time	Base class provides a default implementation that may be either overridden by the derived classes or accepted unchanged by the derived classes.

Figure 4.20   Four types of class methods

This chapter concludes the first part of the text, which provided an overview of Java and object-oriented programming. We will now go on to look at algorithms and the building blocks of problem-solving programming.

 Objects of the Game

abstract class A class that cannot be constructed but serves to specify functionality of derived classes. (83)

abstract method A method that has no meaningful definition and is thus always defined in the derived class. (82)

base class The class on which the inheritance is based. (77)

composition Preferred mechanism to inheritance when an IS-A relationship does not hold. Instead, we say that an object of class *B* is composed of an object of class *A* (and other objects). (75)

derived class A completely new class that nonetheless has some compatibility with the class from which it was derived. (77)

dynamic binding A run-time decision to apply the method corresponding to the actual referenced object. (76)

extends clause A clause used to declare that a new class is a subclass of another class. (78)

final class A class that may not be extended. (81)

final method A method that may not be overridden and is invariant over the inheritance hierarchy. Static binding is used for final methods. (80)

generic programming Used to implement type-independent logic. (94)

HAS-A relationship A relationship in which the derived class has a (property of the) base class. (75)

implements clause A clause used to declare that a class implements the methods of an interface. (91)

inheritance The process whereby we may derive a class from a base class without disturbing the implementation of the base class. Also allows the design of class hierarchies, such as `Exception` and `Component`. (77)

insertion sort A simple sorting algorithm that is appropriate for small inputs. (86)

interface A special kind of abstract class that contains no implementation details. (90)

IS-A relationship A relationship in which the derived class is a (variation of the) base class. (75)

leaf class A final class. (81)

multiple inheritance The process of deriving a class from several base classes. Multiple inheritance is not allowed in Java. However, the alternative, multiple interfaces, is allowed. (90)

partial overriding The act of augmenting a base class method to perform additional, but not entirely different, tasks. (81)

polymorphism The ability of a reference variable to reference objects of several different types. When operations are applied to the variable, the operation that is appropriate to the actual referenced object is automatically selected. (76)

protected class member Accessible by the derived class but private to everyone else. (79)

static binding/overloading The decision on which method to use is made at compile time. Is only used for static or final methods. (81)

subclass/superclass relationships If X IS-A Y, then X is a subclass of Y and Y is a superclass of X. These relationships are transitive. (75)

`super` constructor call A call to the base class constructor. (80)

`super` object An object used in partial overloading to apply a base class method. (81)

wrapper class A class that provides an `Object` that stores a primitive type; e.g., `Integer`. (95)

Common Errors

1. Private members of a base class are not visible in the derived class.
2. Objects of an abstract class cannot be instantiated.
3. If the derived class fails to implement any inherited abstract method, then the derived class becomes abstract. If this was not intended, a compiler error will result.
4. Final methods may not be overridden. Final classes may not be extended.
5. Static methods use static binding, even if they are overridden in a derived class.
6. In a derived class, the inherited base class members should only be initialized as an aggregate by using the `super` method. If these members are

public or protected, they may later be read or assigned to individually.

7. The throws list for a method in a derived class cannot be redefined to throw an exception not thrown in the base class. Return types must also match.

8. If a generic method returns a generic reference, then typically a type conversion must be used to obtain the actual returned object.

On the Internet

Code is provided for the `Shape` case study, all of which is in directory **Chapter04**. `Sort.java` is part of the package `DataStructures`, and thus is in directory **DataStructures**. Code that illustrates the generic `MemoryCell` is also available in **Chapter04**. Finally, the interfaces illustrated in Figures 4.12, 4.14, and 4.15 can all be found in the **Supporting** directory.

Circle.java	The `Circle` class.
Comparable.java	The `Comparable` interface in Figure 4.12, as part of the package `Supporting`.
Hashable.java	The `Hashable` interface in Figure 4.14, as part of the package `Supporting`.
MemoryCell.java	The `MemoryCell` class in Figure 4.16.
MyInteger.java	The `MyInteger` interface in Figure 4.15, as part of the package `Supporting`.
Rectangle.java	The `Rectangle` class.
Shape.java	The abstract `Shape` class.
Sort.java	A collection of generic sorting routines, in the package `DataStructures`.
SortInts.java	Contains the code in Figure 4.19.
Square.java	The `Square` class.
TestMemoryCell.java	The test program for the memory cell class shown in Figure 4.17.
TestShape.java	A test program for the `Shape` example.
Underflow.java	The `Underflow` exception class in Figure 4.3, as part of the package `Supporting`.

Exercises

In Short

4.1. What members of an inherited class can be used in the derived class? What members become public for users of the derived class?

4.2. What is composition?

4.3. Explain polymorphism.

4.4. Explain dynamic binding. When is dynamic binding not used?

4.5. What is a final method?

4.6. Consider the program to test visibility in Figure 4.21.

    a. Which accesses are illegal?

    b. Make `main` a method in `Base`. Which accesses are illegal?

    c. Make `main` a method in `Derived`. Which accesses are illegal?

    d. How do these answers change if `protected` is removed from line 4?

    e. Write a three-parameter constructor for `Base`. Then write a five-parameter constructor for `Derived`.

    f. The class `Derived` consists of five integers. Which are accessible to the class `Derived`?

    g. A method in the class `Derived` is passed a `Base` object. Which of the `Base` object members can the `Derived` class access?

4.7. What is the difference between a final class and other classes? Why are final classes used?

4.8. What is an abstract method?

4.9. What is an abstract class?

```
 1  public class Base
 2  {
 3      public     int bPublic;
 4      protected int bProtect;
 5      private    int bPrivate;
 6      // Public methods omitted
 7  }
 8
 9  public class Derived extends Base
10  {
11      public     int dPublic;
12      private    int dPrivate;
13      // Public methods omitted
14  }
15
16  public class Tester
17  {
18      public static void main( String [ ] args )
19      {
20          Base b    = new Base( );
21          Derived d = new Derived( );
22
23          System.out.println( b.bPublic + " " + b.bProtect + " "
24                            + b.bPrivate + " " + d.dPublic + " "
25                            + d.dPrivate );
26      }
27  }
```

Figure 4.21 Program to test visibility

4.10. What is an interface? How does the interface differ from an abstract class? What members may be in an interface?

4.11. How are generic algorithms implemented in Java?

In Practice

4.12. Write generic methods `min` and `max`, each of which accepts two `Comparable` parameters. Then use those methods on the `MyInteger` type.

4.13. Write generic methods `min` and `max`, each of which accepts an array of `Comparable`. Then use those methods on the `MyInteger` type.

4.14. For the `Shape` example, modify `readShape` and `main` by throwing and catching an exception (instead of creating a circle of radius zero) when an input error is detected.

4.15. Modify the `Shape` class so that it can use a generic sorting algorithm.

4.16. A `SingleBuffer` supports `get` and `put`: The `SingleBuffer` stores a single item and a data member that indicates whether the `SingleBuffer` is logically empty. A `put` may be applied only to an empty buffer, and it inserts an item into the buffer. A `get` may be applied only to a nonempty buffer, and it deletes and returns the contents of the buffer. Write a generic class to implement `SingleBuffer`. Define an exception to signal errors.

Programming Projects

4.17. Rewrite the `Shape` hierarchy to store the area as a data member and have it computed by the `Shape` constructor. The constructors in the derived classes should compute an area and pass the result to the `super` method. Make `area` a final method that returns only the value of this data member.

4.18. Add the concept of a position to the `Shape` hierarchy by including coordinates as data members. Then add a `distance` method.

4.19. Write an abstract class for `Date` and its derived class `GregorianDate`.

4.20. Implement a taxpayer hierarchy that consists of a `TaxPayer` interface and the classes `SinglePayer` and `MarriedPayer` that implement the interface.

References

The following books describe the general principles of object-oriented software development:

1. B. Meyer, *Object-Oriented Software Construction*, Prentice-Hall, Englewood Cliffs, NJ (1988).

2. B. Booch, *Object-Oriented Design and Analysis with Applications (Second Edition)*, Benjamin/Cummings, Redwood City, Calif. (1994).

3. I. Jacobson, M. Christerson, P. Jonsson, and G. Overgaard, *Object-Oriented Software Engineering: A Use Case Driven Approach* (revised fourth printing), Addison-Wesley, Reading, Mass. (1992).

4. D. de Champeaux, D. Lea, and P. Faure, *Object-Oriented System Development*, Addison-Wesley, Reading, Mass. (1993).

Part II
Algorithms and Building Blocks

5 *Algorithm Analysis*

PART I examined how object-oriented programming can help in the design and implementation of large systems. This is only half the story, however. Generally, we use a computer because we need to process a large amount of data. When we run a program on large amounts of input, we must be certain that the program terminates within a reasonable amount of time. This is almost always independent of the programming language we use or even the methodology (such as procedural versus object-oriented).

An *algorithm* is a clearly specified set of instructions the computer will follow to solve a problem. Once an algorithm is given for a problem and determined to be correct, the next step is to determine the amount of resources, such as time and space, that the algorithm will require. This step is called *algorithm analysis*. An algorithm that requires several gigabytes of main memory is not useful for most current machines, even if it is completely correct.

In this chapter, we will see:

- How to estimate the time required for an algorithm
- Techniques that drastically reduce the running time of an algorithm
- A mathematical framework that more rigorously describes the running time of an algorithm
- How to write a simple *binary search* routine

5.1   What Is Algorithm Analysis?

The amount of time that any algorithm takes to run almost always depends on the amount of input it must process. We expect, for instance, that sorting 10,000 elements requires more time than sorting 10 elements. The running time of an algorithm is thus a function of the input size. The exact value of the function depends on many factors, such as the speed of the host machine, the quality of the compiler, and in some cases, the quality of the program. For a given program on a given computer, we can plot the graph that represents the running time function. Figure 5.1 illustrates such a plot for four programs. The curves represent four common functions that are encountered in algorithm analysis: linear, $O(N \log N)$, quadratic, and cubic. The input size N ranges from 1 to 100 items,

More data means the program takes more time.

and the running times range from 0 to 10 milliseconds. A quick glance at Figure 5.1 and its companion, Figure 5.2, suggests that the linear, O(*N* log *N*), quadratic, and cubic curves represent running times in order of decreasing preference.

An example is the problem of downloading a file over the Internet. Suppose there is an initial 2-sec delay (to set up a connection), after which the download proceeds at 1.6 K/sec. Then if the file is *N* kilobytes, the time to download is described by the formula $T(N) = N/1.6 + 2$. This is a *linear function*. We can see that downloading an 80K file takes approximately 52 sec, while downloading a file twice as large (160K) takes about 102 sec, or roughly twice as long. This property, in which time essentially is directly proportional to amount of input, is the signature of a *linear algorithm*, and is the preferred scenario.

As can be seen from the graphs, some of the nonlinear curves lead to large running times. This shows, for instance, that linear is much better than cubic.

This chapter addresses several important questions:

Of the common functions encountered in algorithm analysis, linear represents the most efficient algorithm.

- Is it always important to be on the most preferred curve?
- How much better is one curve than another?
- How do we decide which curve a particular algorithm lies on?
- How do we design algorithms that avoid being on the bad curves?

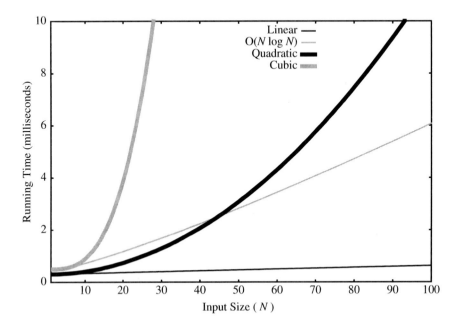

Figure 5.1 Running times for small inputs

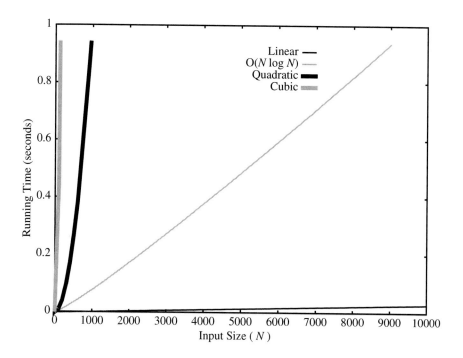

Figure 5.2   Running time for moderate inputs

A *cubic function* is a function whose dominant term is some constant times N^3. As an example, $10N^3 + N^2 + 40N + 80$ is a cubic function. Similarly, a quadratic function has a dominant term that is some constant times N^2, and a linear function has a dominant term that is some constant times N. $O(N \log N)$ represents a function whose dominant term is N times the logarithm of N. The logarithm is a slowly growing function; for instance, the logarithm of 1,000,000 (with the typical base 2) is only 20. The logarithm grows more slowly than a square or cube (or any) root. The logarithm is discussed in more depth in Section 5.5.

Either of two functions may be smaller than the other at any given point, so it does not make sense to claim, for instance, that $F(N) < G(N)$. Instead, we measure the functions' rates of growth. This is justified for three reasons. First, for cubic functions such as the one shown in Figure 5.2, when N is 1,000 the value of the cubic function is almost entirely determined by the cubic term. In the function $10N^3 + N^2 + 40N + 80$, for $N = 1,000$, the value of the function is 10,001,040,080, of which 10,000,000,000 is due to the $10N^3$ term. If we were to use only the cubic term to estimate the entire function, an error of about 0.01 percent would result. For sufficiently large N, the value of a function is largely determined by its dominant term (the meaning of the term *sufficiently large* varies by function).

> The growth rate of a function is most important when *N* is sufficiently large.

The second reason we measure the functions' growth rates is that the exact value of the leading constant of the dominant term is not meaningful across different machines (although the relative values of the leading constant for identically growing functions might be). For instance, the quality of the compiler could have a large influence on the leading constant. And third, small values of N generally are not important. For $N = 20$, Figure 5.1 shows that all algorithms terminate within 5 ms. The difference between the best and worst algorithm is less than a blink of the eye.

Big-Oh notation is used to capture the most dominant term in a function.

We use *Big-Oh* notation to represent growth rate. For instance, the running time of a quadratic algorithm is specified as $O(N^2)$ (pronounced "order N-squared"). Big-Oh notation allows us to establish a relative order among functions by comparing dominant terms. Big-Oh notation is discussed more formally in Section 5.4.

For small values of N (for instance, those less than 30), Figure 5.1 shows that there are points at which one curve is initially better than another, even though eventually this does not prove to be true. For example, initially the quadratic curve is better than the $O(N \log N)$ curve, but as N gets sufficiently large, the quadratic algorithm loses its advantage. For small amounts of input, it is difficult to make comparisons between functions because leading constants become very significant. The function $N + 2,500$ is larger than N^2 when N is less than 50. Eventually, the linear function will always be less than the quadratic function. Most important, for small input sizes the running times are generally inconsequential, so we need not worry about them. For instance, Figure 5.1 shows that when N is less than 25, all the algorithms described for this problem run in less than 10 ms. Consequently, when input sizes are very small, a good rule of thumb is to use the simplest algorithm.

Figure 5.2 clearly demonstrates the differences between the various curves for large input sizes. A linear algorithm solves a problem of size 10,000 in a small fraction of a second. The $O(N \log N)$ algorithm uses roughly ten times as much time. Note that the actual time differences depend on the constants involved and thus might be more or less. Depending on these constants, an $O(N \log N)$ algorithm might be faster than a linear algorithm for fairly large input sizes. For equally complex algorithms, however, linear algorithms tend to win over $O(N \log N)$ algorithms in practice.

Quadratic algorithms are impractical for input sizes exceeding a few thousand.

Cubic algorithms are impractical for input sizes as small as a few hundred.

This is not true, however, for the quadratic and cubic algorithms. Quadratic algorithms are almost always impractical when the input size is more than a few thousand, and cubic algorithms are impractical for input sizes as small as a few hundred. To see this at work, try to run the `insertionSort` algorithm given in Section 4.6 for 100,000 items. Be prepared to wait a long time because an insertion sort is a quadratic algorithm. The sorting algorithms discussed in Chapter 8 run in *subquadratic* time (that is, better than $O(N^2)$), thus making sorting large arrays practical.

Function	Name
c	Constant
$\log N$	Logarithmic
$\log^2 N$	Log-squared
N	Linear
$N \log N$	$N \log N$
N^2	Quadratic
N^3	Cubic
2^N	Exponential

Figure 5.3   Functions in order of increasing growth rate

The most striking feature of these curves is that the quadratic and cubic algorithms are not competitive with the others for reasonably large inputs. We can code the quadratic algorithm in highly efficient machine language and do a poor job coding the linear algorithm, and the quadratic algorithm will still lose badly. Even the most clever programming tricks cannot make an inefficient algorithm fast. Thus, before we waste effort attempting to optimize code, we need to optimize the algorithm. Figure 5.3 arranges functions that commonly describe algorithm running times in order of increasing growth rate.

5.2   Examples of Algorithm Running Times

This section examines three problems. It also sketches possible solutions and determines what kind of running times the algorithms will exhibit, without providing detailed programs. The goal in this section is to provide you with some intuition about algorithm analysis. The next section provides more details on the process, while Section 5.4 formally approaches an algorithm analysis problem.

Here are the problems we look at in this section:

MINIMUM ELEMENT IN AN ARRAY

Given an array of N items, find the smallest item.

CLOSEST POINTS IN THE PLANE

Given N points in a plane (that is, an x-y coordinate system), find the pair of points that are closest together.

COLINEAR POINTS IN THE PLANE

Given N points in a plane (that is, an x-y coordinate system), determine if any three form a straight line.

The minimum element problem is fundamental in computer science. It can be solved as follows:

1. Maintain a variable `min` that stores the minimum element.
2. Initialize `min` to the first element.
3. Make a sequential scan through the array and update `min` as appropriate.

The running time of this algorithm will be $O(N)$, or linear, because we will repeat a fixed amount of work for each element in the array. A linear algorithm is as good as we can hope for. This is because we have to examine every element in the array, a process that requires linear time.

The closest points problem is a fundamental problem in graphics that can be solved as follows:

1. Calculate the distance between each pair of points.
2. Retain the minimum distance.

This is an expensive calculation, however, because there are $N(N-1)/2$ pairs of points.[1] Thus there are roughly N^2 pairs of points. Examining all these pairs and finding the minimum distance among them will take quadratic time. There is an improved algorithm that runs in $O(N \log N)$ time and works by avoiding the computation of all distances. There is also an algorithm that is expected to take $O(N)$ time. These last two algorithms use subtle observations to provide faster results and are beyond the scope of this text.

The colinear points problem is important for many graphics algorithms. This is because the existence of colinear points introduces a degenerate case that requires special handling. It can be directly solved by enumerating all groups of three points. This solution is even more computationally expensive than that for the closest points problem because the number of different groups of three points is $N(N-1)(N-2)/6$ (using reasoning similar to that used for the closest points problem). This tells us that the direct approach will yield a cubic algorithm. There is also a more clever strategy (also beyond the scope of this text) that solves the problem in quadratic time (and further improvement is an area of continuously active research).

The next section looks at a problem that illustrates the differences between linear, quadratic, and cubic algorithms. It also shows how the performance of these algorithms compares to a mathematical prediction. Finally, after discussing the basic ideas, it examines Big-Oh notation more formally.

---

[1] To see this, note that each of N points can be paired with $N-1$ points, for a total of $N(N-1)$ pairs. However, this double counts pairs A, B and B, A, so we must divide by two.

5.3 The Maximum Contiguous Subsequence Sum Problem

In this section, we consider the following problem:

MAXIMUM CONTIGUOUS SUBSEQUENCE SUM PROBLEM

Given (possibly negative) integers $A_1, A_2, ..., A_N$, find (and identify the sequence corresponding to) the maximum value of $\sum_{k=i}^{j} A_k$. The maximum contiguous subsequence sum is zero if all the integers are negative.

As an example, if the input is $\{-2, \mathbf{11}, \mathbf{-4}, \mathbf{13}, -5, 2\}$, then the answer is 20. This represents the contiguous subsequence encompassing items 2 through 4 (that is shown in boldface type). As a second example, for the input $\{ 1, -3, \mathbf{4}, \mathbf{-2}, \mathbf{-1}, \mathbf{6} \}$, the answer is 7 for the subsequence encompassing the last four items.

In Java, arrays begin at zero, so a Java program would represent the input as a sequence A_0 to A_{N-1}. This is a programming detail and not part of the algorithm design.

Programming details are considered after the algorithm design.

Before the discussion of the algorithms for this problem, it is worth commenting on the degenerate case in which all input integers are negative. The problem statement gives a maximum contiguous subsequence sum of zero for this case. One might wonder why we do this, rather than just returning the largest (that is, the smallest in magnitude) negative integer in the input. The reason for this is that the empty subsequence, consisting of zero integers, is also a subsequence, and its sum is clearly zero. Since the empty subsequence is contiguous, we see that there is always a contiguous subsequence whose sum is zero. This is analogous to the empty set being a subset of any set. It is important to be cognizant of the fact that emptiness is always a possibility and that in many instances it is not a special case at all.

Always consider emptiness.

The maximum contiguous subsequence sum problem is interesting mainly because there are so many algorithms to solve it — and the performance of these algorithms varies drastically. This section discusses three such algorithms. The first is an obvious exhaustive search algorithm. However, it is also very inefficient. The second is an improvement on the first one accomplished by a simple observation. The third is a very efficient, but not obvious, algorithm. We prove that its running time is linear.

There are lots of drastically different algorithms (in terms of efficiency) that can be used to solve the maximum contiguous subsequence sum problem.

Chapter 7 presents a fourth algorithm, which has $O(N \log N)$ running time. That algorithm is not as efficient as the linear algorithm, but it is much more efficient than the other two and is typical of the kinds of algorithms that result in $O(N \log N)$ running times. The graphs shown in Figures 5.1 and 5.2 are representative of these four algorithms.

5.3.1 The Obvious $O(N^3)$ Algorithm

A brute force algorithm is generally the least efficient but most simple method to code.

The simplest algorithm is a direct exhaustive search, or a brute force algorithm, as shown in Figure 5.4. Lines 9 and 10 control a pair of loops that iterate over all possible subsequences. For each possible subsequence, the value of its sum is computed at lines 12 to 15. If that sum is the best sum seen, then we update the value of maxSum, which is eventually returned at line 25. Two ints — seqStart and seqEnd (which are static class fields) — are also updated whenever a new best sequence is encountered.

The direct exhaustive search algorithm has the merit of extreme simplicity; the less complex an algorithm is, the more likely it is to be programmed correctly. However, exhaustive search algorithms are usually not as efficient as possible. The remainder of this section shows that the running time of the algorithm is cubic. We count how many times (as a function of the input size) the expressions in Figure 5.4 are evaluated. We require only a Big-Oh result, so once we find a dominant term, we can ignore lower-order terms and leading constants.

```
1    /**
2     * Cubic maximum contiguous subsequence sum algorithm.
3     * seqStart and seqEnd represent the actual best sequence.
4     */
5    public static int maxSubsequenceSum( int [ ] a )
6    {
7        int maxSum = 0;
8
9        for( int i = 0; i < a.length; i++ )
10           for( int j = i; j < a.length; j++ )
11           {
12               int thisSum = 0;
13
14               for( int k = i; k <= j; k++ )
15                   thisSum += a[ k ];
16
17               if( thisSum > maxSum )
18               {
19                   maxSum = thisSum;
20                   seqStart = i;
21                   seqEnd   = j;
22               }
23           }
24
25       return maxSum;
26   }
```

Figure 5.4   Cubic maximum contiguous subsequence sum algorithm

The running time of the algorithm is entirely dominated by the innermost `for` loop in lines 14 and 15. Four expressions there are repeatedly executed:

1. The initialization `k = i`
2. The test `k <= j`
3. The increment `thisSum += a[ k ]`
4. The adjustment `k++`

The number of times expression 3 is executed makes it the dominant term among the four expressions. To see this, first notice that each initialization is accompanied by at least one test. We are ignoring constants, so we may disregard the cost of the initializations; the initializations cannot be the single dominating cost of the algorithm. Because the test given by expression 2 is unsuccessful exactly once per loop, the number of unsuccessful tests performed by expression 2 is exactly equal to the number of initializations. Consequently, it is not dominant. The number of successful tests at expression 2, the number of increments performed by expression 3, and the number of adjustments at expression 4 are all identical. Thus the number of increments (that is, the number of times that line 15 is executed) is a dominant measure of the work performed in the innermost loop.

A mathematical analysis is used to count the number of times certain statements are executed.

The number of times line 15 is executed is exactly equal to the number of ordered triplets (i, j, k) that satisfy $1 \le i \le k \le j \le N$.[2] This is because the index i runs over the entire array, j runs from i to the end of the array, and k runs from i to j. A quick and dirty estimate is that the number of triplets is somewhat less than $N \times N \times N$, or N^3, because i, j, and k can each assume one of N values. The additional restriction $i \le k \le j$ serves to reduce this. A precise calculation is somewhat difficult to obtain and is performed in Theorem 5.1.

The most important part of Theorem 5.1 is not the proof, but rather the result. There are two ways to evaluate the number of triplets. One is to evaluate the sum $\sum_{i=1}^{N} \sum_{j=i}^{N} \sum_{k=i}^{j} 1$. We could evaluate this sum inside out (see Exercise 5.8). Instead, we will use an alternative way.

The number of integer ordered triplets (i, j, k) that satisfy $1 \le i \le k \le j \le N$ is $N(N + 1)(N + 2)/6$.

Theorem 5.1

[2.] In Java, the indices run from 0 to $N - 1$. We have used the algorithmic equivalent 1 to N to simplify the analysis.

Proof

Place the following N + 2 balls in a box: N balls numbered 1 to N, one unnumbered red ball, and one unnumbered blue ball. Remove three balls from the box. If a red ball is drawn, number it as the lowest of the numbered balls drawn. If a blue ball is drawn, number it as the highest of the numbered balls drawn. Notice that if we draw both a red and blue ball, then the effect is to have three balls identically numbered. Order the three balls. Each possible order corresponds to a triplet solution to the equation in Theorem 5.1. The number of possible orders is the number of distinct ways to draw three balls without replacement from a collection of N + 2 balls. This is similar to the problem of selecting three points from a group of N that we evaluated in Section 5.2, so we immediately obtain the stated result.

The result of Theorem 5.1 is that the innermost `for` loop accounts for cubic running time. The remaining work in the algorithm is inconsequential because it is done, at most, once per iteration of the inner loop. Put another way, the cost of lines 17 to 22 is inconsequential because it is done only as often as the initialization of the inner `for` loop, rather than as often as the repeated body of the inner `for` loop. Consequently, the algorithm is $O(N^3)$.

We do not need precise calculations for a Big-Oh estimate. In many cases, we can use the simple rule of multiplying the size of all the nested loops. Note carefully that consecutive loops do not multiply.

The previous combinatoric argument allows us to obtain precise calculations on the number of iterations in the inner loop. For a Big-Oh calculation, this is not really necessary; we need to know only that the leading term is some constant times N^3. Looking at the algorithm, we see a loop that is potentially of size N inside a loop that is potentially of size N inside another loop that is potentially of size N. This tells us that the triple loop has the potential for $N \times N \times N$ iterations. This potential is only about six times higher than what our precise calculation shows actually occurs. Since constants are ignored anyway, we can adopt the general rule that when we have nested loops, we should multiply the cost of the innermost statement by the size of each loop in the nest to obtain an upper bound. In most cases, the upper bound will not be a gross overestimate.[3] Thus a program with three nested loops, each running sequentially through large portions of an array, is likely to exhibit $O(N^3)$ behavior. Note that three consecutive (non-nested) loops exhibit linear behavior; it is nesting that leads to a combinatoric explosion. Consequently, to improve the algorithm, we need to remove a loop. This is done in the next section.

[3.] Exercise 5.15 illustrates a case in which the multiplication of loop sizes yields an overestimate in the Big-Oh result.

5.3.2 An Improved $O(N^2)$ Algorithm

If we can remove a loop from the algorithm, we genereally can lower the running time. How do we remove a loop? Obviously, we cannot always do so. However, the previous algorithm has many unnecessary computations. The inefficiency that the improved algorithm corrects can be seen by noticing that since $\sum_{k=i}^{j} A_k = A_j + \sum_{k=i}^{j-1} A_k$ the computation in the inner `for` loop in Figure 5.4 is unduly expensive. Put another way, suppose we have just calculated the sum for the subsequence extending from i to $j-1$. Then computing the sum for the subsequence extending from i to j should not take long because we need only one more addition. However, the cubic algorithm throws away this information. If we use this observation, we obtain the improved algorithm shown in Figure 5.5. We have two rather than three nested loops, and the running time is $O(N^2)$.

When we remove a deeply nested loop from an algorithm, we generally lower the running time.

```
1      /**
2       * Quadratic maximum contiguous subsequence sum algorithm.
3       * seqStart and seqEnd represent the actual best sequence.
4       */
5      public static int maxSubsequenceSum( int [ ] a )
6      {
7          int maxSum = 0;
8
9          for( int i = 0; i < a.length; i++ )
10         {
11             int thisSum = 0;
12
13             for( int j = i; j < a.length; j++ )
14             {
15                 thisSum += a[ j ];
16
17                 if( thisSum > maxSum )
18                 {
19                     maxSum = thisSum;
20                     seqStart = i;
21                     seqEnd   = j;
22                 }
23             }
24         }
25
26         return maxSum;
27     }
```

Figure 5.5   Quadratic maximum contiguous subsequence sum algorithm

5.3.3 A Linear Algorithm

If we remove another loop, we are down to a linear algorithm.

To move from a quadratic algorithm down to a linear algorithm, we need to remove yet another loop. However, unlike the reduction illustrated in Figures 5.4 and 5.5, where loop removal was simple, it is not so easy to get rid of another loop. The problem is that the quadratic algorithm is still an exhaustive search; that is, we are trying all possible subsequences. The only difference between the quadratic and cubic algorithms is that the cost of testing each successive subsequence is a constant $O(1)$ instead of linear $O(N)$. Because a quadratic number of subsequences are possible, the only way we can attain a subquadratic bound is to find a clever way to eliminate from consideration a large number of subsequences, without actually computing their sum and testing to see if that sum is a new maximum. This section shows how this is done.

The algorithm is tricky. It uses a clever observation to step quickly over large numbers of subsequences that cannot be the best.

First, we eliminate a large number of possible subsequences from consideration. Let $A_{i,j}$ be the subsequence encompassing elements from i to j, and let $S_{i,j}$ be its sum.

Theorem 5.2   *Let $A_{i,j}$ be any sequence with $S_{i,j} < 0$. If $q > j$, then $A_{i,q}$ is not the maximum contiguous subsequence.*

Proof   *The sum of A's elements from i to q is the sum of A's elements from i to j added to the sum of A's elements from j + 1 to q. Thus we have $S_{i,q} = S_{i,j} + S_{j+1,q}$. Since $S_{i,j} < 0$, we know that $S_{i,q} < S_{j+1,q}$. We can thus see that $A_{i,q}$ is not a maximum contiguous subsequence.*

An illustration of the sums generated by i, j, and q is shown on the first two lines in Figure 5.6. Theorem 5.2 demonstrates that it is possible to avoid examination of several subsequences by incorporating an additional test: If `thisSum` is less than zero, then we can `break` from the inner loop in Figure 5.5. Intuitively, if we see a subsequence whose sum is negative, then it cannot be part of the maximum contiguous subsequence. This is because we can get a large contiguous subsequence by not including it. This observation by itself is not sufficient to reduce the running time below quadratic. A similar observation also holds: All contiguous subsequences that border the maximum contiguous subsequence must have negative (or zero) sums (otherwise, we would include them). This also does not reduce the running time to below quadratic. However, a third observation, illustrated in Figure 5.7, does. We can formalize this with Theorem 5.3.

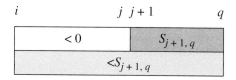

Figure 5.6   The subsequences used in Theorem 5.2

For any i, let $A_{i,j}$ be the first sequence, with $S_{i,j} < 0$. Then, for any   ***Theorem 5.3***
$i \le p \le j$ and $p \le q$, $A_{p,q}$ either is not a maximum contiguous subse-
quence or is equal to an already seen maximum contiguous subsequence.

If $p = i$, then Theorem 5.2 applies. Otherwise, as in Theorem 5.2, we   ***Proof***
have $S_{i,q} = S_{i,p-1} + S_{p,q}$. Since j is the lowest index for which $S_{i,j} < 0$,
it follows that $S_{i,p-1} \ge 0$. Thus $S_{p,q} \le S_{i,q}$. If $q > j$ (shown on the left-
hand side in Figure 5.7), then Theorem 5.2 implies that $A_{i,q}$ is not a
maximum contiguous subsequence, so neither is $A_{p,q}$. Otherwise, as
shown on the right in Figure 5.7, the subsequence $A_{p,q}$ has a sum equal
to, at most, that of the already seen subsequence $A_{i,q}$.

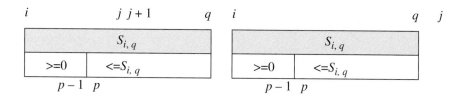

Figure 5.7   The subsequences used in Theorem 5.3. The sequence from p to
q has a sum that is, at most, that of the subsequence from i to q.
On the left-hand side the sequence from i to q is itself not the
maximum (by Theorem 5.2). On the right-hand side, the
sequence from i to q has already been seen

```
1      /**
2       * Linear maximum contiguous subsequence sum algorithm.
3       * seqStart and seqEnd represent the actual best sequence.
4       */
5      public static int maximumSubsequenceSum( int [ ] a )
6      {
7          int maxSum = 0;
8          int thisSum = 0;
9
10         for( int i = 0, j = 0; j < a.length; j++ )
11         {
12             thisSum += a[ j ];
13
14             if( thisSum > maxSum )
15             {
16                 maxSum = thisSum;
17                 seqStart = i;
18                 seqEnd   = j;
19             }
20             else if( thisSum < 0 )
21             {
22                 i = j + 1;
23                 thisSum = 0;
24             }
25         }
26
27         return maxSum;
28     }
```

Figure 5.8   Linear maximum contiguous subsequence sum algorithm

If we detect a negative sum, we can move *i* all the way past *j*.

If an algorithm is complex, a correctness proof is required.

Theorem 5.3 tells us that when a negative subsequence is detected, not only can we break the inner loop; we also can advance i to j+1. Figure 5.8 shows that we can rewrite the algorithm using only a single loop. Clearly, the running time of this algorithm is linear: At each step in the loop, we advance j, so the loop iterates at most N times. The correctness of this algorithm is much less obvious than for the previous algorithms. This is typical. That is, algorithms that use the structure of a problem to beat an exhaustive search generally require some sort of correctness proof. We have proven that the algorithm (although not the resulting Java program) is correct using a short mathematical argument. The purpose is not to make the discussion entirely mathematical, but rather to give a flavor of the techniques that might be required in advanced work.

5.4   General Big-Oh Rules

Now that we have the basic ideas of algorithm analysis, we can adopt a slightly more formal approach. This section outlines the general rules for using Big-Oh notation. Although Big-Oh notation is used almost exclusively throughout this text, three other types of algorithm notation are also defined that are related to Big-Oh and used occasionally later on in the text.

> **DEFINITION:** (Big-Oh) $T(N)$ is $O(F(N))$ if there are positive constants c and N_0 such that $T(N) \le cF(N)$ when $N \ge N_0$.

> **DEFINITION:** (Big-Omega) $T(N)$ is $\Omega(F(N))$ if there are positive constants c and N_0 such that $T(N) \ge cF(N)$ when $N \ge N_0$.

> **DEFINITION:** (Big-Theta) $T(N)$ is $\Theta(F(N))$ if and only if $T(N)$ is $O(F(N))$ and $T(N)$ is $\Omega(F(N))$.

> **DEFINITION:** (Little-Oh) $T(N)$ is $o(F(N))$ if and only if $T(N)$ is $O(F(N))$ and $T(N)$ is not $\Theta(F(N))$.

The first definition, *Big-Oh* notation, states that there is a point N_0 such that for all values of N that are past this point, $T(N)$ is bounded by some multiple of $F(N)$. This is the sufficiently large N mentioned earlier. Thus, if the running time $T(N)$ of an algorithm is $O(N^2)$, then, ignoring constants, we are guaranteeing that at some point we can bound the running time by a quadratic function. Notice that if the true running time is linear, then the statement that the running time is $O(N^2)$ is technically correct because the inequality holds. However, $O(N)$ would be the more precise claim.

If we use the traditional inequality operators to compare growth rates, then the first definition says that the growth rate of $T(N)$ is less than or equal to that of $F(N)$.

Big-Oh is similar to less than or equal to, when considering growth rates.

The second definition, $T(N) = \Omega(F(N))$, called *Big-Omega*, says that the growth rate of $T(N)$ is greater than or equal to that of $F(N)$. For instance, we might say that any algorithm that works by examining every possible subsequence in the maximum subsequence sum problem must take $\Omega(N^2)$ time because a quadratic number of subsequences are possible. This is a lower-bound argument that is used in more-advanced analysis. Later in the text, we will see one example of this, where it is demonstrated that any general-purpose sorting algorithm requires $\Omega(N \log N)$ time.

Big-Omega is similar to greater than or equal to when considering growth rates.

The third definition, $T(N) = \Theta(F(N))$, called *Big-Theta*, says that the growth rate of $T(N)$ equals the growth rate of $F(N)$. For instance, the maximum subsequence algorithm shown in Figure 5.5 runs in $\Theta(N^2)$ time. This means that the running time is bounded by a quadratic function and that this bound cannot be improved because it is also lower-bounded by another quadratic function. When we use Big-Theta notation, we are providing not only an upper bound on an algorithm but also assurances that the analysis that leads to the upper bound is as good

Big-Theta is similar to equal to when considering growth rates.

Little-Oh is similar to less than when considering growth rates.

(tight) as possible. In spite of the additional precision offered by Big-Theta, however, Big-Oh is more commonly used, except by researchers in the algorithm analysis field.

The final definition, $T(N) = o(F(N))$, called *Little-Oh*, says that the growth rate of $T(N)$ is strictly less than the growth rate of $F(N)$. This is different from Big-Oh because Big-Oh allows the possibility that the growth rates are the same. For instance, if the running time of an algorithm is $o(N^2)$, then it is guaranteed to be growing at a slower rate than quadratic (that is, it is *subquadratic*). Thus a bound of $o(N^2)$ is a better bound than $\Theta(N^2)$. Figure 5.9 illustrates the meanings of these four definitions.

Throw out leading constants, lower-order terms, and relational symbols when using Big-Oh.

A couple of stylistic notes are in order. It is bad style to include constants or low-order terms inside a Big-Oh. Do not say $T(N) = O(2N^2)$ or $T(N) = O(N^2 + N)$. In both cases, the correct form is $T(N) = O(N^2)$. Remember that in any analysis that requires a Big-Oh answer, all sorts of shortcuts are possible. Lower-order terms, leading constants, and relational symbols are all thrown away.

Now that the mathematics have formalized, we can relate it to the analysis of algorithms. The most basic rule is that *the running time of a loop is at most the running time of the statements inside the loop (including tests) times the number of iterations*. As shown earlier, the initialization and testing of the loop condition is usually no more dominant than are the statements encompassing the body of the loop.

A *worst-case bound* is a guarantee over all inputs of some size.

The running time of statements inside a group of nested loops is the running time of the statements (including tests in the innermost loop) multiplied by the sizes of all the loops. The running time of a sequence of consecutive loops is equal to the running time of the dominant loop. The time difference between a nested loop in which both indices run from 1 to N and two consecutive loops that are not nested but run over the same indices is the same as the space difference between a two-dimensional array and two one-dimensional arrays. The first case is quadratic. The second case is linear because $N + N$ is $2N$, which is still $O(N)$. Occasionally, this simple rule can overestimate the running time, but in most cases it does not. Even if it does, Big-Oh does not guarantee an exact asymptotic answer, just an upper bound.

Mathematical Expression	Relative Rates of Growth
$T(N) = O(F(N))$	Growth of $T(N)$ is $\leq$ growth of $F(N)$.
$T(N) = \Omega(F(N))$	Growth of $T(N)$ is $\geq$ growth of $F(N)$.
$T(N) = \Theta(F(N))$	Growth of $T(N)$ is $=$ growth of $F(N)$.
$T(N) = o(F(N))$	Growth of $T(N)$ is $<$ growth of $F(N)$.

Figure 5.9 Meanings of the various growth functions

	Figure 5.4	Figure 5.5	Figure 7.18	Figure 5.8
N	$O(N^3)$	$O(N^2)$	$O(N \log N)$	$O(N)$
10	0.00103	0.00045	0.00066	0.00034
100	0.47015	0.01112	0.00486	0.00063
1,000	448.77	1.1233	0.05843	0.00333
10,000	NA	111.13	0.68631	0.03042
100,000	NA	NA	8.01130	0.29832

Figure 5.10   Observed running times (in seconds) for various maximum contiguous subsequence sum algorithms

The analyses we have performed thus far are *worst-case bounds*, which are guarantees over all inputs of some size. Another form of analysis is the *average-case bound*. In this case, the running time is measured as an average over all of the possible inputs of size N. The average might differ from the worst case if, for example, a conditional statement that depends on the particular input causes an early exit from a loop. Average-case bounds are discussed in more detail in Section 5.8. For now, note that the fact that one algorithm has a better worst-case bound than another algorithm does not imply anything about their relative average-case bounds. However, in many cases average-case and worst-case bounds are closely correlated. When they are not, the bounds are discussed separately.

In an *average-case bound*, the running time is measured as an average over all of the possible inputs of size N.

The last Big-Oh item we examine is how the running time grows for each type of curve. We already saw this in the graphs in Figures 5.1 and 5.2. We want a more quantitative answer to this question: If an algorithm takes $T(N)$ time to solve a problem of size N, how long does it take to solve a larger problem? For instance, how long does it take to solve a problem when there is ten times as much input? The answers are shown in Figure 5.10. However, we want to answer the question without running the program. We hope our analytical answers will agree with the observed behavior.

We begin by examining the cubic algorithm. By assumption, we may assume that the running time is reasonably approximated by $T(N) = cN^3$. Consequently, $T(10N) = c(10N)^3$. Mathematical manipulation yields

$$T(10N) = 1000cN^3 = 1000T(N).$$

Thus the running time of a cubic program increases by a factor of 1,000 (assuming N is sufficiently large) when the amount of input is increased by a factor of 10. This is roughly confirmed by examining the increase in running time from $N = 100$ to 1,000 in Figure 5.10. Remember that we do not expect an exact answer, just a reasonable approximation. We would also expect that for $N = 10,000$, there would be another thousand-fold increase in running time. The result

If the size of the input increases by a factor of f, the running time of a cubic program increases by a factor of roughly f^3.

would be that using a cubic algorithm would require roughly two weeks of computation time. In general, if the amount of the input increases by a factor of f, then the cubic algorithm's running time increases by a factor of f^3.

If the size of the input increases by a factor of f, the running time of a quadratic program increases by a factor of roughly f^2.

We can perform similar calculations for quadratic and linear algorithms. For the quadratic algorithm, we assume that $T(N) = cN^2$. It follows that $T(10N) = c(10N)^2$. When we expand, we obtain

$$T(10N) = 100cN^2 = 100T(N).$$

So when the input size increases by a factor of ten, the running time of a quadratic program increases by a factor of approximately 100. This is also confirmed in Figure 5.10. In general, an f-fold increase in input size yields an f^2-fold increase in running time for a quadratic algorithm.

If the size of the input increases by a factor of f, then the running time of a linear program also increases by a factor of f. This is the preferred running time for an algorithm.

Finally, for a linear algorithm, a similar calculation will show that a ten-fold increase in input size results in a ten-fold increase in running time. Once again, this is confirmed experimentally. Notice, however, that for a linear program the term *sufficiently large* means a somewhat higher input size than for the other programs. This is because of the overhead of 0.0003 sec that is used in all cases. For a linear program, this term is still significant for moderate input sizes.

The analysis used here does not work when there are logarithmic terms. When an $O(N \log N)$ algorithm is presented with ten times as much input, the running time increases by a factor that is slightly larger than ten. Specifically, we have $T(10N) = c(10N)\log(10N)$. When we expand we obtain

$$T(10N) = 10cN\log(10N) = 10cN\log N + 10cN\log 10 = 10T(N) + c'N.$$

Here $c' = 10c\log 10$. As N gets very large, the ratio $T(10N)/T(N)$ gets closer and closer to 10 because $c'N/T(N) \approx (10\log 10)/\log N$ gets smaller and smaller with increasing N. Consequently, if the algorithm is competitive with a linear algorithm for very large N, it is likely to remain competitive for slightly larger N.

Does all this mean that quadratic and cubic algorithms are useless? The answer is no. In some cases, the most efficient algorithms known are quadratic or cubic. In others, the most efficient algorithm is even worse (exponential). Furthermore, when the amount of input is small, any algorithm will do, and frequently the algorithms that are not asymptotically efficient are nonetheless easy to program. For small inputs, that is the way to go. Finally, it should be pointed out that a good way to test a complex linear algorithm is to compare its output with an exhaustive search algorithm. Section 5.8 discusses some other limitations of the Big-Oh model.

5.5   The Logarithm

The list of typical growth rate functions includes several entries containing the *logarithm*. This section looks in more detail at the mathematics behind the logarithm. The next section illustrates how it shows up in a simple algorithm.

We begin with the formal definition and then follow with more intuitive viewpoints.

> **DEFINITION:** For any $B, N > 0$, $\log_B N = K$ if $B^K = N$.

In this definition, B is the base of the logarithm. In computer science, when the base is omitted, it defaults to 2. This is natural for several reasons, as is shown later in the chapter. We will prove one mathematical theorem, Theorem 5.4, to show that, as far as Big-Oh notation is concerned, the base is unimportant, and also to show how relations that involve logarithms can be derived.

The logarithm of N (to the base 2) is the value X such that 2 raised to the power of X equals N. By default, the base of the logarithm is 2.

The base does not matter. For any constant $B > 1$, $\log_B N = O(\log N)$.   **Theorem 5.4**

Let $\log_B N = K$. Then $B^K = N$. Let $C = \log B$. Then $2^C = B$. Thus $B^K = (2^C)^K = N$. Hence, we have $2^{CK} = N$, which implies that $\log N = CK = C \log_B N$. Therefore $\log_B N = (\log N)/(\log B)$, thus completing the proof.   ***Proof***

In the rest of the text, base 2 logarithms are used exclusively. An important fact about the logarithm is that it grows slowly. Because $2^{10} = 1{,}024$, $\log 1{,}024 = 10$. Additional calculations show that the logarithm of one million is roughly 20, and the logarithm of one billion is only 30. Consequently, performance of an $O(N \log N)$ algorithm is much closer to a linear $O(N)$ algorithm than to a quadratic $O(N^2)$ algorithm for even moderately large amounts of input. Before we see a realistic algorithm whose running time includes the logarithm, let us look at a few examples of how the logarithm comes into play.

BITS IN A BINARY NUMBER

How many bits are required to represent N consecutive integers?

A 16-bit `short` integer represents the 65,536 integers in the range –32,768 to 32,767. In general, B bits are sufficient to represent 2^B different integers. Thus the number of bits B required to represent N consecutive integers satisfies the equation $2^B \geq N$. Hence, we obtain $B \geq \log N$. The minimum number of bits is thus $\lceil \log N \rceil$. (Here $\lceil X \rceil$ is the ceiling function and represents the smallest integer that is at least as large as X. The corresponding floor function $\lfloor X \rfloor$ represents the largest integer that is at least as small as X.)

The number of bits required to represent numbers is logarithmic.

REPEATED DOUBLING

Starting from X = 1, how many times should X be doubled before it is at least as large as N?

Starting at 1, we can repeatedly double only logarithmically many times until we reach N.

Suppose we start with $1 and double it every year. How long would it take to save a million dollars? In this case, after 1 yr we would have $2; after 2 yr, $4; after 3 yr, $8, and so on. In general, after K years we would have 2^K dollars, so we want to find the smallest K satisfying $2^K \geq N$. This is the same equation as before, so $K = \lceil \log N \rceil$. After 20 yr, we would have over a million dollars. The *repeated doubling principle* states that starting from 1, we can repeatedly double only $\lceil \log N \rceil$ times until we reach N.

REPEATED HALVING

Starting from X = N, if N is repeatedly halved, how many iterations must be applied to make N smaller than or equal to 1?

We can halve only logarithmically many times. Doing this is used to obtain logarithmic routines for searching.

If the division rounds up to the nearest integer (or is real, not integer, division), we have the same problem as with repeated doubling, except that we are going in the opposite direction. Once again the answer is $\lceil \log N \rceil$ iterations. If the division rounds down, the answer is $\lfloor \log N \rfloor$. The difference can be seen by starting with $X = 3$. Two divisions are necessary, unless the division rounds down, in which case only one is needed.

Many of the algorithms examined in this text will have logarithms introduced because of the *repeated halving principle*. That principle is that an algorithm is $O(\log N)$ if it takes constant ($O(1)$) time to cut the problem size by a constant fraction (which is usually $1/2$). This follows directly from the fact that there will be $O(\log N)$ iterations of the loop. Any constant fraction will do because the fraction is reflected in the base of the logarithm, and Theorem 5.4 tells us that the base does not matter.

The Nth *harmonic number* is the sum of the reciprocals of the first N positive integers. The growth rate of the harmonic number is logarithmic.

All of the remaining occurrences of logarithms are introduced (either directly or indirectly) by applying Theorem 5.5. The proof uses calculus, but an understanding of the proof is not needed to use the theorem.

Theorem 5.5   Let $H_N = \sum_{i=1}^{N} 1/i$. Then $H_N = \Theta(\log N)$. A more precise estimate is $\ln N + 0.577$.

Proof   *The intuition of the proof is that a discrete sum is well approximated by the (continuous) integral. The proof uses a construction to show that the sum H_N can be bounded above and below by $\int \frac{dx}{x}$, with appropriate limits. Details are left as Exercise 5.17. H_N is known as the Nth harmonic number.*

The next section shows how the repeated halving principle leads to an efficient searching algorithm.

5.6   Static Searching Problem

An important use of computers is looking up data. If the data is not allowed to change (for instance, it is stored on a CD-ROM), we say that it is static. A *static search* accesses static data. The static searching problem is naturally formulated as follows.

> **STATIC SEARCHING PROBLEM**
> *Given an integer X and an array A, return the position of X in A or an indication that it is not present. If X occurs more than once, return any occurrence. The array A is never altered.*

An example of static searching is looking up a person in the telephone book. The efficiency of a static searching algorithm depends on whether the array being searched is sorted. In the case of the telephone book, searching by name is fast, but searching by phone number is hopeless (for humans). In this section, we examine some solutions to the static searching problem.

5.6.1   Sequential Search

When the input array is not sorted, we have little choice but to do a linear *sequential search*, stepping through the array sequentially until a match is found. The complexity of the algorithm is analyzed in three ways. First, we provide the cost of an unsuccessful search. Then, we give the worst-case cost of a successful search. Finally, we find the average cost of a successful search. Analyzing successful and unsuccessful searches separately is typical. It is also typical that unsuccessful searches are more time-consuming than are successful searches (just think about the last time you lost something in your house). For sequential searching, the analysis is straightforward.

An unsuccessful search requires the examination of every item in the array, so the time will be $O(N)$. In the worst case, a successful search, too, requires the examination of every item in the array because we might not find a match until the last item. Thus the worst-case running time for a successful search is also linear. On average, however, we search only half of the array. That is, for every successful search in position i, there is a corresponding successful search in position $N - i$ (assuming we number starting from 1). However, $N/2$ is still $O(N)$. As mentioned earlier in the chapter, all of these Big-Oh terms should correctly be Big-Theta terms. However, the use of Big-Oh is more popular.

A sequential search is linear.

5.6.2 Binary Search

If the input array is sorted, we can use the *binary search,* which we perform from the middle of the array rather than the end.

If the input array is sorted, then we have an alternative to the sequential search, the *binary search.* We perform a binary search from the middle of the array rather than the end.

At any point in time we keep track of `low` and `high`, which delimit the portion of the array in which an item, if present, must reside. Initially, the range is from 0 to $N - 1$. If `low` is larger than `high`, we know that the item is not present, so we throw an exception. Otherwise, we let `mid` be the halfway point of the range (rounding down if the range has an even number of elements) and compare the item we are searching for with the item in position `mid`. If we find a match, we are done and can return. If the item we are searching for is less than the item in position `mid`, then it must reside in the range `low` to `mid-1`. If it is greater, then it must reside in the range `mid+1` to `high`. In Figure 5.11, lines 18 to 21 alter the possible range, essentially cutting it in half. By the repeated halving principle, we know that the number of iterations will be $O(\log N)$.

The *binary search* is logarithmic because the search range is halved in each iteration.

For an unsuccessful search, the number of iterations in the loop is $\lfloor \log N \rfloor + 1$. This is because we halve the range in each iteration (rounding down if the range has an odd number of elements); we add 1 because the final range encompasses zero elements. For a successful search, the worst case is $\lfloor \log N \rfloor$ iterations because in the worst case we get down to a range of only one element. The average case is only one iteration better. This is because half of the elements require the worst case for their search, a quarter of the elements save one iteration, and only one in 2^i elements will save i iterations from the worst case. The mathematics involves computing the weighted average by calculating the sum of a finite series. The bottom line, however, is that the running time for each search is $O(\log N)$. Exercise 5.19 asks you to complete the calculation.

For reasonably large values of N, the binary search outperforms the sequential search. For instance, if N is 1,000, then on average a successful sequential search requires about 500 comparisons. The average binary search, using the previous formula, requires eight iterations for a successful search. Since each iteration uses 1.5 comparisons on average (sometimes 1, other times 2), the total is 12 comparisons for a successful search. The binary search wins by even more in the worst case or when searches are unsuccessful.

Optimizating the binary search can cut the number of comparisons roughly in half.

If we want to make the binary search even faster, we need to make the inner loop tighter. A possible strategy is to remove the (implicit) test for a successful search from that inner loop and shrink the range down to one item in all cases. Then we can use a single test outside of the loop to determine if the item is in the array or is not found, as shown in Figure 5.12 (page 130). If the item we are searching for in Figure 5.12 is not larger than the item in the `mid` position, then it is in the range that includes the `mid` position. When we break the loop, the subrange is 1, and we can test to see if we have a match.

In the revised algorithm, the number of iterations is always $\lfloor \log N \rfloor$ because we always shrink the range in half, possibly by rounding down. The number of comparisons that are used thus is always $\lfloor \log N \rfloor + 1$.

```
1       /**
2        * Performs the standard binary search
3        * using two comparisons per level.
4        * @exception ItemNotFound if appropriate.
5        * @return index where item is found.
6        */
7       public static int binarySearch( Comparable [ ] a,
8                           Comparable x ) throws ItemNotFound
9       {
10          int low = 0;
11          int high = a.length - 1;
12          int mid;
13
14          while( low <= high )
15          {
16              mid = ( low + high ) / 2;
17
18              if( a[ mid ].compares( x ) < 0 )
19                  low = mid + 1;
20              else if( a[ mid ].compares( x ) > 0 )
21                  high = mid - 1;
22              else
23                  return mid;
24          }
25
26          throw new ItemNotFound( "BinarySearch fails" );
27      }
```

Figure 5.11   Basic binary search that uses three-way comparisons

Binary search is surprisingly tricky to code. Exercise 5.5 illustrates some common errors.

Notice that for small *N*, such as values smaller than 6, the binary search might not be worth using. It uses roughly the same number of comparisons for a typical successful search, but it has the overhead of line 19 in each iteration. Indeed, the last few iterations of the binary search progress slowly. One can adopt a hybrid strategy in which the binary search loop terminates when the range is small and applies a sequential scan to finish. Similarly, people search a phone book nonsequentially. Once they have narrowed the range down to a column, they perform a sequential scan. The scan of a telephone book is not sequential, but it also is not a binary search. This is discussed in the next section.

5.6.3   Interpolation Search

The binary search is very fast searching a sorted static array. In fact, it is so fast that we would rarely use anything else. A static searching method that is sometimes faster, however, is an *interpolation search*. For an interpolation search to be practical, two assumptions must be satisfied:

```
1      /**
2       * Performs the standard binary search
3       * using one comparison per level.
4       * @exception ItemNotFound if appropriate.
5       * @return index where item is found.
6       */
7      public static int binarySearch( Comparable [ ] a,
8                                Comparable x ) throws ItemNotFound
9      {
10         if( a.length == 0 )
11             throw new ItemNotFound( "BinarySearch fails" );
12
13         int low = 0;
14         int high = a.length - 1;
15         int mid;
16
17         while( low < high )
18         {
19             mid = ( low + high ) / 2;
20
21             if( a[ mid ].compares( x ) < 0 )
22                 low = mid + 1;
23             else
24                 high = mid;
25         }
26
27         if( a[ low ].compares( x ) == 0 )
28             return low;
29
30         throw new ItemNotFound( "BinarySearch fails" );
31     }
32 }
```

Figure 5.12   Binary search using two-way comparisons

1. Each access must be very expensive compared to a typical instruction. For example, the array might be on a disk instead of in memory, and each comparison requires a disk access.
2. The data must not only be sorted; it must also be fairly uniformly distributed. For example, a phone book is fairly uniformly distributed. If the input items are {1, 2, 4, 8, 16, …}, then the distribution is not uniform.

These assumptions are quite restrictive, so you might never use an interpolation search. But it is interesting to see that there is more than one way to solve a problem and that no algorithm, not even the classic binary search, is the best in all situations.

The idea of the interpolation search is that we are willing to spend more time to make an accurate guess regarding where the item might be. The binary search always uses the midpoint. However, it would be silly to search for *Hank Aaron* in the middle of the phone book; somewhere near the start clearly would be more appropriate. Thus, instead of `mid`, we use `next` to indicate the next item we will try to access.

Here's an example of what might be good. Suppose the range contains 1,000 items, the low item in the range is 1,000, the high item in the range is 1,000,000, and we are searching for an item of value 12,000. If the items are uniformly distributed, then we expect to find a match somewhere near the twelfth item. The applicable formula is

$$next = low + \left\lceil \frac{x - a[low]}{a[high] - a[low]} \times (high - low - 1) \right\rceil.$$

The subtraction of 1 is a technical adjustment that has been shown to perform well in practice. Clearly, this calculation is more costly then the binary search calculation. It involves an extra division (the division by 2 in the binary search is really just a bit shift, just as dividing by 10 is easy for humans), multiplication, and four subtractions. These calculations need to be done using floating-point operations. One iteration may be slower than the complete binary search. However, if the cost of these calculations is insignificant when compared to the cost of accessing an item, this is immaterial; we care only about the number of iterations.

In the worst case, where data is not uniformly distributed, the running time could be linear and every item might be examined. Exercise 5.18 asks you to construct such a case. However, under the assumption that the items are reasonably distributed, as with a phone book, the average number of comparisons has been shown to be $O(\log\log N)$. This means that we apply the logarithm twice in succession. For $N = 4$ billion, $\log N$ is about 32 and $\log\log N$ is roughly 5. Of course, there are some hidden constants in Big-Oh notation, but the extra logarithm can lower the number of iterations considerably, as long as a bad case does not crop up. Proving the result rigorously, however, is quite complicated.

Interpolation search has a better Big-Oh bound on average than does binary search, but it has limited practicality and a bad worst case.

5.7   Checking an Algorithm Analysis

Once we have performed an algorithm analysis, we want to see if it is correct and as good as possible. One way to do this is to code the program and see if the empirically observed running time matches the running time predicted by the analysis.

When N increases by a factor of ten, the running time goes up by a factor of ten for linear programs, 100 for quadratic programs, and 1,000 for cubic programs. Programs that run in $O(N \log N)$ take slightly more than ten times as long to run under the same circumstances. These increases can be hard to spot if the lower-order terms have relatively large coefficients and N is not large enough. An example is the jump from $N = 10$ to $N = 100$ in the running time for the various implementations of the maximum contiguous subsequence sum problem. It also can be very difficult to differentiate linear programs from $O(N \log N)$ programs based purely on empirical evidence.

Another commonly used trick to verify that some program is $O(F(N))$ is to compute the values $T(N)/F(N)$ for a range of N (usually spaced out by factors of two), where $T(N)$ is the empirically observed running time. If $F(N)$ is a tight answer for the running time, then the computed values converge to a positive constant. If $F(N)$ is an overestimate, the values converge to zero. If $F(N)$ is an underestimate, and hence wrong, the values diverge.

As an example, suppose we write a program to perform N random searches using the binary search algorithm. Since each search is logarithmic, we expect the total running time of the program to be $O(N \log N)$. Figure 5.13 shows the actual observed running time for the routine for various input sizes on a real computer. The table shows that the last column is most likely the converging column and thus confirms our analysis, whereas the increasing numbers for T/N suggest that $O(N)$ is an underestimate and the quickly decreasing values for T/N^2 suggest that $O(N^2)$ is an overestimate.

Note in particular that we do not have definitive convergence. One problem is that the clock that we used to time the program ticks only every 10 ms. Note also that there is not a great difference between $O(N)$ and $O(N \log N)$. Certainly an $O(N \log N)$ algorithm is much closer to being linear than being quadratic. Finally, note that the machine in this example has enough memory to store 640,000 objects (in the case of this experiment, integers). If this is not true on your machine, then you will not be able to reproduce similar results.

The next section discusses some of the limitations of the Big-Oh analysis.

N	CPU Time T (milliseconds)	T/N	T/N^2	$T/(N \log N)$
10,000	100	0.01000000	0.00000100	0.00075257
20,000	200	0.01000000	0.00000050	0.00069990
40,000	440	0.01100000	0.00000027	0.00071953
80,000	930	0.01162500	0.00000015	0.00071373
160,000	1,960	0.01225000	0.00000008	0.00070860
320,000	4,170	0.01303125	0.00000004	0.00071257
640,000	8,770	0.01370313	0.00000002	0.00071046

Figure 5.13 Empirical running time for N binary searches in an N-item array

5.8 Limitations of Big-Oh Analysis

Big-Oh analysis is a very effective tool, but it is important to be aware of its limitations. As already mentioned, it is not appropriate for small amounts of input. With small inputs, use the simplest algorithm. Also, for a particular algorithm, the constant implied by the Big-Oh may be too large to be practical. For example, if one algorithm's running time is governed by the formula $2N \log N$ and another has a running time of $1000N$, then the first algorithm would most likely be better, even though its growth rate is larger. Large constants can come into play when an algorithm is excessively complex. They also come into play because our analysis disregards constants and thus cannot differentiate between things like memory access (which is cheap) and disk access (which typically is many thousand times more expensive). Our analysis assumes infinite memory, but in applications involving large data sets, lack of sufficient memory can be a severe problem.

Sometimes, even when constants and lower-order terms are considered, the analysis is shown empirically to be an overestimate. In this case, then the analysis needs to be tightened (usually by a clever observation). Or the average-case running time bound may be significantly less than the worst-case running time bound, and so no improvement in the bound is possible. There are many complicated algorithms for which the worst-case bound is achievable by some bad input, but in practice it is usually an overestimate. Two examples are the sorting algorithms Shellsort and quicksort (both are described in Chapter 8).

Worse case is sometimes uncommon and can be safely ignored. At other times, it is very common and cannot be ignored.

However, worst-case bounds are usually easier to obtain than their average-case counterparts. For example, a mathematical analysis of the average-case running time of Shellsort has not been obtained. Sometimes, merely defining what "average" means is difficult. We use a worst-case analysis because it is expedient and also because, in most instances, the worst-case analysis is very meaningful. In the course of performing the analysis, we frequently can tell if it will apply to the average case.

Average-case analysis is almost always much more difficult than worst-case analysis.

Summary

This chapter introduced the broad subject of algorithm analysis and showed that algorithmic decisions generally influence the running time of a program much more than programming tricks. It also showed the huge difference between quadratic and linear programs and illustrated that cubic algorithms are, for the most part, unsatisfactory. An algorithm was examined that could be viewed as the basis for our first data structure. The binary search efficiently supports static operations (that is, searching but not updating), thereby providing a logarithmic worst-case search. Later chapters in the text examine dynamic data structures that will efficiently support updates (both insertion and deletion).

The next chapter defines data structures and their allowable operations. Also, it looks at some applications of data structures and discusses their efficiency.

Objects of the Game

average-case bound The bound in which the running time is measured as an average over all of the possible inputs of size N. (123)

Big-Oh The notation used to capture the most dominant term in a function. Big-Oh is similar to less than or equal to when considering growth rates. (110)

Big-Omega The notation similar to greater than or equal to when considering growth rates. (121)

Big-Theta The notation similar to equal to when considering growth rates. (121)

binary search The search method used if the input array is sorted. Searches are performed from the middle rather than the end. The binary search is logarithmic because the search range is halved in each iteration. (128)

harmonic numbers The Nth harmonic number is the sum of the reciprocals of the first N positive integers. The growth rate of the harmonic numbers is logarithmic. (126)

interpolation search A static searching algorithm that has better Big-Oh performance on average than binary search but has limited practicality and a bad worst case. (131)

linear time algorithm An algorithm that causes the running time to grow as $O(N)$. If the size of the input increases by a factor of f, then the running time also increases by a factor of f. This is the preferred running time for an algorithm. (124)

Little-Oh The notation similar to less than when considering growth rates. (122)

logarithm The logarithm of N (to the base 2) is the value X such that 2 raised to the power of X equals N. (125)

repeated-doubling principle The principle whereby if we start at 1, we can repeatedly double only logarithmically many times until we reach N. (126)

repeated-halving principle The principle whereby if we start at N, we can repeatedly halve only logarithmically many times until we reach 1. This is used to obtain logarithmic routines for searching. (126)

sequential search A linear search method that steps through an array until a match is found. (127)

static search Finds an item in data that is never altered. (127)

subquadratic An algorithm whose running time is strictly slower than quadratic. The running time can be written as $o(N^2)$. (122)

worst-case bound A guarantee over all inputs of some size. (122)

 Common Errors

1. For nested loops, the total time is affected by the product of the loop sizes. For consecutive loops, it is not.

2. Do not just blindly count the number of loops. A pair of nested loops that each run from 1 to N^2 accounts for $O(N^4)$ time.

3. Do not write expressions such as $O(2N^2)$ or $O(N^2 + N)$. Only the dominant term, with the leading constant removed, is needed.

4. Use equalities with Big-Oh, Big-Omega, and so on. Do not write that the running time is $> O(N^2)$; this makes no sense because Big-Oh is an upper bound. Do not write that the running time is $< O(N^2)$; if the intention is to say that the running time is strictly less than quadratic, use Little-Oh notation.

5. Use Big-Omega, not Big-Oh, to express a lower bound.

6. Use the logarithm to describe the running time for a problem that is solved by halving its size in constant time. If it takes more than constant time to halve the problem, the logarithm does not apply.

7. The base of the logarithm is irrelevant for the purposes of Big-Oh. It is an error to include it.

On the Internet

The three maximum contiguous subsequence sum algorithms, as well as a fourth taken from Section 7.5, are available, along with a `main` that conducts the timing tests. Also provided is a binary search algorithm in the `DataStructures` package. Here are the file names and the directories:

BinarySearch.java   Contains the binary search shown in Figure 5.12, except it is slightly modified. Found in directory **DataStructures**. Figure 5.11 is found in directory **Chapter05**.

MaxSumTest.java   Contains four algorithms for the maximum subsequence sum problem. Found in directory **Chapter05**.

Exercises

In Short

5.1. Balls are drawn from a box as specified in Theorem 5.1 in the combinations given in (a) to (d). What are the corresponding values of i, j, and k?
   a. Red, 5, 6
   b. Blue, 5, 6
   c. Blue, 3, Red
   d. 6, 5, Red

5.2. Why isn't an implementation based solely on Theorem 5.2 sufficient to obtain a subquadratic running time for the maximum contiguous subsequence sum problem?

5.3. Suppose $T_1(N) = O(F(N))$ and $T_2(N) = O(F(N))$. Which of the following are true:

a. $T_1(N) + T_2(N) = O(F(N))$
b. $T_1(N) - T_2(N) = O(F(N))$
c. $T_1(N) / T_2(N) = O(1)$
d. $T_1(N) = O(T_2(N))$

5.4. Programs A and B are analyzed and are found to have worst-case running times no greater than $150N \log N$ and N^2, respectively. Answer the following questions, if possible:

a. Which program has the better guarantee on the running time for large values of N ($N > 10,000$)?
b. Which program has the better guarantee on the running time for small values of N ($N < 100$)?
c. Which program will run faster *on average* for $N = 1,000$?
d. Is it possible that program B will run faster than program A on *all* possible inputs?

5.5. For the binary search routine in Figure 5.11, show the consequences of the following replacement code fragments:

a. Line 14: using the test `low < high`
b. Line 16: assigning `mid = low + high / 2`
c. Line 19: assigning `low = mid`
d. Line 21: assigning `high = mid`

In Theory

5.6. Determine, for the typical algorithms that you use to perform calculations by hand, the running time to do the following:

a. Add two N-digit integers.
b. Multiply two N-digit integers.
c. Divide two N-digit integers.

5.7. In terms of N, what is the running time of the following algorithm to compute X^N:

```
public static double power( double x, int n )
{
    double result = 1.0;

    for( int i = 0; i < n; i++ )
        result *= x;
    return result;
}
```

5.8. Directly evaluate the triple summation that precedes Theorem 5.1. Verify that the answers are identical.

5.9. For the quadratic algorithm, determine precisely how many times the innermost statement is executed.

5.10. An algorithm takes 0.5 ms for input size 100. How long will it take for input size 500 if the running time is the following (assume low-order terms are negligible):
a. linear
b. $O(N \log N)$
c. quadratic
d. cubic

5.11. An algorithm takes 0.5 ms for input size 100. How large a problem can be solved in 1 min if the running time is the following (assume low-order terms are negligible):
a. linear
b. $O(N \log N)$
c. quadratic
d. cubic

5.12. Complete the table in Figure 5.10 with estimates for the running times that were too long to simulate. Interpolate the running times for all four algorithms and estimate the time required to compute the maximum contiguous subsequence sum of one million numbers. What assumptions have you made?

5.13. Order the following functions by growth rate: N, $\sqrt{N}$, $N^{1.5}$, N^2, $N \log N$, $N \log \log N$, $N \log^2 N$, $N \log(N^2)$, $2/N$, 2^N, $2^{N/2}$, 37, N^3, and $N^2 \log N$. Indicate which functions grow at the same rate.

5.14. For each of the following six program fragments, do the following:
a. Give a Big-Oh analysis of the running time.
b. Implement the code and run for several values of N.
c. Compare your analysis with the actual running times.

```
// Fragment #1
for( int i = 0; i < n; i++ )
    sum++;

// Fragment #2
for( int i = 0; i < n; i++ )
    for( int j = 0; j < n; j++ )
        sum++;

// Fragment #3
for( int i = 0; i < n; i++ )
    sum++;
for( int j = 0; j < n; j++ )
    sum++;

// Fragment #4
for( int i = 0; i < n; i++ )
    for( int j = 0; j < n * n; j++ )
        sum++;
```

```
// Fragment #5
for( int i = 0; i < n; i++ )
    for( int j = 0; j < i; j++ )
        sum++;

// Fragment #6
for( int i = 0; i < n; i++ )
    for( int j = 0; j < n * n; j++ )
        for( int k = 0; k < j; k++ )
            sum++;
```

5.15. Occasionally, multiplying the sizes of nested loops can give an overestimate for the Big-Oh running time. This happens when an innermost loop is infrequently executed. Repeat Exercise 5.14 for the following program fragment:

```
for( int i = 1; i < n; i++ )
    for( int j = 0; j < i * i; j++ )
        if( j % i == 0 )
            for( int k = 0; k < j; k++ )
                sum++;
```

5.16. In a recent court case, a judge cited a city for contempt and ordered a fine of $2 for the first day. Each subsequent day, until the city followed the judge's order, the fine was squared (that is, the fine progressed as follows: $2, $4, $16, $256, $65536, ...).
   a. What would be the fine on day N?
   b. How many days would it take for the fine to reach D dollars (a Big-Oh answer will do)?

5.17. Prove Theorem 5.5. *Hint*: Show that $\sum_2^N \frac{1}{i} < \int_1^N \frac{dx}{x}$. Then show a similar lower bound.

5.18. Construct an example whereby an interpolation search examines every element in the input array.

5.19. Analyze the cost of an average successful search for the binary search algorithm.

In Practice

5.20. Give an efficient algorithm to determine if there exists an integer i such that $A_i = i$ in an array of increasing integers. What is the running time of your algorithm?

5.21. A prime number has no factors besides 1 and itself. Do the following:
   a. Write a program to determine if a positive integer N is prime. In terms of N, what is the worst-case running time of your program?
   b. Let B equal the number of bits in the binary representation of N. What is the value of B?
   c. In terms of B, what is the worst-case running time of your program?

     d. Compare the running times to determine if a 20-bit number and a 40-bit number are prime.

5.22. An important problem in numerical analysis is to find a solution to the equation $F(X) = 0$ for some arbitrary F. If the function is continuous and has two points *low* and *high* such that $F(low)$ and $F(high)$ have opposite signs, then a root must exist between *low* and *high* and can be found by either a binary search or an interpolation search. Write a function that takes as parameters F, *low*, and *high* and solves for a zero. What must you do to ensure termination?

5.23. A majority element in an array A of size N is an element that appears more than $N/2$ times (thus there is at most one). For example, the array

     3, 3, 4, 2, 4, 4, 2, 4, 4

has a majority element (4), whereas the array

     3, 3, 4, 2, 4, 4, 2, 4

does not. Give an algorithm to find a majority element if one exists, or report that one does not. What is the running time of your algorithm? (There is an $O(N)$ solution.)

Programming Projects

5.24. The Sieve of Eratosthenes is a method used to compute all primes less than N. Begin by making a table of integers 2 to N. Find the smallest integer, i, that is not crossed out. Then print i and cross out $i, 2i, 3i, \ldots$. When $i > \sqrt{N}$, the algorithm terminates. The running time has been shown to be $O(N \log \log N)$. Write a program to implement the Sieve and verify that the running time is as claimed. How difficult is it to differentiate the running time from $O(N)$ and $O(N \log N)$?

5.25. The equation $A^5 + B^5 + C^5 + D^5 + E^5 = F^5$ has exactly one integral solution that satisfies $0 < A \le B \le C \le D \le E \le F \le 75$. Write a program to find the solution. *Hint:* First, precompute all values of X^5 and store them in an array. Then, for each tuple (A, B, C, D, E), you only need to check that there exists some F in the array. There are several ways to check for F. One method is to use a binary search to check for F. Other methods might prove to be more efficient.

5.26. Implement the maximum contiguous subsequence sum algorithms to obtain data equivalent to the data in Figure 5.10. Compile the programs with the highest optimization settings.

References

The maximum contiguous subsequence sum problem is from [5]. Books [4], [5], and [6] show how to optimize programs for speed. Interpolation search was first suggested in [14] and was analyzed in [13]. Books [1], [8], and [17] provide a more rigorous treatment of algorithm analysis. The three-part series [10], [11], and [12], newly updated, remains the foremost reference work on the topic. The mathematical background required for more advanced algorithm analysis is provided by [2], [3], [7], [15], and [16]. An especially good book for advanced analysis is [9].

1. A. V. Aho, J. E. Hopcroft, and J. D. Ullman, *The Design and Analysis of Computer Algorithms*, Addison-Wesley, Reading, Mass. (1974).

2. M. O. Albertson and J. P. Hutchinson, *Discrete Mathematics with Algorithms*, John Wiley & Sons, New York, NY (1988).

3. Z. Bavel, *Math Companion for Computer Science*, Reston Publishing Company, Reston, Va, (1982).

4. J. L. Bentley, *Writing Efficient Programs*, Prentice-Hall, Englewood Cliffs, NJ (1982).

5. J. L. Bentley, *Programming Pearls*, Addison-Wesley, Reading, Mass. (1986).

6. J. L. Bentley, *More Programming Pearls*, Addison-Wesley, Reading, Mass. (1988).

7. R. A. Brualdi, *Introductory Combinatorics*, North-Holland, New York, NY (1977).

8. T. H. Cormen, C. E. Leiserson, and R. L. Rivest, *Introduction to Algorithms*, MIT Press, Cambridge, Mass. (1990).

9. R. L. Graham, D. E. Knuth, and O. Patashnik, *Concrete Mathematics*, Addison-Wesley, Reading, Mass. (1989).

10. D. E. Knuth, *The Art of Computer Programming, Vol 1: Fundamental Algorithms*, 3d ed., Addison-Wesley, Reading, Mass (1997).

11. D. E. Knuth, *The Art of Computer Programming, Vol 2: Seminumerical Algorithms,* 3d ed., Addison-Wesley, Reading, Mass. (1997).

12. D. E. Knuth, *The Art of Computer Programming, Vol 3: Sorting and Searching*, 2d ed., Addison-Wesley, Reading, Mass. (1997).

13. Y. Pearl, A. Itai, and H. Avni, "Interpolation Search – A log log N Search," *Communications of the ACM* **21** (1978), 550–554.

14. W. W. Peterson, "Addressing for Random Storage," *IBM Journal of Research and Development* **1** (1957), 131–132.

15. F. S. Roberts, *Applied Combinatorics*, Prentice-Hall, Englewood Cliffs, NJ (1984).

16. A. Tucker, *Applied Combinatorics*, 2d ed., John Wiley & Sons, New York, NY (1984).

17. M. A. Weiss, *Data Structures and Algorithm Analysis in C*, 2d ed., Benjamin/Cummings, Redwood City, Calif. (1997).

6   *Data Structures*

M ANY algorithms require that we use a proper representation of data to achieve efficiency. This representation and the operations that are allowed for it are called a *data structure*. Each data structure allows arbitrary insertion. Data structures vary in how they allow access to members in the group. Some allow arbitrary access and deletions. Others impose restrictions, such as allowing access only to the most-recently inserted or least-recently inserted item in the group.

This chapter discusses seven of the most common data structures: stacks, queues, linked lists, trees, binary search trees, hash tables, and priority queues. The goal is to define each data structure as well as give an intuitive feel for the time complexity of efficient insertion, deletion, and access operations. An efficient implementation is deferred until Parts IV and V.

In this chapter, we will see:

- Descriptions of common data structures, their allowed operations, and their running times
- For each data structure, a Java class interface containing the protocol that must be implemented
- Some applications of the data structures

These data structures are used in the case studies in Part III of the book and implemented in Part IV. The goal is to show that the specification, which describes the functionality, is independent of the implementation. We do not need to know *how* something is implemented as long as we know that it *is* implemented.

6.1   Why Do We Need Data Structures?

Data structures allow us to achieve an important object-oriented programming goal: component reuse. As is shown later in the chapter, the data structures described in this section (and implemented later) have recurring uses. Once each data structure has been implemented once, it can be used over and over again in various applications. In this chapter only the interface is provided. Consideration of efficient implementation is deferred to Part IV.

A *data structure* is a representation of data and the operations allowed on that data.

```
 1  // MemCell interface: simulate one generic RAM cell
 2  //
 3  // ******************PUBLIC OPERATIONS********************
 4  // Object read( )          --> Returns the stored value
 5  // void write( Object x ) --> Stores x
 6
 7  public interface MemCell
 8  {
 9      Object read( );
10      void write( Object x );
11  }
```

Figure 6.1   Interface for the abstract memory cell class

Data structures al-
low us to achieve
component reuse.

This approach — the separation of the interface and implementation — is part of the object-oriented paradigm. The user of the data structure does not need to see the implementation, only the available operations. This is the encapsulation and information-hiding part of object-oriented programming. However, another important part of object-oriented programming is *abstraction*. We must think more carefully about the design of the data structures because we must write programs that use these data structures without having their implementations. This in turn makes the interface cleaner, more flexible (that is, more reusable), and generally easier to implement.

All the data structures are easy to implement if we are not concerned about performance. This allows us to plug "cheap" components into our program for the purposes of debugging. The exercises at the end of this chapter ask you to write inefficient implementations that are suitable for processing small amounts of data. Later, we replace the "cheap" data structure implementations with implementations that have better time-performance and/or space-performance properties and that are suitable for processing large amounts of data. Because the interfaces are fixed, these changes require virtually no change to the programs that use the data structures.

This chapter describes data structures by using interfaces. In Parts IV and V we implement the interface and at that time derive a new class. For instance, the stack is specified by the interface Stack. When we implement it in Chapter 15, a resulting class will be named StackAr (for an array-based implementation). In all cases, the new class will implement the specifications of the interface and may include some additional functionality.

As an example, in Figure 6.1 is an interface for the memory cell described in Section 4.6. The interface describes the available functions; the concrete derived class must provide a definition. The implementation is shown in Figure 6.2 and is identical to that in Figure 4.16, except for the implements clause. The main routine in Figure 4.17 can be used without change.

```
1  // MemoryCell class
2  //
3  // *****************PUBLIC OPERATIONS*********************
4  //
5  //   Object read( )           --> Returns the stored value
6  //   void write( Object x ) --> Stores x
7
8  public class MemoryCell implements MemCell
9  {
10         // Public methods
11     public Object read( )           { return storedValue; }
12     public void write( Object x ) { storedValue = x; }
13
14         // Private internal data representation
15     private Object storedValue;
16 }
```

Figure 6.2   Implementation of the concrete memory cell class

To save space, the interfaces shown in this text contain concise comments prior to the start of the class rather than the more verbose javadoc comments. The online code has both types of comments. It is important to notice that the data structures implemented here store references to the inserted items and do not make internal copies. Hence, it is good practice to place immutable objects into these data structures so that an external agent cannot change the state of an object that is referenced inside a data structure container.

It is important to notice that the data structures implemented here store references to the inserted items and do not make internal copies.

6.2   Stacks

A *stack* is a data structure in which all access is restricted to the most-recently-inserted elements. It behaves very much like the common stack of bills, stack of plates, or stack of newspapers. The last item added to the stack is placed on the top and is easily accessible, while items that have been in the stack for a while are more difficult to access. Thus the stack is appropriate if we expect to access only the top item; all other items are inaccessible.

*A *stack* restricts access to the most-recently-inserted item.*

In a stack, the three natural operations of `insert`, `delete`, and `find` are renamed `push`, `pop`, and `top`. These basic operations are illustrated in Figure 6.3. A Java interface for an abstract stack is shown in Figure 6.4. It includes a `topAndPop` method that combines two operations. There are no new Java features introduced there. Figure 6.5 shows how a `Stack` class is used and provides corresponding output. Notice that the stack can be used to reverse things.

Each stack operation should take a constant amount of time, independent of the number of items in the stack. By analogy, finding today's newspaper in a stack of newspapers is fast, no matter how deep the stack is. However, arbitrary access in a stack is not efficiently supported, so we do not list it as an option.

Stack operations should take a constant amount of time.

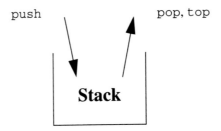

Figure 6.3 Stack model: Input to a stack is by `push`, access is by `top`, deletion is by `pop`

What makes the stack useful is that there are many applications for which we need to access only the most-recently-inserted item. As an illustration, an important use of stacks in compiler design is described in the next section.

```
 1 package DataStructures;
 2
 3 import Exceptions.*;
 4
 5 // Stack interface
 6 //
 7 // ****************PUBLIC OPERATIONS********************
 8 // void push( x )          --> Insert x
 9 // void pop( )             --> Remove most recently inserted item
10 // Object top( )           --> Return most recently inserted item
11 // Object topAndPop( )     --> Return and remove most recent item
12 // boolean isEmpty( )      --> Return true if empty; else false
13 // void makeEmpty( )       --> Remove all items
14 // ****************ERRORS*******************************
15 // top, pop, or topAndPop on empty stack
16
17 public interface Stack
18 {
19     void    push( Object x );
20     void    pop( )          throws Underflow;
21     Object  top( )          throws Underflow;
22     Object  topAndPop( ) throws Underflow;
23     boolean isEmpty( );
24     void    makeEmpty( );
25 }
```

Figure 6.4 Interface for the stack

```
1  import DataStructures.*;
2  import Exceptions.*;
3
4  // Simple test program for stacks
5
6  public final class TestStack
7  {
8      public static void main( String [ ] args )
9      {
10         Stack s = new StackAr( );
11
12         for( int i = 0; i < 5; i++ )
13             s.push( new Integer( i ) );
14
15         System.out.print( "Contents:" );
16         try
17         {
18             for( ; ; )
19                 System.out.print( " " + s.topAndPop( ) );
20         }
21         catch( Underflow e ) { }
22
23         System.out.println( );
24     }
25 }
```

Figure 6.5   Sample stack program: Output is
`Contents:  4  3  2  1  0`

6.2.1   Stacks and Computer Languages

Compilers check your programs for syntax errors. Often, however, a lack of one symbol (such as a missing comment ender */ or }) will cause the compiler to spill out a hundred lines of diagnostics without identifying the real error.

A useful tool in this situation is a program that checks whether everything is balanced; that is, that every { corresponds to a }, every [to a], and so on. The sequence [( )] is legal, but [( ]) is not, so simply counting the numbers of each symbol is insufficient. (Assume for now that we are processing only a sequence of tokens and will not worry about problems such as the character constant ' { ' not needing a matching ' } '.)

A stack is useful for checking unbalanced symbols because we know that when a closing symbol such as) is seen, it matches the most-recently-seen unclosed (. Therefore, by placing opening symbols on a stack, we can easily

A stack can be used to check for unbalanced symbols.

check that a closing symbol makes sense. Specifically, we have the following algorithm:

1. Make an empty stack.
2. Read symbols until the end of the file.
   a. If the symbol is an opening symbol, push it onto the stack.
   b. If it is a closing symbol and if the stack is empty, then report an error.
   c. Otherwise, pop the stack. If the symbol popped is not the corresponding opening symbol, then report an error.
3. At the end of the file, if the stack is not empty, report an error.

In Section 11.1, we will develop this algorithm to work for (almost) all Java programs. Details include error reporting, as well as the processing of comments, strings, character constants, and escape sequences.

The stack is used to implement method calls in most languages.

The algorithm to check balanced symbols suggests a way to implement method calls. The problem is that when a call is made to a new method, all the variables local to the calling method need to be saved by the system; otherwise, the new method would overwrite the calling routine's variables. Furthermore, the current location in the calling routine must be saved so that the new method knows where to go after it is done. This problem is similar to balancing symbols because a method call and a method return are essentially the same as an open parenthesis and a close parenthesis, so the same ideas should apply. This indeed is the case. As discussed in Section 7.3, the stack is used to implement method calls in many programming languages.

The operator precedence parsing algorithm uses a stack to evaluate expressions.

A final important application of the stack is the evaluation of expressions in computer languages. In the expression $1+2*3$, at the point that the $*$ is encountered, the operator $+$ and the operands 1 and 2 have already been read. Does $*$ operate on 2, or on $1+2$? Precedence rules tell us that $*$ operates on 2, which is the most-recently-seen operand. After the 3 is seen, we can evaluate $2*3$ as 6 and then apply the $+$ operator. This suggests that operands and intermediate results should be saved on a stack. It also suggests that the operators be saved on the stack (since the $+$ is held until the higher precedence $*$ is evaluated). An algorithm that uses this strategy is *operator precedence parsing*. This process is described in Section 11.2.

6.3   Queues

The queue restricts access to the least-recently-inserted item.

Another simple data structure is the *queue*. In many cases, it is important to be able to find and/or remove the most-recently-inserted item. But in an equal number of cases, it is not only unimportant — it is actually the wrong thing to do. In a multiprocessing system, for example, when jobs are submitted to a printer, we expect the least-recent or more-senior job to be printed first. This is not only fair but also required in order to guarantee that the first job does not wait forever. Thus printer queues can be expected to be found on all large systems.

enqueue   dequeue

Queue

getFront

Figure 6.6   Queue model: Input is by `enqueue`, output is by `getFront`, deletion is by `dequeue`

The basic operations supported by queues are

- `enqueue` – insertion at the back of the line,
- `dequeue` – removal of the item from the front of the line, and
- `getFront` – access of the item at the front of the line

Figure 6.6 illustrates these queue operations. Historically, `dequeue` and `getFront` have been combined into one operation. This is what is done here. `dequeue` gives the front item, and then removes it from the queue.

```
1  package DataStructures;
2
3  import Exceptions.*;
4
5  // Queue interface
6  //
7  // ******************PUBLIC OPERATIONS********************
8  // void enqueue( x )      --> Insert x
9  // Object getFront( )     --> Return least recently inserted item
10 // Object dequeue( )      --> Return and remove least recent item
11 // boolean isEmpty( )     --> Return true if empty; else false
12 // void makeEmpty( )      --> Remove all items
13 // ******************ERRORS*******************************
14 // getFront or dequeue on empty queue
15
16 public interface Queue
17 {
18     void     enqueue( Object x );
19     Object   getFront( ) throws Underflow;
20     Object   dequeue( )  throws Underflow;
21     boolean  isEmpty( );
22     void     makeEmpty( );
23 }
```

Figure 6.7   Interface for the queue

```
 1  import DataStructures.*;
 2  import Exceptions.*;
 3
 4  // Simple test program for queues
 5
 6  public final class TestQueue
 7  {
 8      public static void main( String [ ] args )
 9      {
10          Queue q = new QueueAr( );
11
12          for( int i = 0; i < 5; i++ )
13              q.enqueue( new Integer( i ) );
14
15          System.out.print( "Contents:" );
16          try
17          {
18              for( ; ; )
19                  System.out.print( " " + q.dequeue( ) );
20          }
21          catch( Underflow e ) { }
22
23          System.out.println( );
24      }
25  }
```

Figure 6.8   Sample queue program; output is

Contents: 0 1 2 3 4

Queue operations take a constant amount of time per query.

Figure 6.7 (page 149) illustrates the interface for a queue, and Figure 6.8 shows how the queue is used and gives sample output. Because the queue operations are restricted in a way similar to the stack operations, we expect that they should also take a constant amount of time per query. This is indeed the case. All of the basic queue operations take $O(1)$ time. We will see several applications of queues in the case studies.

6.4 Linked Lists

The linked list is used to avoid large amounts of data movement. It stores items with an additional one reference per item overhead.

In a linked list, we store items noncontiguously rather than in the usual contiguous array. To do this, we store each object in a *node* that contains the object and a reference to the next node in the list, as shown in Figure 6.9. In this scenario, we maintain references to both the first and last node in the list. To be more concrete, a typical node looks like this:

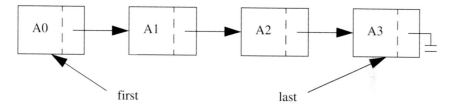

Figure 6.9   A simple linked list

```
class ListNode
{
    Object   data;    // Some element
    ListNode next;
}
```

At any point, we can add a new last item x by doing this:

```
last.next = new ListNode( ); // Attach a new ListNode
last = last.next;            // Adjust last
last.data = x;               // Place x in the node
last.next = null;            // It's the last; adjust next
```

Now, an arbitrary item can no longer be found in one access. Instead, we must scan down the list. This is similar to the difference between accessing an item on a compact disk (one access) or a tape (sequential). While this may appear to make linked lists less attractive than arrays, they still have advantages. First, an insertion into the middle of the list does not require moving all of the items that follow the insertion point. Data movement is very expensive in practice, and the linked list allows insertion with only a constant amount of assignment statements.

It is worth noting that if we allow access only at `first`, then we have a stack, and if we allow insertions only at `last` and access only at `first`, we have a queue.

Typically, we need more-general operations, such as finding or removing any named item in the list. We also need to be able to insert a new item at any point. This is far more than either a stack or a queue allows. Figure 6.10 illustrates these linked list operations.

To access items in the list, we need a reference to the corresponding node. Clearly, however, granting this access is a violation of information-hiding principles. We need to ensure that any access to the list through a reference is safe. To do this, we define the list in two parts: a list class and an iterator class. Figure 6.11 gives the basic linked list interface, supplying methods that describe only the state of the list.

Access to the list is done through an iterator class. The list class has operations that reflect the state of the list. All other operations are in the iterator class.

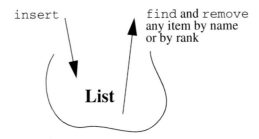

insert

find and remove
any item by name
or by rank

List

Figure 6.10   Link list model: Inputs are arbitrary and ordered, any item may be
output, and iteration is supported, but this data structure is not
time-efficient

Figure 6.12 defines an iterator class that is used for all access into the list. To
see how it is used, let us look at the standard code to output each element in a list.
If the list is stored contiguously in an array, typical code would look like this:

```
// Step through array a, outputting each item
for( int index = 0; index < size; index++ )
    System.out.println( a[ index ] );
```

In basic Java, the code to iterate through the linked list is

```
// Step through List theList, outputting each item
for( ListNode p = theList.first; p != null; p = p.next )
    System.out.println( p.data );
```

```
 1 package DataStructures;
 2
 3 // List interface
 4 //
 5 // Access is via ListItr class
 6 //
 7 // ****************PUBLIC OPERATIONS********************
 8 // boolean isEmpty( )       --> Return true if empty; else false
 9 // void makeEmpty( )        --> Remove all items
10 // ****************ERRORS*******************************
11 // No special errors
12
13 public interface List
14 {
15     boolean isEmpty( );
16     void    makeEmpty( );
17 }
```

Figure 6.11   Interface for the abstract list

```
 1  package DataStructures;
 2
 3  import Exceptions.*;
 4
 5  // ListItr interface; maintains "current position"
 6  //
 7  // ******************PUBLIC OPERATIONS********************
 8  // void insert( x )      --> Insert x after current position
 9  // void remove( x )      --> Remove x
10  // boolean find( x )     --> Set current position to view x
11  // void zeroth(          --> Set position prior to first
12  // void first( )         --> Set current position to first
13  // void advance( )       --> Advance
14  // boolean isInList( )   --> True if at valid position in list
15  // Object retrieve( )    --> Return item in current position
16  // ******************ERRORS*****************************
17  // Exceptions thrown for illegal access, insert, or remove.
18
19  public interface ListItr
20  {
21      void     insert( Object x ) throws ItemNotFound;
22      boolean find( Object x );
23      void     remove( Object x ) throws ItemNotFound;
24      boolean isInList( );
25      Object  retrieve( );
26      void     zeroth( );
27      void     first( );
28      void     advance( );
29  }
```

Figure 6.12   Interface for the abstract list iterator

The iteration mechanism that Java would use is similar to the following (since
ListItr is an interface, the ListItr that follows new would be replaced by
some class that implements the ListItr interface)

```
// Step through List, using abstraction and an iterator
ListItr itr = new ListItr( theList );
for( itr.first( ); itr.isInList( ); itr.advance( ) )
    System.out.println( itr.retrieve( ) );
```

The initialization prior to the for loop is obtained by calling the constructor for
ListItr. The test uses the isInList method defined for the ListItr class.
The advance method advances to the next node in the linked list. We can access
the item that is "current" by making a call to the retrieve method defined for
ListItr. The general principle is that since all access to the list is through the
ListItr class, we have guarantees of safety. Also, we can have multiple itera-
tors traversing a single list.

```
1  import DataStructures.*;
2  import Exceptions.*;
3
4  // Simple test program for lists
5
6  public final class TestList
7  {
8      public static void main( String [ ] args )
9      {
10         List    theList   = new LinkedList( );
11         ListItr itr = new LinkedListItr( theList );
12
13             // Repeatedly insert new items as first elements
14         for( int i = 0; i < 5; i++ )
15         {
16             try
17               { itr.insert( new Integer( i ) ); }
18             catch( ItemNotFound e ) { }        // Cannot happen
19             itr.zeroth( );               // Reset itr to the start
20         }
21
22         System.out.print( "Contents:" );
23         for( itr.first( ); itr.isInList( ); itr.advance( ) )
24             System.out.print( " " + itr.retrieve( ) );
25         System.out.println( " end" );
26      }
27 }
```

Figure 6.13   Sample list program: Output is
Contents: 4 3 2 1 0 end

To make this work, the `ListItr` class must maintain two internal objects. First, it needs a reference to the "current" node. Second, it needs a reference to the `List`; this reference is initialized once (and only once) in the constructor. Figure 6.13 shows the interaction of the list and its iterator. The details of the linked list implementation are shown in Chapter 16; its use in stack and queue implementations is shown in Chapter 15.

Although we began this discussion by using linked lists, the interfaces in Figures 6.11 and 6.12 can be used for any list, regardless of the underlying implementation. The interface does not specify that linked lists must be used.

6.5   General Trees

A *tree* is a widely used data structure that consists of a set of nodes and a set of
edges that connect pairs of nodes. Throughout this book only *rooted trees* are
considered. A rooted tree has the following properties:

A *tree* consists of a set of nodes and a set of edges that connect pairs of nodes.

- One node is distinguished as the root.
- Every node *c* except the root is connected by an edge from exactly one other node *p*. *p* is *c*'s parent. *c* is one of *p*'s children.
- There is a unique path from the root to each node. The number of edges that we must follow is the *path length*.

Figure 6.14 illustrates a tree. The root node is *A*. *A*'s children are *B*, *C*, *D*, and
E. Because *A* is the root, it has no parent. All other nodes have parents. For
instance, *B*'s parent is *A*. Nodes that have no children are called *leaves*. The
leaves in this tree are *C*, *F*, *G*, *H*, *I*, and *K*. The length of the path from *A* to *K* is
three (edges). The length of the path from *A* to *A* is zero edges. Properties such as
ancestor, descendant, and sibling can also be defined in the usual manner. *C*'s siblings are *B*, *D*, and *E*.

Various relation-ships exist among the tree nodes.

The tree is a fundamental data structure in computer science. Almost all operating systems store files in trees or treelike structures. Under DOS, VMS, and
Unix, for instance, directories are stored as the internal, nonleaf nodes of the tree,
while all other files are each stored in a leaf. Traversing an edge is then the same
as descending to a subdirectory. A special edge that connects back to the parent
(namely, the . . entry) allows easy traversal up the tree (although by creating a
cycle, the . . entry makes the structure only treelike rather than a formal tree).

Trees are used for file systems.

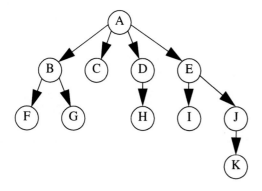

Figure 6.14   A tree

```
1   // Tree interface; details are similar to List
2
3   public interface Tree
4   {
5       boolean isEmpty( );
6       void    makeEmpty( );
7   }
8
9
10  // TreeItr interface; maintains "current position"
11
12  public interface TreeItr
13  {
14      void    insert( Object x ) throws DuplicateItem;
15      boolean find( Object x );
16      void    remove( Object x ) throws ItemNotFound;
17
18      void    gotoRoot( );
19      void    firstChild( );
20      void    nextSibling( );
21      boolean isValid( );
22      Object  retrieve( );
23  }
```

Figure 6.15   Interfaces for the abstract tree class and iterator

Expression trees are used in parsing. In an expression tree, the value of a node is the result of applying the operand at the node, using the children as operands.

A *binary tree* has at most two children per node.

With this in mind we can see what kinds of operations a tree supports. We want to add, search, and remove from the tree. Much like the linked list, we want to define an iterator that allows us access to do this by maintaining the notion of a current internal node. We need to provide methods that allow us to traverse the tree in an orderly manner. Thus, in Figure 6.15, we define the tree and iterator interfaces using the same method as for linked lists. The operations gotoRoot, firstChild, and nextSibling are sufficient to allow us to traverse the tree in one of several orders. In Chapter 17, we describe a hierarchy of classes that supports traversal of trees using only the (logical) methods firstChild, retrieve, isValid, and nextSibling. This includes the classes InOrder, PreOrder, PostOrder, and LevelOrder.

A second application of trees, called the *expression tree*, is shown in Figure 6.16. In an expression tree, the value of a node is the result of applying the operator at the node, using the children as operands. Leaves evaluate to themselves. Consequently, the expression tree shown in Figure 6.16 evaluates to (a+b) * (c-d). Expression trees and the related parse tree are crucial data structures in the parsing and code-generation stages of the compiler. More details are in Section 11.2.

The expression tree in Figure 6.16 is a *binary tree* because the number of children is limited to at most two per node. An important use of the binary tree is examined in the next section.

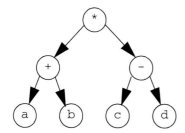

Figure 6.16   Expression tree for `(a+b) * (c-d)`

6.6 Binary Search Trees

In Section 5.6, we examined the static searching problem and saw that if the items are presented to us in sorted order, then we can support the `find` operation in logarithmic worst-case time. This is static searching because once we are presented with the items, we cannot add or remove items.

Suppose, however, that we do want to add and remove items. One data structure that does this is the *binary search tree*. Figure 6.17 shows the basic operations that are allowed in a binary search tree. An interface is shown in Figure 6.18. Notice that only objects that implement the `Comparable` interface can be stored in a binary search tree.

The set of allowed operations is now extended to allow arbitrary `find` (by name) as well as `insert` and `remove`. The `find` method returns a reference to an object that matches the searched-for item. This match is based on the `compares` method that must be implemented by `Comparable` objects. If there is no match, `find` throws an exception. This is a design decision. Another possibility would have been to simply return `null` if there is no match. The basic difference in these two approaches is that our approach requires that the programmer explicitly provide code to test for the possibility that a search fails. In the alternate approach, if `null` is returned and no test was written, the result would be a run-time `NullPointerException` when the return value was used. In terms of efficiency, the exception version may be less efficient, but it is not likely that the result would be observable, except perhaps in some often-executed critical code section. If it were, changes to the code could be made. However, by forcing the programmer to handle this case, we have made the code less susceptible to a run-time error.

In a similar vein, insertion of an item already in the search tree is signaled by a `DuplicateItem` exception. Other alternatives are possible. One is to allow the new insertion to override the stored value; this is done in Section 6.7 when we discuss hash tables.

The binary search tree supports insertion, removal, and searching.

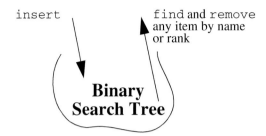

insert   find and remove
              any item by name
              or rank

**Binary
Search Tree**

Figure 6.17   Binary search tree model. The binary search is extended to allow
insertions and deletions

```
1  package DataStructures;
2
3  import Supporting.*;
4  import Exceptions.*;
5
6  // SearchTree interface
7  //
8  // ******************PUBLIC OPERATIONS*********************
9  // void insert( x )        --> Insert x
10 // void remove( x )        --> Remove x
11 // void removeMin( )       --> Remove smallest item
12 // Comparable find( x )    --> Return item that matches x
13 // Comparable findMin( )   --> Return smallest item
14 // Comparable findMax( )   --> Return largest item
15 // boolean isEmpty( )      --> Return true if empty; else false
16 // void makeEmpty( )       --> Remove all items
17 // void printTree( )       --> Print tree in sorted order
18 // ******************ERRORS*******************************
19 // Most routines throw ItemNotFound on various
20 //     degenerate conditions
21 // insert throws DuplicateItem if item is already in the tree
22
23 public interface SearchTree
24 {
25     void       insert( Comparable x ) throws DuplicateItem;
26     void       remove( Comparable x ) throws ItemNotFound;
27     void       removeMin( )           throws ItemNotFound;
28     Comparable find( Comparable x )   throws ItemNotFound;
29     Comparable findMin( )             throws ItemNotFound;
30     Comparable findMax( )             throws ItemNotFound;
31     boolean    isEmpty( );
32     void       makeEmpty( );
33     void       printTree( );
34 }
```

Figure 6.18   Interface for the binary search tree

We illustrate a binary search tree that stores strings. Since only `Comparable` objects can be used, we cannot use `String` directly. Thus we write a `MyString` class, shown in Figure 6.19 (this class also implements the `Hashable` interface, which is needed in Section 6.7). Figure 6.20 shows how binary search tree works for `MyString` objects.

Our `SearchTree` interface also provides two additional methods: one to find the smallest item and another to find the largest item. It turns out that with some additional work, we can also efficiently support access of the *K*th smallest item, for any *K* provided as a parameter. This is known as *searching by rank*.

Here is a summary of the running time of these operations. We are hoping that the worst-case cost of the `find`, `insert`, and `remove` operations is $O(\log N)$ because that would match the bound obtained for the static binary search. Unfortunately, for the simplest implementation of the binary search tree, this is not the case. The average case is logarithmic, but the worst case is $O(N)$ and this occurs quite frequently. However, by applying some algorithmic tricks, we can obtain a more complex structure that does indeed have $O(\log N)$ cost per operation.

Using a binary search tree, we can access the Kth smallest item. The cost is logarithmic average-case time for a simple implementation and logarithmic worst-case time for a more careful implementation.

```
 1  import Supporting.*;
 2  import DataStructures.*;
 3
 4  public final class MyString implements Comparable, Hashable
 5  {
 6      public MyString( String x )
 7        { value = x; }
 8
 9      public String toString( )
10        { return value; }
11
12      public int compares( Comparable rhs )
13        { return value.compareTo( ((MyString)rhs).value ); }
14
15      public boolean lessThan( Comparable rhs )
16        { return compares( rhs ) < 0; }
17
18      public boolean equals( Object rhs )
19        { return value.equals( ((MyString)rhs).value ); }
20
21      public int hash( int tableSize )
22        { return QuadraticProbingTable.hash( value,
23                                             tableSize ); }
24
25      private String value;
26  }
```

Figure 6.19 `MyString` class for test programs in Figures 6.20 and 6.23

What about `findMin`, `findMax`, and a general `findKth` procedure? In the binary search, these are clearly constant-time operations because we merely index an array. In Chapter 18, we will show that these operations take the same time in a binary search tree as does an arbitrary `find`: $O(\log N)$ per operation on average, although $O(N)$ in the worst-case. With sufficient care, the worst-case bound can be reduced to $O(\log N)$ per operation. As the name of the data structure suggests, the binary search tree is implemented as a binary tree and thus requires the overhead of two references per item. A more careful variant that supports efficient worst-case access requires additional space per item. Chapter 18 gives more details on the implementation of a binary search tree.

```
 1  import DataStructures.*;
 2  import Exceptions.*;
 3
 4  // Simple test program for search trees
 5
 6  public final class TestSearchTree
 7  {
 8      public static void main( String [ ] args )
 9      {
10          SearchTree t = new BinarySearchTree( );
11          MyString result = null;
12
13          try { t.insert( new MyString( "Becky" ) ); }
14          catch( DuplicateItem e ) { }  // Cannot happen
15
16          try
17          {
18              result =
19                  (MyString) t.find( new MyString( "Becky" ) );
20              System.out.print( "Found " + result + ";" );
21          }
22          catch( ItemNotFound e )
23            { System.out.print( "Becky not found;" ); }
24
25          try
26          {
27              result =
28                  (MyString) t.find( new MyString( "Mark" ) );
29              System.out.print( " Found " + result + ";" );
30          }
31          catch( ItemNotFound e )
32            { System.out.print( " Mark not found;" ); }
33
34          System.out.println( );
35      }
36  }
```

Figure 6.20   Sample search tree program:
Output is `Found Becky; Mark not found;`

6.7   Hash Tables

Many applications require dynamic searching based only on a name. The classic application is the compiler's *symbol table*. As it compiles a program, the compiler must record the names (including types, scope, and memory assignment) of all declared identifiers. When it sees an identifier outside of a declaration statement, the compiler checks to see that it has been declared. If it has, the compiler looks up the appropriate information in the symbol table.

Since the binary search tree supports logarithmic time access of arbitrary named items, why do we need a new data structure? The answer is that a binary search tree could give linear-time cost per access, and ensuring logarithmic cost requires more sophisticated algorithms.

The *hash table* is a data structure that will avoid this worst case and instead support operations in constant time almost certainly. Degenerative performance is possible but extremely unlikely. Thus the access time for any one item does not depend on the number of items that are in the table. The hash table also avoids repeated calls to memory management routines. This makes it fast in practice. An additional benefit of the hash table is that, unlike the binary search tree, it does not require that the stored objects implement the `Comparable` interface.

The allowed operations are illustrated in Figure 6.21, and an interface is shown in Figure 6.22. Here, insertion of a duplicate item does not throw an exception. Instead, it causes the new item to replace the old item. This is an alternative to what was seen in the binary search tree. The hash table works only for objects that implement the `Hashable` interface. The `Hashable` interface requires a *hash function*, which converts the `Hashable` object to an integer. It has the following declaration:

```
// Return an integer between 0 and tableSize - 1
int hash( int tableSize );
```

The hash table *supports constant average-time insertions, removals, and searches.*

The hash table is not as susceptible to the worst case as is a simple binary search tree.

To use the hash table, we must provide a hash function, which converts a specific object to an integer.

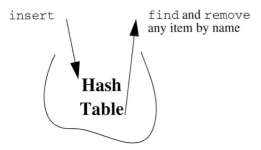

insert   find and remove any item by name

Hash Table

Figure 6.21   The hash table model: Any named item can be accessed or deleted in essentially constant time

```
1  package DataStructures;
2
3  import Supporting.*;
4  import Exceptions.*;
5
6  // HashTable interface
7  //
8  // *****************PUBLIC OPERATIONS********************
9  // void insert( x )        --> Insert x
10 // void remove( x )        --> Remove x
11 // Hashable find( x )      --> Return item that matches x
12 // void makeEmpty( )       --> Remove all items
13 // *****************ERRORS*******************************
14 // find and remove throw ItemNotFound
15 // insert overrides previous value if duplicate; not an error
16
17 public interface HashTable
18 {
19     void        insert( Hashable x );
20     void        remove( Hashable x ) throws ItemNotFound;
21     Hashable    find( Hashable x )   throws ItemNotFound;
22     void        makeEmpty( );
23 }
```

Figure 6.22   Interface for the hash table class

```
1  import DataStructures.*;
2  import Exceptions.*;
3
4  // Simple test program for hash tables
5
6  public final class TestHashTable
7  {
8      public static void main( String [ ] args )
9      {
10         HashTable h = new QuadraticProbingTable( );
11         MyString result = null;
12
13         h.insert( new MyString( new String( "Becky" ) ) );
14
15         try
16         {
17             result = (MyString)
18                           h.find( new MyString( "Becky" ) );
19             System.out.println( "Found " + result );
20         }
21         catch( ItemNotFound e )
22           { System.out.println( "Becky not found" ); }
23     }
24 }
```

Figure 6.23   Sample hash table program. Output is Found Becky

(Details on implementing the hash function are given in Chapter 19, where a function that works for a `String` is provided.) The `equals` method must also be overridden. Figure 6.19 shows how the `MyString` object implements the `Hashable` interface by providing `hash` and `equals`. An example of the use of the hash table — in this case — of `MyString` objects is shown in Figure 6.23.

A common use of the hash table is as a *dictionary*. A dictionary stores objects that consist of a key, which is looked up in the dictionary, and its definition, which is returned. We can use the hash table to implement the dictionary because we can instantiate it as follows:

A dictionary stores keys and definitions.

1. The stored object is a class that stores both key and definition.
2. Equality, inequality, and the hash function are based only on the key portion of the stored object.
3. A lookup is performed by constructing a stored object e with the key and performing a hash table `find`.
4. The definition is obtained by using a reference f, which is assigned the return value of the `find`. f's definition field is what we are looking for.

6.8 Priority Queues

Although jobs sent to a printer are generally placed in a queue, this might not always be best. For instance, one job might be particularly important, so we might want that job to be run as soon as the printer is available. Conversely, when the printer finishes a job and several one-page jobs and one 100-page job are waiting, it might be reasonable to print the long job last, even if it is not the last job submitted. (Unfortunately, most systems do not do this. This can be particularly annoying at times.)

The priority queue supports access of the minimum item only.

Similarly, in a multiuser environment, the operating system scheduler must decide which of several processes to run. Generally, a process is allowed to run only for a fixed time period. One algorithm uses a queue. Jobs are initially placed at the end of the queue. The scheduler will repeatedly take the first job on the queue, run it until either it finishes or its time limit is up, and place it at the end of the queue if it does not finish. Generally, this strategy is not appropriate because short jobs must wait and thus seem to take a long time to run. Clearly, users that are running an editor should not see a visible delay in the echoing of typed characters. Thus short jobs (that is, those using fewer resources) should have precedence over jobs that have already consumed large amounts of resources. Furthermore, some resource-intensive jobs, such as jobs run by the system administrator, might be important and should also have precedence.

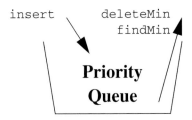

Figure 6.24   Priority queue model: Only the minimum element is accessible

If we give each job a number to measure its priority, then the smaller number (pages printed, resources used) tends to indicate greater importance. Thus we want to be able to access the smallest item in a collection of items and remove it from the collection. These are the findMin and deleteMin operations. The data structure that supports these operations is the aptly named *priority queue*. Figure 6.24 illustrates the basic priority queue operations.

```
 1 package DataStructures;
 2
 3 import Supporting.*;
 4 import Exceptions.*;
 5
 6 // PriorityQueue interface
 7 //
 8 // *****************PUBLIC OPERATIONS********************
 9 // void insert( x )         --> Insert x
10 // Comparable deleteMin( )--> Return and remove smallest item
11 // Comparable findMin( )  --> Return smallest item
12 // void makeEmpty( )        --> Remove all items
13 // boolean isEmpty( )       --> Return true if empty; else false
14 // *****************ERRORS*******************************
15 // findMin and deleteMin throw Underflow when empty.
16
17 public interface PriorityQueue
18 {
19     void       insert( Comparable x );
20     Comparable deleteMin( ) throws Underflow;
21     Comparable findMin( )   throws Underflow;
22     void       makeEmpty( );
23     boolean    isEmpty( );
24 }
```

Figure 6.25   Interface for the priority queue

```
1  import DataStructures.*;
2  import Exceptions.*;
3  import Supporting.*;
4
5  // Simple test program for priority queues
6  public final class TestPriorityQueue
7  {
8      public static void main( String [ ] args )
9      {
10          PriorityQueue pq = new PairHeap( );
11
12          pq.insert( new MyInteger( 4 ) );
13          pq.insert( new MyInteger( 2 ) );
14          pq.insert( new MyInteger( 1 ) );
15          pq.insert( new MyInteger( 3 ) );
16          pq.insert( new MyInteger( 0 ) );
17
18          System.out.print( "Contents: " );
19          try
20          {
21              for( ; ; )
22                  System.out.print( " " + pq.deleteMin( ) );
23          }
24          catch( Underflow e ) { }
25
26          System.out.println( );
27      }
28 }
```

Figure 6.26   Sample program for priority queues:
Output is Contents: 0 1 2 3 4

The priority queue interface is shown in Figure 6.25, and a sample program that illustrates its use is provided in Figure 6.26. The sample program uses a very advanced priority queue, called the *pairing heap* (which is discussed in Chapter 22). As usual, one does not need to know anything about the pairing heap, except that it implements the priority queue interface.

Once again, we must ask: Why not use a binary search tree? And once again, the answer is that a binary search tree is overly powerful, has poor worst-case performance, and requires the overhead of two node references per item. Using a sophisticated binary search tree allows logarithmic worst-case performance. However, then the coding is excessive, thereby leading to sluggish performance in practice.[1] Since the priority queue supports only the deleteMin and findMin operations, we might expect performance that is a compromise between the constant-time queue and the logarithmic-time binary search tree.

[1.] However, the *splay tree*, discussed in Chapter 21, is a notable exception in some applications.

The *binary heap* implements the priority queue in logarithmic time per operation using an array.

An important use of priority queues is *event-driven simulations*.

Indeed, this is the case. The basic priority queue supports all operations in logarithmic worst-case time, does not require the overhead of two references to other nodes per item, supports insertion in constant average time, and is very simple to implement. The resulting structure is known as the *binary heap* and is one of the most elegant data structures known. Chapter 20 gives details on the implementation of the binary heap.

The pairing heap, used in Figure 6.26, is a complicated alternative that is useful when additional functionality is needed, including the ability to efficiently combine two separate priority queues.

An important application of the priority queue is in the area of *event-driven simulation*. Consider, for example, a system such as a bank in which customers arrive and wait in line until one of K tellers is available. Customer arrival is governed by a probability distribution function, as is the service time (the amount of time it takes a teller to provide complete service to one customer). We are interested in statistics such as how long on average a customer has to wait or how long a line might be.

With certain probability distributions and values of K, we can compute these statistics exactly. However, as K gets larger, the analysis becomes considerably more difficult, so it is appealing to use a computer to simulate the operation of the bank. In this way, the bank officers can determine how many tellers are needed to ensure reasonably smooth service. An *event-driven simulation* consists of processing events. The two events here are (1) a customer arriving and (2) a customer departing, thus freeing up a teller. At any point we have a collection of events waiting to happen. To run the simulation, we need to determine the *next* event. This is the event whose time of occurrence is minimum; hence, a priority queue that extracts the event of minimum time is used to process the event list efficiently. A complete discussion and implementation of event-driven simulation is in Section 13.2.

Summary

This chapter examined the basic data structures that are used throughout the rest of this text. An interface was provided and what the running time ought to be for each data structure was explained. Future chapters show how these data structures are used. In Part IV, we will give an implementation of each data structure that meets the time bounds we have claimed here. Figure 6.27 summarizes the results that will be obtained.

The next chapter describes an important problem-solving tool called *recursion*. Recursion allows many problems to be efficiently solved using short algorithms and is central to the implementation of the binary search tree.

Data Structure	Access	Comments
Stack	Most-recent only, pop, $O(1)$	Very, very fast
Queue	Least-recent only, dequeue, $O(1)$	Very, very fast
Linked List	Any item	$O(N)$
Search Tree	Any item by name or rank, $O(\log N)$	Average case; can be made worst case
Hash Table	Any named item, $O(1)$	Almost certain
Priority Queue	findMin, $O(1)$, deleteMin, $O(\log N)$	insert is $O(1)$ on average $O(\log N)$ worst case

Figure 6.27   Summary of some data structures

Objects of the Game

binary heap Implements the priority queue in logarithmic time per operation in an array. (164)

binary search tree A tree that supports insertion, removal, and searching. We can also use it to access the *K*th smallest item. The cost is logarithmic average-case time for a simple implementation and logarithmic worst-case time for a more careful implementation. (157)

binary tree A tree with at most two children per node. (156)

data structure A representation of data and the operations allowed on that data. Data structures allow us to achieve component reuse. (143)

dictionary Stores keys that are looked up in the dictionary and their corresponding definitions. (162)

expression tree A tree used in parsing in which the value of a node is the result of applying the operator at the node, using the children as operands. (156)

hash function A function that converts a Hashable object to an integer. Only Hashable objects can use a hash table, and they must implement a hash function. (161)

hash table A data structure that supports constant average-time insertions, removals, and searches. (161)

iterator class A class that enables access to a list. The list class has operations that reflect the state of the list. All other operations are in the iterator class. (151)

leaf In a tree, a node with no children. (155)

operator precedence parsing An algorithm that uses a stack to evaluate expressions. (148)

path length In a tree, the number of edges that must be followed from the root to reach a node. (155)

priority queue A data structure that supports access of the minimum item only. (163)

queue A data structure that restricts access to the least-recently-inserted item. (148)

rooted tree A tree with a node that is designated as the root. (155)

stack A data structure that restricts access to the most-recently-inserted item. (145)

symbol table A data structure used by the compiler to keep track of identifiers. Generally implemented by a hash table. (161)

tree A widely used data structure that consists of a set of nodes and a set of edges that connect pairs of nodes. Throughout the text, we assume the tree is rooted. (155)

Common Errors

1. Failure to adequately document the characteristics of the class interface is a serious error.

2. It is an error to access or delete from an empty stack, queue, or priority queue. The class implementor must make sure that the error is detected and an exception is thrown. Access and remove operations are allowed for empty trees and hash tables because access on an empty tree or hash table is a subset of the unsuccessful search.

3. Several errors can occur during list or tree access. These must be signaled by the class.

4. The implementor of a `Hashable` object must supply a good hash function; otherwise, performance deteriorates.

5. `equals` (which must take an `Object` as a parameter) should be written for objects inserted into hash tables and search trees.

6. A priority queue is not a queue. It just sounds like it is.

On the Internet

Some of the test programs, including the `MyString` class and the test programs, are in the **Chapter06** directory (but are not listed next). The interfaces for the classes that will be implemented in Parts IV and V are in the **DataStructures** directory and are part of package DataStructures. They are as follows:

Stack.java	The Stack interface in Figure 6.4
Queue.java	The Queue interface in Figure 6.7
List.java	The List interface in Figure 6.11
ListItr.java	The ListItr interface in Figure 6.12
SearchTree.java	The SearchTree interface in Figure 6.18
HashTable.java	The HashTable interface in Figure 6.22
PriorityQueue.java	The PriorityQueue interface in Figure 6.25

Exercises

In Short

6.1. Show the results of the following sequence: add(4), add(8), add(1), add(6), remove(), and remove() when the add and remove operations correspond to the basic operations in the following:
   a. stack
   b. queue
   c. priority queue

In Theory

6.2. Suppose you want to support the following three operations exclusively: insert, findMax, and deleteMax. How fast do you think these operations can be performed?

6.3. Can all of the following be supported in logarithmic time: insert, deleteMin, deleteMax, findMin, and findMax?

6.4. Which of the data structures in Figure 6.27 lead to sorting algorithms that could run in less than quadratic time?

6.5. Show that the following operations can be supported in constant time simultaneously: push, pop, and findMin. Note that deleteMin is not part of the repertoire. *Hint*: Maintain two stacks: One to store items and the other to store minimums as they occur.

6.6. A double-ended queue supports insertions and deletions at both the front and end of the line. What do you think is the running time per operation?

In Practice

6.7. Write a routine that prints out the items in a linked list in reverse order. To do this, have a ListItr go down the linked list and push onto a stack each item that is seen. When the end of the linked list is reached, repeatedly pop the stack until it is empty.

6.8. A deletion in a linked list or a binary search tree leaves the following problem: If the "current" element is deleted, what becomes the new "current" element? Discuss some alternatives.

6.9. Show how to implement a `Stack` efficiently by using a linked list as a data field.

6.10. Show how to implement a `Queue` efficiently by using a linked list as a data field and maintaining a `ListItr` object that is fixed to the last element in the linked list.

6.11. Implement a class `Dictionary` that supports the `insert` and `lookup` operations. Following are some of the lines of the `Dictionary` class. Assume you have a hash table class.

```
public class Dictionary
{
        // Some of the methods
    void insert( Hashable key, Object definition );
    Object lookup( Hashable key ) throws ItemNotFound;
}
```

Programming Projects

6.12. A stack can be implemented by using an array and maintaining the current size. The stack elements are stored in consecutive array positions, with the top item always in position 0. Note that this is not the most efficient method. Do the following:
   a. Describe the algorithms for `push`, `pop`, and `top`.
   b. What is the Big-Oh running time for each of `push`, `pop`, and `top` using these algorithms?
   c. Write an implementation that uses these algorithms.

6.13. A queue can be implemented by using an array and maintaining the current size. The queue elements are stored in consecutive array positions, with the front item always in position 0. Note that this is not the most efficient method. Do the following:
   a. Describe the algorithms for `getFront`, `enqueue`, and `dequeue`.
   b. What is the Big-Oh running time for each of `getFront`, `enqueue`, and `dequeue` using these algorithms?
   c. Write an implementation that uses these algorithms.

6.14. The operations that are supported by the search tree can also be implemented by using an array and maintaining the current size. The array elements are stored in sorted order in consecutive array positions. Thus `find` can be implemented by a binary search. Do the following:
   a. Describe the algorithms for `insert` and `remove`.
   b. What is the running time for these algorithms?
   c. Write an implementation that uses these algorithms.

6.15. A hash table can be implemented by using an array and maintaining the current size. The elements are stored in consecutive locations but are not kept sorted. Instead, they are inserted in the next available array position. Do the following:

   a. Describe the algorithms for `insert`, `remove`, and `find`.

   b. What is the Big-Oh running time for each of `insert`, `remove`, and `find` using these algorithms?

   c. Write an implementation that uses these algorithms.

6.16. A priority queue can be implemented by using a sorted array (as in Exercise 6.14). Do the following:

   a. Describe the algorithms for `findMin`, `deleteMin`, and `insert`.

   b. What is the Big-Oh running time for each of `findMin`, `deleteMin`, and `insert` using these algorithms?

   c. Write an implementation that uses these algorithms.

6.17. A priority queue can be implemented by storing items in an unsorted array and inserting items in the next available location (as in Exercise 6.15). Do the following:

   a. Describe the algorithms for `findMin`, `deleteMin`, and `insert`.

   b. What is the Big-Oh running time for each of `findMin`, `deleteMin`, and `insert` using these algorithms?

   c. Write an implementation that uses these algorithms.

6.18. By adding an extra field to the priority queue class in Exercise 6.17, you can implement both `insert` and `findMin` in constant time. The extra field will store the array position where the minimum is stored. However, `deleteMin` will still be expensive. Do the following:

   a. Describe the algorithms for `insert`, `findMin`, and `deleteMin`.

   b. What is the Big-Oh running time for `deleteMin`?

   c. Write an implementation that uses these algorithms.

6.19. By maintaining the invariant that the elements in the priority queue are sorted in nonincreasing order (that is, the largest item is first, the smallest is last), you can implement both `findMin` and `deleteMin` in constant time. However, `insert` will be expensive. Do the following:

   a. Describe the algorithms for `insert`, `findMin`, and `deleteMin`.

   b. What is the Big-Oh running time for `insert`?

   c. Write an implementation that uses these algorithms.

6.20. A double-ended priority queue allows access to both the minimum and maximum elements. In other words, all of the following are supported: `findMin`, `deleteMin`, `findMax`, and `deleteMax`. Do the following:

   a. Describe the algorithms for `findMin`, `deleteMin`, `findMax`, `deleteMax`, and `insert`.

   b. What is the Big-Oh running time for each of `findMin`, `deleteMin`, `findMax`, `deleteMax`, and `insert` using these algorithms?

   c. Write an implementation that uses these algorithms.

6.21. A median heap supports the following operations: `insert`, `findKth`, and `removeKth`. The last two find and remove, respectively, the Kth smallest element. The simplest implementation maintains the data in sorted order. Do the following:

a. Describe the algorithms that can be used to support median heap operations.

b. What is the Big-Oh running time for each of the basic operations using these algorithms?

c. Write an implementation that uses these algorithms.

References

References for these data structures are provided in Part IV.

7

Recursion

A method that is partially defined in terms of itself is called *recursive*. Like many languages, Java supports recursive methods. Recursion, which is the use of recursive methods, is a powerful programming tool that in many cases can yield both short and efficient algorithms. This chapter explores how recursion works, thus providing some insight into its variations, its limitations, and some of its many uses. The discussion of recursion begins with an examination of the mathematical principle on which it is based: *mathematical induction*. Then it gives examples of simple recursive methods and proves that they generate correct answers.

In this chapter, we will see:

- The four basic rules of recursion, and several basic examples
- Numerical applications of recursion that lead to implementation of an encryption algorithm
- A general technique called *divide and conquer*
- A general technique called *dynamic programming* that is similar to recursion but uses tables instead of recursive methods
- A general technique called *backtracking* that amounts to a careful, exhaustive search

7.1 What Is Recursion?

A *recursive method* is a method that either directly or indirectly makes a call to itself. This may seem to be circular logic: How can a method *F* solve a problem by calling itself? The key is that the method *F* calls itself on a different, generally simpler, instance. Here are some examples:

- Files on a computer are generally stored in directories. Users may create subdirectories that store more files and directories. Suppose we want to examine every file in a directory *D*, including all files in all subdirectories (and subsubdirectories, and so on). This is done by recursively examining

A recursive method is a method that directly or indirectly makes a call to itself.

every file in each subdirectory and then examining all files in the directory *D* (this is discussed in Chapter 17).

- Suppose we have a large dictionary. Words in dictionaries are defined in terms of other words. When we look up the meaning of a word, we might not always understand the definition, so we might have to look up words in the definition. Likewise, we might not understand some of those, so we might have to continue this search for a while. As the dictionary is finite, eventually either we will come to a point where we understand all of the words in some definition (and thus understand that definition and can retrace our path through the other definitions) or we will find that the definitions are circular and we are stuck, or that some word we need to understand is not defined in the dictionary. Our recursive strategy to understand words is as follows. If we know the meaning of a word, we are done; otherwise, we look up the word in the dictionary. If we understand all the words in the definition, we are done. Otherwise, we figure out what the definition means by recursively looking up the words we do not know. This procedure will terminate if the dictionary is well-defined, but it can loop indefinitely if a word is circularly defined.

- Computer languages are frequently defined recursively. For instance, an (arithmetic) expression is either a primitive variable, or a parenthesized expression, or two expressions added to each other, and so on.

Recursion is a powerful problem-solving tool. Many algorithms are most easily expressed using a recursive formulation. Furthermore, there are many problems whose most efficient solutions use this natural recursive formulation. But we must be careful not to create circular logic that would result in infinite loops.

This chapter discusses the general conditions that must be satisfied by recursive algorithms and offers several practical examples. It also shows that sometimes algorithms that are naturally expressed recursively must be rewritten without recursion.

7.2 Background: Proofs by Mathematical Induction

Induction is an important proof technique used to establish theorems that hold for positive integers.

This section discusses proof by *mathematical induction*. (Throughout this chapter, the word *mathematical* is omitted when this technique is described.) Induction proofs are commonly used to establish theorems that hold for positive integers. We will start by proving a simple theorem. It is easy to establish this particular theorem using other methods, but often it turns out that a proof by induction is the simplest mechanism.

> For any integer $N \geq 1$, the sum of the first N integers, given by
> $\sum_{i=1}^{N} i = 1 + 2 + \ldots + N$, is equal to $N(N+1)/2$.

Theorem 7.1

It is easy to see that the theorem is true for $N = 1$ because both the left-hand and right-hand sides evaluate to 1. Further checking shows that it is true for $2 \leq N \leq 10$. However, the fact that the theorem holds for all N that are easy to check by hand does not imply that it is true for all N. Consider, for instance, numbers of the form $2^{2^k} + 1$. The first five numbers (corresponding to $0 \leq k \leq 4$) are 3, 5, 17, 257, and 65,537. These numbers are all prime. Indeed, at one time it was conjectured that all numbers of this form are prime. This is not the case; it is easy to check by computer that $2^{2^5} + 1 = 641 \times 6{,}700{,}417$. In fact, no other prime of the form $2^{2^k} + 1$ is known.

A proof by induction works in two steps. First, as previously, we show that the theorem is true for the smallest cases. Second, we show that if the theorem is true for the first few cases, then it can be extended to include the next case. For instance, we show that a theorem that is true for all $1 \leq N \leq k$ must be true for $1 \leq N \leq k + 1$. Once we show how to extend the range of true cases, we have shown that it is true for all cases. This is because we can extend the range of true cases indefinitely. This technique is used to prove Theorem 7.1.

A proof by induction shows that the theorem is true for some simple cases and then shows how to extend the range of true cases indefinitely.

> Clearly, the theorem is true for $N = 1$. Suppose that the theorem is true for all $1 \leq N \leq k$. Then

Proof (of Theorem 7.1)

$$\sum_{i=1}^{k+1} i = (k+1) + \sum_{i=1}^{k} i. \qquad \textbf{(7.1)}$$

> Since by assumption the theorem is true for k, we may replace the sum on the right side of Equation 7.1 with $k(k+1)/2$, obtaining

$$\sum_{i=1}^{k+1} i = (k+1) + k(k+1)/2. \qquad \textbf{(7.2)}$$

> Algebraic manipulation of the right-hand side of Equation 7.2 now yields

$$\sum_{i=1}^{k+1} i = (k+1)(k+2)/2.$$

> This confirms the theorem for the case $k + 1$. Thus by induction, the theorem is true for all integers $N \geq 1$.

In a proof by induction, the *basis* is the easy case that can be shown by hand.

The *inductive hypothesis* assumes that the theorem is true for some arbitrary case and shows that, under this assumption, it is true for the next case.

Why does this constitute a proof? First, the theorem is true for $N = 1$. This is called the *basis*. One can view it as being the basis for our belief that the theorem is true in general. The basis is the easy case(s) that can be shown by hand. Once we have established the basis, we can hypothesize that the theorem is true for some arbitrary k. This is called the *inductive hypothesis*. We show that if the theorem is true for k, then it is true for $k + 1$. In our case, since we know the theorem is true for the basis $N = 1$, we know that it is true for $N = 2$. Since it is true for $N = 2$, it must be true for $N = 3$. And since it is true for $N = 3$, it must be true for $N = 4$. Extending this logic, we see that the theorem is true for every positive integer beginning with $N = 1$.

Let us apply proof by induction to a second problem, one that is not quite as simple as the first. First, we examine the sequence of numbers 1^2, $2^2 - 1^2$, $3^2 - 2^2 + 1^2$, $4^2 - 3^2 + 2^2 - 1^2$, $5^2 - 4^2 + 3^2 - 2^2 + 1^2$, and so on. Each member represents the sum of the first N squares, with alternating signs. The sequence evaluates to 1, 3, 6, 10, and 15. It seems that, in general, the sum is exactly equal to the sum of the first N integers, which, as we know from Theorem 7.1, would be $N(N+1)/2$. Theorem 7.2 proves this.

Theorem 7.2

The sum $\sum_{i=N}^{1}(-1)^{N-i}i^2 = N^2 - (N-1)^2 + (N-2)^2 \ldots$ *is* $N(N+1)/2$.

Proof

The proof is by induction.

Basis: Clearly, the theorem is true for $N = 1$.

Inductive hypothesis: First, we assume the theorem is true for k:
$\sum_{i=k}^{1}(-1)^{k-i}i^2 = \dfrac{k(k+1)}{2}$. *Then, we must show that it is true for $k + 1$; namely, that* $\sum_{i=k+1}^{1}(-1)^{k+1-i}i^2 = \dfrac{(k+1)(k+2)}{2}$. *We write*

$$\sum_{i=k+1}^{1}(-1)^{k+1-i}i^2 = (k+1)^2 - k^2 + (k-1)^2 \ldots . \qquad (7.3)$$

If we rewrite the right-hand side of Equation 7.3, we obtain

$$\sum_{i=k+1}^{1}(-1)^{k+1-i}i^2 = (k+1)^2 - (k^2 - (k-1)^2 \ldots).$$

This allows a substitution to yield

$$\sum_{i=k+1}^{1}(-1)^{k+1-i}i^2 = (k+1)^2 - \left(\sum_{i=k}^{1}(-1)^{k-i}i^2\right)$$

(7.4) *Proof (continued)*

If we apply the inductive hypothesis, then we can replace the summation on the right-hand side of Equation 7.4, thus obtaining

$$\sum_{i=k+1}^{1}(-1)^{k+1-i}i^2 = (k+1)^2 - k(k+1)/2.$$

(7.5)

Simple algebraic manipulation of the right-hand side of Equation 7.5 then yields

$$\sum_{i=k+1}^{1}(-1)^{k+1-i}i^2 = (k+1)(k+2)/2,$$

which establishes the theorem for $N = k+1$. Thus, by induction, the theorem is true for all $N \geq 1$.

7.3   Basic Recursion

Proofs by induction show us that if we know that a statement is true for a smallest case and we can show that one case implies the next case, then we know the statement is true for all cases.

Sometimes mathematical functions are defined recursively. For instance, let $S(N)$ be the sum of the first N integers. Then $S(1) = 1$, and we can write $S(N) = S(N-1)+N$. Here, we have defined the function S in terms of a smaller instance of itself. The recursive definition of $S(N)$ is identical to the closed form $S(N) = N(N+1)/2$, except that the recursive definition is only defined for positive integers and is less directly computable.

Sometimes it is easier to write a formula recursively than in closed form. Figure 7.1 shows a straightforward implementation of the recursive function. If $N = 1$, then we have the basis, for which we know $S(1) = 1$. We take care of this case at lines 5 and 6. This is the *base case* of the recursion, which is the instance that can be solved without a recursive call. Otherwise, we follow the recursive definition $S(N) = S(N-1) + N$ precisely at line 8. It is hard to imagine that we could implement the recursive function any more simply than this, so the natural question is, does this actually work?

The answer is yes. Except as noted shortly, this routine works. Let us see how the call to s(4) is evaluated. When the call to s(4) is made, the test at line 5 fails. We then execute line 8, where we evaluate s(3). Like any other method, this requires a call to s. In that call, we get to line 5, where the test fails; thus we

A recursive method is defined in terms of a smaller instance of itself. There must be some base case that can be computed without recursion.

go to line 8. At this point, we call `s(2)`. Once again, we call `s`, and now `n` is 2. The test at line 5 still fails, and so we call `s(1)` at line 8. Now we have `n` equal to 1, so `s(1)` returns 1. At this point, `s(2)` can continue, adding the return value from `s(1)` to 2; thus `s(2)` returns 3. Now `s(3)` continues, adding the value of 3 that was returned by `s(2)` to `n`, which is 3; thus `s(3)` returns 6. This enables the completion of the call to `s(4)`, which finally returns 10.

Notice here that although it seems that `s` is calling itself, in reality it is calling a *clone* of itself. That clone is simply another method with different parameters. At any instant, only one clone is active; the rest are pending. It is the computer's job to handle all the bookkeeping, not yours. If there was too much bookkeeping even for the computer, then it would be time to worry. These details are discussed later in this chapter.

The *base case* is an instance that can be solved without recursion. Any recursive call must make progress toward a base case.

If we have a base case and if our recursive calls make progress toward reaching the base case, then eventually we terminate. We thus have our first two fundamental rules of recursion:

1. *Base cases*: Always have at least one case that can be solved without using recursion.

2. *Make progress*: Any recursive call must make progress toward a base case.

The routine does have a few problems. One problem is the call `s(0)`, for which the method behaves poorly.[1] This is natural because the recursive definition of $S(N)$ does not allow for $N < 1$. We can fix this problem by extending the definition of $S(N)$ to include $N = 0$. Since there are no numbers to add in this case, a natural value for $S(0)$ would be 0. This makes sense because the recursive definition can apply for $S(1)$, since $S(0) + 1$ is 1. To implement this change, we just replace 1 with 0 on lines 5 and 6. Negative N also causes errors, but this can be fixed in a similar manner (and is left as Exercise 7.2).

A second problem is that if the parameter `n` is large, the program may crash or hang. On our system, for instance, $N \geq 9410$ cannot be handled.

```
1      // Evaluate the sum of the first n integers
2
3      public static long s( int n )
4      {
5          if( n == 1 )
6              return 1;
7          else
8              return s( n - 1 ) + n;
9      }
```

Figure 7.1   Recursive evaluation of the sum of the first N integers

---

[1.] A call to `s(-1)` is made, and then the program eventually crashes because there are too many pending recursive calls. We have the problem of not progressing toward a base case.

This is because, as already shown, the implementation of recursion requires some bookkeeping to keep track of the pending recursive calls, and for sufficiently long chains of recursion, the computer simply runs out of memory. This is explained in more detail later in the chapter. This routine also is somewhat more time-consuming than an equivalent loop because the bookkeeping also uses up some time.

Suffice it to say that this particular example does not demonstrate the best use of recursion, since it is so easy to solve the problem without recursion. Most of the good uses of recursion will not exhaust the computer's memory and will be only slightly more time-consuming than nonrecursive implementations. However, recursion will almost always lead to more compact code.

7.3.1   Printing Numbers in Any Base

A good example of how recursion simplifies the coding of routines is number printing. Suppose we want to print out a nonnegative number N in decimal, but we do not have a number output method available. However, we can print out one digit at a time. Consider, for instance, how we would print the number 1369. We would need to print first a 1, then a 3, then a 6, and then a 9. The problem is that obtaining the first digit is a bit sloppy: Given a number n, we need a loop to determine the first digit of n. This is in contrast to obtaining the last digit, which is immediately available as n%10 (which is n for n less than 10).

Recursion provides a nifty solution. To print out 1369, we print out 136, followed by the last digit, 9. As mentioned, it is easy to print out the last digit using the % operator. Printing out all but the number represented by eliminating the last digit is also easy; this is the same problem as printing out n/10. Thus it can be done by a recursive call.

The routine in Figure 7.2 implements this printing routine. If n is smaller than 10, then line 6 is not executed and only the one digit n%10 is printed. Otherwise, all but the last digit is printed recursively, and then the last digit is printed.

```
1       // Print n as a Decimal Number
2
3       public static void printDecimal( int n )
4       {
5           if( n >= 10 )
6               printDecimal( n / 10 );
7           printDigit( n % 10 );
8       }
```

Figure 7.2   Recursive routine to print *N* in decimal

```
1        // Print n in any base
2        // Assumes 2 <= base <= 16
3
4        final static String digitTable = "0123456789abcdef";
5
6        public static void printInt( int n, int base )
7        {
8            if( n >= base )
9                printInt( n / base, base );
10           System.out.print( digitTable.charAt( n % base ) );
11       }
```

Figure 7.3   Recursive routine to print *N* in any base

Notice how we have a base case (n is a one-digit integer) and that all recursive calls make progress toward the base case because the recursive problem has one less digit. Thus we have satisfied the first two fundamental rules of recursion.

To make our printing routine useful, we extend it to print in any base between 2 and 16.[2] This modification is shown in Figure 7.3. We have introduced an array of characters to make the printing of a through f easier. Each digit is now output by indexing into the digitTable array. The printInt routine is not robust. If base is more than 16, then the index into digitTable will be out of the digitTable array. If base is 0, then an arithmetic error will result when a division by 0 is attempted at line 9.

Failure to make progress means the program does not work.

The most interesting error occurs when base is 1. When that happens, the recursive call at line 9 fails to make progress. This is because the two parameters to the recursive call will be identical to the original call. Thus the system will make recursive calls until it eventually runs out of bookkeeping space (and exits less than gracefully with an exception).

A *driver routine* tests the validity of the first call and then calls the recursive routine.

We can make the routine more robust by adding an explicit test for base. The problem with that strategy is that the test would be executed during each of the recursive calls to printInt, and not just during the first call. Once base is valid in the first call, it is silly to retest it, since it does not change in the course of the recursion, and thus must still be valid. One way to avoid this inefficiency is to set up a driver routine. A *driver routine* tests the validity of base and then calls the recursive routine. This is shown in Figure 7.4. The use of driver routines for recursive programs is a common technique.

7.3.2   Why It Works

This section shows, somewhat rigorously, that the printDecimal algorithm works. Our goal is to verify that the algorithm is correct, so the proof will assume that we have made no syntax errors.

[2.] Java's toString method can take any base, but many languages do not have this built-in capability.

```
1          // Print n in any base
2
3      static final String digitTable = "0123456789abcdef";
4      private static final int maxBase = digitTable.length( );
5
6          // Recursive routine
7      public static void printIntRec( int n, int base )
8      {
9          if( n >= base )
10             printIntRec( n / base, base );
11         System.out.print( digitTable.charAt( n % base ) );
12     }
13
14         // Driver routine
15     public static void printInt( int n, int base )
16     {
17         if( base <= 1 || base > maxBase )
18             System.err.println( "Illegal base: " + base );
19         else
20         {
21             if( n < 0 )
22             {
23                 n = -n;
24                 System.out.print( "-" );
25             }
26             printIntRec( n, base );
27         }
28     }
```

Figure 7.4   Robust number printing program

The algorithm `printDecimal` *shown in Figure 7.2 correctly prints* n *in base 10*   **Theorem 7.3**

Let k be the number of digits in n*. The proof is by induction on k.*   **Proof**

Basis: If k = 1, then no recursive call is made, and line 7 correctly outputs the one digit of n*.*

Inductive Hypothesis: Assume that `printDecimal` *works correctly for all k ≥ 1 digit integers. We show that this assumption implies correctness for any k + 1 digit integer* n*. Because k ≥ 1, the* `if` *statement at line 5 is satisfied for a k + 1 digit integer* n*.*

Proof (continued)   *By the inductive hypothesis, the recursive call at line 6 prints the first k digits of n. Then the call at line 7 prints the final digit. Thus if any k-digit integer can be printed, then so can a k + 1-digit integer. By induction, we conclude that* `printDecimal` *works for all k, and thus all n.*

Recursive algorithms can be proven correct with mathematical induction.

    The proof of Theorem 7.3 illustrates an important principle. When designing a recursive algorithm, we can always assume that the recursive calls work because when a proof is performed, this assumption will be used as the inductive hypothesis.

    At first glance, such an assumption seems strange. However, recall that we always assume method calls work, and thus the assumption that the recursive call works is really no different. Just like any method, a recursive routine needs to combine solutions from calls to other methods to obtain a solution. It is just that other methods may include easier instances of the original method.

    This observation leads to the third fundamental rule of recursion:

    3.   *"You gotta believe"*: Always assume that the recursive call works.

The third fundamental rule of recursion: Always assume that the recursive call works. Use this rule to design your algorithms.

    Rule 3 tells us that when we design a recursive method, we do not have to attempt to trace the possibly long path of recursive calls. As we saw earlier, this can be a daunting task and tends to make the design and verification more difficult. A good use of recursion makes such a trace almost impossible to understand. Intuitively, we are letting the computer handle the bookkeeping that would result in much longer code if we were to do it ourselves.

    This principle is so important that it is restated: *Always assume that the recursive call works.*

7.3.3 How It Works

Recall that the implementation of recursion requires additional bookkeeping on the part of the computer. Said another way, the implementation of any method requires bookkeeping and a recursive call is not particularly special (except that it can overload the computer's bookkeeping limitations by calling itself too many times).

The bookkeeping in a procedural or object-oriented language is done by using a stack of *activation records*. Recursion is a natural by-product.

    Java, like other languages such as C++ and Ada, implements methods using an internal stack of *activation records*. We can view an activation record as a piece of paper containing relevant information about the method. This includes, for instance, the values of the parameters and local variables. The actual contents of the activation record is system-dependent.

Method calling and method return sequences are stack operations.

    The stack of activation records is used because methods return in reverse order of their invocation. Recall that stacks are great for reversing things. In the most popular scenario, the top of the stack stores the activation record for the currently active method. When method *G* is called, an activation record for *G* is pushed onto the stack; this makes G the currently active method. When a method returns, the stack is popped and the activation record that is the new top of the stack contains the restored values.

As an example, Figure 7.5 shows a stack of activation records that occurs in the course of evaluating `s(4)`. At this point, we have the calls to `main`, `s(4)`, and `s(3)` pending and we are actively processing `s(2)`.

The space overhead is the memory used to store an activation record for each currently active method. Thus, in the earlier example in which `s(9410)` crashes, the system has room for roughly 9,410 activation records. (Note that `main` generates an activation record itself.) The pushing and popping of the internal stack also represents the overhead of executing a method call.

The close relation between recursion and stacks tells us that recursive programs can always be implemented iteratively with an explicit stack. Presumably the stack will store items that are smaller than an activation record, so we can also reasonably expect to use less space. The result is slightly faster but longer code. Modern optimizing compilers have lessened the costs associated with recursion to such a degree that, for the purposes of speed, it is rarely worth removing recursion from an application that uses it well.

Recursion can always be removed by using a stack. This is occasionally required to save space.

7.3.4 Too Much Recursion Can Be Dangerous

In this text are many examples that illustrate the power of recursion. However, before we look at those examples, it is important to realize that recursion is not always appropriate. For instance, the use of recursion in Figure 7.1 is poor because a loop would do just as well. A practical liability is that the overhead of the recursive call takes time and limits the value of n for which the program is correct. A good rule of thumb is that you should never use recursion as a substitute for a simple loop.

Do not use recursion as a substitute for a simple loop.

A much more serious problem is illustrated by an attempt to calculate the Fibonacci numbers recursively. The *Fibonacci numbers* $F_0, F_1, ..., F_i$ are defined as follows: $F_0 = 0$ and $F_1 = 1$. The ith Fibonacci number is equal to the sum of the $(i-1)^{th}$ and $(i-2)^{th}$ Fibonacci numbers. Thus $F_i = F_{i-1} + F_{i-2}$. From this definition, we can determine that the series of Fibonacci numbers continues: 1, 2, 3, 5, 8, 13, 21, 34, 55, 89, ...

The ith Fibonacci number is the sum of the two previous Fibonacci numbers.

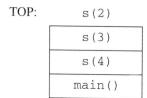

TOP: `s(2)`

| `s(3)` |
| `s(4)` |
| `main()` |

Figure 7.5   Stack of activation records

```
1       // Compute the nth Fibonacci Number
2       // Bad algorithm
3       public static long fib( int n )
4       {
5           if( n <= 1 )
6               return n;
7           else
8               return fib( n - 1 ) + fib( n - 2 );
9       }
```

Figure 7.6   Recursive routine for Fibonacci numbers: a bad idea

The Fibonacci numbers have an incredible number of properties that seem to always crop up. In fact, one journal, *The Fibonacci Quarterly*, exists solely for the purpose of publishing theorems involving the Fibonacci numbers. For instance, the sum of the squares of two consecutive Fibonacci numbers is another Fibonacci number. The sum of the first N Fibonacci numbers is one less than F_{N+2} (see Exercise 7.9 for some other interesting identities).

Because the Fibonacci numbers are recursively defined, it seems natural to write a recursive routine to determine F_N. This recursive routine, shown in Figure 7.6, works but has a serious problem. This routine, on our relatively fast machine, takes several minutes to compute F_{40}. This is an absurd amount of time considering that the basic calculation requires only 39 additions.

> Do not do redundant work recursively; the program will be incredibly inefficient.

The underlying problem is that this particular recursive routine performs redundant calculations. To compute `fib(n)`, we recursively compute `fib(n-1)`. When the recursive call returns, we compute `fib(n-2)` by using another recursive call. But we have already computed `fib(n-2)` in the process of computing `fib(n-1)`, so the call to `fib(n-2)` is a wasted, redundant calculation. In effect, we make two calls to `fib(n-2)` instead of only one.

Normally, making two method calls instead of one would only double the running time of a program. However, it is worse than that. This is because each call to `fib(n-1)` and each call to `fib(n-2)` makes a call to `fib(n-3)`. Thus there are actually three calls to `fib(n-3)`. In fact, it just keeps getting worse: Each call to `fib(n-2)` or `fib(n-3)` results in a call to `fib(n-4)`, so there are five calls to `fib(n-4)`. Thus we get a compounding effect: Each recursive call does more and more redundant work.

> The recursive routine `fib` is exponential.

Let $C(N)$ be the number of calls to `fib` made during the evaluation of `fib(n)`. Clearly, $C(0) = C(1) = 1$ call. For $N \geq 2$, we make the call for `fib(n)`, plus all the calls needed to evaluate `fib(n-1)` and `fib(n-2)` recursively and independently. Thus $C(N) = C(N-1) + C(N-2) + 1$. By induction, we can easily verify that for $N \geq 3$ the solution to this recurrence is $C(N) = F_{N+2} + F_{N-1} - 1$. Thus the number of recursive calls is larger than the Fibonacci number we are trying to compute and is exponential. For $N = 40$, $F_{40} = 102{,}334{,}155$, while the total number of recursive calls is over 300 million. No wonder the program takes forever. The explosive growth of the number of recursive calls is illustrated in Figure 7.7.

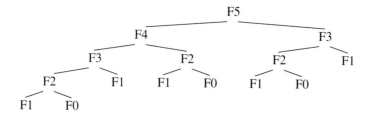

Figure 7.7   Trace of the recursive calculation of the Fibonacci numbers

This example illustrates the fourth and final basic rule of recursion:

4. *Compound interest rule*: Never duplicate work by solving the same instance of a problem in separate recursive calls.

The last fundamental rule of recursion: Never duplicate work by solving the same instance of a problem in separate recursive calls.

7.3.5 Additional Examples

Perhaps the best way to understand recursion is to see examples. In this section, we look at four more examples of recursion. The first two are easily implemented nonrecursively, but the last two show off some of the power of recursion.

Factorials

Recall that $N!$ is the product of the first N integers. Thus we can express $N!$ as N times $(N-1)!$. Combined with the base case $1! = 1$, this immediately provides all that is needed for a recursive implementation. This is shown in Figure 7.8.

Binary Search

Section 5.6.2 described the binary search. Recall that in a binary search, we perform a search in a sorted array A by examining the middle element. If we have a match, we are done. Otherwise, if the item that is being searched for is smaller than the middle element, we search in the subarray that is to the left of the middle element. Otherwise, we search in the subarray that is to the right of the middle element. This presumes that the subarray is not empty; if it is, the item is not found.

```
1       // Evaluate n!
2       public static long factorial( int n )
3       {
4           if( n <= 1 )     // base case
5               return 1;
6           else
7               return n * factorial( n - 1 );
8       }
```

Figure 7.8   Recursive implementation of `factorial` function

```
1    /**
2     * Performs the standard binary search
3     * using two comparisons per level.
4     * This is a driver that calls the recursive method.
5     */
6    public static int binarySearch( Comparable [ ] a,
7                           Comparable x ) throws ItemNotFound
8    {
9        return binarySearch( a, x, 0, a.length - 1 );
10   }
11
12   /**
13    * Hidden recursive routine.
14    */
15   private static int binarySearch( Comparable [ ] a,
16                          Comparable x, int low, int high )
17                                      throws ItemNotFound
18   {
19       if( low > high )
20           throw new ItemNotFound( "BinarySearch fails" );
21       int mid = ( low + high ) / 2;
22       if( a[ mid ].compares( x ) < 0 )
23           return binarySearch( a, x, mid + 1, high );
24       else if( a[ mid ].compares( x ) > 0 )
25           return binarySearch( a, x, low, mid - 1 );
26       else
27           return mid;
28   }
```

Figure 7.9   Binary search routine using recursion

This translates directly into the recursive method shown in Figure 7.9. The code illustrates a thematic technique in which the public driver routine makes an initial call to a private recursive routine, and if necessary, passes on the return value (or thrown exception). Here, the driver sets the low and high points of the subarray, namely, 0 and a.length-1.

In the recursive method, the base case at lines 19 and 20 handles an empty subarray. Otherwise, we follow the description given previously by making a recursive call on the appropriate subarray (line 23 or 25) if a match has not been detected. When a match is detected, the matching index is returned at line 27.

Note that the running time, in terms of Big-Oh, is unchanged from the non-recursive implementation because, here, we are performing the same work. In practice, the running time would be expected to be slightly larger because of the hidden costs of recursion.

Figure 7.10   A recursively drawn ruler

Drawing a Ruler

Figure 7.10 shows the result of running a Java program that draws ruler markings. Here, we consider the problem of marking 1 inch. In the middle is the longest mark. In Figure 7.10, to the left of the middle is a miniaturized version of the ruler and to the right of the middle is a second miniaturized version. This suggests a recursive algorithm that first draws the middle line and then draws the left and right halves.

Appendix D provides the details of drawing lines and shapes in Java. Suffice it to say that the programmer must provide a `paint` method, and this `paint` method can call other methods. The `drawRuler` method in Figure 7.11 is our recursive routine that is called from `paint`. It uses the `drawLine` method, which is part of the Java library. `drawLine` draws a line from one x, y coordinate to another x, y coordinate, where coordinates are offset from the top-left corner.

Our routine draws markings at `level` different heights; each recursive call is one level deeper (in Figure 7.10 there are eight levels). It first disposes of the base case at lines 4 and 5. Then the midpoint mark is drawn at line 9. Finally, the two miniatures are drawn recursively at lines 11 and 12. In the online code, we include extra code to slow down the drawing. In that way, we can see the order in which the lines are drawn by the recursive algorithm.

```
1      private void
2      drawRuler( Graphics g, int left, int right, int level)
3      {
4          if( level < 1 )
5              return;
6
7          int mid = ( left + right ) / 2;
8
9          g.drawLine( mid, 80, mid, 80 - level * 5 );
10
11          drawRuler( g, left, mid - 1, level- 1 );
12          drawRuler( g, mid + 1, right, level - 1 );
13      }
```

Figure 7.11   Recursive method to draw a ruler

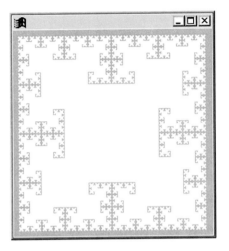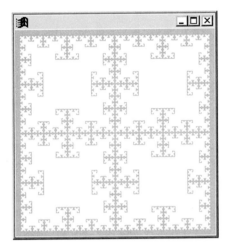

Figure 7.12   On the left-hand side is a fractal star outline drawn by Figure 7.13. On the right-hand side is the same star immediately prior to the last square being added

```
1     // Draw picture in Figure 7.12
2     private void drawFractal( Graphics g, int xCenter,
3                               int yCenter, int boundingDim )
4     {
5         int side = boundingDim / 2;
6
7         if( side < 1 )
8             return;
9
10            // Compute corners
11        int left =   xCenter - side / 2;
12        int top =    yCenter - side / 2;
13        int right =  xCenter + side / 2;
14        int bottom = yCenter + side / 2;
15
16            // Recursively draw four quadrants
17        drawFractal( g, left, top, boundingDim / 2 );
18        drawFractal( g, left, bottom, boundingDim / 2 );
19        drawFractal( g, right, top, boundingDim / 2 );
20        drawFractal( g, right, bottom, boundingDim / 2 );
21
22            // Draw central square, overlapping quadrants
23        g.fillRect( left, top, right - left, bottom - top );
24    }
```

Figure 7.13   Code to draw fractal star outline in Figure 7.12

Fractal Star

On the left of Figure 7.12 is a seemingly complex pattern, called a *fractal star*, that is easily drawn using recursion. The entire canvas is initially grey (not shown in the figure). The pattern is formed by drawing white squares onto the grey background. The last square drawn is over the center; the picture on the right-hand side shows the drawing immediately before the last square is added. From this, it becomes apparent that prior to the last square being drawn, four miniature versions have been drawn, one in each of the four quadrants. This provides the necessary information to derive the recursive algorithm.

As was the case with the previous example, the method `drawFractal` will be called from `paint` and it uses a Java library routine. In this case, `fillRect` draws a rectangle; its upper left-hand corner and dimensions must be specified. The code is shown in Figure 7.13. The parameters to `drawFractal` include the center of the fractal and the overall dimension. From this, we can compute, at line 5, the size of the large central square. After handling the base case at lines 7 and 8, we compute the boundaries of the central rectangle. We can then draw the four miniature fractals at lines 17 to 20. Finally, we draw the central square at line 23. Notice that the square must be drawn after the recursive calls. Otherwise, we obtain a different picture (Exercise 7.28 asks you to describe the difference).

7.4   Numerical Applications

This section looks at three problems drawn primarily from number theory. Number theory used to be considered an interesting but useless branch of mathematics. However, in the last 20 years, an important application for number theory has emerged: data security. The discussion begins with a small amount of mathematics background and then shows recursive algorithms to solve three problems. We can combine these routines, in conjunction with a fourth algorithm that is more complex and is described in Chapter 9, to implement an algorithm that can be used to encode and decode messages. To date, nobody has been able to show that the encryption scheme described here is not secure.

Here are the four problems we examine:

1. *Modular exponentiation*: Compute $X^N (\bmod\ P)$.
2. *Greatest common divisor*: Compute $gcd(A, B)$.
3. *Multiplicative inverse*: Solve $AX \equiv 1 (\bmod\ P)$ for X.
4. *Primality testing*: Determine if N is prime (this is deferred to Chapter 9).

The integers we expect to deal with are all large, requiring at least 100 digits each. So we must already have a way to represent such integers, along with a complete set of algorithms for basic operations such as addition, subtraction, multiplication, division, and so on. Java 1.1 provides a class named `BigDecimal` for this purpose. Implementing it efficiently is no trivial matter, and in fact there is an extensive literature on the subject.

The algorithms described here have the property that they work with these objects but still execute in a reasonable amount of time. The methods that we code will work with `long` types so that we can test the basic algorithms. Because Java does not allow operator overloading, this code would need to be rewritten to use named methods (instead of operators) with `BigDecimal` objects.

7.4.1 Modular Arithmetic

The problems in this section, as well as the implementation of the hash table data structure (Section 6.7 and Chapter 19), require the use of the Java mod operator, denoted as `operator%`. `operator%` computes the remainder of two integral types. As an example, `13%10` evaluates to 3, as does `3%10` and `23%10`. When we compute the remainder of a division by 10, the possible results range from 0 to 9. This makes `operator%` useful when small integers need to be generated.

If two numbers A and B give the same remainder when divided by N, we say that they are congruent modulo N. This is written as $A \equiv B(\bmod N)$. In this case, it must be true that N divides $A - B$. Furthermore, the converse is true: If N divides $A - B$, then $A \equiv B(\bmod N)$. Because there are only N possible remainders — 0, 1, ..., $N - 1$ — we say that the integers are divided into congruence classes modulo N. In other words, every integer can be placed in one of N classes, and those in the same class are congruent to each other, modulo N. There are three important facts that we use in our algorithms (we leave their proofs as Exercise 7.10):

1. If $A \equiv B(\bmod N)$, then for any C, $A + C \equiv B + C(\bmod N)$.
2. If $A \equiv B(\bmod N)$, then for any D, $AD \equiv BD(\bmod N)$.
3. If $A \equiv B(\bmod N)$, then for any P, $A^P \equiv B^P(\bmod N)$.

These theorems allow certain calculations to be done with less effort. For instance, suppose we want to know the last digit in 3333^{5555}. Since this number has over 15,000 digits, it is expensive to directly compute the answer. However, what we want is to determine $3333^{5555}(\bmod 10)$. Since $3333 \equiv 3(\bmod 10)$, it suffices to compute $3^{5555}(\bmod 10)$. Since $3^4 = 81$, we know that $3^4 \equiv 1(\bmod 10)$, and raising both sides to the power of 1388 tells us that $3^{5552} \equiv 1(\bmod 10)$. If we multiply both sides by $3^3 = 27$, then we obtain $3^{5555} \equiv 27 \equiv 7(\bmod 10)$, thereby completing the calculation. The next section shows how this procedure is generalized.

7.4.2 Modular Exponentiation

This section shows how to efficiently compute $X^N(\bmod P)$. This can be done by initializing `result` to 1 and then repeatedly multiplying `result` by X and applying `operator%` after every multiplication. Applying `operator%` in this way instead of after just the last multiplication makes each multiplication easier because it keeps `result` small.

After N multiplications, `result` is the answer we are seeking. However, doing N multiplications is impractical if N is a 100-digit number. In fact, if N is one billion it is impractical on all but the fastest machines.

A faster algorithm is based on the following observation. That is, if N is even, then $X^N = (X \cdot X)^{\lfloor N/2 \rfloor}$ and if N is odd, $X^N = X \cdot X^{N-1} = X \cdot (X \cdot X)^{\lfloor N/2 \rfloor}$. (Recall that $\lfloor X \rfloor$ is the largest integer that is smaller than or equal to X.) As before, to perform modular exponentiation, apply an `operator%` after every multiplication.

The recursive algorithm in Figure 7.14 represents a direct implementation of this strategy. Lines 7 and 8 handle the base case: X^0 is 1, by definition.[3] At line 10, we make a recursive call based on the identity stated in the previous paragraph. If N is even, then this computes the desired answer. If N is odd, we need to multiply by an extra X (and use `operator%`).

This algorithm is faster than the simple algorithm proposed earlier. If $M(N)$ is the number of multiplications that are used by `power`, then we have $M(N) \le M\lfloor N/2 \rfloor + 2$. This is because if N is even, we perform one multiplication, plus those done recursively, and if N is odd, we perform two multiplications, plus those done recursively. Since $M(0) = 0$, we can show that $M(N) < 2\log N$. The logarithmic factor can be seen without direct calculation by application of the halving principle (see Section 5.5), which tells us the number of recursive invocations of `power`. Moreover, an average value of $M(N)$ is $(3/2)\log N$. This is because in each recursive step, N is equally likely to be even or odd. If N is a 100-digit number, then in the worst case, only about 665 multiplications (and typically only 500 on average) are needed.

Exponentiation can be done in a logarithmic number of multiplications.

```
1      /**
2       * Return x^n (mod p)
3       * Assumes that p is positive and power( 0, 0, p ) is 1
4       */
5      public static long power( long x, long n, long p )
6      {
7          if( n == 0 )
8              return 1;
9
10         long tmp = power( ( x * x ) % p, n / 2, p );
11         if( n % 2 != 0 )
12             tmp = ( tmp * x ) % p;
13
14         return tmp;
15     }
```

Figure 7.14   Modular exponentiation routine

[3.] For the purposes of this algorithm, $0^0 = 1$, N is nonnegative, and P is positive.

7.4.3 Greatest Common Divisor and Multiplicative Inverses

The greatest common divisor (gcd) of two integers is the largest integer that divides both of them.

Consider two nonnegative integers A and B. Their greatest common divisor, $gcd(A, B)$, is the largest integer D that divides both A and B. For instance, $gcd(70, 25)$ is 5.

It is easy to verify that $gcd(A, B) \equiv gcd(A - B, B)$. If D divides both A and B, it must also divide $A - B$; and if D divides both $A - B$ and B, then it must also divide A.

This observation leads to a simple algorithm in which we repeatedly subtract B from A, thereby transforming the problem into a smaller one. Eventually A becomes less than B, and then we can switch roles for A and B and continue from there. At some point, B will become 0. Then we know that $gcd(A, 0) \equiv A$, and since each transformation preserves the gcd of the original A and B, we have our answer. This algorithm is called Euclid's algorithm and was first described over 2,000 years ago. Although correct, it is unusable for `BigDecimals` because a huge number of subtractions are likely to be required.

A computationally efficient modification is that the repeated subtractions of B from A until A is smaller than B is equivalent to the conversion of A to precisely $A \bmod B$. Thus $gcd(A, B) \equiv gcd(B, A \bmod B)$. This recursive definition, along with the base case in which $B = 0$, is directly used to obtain the routine in Figure 7.15. To see how this works, note that in the previous example, the following sequence of recursive calls is used to deduce that the gcd of 70 and 25 is 5: $gcd(70, 25) \Rightarrow gcd(25, 20) \Rightarrow gcd(20, 5) \Rightarrow gcd(5, 0) \Rightarrow 5$.

The number of recursive calls that are used is proportional to the logarithm of A, which is the same order of magnitude as the other routines discussed in this section. The reason for this is that in two recursive calls, the problem is reduced at least in half. The proof of this is left as Exercise 7.11.

The gcd and multiplicative inverse can also be calculated in logarithmic time using a variant of Euclid's algorithm.

The gcd algorithm is used implicitly to solve a similar mathematical problem. The solution $1 \leq X < N$ to the equation $AX \equiv 1 (\bmod N)$ is called the *multiplicative inverse* of A, $\bmod N$. Also assume that $1 \leq A < N$. As an example, the inverse of 3, mod 13 is 9: $3 \cdot 9 \bmod 13$ yields 1.

```
1     /**
2      * Return the greatest common divisor.
3      */
4     public static long gcd( long a, long b )
5     {
6         if( b == 0 )
7             return a;
8         else
9             return gcd( b, a % b );
10    }
```

Figure 7.15 Computation of greatest common divisor

The ability to compute multiplicative inverses is important because equations such as $3i \equiv 7 (\text{mod } 13)$ are easily solved if we know the multiplicative inverse. These equations arise in many applications, including the encryption algorithm discussed at the end of this section. In this example, if we multiply by the inverse of 3 (namely 9), we obtain $i \equiv 63 (\text{mod } 13)$, so $i = 11$ is a solution. If

$$AX \equiv 1 (\text{mod } N)$$

then

$$AX + NY \equiv 1 (\text{mod } N)$$

is true for any Y. For some Y, the left-hand side must be exactly 1. Thus the equation

$$AX + NY = 1$$

is solvable if (and only if) A has a multiplicative inverse.

Given A and B, we show how to find X and Y to satisfy

$$AX + BY = 1.$$

We assume $0 \le |B| < |A|$. To do this, we extend the gcd algorithm to compute X and Y.

First, consider the base case $B \equiv 0$. In this case, we have to solve $AX = 1$, which implies both A and X are 1. In fact, if A is not 1, then there is no multiplicative inverse. A consequence of this fact is that A has a multiplicative inverse modulo N if and only if $gcd(A, N) = 1$.

Otherwise, B is not zero. Recall that $gcd(A, B) = gcd(B, A \bmod B)$. So let $A = BQ + R$. Here, Q is the quotient and R is the remainder, and thus the recursive call is $gcd(B, R)$. Suppose we can recursively solve

$$BX_1 + RY_1 = 1.$$

Since $R = A - BQ$, we have

$$BX_1 + (A - BQ)Y_1 = 1,$$

which means that

$$AY_1 + B(X_1 - QY_1) = 1.$$

Thus $X = Y_1$ and $Y = X_1 - \lfloor A/B \rfloor Y_1$ is a solution to $AX + BY = 1$. This is directly coded as fullGcd in Figure 7.16. inverse just calls fullGcd, where X and Y are static class variables. The only detail left is that the value given for X may be negative. If it is, line 35 of inverse will make it positive. A proof of that fact is left as Exercise 7.14. The proof can be done by induction.

```
 1          // Internal variables for fullGCD
 2      private static long x;
 3      private static long y;
 4
 5      /**
 6       * Works back through Euclid's algorithm to find
 7       * x and y such that if gcd(a,b) = 1,
 8       * ax + by = 1.
 9       */
10      private static void fullGcd( long a, long b )
11      {
12          long x1, y1;
13
14          if( b == 0 )
15          {
16              x = 1;          // If a != 1, there is no inverse
17              y = 0;          // We omit this check
18          }
19          else
20          {
21              fullGcd( b, a % b );
22              x1 = x; y1 = y;
23              x = y1;
24              y = x1 - ( a / b ) * y1;
25          }
26      }
27
28      /**
29       * Solve ax == 1 (mod n), assuming gcd( a, n ) = 1.
30       * @return x.
31       */
32      public static long inverse( long a, long n )
33      {
34          fullGcd( a, n );
35          return x > 0 ? x : x + n;
36      }
```

Figure 7.16   Routine to determine multiplicative inverse

7.4.4 The RSA Cryptosystem

Number theory is used in cryptography because factoring appears to be a much harder process than multiplication.

For centuries, number theory was thought to be a completely impractical branch of mathematics. Recently, however, it has emerged as an important field because of its applicability in cryptography.

The problem we consider has two parts. Suppose Alice wants to send a message to Bob, but she is worried that the transmission may be compromised. For instance, if the transmission is over a phone line and the phone is tapped, then somebody else may be reading the message. We assume that even if there is eavesdropping on the phone line, there is no maliciousness (that is, damage to the signal) — Bob gets whatever Alice sends.

A solution to this problem is to use an encryption scheme which consists of two parts. First, Alice *encrypts* the message and sends the result, which is no longer plainly readable. When Bob receives Alice's transmission, he *decrypts* it to obtain the original. The security of the algorithm is based on the fact that nobody else besides Bob should be able to perform the decryption, including Alice (if she did not save the original message).

Encryption is used to transmit messages so that they cannot be read by other parties.

Thus Bob must provide Alice with a method of encryption that only he knows how to reverse. This is an extremely challenging problem. Many proposed algorithms can be compromised by subtle code-breaking techniques. One method, described here, is the *RSA cryptosystem* (named after the initials of its authors) and is a very elegant implementation of an encryption strategy.

The *RSA cryptosystem* is a popular encryption method.

The goal here is to give only a high-level overview showing how the methods written in this section interact in a practical way. The references contain pointers to more detailed descriptions, as well as proofs of the key properties of the algorithm.

First, however, note that a message consists of a sequence of characters and each character is just a sequence of bits. Thus a message is a sequence of bits. If we break up the message into blocks of B bits, then we can interpret the message as a series of very large numbers. Thus the basic problem is reduced to encrypting a large number and then decrypting the result.

Computation of the RSA Constants

The RSA algorithm begins by having the receiver determine some constants. First, two large primes p and q are randomly chosen. Typically, these would be 100 or so digits each. For the purposes of this example, suppose $p = 127$ and $q = 211$. Note that Bob is the receiver and thus is performing these computations. Note, also, that primes are plentiful. Bob can thus keep trying random numbers until two of them pass the primality test (which is discussed in Chapter 9).

Next, Bob computes $N = pq$ and $N' = (p-1)(q-1)$. For this example, this gives $N = 26,797$ and $N' = 26,460$. The receiver, Bob, continues by choosing any $e > 1$ such that $gcd(e, N') = 1$. In mathematical terms, he chooses any e that is relatively prime to N'. Bob can keep trying different values of e by using the routine shown in Figure 7.15 until one is found that satisfies the property. Since any prime e would work, finding e is at least as easy as finding a prime number. In our case, $e = 13,379$ is one of many valid choices. Next, d, the multiplicative inverse of e, mod N' is computed using the routine in Figure 7.16. In this example, $d = 11,099$.

Once Bob has computed all of these constants, he does the following. First, he destroys p, q, and N'. The security of the system is compromised if any of these values are discovered. Bob then tells anybody who wants to send him an encrypted message what the values of e and N are, but he keeps d secret.

Encryption and Decryption Algorithms

To encrypt an integer M, the sender computes $M^e(\bmod N)$ and sends it. In our case, if $M = 10,237$, then the value sent is 8,422. When an encrypted integer R is received, all Bob has to do is compute $R^d(\bmod N)$. For $R = 8{,}422$, it can be verified that he gets back the original $M = 10{,}237$ (this is not accidental). Both encryption and decryption can thus be carried out by using the modular exponentiation routine in Figure 7.14.

Why the algorithm works: The choices of e, d, and N guarantee (via a number theory proof that is beyond the scope of this text) that $M^{ed} \equiv M(\bmod N)$, as long as M and N share no common factors. Since the only factors of N are two 100-digit primes, it is virtually impossible for that to occur.[4] Thus decryption of the encrypted text gets the original back.

What makes the scheme seem secure is that knowledge of d is apparently required in order to decode. Now N and e uniquely determine d. For instance, if we factor N, we get p and q and can then reconstruct d. The caveat is that factoring is apparently very hard to do for large numbers. Thus the security of the RSA system is based on the fact that it is thought that factoring large numbers is intrisically very difficult. So far it has held up well.

In public key cryptography, each participant publishes the code others can use to send encrypted messages, but keeps the decrypting code secret.

This general scheme is known as *public key cryptography*. Anybody who wants to receive messages publishes encryption information for anybody else to use. In the RSA system, e and N would be computed once by each enrolled person and listed in a publicly readable place.

The RSA algorithm is widely used to implement secure email, as well as secure Internet transactions. When you see a closed lock (🔒) at the bottom of a Netscape Navigator Web page, then a secure transaction is being performed via cryptography. The method that is actually employed is more complex than what is described here. One problem is that the RSA algorithm is somewhat slow for sending large messages.

In practice, RSA is used to encrypt the key that is used by a single-key encryption algorithm, such as DES.

A faster method is called *DES*. Unlike the RSA algorithm, DES is a single-key algorithm, meaning that the same key serves to both encode and decode. This is like the typical lock on your house door. The problem with single-key algorithms is that both parties need to share the single key. How does one party make sure the other party has the single key? It turns out that this is solved by using the RSA algorithm. A typical solution is that, say, Alice will randomly generate a single key for DES encryption. She then encrypts her message using DES, which is much faster than using RSA. She transmits the encrypted message to Bob. For Bob to decode the encrypted message, he needs to get the DES key that was just used. Since a DES key is relatively short, Alice can use RSA to encrypt the DES key and then send it in a second transmission to Bob. Bob next decrypts Alice's second transmission, thus obtaining the DES key, at which point the original message can be decoded. These types of protocols, with enhancements, form the basis of most practical encryption implementations.

---

4. You are more likely to win a typical state lottery 13 weeks in a row. However, if this does happen, the system is compromised because the gcd will be a factor of N.

7.5   Divide-and-Conquer Algorithms

An important problem-solving technique that makes use of recursion is *divide-and-conquer*. Divide-and-conquer algorithms are recursive algorithms that consist of two parts:

Divide-and-conquer algorithms are recursive algorithms that are generally very efficient.

- *Divide*: Smaller problems are solved recursively (except, of course, base cases).
- *Conquer*: The solution to the original problem is then formed from the solutions to the subproblems.

Traditionally, routines in which the algorithm contains at least two recursive calls are called divide-and-conquer algorithms, while routines whose text contains only one recursive call are not. Consequently, the recursive routines seen thus far in this chapter are not divide-and-conquer algorithms. Also, the subproblems usually must be disjoint (that is, essentially nonoverlapping) so as to avoid the excessive costs seen in the sample recursive computation of the Fibonacci numbers.

This section gives an example of the divide-and-conquer paradigm. First, it shows how to use recursion to solve the maximum subsequence sum problem. Then it provides an analysis to show that the running time is $O(N \log N)$. Although we have already seen a linear algorithm for this problem, the solution used here is thematic of others in a wide range of applications, including the sorting algorithms, such as mergesort and quicksort, that are discussed in Chapter 8. Consequently, the technique is important to learn. Finally, this section shows the general form for the running time of a wide class of divide-and-conquer algorithms.

7.5.1   The Maximum Contiguous Subsequence Sum Problem

Recall from Section 5.3 the problem of finding, in a sequence of numbers, a contiguous subsequence of maximum sum. For convenience, the problem is restated here.

MAXIMUM CONTIGUOUS SUBSEQUENCE SUM PROBLEM

Given (possibly negative) integers $A_1, A_2, ..., A_N$, find (and identify the sequence corresponding to) the maximum value of $\sum_{k=i}^{j} A_k$. The maximum contiguous subsequence sum is zero if all the integers are negative.

The maximum con-
tiguous subse-
quence sum prob-
lem can be solved
with a divide-and-
conquer algorithm.

Three algorithms of various complexities were presented. One was a cubic algorithm that was based on an exhaustive search: We calculated the sum of each possible subsequence and selected the maximum. A quadratic improvement was described that takes advantage of the fact that each new subsequence can be computed in constant time from a previous subsequence. Since we have $O(N^2)$ subsequences, this is the best bound that can be achieved using an approach that directly examines all subsequences. We also saw a linear-time algorithm that works by examining only a few subsequences. However, its correctness was not obvious.

Let us consider a divide-and-conquer algorithm. Suppose the sample input is { 4, –3, 5, –2, –1, 2, 6, –2 }. We divide this input into two halves, as shown in Figure 7.17. Then the maximum contiguous subsequence sum can occur in one of three ways:

- *Case 1*: It resides entirely in the first half.
- *Case 2*: It resides entirely in the second half.
- *Case 3*: It begins in the first half but ends in the second half.

We will show how to find the maximums for each of these three cases more efficiently than by using an exhaustive search.

We begin by looking at case 3. We want to avoid the nested loop that results from considering all $N/2$ starting points and $N/2$ ending points independently. The idea is to replace two nested loops by two consecutive loops. The consecutive loops, each of size $N/2$, combine to require only linear work. We can do this because any contiguous subsequence that begins in the first half and ends in the second half must include both the last element of the first half and the first element of the second half.

Figure 7.17 shows that we can calculate, for each element in the first half, the contiguous subsequence sum that ends at the rightmost item. We do this with a right-to-left scan, starting from the border between the two halves. Similarly, we can calculate the contiguous subsequence sum for all sequences that begin with the first element in the second half. These two subsequences can then be combined to form the maximum contiguous subsequence that spans the dividing border. In the example in Figure 7.17, the resulting sequence spans from the first element in the first half to the next to last element in the second half. The total sum is the sum of the two subsequences, $4 + 7 = 11$.

First Half				Second Half				
4	–3	5	–2	–1	2	6	–2	Values
4*	0	3	–2	–1	1	7*	5	Running Sums

Running Sum from the Center (*denotes maximum for each half)

Figure 7.17   Dividing the maximum contiguous subsequence problem into halves

This analysis shows us that case 3 can be solved in linear time. But what about cases 1 and 2? Because there are $N/2$ elements in each half, an exhaustive search applied to each half will still require quadratic time per half. Specifically, all we have done is eliminate roughly half of the work; half of quadratic is still quadratic. In cases 1 and 2, we can apply the same strategy, that of dividing into more halves. We can keep dividing those quarters further and further until splitting is impossible. This is succinctly stated as follows: *Solve cases 1 and 2 recursively.* As will be shown later in the chapter, this will lower the running time below quadratic because the savings will compound throughout the algorithm. The following is a summary of the main portion of the algorithm:

In *divide and conquer*, the recursion is the *divide*, the overhead is the *conquer*.

1. Recursively compute the maximum contiguous subsequence sum that resides entirely in the first half.
2. Recursively compute the maximum contiguous subsequence sum that resides entirely in the second half.
3. Compute, via two consecutive loops, the maximum contiguous subsequence sum that begins in the first half but ends in the second half.
4. Choose the largest of the three sums.

A recursive algorithm requires us to specify a base case. When the size of the problem reaches one element, we do not use recursion. The Java method that results is coded in Figure 7.18.

The general form for the recursive call is to pass the input array along with the left and right borders, which delimit the portion of the array that is being operated on. A one-line driver routine sets this up by passing the borders 0 and $N - 1$ along with the array.

Lines 13 and 14 handle the base case. If `left==right`, there is one element, and it is the maximum contiguous subsequence if the element is nonnegative (otherwise, the empty sequence with sum 0 is maximum). Lines 16 and 17 perform the two recursive calls. We can see that the recursive calls are always on a problem that is smaller than the original; thus we make progress toward the base case. Lines 19 to 24 and then 25 to 30 calculate the maximum sums that touch the center border. The sum of these two values is the maximum sum that spans both halves. The routine `max3` (not shown) returns the largest of the three possibilities.

7.5.2 Analysis of a Basic Divide-and-Conquer Recurrence

The recursive maximum contiguous subsequence sum algorithm works by performing linear work to compute a sum that spans the center border and then performing two recursive calls. These recursive calls collectively compute a sum that spans the center border, and then do further recursive calls, and so on. The total work performed by the algorithm is then proportional to the scanning done over all of the recursive calls.

Intuitive analysis of the maximum contiguous subsequence sum divide-and-conquer algorithm: We spend $O(N)$ per level.

```
 1    /**
 2     * Recursive maximum contiguous subsequence sum algorithm.
 3     * Finds maximum sum in subarray spanning a[left..right].
 4     * Does not attempt to maintain actual best sequence.
 5     */
 6    private static int maxSumRec( int [ ] a, int left,
 7                                            int right )
 8    {
 9        int maxLeftBorderSum = 0, maxRightBorderSum = 0;
10        int leftBorderSum = 0, rightBorderSum = 0;
11        int center = ( left + right ) / 2;
12
13        if( left == right )   // Base case
14            return a[ left ] > 0 ? a[ left ] : 0;
15
16        int maxLeftSum  = maxSumRec( a, left, center );
17        int maxRightSum = maxSumRec( a, center + 1, right );
18
19        for( int i = center; i >= left; i-- )
20        {
21            leftBorderSum += a[ i ];
22            if( leftBorderSum > maxLeftBorderSum )
23                maxLeftBorderSum = leftBorderSum;
24        }
25        for( int j = center + 1; j <= right; j++ )
26        {
27            rightBorderSum += a[ j ];
28            if( rightBorderSum > maxRightBorderSum )
29                maxRightBorderSum = rightBorderSum;
30        }
31
32        return max3( maxLeftSum, maxRightSum,
33                    maxLeftBorderSum + maxRightBorderSum );
34    }
35
36    // Publicly visible routine
37    public static int maxSubSum4( int [ ] a )
38    {
39        return maxSumRec( a, 0, a.length - 1 );
40    }
```

Figure 7.18   Divide-and-conquer algorithm for maximum contiguous subsequence sum problem

Figure 7.19 graphically illustrates how the algorithm works for $N = 8$ elements. Each rectangle represents a call to maxSumRec, and the length of the rectangle is proportional to the size of the subarray (and hence the cost of the scanning of the subarray) being operated on by the invocation. The initial call is shown on the first line. Notice that the size of the subarray is N. This represents the cost of the scanning for the third case. The initial call then makes two recursive calls, yielding two subarrays of size $N/2$. The cost of each scan in case 3 is half the original cost, but since there are two such recursive calls, the combined cost of these recursive calls is also N. Each of those two recursive instances themselves make two recursive calls, thus yielding four subproblems that are a quarter of the original size. So the total of all of those case 3 costs is also N.

Eventually, we reach the base case. Each base case has size 1, and there are N of them. Of course, there are no case 3 costs in this case, but we charge 1 unit to perform the check that determines if the sole element is positive or negative. The total cost then, shown in Figure 7.19, is N per level of recursion. Each level halves the size of the basic problem, so the halving principle tells us that there are approximately $\log N$ levels. In fact, the number of levels is $1 + \lceil \log N \rceil$ (which is 4 when N is equal to 8). Thus we expect that the total running time is $O(N \log N)$.

This analysis gives an intuitive explanation of why the running time is $O(N \log N)$. In general, however, expanding a recursive algorithm to examine behavior is a bad idea; it violates the third rule of recursion. We next consider a more formal mathematical treatment.

Let $T(N)$ represent the time it takes to solve a maximum contiguous subsequence sum problem of size N. If $N = 1$, then the program takes some constant amount of time to execute lines 13 to 14, which we shall call 1 unit. Thus $T(1) = 1$. Otherwise, the program must perform two recursive calls plus the linear work involved in computing the maximum sum for case 3. The constant overhead is absorbed by the $O(N)$ term. How long do the two recursive calls take? Since they solve problems of size $N/2$, we know they must each require $T(N/2)$ units of time; consequently, the total recursive work is $2T(N/2)$. This gives the equations

> A more formal analysis. Note carefully that it holds for all classes of algorithms that recursively solve two halves and use linear additional work.

$$T(1) = 1,$$
$$T(N) = 2T(N/2) + O(N).$$

Of course, for the second equation to make sense, N must be a power of two. Otherwise, at some point $N/2$ will not be even. A more precise equation would be

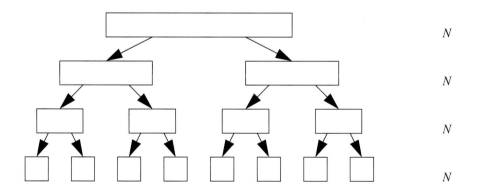

N

N

N

N

Figure 7.19 Trace of recursive calls for recursive maximum contiguous subsequence sum algorithm; $N = 8$ elements

$$T(N) = T(\lfloor N/2 \rfloor) + T(\lceil N/2 \rceil) + O(N).$$

To simplify the calculations, we assume N is a power of 2 and replace the $O(N)$ term with N. These assumptions are minor and do not affect the Big-Oh result. Consequently, assuming N is a power of 2, we need to obtain a closed form solution for $T(N)$ from

$$T(1) = 1,$$
$$T(N) = 2T(N/2) + N. \tag{7.6}$$

This is exactly the equation that is illustrated in Figure 7.19, so we know that the answer will be $N \log N + N$. This is easily verified by examining a few values: $T(1) = 1$, $T(2) = 4$, $T(4) = 12$, $T(8) = 32$, and $T(16) = 80$. We now prove this result (Theorem 7.4) mathematically by using two different methods.

Theorem 7.4   *Assuming N is a power of 2, the solution to the equation*
$T(N) = 2T(N/2) + N$, with initial condition $T(1) = 1$ is
$T(N) = N \log N + N$.

Proof (Method 1)   *For sufficiently large N, we have $T(N/2) = 2T(N/4) + N/2$ because*
we can use Equation 7.6 with $N/2$ instead of N. Consequently, we have

$$2T(N/2) = 4T(N/4) + N.$$

Substituting this into Equation 7.6 yields

$$T(N) = 4T(N/4) + 2N. \tag{7.7}$$

If we use Equation 7.6 for $N/4$ and multiply by 4, we obtain

$$4T(N/4) = 8T(N/8) + N,$$

which we can substitute into the right side of Equation 7.7 to obtain

$$T(N) = 8T(N/8) + 3N.$$

Continuing in this manner, we obtain

$$T(N) = 2^k T(N/2^k) + kN.$$

Finally, using $k = \log N$ (which makes sense, since then $2^k = N$), we obtain **Proof (continued)**

$$T(N) = NT(1) + N \log N = N \log N + N.$$

Although this proof method appears to work well, it can be difficult to apply in more complicated cases because it tends to give very long equations. Following is a second method that appears to be easier because it generates equations vertically, which are more easily manipulated.

We divide Equation 7.6 by N, yielding a new basic equation: **Proof (Method 2)**

$$\frac{T(N)}{N} = \frac{T(N/2)}{N/2} + 1.$$

This equation is now valid for any N that is a power of 2, so we may also write the following equations:

$$\frac{T(N)}{N} = \frac{T(N/2)}{N/2} + 1$$

$$\frac{T(N/2)}{N/2} = \frac{T(N/4)}{N/4} + 1$$

$$\frac{T(N/4)}{N/4} = \frac{T(N/8)}{N/8} + 1 \qquad \textbf{(7.8)}$$

$$\cdots$$

$$\frac{T(2)}{2} = \frac{T(1)}{1} + 1$$

Next, we add up the collective in Equation 7.8. This means that we add all of the terms on the left-hand side and set the result equal to the sum of all the terms on the right-hand side. Observe that the term $T(N/2)/(N/2)$ appears on both sides and thus cancels. In fact, virtually all the terms appear on both sides and cancel. This is called a telescoping sum. After everything is added, the final result is

Telescoping sums generate large numbers of canceling terms.

Proof (continued)

$$\frac{T(N)}{N} = \frac{T(1)}{1} + \log N$$

because all of the other terms cancel and there are $\log N$ *equations. Thus all the 1s at the end of these equations add up to* $\log N$. *Multiplying through by* N *gives the final answer, as before.*

Notice that if we did not divide through by N at the start of the solution, the sum would not telescope. Deciding on the division required to ensure a telescoping sum requires some experience and makes the method a little more difficult to apply than the first alternative. However, once you have found the correct divisor, the second alternative tends to produce scrap work that fits better on a standard sheet of paper, thereby leading to fewer mathematical errors. In contrast, the first method is more of a brute force approach.

Notice carefully that whenever we have a divide-and-conquer algorithm that solves two half-sized problems with linear additional work, we will always have $O(N \log N)$ running time. The next section examines what happens in a more general setting.

7.5.3   A General Upper Bound for Divide-and-Conquer Running Times

This section gives a general formula that allows the number of subproblems, the size of the subproblems, and the amount of additional work to assume general forms. The result can be used without understanding of the proof.

The analysis in the previous section showed that when a problem is divided into two equal halves that are solved recursively, with $O(N)$ overhead, the result is an $O(N \log N)$ algorithm. What if we divide into three half-sized problems with linear overhead, or seven half-sized problems with quadratic overhead (see Exercise 7.17)? This section provides a general formula to compute the running time of a divide-and-conquer algorithm. The formula requires three parameters:

- A, which is the number of subproblems
- B, which is the relative size of the subproblems (for instance, $B = 2$ represents half-sized subproblems)
- k, which is representative of the fact that the overhead is $\Theta(N^k)$

The proof of the formula requires familiarity with geometric sums. However, knowledge of the proof is not needed to use the formula.

The solution to the equation $T(N) = AT(N/B) + O(N^k)$, *where* $A \geq 1$ *and* $B > 1$, *is*	***Theorem 7.5***

$$T(N) = \begin{cases} O(N^{\log_B A}) & \text{if } A > B^k \\ O(N^k \log N) & \text{if } A = B^k. \\ O(N^k) & \text{if } A < B^k \end{cases}$$

Before proving Theorem 7.5, let us see some applications. For the maximum contiguous subsequence sum problem, we have two problems, two halves, and linear overhead. The applicable values are $A = 2$, $B = 2$, and $k = 1$. Consequently, the second case in Theorem 7.5 applies, and we get $O(N \log N)$, in agreement with our previous calculations. If we recursively solve three half-sized problems with linear overhead, then we have $A = 3$, $B = 2$, and $k = 1$, and the first case applies. The result is $O(N^{\log_2 3}) = O(N^{1.59})$. Here, we see that the overhead does not contribute to the total cost of the algorithm. Any overhead smaller than $O(N^{1.59})$ would give the same running time for the recursive algorithm. An algorithm that solved three half-sized problems but required quadratic overhead would have $O(N^2)$ running time because the third case would apply. In effect, the overhead dominates once it exceeds the $O(N^{1.59})$ threshold. At the threshold, the penalty is the logarithmic factor shown in the second case. We can now prove Theorem 7.5.

Following the second proof of Theorem 7.4, we assume N is a power of B. Thus let $N = B^M$. *Then* $N/B = B^{M-1}$ *and* $N^k = (B^M)^k = (B^k)^M$. *We assume* $T(1) = 1$, *and ignore the constant factor in* $O(N^k)$. *Then we have the basic equation*	***Proof (of Theorem 7.5)***

$$T(B^M) = AT(B^{M-1}) + (B^k)^M.$$

If we divide through by A^M, *we obtain the new basic equation*

$$\frac{T(B^M)}{A^M} = \frac{T(B^{M-1})}{A^{M-1}} + \left(\frac{B^k}{A}\right)^M.$$

Proof (continued)   *Now we can write this equation for all M to obtain the following:*

$$\frac{T(B^M)}{A^M} = \frac{T(B^{M-1})}{A^{M-1}} + \left(\frac{B^k}{A}\right)^M$$

$$\frac{T(B^{M-1})}{A^{M-1}} = \frac{T(B^{M-2})}{A^{M-2}} + \left(\frac{B^k}{A}\right)^{M-1}$$

$$\frac{T(B^{M-2})}{A^{M-2}} = \frac{T(B^{M-3})}{A^{M-3}} + \left(\frac{B^k}{A}\right)^{M-2} \qquad (7.9)$$

$$\cdots$$

$$\frac{T(B^1)}{A^1} = \frac{T(B^0)}{A^0} + \left(\frac{B^k}{A}\right)^1$$

If we add up the collective denoted by Equation 7.9, once again virtually all of the terms on the left-hand side cancel the leading terms on the right-hand side, thus yielding

$$\frac{T(B^M)}{A^M} = 1 + \sum_{i=1}^{M} \left(\frac{B^k}{A}\right)^i$$

$$= \sum_{i=0}^{M} \left(\frac{B^k}{A}\right)^i$$

Thus

$$T(N) = T(B^M) = A^M \sum_{i=0}^{M} \left(\frac{B^k}{A}\right)^i . \qquad (7.10)$$

If $A > B^k$, then the sum is a geometric series with a ratio smaller than 1. Since the sum of an infinite series would converge to a constant, this finite sum is also bounded by a constant. Thus we obtain Equation 7.11.

$$T(N) = O(A^M) = O(N^{\log_B A}). \qquad (7.11)$$

If $A = B^k$, then each term in the sum in Equation 7.10 is 1. Since the sum contains $1 + \log_B N$ terms and $A = B^k$ implies $A^M = N^k$,

$$T(N) = O(A^M \log_B N) = O(N^k \log_B N) = O(N^k \log N).$$

Finally, if $A < B^k$, then the terms in the geometric series are larger than 1. We can compute the sum using a standard formula, thereby obtaining

$$T(N) = A^M \frac{\left(\frac{B^k}{A}\right)^{M+1} - 1}{\frac{B^k}{A} - 1} = O\left(A^M \left(\frac{B^k}{A}\right)^M\right) = O((B^k)^M) = O(N^k)$$

and proving the last case of Theorem 7.5.

7.6 Dynamic Programming

A problem that can be mathematically expressed recursively can also be expressed as a recursive algorithm. In many cases, doing this yields a significant performance improvement over a more naive exhaustive search. Any recursive mathematical formula could be directly translated to a recursive algorithm, but often the compiler may not do justice to the recursive algorithm and an inefficient program results. Such is the case for the recursive computation of the Fibonacci numbers described in Section 7.3.4. In such a case, we can rewrite the recursive algorithm as a nonrecursive algorithm that systematically records the answers to the subproblems in a table. One technique that makes use of this approach is *dynamic programming*. This technique is illustrated with the following problem:

Dynamic programming solves subproblems nonrecursively by recording answers in a table.

CHANGE-MAKING PROBLEM

For a currency with coins $C_1, C_2, ..., C_N$ (cents) what is the minimum number of coins needed to make K cents of change?

U.S. currency has coins in 1-, 5-, 10-, and 25-cent denominations (ignore the less-frequently occurring 50-cent piece). We can make 63 cents by using two 25-cent pieces, one 10-cent piece, and three 1-cent pieces, for a total of six coins. Change-making in this currency is relatively simple: We repeatedly use the largest coin that is available to us. One can show that for U.S. currency, this always minimizes the total number of coins used. This is an example of a so-called greedy algorithm. In a greedy algorithm, during each phase, a decision is made that appears to be good, without regard for future consequences. This "take what you can get now" strategy is the source of the name for this class of algorithms. When a problem can be solved with a greedy algorithm, we are usually quite happy: Greedy algorithms often match our intuition and make for relatively painless coding. Unfortunately, greedy algorithms do not always work. If the U.S. currency included a 21-cent piece, then the greedy algorithm would still give a solution that uses six coins, while the optimal solution uses three coins (all 21-cent pieces).

Greedy algorithms make locally optimal decisions at each step. This is simple, but not always the correct thing to do.

The question then becomes how do we solve the problem for an arbitrary coin set. We assume that there is always a 1-cent coin so that the solution always exists. A simple strategy to make K cents in change uses recursion as follows:

1. If we can make change using exactly one coin, that is the minimum.
2. Otherwise, for each possible value i we can compute the minimum number of coins needed to make i cents in change and $K - i$ cents in change independently. We then choose the i that minimizes this sum.

A simple recursive algorithm for change-making is easily written, but it is inefficient.

As an example, let us see how we can make 63 cents in change. Clearly, one coin will not suffice. We can compute the number of coins required to make 1 cent of change and 62 cents of change independently (these are 1 and 4, respectively). These results are obtained recursively, so they must be taken as optimal (it happens that the 62 cents is given as two 21-cent pieces and two 10-cent pieces). Thus we have a method that uses five coins. If we split into 2 cents and 61 cents, the recursive solutions yield 2 and 4, respectively, for a total of six coins. We continue trying all the possibilities. Some of these possibilities are shown in Figure 7.20. Eventually, we see a split into 21 cents and 42 cents, which is changeable in one and two coins, respectively, thus allowing change to be made in three coins.

The last split we need to try is 31 cents and 32 cents. We can change 31 cents in two coins, and we can change 32 cents in three coins for a total of five coins. But the minimum remains the three coins.

Again, each of these subproblems is solved recursively. This yields the natural algorithm shown in Figure 7.21. If we run the algorithm to make small change, it works perfectly. But like the Fibonacci calculations, there is too much redundant work. It will not terminate in a reasonable amount of time for the 63-cent case.

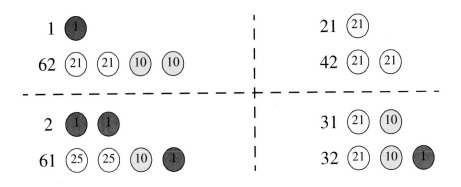

Figure 7.20   Some of the subproblems that are solved recursively in Figure 7.21

```
1       // Return minimum coins to make change
2       // Simple recursive algorithm that is very inefficient
3
4       public static int makeChange( int [ ] coins, int change,
5                                     int differentCoins )
6       {
7           int minCoins = change;
8
9               // Look for exact match with any single coin
10          for( int i = 0; i < differentCoins; i++ )
11              if( coins[ i ] == change )
12                  return 1;
13
14              // No match; solve recursively
15          for( int j = 1; j <= change / 2; j++ )
16          {
17              int thisCoins =
18                makeChange( coins, j, differentCoins ) +
19                makeChange( coins, change - j, differentCoins );
20              if( thisCoins < minCoins )
21                  minCoins = thisCoins;
22          }
23
24          return minCoins;
25      }
```

Figure 7.21   Inefficient recursive method to solve the change-making problem

An alternative algorithm is to reduce the problem recursively by specifying one of the coins. For example, for 63 cents, we can give change in the following ways shown in Figure 7.22:

An alternative recursive change-making algorithm is still inefficient.

- One 1-cent piece plus 62 cents recursively distributed
- One 5-cent piece plus 58 cents recursively distributed
- One 10-cent piece plus 53 cents recursively distributed
- One 21-cent piece plus 42 cents recursively distributed
- One 25-cent piece plus 38 cents recursively distributed

Instead of solving 62 recursive problems, as was done in Figure 7.20, we get by with only five recursive calls, one for each different coin. Once again, a naive recursive implementation would be very inefficient because it would recompute answers. For example, in the first case we are left with a problem of making 62 cents in change. In this subproblem, one of the recursive calls that is made chooses a 10-cent piece and recursively solves for 52 cents. In the third case, we are left with 53 cents. One of its recursive calls removes the 1-cent piece and also recursively solves for 52 cents. This redundant work again leads to a wildly large running time. If we are careful, however, we can make the algorithm reasonably fast.

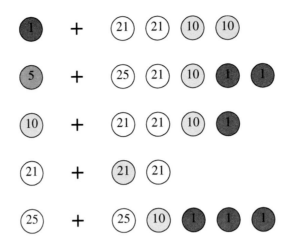

Figure 7.22   Alternative recursive algorithm for the change-making problem

The trick is to save answers to the subproblems in an array. This *dynamic programming* technique forms the basis of many algorithms. Since a large answer depends only on smaller answers, we can compute the optimal way to change 1 cent, then 2 cents, then 3 cents, and so on. This strategy is shown in the program in Figure 7.23.

First, at line 11, note that 0 cents can be changed using zero coins. The `lastCoin` array is used to tell us which coin was last used to make the optimal change. Otherwise, we attempt to make `cents` cents worth of change, for `cents` ranging from 1 to the final `maxChange`. To make `cents` worth of change, we try each coin in succession as indicated by the `for` statement beginning at line 18. If the amount of the coin is larger than the amount of change we are trying to make, then there is nothing to do. Otherwise, we test at line 22 to determine whether the number of coins used to solve the subproblem plus the one coin combine to be fewer than the minimum number of coins we have used thus far; if so, we perform an update at lines 25 to 27. When the loop ends for the current number of `cents`, the minimums can be inserted in the arrays. This is done at lines 30 and 31.

At the end of the algorithm, `coinsUsed[i]` represents the minimum number of coins needed to make change for i cents (`i==maxChange` is the particular solution we are looking for). By tracing back through `lastCoin`, we can figure out the coins that are needed to achieve the solution. The running time is that of two nested `for` loops and is thus $O(NK)$, where N is the number of different denominations of coins and K is the amount of change we are trying to make.

```
1      // Dynamic programming algorithm for change making
2      // problem.  As a result, the coinsUsed array is filled
3      // with the minimum number of coins needed for change
4      // from 0 -> maxChange and lastCoin contains one of the
5      // coins needed to make the change.
6
7      public static void makeChange( int [ ] coins,
8                    int differentCoins, int maxChange,
9                    int [ ] coinsUsed, int [ ] lastCoin )
10     {
11         coinsUsed[ 0 ] = 0; lastCoin[ 0 ] = 1;
12
13         for( int cents = 1; cents <= maxChange; cents++ )
14         {
15             int minCoins = cents;
16             int newCoin  = 1;
17
18             for( int j = 0; j < differentCoins; j++ )
19             {
20                 if( coins[ j ] > cents )    // Can't use coin j
21                     continue;
22                 if( coinsUsed[ cents - coins[ j ] ] + 1
23                                             < minCoins )
24                 {
25                     minCoins =
26                         coinsUsed[ cents - coins[ j ] ] + 1;
27                     newCoin  = coins[ j ];
28                 }
29             }
30             coinsUsed[ cents ] = minCoins;
31             lastCoin [ cents ] = newCoin;
32         }
33     }
```

Figure 7.23   Dynamic programming algorithm to solve change-making problem by computing optimal change for all amounts from 0 to maxChange and maintaining information to construct the actual coin sequence

7.7   Backtracking Algorithms

This section sets out the last application of recursion. It shows how to write a routine to have the computer select an optimal move in the game tic-tac-toe. The class Best, shown in Figure 7.24, is used to store the optimal move that is returned by the move selection algorithm. The skeleton for a TicTacToe class is shown in Figure 7.25 (page 213). This class has a data object board that represents the current game position. A host of trivial methods are specified, includ-

Backtracking algorithms use recursion to try all the possibilities.

ing routines to clear the board, to test if a square is occupied, to place something on a square, and to test whether a tic-tac-toe win has been achieved. The implementation details are provided in the online code.

The challenging routine is to decide, for any position, what the best move is. This is the routine `chooseMove`. The general strategy uses a backtracking algorithm. A *backtracking algorithm* uses recursion to try all the possibilities.

The basis for making this decision is the routine `positionValue`, which is shown in Figure 7.26 (page 214). `positionValue` returns either HUMAN_WIN, DRAW, COMPUTER_WIN, or UNCLEAR, depending on what the board represents.

The minimax strategy is used for tic-tac-toe. It assumes optimal play by both players.

The strategy often used is the *minimax strategy,* which assumes optimal play by both players. The value of a position is a COMPUTER_WIN if optimal play implies that the computer can force a win. If the computer can force a draw but not a win, the value is DRAW; if the human can force a win, the value is HUMAN_WIN. Since we want the computer to win, we have HUMAN_WIN < DRAW < COMPUTER_WIN.

For the computer, the value of the position is the maximum of all the values of the positions that can result from making a move. Thus suppose one move leads to a winning position, two lead to a drawing position, and six lead to a losing position. Then the starting position is a winning position because the computer can force the win. Moreover, the move that leads to the winning position is the move to make. For the human, we use minimum instead of the maximum.

This suggests a recursive algorithm to determine the value of a position. Keeping track of the best move is a matter of bookkeeping, once the basic algorithm to find the value of the position is written. If the position is a terminal position (that is, we can see right away that tic-tac-toe has been achieved or the board is full without tic-tac-toe), the position's value is immediate. Otherwise, we recursively try all moves, computing the value of each resulting position, and choose the maximum value. The recursive call will then require that the human player evaluate the value of the position. For the human, the value is the minimum of all the possible next moves, since the human is trying to force the computer to lose. Thus the recursive method `chooseMove`, shown in Figure 7.27 (page 215), takes a parameter `side`, which indicates whose turn it is to move.

```
1  final class Best
2  {
3      int row;
4      int column;
5      int val;
6
7      public Best( int v )
8        { this( v, 0, 0 ); }
9      public Best( int v, int r, int c )
10       { val = v; row = r; column = c; }
11 }
```

Figure 7.24   Class to store an evaluated move

```
 1  class TicTacToe
 2  {
 3      public static final int HUMAN        = 0;
 4      public static final int COMPUTER     = 1;
 5      public static final int EMPTY        = 2;
 6
 7      public static final int HUMAN_WIN    = 0;
 8      public static final int DRAW         = 1;
 9      public static final int UNCLEAR      = 2;
10      public static final int COMPUTER_WIN = 3;
11
12          // Constructor
13      public TicTacToe( )
14        { clearBoard( ); }
15
16          // Compute optimal move
17      public Best chooseMove( int side )
18        { /* Implementation in Figure 7.27 */ }
19
20          // Compute static value of the position
21      private int positionValue( )
22        { /* Implementation in Figure 7.26 */ }
23
24          // Play move, including checking legality
25      public boolean playMove( int side, int row, int column )
26        { /* Implementation in online code */ }
27
28          // Make board empty
29      public void clearBoard( )
30        { /* Implementation in online code */ }
31
32          // Return true if board is full
33      public boolean boardIsFull( )
34        { /* Implementation in online code */ }
35
36          // Return true if board shows a win
37      boolean isAWin( int side )
38        { /* Implementation in online code */ }
39
40          // Play a move, possibly clearing a square
41      private void place( int row, int column, int piece )
42        { board[ row ][ column ] = piece; }
43
44          // Test if a square is empty
45      private boolean squareIsEmpty( int row, int column )
46        { return board[ row ][ column ] == EMPTY; }
47
48      private int [ ][ ] board = new int[ 3 ][ 3 ];
49  }
```

Figure 7.25   Skeleton for class `TicTacToe`

```
1              // Compute static value of current position
2         private int positionValue( )
3         {
4             return isAWin( COMPUTER ) ? COMPUTER_WIN :
5                    isAWin( HUMAN )    ? HUMAN_WIN :
6                    boardIsFull( )     ? DRAW : UNCLEAR;
7         }
```

Figure 7.26   Supporting routine to evaluate positions

Lines 12 and 13 handle the base case of the recursion. If we have an immediate answer, we can return. Otherwise, we set some values at lines 15 to 22, depending on which side is moving. The code in lines 28 to 38 is executed once for each available move. We try the move at line 28, recursively evaluate the move at line 29 (saving the value), and then undo the move at line 30. Lines 33 and 34 test to see if this is the best move seen so far. If so, we adjust value at line 36 and record the move at line 37. At line 41, we return the value of the position in a Best object.

Alpha-beta pruning is an improvement to the minimax algorithm.

Although the routine in Figure 7.27 optimally solves tic-tac-toe, it performs a lot of searching. Specifically, to choose the first move on an empty board, it makes 549,946 recursive calls (this number is obtained by running the program). By using some algorithmic tricks, we can compute exactly the same information using fewer searches. One such trick is known as *alpha-beta pruning*, and is described in detail in Chapter 10. The application of alpha-beta pruning reduces the number of recursive calls to only 18,297.

Summary

This chapter examined recursion and showed that it is a powerful problem-solving tool. Following are the fundamental rules of recursion, which you should never forget:

1. *Base case*: Always have at least one case that can be solved without using recursion.
2. *Make progress*: Any recursive call must make progress toward the base case.
3. *"You gotta believe"*: Always assume that the recursive call works.
4. *Compound interest rule*: Never duplicate work by solving the same instance of a problem in separate recursive calls.

Recursion has many uses, some of which were discussed in this chapter. Three important algorithm design techniques that are based on recursion are divide-and-conquer, dynamic programming, and backtracking.

The next chapter examines sorting. The fastest known sorting algorithm is recursive.

```
1              // Find optimal move
2         public Best chooseMove( int side )
3         {
4             int opp;            // The other side
5             Best reply;         // Opponent's best reply
6             int simpleEval;     // Result of an immediate evaluation
7             Position thisPosition = new Position( board );
8             int bestRow = 0;
9             int bestColumn = 0;
10            int value;
11
12            if( ( simpleEval = positionValue( ) ) != UNCLEAR )
13                return new Best( simpleEval );
14
15            if( side == COMPUTER )
16            {
17                opp = HUMAN; value = HUMAN_WIN;
18            }
19            else
20            {
21                opp = COMPUTER; value = COMPUTER_WIN;
22            }
23
24            for( int row = 0; row < 3; row++ )
25                for( int column = 0; column < 3; column++ )
26                    if( squareIsEmpty( row, column ) )
27                    {
28                        place( row, column, side );  // Try a move
29                        reply = chooseMove( opp );   // Evaluate
30                        place( row, column, EMPTY ); // Undo
31
32                            // Update if side gets better position
33                        if( side == COMPUTER && reply.val > value
34                            || side == HUMAN && reply.val < value )
35                        {
36                            value = reply.val;
37                            bestRow = row; bestColumn = column;
38                        }
39                    }
40
41            return new Best( value, bestRow, bestColumn );
42        }
```

Figure 7.27   Recursive routine to find an optimal tic-tac-toe move

Objects of the Game

activation record The method by which the bookkeeping in many programming languages is done. A stack of activation records is used. (182)
alpha-beta pruning An improvement to the minimax algorithm. (214)

backtracking algorithm An algorithm that uses recursion to try all possibilities. (212)

base case An instance that can be solved without recursion. Any recursive call must make progress toward a base case. (178)

basis In a proof by induction, the easy case that can be shown by hand. (176)

divide-and-conquer algorithm A type of recursive algorithm that is generally very efficient. The recursion is the *divide* part, and the combining of recursive solutions is the *conquer* part. (197)

driver routine A routine that tests the validity of the first case and then calls the recursive routine. (180)

dynamic programming A technique that avoids the recursive explosion by recording answers in a table. (207)

encryption An encoding scheme used in the transmitting of messages that cannot be read by other parties. (195)

Fibonacci numbers A sequence of numbers in which the ith number is the sum of the two previous numbers. Fibonacci numbers are widely encountered. (183)

greatest common divisor (gcd) The greatest common divisor of two integers is the largest integer that divides both of them. (192)

greedy algorithm An algorithm that makes locally optimal decisions at each step. Doing this is simple but not always correct. (207)

induction A proof technique used to establish theorems that hold for positive integers. (175)

inductive hypothesis The hypothesis that a theorem is true for some arbitrary case and shows that, under this assumption, it is true for the next case. (176)

minimax strategy A strategy used for tic-tac-toe and other strategic games that assumes optimal play by both players. (212)

multiplicative inverse The solution $1 \le X < N$ to the equation $AX \equiv 1 \pmod{N}$. (192)

public key cryptography A type of cryptography in which each participant publishes the code others can use to send the participant encrypted messages but keeps the decrypting code secret. (196)

recursive method A method that directly or indirectly makes a call to itself. (177)

RSA cryptosystem A popular encryption method. (195)

rules of recursion 1. Base case: Always have at least one case that can be solved without using recursion. (178); 2. Make progress: Any recursive call must make progress toward a base case. (178); 3. "You gotta believe": Always assume that the recursive call works. (182); 4. Compound Interest Rule: Never duplicate work by solving the same instance of a problem in separate recursive calls. (185)

telescoping sum Generates large numbers of canceling terms. (203)

Common Errors

1. The most common error when using recursion is forgetting to establish a base case.
2. Make sure that each recursive call makes progress toward a base case. Otherwise, the recursion is not correct.
3. Overlapping recursive calls must be avoided because they tend to yield exponential algorithms.
4. It is bad style to use recursion in place of a simple loop.
5. Recursive algorithms are analyzed by using a recursive formula. Do not assume that a recursive call takes linear time.
6. Violating copyright laws is another bad error. RSA is patented, but some uses are allowed. See the references for more information.

On the Internet

All of the chapter's code is provided, including a tic-tac-toe program. An improved version of the tic-tac-toe algorithm that uses fancier data structures is discussed in Chapter 10. All routines are in directory **Chapter07** unless otherwise indicated. Here are the filenames:

RecSum.java	The routine in Figure 7.1 with a simple main.
PrintInt.java	The routine in Figure 7.4 to print a number in any base, plus a `main`.
Factorial.java	The routine in Figure 7.8 with a simple `main`.
BinarySearch.java	The routine in Figure 7.9, plus a `main`.
Ruler.java	The routine in Figure 7.11, ready to run. Contains code that forces the drawing to be slow.
FractalStar.java	The routine in Figure 7.13, ready to run. Contains code that allows the drawing to be slow.
Numerical.java	The math routines in Section 7.4, a primality testing routine, and `main`, all in directory **Supporting**.
RSA.java	Demonstrates the RSA algorithm.
MaxSum.java	The four maximum contiguous subsequence sum routines (in directory **Chapter05**).
MkChnge.java	The routine in Figure 7.23 with a simple `main`.
Best.java	`Best` class used in tic-tac-toe algorithm.
TicTacToe.java	The basic tic-tac-toe algorithm.
TicTacMain.java	Simple GUI to run the tic-tac-toe program.

Exercises

In Short

7.1. What are the four fundamental rules of recursion?

7.2. Modify the program in Figure 7.1 so that zero is returned for negative n. Make the minimum number of changes.

7.3. Following are four alternatives for line 10 of the routine `power`. Why is each wrong?

```
long tmp = power( x * x, n/2, p );
long tmp = power( power( x, 2, p ), n/2, p );
long tmp = power( power( x, n/2, p ), 2, p );
long tmp = power( x, n/2, p ) * power( x, n/2, p ) % p;
```

7.4. Show how the recursive calls are processed in the calculation $2^{63} \bmod 37$.

7.5. Compute $gcd(1995,1492)$.

7.6. Bob chooses p and q equal to 37 and 41, respectively. Determine acceptable values for the remaining parameters in the RSA algorithm.

7.7. Show that the greedy change-making algorithm fails if 5-cent pieces are not part of the U.S. currency.

In Theory

7.8. Prove by induction the formula for F_N:

$$F_N = \frac{1}{\sqrt{5}}\left(\left(\frac{(1+\sqrt{5})}{2}\right)^N - \left(\frac{1-\sqrt{5}}{2}\right)^N\right)$$

7.9. Prove the following identities relating to the Fibonacci numbers:
a. $F_1 + F_2 + \ldots + F_N = F_{N+2} - 1$
b. $F_1 + F_3 + \ldots + F_{2N-1} = F_{2N}$
c. $F_0 + F_2 + \ldots + F_{2N} = F_{2N+1} - 1$
d. $F_{N-1}F_{N+1} = (-1)^N + F_N^2$
e. $F_1F_2 + F_2F_3 + \ldots + F_{2N-1}F_{2N} = F_{2N}^2$
f. $F_1F_2 + F_2F_3 + \ldots + F_{2N}F_{2N+1} = F_{2N+1}^2 - 1$
g. $F_N^2 + F_{N+1}^2 = F_{2N+1}$

7.10. Show that if $A \equiv B(\bmod N)$, then for any C, D, and P, the following are true:
a. $A + C \equiv B + C(\bmod N)$
b. $AD \equiv BD(\bmod N)$
c. $A^P \equiv B^P(\bmod N)$

7.11. Prove that if $A \geq B$, then $A \bmod B < A/2$. (*Hint:* Consider the cases $B \leq A/2$ and $B > A/2$ separately.) How does this show that the running time of `gcd` is logarithmic?

7.12. Prove by induction the formula for the number of calls to the recursive method `fib` in Section 7.3.4.

7.13. Prove by induction that if $A > B \geq 0$ and the invocation `gcd(a,b)` performs $k \geq 1$ recursive calls, then $A \geq F_{k+2}$ and $B \geq F_{k+1}$.

7.14. Prove by induction that in the extended *gcd* algorithm, $|X| < B$ and $|Y| < A$.

7.15. Write an alternative `gcd` algorithm based on the following observations (arrange that $A > B$):

   a. $gcd(A, B) = 2gcd(A/2, B/2)$ if A and B are both even.
   b. $gcd(A, B) = gcd(A/2, B)$ if A is even and B is odd.
   c. $gcd(A, B) = gcd(A, B/2)$ if A is odd and B is even.
   d. $gcd(A, B) = gcd((A + B)/2, (A - B)/2)$ if A and B are both odd.

7.16. Solve the following equation. Assume $A \geq 1$, $B > 1$, and $P \geq 0$.
$$T(N) = AT(N/B) + O(N^k \log^P N)$$

7.17. Strassen's algorithm for matrix multiplication multiplies two $N \times N$ matrices by performing seven recursive calls to multiply two $N/2 \times N/2$ matrices. The additional overhead is quadratic. What is the running time of Strassen's algorithm?

In Practice

7.18. The `printInt` method in Figure 7.4 incorrectly handles the case where $N = $ `Integer.MIN_VALUE`. Explain why and provide a fix.

7.19. Write a recursive method that returns the number of 1's in the binary representation of N. Use the fact that this is equal to the number of 1's in the representation of $N/2$, plus 1, if N is odd.

7.20. Implement the one-comparison-per-level binary search recursively.

7.21. The maximum contiguous subsequence sum algorithm in Figure 7.18 does not give any indication of the actual sequence. Modify it so that it returns in a single object the value of the maximum subsequence and the indices of the actual sequence (as was done in `chooseMove`). Then have the driver set the static fields as was done in Section 5.3.

7.22. For the coin problem, give an algorithm that computes the number of different ways to give exactly K cents in change.

7.23. The *subset sum problem* is as follows: Given N integers $A_1, A_2, ..., A_N$ and an integer K, is there a group of integers that sums to exactly K? Give an $O(NK)$ algorithm to solve the subset sum problem.

7.24. Give an $O(2^N)$ algorithm for the subset sum problem described in Exercise 7.23. *Hint*: Use recursion.

7.25. Write the routines with the following declarations:

```
public  void permute( String str );
private void permute( char [ ] str, int low, int high );
```

The first routine is a driver that calls the second and prints all the permutations of the characters in `String str`. If `str` is `"abc"`, then the strings that are output are abc, acb, bac, bca, cab, and cba. Use recursion for the second routine.

7.26. Write a program that computes the maximum value of N that can be handled by the program in Figure 7.1 on your machine. *Hint*: Use the idea of a binary search to determine N; the actual mechanism for deciding if the call to s succeeds is to test if any Throwable objects are thrown.

7.27. Write a program that draws Figure 7.7.

7.28. Explain what happens if in Figure 7.13, we draw the central square prior to making the recursive calls.

Programming Projects

7.29. The binomial coefficients $C(N, k)$ can be defined recursively as follows: $C(N, 0) = 1$, $C(N, N) = 1$, and, for $0 < k < N$, $C(N, k) = C(N-1, k) + C(N-1, k-1)$. Write a method and give an analysis of the running time to compute the binomial coefficients as follows:
  a. recursively
  b. using dynamic programming

7.30. Implement the RSA cryptosystem using a library BigDecimal class.

7.31. Improve the tic-tac-toe implementation by making the supporting routines more efficient and the GUI fancier than what is provided in the online code.

7.32. Let A be a sequence of N distinct sorted numbers $A_1, A_2, ..., A_N$ with $A_1 = 0$. Let B be a sequence of $N(N-1)/2$ numbers, defined by $B_{i,j} = A_i - A_j$ $(i < j)$. Let D be the sequence obtained by sorting B. Both B and D may contain duplicates. *Example*: $A = 0, 1, 5, 8$. Then $D = 1, 3, 4, 5, 7, 8$. Do the following:
  a. Write a program that constructs D from A. This part is easy.
  b. Write a program that constructs some sequence A that corresponds to D. Note that A is not unique. Use a backtracking algorithm.

7.33. Consider an N-by-N grid in which some squares are occupied by black circles. Two squares belong to the same group if they share a common edge. In Figure 7.28, there is one group of four occupied squares, three groups of two occupied squares, and two individual occupied squares. Assume that the grid is represented by a two-dimensional array. Write a program that does the following:
  a. Computes the size of a group when a square in the group is given.
  b. Computes the number of different groups.
  c. Lists all groups.

7.34. Write a program that expands a C or C++ source file's #include directives (recursively). Do this by replacing lines of the form

```
#include "filename"
```

with the contents of filename.

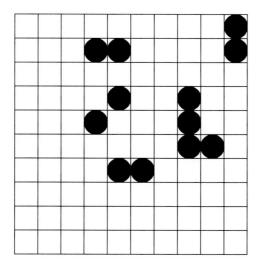

Figure 7.28   Grid for Exercise 7.33

References

Much of this chapter is based on the discussion in [4]. A description of the RSA algorithm, with proof of correctness, can be found in [1]. That text also devotes a chapter to dynamic programming. The RSA algorithm is patented, and its commercial use requires payment of a licensing fee. However, an implementation of RSA, namely *PGP* (pretty good privacy), is widely available, and noncommercial use is allowed for free. More details can be found in [3]. The shape-drawing examples are adapted from [2].

1. T. H. Cormen, C. E. Leiserson, and R. L. Rivest, *Introduction to Algorithms*, The MIT Press, Cambridge, Mass. (1990).

2. R. Sedgewick, *Algorithms in C++*, Addison-Wesley, Reading, Mass. (1992).

3. W. Stallings, *Protect Your Privacy: A Guide for PGP Users,* Prentice-Hall, Englewood Cliffs, NJ (1995).

4. M. A. Weiss, *Efficient C Programming: A Practical Approach*, Prentice-Hall, Englewood Cliffs, NJ (1995).

8

Sorting Algorithms

S ORTING is a fundamental application for computers. Much of the output that is eventually produced by a computation is sorted in some way, and many computations are made efficient by invoking a sorting procedure internally. Thus sorting is perhaps the most well-studied and important operation in computer science.

This chapter discusses the problem of sorting an array of elements. It describes and analyzes the various sorting algorithms. The sorts in this chapter can be done entirely in main memory, so the number of elements is relatively small (less than a few million). Sorts that cannot be performed in main memory and must be done on disk or tape are also quite important. This type of sorting, called *external sorting*, is discussed in Section 20.6.

This discussion of sorting is a blend of theory and practice. It includes several algorithms with different performances and shows how an analysis of an algorithm's performance properties can guide us as we make implementation decisions that are not obvious.

In this chapter, we will see:

- That the insertion sort, previously shown in Figure 4.18, runs in quadratic time
- How to code Shellsort, which is a simple and efficient algorithm that runs in subquadratic time
- How to write the slightly more complicated $O(N \log N)$ mergesort and quicksort algorithms
- That $\Omega(N \log N)$ comparisons are required for any general-purpose sorting algorithm

8.1 Why Is Sorting Important?

Recall from Section 5.6 that searching a sorted array is much easier than searching an unsorted array. This is especially true for people. That is, finding a person's name in a phone book is easy, for example, but finding a phone number without knowing the person's name is virtually impossible. As a result, any significant amount of computer output is generally arranged in some sorted order so that it can be interpreted. Here are some more examples:

- Words in a dictionary are sorted (and case distinctions are ignored).
- Files in a directory are often listed in sorted order.
- The index of a book is sorted (and case distinctions are ignored).
- The card catalog in a library is sorted by both author and title.
- A listing of course offerings at a university is sorted, first by department and then by course number.
- Many banks provide statements that list checks in increasing order by check number.
- In a newspaper, the calendar of events in a schedule is generally sorted by date.
- Musical compact disks in a record store are generally sorted by recording artist.
- In the programs that are printed for graduation ceremonies, departments are listed in sorted order and then students in those departments are listed in sorted order.

An initial sort of the data can significantly enhance the performance of an algorithm.

It is not surprising that much of the work in computing involves sorting. However, there are also indirect uses of sorting. For instance, suppose we want to decide if an array has any duplicates. Figure 8.1 shows a simple method that is immediately seen to require quadratic worst-case time. Sorting provides an alternative algorithm. That is, if we sort a copy of the array, then any duplicates will be adjacent and can be detected in a single linear-time scan of the array. The cost of this algorithm is dominated by the time to sort, so if we can sort in subquadratic time, we have an improved algorithm. There are many other algorithms whose performance is significantly enhanced when we initially sort the data.

The vast majority of significant programming projects use a sort somewhere, and in many cases, the sorting cost determines the running time. Thus we want to be able to implement a fast and reliable sort.

```
1    // Return true if array a has duplicates; false otherwise
2
3    public static boolean duplicates( Object [ ] a )
4    {
5        for( int i = 0; i < a.length; i++ )
6            for( int j = i + 1; j < a.length; j++ )
7                if( a[ i ].equals( a[ j ] ) )
8                    return true;     // Duplicate found
9
10       return false;               // No duplicates found
11   }
```

Figure 8.1 Simple quadratic algorithm to detect duplicates

8.2   Preliminaries

The algorithms described in this chapter are all interchangeable. Each is passed an array containing the elements, and only objects that implement the `Comparable` interface may be sorted. Thus the only operations that can be used to obtain ordering information on the input data are the methods `lessThan` and `compares`. Algorithms that sort under these conditions are *comparison-based sorting algorithms*. All of the sorting algorithms here are static methods in class `Sorting` (in package `DataStructures`). In this chapter, N is the number of elements being sorted.

Comparison-based sorting algorithms make ordering decisions only on the basis of comparisons.

8.3   Analysis of the Insertion Sort and Other Simple Sorts

The simplest sort, *insertion sort*, was discussed in Section 4.3.1. The implementation in Figure 8.2 duplicates Figure 4.18. Because of the nested loops, each of which can take N iterations, the insertion sort algorithm is $O(N^2)$. Furthermore, this bound is achievable because input in reverse order really does take quadratic time. A precise calculation shows that the tests at line 10 in Figure 8.2 can be executed, at most, $P + 1$ times for each value of P. Summing over all P gives a total of

The insertion sort is quadratic in the worst and average cases. It is fast if the input is already sorted.

$$\sum_{P=1}^{N-1}(P+1) = 2 + 3 + 4 + \ldots + N = \Theta(N^2).$$

```
 1  // InsertionSort: sort array a
 2
 3      public static void insertionSort( Comparable[ ] a )
 4      {
 5          for( int p = 1; p < a.length; p++ )
 6          {
 7              Comparable tmp = a[ p ];
 8              int j = p;
 9
10              for( ; j > 0 && tmp.lessThan( a[ j - 1 ] ); j-- )
11                  a[ j ] = a[ j - 1 ];
12              a[ j ] = tmp;
13          }
14      }
```

Figure 8.2   Generic insertion sort

On the other hand, if the input is presorted, the running time is $O(N)$ because the test at the top of the inner `for` loop always fails immediately. Indeed, if the input is almost sorted (almost sorted will be more rigorously defined shortly), the insertion sort will run quickly. This means that the running time depends not only on the amount of input but also on the specific ordering of the input. Because of this wide variation, it is worth analyzing the average-case behavior of this algorithm. And it turns out that the average case is $\theta(N^2)$ for the insertion sort as well as for a variety of other simple sorting algorithms.

Inversions measure unsortedness.

An *inversion* in an array of numbers is any ordered pair (i, j) having the property that $i < j$ but $A_i > A_j$. For example, the sequence $\{8, 5, 9, 2, 6, 3\}$ has ten inversions that correspond to the pairs $(8, 5)$, $(8, 2)$, $(8, 6)$, $(8, 3)$, $(5, 2)$, $(5, 3)$, $(9, 2)$, $(9, 6)$, $(9, 3)$, and $(6, 3)$. Notice that the number of inversions is equal to the total number of times that line 11 in Figure 8.2 is executed. This is always the case because the effect of the assignment statement is to swap the two items `a[j]` and `a[j-1]`. (We avoid the actual excessive swapping by using the temporary variable, but nonetheless it is an abstract swap.) Swapping two elements that are out of place removes exactly one inversion, and a sorted array has no inversions. Thus, if there are I inversions at the start of the algorithm, we must have I implicit swaps. Since there is $O(N)$ other work involved in the algorithm, the running time of the insertion sort is $O(I + N)$, where I is the number of inversions in the original array. Thus the insertion sort runs in linear time if the number of inversions is $O(N)$.

We can compute precise bounds on the average running time of the insertion sort by computing the average number of inversions in an array. Defining "average" is a difficult proposition. We can assume that there are no duplicate elements (if we allow duplicates, it is not even clear what the average number of duplicates is). We can also assume that the input is some arrangement of the first N integers (since only relative ordering is important); these arrangements are called *permutations*. We can further assume that all these permutations are equally likely. Under these assumptions, we can establish Theorem 8.1.

Theorem 8.1

The average number of inversions in an array of N distinct numbers is $N(N-1)/4$.

Proof

For any array A of numbers, consider A_r, *which is the array in reverse order. For example, the reverse of array 1, 5, 4, 2, 6, 3 is 3, 6, 2, 4, 5, 1. Consider any two numbers (x, y) in the array, with $y > x$. In exactly one of A and A_r, this ordered pair represents an inversion. The total number of these pairs in an array A and its reverse A_r is $N(N-1)/2$. Thus an average list has half this amount, or $N(N-1)/4$ inversions.*

Theorem 8.1 implies that insertion sort is quadratic on average. It also can be used to provide a very strong lower bound about any algorithm that exchanges adjacent elements only. This is expressed as Theorem 8.2.

Any algorithm that sorts by exchanging adjacent elements requires $\Omega(N^2)$ *time on average.*

Theorem 8.2

The average number of inversions is initially $N(N-1)/4$. *Each swap removes only one inversion, so* $\Omega(N^2)$ *swaps are required.*

Proof

This is an example of a *lower-bound proof*. It is valid not only for the insertion sort, which performs adjacent exchanges implicitly, but also for other simple algorithms such as the bubble sort and the selection sort, which are not described here. In fact, it is valid over an entire *class* of algorithms, including undiscovered ones, that perform adjacent exchanges only.

Unfortunately, any computational confirmation of a proof applying to a class of algorithms would require running all algorithms in the class. This is impossible because the number of possible algorithms is infinite. Any attempt at confirmation would apply only to the algorithms that are run. This makes the confirmation of the validity of lower-bound proofs more difficult than confirming the validity of the usual single-algorithm upper bounds to which we are accustomed. A computation could only *disprove* a lower-bound conjecture; it could never prove it in general.

Although this lower-bound proof is rather simple, proving lower bounds is in general much more complicated than proving upper bounds. Lower-bound arguments are much more abstract than their upper-bound counterparts.

This lower bound shows us that for a sorting algorithm to run in subquadratic or $o(N^2)$ time, it must do comparisons and, in particular, exchanges between elements that are far apart. A sorting algorithm makes progress by eliminating inversions. To run efficiently, it must eliminate more than just one inversion per exchange.

The *lower-bound proof* shows that quadratic performance is inherent in any algorithm that sorts by performing adjacent comparisons.

8.4 Shellsort

The first algorithm to improve on the insertion sort substantially was *Shellsort*. Shellsort was developed in 1959 by Donald Shell. Although it is not the fastest algorithm known, it is only slightly longer than the insertion sort, thus making it the simplest of the faster algorithms.

Shell's idea was to avoid the large amount of data movement first by comparing elements that were far apart and then by comparing elements that were less far apart, and so on, gradually shrinking toward the basic insertion sort. Shellsort uses a sequence $h_1, h_2, ..., h_t$ called the increment sequence. Any increment sequence will do as long as $h_1 = 1$, but some choices are better than others. After

Shellsort is a subquadratic algorithm that works well in practice and is simple to code. The performance of Shellsort is highly dependent on the increment sequence.

a phase, using some increment h_k, we will have $a[i] \le a[i + h_k]$ for every i where this makes sense; all elements spaced h_k apart are sorted. The array is then said to be h_k-*sorted*.

For example, Figure 8.3 shows an array after several phases of Shellsort. After a 5-sort, elements spaced five apart are guaranteed to be in correct sorted order. In the figure, elements spaced five apart are identically shaded. As you can see, they are sorted relative to each other. Similarly, after a 3-sort, elements spaced three apart are guaranteed to be in sorted order, relative to each other. An important property of Shellsort (which we state without proof) is that an h_k-sorted array that is then h_{k-1}-sorted remains h_k-sorted. If this were not the case, the algorithm would likely be of little value because work done by early phases would be undone by later phases.

A *diminishing gap sort* is another name for Shellsort.

In general, an h_k-sort requires that for each position i in h_k, h_{k+1}, ..., $N - 1$, we place the element in the correct spot among $i, i - h_k, i - 2h_k$, and so on. Although this does not affect the implementation, a careful examination shows that the action of an h_k-sort is to perform an insertion sort on h_k independent sub-arrays (shown in different shades in Figure 8.3). Consequently, it should be no surprise that in Figure 8.4, lines 9 to 19 represent a *gap insertion sort*. In a gap insertion sort, after the loop is executed elements separated by a distance of gap in the array are sorted. For instance, when gap is 1, the loop is identical, statement by statement, to an insertion sort. Thus Shellsort is also known as *diminishing gap sort*.

It is easy to show several facts. First, when gap is 1 the inner loop is guaranteed to sort the array a. If gap is never 1, then there is always some input for which the array cannot be sorted. Thus Shellsort always sorts as long as we eventually have gap equal to 1, and at that point we can stop. The only issue remaining, then, is to choose the increment sequence.

Shell's increment sequence is an improvement over the insertion sort (although better sequences are known).

Shell suggested starting gap at $N/2$ and halving it until it reaches 1, after which the program can terminate. Using these increments, Shellsort represents a substantial improvement over the insertion sort, despite the fact that it nests three for loops instead of two, which is usually inefficient. By altering the sequence of gaps, one can further improve the algorithm's performance. A summary of Shellsort's performance with three different choices of increment sequences is shown in Figure 8.5.

Original	81	94	11	96	12	35	17	95	28	58	41	75	15
After 5-sort	35	17	11	28	12	41	75	15	96	58	81	94	95
After 3-sort	28	12	11	35	15	41	58	17	94	75	81	96	95
After 1-sort	11	12	15	17	28	35	41	58	75	81	94	95	96

Figure 8.3   Shellsort after each pass, if the increment sequence is {1, 3, 5}

```
1      /**
2       * Shellsort, using a sequence suggested by Gonnet.
3       * @param a an array of Comparable items.
4       */
5      public static void shellsort( Comparable [ ] a )
6      {
7          for( int gap = a.length / 2; gap > 0;
8                      gap = gap == 2 ? 1 : (int) ( gap / 2.2 ) )
9              for( int i = gap; i < a.length; i++ )
10             {
11                 Comparable tmp = a[ i ];
12                 int j = i;
13
14                 for( ; j >= gap &&
15                         tmp.lessThan( a[ j - gap ] );
16                                             j -= gap )
17                     a[ j ] = a[ j - gap ];
18                 a[ j ] = tmp;
19             }
20     }
```

Figure 8.4   Shellsort implementation with divide by 2.2 instead of 2

8.4.1 Performance of Shellsort

The running time of Shellsort depends heavily on the choice of increment sequences, and in general the proofs can be rather involved. The average-case analysis of Shellsort is a longstanding open problem, except for the most trivial increment sequences.

N	Insertion Sort	Shellsort		
		Shell's	Odd Gaps Only	Dividing by 2.2
1,000	122	11	11	9
2,000	483	26	21	23
4,000	1,936	61	59	54
8,000	7,950	153	141	114
16,000	32,560	358	322	269
32,000	131,911	869	752	575
64,000	520,000	2,091	1,705	1,249

Figure 8.5   Running time (milliseconds) of the insertion sort and Shellsort with various increment sequences

In the worst case, Shell's increments give quadratic behavior.

When Shell's increments are used, the worst case can be proven to be $O(N^2)$. This bound is achievable if N is an exact power of 2, all the large elements are in even-indexed array positions, and all the small elements are in odd-indexed array positions. When the final pass is reached, all the large elements will still be in the even-indexed array positions, and all the small elements will still be in the odd-indexed array positions. A calculation of the number of remaining inversions shows that the final pass will require quadratic time. The fact that this is the worst that can happen follows from the fact that an h_k-sort consists of h_k insertion sorts of roughly N/h_k elements. Consequently, the cost of each pass is $O(h_k(N/h_k)^2)$, or $O(N^2/h_k)$. When we sum this over all the passes, we obtain $O(N^2 \Sigma h_k)$. Since the increments are roughly a geometric series, the sum is bounded by a constant. The result is a quadratic worst-case running time. One can also prove via a complex argument that when N is an exact power of 2, the average running time is $O(N^{3/2})$. Thus, on average, Shell's increments give a significant improvement over insertion sort.

If consecutive increments are relatively prime, the performance of Shellsort is improved.

A minor change to the increment sequence can prevent the quadratic worst case from occurring. If we divide gap by 2 and it becomes even, then we can add 1 to make it odd. We can then prove that the worst case is not quadratic but only $O(N^{3/2})$. Although the proof is complicated, the basis for it is that in this new increment sequence, consecutive increments share no common factors (whereas in Shell's increment sequence they do). Any sequence that satisfies this property (and whose increments decrease roughly geometrically) will have a worst-case running time of at most $O(N^{3/2})$.[1] The average performance of the algorithm with these new increments is unknown but seems to be $O(N^{5/4})$, based on simulations.

Dividing by 2.2 gives excellent performance in practice.

A third sequence, which performs well in practice but has no theoretical basis, is to divide by 2.2 instead of 2. This appears to bring the average running time to below $O(N^{5/4})$ (perhaps to $O(N^{7/6})$), but this is completely unresolved. For 100,000 to 1,000,000 items, it typically improves performance by about 25 to 35 percent, although nobody knows why. A Shellsort implementation with this increment sequence is coded in Figure 8.4. The complicated code at line 8 is necessary to avoid prematurely setting gap equal to 0. If that happens, then the algorithm is broken because we never see a 1-sort. Line 8 ensures that if gap is 2 and is about to be set to 0, it is reset to 1.

The table in Figure 8.5 compares the performance of insertion sort and Shellsort, with various gap sequences. These results were obtained on a reasonably fast machine. The test is clearly biased against the original gap sequence because N is chosen to be 125 times an exact power of 2. Thus, rounding up to an odd number is particularly beneficial, especially as N gets large. We could easily conclude that Shellsort, even with the simplest gap sequence, provides a significant improvement over the insertion sort, at a cost of little additional code complexity. A simple change to the gap sequence can further improve performance.

[1.] To appreciate the subtlety involved, note that subtracting 1 instead of adding 1 does not work. For instance, if N is 186, the resulting sequence is 93, 45, 21, 9, 3, 1, all of which share the common factor 3.

More improvement is possible (as you will see in Exercise 8.18). Some of these improvements have theoretical backing, but no known sequence markedly improves the program shown in Figure 8.4.

The performance of Shellsort is quite acceptable in practice, even for N in the tens of thousands. The simplicity of the code makes it the algorithm of choice for sorting up to moderately large input. It is also a fine example of a very simple algorithm with an extremely complex analysis.

Shellsort is a good choice for moderate amounts of input.

8.5 Mergesort

Recall from Section 7.5 that recursion can be used to develop subquadratic algorithms. Specifically, a divide-and-conquer algorithm in which two half-size problems are solved recursively with an $O(N)$ overhead results in an $O(N \log N)$ algorithm. Mergesort is such an algorithm. It offers a better bound, at least theoretically, than the bounds claimed for Shellsort.

Mergesort uses divide-and-conquer to obtain an $O(N \log N)$ running time.

The mergesort algorithm involves three steps:

1. If the number of items to sort is 0 or 1, return.
2. Recursively sort the first and second halves separately.
3. Merge the two sorted halves into a sorted group.

To claim an $O(N \log N)$ algorithm, we need to show only that the merging of two sorted groups can be performed in linear time. This section shows how to merge two input arrays A and B, with the result placed in a third array C. We then provide a simple implementation of mergesort. The merge routine is the cornerstone of most external sorting algorithms. This is demonstrated in in Section 20.6.

Merging of sorted arrays can be done in linear time.

8.5.1 Linear-time Merging of Sorted Arrays

The basic merge algorithm takes two input arrays A and B, output array C, and three counters $Actr$, $Bctr$, and $Cctr$, which are initially set to the beginning of their respective arrays. The smaller of $A[Actr]$ and $B[Bctr]$ is copied to the next entry in C, and the appropriate counters are advanced. When either input array is exhausted, the rest of the other array is copied to C.

An example of how the merge routine works is provided for the following input:

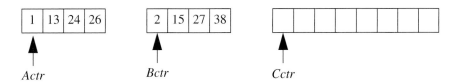

If the array A contains 1, 13, 24, 26, and B contains 2, 15, 27, 38, then the algorithm proceeds as follows: First, a comparison is done between 1 and 2, 1 is added to C, and then 13 and 2 are compared:

2 is added to C, and then 13 and 15 are compared:

13 is added to C, and then 24 and 15 are compared:

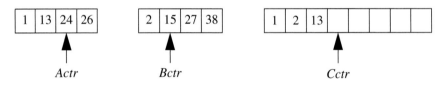

The process continues until 26 and 27 are compared:

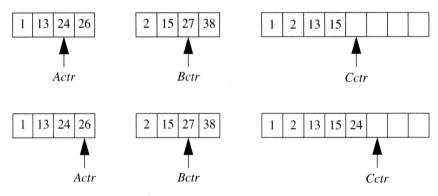

26 is added to C, and the A array is exhausted:

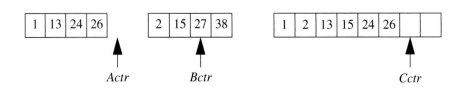

The rest of the *B* array is then copied to *C*.

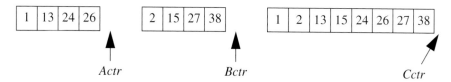

Actr   Bctr   Cctr

The time needed to merge two sorted arrays is linear because each comparison advances *Cctr* (thus limiting the number of comparisons). As a result, a divide-and-conquer algorithm that uses a linear merging procedure will run in $O(N \log N)$ worst-case time. This running time will also be the average-case and best-case times because the merging step is always linear.

An example of the mergesort algorithm would be sorting the 8-element array 24, 13, 26, 1, 2, 27, 38, 15. After recursively sorting the first four and last four elements, we obtain 1, 13, 24, 26, 2, 15, 27, 38. Then we merge the two halves, thus obtaining the final array 1, 2, 13, 15, 24, 26, 27, 38.

```
1      /**
2       * Internal method that makes recursive calls.
3       * @param a an array of Comparable items.
4       * @param tmpArray an array to place the merged result.
5       * @param left the left-most index of the subarray.
6       * @param right the right-most index of the subarray.
7       */
8      private static void mergeSort( Comparable [ ] a,
9                  Comparable [ ] tmpArray, int left, int right )
10     {
11         if( left < right )
12         {
13             int center = ( left + right ) / 2;
14             mergeSort( a, tmpArray, left, center );
15             mergeSort( a, tmpArray, center + 1, right );
16             merge( a, tmpArray, left, center + 1, right );
17         }
18     }
19
20     /**
21      * Mergesort algorithm.
22      * @param a an array of Comparable items.
23      */
24     public static void mergeSort( Comparable [ ] a )
25     {
26         Comparable [ ] tmpArray = new Comparable[ a.length ];
27
28         mergeSort( a, tmpArray, 0, a.length - 1 );
29     }
```

Figure 8.6   Basic mergeSort routines

8.5.2 The Mergesort Algorithm

Mergesort uses lin-
ear extra memory,
which is a practical
liability.

A straightforward implementation of mergesort is shown in Figure 8.6
(page 233). The public `mergeSort` is a simple driver that declares a temporary
array and calls recursive `mergeSort` with the boundaries of the array. The
`merge` routine follows the description given in the previous section. It uses the
first half of the array (indexed from `left` to `center`) as *A*, the second half
(indexed from `center+1` to `right`) as *B*, and the temporary as *C*. Figure 8.7
implements the `merge` routine. The temporary is then copied back into the original array.

```
1      /**
2       * Method that merges two sorted halves of a subarray.
3       * @param a an array of Comparable items.
4       * @param tmpArray an array to place the merged result.
5       * @param leftPos the left-most index of the subarray.
6       * @param rightPos the index of the start of the 2nd half.
7       * @param rightEnd the right-most index of the subarray.
8       */
9      private static void merge( Comparable [ ] a,
10                                 Comparable [ ] tmpArray, int leftPos,
11                                 int rightPos, int rightEnd )
12     {
13         int leftEnd = rightPos - 1;
14         int tmpPos = leftPos;
15         int numElements = rightEnd - leftPos + 1;
16
17         // Main loop
18         while( leftPos <= leftEnd && rightPos <= rightEnd )
19             if( a[ leftPos ].lessThan( a[ rightPos ] ) )
20                 tmpArray[ tmpPos++ ] = a[ leftPos++ ];
21             else
22                 tmpArray[ tmpPos++ ] = a[ rightPos++ ];
23
24         // Copy the rest of the first half
25         while( leftPos <= leftEnd )
26             tmpArray[ tmpPos++ ] = a[ leftPos++ ];
27
28         // Copy the rest of the second half
29         while( rightPos <= rightEnd )
30             tmpArray[ tmpPos++ ] = a[ rightPos++ ];
31
32         // Copy tmpArray back
33         for( int i = 0; i < numElements; i++, rightEnd-- )
34             a[ rightEnd ] = tmpArray[ rightEnd ];
35     }
```

Figure 8.7   `merge` routine

Although mergesort's running time is $O(N \log N)$, it is hardly ever used for main memory sorts. This is because merging two sorted lists uses linear extra memory and the additional work involved in copying to the temporary array and back, throughout the algorithm, slows down the sort considerably. This copying can be avoided by judiciously switching the roles of `a` and `tmpArray` at alternate levels in the recursion.

We can avoid excessive copying with more work, but the linear extra memory cannot be removed without excessive time penalties.

A variant of mergesort can also be implemented nonrecursively. For serious internal sorting applications, however, the algorithm of choice is quicksort, which is described in the next section.

8.6 Quicksort

As its name implies, *quicksort* is the fastest-known sorting algorithm. Its average running time is $O(N \log N)$. Its speed is due mainly to a very tight and highly optimized inner loop. It has quadratic worst-case performance, but this can be made statistically impossible with a little effort. The quicksort algorithm is relatively simple to understand and prove correct because it relies on recursion. It is a tricky algorithm to implement because minute changes in the code can make significant differences in the running time. This section first describes the algorithm in broad terms. It then provides an analysis that shows its best-, worst-, and average-case running times. We use this analysis to make decisions on how certain details, are implemented in Java, such as the handling of duplicate items.

Quicksort is a fast divide-and-conquer algorithm, when properly implemented. In practice, it is the fastest comparison-based sorting algorithm.

8.6.1 The Quicksort Algorithm

The basic algorithm *Quicksort(S)* is recursive and consists of the following four steps:

The basic quicksort algorithm is recursive. Details include choosing the pivot, deciding how to partition, and dealing with duplicates.

1. If the number of elements in *S* is 0 or 1, then return.
2. Pick *any* element *v* in *S*. This element is called the *pivot*.
3. *Partition* $S - \{v\}$ (the remaining elements in *S*) into two disjoint groups: $L = \{x \in S - \{v\} | x \leq v\}$ and $R = \{x \in S - \{v\} | x \geq v\}$.
4. Return the result of *Quicksort(L)*, followed by *v*, followed by *Quicksort(R)*.

Several points stand out when we look at these steps. First, the base case of the recursion includes the possibility that *S* might be an empty set. This is needed because the recursive calls could generate empty subsets. Second, the algorithm allows any element to be used as the *pivot*. The pivot divides array elements into two groups: those that are smaller than the pivot and those that are larger than the pivot. The analysis performed here shows that some choices for the pivot are better than others. Thus, when we provide an actual implementation, we will not use just any pivot. Instead, we will try to make an educated choice.

The pivot divides array elements into two groups: those smaller than the pivot and those larger than the pivot.

The *partition* step places every element except the pivot in one of two groups.

In the *partition* step, every element in S, except for the pivot, is placed in either L (which stands for the left-hand part of the array) or R (which stands for the right-hand part of the array). The intent is that elements that are smaller than the pivot go to L, while elements that are larger than the pivot go to R. The description in the algorithm, however, ambiguously describes what to do with elements equal to the pivot. It allows each instance of a duplicate to go into either subset, specifying only that it must go to one or the other. Part of a good Java implementation is handling this case as efficiently as possible. Once again, the analysis will allow us to make an informed decision.

Figure 8.8 shows the action of quicksort on a set of numbers. The pivot is chosen (by chance) to be 65. The remaining elements in the set are partitioned into two smaller subsets. Each of these groups is then sorted recursively. By the third rule of recursion, we can assume that this step works. The sorted arrangement of the entire group is then trivially obtained. In a Java implementation, the items would be stored in a part of an array delimited by `low` and `high`. After the partitioning step, the pivot would wind up in some array cell `p`. The recursive calls would then be on the parts from `low` to `p-1` and then `p+1` to `high`.

Because recursion allows us to take the giant leap of faith, the correctness of the algorithm is guaranteed as follows:

- The group of small elements is sorted, by virtue of the recursion.
- The largest element in the group of small elements is not larger than the pivot, by virtue of the partition.
- The pivot is not larger than the smallest element in the group of large elements, by virtue of the partition.
- The group of large elements is sorted, by virtue of the recursion.

Quicksort is fast because the partitioning step can be performed quickly and in place.

Although the correctness of the algorithm is easily established, it is not clear why it is any faster than mergesort. Like mergesort, it recursively solves two subproblems and requires linear additional work (in the form of the partitioning step). Unlike with mergesort, however, the subproblems are not guaranteed to be of equal size. This is bad for performance. Quicksort is faster than mergesort because the partitioning step can be performed significantly faster than the merging step can. In particular, the partitioning step can be performed without using an extra array and the code to implement it is very compact and efficient. This makes up for the lack of equal-sized subproblems.

8.6.2 Analysis of Quicksort

The algorithm description leaves several questions unanswered. How do we choose the pivot? How do we perform the partition? What do we do if we see an element that is equal to the pivot? All these questions can dramatically affect the running time of the algorithm. We will perform an analysis to help us decide how we should implement the unspecified steps in quicksort.

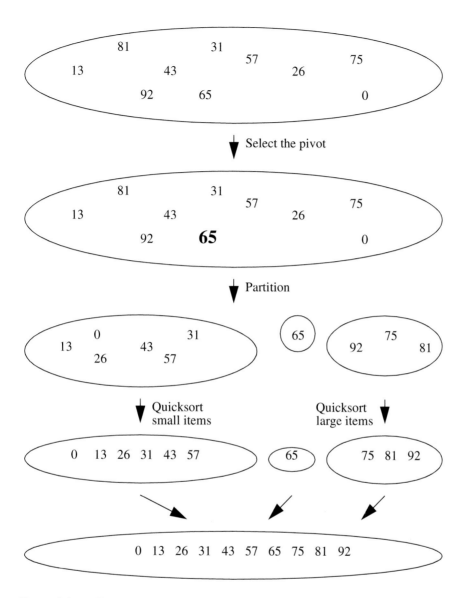

Figure 8.8 The steps of quicksort

Best Case

The best case for quicksort is that the pivot partitions the set into two equal-sized subsets and that this happens at each stage of the recursion. We then have two half-sized recursive calls plus linear overhead, which matches the performance of mergesort. The running time, for this case, is $O(N \log N)$. (We have not actually proved that this is the best case. Such a proof is possible; however, we omit the details.)

The best case occurs when the partition always splits into equal subsets. The running time is $O(N \log N)$.

Worst Case

Since equal-sized subsets are good for quicksort, one might expect that unequal-sized subsets are bad. This is indeed the case. Suppose that in each step of the recursion, the pivot happens to be the smallest element. Then the set of small elements L will be empty and the set of large elements R will have all the elements except for the pivot. We will then have to recursively call quicksort on subset R. Suppose $T(N)$ is the running time to quicksort N elements and we assume that the time to sort 0 or 1 element is just 1 time unit. Suppose also that we charge N units to partition a set that contains N elements. Then for $N > 1$, we obtain a running time that satisfies

$$T(N) = T(N-1) + N. \tag{8.1}$$

In other words, Equation 8.1 states that the time to quicksort N items is equal to the time to recursively sort the $N-1$ items in the subset of larger elements plus the N units of cost to perform the partition. This assumes that in each step of the iteration, we are unfortunate enough to pick the smallest element as the pivot. To simplify the analysis, we normalize by throwing out constant factors. We can solve this recurrence by telescoping Equation 8.1 repeatedly:

$$T(N) = T(N-1) + N$$
$$T(N-1) = T(N-2) + (N-1)$$
$$T(N-2) = T(N-3) + (N-2) \tag{8.2}$$
$$\dots$$
$$T(2) = T(1) + 2$$

When we add up everything in Equation 8.2, we obtain massive cancellations, yielding

$$T(N) = T(1) + 2 + 3 + \dots + N = N(N+1)/2 = O(N^2). \tag{8.3}$$

This analysis verifies the intuition that an uneven split is bad. We spend N units of time to partition and then have to make a recursive call for $N-1$. Then we spend $N-1$ units to partition that group, only to have to make a recursive call for $N-2$ elements. In that call, we spend $N-2$ units performing the partition, and so on. The total time to perform all the partitions throughout the recursive calls exactly matches what is obtained in Equation 8.3. This tells us that when implementing the selection of the pivot and the partitioning step, we do not want to do anything that might encourage the subsets to be unbalanced in size.

Average Case

The first two analyses tell us that the best and worst cases are wildly different. Naturally, we want to know what happens in the average case. We would expect that since each subproblem is half of the original on average, the $O(N \log N)$ would now become an average-case bound. Such expectation, while correct for the particular quicksort application we examine here, does not constitute a formal proof. Averages cannot be thrown around lightly. For example, suppose we have a pivot algorithm that is guaranteed to select only the smallest or largest element, each with probability 1/2. Then the average size of the small group of elements is roughly $N/2$, as is the average size of the large group of elements (because each is equally likely to have 0 or $N-1$ elements). But the running time of quicksort with that pivot selection will always be quadratic because we always get a poor split of elements. We must be careful how we assign the label "average." We can argue that the group of small elements is as likely to contain 0, 1, 2, ..., or $N-1$ elements. This is also true for the group of large elements. Under this assumption, we can establish that the average-case running time is indeed $O(N \log N)$.

Since the cost of quicksort of N items is equal to N units for the partitioning step plus the cost of the two recursive calls, we need to determine the average cost of each of the recursive calls. If $T(N)$ represents the average cost to quicksort N elements, the average cost of each recursive call is equal to the average, over all possible subproblem sizes, of the average cost of a recursive call on the subproblem:

The average cost of a recursive call is obtained by averaging the costs of all possible subproblem sizes.

$$T(L) = T(R) = \frac{T(0) + T(1) + T(2) + \ldots + T(N-1)}{N} \tag{8.4}$$

Equation 8.4 states that we are looking at the costs for each possible subset size and averaging them. Since we have two recursive calls plus linear time to perform the partition, we obtain

$$T(N) = 2\left(\frac{T(0) + T(1) + T(2) + \ldots + T(N-1)}{N}\right) + N. \tag{8.5}$$

To solve Equation 8.5, we begin by multiplying both sides by N, obtaining

$$NT(N) = 2(T(0) + T(1) + T(2) + \ldots + T(N-1)) + N^2. \tag{8.6}$$

The average running time is given by $T(N)$. We solve Equation 8.5 by removing all but the most recent recursive value of T.

We then write Equation 8.6 for the case $N-1$, with the idea being that we can perform a subtraction and greatly simplify the equation. If we do this, we obtain

$$(N-1)T(N-1) = 2(T(0) + T(1) + T(2) + \ldots + T(N-2)) + (N-1)^2. \tag{8.7}$$

Now if we subtract Equation 8.7 from Equation 8.6, we obtain

$$NT(N) - (N-1)T(N-1) = 2T(N-1) + 2N - 1.$$

We rearrange terms and drop the insignificant -1 on the right to obtain

$$NT(N) = (N+1)T(N-1) + 2N. \tag{8.8}$$

We now have a formula for $T(N)$ in terms of $T(N-1)$ only. Again, the idea is to telescope, but Equation 8.8 is in the wrong form. If we divide Equation 8.8 by $N(N+1)$, we obtain

Once we have $T(N)$ in terms of $T(N-1)$ only, we attempt to telescope.

$$\frac{T(N)}{N+1} = \frac{T(N-1)}{N} + \frac{2}{N+1}.$$

Now we can telescope:

$$\frac{T(N)}{N+1} = \frac{T(N-1)}{N} + \frac{2}{N+1}$$

$$\frac{T(N-1)}{N} = \frac{T(N-2)}{N-1} + \frac{2}{N}$$

$$\frac{T(N-2)}{N-1} = \frac{T(N-3)}{N-2} + \frac{2}{N-1} \qquad \textbf{(8.9)}$$

$$\cdots$$

$$\frac{T(2)}{3} = \frac{T(1)}{2} + \frac{2}{3}$$

If we add all the equations in Equation 8.9, we obtain

$$\frac{T(N)}{N+1} = \frac{T(1)}{2} + 2\left(\frac{1}{3} + \frac{1}{4} + \cdots + \frac{1}{N} + \frac{1}{N+1}\right)$$

$$= 2\left(1 + \frac{1}{2} + \frac{1}{3} + \cdots + \frac{1}{N+1}\right) - \frac{5}{2} \qquad \textbf{(8.10)}$$

$$= O(\log N)$$

We use the fact that the N th harmonic number is O(log N).

The last line in Equation 8.10 follows from Theorem 5.5. When we multiply both sides by $N + 1$, we obtain the final result of

$$T(N) = O(N \log N). \qquad \textbf{(8.11)}$$

8.6.3 Picking the Pivot

Now that we have established that quicksort will run in $O(N \log N)$ time on average, our primary concern is to ensure that the worst case does not occur. By performing a complex analysis, we can compute the standard deviation of quicksort's running time. The result is that if a single random permutation is presented, it is almost certain that the running time used to sort it will be close to the average. Thus we must be careful that degenerate inputs do not result in bad running times. Degenerate inputs include data that is already sorted and data that contains only N completely identical elements. As we will see below, sometimes it is the easy cases that give algorithms trouble.

A Wrong Way

Picking the pivot is crucial to good performance. Never choose the first element as the pivot.

The popular, uninformed choice is to use the first element (that is, the element that is in position `low`) as the pivot. This is acceptable if the input is random, but if the input is presorted or in reverse order, then the pivot provides a poor partition because it will be an extreme element. Furthermore, this behavior will continue recursively. As we saw earlier in the chapter, we would get quadratic running time to do absolutely nothing. This, needless to say, is embarrassing. *Never* use the first element as the pivot.

Another popular alternative is to choose the larger of the first two distinct keys as the pivot, but this has the same bad effects as choosing the first key. Stay away from any strategy that looks only at some key near the front or end of the input group.

A Safe Choice

A perfectly reasonable choice for the pivot is the middle element (that is, the element in array cell `(low+high)/2`). When the input is already sorted, this gives the perfect pivot in each recursive call. Of course, we could construct an input sequence that forces quadratic behavior for this strategy (see Exercise 8.8), but the chances of randomly running into a case that took even twice as long as the average case is astronomically small.

The middle element is a reasonable but passive choice.

Median-of-three Partitioning

Choosing the middle element as the pivot avoids the degenerate cases that arise from nonrandom inputs. Notice that this is a passive choice, however. That is, we do not attempt to choose a good pivot. Instead, we merely try to avoid picking a bad pivot. *Median-of-three partitioning* is an attempt to pick a better than average pivot.

The median of a group of N numbers is the $\lceil N/2 \rceil$th smallest number. The best choice for the pivot would clearly be the median because it would guarantee an even split of the elements. Unfortunately, the median is hard to calculate and would slow down quicksort considerably. So we want to get a good estimate of the median without spending too much time. Such an estimate can be obtained by sampling: That is, we pick a subset of these numbers and find their median. This is the classic method used in opinion polls. The larger the sample, the more accurate the estimate. However, the larger sample takes longer to evaluate. It has been shown that a sample size of three gives a small improvement in the average running time of quicksort and also simplifies the resulting partitioning code by eliminating some special cases. It has also been shown that large sample sizes do not significantly improve performance and thus are not worth using.

The three elements that are used in the sample are the first, middle, and last. For instance, with input 8, 1, 4, 9, 6, 3, 5, 2, 7, 0, the leftmost element is 8, the rightmost element is 0, and the center element is 6; thus the pivot would be 6 (when there are two center elements, as in this case, the leftmost of the two is used). Note that for already-sorted items, we keep the middle element as the pivot; this is the best case.

In median-of-three partitioning, the median of the first, middle, and last elements is used as the pivot. This simplifies the partitioning stage of quicksort.

8.6.4 A Partitioning Strategy

There are several commonly used partitioning strategies. The one described in this section is known to give good results. The simplest partitioning strategy is discussed now. It occurs in three steps. Section 8.6.6 shows the improvements that occur when median-of-three pivot selection is used.

Step 1: Swap the pivot with the element at the end.

The first step in the partitioning algorithm is to get the pivot element out of the way by swapping it with the last element. The result for our sample input is shown in Figure 8.9. The pivot element is shown in the darkest shade at the end of the array.

For now, we assume that all the elements are distinct and leave for later what to do in the presence of duplicates. As a limiting case, our algorithm must work properly when *all* the elements are identical.

Step 2: Run i from left to right, and j from right to left. When i sees a large element, i stops. When j sees a small element, j stops. If i and j have not crossed, swap their items and continue. Otherwise, stop this loop.

In step 2, we use our partitioning strategy to move all the small elements to the left part of the array and all the large elements to the right part. *Small* and *large* are relative to the pivot. In Figures 8.10 – 8.15, white cells are cells that we know are correctly placed. The cells that are almost as dark as the pivot are not known to be correctly placed.

We search from left to right looking for a large element. To do this we use a counter i, initialized at position low. We also search from right to left looking for a small element. We do this by using a counter j, initialized to start at high-1. Figure 8.10 shows that the search for a large element stops at 8 and the search for a small element stops at 2. These cells have been lightly shaded. Notice that by skipping past 7, we know that 7 is not small and thus is correctly placed. Thus it is colored white. Now we have a large element, 8, on the left-hand side of the array and a small element, 2, on the right-hand side of the array. We must swap these two elements to correctly place them, as shown in Figure 8.11.

Figure 8.9   Partitioning algorithm: The pivot element 6 is placed at the end

Figure 8.10   Partitioning algorithm: i stops at large element 8; j stops at small element 2

Figure 8.11   Partitioning algorithm: The out-of-order elements 8 and 2 are swapped

Figure 8.12   Partitioning algorithm: `i` stops at large element 9; `j` stops at small element 5

Figure 8.13   Partitioning algorithm: The out-of-order elements 9 and 5 are swapped

Figure 8.14   Partitioning algorithm: `i` stops at large element 9; `j` stops at small element 3

Figure 8.15   Partitioning algorithm: Swap pivot and element in position `i`

As the algorithm continues, `i` stops at large element 9 and `j` stops at small element 5. Once again, elements that `i` and `j` skip during the scan are guaranteed to be correctly placed. Figure 8.12 shows the result: The ends of the array (not counting the pivot) become filled with correctly placed elements.

Next, swap the elements that `i` and `j` are indexing, as shown in Figure 8.13. The scan continues, with `i` stopping at large element 9 and `j` stopping at small element 3. However, at this point `i` and `j` have crossed positions in the array. Consequently, a swap would be useless. This is shown in Figure 8.14, which shows that the item being accessed by `j` is already correctly placed and should not move.

Figure 8.14 shows that all but two items are correctly placed. Wouldn't it be nice if we could just swap them and be done? Well, we can. All we need to do is swap the element in position `i` and the element in the last cell (the pivot). This is shown in Figure 8.15. The element that `i` is indexing was clearly large, so moving it to the last position is fine.

Step 3: Swap the element in position `i` with the pivot.

Notice that the partitioning algorithm requires no extra memory and that each element is compared exactly once with the pivot. When the code is written, this translates to a very tight inner loop.

8.6.5 Keys Equal to the Pivot

One important detail that we must consider is how to handle keys that are equal to the pivot. The questions are whether i should stop when it sees a key equal to the pivot and whether j should stop when it sees a key equal to the pivot. i and j should do the same thing; otherwise, the partitioning step is biased. For instance, if i stops and j does not, then all keys that are equal to the pivot wind up on the right-hand side.

Let us consider the case in which all elements in the array are identical. If both i and j stop, there will be many swaps between identical elements. Although this seems useless, the positive effect is that i and j cross in the middle, so when the pivot is replaced, the partition creates two nearly equal subsets. Thus the best-case analysis applies, and the running time is $O(N \log N)$.

If neither i nor j stops, then i winds up at the last position (assuming, of course, that it does stop at the boundary) and no swaps are performed. This seems great until we realize that the pivot will then be placed as the last element because that is the last cell that i touches. The result is wildly uneven subsets and a running time that matches the worst-case bound of $O(N^2)$. The effect is the same as using the first element as a pivot for presorted input. It takes quadratic time to do nothing.

We can conclude that it is better to do the unnecessary swaps and create even subsets than to risk wildly uneven subsets. So, we will have both i and j stop if they encounter an element equal to the pivot. This turns out to be the only one of the four possibilities that does not take quadratic time for this input.

At first glance, it may seem that worrying about an array of identical elements is silly. After all, why would anyone want to sort 5,000 identical elements? However, recall that quicksort is recursive. Suppose there are 100,000 elements, of which 5,000 are identical. Eventually quicksort could make the recursive call on only the 5,000 identical elements. Then it really will be important to make sure that 5,000 identical elements can be sorted efficiently.

8.6.6 Median-of-three Partitioning

When we do median-of-three partitioning, we can do a simple optimization that saves a few comparisons and also greatly simplifies the code. Figure 8.16 shows the original array.

Median-of-three partitioning requires that we find the median of the first, middle, and last elements. The easiest way to do this is to sort them in the array. The result is shown in Figure 8.17. Notice the resulting shading: The element that winds up in the first position is guaranteed to be smaller than (or equal to) the pivot, and the element in the last position is larger than (or equal to) the pivot. This tells us four things:

1. We should not swap the pivot with the element in the last position. Instead, we should swap it with the element in the next-to-last position. This is shown in Figure 8.18.

Figure 8.16 Original array

Figure 8.17 Result of sorting three elements (first, middle, and last)

Figure 8.18 Result of swapping the pivot with next-to-last element

2. We can start i at low+1 and j at high-2.
3. We are guaranteed that whenever i searches for a large element, it will stop because in the worst case, it will encounter the pivot (and we stop on equality).
4. We are guaranteed that whenever j searches for a small element, it will stop because in the worst case, it will encounter the first element (and we stop on equality).

All of these optimizations will be incorporated into the final Java code.

8.6.7 Small Arrays

Our final optimization concerns small arrays. Is it worth using a high-powered routine like quicksort when there are only ten elements to sort? The answer is, of course not. A simple routine, such as the insertion sort, will probably be faster for small arrays. The recursive nature of quicksort tells us that we will generate many calls that have only small subsets. Thus it is worthwhile to test the size of the subset. If it is smaller than some cutoff, we apply insertion sort; otherwise, we do the quicksort.

Sort ten or fewer items by insertion sort. Place this test in the recursive quicksort routine.

It has been shown that a good cutoff is ten elements, although any cutoff between 5 and 20 is likely to produce similar results. The actual best cutoff is machine-dependent. Using a cutoff saves us from degenerate cases. For example, finding the median of three elements does not make much sense when there are not three elements.

In the past, it was thought that an even better alternative was to leave the array slightly unsorted by doing absolutely nothing when the subset size was below the cutoff. Because the insertion sort is so efficient for nearly sorted arrays, we could show mathematically that running a final insertion sort to clean up the array was faster than running all the smaller insertion sorts. The savings was roughly the overhead of the insertion sort method calls.

Now method calls are not as expensive as they used to be. Furthermore, a second scan of the array for the insertion sort is expensive. Because of a technique called *caching*, we are better off doing the insertion sort on the small subarrays. Localized memory accesses are faster than nonlocalized accesses. On many machines, touching memory twice in one scan is faster than touching memory once in each of two separate scans.

8.6.8 Java Quicksort Routine

We use a driver to set things up.

The actual implementation of quicksort is shown in Figure 8.19. The visible quicksort, declared at lines 46 to 49 in the figure, is merely a driver that calls the recursive quicksort. Thus we discuss only the implementation of the recursive quicksort.

At line 7, we test for small subarrays and call an insertion sort (not shown) when the problem instance is below some specified value given by the constant CUTOFF. Otherwise, we proceed with the recursive procedure. Lines 12 to 18 sort the low, middle, and high elements in place. In keeping with our previous discussion, the middle element is used as the pivot and is swapped (using swapReferences, not shown) with the element in the next to last position at lines 21 and 22. We then do the partitioning phase. We initialize the counters i and j to 1 past their true initial values because the prefix increment and decrement operators will immediately adjust them before the array accesses at lines 28 and 30. When the first while loop at line 28 exits, i will be indexing an element that is greater than or possibly equal to the pivot. Likewise, when the second loop ends, j will be indexing an element that is less than or possibly equal to the pivot. If i and j have not crossed, these elements are swapped and we continue scanning. Otherwise, the scan is terminated and the pivot is restored at line 39. The sort is finished when the two recursive calls are made at lines 41 and 42.

The inner loop of quicksort is very tight and efficient.

The fundamental operations occur at lines 28 through 35. The scans consist of simple operations: increments, array accesses, and simple comparisons. This accounts for the "quick" in quicksort. To ensure that the inner loops are tight and efficient, we want to make sure that the swap at line 33 comprises the three assignments that we expect and does not incur the overhead of a method call. A good optimizing compiler might do this, since all methods in the Sort package are final, and inline optimization is thus allowable. However, it may be necessary to manually inline the code if the compiler is unwilling to perform the optimization.

Quicksort is a classic example of using an analysis to guide the program implementation.

Although the code looks straightforward now, it is important to keep in mind that this is only because of the analysis we performed prior to coding. Also there are still some traps lurking (see Exercise 8.12). Quicksort is a classic example of using an analysis to guide the program implementation.

```
1      // Quicksort algorithm that uses median-of-three
2      // partitioning and a cutoff for small subarrays.
3
4      private static void
5      quicksort( Comparable [ ] a, int low, int high )
6      {
7          if( low + CUTOFF > high )
8              insertionSort( a, low, high );
9          else
10         {
11                 // Sort low, middle, high
12             int middle = ( low + high ) / 2;
13             if( a[ middle ].lessThan( a[ low ] ) )
14                 swapReferences( a, low, middle );
15             if( a[ high ].lessThan( a[ low ] ) )
16                 swapReferences( a, low, high );
17             if( a[ high ].lessThan( a[ middle ] ) )
18                 swapReferences( a, middle, high );
19
20                 // Place pivot at position high - 1
21             swapReferences( a, middle, high - 1 );
22             Comparable pivot = a[ high - 1 ];
23
24                 // Begin partitioning
25             int i, j;
26             for( i = low, j = high - 1; ; )
27             {
28                 while( a[ ++i ].lessThan( pivot ) )
29                     ;
30                 while( pivot.lessThan( a[ --j ] ) )
31                     ;
32                 if( i < j )
33                     swapReferences( a, i, j );
34                 else
35                     break;
36             }
37
38                 // Restore pivot
39             swapReferences( a, i, high - 1 );
40
41             quicksort( a, low, i - 1 ); // Sort small elements
42             quicksort( a, i + 1, high );// Sort large elements
43         }
44     }
45
46     public static void quicksort( Comparable [ ] a )
47     {
48         quicksort( a, 0, a.length - 1 );
49     }
```

Figure 8.19   Quicksort with median-of-three partitioning and cutoff for small subarrays

8.7 Quickselect

Selection is finding the kth smallest element of an array.

A problem closely related to sorting is *selection*, that is, given an array of N items, we must find the kth smallest item. An important special case is finding the median, or the $N/2$th smallest element. Obviously, we can sort the items, but we would hope that since selection requests less information than sorting, selection would be a faster process. It turns out that this is true. By making a small change to quicksort, we can solve the selection problem in linear time, on average. We call this algorithm *quickselect*. The steps for *Quickselect(S, k)* are as follows:

1. If the number of elements in S is 1, then presumably k is also 1, so we can return the single element in S.
2. Pick any element v in S. This is the pivot.
3. *Partition $S - \{v\}$ into L and R*, exactly as was done for quicksort.
4. If k is less than or equal to the number of elements in L, then the item we are searching for must be in L. Call *Quickselect(L, k)* recursively. Otherwise, if k is exactly equal to one more than the number of items in L, then the pivot is the kth smallest element and we can return it as the answer. Otherwise, the kth smallest element lies in R, and it is the $(k - |L| - 1)$th smallest element in R. Again, we can make a recursive call and return the result.

Quickselect is used to perform a selection. It is similar to quicksort but makes only one recursive call. The average running time is linear.

Quickselect makes only one recursive call compared to quicksort's two. The worst case of quickselect is identical to that of quicksort and is quadratic. It occurs when one of the recursive calls is on an empty set. In such cases, quickselect does not save much. We can show that the average time is linear, however, by using an analysis that is similar to quicksort's (see Exercise 8.9).

The implementation of quickselect is even simpler than our abstract description might imply. A complete implementation is shown in Figure 8.20. Except for the extra parameter (k) and the recursive calls, the algorithm is identical to quicksort. When it terminates, the kth smallest element is in its correct position in the array. Note that since the array begins at index 0, the fourth smallest element is in position three; the original ordering is destroyed. If this situation is undesirable, we can have the driver routine pass a copy of the array instead.

The linear worst-case algorithm is a classic result even though it is impractical.

Using median-of-three partitioning makes the chance of the worst case occurring almost negligible. By carefully choosing the pivot, it can be shown that the worst case never occurs and that the running time is linear even in the worst-case scenario. The resulting algorithm is entirely of theoretical interest, however, because the constant that the Big-Oh notation hides is much larger than the constant seen in the normal median-of-three implementation.

```
1      // Internal selection method that makes recursive calls.
2      // Places the kth smallest item in a[k-1].
3      // Initial call is quickSelect( a, 0, a.length, k )
4
5      private static void
6      quickSelect( Comparable [ ] a, int low, int high, int k )
7      {
8          if( low + CUTOFF > high )
9              insertionSort( a, low, high );
10         else
11         {
12                 // Sort low, middle, high
13             int middle = ( low + high ) / 2;
14             if( a[ middle ].lessThan( a[ low ] ) )
15                 swapReferences( a, low, middle );
16             if( a[ high ].lessThan( a[ low ] ) )
17                 swapReferences( a, low, high );
18             if( a[ high ].lessThan( a[ middle ] ) )
19                 swapReferences( a, middle, high );
20
21                 // Place pivot at position high - 1
22             swapReferences( a, middle, high - 1 );
23             Comparable pivot = a[ high - 1 ];
24
25                 // Begin partitioning
26             int i, j;
27             for( i = low, j = high - 1; ; )
28             {
29                 while( a[ ++i ].lessThan( pivot ) )
30                     ;
31                 while( pivot.lessThan( a[ --j ] ) )
32                     ;
33                 if( i < j )
34                     swapReferences( a, i, j );
35                 else
36                     break;
37             }
38
39                 // Restore pivot
40             swapReferences( a, i, high - 1 );
41
42                 // Recurse; only this part changes
43             if( k - 1 < i )
44                 quickSelect( a, low, i - 1, k );
45             else if( k - 1 > i )
46                 quickSelect( a, i + 1, high, k );
47         }
48     }
```

Figure 8.20   Quickselect with median-of-three partitioning and cutoff for
small subarrays

8.8 A Lower Bound for Sorting

Any comparison-based sorting algorithm must use roughly N log N comparisons on average and in the worst case.

The proofs are abstract; we show the worst-case lower bound.

Although we have $O(N \log N)$ algorithms for sorting, it is not clear that this is as good as we can do. In this section, we prove that any algorithm for sorting that uses only comparisons requires $\Omega(N \log N)$ comparisons (and hence time) in the worst case. This means that *any algorithm that sorts by using element comparisons must use at least roughly N log N comparisons for some input sequence.* A similar technique can be used to show that this is also true on average.

Must every sorting algorithm work by using comparisons? The answer is no. However algorithms that do not use general comparisons are likely to work only for restricted types, such as integers. Although we may often need to sort only integers (see Exercise 8.13), a general-purpose sorting algorithm cannot make such sweeping assumptions about its input. It may only assume the given, namely that since the items need to be sorted, we can assume that any two items can be compared.

Next, we prove one of the most fundamental theorems in computer science (see Theorem 8.3). Recall first that the product of the first N positive integers is $N!$. The proof is an existence proof, which is somewhat abstract. It shows that some bad input must always exist.

Theorem 8.3

Any algorithm that sorts by using element comparisons only must use at least $\lceil \log(N!) \rceil$ comparisons for some input sequence.

Proof

We may regard the possible inputs as any of the permutations of 1, 2, ..., N. This is because only the relative order of the input items matters, not their actual values. Thus the number of possible inputs is the number of different arrangements of N items, which is exactly N!. Let P_i be the number of permutations that are consistent with the results after the algorithm has processed i comparisons. Let F be the number of comparisons processed when the sort terminates. We know the following: (a) $P_0 = N!$ because all permutations are possible before the first comparison; (b) $P_F = 1$, because if more than one permutation was possible, the algorithm could not terminate with confidence that it produced the correct output; (c) there exists a permutation such that $P_i \geq P_{i-1}/2$, because after a comparison, each permutation goes into one of two groups: the still-possible group and the no-longer-possible group. The larger of these two groups must have at least half the permutations. Furthermore, there

is at least one permutation for which we can apply this logic throughout the   ***Proof (continued)***
comparison sequence. The action of a sorting algorithm is thus to go from
the state P_0, in which all N! permutations are possible, to the final state
P_F, in which only one permutation is possible, with the restriction that
there exists an input such that in each comparison, only half of the permuta-
tions can be eliminated. By the halving principle, we know that at least
$\lceil \log(N!) \rceil$ comparisons are required for that input.

How large is $\lceil \log(N!) \rceil$? It is approximately $N \log N - 1.44N$.

Summary

For most general internal sorting applications, either an insertion sort, Shellsort, or quicksort is the method of choice. The decision regarding which to use depends on the size of the input.

Insertion sort is appropriate for very small amounts of input. Shellsort is a good choice for sorting moderate amounts of input. With a proper increment sequence, it gives excellent performance using only a few lines of code. Quicksort gives the best performance but is trickier to code. Asymptotically, it has almost certain $O(N \log N)$ performance with a careful implementation, and this chapter showed that this is essentially as good as we can expect. Section 20.5 discusses another popular internal sort, *heapsort*.

When we are sorting input that does not fit entirely in main memory, different techniques are needed. The general technique is discussed in Section 20.6. It makes use of the merge algorithm discussed in Section 8.5.

To test and compare the merits of the various sorting algorithms, we need to be able to generate random inputs. Randomness is an important topic in general and is discussed in the next chapter.

Objects of the Game

comparison-based sorting algorithm An algorithm that makes ordering decisions only on the basis of comparisons. (225)

diminishing gap sort Another name for Shellsort. (228)

inversion A pair of elements in an array that are out of order. Used to measure unsortedness. (226)

lower-bound proof for sorting Confirms that any comparison-based sorting algorithm must use at least roughly $N \log N$ comparisons on the average and in the worst case. (250)

median-of-three partitioning The median of the first, middle, and last elements is used as the pivot. This simplifies the partitioning stage of quicksort. (241)

mergesort A method of sorting that uses divide-and-conquer to obtain an $O(N \log N)$ sort. (231)

partition The step of quicksort that places every element except the pivot in one of two groups, one consisting of elements that are smaller than the pivot and one consisting of elements that are larger than the pivot. (236)

pivot For quicksort, an element that splits the array into two groups, one that is smaller than the pivot and one that is larger than the pivot. (235)

quickselect An algorithm used to perform a selection that is similar to quicksort but makes only one recursive call. The average running time is linear. (248)

quicksort A fast divide-and-conquer algorithm when properly implemented. In practice, the fastest comparison-based sorting algorithm. (235)

selection The process of finding the kth smallest element of an array. (248)

Shellsort A subquadratic algorithm that works well in practice and is simple to code. The performance of Shellsort is highly dependent on the increment sequence and requires a challenging (and not completely resolved) analysis. (227)

Common Errors

1. The sorts coded in this chapter begin at array position 0, not position 1.
2. Using the wrong increment sequence for Shellsort is a common error. Make sure the increment sequence terminates with 1 and avoid sequences that are known to give poor performance.
3. Quicksort has a host of traps. The most common errors deal with sorted inputs, duplicate elements, and degenerate partitions.
4. For small inputs, an insertion sort is appropriate. But it is wrong to use it for large inputs.

On the Internet

All the sorting algorithms and an implementation of quickselect are in a single file as part of package `DataStructures`.

DuplicateTest.java	The method in Figure 8.1 with a test program, in directory **Chapter08**.
Sort.java	The sorting class in the **DataStructures** directory.
TestSort.java	A class in directory **Chapter08** that tests all the sorting methods.

Exercises

In Short

8.1. Sort the sequence 8, 1, 4, 1, 5, 9, 2, 6, 5 using the following:
  a. insertion sort
  b. shellsort, using the increments {1, 3, 5}
  c. mergesort
  d. quicksort, using the middle element as the pivot and no cutoff (show all steps)
  e. quicksort, using median-of-three pivot selection and a cutoff of three

8.2. A sorting algorithm is *stable* if elements with equal keys are left in the same order as they occur in the input. Which of the sorting algorithms in this chapter are stable and which are not? Why?

8.3. Explain why the elaborate quicksort in the text is typically better than randomly permuting the input and choosing the middle element as the pivot.

In Theory

8.4. When all keys are equal, what is the running time of the following:
  a. insertion sort
  b. shellsort
  c. mergesort
  d. quicksort

8.5. When the input is already sorted, what is the running time of the following:
  a. insertion sort
  b. shellsort
  c. mergesort
  d. quicksort

8.6. When the input is already sorted in reverse order, what is the running time of the following:
  a. insertion sort
  b. shellsort
  c. mergesort
  d. quicksort

8.7. Suppose we exchange elements `a[i]` and `a[i+k]`, which were originally out of order. Prove that at least 1 and at most $2k - 1$ inversions are removed.

8.8. Construct a worst-case input for quicksort with the following:
  a. the middle element as pivot
  b. median-of-three pivot partitioning

8.9. Show that the quickselect has linear average performance. Do this by solving Equation 8.5 with the constant 2 replaced by 1.

8.10. Using Stirling's formula, $N! \geq (N/e)^N \sqrt{2\pi N}$, derive an estimate for $\log(N!)$.

8.11. Prove that any comparison-based algorithm used to sort four elements requires at least five comparisons for some input. Then show that an algorithm that sorts four elements using at most five comparisons does indeed exist.

In Practice

8.12. A student alters the `quicksort` routine in Figure 8.19 by making the following changes to lines 26 to 31. Is the result equivalent to the original routine?

```
for( i = low + 1, j = high - 2; ; )
{
    while( a[ i ].lessThan( pivot ) )
        i++;
    while( pivot.lessThan( a[ j ] ) )
        j--;
```

8.13. If you know more information about the items being sorted, you can sort them in linear time. Show that a collection of N `short` integers can be sorted in $O(N)$ time. *Hint*: Maintain an array indexed from 0 to 65,535.

8.14. We are given an array that contains N numbers. We want to determine if there are two numbers whose sum equals a given number K. For instance, if the input is 8, 4, 1, 6, and K is 10, then the answer is yes (4 and 6). A number may be used twice. Do the following:
  a. Give an $O(N^2)$ algorithm to solve this problem.
  b. Give an $O(N \log N)$ algorithm to solve this problem. *Hint*: Sort the items first. After that is done, you can solve the problem in linear time.
  c. Code both solutions and compare the running times of your algorithms.

8.15. Repeat Exercise 8.14 for four numbers. Try to design an $O(N^2 \log N)$ algorithm. *Hint*: Compute all possible sums of two elements. Sort these possible sums. Then proceed as in Exercise 8.14.

8.16. Repeat Exercise 8.14 for three numbers. Try to design an $O(N^2)$ algorithm.

8.17. Exercise 5.25 asked you to find the single integral solution to the equation $A^5 + B^5 + C^5 + D^5 + E^5 = F^5$ satisfying $0 < A \le B \le C \le D \le E \le F \le N$, where N is 75. Use the ideas explored in Exercise 8.15 to obtain a solution relatively quickly by sorting all possible values of $A^5 + B^5 + C^5$ and $F^5 - (D^5 + E^5)$ and then seeing if a number in the first group is equal to a number in the second group. In terms of N, how much space and time does the algorithm require?

Programming Projects

8.18. Compare the performance of Shellsort with various increment sequences, as follows. Obtain an average time for some input size N by generating several random sequences of N items. Use the same input for all increment sequences. In a separate test, obtain the average number of `Comparable` comparisons and `Comparable` reference assignments. Set the number of repeated trials to be large but doable within 1 hour of CPU time. The increment sequences are the following:
   a. Shell's original sequence (repeatedly divide by 2)
   b. Shell's original sequence, adding 1 if the result is nonzero but even
   c. Gonnet's sequence shown in the text, in which we repeatedly divide by 2.2
   d. Hibbard's increments: 1, 3, 7, ... , $2^k - 1$
   e. Knuth's increments: 1, 4, 13, ... , $(3^k - 1)/2$
   f. Sedgewick's increments: 1, 5, 19, 41, 109, ... ; each term is of the form either $9 \cdot 4^k - 9 \cdot 2^k + 1$ or $4^k - 3 \cdot 2^k + 1$

8.19. Code both Shellsort and quicksort and compare their running times. Use the implementations in the text. Run on the following objects:
   a. integers
   b. real numbers of type `double`
   c. strings

8.20. Write a method that removes all duplicates in an array A of N items. Return the number of items that remain in A. Your method must run in $O(N \log N)$ average time (use quicksort as a preprocessing step).

8.21. Exercise 8.2 discussed stable sorting. Write a generic method that performs a stable quicksort. To do this, create an array of entries in which each entry contains a reference to a data item and its initial position in the array. The array of entries is sorted; if two entries have identical data items, use the initial position to break the tie. After the array of entries is sorted, rearrange the original array.

8.22. Write a simple sorting utility, `Sort`. The `Sort` command takes a file name as a parameter. The file contains one item per line. By default, the lines are considered strings and are sorted by normal lexicographic order (in a case-sensitive manner). Add two options. The `-c` option means that the sort should be case insensitive. The `-n` option means that the lines are to be considered integers for the purpose of the sort.

8.23. Suppose you have K files that are each sorted. Each line contains a `Line` object, where `Line` is an interface that implements the `Comparable` interface and a specifies a `getLine` method that reads the line into the object.
   a. Write a method `readFile` that reads the elements of a single file into a queue created by `readFile`. A reference to the queue is returned.

Notice that the elements in the queue will be sorted. The declaration is

```
Queue readFile( String fileName );
```

b. Write a method named `mergeTwo` that takes two queues and creates a third queue with the merged result. A reference to the newly created queue is returned, and the originals are made empty. The declaration is

```
Queue mergeTwo( Queue q1, Queue q2 );
```

c. The algorithm to produce a sorted file is as follows. Declare a queue of queues `theItems`. Call `readFile` for each of K files and insert the returned result onto `theItems`. Then $K - 1$ times, remove two elements from `theItems`, merge the two queues, and `enqueue` the result. The result is that `theItems` will contain only a single queue entry that has all the items in sorted order. Write the method.

d. Write a complete program to implement the merging of K sorted files.

e. Show that declaring `theItems` as a stack of queues can lead to poor performance. *Hint*: Consider the case in which the first file has N elements and all the others have one element each.

References

The classic reference for sorting algorithms is [5]. A more recent reference, complete with up-to-date results, is [3]. The Shellsort algorithm first appeared in [7]. An empirical study of its running time was done in [8]. Quicksort was discovered by Hoare [4]. The paper also includes the quickselect algorithm and details many of the important implementation issues. A thorough study of the quicksort algorithm, including analysis for the median-of-three variant, appears in [6]. A detailed C implementation that includes additional improvements can be found in [1]. The $\Omega(N \log N)$ lower bound for comparison-based sorting is taken from [2]. The presentation of Shellsort is adapted from [9].

1. J. L. Bentley and M. D. McElroy, "Engineering a Sort Function," *Software-Practice and Experience* **23** (1993), 1249–1265.

2. L. R. Ford and S. M. Johnson, "A Tournament Problem," *American Mathematics Monthly* **66** (1959), 387–389.

3. G. H. Gonnet and R. Baeza-Yates, *Handbook of Algorithms and Data Structures*, 2d ed., Addison-Wesley, Reading, Mass. (1991).

4. C. A. R. Hoare, "Quicksort," *Computer Journal* **5** (1962), 10–15.

5. D. E. Knuth, *The Art of Computer Programming, Volume 3: Sorting and Searching*, 2d ed., Addison-Wesley, Reading, Mass. (1997).

6. R. Sedgewick, *Quicksort*, Garland Publishing, New York, NY (1978). (Originally presented as the author's Ph.D. thesis, Stanford University, 1975.)

7. D. L. Shell, "A High-Speed Sorting Procedure," *Communications of the ACM* **2** 7 (1959), 30–32.

8. M. A. Weiss, "Empirical Results on the Running Time of Shellsort," *Computer Journal* **34** (1991), 88–91.

9. M. A. Weiss, *Efficient C Programming: A Practical Approach*, Prentice-Hall, Englewood Cliffs, NJ (1995).

9 *Randomization*

M ANY situations in computing require the use of random numbers. For example, modern cryptography, simulation systems, and, surprisingly, even searching and sorting algorithms rely on random-number genera- tors. Yet good random-number generators are difficult to implement. This chapter discusses the generation and use of random numbers.

In this chapter, we will see:

- How random numbers are generated
- How random permutations are generated
- How random numbers allow us to design efficient algorithms using a gen- eral technique known as the *randomized algorithm*

9.1   Why Do We Need Random Numbers?

Random numbers are used in many applications. This section discusses a few of the most common ones.

One important application of random numbers is in program testing. Sup- pose, for example, that we want to test if the sorting algorithms that were written in Chapter 8 work. Of course, we can provide some small amount of input, but if we want to test the algorithms for the large data sets they were designed for, we need lots of input. Providing sorted data as input tests one case, but more con- vincing tests would be preferable. For instance, we would want to test the pro- gram by perhaps running 5,000 sorts for inputs of size 1,000. This requires writing a routine to generate the test data, which in turn requires the use of ran- dom numbers.

Continuing this example, once we have random inputs, how do we know if the sorting algorithm works? One test of this is that the result of the sort is that the array is arranged in nondecreasing order. This can be done in a linear-time sequential scan. But how do we know that the items present after the sort are the same as those prior to the sort? One method is to fix the items into an arrange- ment of 1, 2, ..., N. In other words, we start with a random *permutation* of the first N integers. Recall from Chapter 8 that a permutation of 1, 2, ..., N is a sequence of N integers that includes each of 1, 2, ..., N exactly once. Then, no

Random numbers have many impor- tant uses including cryptography, simu- lation, and program testing.

A permutation of 1, 2, ..., N is a se- quence of N inte- gers that includes each of 1, 2, ..., N exactly once.

matter what permutation we start with, the result of the sort will be the sequence 1, 2, ..., N; this is easily tested as well.

In addition to helping us generate test data to verify program correctness, random numbers are useful in comparing the performance of various algorithms. This is because, once again, they can be used to provide a host of inputs.

Another use of random numbers is in simulations. If we want to know the average time it takes a service system (such as teller service in a bank) to process a sequence of requests, we can model the system by using a computer. In this computer simulation, the request sequence is generated using random numbers.

Still another use of random numbers is in the general technique called the *randomized algorithm*: A random number is used to determine the next step performed in the algorithm. The most common type of randomized algorithm involves selecting from among several possible alternatives that are more or less indistinguishable. For instance, in a commercial computer chess program, the computer generally chooses its first move randomly rather than playing deterministically (that is, rather than always playing the same move). This chapter looks at several problems that can be solved more efficiently by using a randomized algorithm.

9.2 Random-number Generators

Pseudorandom numbers have many properties of random numbers. Good random-number generators are hard to find.

How are random numbers generated? True randomness is impossible to achieve on a computer, since any numbers obtained will depend on the algorithm used to generate them and thus cannot possibly be random. Generally, it is sufficient to produce *pseudorandom numbers* — numbers that *appear* to be random; that is, the numbers should satisfy many of the properties that random numbers do. This is much easier said than done.

Suppose we need only to simulate a coin flip. One way to do this is to examine the system clock. Presumably, the system clock maintains the number of seconds in the current time. If this number is even, we can return 0 (for heads); if it is odd, we can return 1 (for tails). The problem is that this strategy does not work well if we need a sequence of random numbers. One second is a long time, and the clock might not change at all while the program is running. We would expect to generate all 0s or all 1s, which is hardly a random sequence. Even if the time was recorded in units of microseconds and the program was running by itself, the sequence of numbers that would be generated would be far from random because the time between calls to the generator would be essentially identical on every program invocation.

In a *uniform distribution*, all numbers in the specified range are equally likely to occur.

What we really need is a *sequence* of pseudorandom numbers, that is, a sequence with the same properties as a random sequence. Suppose we want random numbers between 0 and 999, uniformly distributed. In a *uniform distribution*, all numbers in the specified range are equally likely to occur. Other distributions are also widely used. The class skeleton in Figure 9.1 supports several distributions. Most distributions can be derived from the uniform distribution, so that is the one considered first. The following properties hold if the sequence 0 ... 999 is a true uniform distribution:

- The first number is equally likely to be 0, 1, 2, ..., 999.
- The *i*th number is equally likely to be 0, 1, 2, ..., 999.
- The average of all the generated numbers is 499.5.

```
1  // Random class
2  //
3  // CONSTRUCTION: with (a) no initializer or (b) an integer
4  //      that specifies the initial state of the generator
5  //
6  // ******************PUBLIC OPERATIONS*******************
7  //      Return a random number according to some distribution:
8  // int randomInt( )                    --> Uniform, 1 to 2^31-1
9  // double randomReal( )                --> Uniform, 0..1
10 // int randomInt( int low, int high ) --> Uniform low..high
11 // int poisson( double expectedVal )  --> Poisson
12 // double negExp( double expectedVal )--> Negative exponential
13 //      A related static method:
14 // void permute( Object [ ] a )        --> Randomly permute
15
16 /**
17  * Random number class, using a 31-bit
18  * linear congruential generator.
19  * Note that java.util contains a class Random,
20  * so watch out for name conflicts.
21  */
22 public class Random
23 {
24     public Random( )
25       { /* Figure 9.2 */ }
26     public Random( int initialState )
27       { /* Figure 9.2 */ }
28     public int randomInt( )
29       { /* Figure 9.3 */ }
30     public double randomReal( )
31       { return randomInt( ) / (double) M; }
32     public int randomInt( int low, int high )
33       { /* Exercise 9.8 */ }
34     public int poisson( double expectedValue )
35       { /* Figure 9.5 */ }
36     public double negExp( double expectedValue )
37       { /* Figure 9.6 */ }
38     public static final void permute( Object [ ] a )
39       { /* Figure 9.7 */}
40
41     private int state;
42 }
```

Figure 9.1   Skeleton for random-number generator class

Typically a random sequence, rather than one random number, is required.

These properties are not particularly restrictive. For instance, we could generate the first number by examining a system clock that was accurate to one millisecond and then using the number of milliseconds. We can generate subsequent numbers by adding one to the previous number. Clearly, after 1,000 numbers are generated, all the previous properties hold. However, stronger properties do not. Some stronger properties that would hold for uniformly distributed random numbers include the following:

- The sum of two consecutive random numbers is equally likely to be even or odd.
- If 1,000 numbers are randomly generated, some will be duplicated. (Roughly 368 numbers will never appear.)

Our numbers do not satisfy these properties. Consecutive numbers always sum to an odd number, and our sequence is duplicate-free. Hence, our simple pseudorandom-number generator has failed two statistical tests. All pseudorandom-number generators fail some statistical tests, but the better generators fail fewer tests than the bad ones do. Exercise 9.14 describes a common statistical test.

The *linear congruential generator* is a good algorithm to generate uniform distributions.

This section describes the simplest uniform generator that passes a reasonable number of statistical tests. By no means is it the best generator. However, it is suitable for use as a reasonable generator in applications in which a good approximation to a random sequence is acceptable. The method used is the linear congruential generator, which was first described in 1951. The *linear congruential generator* is a random-number generator in which numbers X_1, X_2, ... are generated, satisfying

$$X_{i+1} = AX_i(\bmod M). \tag{9.1}$$

This equation states that we can get the $(i + 1)$th number by multiplying the ith number by some constant A and computing the remainder when the result is divided by M. In Java, we would have

```
x[ i + 1 ] = A * x[ i ] % M;
```

The *seed* is the initial value of the random-number generator.

The constants A and M are specified shortly. Notice that all generated numbers will be smaller than M. Some value X_0 must be given to start the sequence. This value is the *seed*. If $X_0 = 0$, then the sequence is not random because it generates all zeros. But if A and M are carefully chosen, then any other seed satisfying $1 \leq X_0 < M$ is equally valid. Figure 9.2 constructs a Random object by initializing the state to the seed. If M is prime, then X_i is never 0. For example, if $M = 11$, $A = 7$, and the seed $X_0 = 1$, then the numbers generated are

7, 5, 2, 3, 10, 4, 6, 9, 8, 1, 7, 5, 2, ...

```
 1     /**
 2      * Construct this Random object with
 3      * initial state obtained from system clock.
 4      */
 5     public Random( )
 6     {
 7         this( (int) ( System.currentTimeMillis( )
 8                         % Integer.MAX_VALUE ) );
 9     }
10
11     /**
12      * Construct this Random object with
13      * specified initial state.
14      * @param initialState the initial state.
15      */
16     public Random( int initialState )
17     {
18         if( initialState < 0 )
19             initialState += M;
20
21         state = initialState;
22         if( state == 0 )
23             state = 1;
24     }
```

Figure 9.2   Constructors for class Random

Generating a number a second time results in a repeating sequence. In our case the sequence repeats after $M - 1 = 10$ numbers. The length of the sequence until a repeated number occurs is called the *period* of the sequence. The period obtained with this choice of A is clearly as good as possible, since all nonzero numbers smaller than M are generated. (We must have a repeated number generated on the 11th iteration.)

A random-number generator with *period* P generates the same sequence of numbers after P iterations.

If M is prime, several choices of A give a full period of $M - 1$. This type of generator is called a *full-period linear congruential generator*. Some choices of A do not give a full period. For instance, if $A = 5$ and $X_0 = 1$, the sequence has a short period of 5:

A *full-period linear congruential generator* has period $M - 1$.

5, 3, 4, 9, 1, 5, 3, 4, ...

If M is chosen to be a large, 31-bit prime, the period should be significantly large for most applications. The 31-bit prime $M = 2^{31} - 1 = 2,147,483,647$ is a common choice. For this prime, $A = 48,271$ is one of the many values that gives a full-period linear congruential generator. Its use has been well-studied and is recommended by experts in the field. As will be shown later in the chapter, tinkering with random number generators usually means breaking, so we are well advised to stick with this formula until told otherwise.

Because of over-
flow, we must rear-
range calculations.

This seems like a simple routine to implement. If `state` represents the last value computed by the `Random` routine, then it would appear that the new value of `state` should be given by

```
state = ( A * state ) % M;      // Incorrect
```

Unfortunately, if this computation is done on 32-bit integers, the multiplication is certain to overflow. Although Java provides a 64-bit `long`, using it is computationally expensive. If we stick with the 32-bit `int`, we could argue that the overflow is part of the randomness. However, overflow is unacceptable because we would no longer have the guarantee of a full period. It turns out that a slight reordering allows the computation to proceed without overflow. Specifically, if Q and R are the quotient and remainder of M/A, then we can rewrite Equation 9.1 as

$$X_{i+1} = A(X_i(\bmod Q)) - R\lfloor X_i/Q \rfloor + M\delta(X_i) \qquad (9.2)$$

and the following are true (see Exercise 9.5):

- The first term can always be evaluated without overflow.
- The second term can be evaluated without overflow if $R < Q$.
- $\delta(X_i)$ evaluates to 0 if the result of the subtraction of the first two terms is positive. It evaluates to 1 if the result of the subtraction is negative.

Stick with these
choice of A and M
unless you know
better.

For the values of M and A, we have $Q = 44,488$ and $R = 3,399$. Consequently, $R < Q$ and a direct application now gives an implementation of a random-number class. The resulting code is shown in Figure 9.3. The routine `randomInt` returns the value of the state.

```
1       private static final int A = 48271;
2       private static final int M = 2147483647;
3       private static final int Q = M / A;
4       private static final int R = M % A;
5
6       /**
7        * Return a pseudorandom int, and change the
8        * internal state.
9        * @return the pseudorandom int.
10       */
11      public int randomInt( )
12      {
13          int tmpState = A * ( state % Q ) - R * ( state / Q );
14          if( tmpState >= 0 )
15              state = tmpState;
16          else
17              state = tmpState + M;
18
19          return state;
20      }
```

Figure 9.3   Random-number generator

Two additional methods are provided in the skeleton in Figure 9.1: one to generate a random real number in the open interval from 0 to 1 and a second to generate a random integer in a specified closed interval (see Exercise 9.8).

Finally, the class provides a generator for the case in which nonuniform random numbers are required. Section 9.3 provides the body for the methods `poisson` and `negExp`.

One might be tempted to assume that all machines have a random number generator at least as good as the one in Figure 9.3. Sadly, this is not true. Many libraries have generators based on the function

$$X_{i+1} = (AX_i + C) \bmod 2^B,$$

where B is chosen to match the number of bits in the machine's integer and C is odd. These libraries, like the `randomInt` routine in Figure 9.3, also return the newly computed `state` directly, instead of (for example) a value between 0 and 1. Unfortunately, these generators always produce values of X_i that alternate between even and odd – obviously an undesirable property. Indeed, the lower k bits cycle with a period of 2^k (at best). Many other random-number generators have much smaller cycles than the one provided here. These are not suitable for any application that requires long sequences of random numbers. The Java library has a generator of this form. However, it uses a 48-bit linear congruential generator and returns only the high 32 bits, thus avoiding the cycling problem in the low-order bits. The constants are $A = 25,214,903,917$, $B = 48$, and $C = 13$.[1]

Finally, it may seem that we can get a better random-number generator by adding a constant to the equation. For instance, we might conclude that

$$X_{i+1} = (48271X_i + 1) \bmod (2^{31} - 1)$$

would somehow be more random. However when we use this equation, we see that

$$(48271 \cdot 179424105 + 1) \bmod (2^{31} - 1) = 179424105.$$

Hence, if the seed is 179,424,105, the generator gets stuck in a cycle of period 1. This illustrates how fragile these generators are.

9.3 Nonuniform Random Numbers

Not all applications require uniformly distributed random numbers. For example, grades in a large course are generally not uniformly distributed. Instead, they satisfy the classic bell curve distribution, more formally known as the *normal* or *Gaussian distribution*. A uniform random-number generator can be used to generate random numbers that satisfy other distributions.

The *Poisson distribution* models the number of occurrences of a rare event and is used in simulations.

[1.] This is the same generator as `drand48` seen on Unix systems.

Winning Tickets	0	1	2	3	4	5
Frequency	0.135	0.271	0.271	0.180	0.090	0.036

Figure 9.4 Distribution of lottery winners if expected number of winners is 2

An important nonuniform distribution that occurs in simulations is the *Poisson distribution*. Occurrences that happen under the following circumstances satisfy the Poisson distribution:

- The probability of one occurrence in a small region is proportional to the size of the region.
- The probability of two occurrences in a small region is proportional to the square of the size of the region and is usually small enough to be ignored.
- The event of getting k occurrences in one region and the event of getting j occurrences in another region disjoint from the first region are independent. (Technically, this statement means that you can get the probability of both events simultaneously occurring by multiplying the probability of individual events.)
- The mean number of occurrences in a region of some size is known.

Then if the mean number of occurrences is the constant a, the probability of exactly k occurrences is $a^k e^{-a}/k!$.

The Poisson distribution generally applies to events that have a low probability of a single occurrence. For example, consider the event of purchasing a winning lottery ticket in Florida, where the odds of winning the jackpot are 14 million to 1. Presumably, the picked numbers are more or less random and independent. If a person buys 100 tickets, the odds of winning become 140,000 to 1 (the odds improve by a factor of 100), so condition 1 holds. The odds of the person holding 2 winning tickets are negligible, so condition 2 holds. If some other person buys 10 tickets, their odds of winning are 1,400,000 to 1, and this is independent of the first person, so condition 3 holds. Suppose 28 million tickets are sold. The mean number of winning tickets in this situation is 2 (this is the number we need for condition 4). The actual number of winning tickets is a random variable with an expected value of 2, and this random variable satisfies the Poisson distribution. Thus the probability that exactly k winning tickets have been sold is $2^k e^{-2}/k!$. This gives the distribution shown in Figure 9.4. If the expected number of winners is the constant a, then the probability of k winning tickets is $a^k e^{-a}/k!$.

To generate a random integer according to a Poisson distribution that has an expected value of a, we can adopt the following strategy (whose mathematical justification is beyond the scope of this book). That is, we repeatedly generate uniformly distributed random numbers in the interval (0, 1) until their product is smaller than (or equal to) e^{-a}. This is done in Figure 9.5.

```
1       /**
2        * Return a double using a Poisson distribution, and
3        * change the internal state.
4        * @param expectedValue the mean of the distribution.
5        * @return the pseudorandom double.
6        */
7       public int poisson( double expectedValue )
8       {
9           double limit = Math.exp( -expectedValue );
10          double product = randomReal( );
11          int count;
12
13          for( count = 0; product > limit; count++ )
14              product *= randomReal( );
15
16          return count;
17      }
```

Figure 9.5   Generation of a random number according to the Poisson
distribution

Another important nonuniform distribution is the *negative exponential distribution*, shown in Figure 9.6. This distribution has the same mean and variance. The negative exponential distribution is used to model the time between occurrences of random events, as in a simulation application shown in Section 13.2.

Many other distributions are common. The main purpose here is to show that most can be generated from the uniform distribution. Consult any book on probability and statistics to find out more about these distributions.

> The *negative exponential distribution* has the same mean and variance. It is used to model the time between occurrences of random events.

```
1       /**
2        * Return an int using a negative exponential
3        * distribution, and change the internal state.
4        * @param expectedValue the mean of the distribution.
5        * @return the pseudorandom int.
6        */
7       public double negExp( double expectedValue )
8       {
9           return expectedValue * Math.log( randomReal( ) );
10      }
```

Figure 9.6   Generation of a random number according to the negative
exponential distribution

9.4 Generating a Random Permutation

Consider the problem of simulating a card game. The deck consists of 52 distinct cards. In the course of a deal, we must generate cards from the deck, without duplicates. In effect, we need to shuffle the cards and then iterate through the deck. We want the shuffle to be fair. That is, each of the 52! possible orderings of the deck should be equally likely as a result of the shuffle.

Random permutations can be generated in linear time using one random number per item.

This type of problem involves *random permutations*. A random permutation uses one distinct random number per item. In general, the problem is the following: Generate a random permutation of 1, 2, ..., *N*. All permutations should be equally likely. The randomness of the random permutation is, of course, limited by the randomness of the pseudorandom-number generator. Thus all permutations being equally likely is contingent on all random numbers' being uniformly distributed and independent. Random permutations can be generated in linear time.

A routine, `permute`, to generate a random permutation is shown in Figure 9.7. Here is how the `permute` routine works. We assume the items in the array are present in some unshuffled order. The loop performs a random shuffling. In each iteration of the loop, we switch a[j] with some array element in positions 0 to j (it is possible to perform no swap). A random permutation of 1, 2, ..., *N* is generated by passing an array containing these items to `permute`.

The correctness of `permute` is subtle.

It is clear that `permute` generates shuffled permutations. But are all permutations equally likely? The answer is both yes and no. The answer, based on the algorithm, is yes. There are *N*! possible permutations, and the number of different possible outcomes of the *N* − 1 calls to `randomInt` at line 11 is also *N*! This is because the first call produces either 0 or 1, so it has two outcomes. The second call produces either 0, 1, or 2, so it has three outcomes. The *i*th call has *N* outcomes. The total number of outcomes is the product of all these possibilities because each random number is independent of the previous one. All we have to show is that each sequence of random numbers corresponds to one and only one permutation. This can be established by working backward (see Exercise 9.6).

```
1    /**
2     * Randomly rearrange an array.
3     * The random numbers used depend on the time and day.
4     * @param a the array.
5     */
6    public static final void permute( Object [ ] a )
7    {
8        Random r = new Random( );
9
10       for( int j = 1; j < a.length; j++ )
11           Sort.swapReferences( a, j, r.randomInt( 0, j ) );
12   }
```

Figure 9.7   Permutation routine

However, the answer is actually no — all permutations are not equally likely — since there are only $2^{31} - 2$ initial states for the random-number generator, so there can be only $2^{31} - 2$ different permutations. This could be a problem in some situations. For instance, a program that generates 1,000,000 permutations (perhaps by splitting the work among many computers) to measure the performance of a sorting algorithm will, unfortunately, almost certainly generate some permutations twice. Better random-number generators are needed to make the practice meet the theory.

Notice, by the way, that rewriting the call to the swap method with the call to `r.randomInt(0,a.length-1)` does not work, even for three elements. There are 3! = 6 possible permutations, and the number of different sequences that could be computed by the three calls to `randomInt` is $3^3 = 27$. Since 6 does not divide 27 exactly, some permutations must be more likely than others.

9.5   Randomized Algorithms

Suppose you are a professor who is giving weekly programming assignments. You want to ensure the students are doing their own programs or, at the very least, that they understand the code they are submitting. One solution is to give a quiz on the day each program is due. However, these quizzes take time out of the available class time, so it might be practical to do this for only roughly half of the programs. Your problem is to decide when to give the quizzes.

Of course, if you announce the quizzes in advance, that could be interpreted as an implicit license to cheat for the 50 percent of the programs that will not get a quiz. You could adopt the unannounced strategy of giving quizzes on alternate programs, but students would quickly figure out that strategy. Another possibility is to give quizzes on what seem like the important programs, but this would likely lead to similar quiz patterns from semester to semester. Student grapevines being what they are, this strategy would probably be worthless after one semester.

One method that seems to eliminate these problems is to flip a coin. You make a quiz for every program (making quizzes is not nearly as time-consuming as grading them), and at the start of class, you flip a coin to decide whether the quiz is to be given. This way it is impossible to know before class whether the quiz will occur. Also, these patterns do not repeat from semester to semester. The students can expect a quiz to occur with 50 percent probability, regardless of previous quiz patterns. The disadvantage of this strategy is that you could end up giving no quizzes during an entire semester. Assuming a large number of programming assignments, however, this is not a likely occurrence unless the coin is suspect. Each semester, the expected number of quizzes is half the number of programs, and with high probability, the number of quizzes will not deviate much from this.

This example illustrates what is called a *randomized algorithm*. At least once during a randomized algorithm, a random number, rather than a deterministic

Randomized algorithms use random numbers to make decisions.

decision, is used to make a decision. The running time of the algorithm depends not only on the particular input but also on the random numbers that occur.

The worst-case running time of a randomized algorithm is almost always the same as the worst-case running time of the nonrandomized algorithm. The important difference is that a good randomized algorithm has no bad inputs but only bad random numbers (relative to the particular input). This may seem like only a philosophical difference, but actually it is quite important, as the following example shows.

The running time of a randomized algorithm depends on the random numbers that occur as well as the particular input.

Consider the following problem. Your boss asks you to write a program to determine the median of a group of 1,000,000 numbers. You are to submit the program and then run it on an input that the boss will choose. If the correct answer is given within a few seconds of computing time (which would be expected for a linear algorithm), your boss will be very happy and you will get a bonus. But if your program does not work or takes too much time, your boss will fire you for incompetence. Your boss already thinks you are overpaid and is hoping to be able to take the second option. What should you do?

The quickselect algorithm described in Section 8.7 might seem like the way to solve this problem. Although the algorithm (see Figure 8.20) is very fast on average, recall that it has quadratic worst-case time if the pivot is continually poor. By using median-of-three partitioning, we have guaranteed that this worst case will not occur for common inputs, such as those that are already sorted or that contain a host of duplicates. However, there is still a quadratic worst case, and as Exercise 8.8 showed, the boss will read your program, realize how you are choosing the pivot, and be able to construct the worst case. Consequently, you will be fired.

Randomized quickselect is statistically guaranteed to work in linear time.

By using random numbers, you can statistically guarantee the safety of your job. You begin the quickselect algorithm by randomly shuffling the input by using Figure 9.7.[2] As a result, your boss has essentially lost control of specifying the input sequence. When you run the quickselect algorithm, it will now be working on random input, so you expect it to take linear time. Can it still take quadratic time? The answer is yes. For any original input, it is possible that the shuffling gets you to the worst case for quickselect: thus the result would be a quadratic-time sort. If you are unfortunate enough to have this happen, you lose your job. However, this is a statistically impossible event: This is because for a million items, the chances of using even twice as much time as the average would indicate is so small, you can essentially ignore the possibility. The computer is much, much more likely to break. Your job is secure.

Instead of using a shuffling technique, we can achieve the same result by choosing the pivot randomly instead of deterministically. We take a random item in the array and swap it with the item in position `low`. We take another random item and swap it with the item in position `high`. We take a third random item and swap it with the item in the middle position. We then continue as usual. As

---

[2.] You do need to make sure that the random-number generator is sufficiently random and its output cannot be predicted by the boss.

before, degenerate partitions are always possible, but this now happens as a result of bad random numbers and not bad inputs.

Here are the differences between the randomized algorithms and nonrandomized algorithms. Thus far we have seen nonrandomized algorithms. When calculating their average running times, we assume that all inputs are equally likely. This assumption is not true, however, because nearly sorted input, for instance, occurs much more often than is statistically expected. This can cause problems for some algorithms, such as quicksort. By our using a randomized algorithm, the particular input is no longer important. The random numbers are important, and we get an *expected* running time, in which we average over all possible random numbers for any particular input. Using quickselect with random pivots (or a shuffle preprocessing step) gives an $O(N)$ expected time algorithm. This means that *for any input*, including already sorted input, the running time is expected to be $O(N)$, based on the statistics of random numbers. An expected time bound is somewhat stronger than an average-case time bound because the assumptions used to generate it are weaker (random numbers versus random input), but it is weaker than the corresponding worst-case time bound. On the other hand, in many instances, solutions that have good worst-case bounds frequently have extra overhead built in to assure that the worst case does not occur. The $O(N)$ worst-case algorithm for selection, for example, is a marvelous theoretical result, but it is not practical.

Randomized algorithms come in two basic flavors. The first, as already shown, always gives a correct answer, but it could take a long time, depending on the luck of the random numbers. The second is what we examine in the remainder of this chapter. Some randomized algorithms work in a fixed amount of time but randomly make mistakes (presumably with low probability). These mistakes are *false positives* or *false negatives*. This is a commonly accepted technique in medicine. False positives and false negatives for most tests are actually fairly common; some tests have surprisingly high error rates. Furthermore, for some tests, the errors depend on the individual and not random numbers, so repeating the test is certain to produce another false result. In randomized algorithms, we can rerun the test on the same input using different random numbers. If we run a randomized algorithm ten times and get ten positives, and if a single false positive is an unlikely occurrence (say 1 chance in 100), then the probability of ten consecutive false positives (1 chance in 100^{10} or one hundred billion billion) is essentially zero.

Some randomized algorithms work in a fixed amount of time, but they randomly make mistakes (presumably with low probability). These mistakes are false positives or false negatives.

9.6   Randomized Primality Testing

Recall that Section 7.4 described some numerical algorithms and showed how they could be used to implement the RSA algorithm encryption scheme. An important step in the RSA algorithm is to produce two prime numbers p and q. We can find a prime number by repeatedly trying successive odd numbers until we find one that is prime. Thus the issue boils down to testing if a given number is prime.

```
1      // Return true if odd integer n is prime
2
3      public static boolean isPrime( long n )
4      {
5          for( long i = 3; i * i <= n; i += 2 )
6              if( n % i == 0 )
7                  return false;      // Not prime
8
9          return true;              // Prime
10     }
```

Figure 9.8   Primality testing by trial division

The simplest algorithm for testing if an odd number N is prime is *trial division*. In this algorithm, an odd number greater than 3 is prime if it is not divisible by any other odd number smaller than or equal to $\sqrt{N}$. A direct implementation of this strategy is shown in Figure 9.8.

Trial division is a simple algorithm for primality testing. It is fast for small (32-bit) numbers but cannot be used for larger numbers.

Trial division is reasonably fast for small (32-bit) numbers, but it is unusable for even 64-bit `long`s because it could require the testing of roughly $\sqrt{N}/2$ divisors, thus using $O(\sqrt{N})$ time. What we want is a test whose running time is of the same order of magnitude as the `power` routine in Section 7.4.2. A well-known theorem, called *Fermat's Little Theorem*, looks very promising. (A proof of this theorem is provided in Theorem 9.1 for completeness, but it is not needed to understand the primality-testing algorithm.)

Theorem 9.1

(Fermat's Little Theorem): If P is prime and $0 < A < P$, then
$$A^{P-1} \equiv 1 \pmod{P}.$$

Proof

Consider any $1 \leq k < P$. $Ak \equiv 0 \pmod{P}$ is impossible, since P is prime and less than A and k. Now consider any $1 \leq i < j < P$. $Ai \equiv Aj \pmod{P}$ would imply $A(j-i) \equiv 0 \pmod{P}$. This is impossible by the previous argument because $1 \leq j - i < P$. Thus the sequence $A, 2A, \ldots, (P-1)A$, when considered $\pmod{P}$, is a permutation of $1, 2, \ldots, P-1$. The product of both sequences $\pmod{P}$ must be equivalent, thus yielding the equivalence $A^{P-1}(P-1)! \equiv (P-1)! \pmod{P}$ from which the theorem follows.

Fermat's Little Theorem is necessary but not sufficient to establish primality.

If the converse of Fermat's Little Theorem was true, then we would have a primality-testing algorithm that would be computationally equivalent to modular exponentiation (that is, $O(\log N)$). Unfortunately, the converse is not true. It is easily verified that $2^{340} \equiv 1 \pmod{341}$, but 341 is composite ($11 \cdot 31$).

To do the primality test, we need an additional theorem, Theorem 9.2.

If P is prime and $X^2 \equiv 1(\bmod P)$, then $X \equiv \pm 1(\bmod P)$.　　　　**Theorem 9.2**

Since $X^2 - 1 \equiv 0(\bmod P)$ implies $(X-1)(X+1) \equiv 0(\bmod P)$ and P is　　**Proof**
prime, $X-1$ or $X+1 \equiv 0(\bmod P)$.

A combination of Theorems 9.1 and 9.2 is useful. Let A be any integer between 2 and $N-2$. If we compute $A^{N-1}(\bmod N)$ and the result is not 1, then we know that N cannot be prime; otherwise, we would contradict Fermat's Little Theorem. We say then that A is a *witness* to N's compositeness, because A proves that N must be composite. Every composite number N has some witnesses A, but for some numbers, called the *Carmichael numbers*, these witnesses are hard to find. We need to make sure that we have a high probability of finding a witness no matter what the choice of N is. To improve our chances, we use Theorem 9.2.

In the course of computing A^i, we compute $(A^{\lfloor i/2 \rfloor})^2$. So we let $X = A^{\lfloor i/2 \rfloor}$ and $Y = X^2$. Notice that X and Y are computed automatically as part of the power routine. If Y is 1 and if X is not $\pm 1(\bmod N)$, then by Theorem 9.2, N cannot be prime. We can return 0 for the value of A^i when this is detected. N will appear to have failed the test of primality implied by Fermat's Little Theorem.

The routine witness, shown in Figure 9.9, computes $A^i(\bmod P)$, which has been augmented to return 0 if a violation of Theorem 9.2 is detected.[3] If witness does not return 1, then A is a witness to the fact that N cannot be prime. Lines 12 to 14 make a recursive call and produce X. We then compute X^2, as is normal for the power computation. We check if Theorem 9.2 is violated and return 0 if it is. Otherwise, we complete the power computation.

The only remaining issue is correctness. If our algorithm declares that N is composite, then N *must* be composite. If N is composite, then is it true that all $2 \le A \le N-2$ are witnesses? The answer, unfortunately, is no. This means that there exist some choices of A that will trick our algorithm into declaring that N is prime. In fact, if we choose A randomly, we have at most a $1/4$ chance of failing to detect a composite number and thus making an error. Note carefully that this is true for *any* N. If it were obtained only by averaging over all N, we would not have a good enough routine. In the analogy with medical tests, our algorithm generates false positives at most 25 percent of the time for any N.

If the algorithm declares a number not to be prime, it is not prime with 100 percent certainty. Each random attempt has at most a 25 percent false positive rate.

---

3. Note that this pseudocode does not work for large longs because of overflow possibilities. We must restrict the numbers tested to be 32 bits.

```
1       /**
2        * Method that implements the basic primality test.
3        * If witness doesn't return 1, n is definitely composite.
4        * Do this by computing a^i (mod n) and looking
5        * for non-trivial square roots of 1 along the way.
6        */
7       private static long witness( long a, long i, long n )
8       {
9           if( i == 0 )
10              return 1;
11
12          long x = witness( a, i / 2, n );
13          if( x == 0 )     // If n is recursively composite, stop
14              return 0;
15
16          // n not prime if find a nontrivial square root of 1
17          long y = ( x * x ) % n;
18          if( y == 1 && x != 1 && x != n - 1 )
19              return 0;
20
21          if( i % 2 != 0 )
22              y = ( a * y ) % n;
23          return y;
24      }
25
26      public static final int TRIALS = 5;
27
28      /**
29       * Randomized primality test.
30       * Adjust TRIALS to increase confidence level.
31       * @param n the number to test.
32       * @return if false, n is definitely not prime.
33       *     If true, n is probably prime.
34       */
35      public static boolean isPrime( long n )
36      {
37          Random r = new Random( );
38
39          for( int counter = 0; counter < TRIALS; counter++ )
40              if( witness( r.randomInt( 2, (int) n - 2 ),
41                                          n - 1, n ) != 1 )
42                  return false;
43
44          return true;
45      }
```

Figure 9.9   Randomized test for primality

This does not seem like very good odds, since a 25-percent error rate is considered very high. However, if we independently use 20 values of A, then the chances that none of these will witness a composite number is $1/4^{20}$, which is about one in a million million. Those odds are much more reasonable and can be made even better by using more trials. The routine `isPrime`, which is also shown in Figure 9.9, uses five trials.[4]

Some composites will pass the test and be declared prime. It is very unlikely that a composite will pass 20 independent random tests.

Summary

This chapter described how random numbers are generated and used. The linear congruential generator is a good choice for simple applications, as long as care is taken in choosing the parameters A and M. Using a uniform random-number generator, we can derive random numbers for other distributions, such as the Poisson and negative exponential distributions.

Random numbers have many uses. Some of these include the empirical study of algorithms, the simulation of real-life systems, and the design of algorithms that probabilistically avoid the worst case. Random numbers are used in other parts of the book, most notably in Section 13.2 and Exercise 20.18.

This chapter concludes Part II of the book. Part III looks at some simple applications, beginning with a discussion of games in Chapter 10 that illustrates three important problem-solving techniques.

Objects of the Game

false positives and false negatives Mistakes randomly made (presumably with low probability) by some randomized algorithms that work in a fixed amount of time. (271)

Fermat's Little Theorem States that if P is prime, and $0 < A < P$, then $A^{P-1} \equiv 1 \pmod P$. A necessary but not sufficient to establish primality. (272)

full-period linear congruential generator A linear congruential random-number generator that has period $M - 1$. (263)

linear congruential generator A good algorithm to generate uniform distributions. (262)

negative exponential distribution A form of distribution used to model the time between occurrences of random events. Its mean equals its variance. (267)

---

[4]. These bounds are typically pessimistic, and the analysis involves number theory that is much too involved for this book.

period A random-number generator with period P generates the same random sequence of random numbers after P iterations. (263)

permutation A permutation of 1, 2, …, N is a sequence of N integers that includes each of 1, 2, …, N exactly once. (259)

Poisson distribution A distribution that models the number of occurrences of a rare event. (265)

pseudorandom numbers Numbers that have many properties of random numbers. Good generators of pseudorandom numbers are hard to find. (260)

random permutation A random arrangement of N items. Can be generated in linear time using one random number per item. (268)

randomized algorithm An algorithm that uses random numbers rather than deterministic decisions to control branching. (269)

seed The initial state of the random-number generator. (262)

trial division A simple algorithm for primality testing. It is fast for small (32-bit) numbers but cannot be used for larger numbers. (272)

uniform distribution A distribution in which all numbers in the specified range are equally likely to occur. (260)

witness to compositeness A value of A that proves that a number is not prime using Fermat's Little Theorem. (273)

Common Errors

1. Using an initial seed of zero will give bad random numbers.

2. Inexperienced users occasionally reinitialize the seed prior to generating a random permutation. This guarantees that the same permutation will be repeatedly produced, which is probably not what is intended.

3. Many random numbers are notoriously bad. For serious applications in which long sequences of random numbers are required, the linear congruential generator is also unsatisfactory.

4. The low-order bits of linear congruential generators are known to be somewhat nonrandom, so avoid using them. As an example, `randomInt()%2` is a bad way to flip a coin.

5. When random numbers are being generated in some interval, a common error is to be slightly off at the boundaries and either allow some number outside of the interval to be generated or not allow the smallest number to be generated with fair probability.

6. Many random permutation generators do not generate all permutations with equal likelihood. As discussed in the text, our algorithm is limited by the random-number generator.

7. Tinkering with a random number generator is likely to weaken its statistical properties.

On the Internet

All code in this chapter is part of package `Supporting`, and is found in the directory **Supporting**. Here are the filenames:

Random.java   Contains the `Random` class.
Numerical.java   Contains the primality-testing routine in Figure 9.9
                      plus the math routines from Section 7.4.

Exercises

In Short

9.1. For the random-number generator described in the text, determine the first 10 values of `state`, assuming it is initialized with a value of 1.

9.2. Show the result of running the primality-testing algorithm for $N = 561$ with values of A ranging from 2 to 5.

9.3. If 42,000,000 Florida lottery tickets are sold, what is the expected number of winners? What are the odds that there will be no winners? Exactly 1 winner?

9.4. Why can't zero be used as a seed for the linear congruential generator?

In Theory

9.5. Prove that Equation 9.2 is equivalent to Equation 9.1 and that the resulting program in Figure 9.3 is correct.

9.6. Complete the proof that each permutation obtained in Figure 9.7 is equally likely.

9.7. Suppose you have a biased coin that comes up heads with probability p and tails with probability $1 - p$. Show how to design an algorithm that uses the coin to generate a 0 or a 1 with equal probability.

In Practice

9.8. Write the methods `randomReal` and `randomInt`. Then write a program that calls `randomInt` 1,000 times to generate numbers between 1 and 1,000. Does it pass the stronger statistical tests given in Section 9.2?

9.9. Run the Poisson generator shown in Figure 9.5 one million times using an expected value of 2. Does the distribution agree with Figure 9.4?

9.10. Consider a two-candidate election in which the winner has a fraction p of the vote. If the votes are counted sequentially, what is the probability that the winner is ahead (or tied) at every stage of the election? This is the so-called *ballot problem*. (The answer is p.) Write a program that verifies this. *Hint*: Simulate an election of 10,000 voters. Generate random arrays of $10000p$ ones and $10000(1-p)$ zeros. Then verify in a sequential scan that the difference between ones and zeros is never negative.

Programming Projects

9.11. An alternative permutation algorithm is to fill the array a from a[0] to a[n-1] as follows. To fill a[i], generate random numbers until you get one that has not been used previously. Use an array of Booleans to perform that test. Give an analysis of the expected running time (this is tricky). Then write a program that compares this running time with both your analysis and the routine shown in Figure 9.7.

9.12. Suppose you want to generate a random permutation of N distinct items drawn from the range 1, 2, ..., M. (The case $M = N$ has, of course, already been discussed.) Floyd's algorithm is the following: Recursively generate a permutation of $N-1$ distinct items drawn from the range $M-1$. Then generate a random integer in the range 1 to M. If the random integer is not already in the permutation add it; otherwise, add M. Do the following:
a. Prove that this algorithm does not add duplicates.
b. Prove that each permutation is equally likely.
c. Give a recursive implementation of the algorithm.
d. Give an iterative implementation of the algorithm.

9.13. A *random walk* in two dimensions is the following game played on the x, y coordinate system. Starting at the origin (that is, (0, 0)), each iteration consists of a random step either 1 unit left, up, right, or down. The walk terminates when the walker returns to the origin. (It can be shown that this happens with probability 1 in two dimensions but with probability less than 1 in three dimensions.) Write a program that performs 100 independent random walks and computes the average number of steps taken in each direction.

9.14. A simple and effective statistical test is the *chi-square test*. Suppose you generate N positive numbers that can assume one of M values (for instance, generate numbers between 1 and M, inclusive). The number of occurrences of each number is a random variable with mean $\mu = N/M$. For the test to work, you should have $\mu > 10$. Let f_i be the number of times i is generated. Then compute the chi-square value $V = \Sigma(f_i - \mu)^2/u$. The result should be close to M. If the result is consistently more than $2\sqrt{M}$ away from M (that is, more than once in ten tries), then the generator has failed the test. Implement the chi-square test and run it on your implementation of the randomInt method (with low=1 and high=100).

References

A good discussion of elementary random-number generators is provided in [3]. The permutation algorithm is due to R. Floyd and can be found in [1]. The randomized primality-testing algorithm is taken from [2] and [4]. More information on random numbers can be found in any good book on statistics or probability.

1. J. Bentley, "Programming Pearls," *Communications of the ACM* **30** (1987), 754–757.

2. G. L. Miller, "Riemann's Hypothesis and Tests for Primality," *Journal of Computer and System Science* **13** (1976), 300–317.

3. S. K. Park and K. W. Miller, "Random Number Generators: Good Ones Are Hard to Find," *Communications of the ACM* **31** (1988) 1192–1201. (See also *Technical Correspondence* in **36** (1993) 105–110.)

4. M. O. Rabin, "Probabilistic Algorithms for Testing Primality," *Journal of Number Theory* **12** (1980), 128–138.

Part III
Applications

CHAPTER

10 *Fun and Games*

T HIS chapter introduces three important algorithmic techniques by showing
their use in the implementation of programs to solve recreational problems.
The first problem is a *word search puzzle* and involves finding words in a
two-dimensional grid of characters. The second is optimal play in the game of tic-
tac-toe.

In this chapter, we will see:

- How to use the binary search algorithm, modified from Figure 5.12, to
  incorporate information from unsuccessful searches and to solve large
  instances of a word search problem in under 1 sec
- How to use the *alpha-beta pruning* algorithm to speed up the recursive
  algorithm in Section 7.7
- How to use hash tables to increase the speed of the tic-tac-toe algorithm

10.1 Word Search Puzzles

The input to the *word search puzzle* problem is a two-dimensional array of characters and a list of words. The object is to find the words in the grid. These words
may be horizontal, vertical, or diagonal in any direction (for a total of eight directions). As an example, the grid shown in Figure 10.1 contains the words this,
two, fat, and that. The word this begins at row 0, column 0 — the point (0,
0) — and extends to (0, 3); two goes from (0, 0) to (2, 0); fat goes from (3, 0) to
(1, 2); and that goes from (3, 3) to (0, 0).

*The word search
puzzle requires
searching for words
in a two-dimen-
sional grid of letters.
Words may be ori-
ented in one of
eight directions.*

10.1.1 Theory

There are several naive algorithms we can use to solve the word search puzzle
problem. The most direct is the following brute force approach:

*The brute force al-
gorithm searches
each word in the
word list.*

	0	1	2	3
0	t	h	i	s
1	w	a	t	s
2	o	a	h	g
3	f	g	d	t

Figure 10.1 Sample word search grid

```
for each word W in the word list
    for each row R
        for each column C
            for each direction D
                check if W exists at row R, column C
                in direction D
```

An alternative algorithm searches from each point in the grid in each direction for each word length and looks to see if the word is in the word list.

Since there are eight directions, this algorithm requires $8WRC$ checks. For the typical puzzles published in magazines, there are 40 or so words and a 16-by-16 grid. This is roughly 80,000 checks, and they are certainly easy to compute on any modern machine. Suppose, however, we consider the variation in which only the puzzle board is given and the word list is essentially an English dictionary. In this case, the number of words might be 40,000 instead of 40, thus resulting in 80 million checks. If the grid is doubled, we would then have 320 million checks, and this is no longer a trivial calculation. We want an algorithm that can solve a puzzle of this size in roughly 1 sec. To do this, we consider an alternative algorithm:

```
for each row R
    for each column C
        for each direction D
            for each word length L
                check if L chars starting at row R column C
                        in direction D form a word
```

The lookups can be done by a binary search.

This algorithm rearranges the loop to avoid searching for every word in the word list. Assume that words are limited to 20 characters. In this case, the number of checks used by the algorithm is $160RC$. For a 32-by-32 puzzle, this is roughly 160,000 checks. The problem, of course, is that we must now decide if a word is in the word list. If we use a linear search, we lose. If we use a good data structure, we can expect an efficient search. If the word list is sorted, which is to be expected for an online dictionary, then we can use a binary search (shown in Figure 5.12) and perform each check in roughly $\log W$ string comparisons. For 40,000 words, this is perhaps 16 comparisons per check, for a total of under 3 million string comparisons. This can certainly be done in a few seconds and is a factor of 100 better than the previous algorithm.

```
1     /**
2      * Performs the binary search for word search puzzle
3      * using one comparison per level.
4      * Return last position examined; this position either
5      * matches x, or x is a prefix of the mismatch, or there
6      * is no word for which x is a prefix.
7      */
8     private static int prefixSearch( String [ ] a,
9                                      String x, int n )
10    {
11        int low = 0;
12        int high = n - 1;
13
14        while( low < high )
15        {
16            int mid = ( low + high ) / 2;
17            if( a[ mid ].compareTo( x ) < 0 )
18                low = mid + 1;
19            else
20                high = mid;
21        }
22
23        return low;
24    }
```

Figure 10.2   Binary search modified to return ending point of search

This algorithm can be further improved. Suppose we are searching in some direction and notice the character sequence qx. An English dictionary will not contain any words beginning with qx. So is it worth continuing the innermost loop (over all word lengths)? The answer is obviously no. If we detect a character sequence that is not a prefix of any word in the dictionary, we can immediately look in another direction. This algorithm is given by the following pseudocode:

If a character sequence is not a prefix of any word in the dictionary, we can terminate searching in that direction.

```
for each row R
    for each column C
        for each direction D
            for each word length L
                check if L chars starting at row R column
                        C in direction D form a word
                if they do not form a prefix,
                    break;   // the innermost loop
```

The only remaining algorithmic detail to handle is the implementation of the prefix test. That is, assuming that the current character sequence is not in the word list, how can we decide if it is a prefix of some word in the word list? The answer turns out to be simple. The binary search algorithm in Figure 5.12 narrows down the search range to one item and then checks to see if a match is found. Suppose that instead of doing the test that verifies the match, we merely

Prefix testing can also be done by binary search.

return the narrowed-down position and let the caller use that information. Then, of course, it is easy for the caller of the binary search to check if a match is found. If a match is not found, then it is also easy to verify if the character sequence is a prefix of some word in the list, because if it is, it must be a prefix of the word in the returned position (Exercise 10.3 asks you to prove this). Thus we write the `prefixSearch` algorithm as shown in Figure 10.2 (page 285).

```
 1  // Puzzle class: solve word search puzzle
 2  //
 3  // CONSTRUCTION: with no initialzier
 4  // ******************PUBLIC OPERATIONS******************
 5  // int solvePuzzle( )    --> Print all words found in the
 6  //                           puzzle; return number of matches
 7
 8  public class WordSrch
 9  {
10      private static final int MAX_ROWS    =      64;
11      private static final int MAX_COLUMNS =      64;
12      private static final int MAX_WORDS   = 100000;
13
14      public wordSrch( )
15        { /* Figure 10.4 */ }
16      public int solvePuzzle( )
17        { /* Figure 10.8 */ }
18
19      private int rows;
20      private int columns;
21      private int numEntries;
22      private String [ ] theWords = new String[ MAX_WORDS ];
23      private BufferedReader puzzleStream;
24      private BufferedReader wordStream;
25      private char theBoard[ ][ ] =
26                      new char[ MAX_ROWS ][ MAX_COLUMNS ];
27      private BufferedReader in = new
28          BufferedReader( new InputStreamReader( System.in ) );
29
30      private static int prefixSearch( String [ ] a,
31                                       String x, int n )
32        { /* Figure 10.2 */ }
33      private BufferedReader openFile( String message )
34        { /* Figure 10.5 */ }
35      private void readWords( )
36        { /* Figure 10.6 */ }
37      private void readPuzzle( )
38        { /* Figure 10.7 */ }
39      private int solveDirection( int baseRow, int baseCol,
40                                  int rowDelta, int colDelta )
41        { /* Figure 10.9 */ }
42  }
```

Figure 10.3   `WordSrch` class skeleton

```
1      /**
2       * Constructor for WordSrch class.
3       * Prompts for and reads puzzle and dictionary files.
4       */
5      public WordSrch( )
6      {
7          puzzleStream = openFile( "Enter puzzle file" );
8          wordStream  = openFile( "Enter dictionary name" );
9          readPuzzle( );
10         readWords( );
11     }
```

Figure 10.4   WordSrch constructor

```
1      /**
2       * Print a prompt and open a file.
3       * Retry until open is successful.
4       * Program exits if end of file is hit.
5       */
6      private BufferedReader openFile( String message )
7      {
8          String fileName = "";
9          FileReader theFile;
10         BufferedReader fileIn = null;
11
12         do
13         {
14             System.out.println( message + ": " );
15
16             try
17             {
18                 fileName = in.readLine( );
19                 if( fileName == null )
20                     System.exit( 0 );
21                 theFile = new FileReader( fileName );
22                 fileIn  = new BufferedReader( theFile );
23             }
24             catch( IOException e )
25                 { System.err.println( "Bad file " + fileName ); }
26         } while( fileIn == null );
27
28         System.out.println( "Opened " + fileName );
29         return fileIn;
30     }
```

Figure 10.5   openFile routine to open both the grid and word list file

10.1.2 Java Implementation

Our implementation follows the algorithm description.

Our Java implementation follows the algorithm description almost verbatim. We design a class named `WordSrch` to store the grid and word list as well as the corresponding input streams. The class skeleton is shown in Figure 10.3 (page 286). For simplicity, we assume a limit of 64 rows and columns and a maximum dictionary size of 100,000 words. We leave the problem of removing these restrictions as Exercise 10.6. The public part of the class consists of a constructor and a single method `solvePuzzle`. The private section includes the data fields and supporting routines.

```
1      /**
2       * Routine to read the dictionary.
3       * Error message is printed if dictionary is not sorted.
4       * Check is made to avoid exceeding MAX_WORDS.
5       */
6      private void readWords( )
7      {
8          numEntries = 0;
9
10         try
11         {
12             while( ( theWords[ numEntries ] =
13                         wordStream.readLine( ) ) != null )
14             {
15                 if( numEntries != 0 && theWords[ numEntries ].
16                   compareTo( theWords[ numEntries - 1 ] ) < 0 )
17                 {
18                     System.err.println( "Dictionary is not " +
19                                         "sorted - skipping" );
20                     continue;
21                 }
22                 else if( ++numEntries >= MAX_WORDS )
23                     break;
24             }
25
26             if( wordStream.ready( ) )
27                 System.err.println( "Warning: unread data " +
28                                     "- increase MAX_WORDS" );
29         }
30         catch( IOException e ) { }
31     }
```

Figure 10.6 `readWords` routine to read the word list

Figure 10.4 (page 287) gives the code for the constructor. It merely opens and reads the two files corresponding to the grid and the word list. The supporting routine, openFile, shown in Figure 10.5 (page 287), repeatedly prompts for a file until an open is successful. The readWords routine, shown in Figure 10.6, reads the word list. Most of the code is concerned with error checks: We do not want to read more than the limit MAX_WORDS, and we make sure that the word list is sorted. Similarly, readPuzzle, shown in Figure 10.7, reads the grid and is also concerned with error handling. We need to make sure that we can handle missing puzzles, and we want to warn the user if the grid is not rectangular. In the interest of brevity, a few error checks have been omitted that really should have been performed. Exercise 10.1 asks you to figure out what is missing.

The constructor opens and reads the data files. For brevity, we skimp on error checks.

```
1      /**
2       * Routine to read the grid.
3       * Checks to ensure that the grid is rectangular.
4       * Check that capacity is not exceeded is omitted.
5       */
6      private void readPuzzle( )
7      {
8          String oneLine;
9
10         try
11         {
12             oneLine = puzzleStream.readLine( );
13             if( oneLine == null )
14             {
15                 rows = 0;
16                 return;
17             }
18             columns = oneLine.length( );
19             for( int i = 0; i < columns; i++ )
20                 theBoard[ 0 ][ i ] = oneLine.charAt( i );
21
22             for( rows = 1;
23                    ( oneLine = puzzleStream.readLine( ) ) != null;
24                            rows++ )
25             {
26                 if( oneLine.length( ) != columns )
27                     System.err.println( "Bad puzzle" );
28
29                 for( int i = 0; i < columns; i++ )
30                     theBoard[ rows ][ i ] = oneLine.charAt( i );
31             }
32         }
33         catch( IOException e ) { }
34     }
```

Figure 10.7   readPuzzle routine to read the grid

We use two loops to iterate over the eight directions.

solvePuzzle, shown in Figure 10.8, nests the row, column, and direction loops and then calls the private routine solveDirection for each possibility. The return value is the number of matches found. A direction is given by indicating a column direction and then a row direction. For instance, south is indicated by cd=0 and rd=1 and northeast by cd=1 and rd=-1. cd can range from -1 to 1 and rd from -1 to 1, except that both cannot be 0 simultaneously. All that remains is solveDirection, and that is coded in Figure 10.9.

solveDirection constructs a string by starting at the base row and column and extending in the appropriate direction.

We also assume that 1-letter matches are not allowed (because any 1-letter match would be reported eight times). At lines 15 and 16, we iterate and extend the string while checking that we do not go past the boundary of the grid. At line 18, we tack on the next character and perform a binary search at lines 19 and 20. If we do not have a prefix, then clearly we can stop looking and return. Otherwise, we know that we will continue after checking at line 26 for a possible exact match. Line 34 returns the number of matches found when it is clear that the call to solveDirection can find no more words. A simple main program is shown in Figure 10.10.

```
1      /**
2       * Routine to solve the word search puzzle.
3       * Performs checks in all eight directions.
4       * @return number of matches
5       */
6      public int solvePuzzle( )
7      {
8          int matches = 0;
9
10         for( int r = 0; r < rows; r++ )
11             for( int c = 0; c < columns; c++ )
12                 for( int rd = -1; rd <= 1; rd++ )
13                     for( int cd = -1; cd <= 1; cd++ )
14                         if( rd != 0 || cd != 0 )
15                             matches += solveDirection( r,
16                                                 c, rd, cd );
17
18         return matches;
19     }
```

Figure 10.8   solvePuzzle routine to search in all directions from all starting points

```
1     /**
2      * Search the grid from a starting point and direction.
3      * @return number of matches
4      */
5     private int solveDirection( int baseRow, int baseCol,
6                                 int rowDelta, int colDelta )
7     {
8         String charSequence = "";
9         int numMatches = 0;
10        int searchResult;
11
12        charSequence += theBoard[ baseRow ][ baseCol ];
13
14        for( int i = baseRow + rowDelta,  j = baseCol + colDelta;
15                 i >= 0 && j >= 0 && i < rows && j < columns;
16                 i += rowDelta, j += colDelta )
17        {
18            charSequence += theBoard[ i ][ j ];
19            searchResult = prefixSearch( theWords,
20                                    charSequence, numEntries );
21
22            if( !theWords[ searchResult ].
23                                startsWith( charSequence ) )
24                break;
25
26            if( theWords[ searchResult ].equals( charSequence ) )
27            {
28                numMatches++;
29                System.out.println( "Found " + charSequence +
30                        " at " + baseRow + " " + baseCol +
31                        " to " + i + " " + j );
32            }
33        }
34        return numMatches;
35    }
```

Figure 10.9   Implementation of a single search

```
1     // Cheap main
2     public static void main( String [ ] args )
3     {
4         WordSrch p = new WordSrch( );
5         System.out.println( "Solving..." );
6         p.solvePuzzle( );
7     }
```

Figure 10.10   Simple `main` routine for the word search puzzle problem

10.2 The Game of Tic-Tac-Toe

The minimax strategy examines lots of positions. We can get by with less without losing any information.

Recall from Section 7.7 a simple algorithm that allows the computer to select an optimal move in a game of tic-tac-toe. This recursive strategy known as the *minimax strategy* is as follows:

1. If the position is *terminal* (that is, can immediately be evaluated), return its value.

2. Otherwise, if it is the computer's turn to move, return the maximum value of all positions reachable by making one move. The reachable values are calculated recursively.

3. Otherwise, it is the human's turn to move. Return the minimum value of all positions reachable by making one move. The reachable values are calculated recursively.

10.2.1 Alpha-beta Pruning

A refutation is a countermove that proves that a proposed move is not an improvement over moves previously considered. If we find a refutation, we do not have to examine any more moves and the recursive call can return.

Although the minimax strategy gives an optimal tic-tac-toe move, it performs a lot of searching. Specifically, to choose the first move, it makes roughly a half million recursive calls. One reason for this is that the algorithm does more searching than is necessary. Suppose that the computer is considering five moves: C_1, C_2, C_3, C_4, and C_5. Suppose that the recursive evaluation of C_1 reveals that C_1 forces a draw. Now C_2 is evaluated. At this stage, we have a position from which it would be the human's turn to move. Suppose that in response to C_2, the human can consider H_{2a}, H_{2b}, H_{2c}, and H_{2d}. Further, suppose that an evaluation of H_{2a} shows a forced draw. Automatically, C_2 is at best a draw and possibly even a loss for the computer (because the human is assumed to play optimally). Because we need to improve on C_1, we do not have to evaluate any of H_{2b}, H_{2c}, and H_{2d}. We say that H_{2a} is a *refutation*, meaning that it proves that C_2 is not a better move than what has already been seen. Thus we return that C_2 is a draw and keep C_1 as the best move seen so far. This is shown in Figure 10.11.

Alpha-beta pruning is used to reduce the number of positions that are evaluated in a minimax search. Alpha is the value that the human has to refute and beta is the value that the computer has to refute.

We do not need to evaluate each node completely; for some nodes, a refutation suffices. This means that some loops can terminate early. Specifically, when the human evaluates a position, such as C_2, a refutation, if found, is just as good as the absolute best move. The same logic applies to the computer. At any point in the search, `alpha` is the value that the human has to refute, and `beta` is the value that the computer has to refute. When a search is done on the human side, any move less than `alpha` is equivalent to `alpha`; when a search is done on the computer side, any move greater than `beta` is equivalent to `beta`. This strategy is commonly called *alpha-beta pruning*.

As Figure 10.12 shows (page 294), alpha-beta pruning requires only a few changes to `chooseMove`. Both `alpha` and `beta` are passed as additional parameters. Initially, `chooseMove` is started with `alpha` and `beta` representing HUMAN_WIN and COMPUTER_WIN, respectively. Lines 16 and 20 reflect a change in the initialization of `value`. The move evaluation is only slightly more complex than the original in Figure 7.27. The recursive call at line 29 includes the parameters `alpha` and `beta`, which are adjusted at line 36 or 38 if needed. The only other change is at line 42, which provides for an immediate return when a refutation is found.

To take full advantage of alpha-beta pruning, game programs usually try to apply heuristics to place the best moves early in the search. This results in even more pruning than one would expect from a random search of positions. In practice, alpha-beta pruning limits the searching to only $O(\sqrt{N})$ nodes, where N is the number of nodes that would be examined without alpha-beta pruning. This results in a huge savings. The tic-tac-toe example is not ideal because there are so many identical values. Even so, the initial search is reduced to roughly 18,000 positions.

Alpha-beta pruning works best when it finds refutations early.

10.2.2 Transposition Tables

Another commonly employed practice is to use a table to keep track of all positions that have been evaluated. For instance, in the course of searching for the first move, the program will examine the positions shown in Figure 10.13. If the values of the positions are saved, the second occurrence of a position need not be recomputed; it essentially becomes a terminal position. The data structure that records this is called a *transposition table*; it is implemented as a simple hash table. In many cases, doing this can save considerable computation.

A transposition table stores previously evaluated positions.

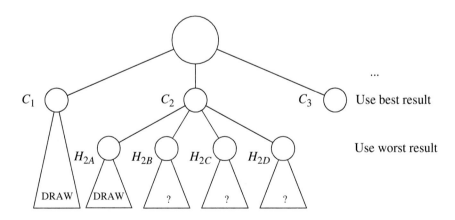

Figure 10.11 Alpha-beta pruning: After H_{2A} is evaluated, C_2, which is the minimum of the H_2's, is at best a draw. Consequently, it cannot be an improvement over C_1. We therefore do not need to evaluate H_{2B}, H_{2C}, and H_{2D} and can proceed directly to C_3

```
1              // Find optimal move
2      private Best chooseMove( int side, int alpha, int beta )
3      {
4          int opp;          // The other side
5          Best reply;       // Opponent's best reply
6          int simpleEval;   // Result of an immediate evaluation
7          int bestRow = 0;
8          int bestColumn = 0;
9          int value;
10
11         if( ( simpleEval = positionValue( ) ) != UNCLEAR )
12             return new Best( simpleEval );
13
14         if( side == COMPUTER )
15         {
16             opp = HUMAN; value = alpha;
17         }
18         else
19         {
20             opp = COMPUTER; value = beta;
21         }
22
23     Outer:
24         for( int row = 0; row < 3; row++ )
25             for( int column = 0; column < 3; column++ )
26                 if( squareIsEmpty( row, column ) )
27                 {
28                     place( row, column, side );
29                     reply = chooseMove( opp, alpha, beta );
30                     place( row, column, EMPTY );
31                     if( side == COMPUTER && reply.val > value
32                         || side == HUMAN && reply.val < value )
33                     {
34                             // Better move found
35                         if( side == COMPUTER )
36                             alpha = value = reply.val;
37                         else
38                             beta = value = reply.val;
39
40                         bestRow = row;
41                         bestColumn = column;
42                         if( alpha >= beta )
43                             break Outer;  // Refutation
44                     }
45                 }
46
47         return new Best( value, bestRow, bestColumn );
48     }
```

Figure 10.12 chooseMove routine to compute optimal tic-tac-toe move using alpha-beta pruning

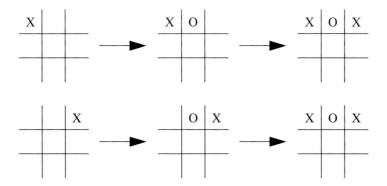

Figure 10.13 Two searches that arrive at identical positions

To implement the transposition table, we first define a `Position` class, shown in Figure 10.14 (page 296), that is used to store each position and its computed value. This class implements the `Hashable` interface. We also provide a constructor that can be initialized with a (two-dimensional) board array.

A hash table is used to implement the transposition table.

The changes that are needed in the `TicTacToe` class are minor and are shown in Figure 10.15 (page 296). The additions are the new data field at line 3 and the new declaration for the internal `chooseMove`. We now pass `alpha` and `beta` (as was done for alpha-beta pruning) and also the `depth` of the recursion, which is zero to start. The initial call to `chooseMove` is shown at line 7.

ChooseMove has three additional parameters: the values of alpha and beta and the current search depth.

We maintain the depth because including all positions in the transposition table is not worthwhile. The overhead of maintaining the table suggests that positions near the bottom of the recursion ought not to be saved, for these reasons:

We do not store in the transposition table the positions that are at the bottom of the recursion.

- There are so many positions.
- The point of alpha-beta pruning and transposition tables is to reduce search times by avoiding recursive calls early in the game: Saving a recursive call very deep in the search does not greatly reduce the number of positions that are examined because that recursive call would examine only a few positions anyway.

Figures 10.16 (page 297) and 10.17 (page 298) show the new `chooseMove`. At line 8, we declare a `Position` object named `thisPosition`. When the time comes this object will be placed in the transposition table. `tableDepth` tells us how deep in the search we will allow positions to be placed in the transposition table. By experimenting, we find that 5 is optimal. Allowing positions at `depth` 6 to be saved hurts because the extra cost of maintaining the larger transposition table is not compensated for by the fewer examined positions.

```
 1  final class Position implements Hashable
 2  {
 3      int [ ][ ] board;
 4      int value;
 5
 6      Position( int theBoard[ ][ ] )
 7      {
 8          board = new int[ 3 ][ 3 ];
 9          for( int i = 0; i < 3; i++ )
10              for( int j = 0; j < 3; j++ )
11                  board[ i ][ j ] = theBoard[ i ][ j ];
12      }
13
14      public boolean equals( Object rhs )
15      {
16          for( int i = 0; i < 3; i++ )
17              for( int j = 0; j < 3; j++ )
18                  if( board[ i ][ j ] !=
19                          ((Position)rhs).board[ i ][ j ] )
20                      return false;
21          return true;
22      }
23
24      public int hash( int tableSize )
25      {
26          int hashVal = 0;
27
28          for( int i = 0; i < 3; i++ )
29              for( int j = 0; j < 3; j++ )
30                  hashVal = hashVal * 4 + board[ i ][ j ];
31
32          return hashVal % tableSize;
33      }
34  }
```

Figure 10.14 Position class

```
 1  class TicTacToe
 2  {
 3      private HashTable transpositions =
 4                              new QuadraticProbingTable( );
 5      Best chooseMove( int side )
 6      {
 7          return chooseMove( side, HUMAN_WIN, COMPUTER_WIN, 0 )
 8      }
 9      ...
10  }
```

Figure 10.15 Changes to the TicTacToe class to incorporate the transposition table and alpha-beta pruning

```
1             // Find optimal move
2         private Best chooseMove( int side, int alpha, int beta,
3                                     int depth )
4         {
5             int opp;            // The other side
6             Best reply;         // Opponent's best reply
7             int simpleEval;     // Result of an immediate evaluation
8             Position thisPosition = new Position( board );
9             int tableDepth = 5;// Max depth placed in Trans. table
10            int bestRow = 0;
11            int bestColumn = 0;
12            int value;
13
14            if( ( simpleEval = positionValue( ) ) != UNCLEAR )
15                return new Best( simpleEval );
16
17            if( depth == 0 )
18                transpositions.makeEmpty( );
19            else if( depth >= 3 && depth <= tableDepth )
20            {
21                try
22                {
23                    Position lookupVal = (Position)
24                            transpositions.find( thisPosition );
25                    return new Best( lookupVal.value );
26                }
27                catch( ItemNotFound e ) { } /* Evaluate below */
28            }
29
30            if( side == COMPUTER )
31            {
32                opp = HUMAN; value = alpha;
33            }
34            else
35            {
36                opp = COMPUTER; value = beta;
37            }
38
39    Outer:
40            for( int row = 0; row < 3; row++ )
41                for( int column = 0; column < 3; column++ )
42                    if( squareIsEmpty( row, column ) )
43                    {
44                        place( row, column, side );
45                        reply = chooseMove( opp, alpha, beta,
46                                                    depth + 1 );
47                        place( row, column, EMPTY );
```

Figure 10.16 Tic-tac-toe algorithm with alpha-beta pruning and a transposition table (part 1)

```
48                        if( side == COMPUTER && reply.val > value
49                            || side == HUMAN && reply.val < value )
50                        {
51                            if( side == COMPUTER )
52                                alpha = value = reply.val;
53                            else
54                                beta = value = reply.val;
55
56                            bestRow = row; bestColumn = column;
57                            if( alpha >= beta )
58                                break Outer;  // Refutation
59                        }
60                    }
61
62                // Insert into transposition table
63            thisPosition.value = value;
64            if( depth <= tableDepth )
65                transpositions.insert( thisPosition );
66
67            return new Best( value, bestRow, bestColumn );
68        }
```

Figure 10.17 Tic-tac-toe algorithm with alpha-beta pruning and a transposition table (part 2)

The code has a few little tricks but nothing major.

Lines 17 to 28 are new. If we are in the first call to `chooseMove`, we initialize the transposition table. Otherwise, if we are at an appropriate depth, we check whether the current position has already been evaluated, and if so, return its value. The code has two tricks. First, we can transpose only at `depth 3` or higher, as Figure 10.13 suggests. The only other difference is from lines 62 onward. Immediately before the return, we store the value of the position in the transposition table.

The use of the transposition table in this tic-tac-toe algorithm removes about half of the positions from consideration, with only a slight cost for the transposition table operations. There is almost a doubling of the program speed.

10.2.3 Computer Chess

Terminal positions cannot be searched in computer chess. In the best programs, considerable knowledge is built into the evaluation function.

In a complex game such as chess or Go, it is infeasible to search all the way to the terminal nodes: Some estimates claim that there are roughly 10^{100} legal chess positions, and all the tricks in the world will not bring this down to a manageable level. In this case, we have to stop the search after a certain depth of recursion is reached. The nodes at which the recursion is stopped become terminal nodes. These terminal nodes are evaluated with a function that estimates the value of the position. For instance, in a chess program, the evaluation function measures such variables as the relative amount and strength of pieces and other positional factors.

Computers are especially adept at playing moves involving deep combinations that result in exchanges of material. This is because the strength of pieces is easily evaluated. However, extending the search depth merely one level requires an increase in processing speed by a factor of about six (because the number of positions increases by about a factor of 36). Each extra level of search greatly enhances the ability of the program, up to a certain limit (which appears to have been reached by the best programs). On the other hand, computers generally are not as good at playing quiet positional games in which more subtle evaluations and knowledge of the game is required. However, this is only apparent when the computer is playing very strong opposition. The mass-marketed computer chess programs are better than all but a small fraction of today's players.

The best computer chess programs play at grandmaster level.

In 1997, the computer program *Deep Blue*, using an enormous amount of computational power (evaluating as many as 200 million moves per second) was able to defeat the reigning chess champion in a six-game match. Its evaluation function, although top secret, is known to have incorporated a large number of factors, was aided by several grandmasters, and was the result of years of experimentation. Writing the top computer chess program is certainly not a trivial task.

Summary

This chapter gave an application of binary search and some algorithmic techniques that are commonly used in game-playing programs such as chess, checkers, and Othello. The top programs for these games are all world class. The game Go, however, appears too complex for computer searching.

Objects of the Game

alpha-beta pruning A technique used to reduce the number of positions that are evaluated in a minimax search. Alpha is the value that the human has to refute, and beta is the value that the computer has to refute. (292)

minimax strategy A recursive strategy that allows the computer to select an optimal move in a game of tic-tac-toe. (292)

refutation A countermove that proves that a proposed move is not an improvement over moves previously considered. If we find a refutation, we do not have to examine any more moves and the recursive call can return. (292)

terminal position A position in a game that can be evaluated immediately. (292)

transposition table A hash table that stores previously evaluated positions. (293)

word search puzzle A program that requires searching for words in a two-dimensional grid of letters. Words may be oriented in one of eight directions. (283)

Common Errors

1. When using a transposition table, limit the number of stored positions to avoid running out of memory.
2. It is important to check that assumptions are satisfied. For instance, in the word search puzzle, check that the dictionary is sorted. It is a common error to forget this check.

On the Internet

Both case studies are completely coded, although the interface for the tic-tac-toe game leaves a little to be desired. Both are in the directory **Chapter10**. Here are the filenames:

WordSrch.java   Contains the word search puzzle algorithm.
Best.java   Contains the Best class that is part of the tic-tac-toe algorithm.
TicTacToe.java   Contains a tic-tac-toe class using the alpha-beta pruning algorithm with a transposition table.
TicTacMain.java   Contains a simple tic-tac-toe GUI.

Exercises

10.1. What error checks are missing in Figure 10.7?
10.2. For the situation in Figure 10.18, determine the following:
a. Which of the responses to move C_2 is a refutation?
b. What is the value of the position?

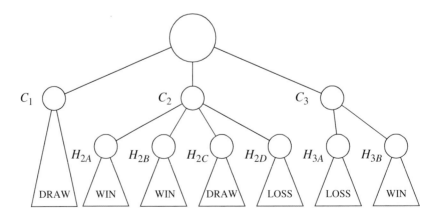

Figure 10.18 Alpha-beta pruning example for Exercise 10.2

In Theory

10.3. Verify that if x is a prefix of some word in array a, then x is a prefix of the word that terminates the binary search.

10.4. Explain how the running time of the word search algorithm changes when the following occurs:
   a. the number of words doubles
   b. the number of rows and columns double (simultaneously)

10.5. Describe the effect of writing an `Equals` method instead of an `equals` method for class `Position`.

In Practice

10.6. Remove restrictions on the grid size and dictionary size that are present in the text implementation of the `Puzzle` class.

10.7. For the word search problem, replace the binary search with a sequential search. How does the change affect performance?

10.8. Compare the performance of the word search algorithm with and without the prefix search.

10.9. Implement a nice GUI for the tic-tac-toe program. Your program should work as both an application and an applet.

10.10. A non-GUI tic-tac-toe program requires additional code to read moves and output the board. Write a user-friendly interface.

10.11. Even if the computer has a move that gives an immediate win, it may not make it if it detects another move that is also guaranteed to win. Some early chess programs had the problem that they would get into a repetition of position when a forced win was detected, thereby allowing the opponent to claim a draw. In tic-tac-toe, this is not a problem because the program eventually will win. Modify the tic-tac-toe algorithm so that when a winning position is found, the move that leads to the shortest win is always taken. You can do this by adding 9-depth to COMPUTER_WIN so that the quickest win gives the highest value.

10.12. Instead of using a two-dimensional array, use an `int` to store the board in 18 bits. Clearly this saves space. Does it save time?

10.13. Compare the performance of the tic-tac-toe program with and without alpha-beta pruning.

10.14. Implement the tic-tac-toe algorithm and measure the performance when various depths are allowed to be stored in the transposition table. Also measure the performance when no transposition table is used. How are the results affected by alpha-beta pruning?

Programming Projects

10.15. Write a program to play 5-by-5 tic-tac-toe, where 4 in a row wins. Can you search to terminal nodes?

10.16. The game of boggle consists of a grid of letters and a word list. The object is to find words in the grid subject to the constraint that two adjacent letters must be adjacent in the grid (that is, north, south, east, or west) of each other and each item in the grid can be used at most once per word. Write a program to play boggle.

10.17. Write a program to play MAXIT. The board is represented as an N-by-N grid of numbers randomly placed at the start of the game. One position is designated as the initial current position. Two players alternate turns. At each turn, a player must select a grid element in the current row or column. The value of the selected position is added to the player's score, and that position becomes the current position and cannot be selected again. Players alternate until all grid elements in the current row and column are already selected, at which point the game ends and the player with the highest score wins.

10.18. Othello played on a 6-by-6 board is a forced win for black. Prove this by writing a program. What is the final score if play on both sides is optimal?

References

If you are interested in computer games, a good starting point for information is the following paper, which is contained in a special issue devoted exclusively to the subject. You will find plenty of information and references to other works covering chess, checkers, and other computer games.

1. K. Lee and S. Mahajan, "The Development of a World Class Othello Program," *Artificial Intelligence* **43** (1990), 21–36.

11 *Stacks and Compilers*

S TACKS are used extensively in compilers. This chapter presents two simple
components of a compiler: a balanced symbol checker and a simple calculator. The goal is to show simple algorithms that use stacks and to see how the
data structures that were described in Chapter 6 are used.

In this chapter, we will see:

- How to use a stack to check for balanced symbols
- How to use a *state machine* to parse symbols in a balanced symbol
  program
- How to use *operator precedence parsing* to evaluate infix expressions in a
  simple calculator program

11.1 Balanced-symbol Checker

As discussed in Section 6.2, compilers check your programs for syntax errors.
However, frequently a lack of one symbol (such as a missing comment ender * /
or }) will cause the compiler to spill out a hundred lines of diagnostics without
identifying the real error. A useful tool to help debug compiler error messages is a
program that checks whether symbols are balanced. In other words, every { must
correspond to a } , every [to a] , and so on. However, simply counting the numbers of each symbol is insufficient. For example, the sequence [( )] is legal, but
[( ]) is wrong.

11.1.1 Basic Algorithm

A stack is useful here because we know that when a closing symbol such as) is
seen, it matches the most recently seen unclosed (. Therefore, by placing opening
symbols on a stack, we can easily check that a closing symbol makes sense. Specifically, we have the following algorithm:

A stack can be
used to detect mis-
matched symbols.

1. Make an empty stack.
2. Read symbols until the end of the file.
    a. If the symbol is an opening symbol, push it onto the stack.
    b. If it is a closing symbol and if the stack is empty, then report an error.
    c. Otherwise, pop the stack. If the symbol popped is not the corresponding opening symbol, then report an error.
3. At the end of the file, if the stack is not empty, report an error.

In this algorithm, illustrated in Figure 11.1, the fourth, fifth, and sixth symbols all generate errors. The } is an error because the symbol popped from the top of stack is an (, so a mismatch is detected. The) is an error because the stack is empty, so there is no corresponding (. The [is an error that is detected when the end of input is seen and the stack is not empty.

Symbols in comments, string constants, and character constants need not be balanced.

To make this work for Java programs, we need to consider all the contexts in which parentheses, braces, and brackets need not match. For example, we should not consider a parenthesis as a symbol if it occurs inside a comment, string constant, or character constant. We thus need routines to skip comments, string constants, and character constants. A character constant in Java can be complex to recognize because of the host of escape sequences, so we will simplify things. The goal is to design a program that will work for the bulk of inputs likely to occur.

Line numbers are needed for meaningful error messages.

For the program to be useful, we must not only report mismatches but also attempt to identify where the mismatches occur. Consequently, we will keep track of the line numbers where the symbols are seen. When an error is seen, obtaining an accurate message is always difficult. If there is an extra }, does that mean the } is extraneous? Or was a { missing earlier? We keep the error handling as simple as possible. Note, however, that once one error is reported, it is possible that the program will be confused and start flagging many errors. Thus only the first error can be considered meaningful. Even so, the program developed here is very useful.

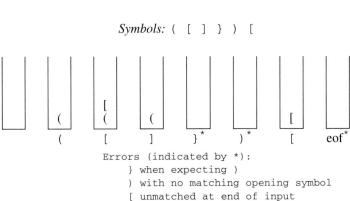

Symbols: ([ ] }) [

Errors (indicated by *):
} when expecting)
) with no matching opening symbol
[unmatched at end of input

Figure 11.1 Stack operations in balanced-symbol algorithm

```
 1  // JavaAnalyzer class: check for balanced symbols
 2  //
 3  // CONSTRUCTION: with a PushbackReader object
 4  // ******************PUBLIC OPERATIONS**********************
 5  // int checkBalance( )    --> Print mismatches
 6  //                            return number of errors
 7  // ******************ERRORS********************************
 8  // Error checking on comments and quotes is performed
 9
10  import java.io.*;
11  import DataStructures.*;
12  import Exceptions.*;
13  import Supporting.*;
14
15  class JavaAnalyzer
16  {
17      public JavaAnalyzer( PushbackReader inStream )
18      {
19          errors = 0;
20          ch = '\0';
21          currentLine = 1;
22          in = inStream;
23          pendingTokens = new StackAr( );
24      }
25
26      public int checkBalance( )
27        { /* Figure 11.8 */ }
28
29      private PushbackReader in;      // The input stream
30      private char ch;               // Current character
31      private int currentLine;       // Current line
32      private Stack pendingTokens;   // Open symbols pending
33      private int errors;            // Number of errors seen
34
35      private boolean nextChar( )
36        { /* Figure 11.4 */ }
37      private void putBackChar( )
38        { /* Figure 11.4 */ }
39      private void skipComment( int start )
40        { /* Figure 11.5 */ }
41      private void skipQuote( char quoteType )
42        { /* Figure 11.6 */ }
43      private boolean getNextSymbol( )
44        { /* Figure 11.7 */ }
45      private void processSlash( )
46        { /* Figure 11.7 */ }
47      private void checkMatch( Symbol opSym, Symbol clSym )
48        { /* Figure 11.9 */ }
49  }
```

Figure 11.2   Class skeleton for balanced-symbol program

```
 1  /**
 2   * Symbol represents what will be placed on the stack.
 3   */
 4  class Symbol
 5  {
 6      char   token;
 7      int    theLine;
 8
 9      Symbol( char tok, int line )
10      {
11          token = tok;
12          theLine = line;
13      }
14  }
```

Figure 11.3   Object that is placed on the stack

11.1.2 Implementation

Figure 11.2 (page 305) shows the `JavaAnalyzer` class that does all the work. In addition to the constructor, the only other publicly visible routine is `checkBalance`, shown at line 26. Everything else is a supporting routine or a class data field. We begin by describing the data fields.

in is a reference to a `PushbackReader` object and is initialized at construction. A `PushbackReader` is like a `BufferedReader`, except that it also provides an `unread` method. The current character being scanned is stored in ch, and the current line number is stored in `currentLine`. The balanced symbol algorithm requires that we place opening symbols on a stack. In order to print diagnostics, we store a line number with each symbol, as shown in the `Symbol` class in Figure 11.3. The stack itself is `pendingTokens`, declared at line 32. Finally, an integer that counts the number of errors is declared at line 33.

The constructor, shown at lines 17 to 24, initializes the error count to 0 and the current line number to 1 and sets the `PushbackReader` reference. The remaining data fields, namely ch and `pendingTokens`, are initialized; in the case of `pendingTokens` a zero-parameter constructor is used to create an empty stack.

Lexical analysis is used to ignore comments and recognize symbols.

We can now examine some of the supporting routines. Many of them are concerned with keeping track of the current line and attempting to differentiate symbols that represent opening and closing tokens with those that are inside comments, character constants, and string constants. This general process is called *lexical analysis*. Figure 11.4 shows a pair of routines, `nextChar` and `putBackChar`. `nextChar` reads the next character, assigns it to ch, and updates `currentLine` if a newline is seen. It returns `false` if the end of the file is reached. The complementary procedure `putBackChar` puts the current character (ch) back onto the input stream and decrements currentLine if the character is a newline. Clearly, putBackChar should be called only once between calls to nextChar. Since it is a private routine, we do not worry about abuse on the part of the class user.

Putting back characters on the input stream is a commonly used technique in parsing. In many instances, we have read one too many characters and it is useful to undo the read. In our case, this occurs after processing a /. We must see if the next character begins the comment start token. However, if it does not, we cannot simply disregard it, because it could be an opening or closing symbol or a quote. Thus we pretend that it was never read.

```
1     /**
2      * nextChar sets ch based on the next character in the
3      * input stream. putBackChar puts the character
4      * back onto the stream. It should only be used once
5      * after a nextChar.
6      */
7     private boolean nextChar( )
8     {
9         try
10        {
11            int readVal = in.read( );
12            if( readVal == -1 )
13                return false;
14            ch = (char) readVal;
15            if( ch == '\n' )
16                currentLine++;
17            return true;
18        }
19        catch( IOException e )
20          { return false; }
21    }
22
23    private void putBackChar( )
24    {
25        if( ch == '\n' )
26            currentLine--;
27        try
28          { in.unread( (int) ch ); }
29        catch( IOException e ) { }
30    }
```

Figure 11.4   nextChar routine to read next character, update currentLine if necessary, and return true if not at the end of file. putBackChar routine to put back ch and update currentLine if necessary

```
1     /**
2      * Precondition: We are about to process a comment; have
3      *                     already seen comment-start token
4      * Postcondition: Stream will be set immediately after
5      *                     comment-ending token
6      */
7     private void skipComment( int start )
8     {
9         if( start == SLASH_SLASH )
10        {
11            while( nextChar( ) && ( ch != '\n' ) )
12                ;
13            return;
14        }
15
16            // Look for */ sequence
17        boolean state = false;    // True if we have seen *
18
19        while( nextChar( ) )
20        {
21            if( state && ch == '/' )
22                return;
23            state = ( ch == '*' );
24        }
25        errors++;
26        System.out.println( "Unterminated comment!" );
27    }
```

Figure 11.5   `skipComment` routine to move past an already started comment

Next up is the routine `skipComment` shown in Figure 11.5. The purpose is to skip over the characters in the comment and position the input stream so that the next read will be the first character after the comment ends. Things are complicated by the fact that comments can begin either with `//`, in which case the line ends the comment, or with `/*`, in which case `*/` ends the comment. When we have the `//` case, we continually get the next character until either the end of file is reached (in which case, the first half of the `&&` operator fails) or we see a newline. At that point, we return. Notice that the line number is updated automatically by `nextChar`. Otherwise, we have the `/*` case, which is processed starting at line 17. `/**` is handled prior to entering this routine (see Figure 11.7 (page 310), lines 17 and 18).

The *state machine* is a common technique used to parse symbols.

The `skipComment` routine uses a simplified *state machine*. The state machine is a common technique used to parse symbols. At any point, it is in some state; each input character takes it to a new state. Eventually, it reaches a state at which a symbol has been recognized.

In `skipComment`, at any point, it has matched either 0, 1, or 2 characters of the * / terminator, corresponding to states 0, 1, and 2. If it matches two characters, it can return. Thus, inside the loop, it can be in only state 0 or 1, since if it is in state 1 and sees a /, it returns immediately. Thus the state can be represented by a Boolean variable that is true if the state machine is in state 1. If it does not return, then it goes back either to state 1 if it sees a * or to state 0 if it does not. This is stated succinctly at line 23.

If we never find the comment-ending token, then eventually `nextChar` returns `false` and the `while` loop terminates, resulting in an error message. `skipQuote`, shown in Figure 11.6, is similar. Here, the parameter is the opening quote character, which is either `"` or `'`. In either case, we need to see that character as the closing quote. However, we must be prepared to handle the \ character; otherwise, our program will report errors when it is run on its own source. Thus we repeatedly digest characters. If the current character is a closing quote, we are done. If it is newline, we have an unterminated character or string constant. And if it is a backslash, we digest an extra character without examining it.

> At any point, it is in some state, and each input character takes it to a new state. Eventually, the state machine reaches a state in which a symbol has been recognized.

```
1     /**
2      * Precondition: We are about to process a quote; have
3      *                already seen beginning quote.
4      * Postcondition: Stream will be set immediately after
5      *                matching quote
6      */
7     private void skipQuote( char quoteType )
8     {
9         while( nextChar( ) )
10        {
11            if( ch == quoteType )
12                return;
13            if( ch == '\n' )
14            {
15                errors++;
16                System.out.println( "Missing quote at line " +
17                                    currentLine );
18                return;
19            }
20            else if( ch == '\\' )
21                nextChar( );
22        }
23    }
```

Figure 11.6   `skipQuote` routine to move past an already-started character or string constant

```
 1      /**
 2       * After the opening slash is seen, deal with next
 3       * character.  If it is a comment starter, process it;
 4       * otherwise putback the next character if it is not a
 5       * newline.
 6       */
 7      private static final int SLASH_SLASH = 0;
 8      private static final int SLASH_STAR  = 1;
 9
10      private void processSlash( )
11      {
12          if( nextChar( ) )
13          {
14              if( ch == '*' )
15              {
16                  // Javadoc comment
17                  if( nextChar( ) && ch != '*' )
18                      putBackChar( );
19                  skipComment( SLASH_STAR );
20              }
21              else if( ch == '/' )
22                  skipComment( SLASH_SLASH );
23              else if( ch != '\n' )
24                  putBackChar( );
25          }
26      }
27
28      /**
29       * Get the next opening or closing symbol.
30       * Return false if end of file.
31       * Skip past comments and character and string constants
32       */
33      private boolean getNextSymbol( )
34      {
35          while( nextChar( ) )
36          {
37              if( ch == '/' )
38                  processSlash( );
39              else if( ch == '\'' || ch == '"' )
40                  skipQuote( ch );
41              else if( ch == '(' || ch == '[' || ch == '{' ||
42                       ch == ')' || ch == ']' || ch == '}' )
43                  return true;
44          }
45          return false;        // End of file
46      }
```

Figure 11.7   getNextSymbol routine to skip comments and quotes and
return the next opening or closing character

```
 1       /**
 2        * Print an error message for unbalanced symbols.
 3        * @return number of errors detected.
 4        */
 5       public int checkBalance( )
 6       {
 7           Symbol match = null;
 8
 9           errors = 0;
10           currentLine = 1;
11           while( getNextSymbol( ) )
12           {
13               char   lastChar = ch;
14               Symbol lastSymbol = new Symbol( lastChar,
15                                               currentLine );
16
17               switch( lastChar )
18               {
19                 case '(': case '[': case '{':
20                   pendingTokens.push( lastSymbol );
21                   break;
22                 case ')': case ']': case '}':
23                   try
24                   {
25                       match = (Symbol)
26                                 pendingTokens.topAndPop( );
27                       checkMatch( match, lastSymbol );
28                   }
29                   catch( Underflow e )
30                   {
31                       errors++;
32                       System.out.println( "Extraneous " +
33                           lastChar +" at line " + currentLine );
34                   }
35                   break;
36                 default: // Cannot happen
37                   break;
38               }
39           }
40
41           while( !pendingTokens.isEmpty( ) )
42           {
43               errors++;
44               try
45                 { match = (Symbol) pendingTokens.topAndPop( ); }
46               catch( Underflow e ) { } // Cannot happen
47               System.out.println( "Unmatched " + match.token +
48                                   " at line " + match.theLine );
49           }
50           return errors;
51       }
```

Figure 11.8   checkBalance, the main algorithm

```
1      // Print an error message if clSym does not match opSym.
2      // Update error.
3      private void checkMatch( Symbol opSym, Symbol clSym )
4      {
5          if( opSym.token == '(' && clSym.token != ')' ||
6              opSym.token == '[' && clSym.token != ']' ||
7              opSym.token == '{' && clSym.token != '}' )
8          {
9              System.out.println( "Found " + clSym.token +
10                 " on line " + currentLine + "; does not match "
11                 + opSym.token + " at line " + opSym.theLine );
12             errors++;
13         }
14     }
```

Figure 11.9   checkMatch routine to check that the close symbol matches the opening symbol

```
1      // main routine for balanced symbol checker.
2      public static void main( String [ ] args )
3      {
4          JavaAnalyzer p;
5
6          if( args.length == 0 )
7          {
8              p = new JavaAnalyzer( new PushbackReader(
9                      new InputStreamReader( System.in ) ) );
10             if( p.checkBalance( ) == 0 )
11                 System.out.println( "No errors!" );
12             return;
13         }
14
15         for( int i = 0; i < args.length; i++ )
16         {
17             try
18             {
19                 FileReader f = new FileReader( args[ i ] );
20
21                 System.out.println( args[ i ] + ": " );
22                 p = new JavaAnalyzer( new
23                                      PushbackReader( f ) );
24                 if( p.checkBalance( ) == 0 )
25                     System.out.println( "   ...no errors!" );
26                 f.close( );
27             }
28             catch( IOException e )
29               { System.err.println( e + " " + args[ i ] ); }
30         }
31     }
```

Figure 11.10   main routine with command-line arguments

Once the skipping routine is written, it is easier to write `getNextSymbol`. If the current character is a `/`, we call `processSlash` to read a second character to check if we have a comment. In `processSlash`, if we have a comment, we call `skipComment`; if not, we undo the second read. If we have a quote, we call `skipQuote`. If we have an opening or closing symbol, we can return. Otherwise, we keep reading until we eventually run out of input or find an opening or closing symbol. The entire routine is shown in Figure 11.7 (page 310).

`checkBalance` is implemented in Figure 11.8 (page 311). It follows the algorithm description almost verbatim. Opening symbols are pushed onto the stack with the current line number. When a closing symbol is seen and the stack is empty, then the closing symbol is extraneous; otherwise, we remove the top item from the stack and check that the opening symbol that was on the stack matches the closing symbol just read. This is done by the routine `checkMatch`, which is shown in Figure 11.9. Once the end of input is seen, any symbols on the stack are unmatched; these are repeatedly output in the `while` loop that begins at line 41. The total number of errors that were detected is then returned.

> `checkBalance` does all the algorithmic work.

Note that the current implementation allows multiple calls to `checkBalance`. However, if the input stream is not reset externally, then all that happens is that the end of the file is immediately detected and we return immediately. Figure 11.10 shows that we expect a `Program` object to be created and then `checkBalance` to be invoked. In our example, if there are no command-line arguments, a `PushbackReader` is associated with `System.in`. Otherwise, we repeatedly use `PushbackReaders` that are associated with the files given in the command-line argument list.

11.2 A Simple Calculator

Some of the techniques used to implement compilers can be used on a smaller scale in the implementation of a typical pocket calculator. Typically, calculators evaluate infix expressions, such as `1+2`, which consists of a binary operator with arguments to its left and right. This format, although often fairly easy to evaluate, can be more complex. Consider the expression

```
1 + 2 * 3
```

Mathematically, this evaluates to 7 because the multiplication operator has higher precedence than addition. Some calculators give the answer 9. This illustrates that a simple left-to-right evaluation is not sufficient; we cannot begin by evaluating `1+2`. Furthermore, consider the expressions

> In an *infix expression*, a binary operator has arguments to its left and right.

```
10 - 4 - 3
2 ^ 3 ^ 3
```

When there are several operators, precedence and associativity determine how the operators are processed.

in which ^ is the exponentiation operator. Which subtraction and which exponentiation get evaluated first? Subtractions are processed left-to-right, meaning the result is 3. On the other hand, exponentiation is generally processed right-to-left, thereby reflecting the mathematical 2^{3^3} rather than $(2^3)^3$. Thus subtraction associates left-to-right, while exponentiation associates from right-to-left. All of these possibilities suggest that evaluating an expression such as

```
1 - 2 - 3 * 4 ^ 5 * 6 / 7 ^ 2 ^ 2
```

would be quite challenging.

If the calculations are performed in integer math (that is, rounding down on division), the answer is -8. To show this, parentheses are inserted to illustrate that the calculations are ordered:

```
( 1 - 2 ) - ( ( ( 3 * ( 4 ^ 5 ) ) * 6 ) / ( 7 ^ ( 2 ^ 2 ) ) )
```

Although the parentheses make the order of evaluations unambiguous, it is difficult to argue that they make the mechanism for evaluation any clearer. It turns out that a different expression form, called a *postfix expression*, provides a direct mechanism for evaluation. The following several sections explain how this works. The first one examines the postfix expression form and shows how postfix expressions can be evaluated in a simple left-to-right scan. The next section shows algorithmically how the previous expressions, which are presented as infix expressions, can be converted to postfix. Finally, a Java program is given that evaluates infix expressions containing additive, multiplicative, and exponentiation operators as well as overriding parentheses. An algorithm called *operator precedence parsing* is used.

11.2.1 Postfix Machines

A *postfix expression* can be evaluated as follows. Operands are pushed onto a single stack. An operator pops its operands and then pushes the result. At the end of the evaluation, the stack should contain exactly one element, which represents the result.

A *postfix expression* is a series of operators and operands. It is evaluated using a *postfix machine* as follows. When an operand is seen, it is pushed onto a stack. When an operator is seen, the appropriate number of operands are popped from the stack, the operator is evaluated, and the result is pushed back onto the stack. For binary operators, which are the most common, two operands are popped. When the complete postfix expression is evaluated, the result should be a single item on the stack that represents the answer. The postfix form represents a natural way to evaluate expressions because precedence rules are not required.

Here is a simple example. Consider the postfix expression

```
1 2 3 * +
```

The evaluation proceeds as follows: 1, then 2, and then 3 are each pushed onto the stack. To process *, we pop the top two items on the stack: 3 and then 2. Note that the first item popped becomes the rhs parameter to the binary operator, and the second item popped is the `lhs` parameter; thus parameters are popped in reverse order. For multiplication, this does not matter, but for subtraction and division, it certainly does. The result of the multiplication is 6, and that is pushed back onto the stack. At this point, the top of the stack is 6; below it is 1. To process the +, the 6 and 1 are popped, and their sum, 7, is pushed. At this point, the expression has been read and the stack has only one item. Thus the final answer is 7.

Every valid infix expression can be converted to postfix form. For example, the earlier long infix expression can be written in postfix notation as

```
1 2 - 4 5 ^ 3 * 6 * 7 2 2 ^ ^ / -
```

Figure 11.11 shows the steps used by the postfix machine to evaluate it. Each step involves exactly one push. Consequently, since there are 9 operands and 8 operators, there are 17 steps and 17 pushes. Clearly, the time to evaluate a postfix expression is linear.

Evaluation of a postfix expression takes linear time.

The remaining detail to handle is an algorithm to convert from infix notation to postfix notation. Once we have one, we have an algorithm to evaluate an infix expression.

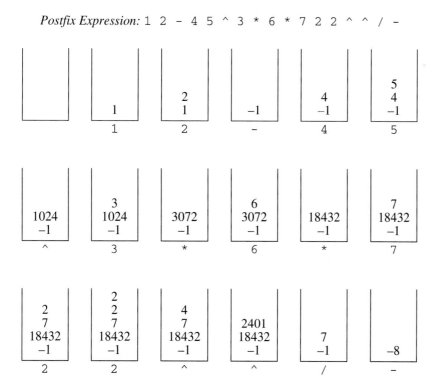

Postfix Expression: 1 2 - 4 5 ^ 3 * 6 * 7 2 2 ^ ^ / -

Figure 11.11   Steps in the evaluation of a postfix expression

11.2.2 Infix to Postfix Conversion

The basic principle involved in the *operator precedence parsing* algorithm, which converts an infix expression to a postfix expression, is the following. When an operand is seen, we can immediately output it. However, when we see an operator, we can never output it because we must wait to see the second operand. Consequently, we must save it. In an expression such as

```
1 + 2 * 3 ^ 4
```

which in postfix form is

```
1 2 3 4 ^ * +
```

a postfix expression in some cases has operators in the reverse order than they appear in an infix expression. Of course, this is true only if the precedence of the involved operators is increasing as we go left-to-right. Even so, this suggests that a stack is appropriate for storing operators. Following this logic, then when we read an operator, it must somehow be placed onto a stack. Consequently, at some point the operator must get off the stack. The rest of the algorithm involves deciding when operators go on and come off the stack.

Here is another simple infix expression:

```
2 ^ 5 - 1
```

When we reach the – operator, 2 and 5 have been output and ^ is on the stack. Because – has lower precedence than ^, ^ needs to be applied to 2 and 5. Thus we must pop the ^ and any other operands of higher precedence than – from the stack. After that is completed, we push the –. The resulting postfix expression is

```
2 5 ^ 1 -
```

In general, when we are processing an operator from the input, we output those operators from the stack that the precedence (and associativity) rules tell us need to be processed.

A second example is the infix expression

```
3 * 2 ^ 5 - 1
```

When we reach the ^ operator, 3 and 2 have been output and * is on the stack. Since ^ has higher precedence than *, nothing is popped and ^ goes on the stack. The 5 is output immediately. Then we see a – operator. Precedence rules tell us that ^ is popped, followed by the *. At this point, there is nothing left to pop, so we are done popping and – goes onto the stack. We then output 1. When we reach the end of the infix expression, we can pop the remaining operators from the stack. The resulting postfix expression is

```
3  2  5  ^  *  1  -
```

Before the algorithm is summarized, a few questions must be answered. First, if the current symbol is a + and the top of the stack is a +, should the + on the stack be popped or should it stay? The answer is determined by deciding if the input + implies that the stack + is completed. Since + associates from left-to-right, the answer is yes. However, if we are talking about the ^ operator, which associates from right-to-left, the answer is no. Therefore, when examining two operators of equal precedence, we look at the associativity to decide, as shown in the following examples:

Infix Expression	Postfix Expression	Associativity
2 + 3 + 4	2 3 + 4 +	Left-associative: Input + is lower than stack +.
2 ^ 3 ^ 4	2 3 4 ^ ^	Right-associative: Input ^ is higher than stack ^.

What about parentheses? A left parenthesis can be considered a high precedence operator when it is an input symbol but a low precedence operator when it is on the stack. Consequently, the input left parenthesis is simply placed on the stack. When a right parenthesis is seen on the input, we pop the operator stack until we see a left parenthesis. The operators are written, but the parentheses are not.

Here is a summary of the various cases in the operator precedence parsing algorithm. Everything that is popped from the stack is output, with the exception of parentheses.

- *Operands*: Immediately output.
- *Close parenthesis*: Pop stack symbols until an open parenthesis is seen.
- *Operator*: Pop all stack symbols until we see a symbol of lower precedence or a right-associative symbol of equal precedence. Then push the operator.
- *End of input*: Pop all remaining stack symbols.

As an example, Figure 11.12 shows how the algorithm processes

```
1  -  2  ^  3  ^  3  -  (  4  +  5  *  6  )  *  7
```

Below each stack is the symbol that is read. To the right in bold is any output.

> A left parenthesis is treated as a high precedence operator when it is an input symbol but as a low precedence operator when it is on the stack. A left parenthesis is removed only by a right parenthesis.

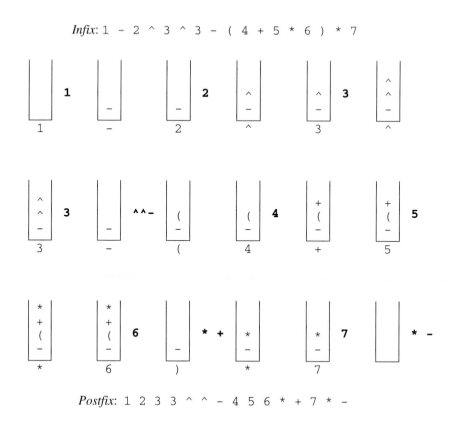

Figure 11.12 Infix to postfix conversion

11.2.3 Implementation

The Evaluator class will parse and evaluate infix expressions.

We now have the theoretical background required to implement a simple calculator. Our calculator supports addition, subtraction, multiplication, division, and exponentiation. Next, we will write a class named Evaluator. First, however, we make a simplifying assumption: Negative numbers are not allowed. Distinguishing between the binary minus operator and the unary minus requires extra work in the scanning routine. It also complicates matters because it introduces a nonbinary operator. Incorporating unary operators is not difficult. However, the extra code does not illustrate any unique concepts and thus is left as an exercise.

```
 1  // Evaluator class: evaluate infix expression
 2  //
 3  // CONSTRUCTION: with a String
 4  //
 5  // ******************PUBLIC OPERATIONS*********************
 6  // int getValue( )       --> Return value of infix expression
 7  // ******************ERRORS********************************
 8  // Some error checking is performed
 9
10  import DataStructures.*;
11  import Exceptions.*;
12  import java.io.*;
13  import java.util.StringTokenizer;
14
15  public class Evaluator
16  {
17      static final int EOL     = 0;
18      static final int VALUE   = 1;
19      static final int OPAREN  = 2;
20      static final int CPAREN  = 3;
21      static final int EXP     = 4;
22      static final int MULT    = 5;
23      static final int DIV     = 6;
24      static final int PLUS    = 7;
25      static final int MINUS   = 8;
26
27      public Evaluator( String s )
28      {
29          opStack      = new StackAr( );
30          postfixStack = new StackAr( );
31          str = new StringTokenizer( s, "+*-/^() ", true );
32          opStack.push( new Integer( EOL ) );
33      }
34
35      public long getValue( )
36        { /* Figure 11.15 */ }
37
38      private Stack opStack;       // Operator stack for conversion
39      private Stack postfixStack;  // Stack for postfix machine
40      StringTokenizer str;         // The character stream
41      long currentValue;           // Current operand
42      int lastToken;               // Last token read
43
44      private int getToken( )
45        { /* Figure 11.16 */ }
46      private void binaryOp( int topOp )
47        { /* Figure 11.18 */ }
48      private void processToken( )
49        { /* Figure 11.20 */ }
50  }
```

Figure 11.13   Evaluator class skeleton

```
 1    /**
 2     * Internal method that hides type-casting.
 3     */
 4    private long postFixTopAndPop( ) throws Underflow
 5    {
 6        return ( (Long)( postfixStack.topAndPop( ) ) ).
 7                                          longValue( );
 8    }
 9
10    /**
11     * Another internal method that hides type-casting.
12     */
13    private int opStackTop( ) throws Underflow
14    {
15        return ( (Integer)( opStack.top( ) ) ).intValue( );
16    }
```

Figure 11.14 Internal methods to hide type-casting in generic stacks

```
 1    /**
 2     * Public routine that performs the evaluation.
 3     * Examine the postfix machine to see if a single result
 4     * is left and if so, return it; otherwise print error.
 5     */
 6    public long getValue( )
 7    {
 8        long theResult = 0;
 9
10        do
11        {
12            lastToken = getToken( );
13            processToken( );
14        } while( lastToken != EOL );
15
16        try
17          { theResult = postFixTopAndPop( ); }
18        catch( Underflow e )
19        {
20            System.err.println( "Missing operand!" );
21            return 0;
22        }
23
24        if( !postfixStack.isEmpty( ) )
25            System.err.println( "Missing operators!" );
26
27        return theResult;
28    }
```

Figure 11.15 `getValue` routine to read and process tokens and then return the item at the top of the stack

```
1       /**
2        * Find the next token, skipping blanks, and return it.
3        * For VALUE token, place processed value in CurrentValue.
4        * Print error message if input is unrecognized.
5        */
6       private int getToken( )
7       {
8           String s = "";
9
10          try
11            { s = str.nextToken( ); }
12          catch( java.util.NoSuchElementException e )
13            { return EOL; }
14
15          if( s.equals( " " ) ) return getToken( );
16          if( s.equals( "^" ) ) return EXP;
17          if( s.equals( "/" ) ) return DIV;
18          if( s.equals( "*" ) ) return MULT;
19          if( s.equals( "(" ) ) return OPAREN;
20          if( s.equals( ")" ) ) return CPAREN;
21          if( s.equals( "+" ) ) return PLUS;
22          if( s.equals( "-" ) ) return MINUS;
23
24          try
25            { currentValue = Long.parseLong( s ); }
26          catch( NumberFormatException e )
27          {
28              System.err.println( "Parse error" );
29              return EOL;
30          }
31          return VALUE;
32      }
```

Figure 11.16   getToken routine to return the next token in the stream

```
1       /*
2        * topAndPop the postfix machine stack; return the result.
3        * If the stack is empty, print an error message.
4        */
5       private long getTop( )
6       {
7           try
8             { return postFixTopAndPop( ); }
9           catch( Underflow e )
10            { System.err.println( "Missing operand" ); }
11          return 0;
12      }
```

Figure 11.17   getTop routine to get the top item in the postfix stack and
remove it

```
 1      /**
 2       * Process an operator by taking two items off the postfix
 3       * stack, applying the operator, and pushing the result.
 4       * Print error if missing parenthesis or division by 0.
 5       */
 6      private void binaryOp( int topOp )
 7      {
 8          if( topOp == OPAREN )
 9          {
10              System.err.println( "Unbalanced parentheses" );
11              try
12                { opStack.pop( ); }
13              catch( Underflow e ) { }  // Cannot happen
14              return;
15          }
16          long rhs = getTop( );
17          long lhs = getTop( );
18
19          if( topOp == EXP )
20              postfixStack.push( new Long( pow( lhs, rhs ) ) );
21          else if( topOp == PLUS )
22              postfixStack.push( new Long( lhs + rhs ) );
23          else if( topOp == MINUS )
24              postfixStack.push( new Long( lhs - rhs ) );
25          else if( topOp == MULT )
26              postfixStack.push( new Long( lhs * rhs ) );
27          else if( topOp == DIV )
28              if( rhs != 0 )
29                  postfixStack.push( new Long( lhs / rhs ) );
30              else
31              {
32                  System.err.println( "Division by zero" );
33                  postfixStack.push( new Long( lhs ) );
34              }
35          try
36            { opStack.pop( ); }
37          catch( Underflow e ) { }
38      }
```

Figure 11.18 binaryOp routine to apply topOp to the postfix stack

We need two
stacks: an operator
stack and a stack
for the postfix
machine.

Figure 11.13 (page 319) shows the Evaluator class skeleton, which is used to read a single string of input. The basic evaluation algorithm requires two stacks. The first stack is used to evaluate the infix expression and generate the postfix expression. It is a stack of operators declared at line 38. Rather than explicitly outputting the postfix expression, we send each postfix symbol to the postfix machine as it is generated. Thus we also need a second stack, one that stores operands. So we have a postfix machine stack, declared at line 39. Notice that if we did not have a workaround for generic programming, we would be in trouble because the two stacks hold items of different types. (Figure 11.14

(page 320) contains two methods that access the two stacks, and perform the needed type conversions.) The remaining data fields are a `StringTokenizer` object that is used to step through the input line and fields to store the current token and, if the token is an operand, the value of the operand.

Lines 17 to 25 show some constants. The constructor, shown at lines 27 to 33, constructs the two stacks and then the `StringTokenizer` object. The parameters for the tokenizer indicate the symbols that are considered delimiters. They also show that these delimiters are tokens that are matched (rather than delimiters that are skipped).[1]

The only publicly visible method is `getValue`. Shown in Figure 11.15 (page 320), `getValue` repeatedly reads a token and processes it until the end of line is detected. At that point, the item at the top of the stack is the answer. Figure 11.16 (page 321) shows the `getToken` routine. We skip any blanks (by calling `getToken` again if a blank is seen). If we have not reached the end of line, then we check to see if we match any of the 1-character operators, and if so, return the appropriate token. Otherwise, we reach line 24. We expect that what remains is an operand, so we get `currentValue`.

```
 1  class Precedence
 2  {
 3      int inputSymbol;
 4      int topOfStack;
 5
 6      Precedence( int inSymbol, int topSymbol )
 7      {
 8          inputSymbol = inSymbol;
 9          topOfStack  = topSymbol;
10      }
11  }
12          // This is part of class Evaluator
13          // precTable matches order of Token enumeration
14      static Precedence [ ] precTable = new Precedence[ 9 ];
15      static
16      {
17          precTable[ 0 ] = new Precedence(   0, -1 );   // EOL
18          precTable[ 1 ] = new Precedence(   0,  0 );   // VALUE
19          precTable[ 2 ] = new Precedence( 100,  0 );   // OPAREN
20          precTable[ 3 ] = new Precedence(   0, 99 );   // CPAREN
21          precTable[ 4 ] = new Precedence(   6,  5 );   // EXP
22          precTable[ 5 ] = new Precedence(   3,  4 );   // MULT
23          precTable[ 6 ] = new Precedence(   3,  4 );   // DIV
24          precTable[ 7 ] = new Precedence(   1,  2 );   // PLUS
25          precTable[ 8 ] = new Precedence(   1,  2 );   // MINUS
26      }
```

Figure 11.19 Table of precedences used to evaluate an infix expression

---

[1.] Appendix C.3.2 describes the `StringTokenizer` class in more detail.

```
 1      /**
 2       * After a token is read, use operator precedence parsing
 3       * algorithm to process it; missing opening parentheses
 4       * are detected here.
 5       */
 6      private void processToken( )
 7      {
 8          int topOp;
 9
10          try
11          {
12              switch( lastToken )
13              {
14                case VALUE:
15                  postfixStack.push( new Long( currentValue ) );
16                  return;
17
18                case CPAREN:
19                  while( ( topOp = opStackTop( ) ) != OPAREN
20                          && topOp != EOL )
21                      binaryOp( topOp );
22                  if( topOp == OPAREN )
23                      opStack.pop( );   // Remove opening paren
24                  else
25                      System.err.println( "Missing (" );
26                  break;
27
28                default:    // General operator case
29                  while( precTable[ lastToken ].inputSymbol <=
30                          precTable[ topOp = opStackTop( ) ].
31                                                      topOfStack )
32                      binaryOp( topOp );
33                  if( lastToken != EOL )
34                      opStack.push( new Integer( lastToken ) );
35                  break;
36              }
37          }
38          catch( Underflow e ) { }  // Cannot happen
39      }
```

Figure 11.20 processToken routine to process lastToken using the operator precedence parsing algorithm

Figures 11.17 (page 321) and 11.18 (page 322) show the routines used to implement the postfix machine. getTop returns and removes the top item in the postfix stack. The routine binaryOp applies topOp (which is expected to be the top item in the operator stack) to the top two items on the postfix stack and replaces them with the result. It also pops the operator stack, thereby signifying that processing for topOp is complete.

Figure 11.19 (page 323) declares a *precedence table*, which stores the operator precedences and is used to decide what is removed from the operator stack. It is allocated when the `Evaluator` class is loaded. The operators are listed in the same order as the basic class constants.

We want to assign a number to each level of precedence. The higher the number, the higher the precedence. We could assign the additive operators precedence 1, multiplicative operators precedence 3, exponentiation precedence 5, and parentheses precedence 99. However, we also need to take into account associativity. To do this, we assign each operator a number that represents its precedence when it is an input symbol and a second number that represents its precedence when it is on the operator stack. A left-associative operator has the operator stack precedence set at 1 higher than the odd number would indicate, while a right-associative operator has the input symbol precedence set at 1 higher than the odd number. Thus the precedence of the + operator that is on the stack is 2.

A consequence of this rule is that any two operators that have different precedences are still correctly ordered. However, if a + is on the operator stack and is also the input symbol, it will appear that the operator that is on the top of the stack has higher precedence. Thus it will be popped. This is what we want for left-associative operators.

A precedence table is used to decide what is removed from the operator stack. Left-associative operators have the operator stack precedence set at 1 higher than the input symbol precedence. Right-associative operators go the other way.

```
1     /**
2      * Quick and dirty main
3      */
4     public static void main( String [ ] args )
5     {
6         String str;
7         BufferedReader in = new BufferedReader( new
8                             InputStreamReader( System.in ) );
9
10        try
11        {
12            System.out.println( "Enter expressions" +
13                                " one per line" );
14            while( ( str = in.readLine( ) ) != null )
15            {
16                System.out.println( "Read: " + str );
17                Evaluator ev = new Evaluator( str );
18                System.out.println( ev.getValue( ) );
19                System.out.println( "Enter next expression" );
20            }
21        }
22        catch( IOException e ) { }
23    }
```

Figure 11.21 A simple `main` to evaluate expressions repeatedly

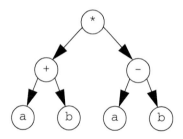

Figure 11.22 Expression tree for `(a+b)*(a-b)`

Similarly, if a ^ is on the operator stack and is also the input symbol, it will appear that the operator that is on the top of the stack has lower precedence. Thus it will not be popped, which is correct for right-associative operators. The token VALUE never gets placed on the stack, so its precedence is meaningless. The end of line token is given lowest precedence because it will be placed on the stack for use as a sentinel (this is done in the constructor). If we treat it as a right-associative operator, then it is covered under the operator case.

The remaining method is `processToken`, which is shown in Figure 11.20 (page 324). When we see an operand, it is pushed onto the postfix stack. If we see a close parenthesis, we repeatedly pop and process the top operator on the operator stack until the opening parenthesis is seen (lines 19 to 21). The open parenthesis is then popped at line 23. (The test at line 22 is used to avoid popping the sentinel in the event of a missing open parenthesis.) Otherwise, we have the general operator case, which is succinctly described by the code in lines 29 to 34. A simple `main` routine is given in Figure 11.21 (page 325). It repeatedly reads a line of input, instantiates an `Evaluator` object, and computes its value.

11.2.4 Expression Trees

In an *expression tree*, the leaves contain operands and the other nodes contain operators.

Figure 11.22 shows an example of an *expression tree*. The leaves of an expression tree are operands such as constants or variable names, and the other nodes contain operators. This particular tree happens to be binary because all of the operations are binary. Although this is the simplest case, it is possible for nodes to have more than two children. It is also possible for a node to have only one child, as is the case with the unary minus operator.

We evaluate an expression tree T by applying the operator at the root to the values obtained by recursively evaluating the left and right subtrees. In this example, the left subtree evaluates to `(a+b)` and the right subtree evaluates to `(a-b)`. The entire tree therefore represents `((a+b)*(a-b))`. It is evident that we can produce an (overly parenthesized) infix expression by recursively producing a parenthesized left expression, then printing out the operator at the root, and finally recursively producing a parenthesized right expression. This general strategy (left, node, right) is called an *inorder traversal*. This type of traversal is easy to remember because of the type of expression it produces.

A second strategy is to recursively print the left subtree, then the right subtree, and then the operator (without parentheses). We obtain the postfix expression. This is called a *postorder traversal of the tree*. A third strategy for evaluating a tree results in a prefix expression. All of these strategies are discussed in Chapter 17. The expression tree (and its generalizations) are useful data structures in compiler design because they allow us to see an entire expression. This makes code generation easier and in some cases greatly enhances optimization efforts.

Of interest is the construction of an expression tree given an infix expression. As already shown, we can always convert an infix expression to postfix, so it suffices to show how to construct an expression tree from a postfix expression. Not surprisingly, this is simple. We maintain a stack of (references to) trees. When we see an operand, we create a single-node tree and push a reference to it onto our stack. When we see an operator, the top two trees on the stack are popped and merged. In the new tree, the node is the operator, the right child is the first tree popped from the stack, and the left child is the second tree popped. A reference to the result is then pushed back onto the stack. This is essentially the same algorithm as that used in a postfix evaluation, with tree creation replacing the binary operator computation.

> Recursive printing of the expression tree can be used to obtain an infix, postfix, or prefix expression.

> Expression trees can be constructed from a postfix expression in a similar manner as postfix evaluation.

Summary

This chapter examined two uses of stacks in the general area of programming language and compiler design. It illustrated that even though the stack is a simple structure, it is very powerful. Stacks can be used to decide if a sequence of symbols is well-balanced. The resulting algorithm uses linear time and, equally important, consists of a single sequential scan of the input. Operator precedence parsing is a technique that can be used to parse infix expressions. It, too, uses linear time and a single sequential scan. Two stacks are used by the operator precedence parsing algorithm. Although the stacks store different types of objects, the generic mechanism allows the use of a single stack implementation for both types of objects.

Objects of the Game

expression tree A tree in which the leaves contain operands and the other nodes contain operators. (326)

infix expression An expression in which a binary operator has arguments to its left and right. When there are several operators, precedence and associativity determine how the operators are processed. (313)

lexical analysis The process of recognizing tokens in a stream of symbols. (306)

operator precedence parsing An algorithm that converts an infix expression to a postfix expression in order to evaluate the infix expression. (316)

postfix expression An expression that can be evaluated by a postfix machine without using any precedence rules. (314)

postfix machine Machine used to evaluate a postfix expression. The algorithm it uses is as follows: Operands are pushed onto a stack and an operator pops its operands and then pushes the result. At the end of the evaluation, the stack should contain exactly one element, which represents the result. (314)

precedence table A table used to decide what is removed from the operator stack. Left-associative operators have the operator stack precedence set at 1 higher than the input symbol precedence. Right-associative operators go the other way. (325)

state machine A common technique used to parse symbols. At any point, the machine is in some state. Each input character takes it to a new state. Eventually, the state machine reaches a state at which a symbol has been recognized. (308)

Common Errors

1. Errors in the input must be handled as carefully as possible. It is a programming error to be lax in this area.
2. For the balanced symbol routine, handling quotes incorrectly is a common error.
3. For the infix to postfix algorithm, the precedence table must reflect the correct precedence and associativity.

On the Internet

Both application programs are available in the directory **Chapter11**. You should probably download the balancing program; it may help you debug other Java programs. Here are the filenames:

JavaAnalyzer.java	Contains the balanced-symbol program. A version that includes a cross-reference generator (see Chapter 12) can be found in directory **Part3**.
Evaluator.java	Contains the expression evaluator.

Exercises

In Short

11.1. Show the result of running the balanced-symbol program on the following inputs:
   a. }
   b. (}
   c. [[[
   d.) (
   e. [ )]

11.2. Show the postfix expression for the following:
   a. 1 + 2 - 3 ^ 4
   b. 1 ^ 2 - 3 * 4
   c. 1 + 2 * 3 - 4 ^ 5 + 6
   d. (1 + 2) * 3 - (4 ^ (5 - 6))

11.3. For the infix expression a + b ^ c * d ^ e ^ f - g - h / (i + j), do the following:
   a. Show how the operator precedence parsing algorithm generates the corresponding postfix expression.
   b. Show how a postfix machine evaluates the resulting postfix expression.
   c. Draw the resulting expression tree.

In Theory

11.4. For the balanced-symbol program, explain how to print out an error message that is likely to reflect the probable cause.

11.5. Explain, in general terms, how unary operators are incorporated into the expression evaluators. Assume that the unary operators precede their operands and have high precedence. Include a description of how they are recognized by the state machine.

In Practice

11.6. The use of the ^ operator for exponentiation is likely to confuse Java programmers (because it is the bitwise exclusive-or operator). Rewrite the `Evaluator` class with ** as the exponentiation operator.

11.7. The infix evaluator accepts illegal expressions in which the operators are misplaced. Do the following:
   a. What will 1 2 3 + * be evaluated as?
   b. How can we detect these illegalities?
   c. Modify the `Evaluator` class to do so.

Programming Projects

11.8. Modify the expression evaluator to handle negative input numbers.

11.9. Implement a complete Java expression evaluator. Handle all Java operators that can accept constants and make arithmetic sense.

11.10. Implement a Java expression evaluator that includes variables. Assume that there are at most 26 variables, namely, a through z, and that a variable can be assigned to by an = operator of low precedence (as in Java).

11.11. Write a program that reads an infix expression and generates a postfix expression.

11.12. Write a program that reads a postfix expression and generates an infix expression.

11.13. Design a calculator applet that uses a keypad for input.

11.14. Write an applet that illustrates how the two stacks change during execution of the infix-expression evaluation.

11.15. Write a Java application that provides a GUI for the balanced-symbol program. Use a file dialog, and place the output in a text area.

References

The infix to postfix algorithm (*operator precedence parsing*) was first described in [3]. Some good books on compiler construction are [1] and [2].

1. A. V. Aho, R. Sethi, and J. D. Ullman, *Compiler Design: Principles, Techniques, and Tools*, Addison-Wesley, Reading, Mass. (1986).

2. C. N. Fischer and R. J. LeBlanc, *Crafting a Compiler with C*, Benjamin/Cummings, Redwood City, Calif. (1991).

3. R. W. Floyd, "Syntactic Analysis and Operator Precedence," *Journal of the ACM* **10:3** (1963), 316–333.

12

Utilities

THIS chapter discusses two utility applications of data structures: data compression and cross referencing. Data compression is an important technique in computer science. It can be used to reduce the size of files stored on disk (in effect increasing the capacity of the disk) and also to increase the effective rate of transmission across modems (by transmitting less data). Virtually all newer modems perform some type of compression. Cross referencing is a scanning and sorting technique that is done, for example, to make an index for a book.

In this chapter, we will see:

- A discussion of a file-compression algorithm called *Huffman's algorithm* and a description of how it can be implemented (an actual implementation is beyond the scope of this text, however)
- An implementation of a cross-referencing program that lists, in sorted order, all identifiers in a Java program and gives the line numbers on which they occur

12.1 File Compression

The ASCII character set consists of roughly 100 printable characters. To distinguish these characters, $\lceil \log 100 \rceil = 7$ bits are required. Seven bits allow the representation of 128 characters, so the ASCII character set adds some other "unprintable" characters. An eighth bit is added to allow parity checks. The important point, however, is that if the size of the character set is C, then $\lceil \log C \rceil$ bits are needed in a standard fixed-length encoding.

A standard encoding of C characters uses $\lceil \log C \rceil$ bits.

Suppose we have a file that contains only the characters a, e, i, s, t, plus blank spaces (*sp*) and newlines (*nl*). Suppose further that the file has 10 a's, 15 e's, 12 i's, 3 s's, 4 t's, 13 blanks, and 1 newline. As the table in Figure 12.1 shows, this file requires 174 bits to represent, since there are 58 characters and each character requires 3 bits.

In real life, files can be quite large. Many very large files are the output of some program, and there is usually a big disparity between the most-frequent and least-frequent characters. For instance, many large data files have an inordinately large number of digits, blanks, and newlines but few q's and x's.

Character	Code	Frequency	Total Bits
a	000	10	30
e	001	15	45
i	010	12	36
s	011	3	9
t	100	4	12
sp	101	13	39
nl	110	1	3
Total			**174**

Figure 12.1 A standard coding scheme

Reducing the amount of bits required for data representation is called *compression*. Compression consists of two phases: the encoding phase (compressing) and the decoding phase (uncompressing).

In a variable-length code, the most-frequent characters have the shortest representation.

There are many situations in which reducing the size of a file is desirable. For instance, since disk space is precious on virtually every machine, decreasing the amount of space that is required for files would increase the effective capacity of the disk. When data is being transmitted across phone lines by a modem, the effective rate of transmission is increased if the amount of data that is transmitted can be reduced. Reducing the amount of bits required for data representation is called *compression*. Actually, compression consists of two phases: the encoding phase (compression) and the decoding phase (uncompression). A simple strategy discussed in this chapter achieves 25 percent savings on typical large files and as much as 50 or 60 percent savings on many large data files. Extensions provide somewhat better compression.

The general strategy is to allow the code length to vary from character to character and to ensure that frequently occurring characters have short codes. Notice that if all characters occur with the same or very similar frequency, we cannot expect any savings.

12.1.1 Prefix Codes

In a *binary trie*, a left branch represents 0 and a right branch represents 1. The path to a node indicates its representation.

The binary code in Figure 12.1 can be represented by the binary tree in Figure 12.2. In that tree, characters are stored only in leaf nodes. The representation of each character can be found by starting at the root and recording the path, using a 0 to indicate the left branch and a 1 to indicate the right branch. For instance, *s* is reached by going left, then right, and finally right. This is encoded as 011. This data structure is sometimes called a *binary trie* (pronounced "try"). If character c_i is at depth d_i and occurs f_i times, then the *cost* of the code is equal to $\sum d_i f_i$.

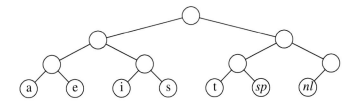

Figure 12.2   Representation of the original code by a tree

A better code than the one given in Figure 12.2 can be obtained by noticing that *nl* is an only child. By placing it one level higher (in place of its parent), we obtain the new tree shown in Figure 12.3. This new tree has a cost of 173 but is still far from optimal.

Notice that the tree in Figure 12.3 is a *full tree* — all nodes either are leaves or have two children. An optimal code will always have this property; otherwise, as already shown, nodes with only one child could move up a level. If the characters are placed only at the leaves, any sequence of bits can always be decoded unambiguously.

For instance, suppose the encoded string is 0100111100010110001000111. Figure 12.3 shows that 0 is not a character code and 01 is not a character code, but 010 represents *i*, so the first character is *i*. Then 011 follows, which is an *s*. Then 11 follows, which is a newline (*nl*). The remainder of the code is *a*, *sp*, *t*, *i*, *e*, and *nl*.

The character codes can be different lengths, as long as no character code is a prefix of another character code. Such an encoding is called a *prefix code*. Conversely, if a character is contained in a nonleaf node, it is no longer possible to guarantee that the decoding will be unambiguous.

Putting these facts together, we see that our basic problem is to find the full binary tree of minimum cost (as defined previously) in which all characters are contained in the leaves. The tree in Figure 12.4 shows the optimal tree for our sample alphabet. As can be seen in Figure 12.5, this code uses only 146 bits. Notice that there are many optimal codes. These can be obtained by swapping children in the encoding tree.

> In a *full tree*, all nodes either are leaves or have two children.

> In a *prefix code*, no character code is a prefix of another character code. This is guaranteed if the characters are only in leaves. A prefix code can be decoded unambiguously.

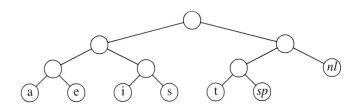

Figure 12.3   A slightly better tree

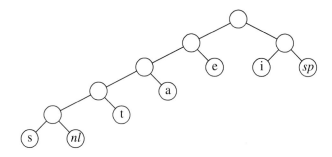

Figure 12.4 Optimal prefix code tree

12.1.2 Huffman's Algorithm

Huffman's algorithm constructs an optimal prefix code. It works by repeatedly merging the two minimum-weight trees.

How is the coding tree constructed? The coding system algorithm was given by Huffman in 1952 and is commonly called *Huffman's algorithm.*

Throughout this section, the number of characters is C. Huffman's algorithm can be described as follows: We maintain a forest of trees. The *weight* of a tree is equal to the sum of the frequencies of its leaves. $C - 1$ times, select the two trees, T_1 and T_2, of smallest weight, breaking ties arbitrarily, and form a new tree with subtrees T_1 and T_2. At the beginning of the algorithm, there are C single-node trees (one for each character). At the end of the algorithm, there is one tree. This is an optimal Huffman tree. Exercise 12.4 asks you to prove that Huffman's algorithm is correct.

Character	Code	Frequency	Total Bits
a	001	10	30
e	01	15	30
i	10	12	24
s	00000	3	15
t	0001	4	16
sp	11	13	26
nl	00001	1	5
Total			**146**

Figure 12.5 Optimal prefix code

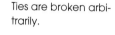

Figure 12.6   Initial stage of Huffman's algorithm

An example will make the operation of the algorithm clear. Figure 12.6 shows the initial forest; the weight of each tree is shown in small type at the root. The two trees of lowest weight are merged together, creating the forest shown in Figure 12.7. The new root is $T1$. We have made s the left child arbitrarily; any tie-breaking procedure can be used. The total weight of the new tree is just the sum of the weights of the old trees and can thus be easily computed.

Now there are six trees, and we again select the two trees of smallest weight, $T1$ and t. They are merged into a new tree with root $T2$ and weight 8. This is shown in Figure 12.8. The third step merges $T2$ and a, creating $T3$, with weight $10 + 8 = 18$. Figure 12.9 shows the result of this operation.

Ties are broken arbitrarily.

Figure 12.7   Huffman's algorithm after the first merge

Figure 12.8   Huffman's algorithm after the second merge

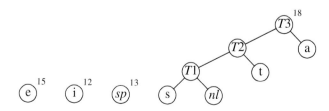

Figure 12.9   Huffman's algorithm after the third merge

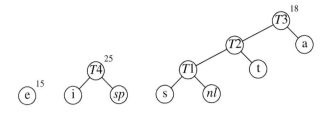

Figure 12.10 Huffman's algorithm after the fourth merge

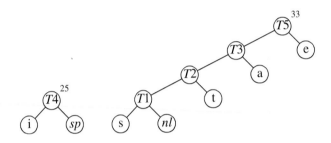

Figure 12.11 Huffman's algorithm after the fifth merge

After the third merge is completed, the two trees of lowest weight are the single-node trees representing i and the blank space. Figure 12.10 shows how these trees are merged into the new tree with root $T4$. The fifth step is to merge the trees with roots e and $T3$, since these trees have the two smallest weights. The result of this step is shown in Figure 12.11.

Finally, an optimal tree, shown previously in Figure 12.4, is obtained by merging the two remaining trees. Figure 12.12 shows the optimal tree, with root $T6$.

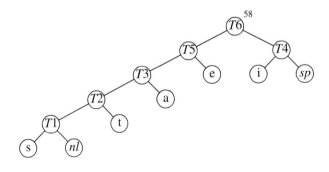

Figure 12.12 Huffman's algorithm after the final merge

12.1.3   The Encoding Phase

Once a tree is built, we must decide on the code for each character. This can be done if every node in the tree stores its parent and an indication of whether it is a left child or right child. If there are C characters, then there will be $2C - 1$ nodes. We can use an array of entries containing the weight, parent, and child status.

The code can be represented in an array.

   The encoding table for our Huffman tree is shown in Figure 12.13. The character is not really stored but rather is used to index into the table (presumably, then 'a' would index into position 97, which is its ASCII value; 'b' would index into 98; and so on). The parent of *nl*, for example, is $T1$, and *nl* is a right child. We can print *nl*'s code by recursively printing $T1$'s code and then the child type. Notice that $T6$ has 0 for a parent. This tells us when to stop the recursion. Since the ASCII set runs from 0 to 127, the array would run from 0 to 254 to represent the fact that at most $C - 1$ internal symbols might be needed.

12.1.4   Decoding Phase

Eventually, we need to uncompress a compressed file. To do this, we must include extra information in the compressed file. Obviously, we want to include as little information as possible. Assume that we are using the ASCII character set.

	Character	Weight	Parent	Child Type
0	a	10	9	1
1	e	15	11	1
2	i	12	10	0
3	s	3	7	0
4	t	4	8	1
5	sp	13	10	1
6	nl	1	7	1
7	T1	4	8	0
8	T2	8	9	0
9	T3	18	11	0
10	T4	25	12	1
11	T5	33	12	0
12	T6	58	0	

Figure 12.13   Encoding table (numbers on left are array indices)

One possibility is to store the character counts. This requires 128 integers. Presumably, 24-bit (that is, 3-byte) integers will suffice (16-bit integers are probably not sufficient because it is possible that some characters occur more than 65,535 times if the file is large). The total storage requirement is 384 bytes.

For the ASCII character set, we can store the tree in 255 bytes.

An alternative is to store the parent and child type information. Since every parent is a newly created node, the value of the parent is a number between 128 and 254. Consequently, we need 7 bits to store the parent. In fact, we can use an 8-bit character: the low 7 bits plus 128 will represent the parent (the root can use 255 as its parent). This leaves the 8th (that is, the most-significant) bit free to represent the child type. Consequently, the total storage requirement for the coding information is 255 bytes.

12.1.5 Practical Considerations

A practical algorithm cannot scan the file twice. There are several alternatives.

Before we can begin compression, we need a frequency count for each character. If the file is small enough to fit in main memory, we can read the file into a character array, compute the character counts, and apply the algorithm. But what if it is too large?

Certainly we do not want to read the file twice; disk I/O is extremely slow. A possibility is to break the file into chunks that can be stored in main memory and then compress each chunk separately. Most modern computers can store several megabytes at a time, so the overhead of 255 bytes for each coding table is not likely to be large.

An alternative is to assume that the input file is "typical." For instance, the distribution of characters in Java programs is well-known. An advantage of this method is that we do not need to store the coding table; this is particularly attractive if the file sizes are not huge. There are many other possibilities that have been explored, as well as more complex compression schemes that perform even better than Huffman coding. See the references for some pointers.

12.2 A Cross-reference Generator

A *cross-reference generator* lists identifiers and their line numbers. It is a common application because it is similar to creating an index.

In this section, we design a program that scans a Java source file and outputs all identifiers, along with the line numbers on which they occur. The identifiers are sorted. This is called a *cross-reference generator*. One compiler application is to list, for each function, the names of all other functions that it directly calls.

However, this is a general problem that occurs in many other contexts. For instance, it generalizes the creation of an index for a book. Another use, spell checking, is described in Exercise 12.16. As a spelling checker detects misspelled words in a document, those words are gathered together with the lines on which they occur. This avoids repeatedly printing out the same misspelled word and provides an indication of where the errors are.

12.2.1 Basic Ideas

Each identifier and the line numbers on which it occurs is stored in an `IdNode` object. We then maintain a sorted collection of `IdNodes`. When the source file has been read, we can iterate over the collection, outputting identifiers and their corresponding line numbers.

One alternative is to use a sorted linked list of `IdNode` objects. When an identifier is read, we check to see if it is already in the list of `IdNode` objects. If so, we add the current line number to the `IdNode` object referenced by a call to `find`. If not, we create a new `IdNode` object with the new identifier and the current line number and insert the `IdNode` into the linked list. After the entire input is read, we can iterate over the linked list and output our answers. However, a sorted linked list has poor asymptotic performance. Consequently, we use a binary search tree and perform an inorder traversal to obtain the final output.

We store the line numbers for each identifier in a queue. We place the identifiers in a binary search tree.

The `IdNode` object stores the identifier and the line numbers on which it occurs. The identifier can be represented by a `String`. The line numbers can be represented by a queue of integers. This makes sense because when we output the line numbers, they will come out in the same order as they went in — increasing order. Thus each `IdNode` stores a reference to a queue that is allocated when the `IdNode` is constructed. The implementation is described in the next subsection.

12.2.2 Java Implementation

Figure 12.14 (page 340) shows the `IdNode` class (which contains only package-friendly members). An `IdNode` consists of a string and a reference to a queue of integers. The `String` field `word` is declared at line 9: `lines`, which is the reference to a queue of integers, is declared at line 10. The constructor implemented at lines 13 to 18 initializes an `IdNode` with a `String` and a line number. The `String` component is initialized in the normal way. `lines` is initialized by creating a queue and enqueueing `currentLine`. The rest of the `IdNode` class implements the `Comparable` interface.

The class shown in Figure 12.15 (page 341) is similar to the one shown in Figure 11.2, which was part of a balanced-symbol program (the online code provides a version that merges these two classes into one). Many of the methods were already seen there, and their implementations are not repeated. We do not use inheritance. The possibility of creating an abstract base class and two derived classes is left as Exercise 12.13.

The new parsing routines deal with recognizing an identifier. At line 31, an `IdNode` object is declared. It will store the identifier that is currently being processed. This is because since we will store a tree of `IdNode` objects, we need an `IdNode` object to pass to the `find` and `insert` routines.

The parsing routines are straightforward, although as usual they require lots of effort.

```
 1  /**
 2   * The basic object that will be stored in a search tree
 3   * for the cross-reference generator.
 4   * It implements the Comparable interface by providing
 5   * compares and lessThan.
 6   */
 7  class IdNode implements Comparable
 8  {
 9      String word;     // An identifier
10      Queue  lines;    // Lines where it occurs
11
12          // Constructor
13      IdNode( String theWord, int currentLine )
14      {
15          word = new String( theWord );
16          lines = new QueueAr( );
17          lines.enqueue( new Integer( currentLine ) );
18      }
19
20          // Ordering methods
21      public boolean lessThan( Comparable rhs )
22      {
23          return word.compareTo( ((IdNode)rhs).word ) < 0;
24      }
25
26      public int compares( Comparable rhs )
27      {
28          return word.compareTo( ((IdNode)rhs).word );
29      }
30  }
```

Figure 12.14 IdNode class

A Java identifier consists of alphanumeric characters and underscores, with the restriction that the first character may not be a digit. Consequently, the routine in Figure 12.16 (page 342) tests if a character is part of an identifier. The get-String routine in Figure 12.17 (page 342) assumes that the first character of an identifier is already read and is stored in the class data field ch. It repeatedly reads characters until one that is not part of an identifier is seen. At that point, we put the character back (at line 12) and then return a String .[1]

getNextID, shown in Figure 12.18 (page 343), is similar to the routine in Figure 11.7. The difference is that here, at line 15, if the first character of an identifier is seen, we fill currentIdNode.word with the identifier.

[1.] Java 1.1 provides methods to test if a character can be part of a Java identifier. See Appendix C.1.1 for details.

```
 1  // JavaAnalyzer class: cross-reference generator
 2  //
 3  // CONSTRUCTION: with a PushbackReader object
 4  // *****************PUBLIC OPERATIONS*********************
 5  // void generateCrossReference( ) --> Name says it all ...
 6  // *****************ERRORS********************************
 7  // Error checking on comments and quotes is performed
 8
 9  import java.io.*;
10  import DataStructures.*;
11  import Exceptions.*;
12  import Supporting.*;
13
14  /**
15   * Class to generate cross reference for Java programs.
16   */
17  class JavaAnalyzer
18  {
19      public JavaAnalyzer( PushbackReader inStream )
20      {
21          errors = 0;
22          ch = '\0';
23          currentLine = 1;
24          in = inStream;
25          currentIdNode = new IdNode( "", 1 );
26      }
27
28      public void generateCrossReference( )
29        { /* Figure 12.19 */ }
30
31      private IdNode currentIdNode;
32
33      private static int isIdChar( ch )
34        { /* Figure 12.16 */ }
35      private String getString( )
36        { /* Figure 12.17 */ }
37      private int getNextID( )
38        { /* Figure 12.18 */ }
39
40          // These are all unchanged from Figure 11.2
41      private PushbackReader in;        // The input stream
42      private char ch;                  // Current character
43      private int currentLine;          // Current line
44      private int errors;               // Number of errors seen
45      private boolean nextChar( )
46      private void putBackChar( )
47      private void skipComment( int start )
48      private void skipQuote( char quoteType )
49      private void processSlash( )
50  }
```

Figure 12.15   Class skeleton for the cross-reference generator

```
1       /**
2        * Return true if ch can be part of a Java identifier
3        */
4       private boolean isIdChar( char ch )
5       {
6           return ch == '_' || Character.isUpperCase( ch )
7                            || Character.isLowerCase( ch )
8                            || Character.isDigit( ch );
9       }
```

Figure 12.16 Routine to test if a character could be part of an identifier

If the item is found, we add to the referenced queue.

With all of the supporting routines written, we can deal with the main method, generateCrossReference, which is shown in Figure 12.19 (page 344). Lines 6 and 7 define a binary search tree of IdNode objects. Lines 10 to 28 process the source file. At lines 14 and 15, a find is performed for each identifier to see if it has already been seen. If the find is successful, then at lines 16 and 17 we can enqueue the current line onto the corresponding queue. Otherwise, we have a new identifier. In that case, we add it to the search tree at lines 21 to 26.

If an item is not found, we create a new IdNode, enqueue the current line, and insert it into the tree.

Recall that the insert method needs an IdNode object. Consequently, we create a new, unnamed IdNode by calling the constructor in Figure 12.14. A reference to the new IdNode will be placed in the search tree. This means that in the IdNode contained in the search tree, its lines field references the queue.

```
1       /**
2        * Return an identifier read from input stream
3        * First character is already read into ch
4        */
5       private String getString( )
6       {
7           String tmpString = "";
8
9           for( tmpString += ch; nextChar( ); tmpString += ch )
10              if( !isIdChar( ch ) )
11              {
12                  putBackChar( );
13                  break;
14              }
15
16          return tmpString;
17      }
```

Figure 12.17 Routine to return a String from input

```
1      /**
2       * Return next identifier, skipping comments,
3       * string constants, and character constants.
4       * Place identifier in currentIdNode.word and return false
5       * only if end of stream is reached.
6       */
7      private boolean getNextID( )
8      {
9          while( nextChar( ) )
10         {
11             if( ch == '/' )
12                 processSlash( );
13             else if( ch == '\'' || ch == '"' )
14                 skipQuote( ch );
15             else if( !Character.isDigit( ch ) &&
16                     isIdChar( ch ) )
17             {
18                 currentIdNode.word = getString( );
19                 return true;
20             }
21         }
22         return false;        // End of file
23     }
```

Figure 12.18   Routine to fill `currentIdNode.word` with the next identifier

Once we have built the search tree, we merely iterate through it using an inorder traversal. To do this, we use the `InOrder` class described in Section 17.4.2. The iterator visits nodes in the binary search tree in their sorted order. It is used in the same way as `ListItr`. The iterator is declared at line 33, while at line 34 the standard iteration methods provided by the `InOrder` class are used. At line 36, `thisNode` is a reference to the `IdNode` object that is stored in the current search tree node. We print the word and the first line number at lines 39 and 40 (we are guaranteed that the queue is not empty) by dequeueing that line number. While the queue is not empty, we repeatedly output line numbers in the loop that extends from line 43 to 45. We print out a newline at line 46. A main program is not provided because it is essentially identical to that in Figure 11.10.

The output is obtained by an inorder traversal using an iterator class.

Summary

This chapter presented the implementations of two important utilities. Text compression is an important technique that allows us to increase both the effective disk capacity and the effective modem speed. It is an area of active research. The simple method described here, namely, Huffman's algorithm, typically achieves compression of 25 percent on text files. Other algorithms and extensions of Huffman's algorithm perform better. The cross-referencing problem is a general problem that also has many applications.

```
1     /**
2      * Output the cross reference.
3      */
4     public void generateCrossReference( )
5     {
6         BinarySearchTree theIdentifiers =
7                                     new BinarySearchTree( );
8
9             // Insert identifiers into the search tree
10        while( getNextID( ) )
11        {
12            try
13            {
14                IdNode thisNode = (IdNode)
15                        theIdentifiers.find( currentIdNode );
16                thisNode.lines.enqueue(
17                        new Integer( currentLine ) );
18            }
19            catch( ItemNotFound e )
20            {
21                try
22                {
23                    theIdentifiers.insert( new IdNode
24                        ( currentIdNode.word, currentLine ) );
25                }
26                catch( DuplicateItem ex ) { } // Cannot happen
27            }
28        }
29            // Iterate through search tree and output
30            // identifiers and their line number.
31        try
32        {
33            InOrder itr = new InOrder( theIdentifiers );
34            for( itr.first( ); itr.isValid( ); itr.advance( ))
35            {
36                IdNode thisNode = (IdNode) itr.retrieve( );
37
38                // Print identifier and first occurrence
39                System.out.print( thisNode.word + ": " +
40                        (Integer) thisNode.lines.dequeue( ) );
41
42                    // Print other lines on which it occurs
43                while( !thisNode.lines.isEmpty( ) )
44                    System.out.print( ", " + (Integer)
45                                    thisNode.lines.dequeue( ) );
46                System.out.println( );
47            }
48        }
49        catch( ItemNotFound e ) { }    // Empty tree
50        catch( Underflow e ) { }       // Cannot happen
51    }
```

Figure 12.19 Main cross-reference algorithm

Objects of the Game

binary trie A data structure in which a left branch represents 0 and a right branch represents 1. The path to a node indicates its representation. (332)

compression The act of reducing the amount of bits required for data representation. There are actually two phases: the encoding phase (compression) and the decoding phase (uncompression). (332)

cross-reference generator Program that lists identifiers and their line numbers. It is a common application because it is similar to creating an index. (338)

full tree A tree whose nodes either are leaves or have two children. (333)

Huffman's algorithm An algorithm that constructs an optimal prefix code. It works by repeatedly merging the two minimum-weight trees. (334)

prefix code Code in which no character code is a prefix of another character code. This is guaranteed in a trie if the characters are only in leaves. A prefix code can be decoded unambiguously. (333)

Common Errors

1. When performing file compression, do not read the input file twice.
2. Using too much memory to store the compression table is a common mistake. This limits the amount of compression that can be achieved.

On the Internet

The cross-reference generator is available in the directory **Chapter12**. Here is the filename:

JavaAnalyzer.java   Contains the source for the cross-reference generator. A program that includes the balanced symbol routine from Chapter 11 is in directory **Part3**.

Exercises

In Short

12.1. Show the Huffman tree that results from the following distribution of punctuation characters and digits: colon (100), space (605), newline (100), comma (705), 0 (431), 1 (242), 2 (176), 3 (59), 4 (185), 5 (250), 6 (174), 7 (199), 8 (205), and 9 (217).

12.2. Most systems come with a compression program. Compress several types of files to determine the typical compression rate on your system. How large do the files have to be to make compression worthwhile?

12.3. What happens if a file compressed using Huffman's algorithm is used to transmit data over a phone line and a single bit is accidentally lost? What can be done about this?

In Theory

12.4. Prove the correctness of Huffman's algorithm by expanding the following steps:
  a. Show that no node has only one child.
  b. Show that the two least-frequent characters must be the two deepest nodes in the tree.
  c. Show that the characters in any two nodes at the same depth can be swapped without affecting optimality.
  d. Use induction: As trees are merged, consider the new character set to be the characters in the tree roots.

12.5. Under what circumstances could a Huffman tree of ASCII characters generate a 2-bit code for some character? Under what circumstances could it generate a 20-bit code?

12.6. Show that if the symbols are already sorted by frequency, Huffman's algorithm can be implemented in linear time.

In Practice

12.7. For the cross-reference generator, use a sorted linked list instead of a binary search tree. How does this affect performance?

12.8. The disadvantage of using a queue to store line numbers is that the queue is emptied in the course of this operation. This could be a liability in some cases. Instead of storing the line numbers in a queue, use a linked list. Implement the following strategies and compare their performances:
  a. Replace an `enqueue` with an insertion at the end of the linked list. A traversal of the list is used.
  b. Store both a linked list and a `ListItr` object that refers to the last item in the linked list. The insertion at the end of the linked list should be more efficient than that in part (a).

12.9. Combine Exercises 12.7 and 12.8 so that the cross-reference generator uses a sorted linked list to store the word information and the word information consists of a `String`, a list of line numbers, and a `ListItr` to the end of the list.

12.10. Modify `IdNode` in the cross-reference generator by adding a `toString` method that outputs the name and line numbers of the `IdNode`. Then simplify the `generateCrossReference` method accordingly. This use of `toString` is misleading because `toString` does not normally alter the state of the object it acts upon. However, here, it makes the object's queue of lines empty. What can be done to repair this incongruity?

12.11. If a word occurs twice on a line, the cross-reference generator will list it twice. Modify the algorithm so that duplicates are listed only once.

```
IX: {Series|()              {2}
IX: {Series!geometric|()  {4}
IX: {Euler's constant}      {4}
IX: {Series!geometric|)}  {4}
IX: {Series!arithmetic|()  {4}
IX: {Series!arithmetic|)}  {5}
IX: {Series!harmonic|()   {5}
IX: {Euler's constant}      {5}
IX: {Series!harmonic|)}   {5}
IX: {Series|)}              {5}
```

Figure 12.20 Sample input for Exercise 12.15

```
Euler's constant: 4, 5
Series: 2-5
   arithmetic: 4-5
   geometric: 4
   harmonic: 5
```

Figure 12.21 Sample ouput for Exercise 12.15

12.12. Modify the cross-reference generator so that if a word appears on consecutive lines, a range is indicated. For example,

```
if: 2, 4, 6-9, 11
```

Programming Projects

12.13. Split the `JavaAnalyzer` into three classes: an abstract base class that handles the common functionality and separate derived classes `CheckBalance` and `GenerateCrossReference`.

12.14. Add a GUI component to the cross-reference generator that includes the option for an advanced query such as reporting specific names (rather than a simple traversal) in the binary search tree.

12.15. Generate an index for a book. The input file consists of a set of index entries. Each line consists of the string `IX:`, followed by an index entry name enclosed in braces, followed by a page number that is enclosed in braces. Each ! in an index entry name represets a sub-level. A | (represents the start of a range and a |) represents the end of the range. Occasionally, this range will be the same page. In that case, output only a single page number. Otherwise, do not collapse or expand ranges on your own. As an example, Figure 12.20 shows sample input and Figure 12.21 shows the corresponding output.

12.16. Implement a spelling checker using a hash table. Assume that the dictionary comes from two sources: an existing large dictionary and a second file containing a personal dictionary. Output all misspelled words and the line numbers on which they occur (note that keeping track of the misspelled words and their line numbers is identical to generating a cross reference). Also, for each misspelled word, list any words in the dictionary that are obtainable by applying any of the following rules:

a. Add one character.

b. Remove one character.

c. Exchange adjacent characters.

12.17. Implement an interactive applet that demonstrates how the Huffman coding tree is constructed.

12.18. Implement a complete file compression program. Do not forget to provide a decompression algorithm. You will need to write a `BitStream` class. Note that if the total number of bits in the output code is not a precise multiple of the number of bits in a byte, then some stray bits will have to appear in the compressed output. You will have to provide a mechanism by which these extraneous bits will be ignored.

References

The original paper on Huffman's algorithm is [3]. Variations on the algorithm are discussed in [2] and [4]. Another popular compression scheme is *Ziv-Lempel encoding*, described in [7] and [6]. It works by generating a series of fixed-length codes. Typically, we would generate 4,096 12-bit codes that represent the most common substrings in the file. [1] and [5] are good surveys of the common compression schemes.

1. T. Bell, I. H. Witten, and J. G. Cleary, "Modelling for Text Compression," *ACM Computing Surveys* **21** (1989) 557–591.

2. R. G. Gallager, "Variations on a Theme by Huffman," *IEEE Transactions on Information Theory* **IT-24** (1978), 668–674.

3. D. A. Huffman, "A Model for the Construction of Minimum Redundancy Codes," *Proceedings of the IRE* **40** (1952), 1098–1101.

4. D. E. Knuth, "Dynamic Huffman Coding," *Journal of Algorithms* **6** (1985), 163–180.

5. D. A. Lelewer and D. S. Hirschberg, "Data Compression," *ACM Computing Surveys* **19** (1987), 261–296.

6. T. A. Welch, "A Technique for High-Performance Data Compression," *Computer* **17** (1984), 8–19.

7. J. Ziv and A. Lempel, "Compression of Individual Sequences via Variable-Rate Coding," *IEEE Transactions on Information Theory* **IT-24** (1978), 530–536.

13

Simulation

A N important use of computers is for *simulation*. In a simulation, the computer emulates the operation of a real system and gathers statistics. As an example, we might want to simulate the operation of a bank with k tellers to determine the minimum value of k that gives reasonable service time. Using a computer would provide many advantages. First, the information would be gathered without involving real customers. Second, a simulation by computer can be faster than the actual implementation because of the speed of the computer. Third, the simulation could be easily replicated. In many cases, the proper choice of data structures can help us improve the efficiency of the simulation.

In this chapter, we will see:

- How to simulate a game modeled on the *Josephus problem*
- How to simulate the operation of a computer modem bank

An important use of computers is simulation. In a simulation, the computer emulates the operation of a real system and gathers statistics.

13.1 The Josephus Problem

The *Josephus problem* is the following game. N people, numbered 1 to N, are sitting in a circle. Starting at person 1, a hot potato is passed. After M passes, the person holding the hot potato is eliminated, the circle closes ranks, and the game continues with the person who was sitting after the eliminated person picking up the hot potato. The last remaining person wins. It is common to assume that M is a constant of the game, although a random-number generator can be used to change M after each elimination.

The Josephus problem arose in the first century AD in a cave on a mountain in Israel where Jewish zealots were being besieged by Roman soldiers. The historian Josephus was among them. To Josephus's consternation, the zealots voted to form a suicide pact rather than surrender to the Romans. He suggested the game mentioned here. The hot potato was the sentence of death to the person next to the one who got the potato. Josephus rigged the game to get the last lot and convinced the intended victim that they should surrender. That is how we know about this game; in effect, Josephus cheated.[1]

In the Josephus *problem, a hot potato is repeatedly passed. When passing terminates, the player holding the potato is eliminated. The game continues, and the last remaining player wins.*

---

[1]. Thanks to David Teague for relaying this story. The version that we solve differs from the historical description. Exercise 13.11 asks you to solve the historical version.

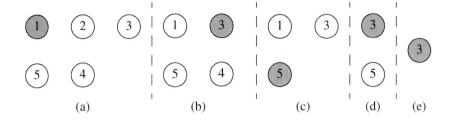

Figure 13.1   The Josephus problem. In each step, the darkest circle represents the initial holder and the lightly shaded circle represents the player who receives the hot potato (and is eliminated). Passes are made clockwise

If $M = 0$, then the players are eliminated in order and the last player always wins. For other values of M, things are not so obvious. Figure 13.1 shows that if $N = 5$ and $M = 1$, then the players are eliminated in the order 2, 4, 1, 5. In this case, player 3 wins. The steps are as follows:

1. At the start, the potato is at player 1. After one pass it is at player 2.
2. Player 2 is eliminated. Player 3 picks up the potato, and after one pass, it is at player 4.
3. Player 4 is eliminated. Player 5 picks up the potato and passes it to player 1.
4. Player 1 is eliminated. Player 3 picks up the potato and passes it to player 5.
5. Player 5 is eliminated, so player 3 wins.

First, we will write a program that simulates, pass for pass, a game for any values of N and M. The running time of the simulation is $O(MN)$, which is acceptable if the number of passes is small. Each step takes $O(M)$ time because it performs M passes. We will then show how to implement each step in $O(\log N)$ time, regardless of the number of passes that are performed. The running time of the simulation becomes $O(N \log N)$.

13.1.1   The Simple Solution

We can represent the players by a linked list and use the iterator to simulate the passing.

The passing stage in the Josephus problem suggests that we represent the players in a linked list. We create a linked list in which the elements 1, 2, ..., N are inserted in order. We then set an iterator to the front element. Each pass of the potato corresponds to an advance operation on the iterator. When we are at the last player (currently remaining) in the list, we implement the pass by resetting the iterator to the first element. This action mimics the circle. When we are done passing, we remove the element on which the iterator has landed.

```
1    /**
2     * Return the winner in the Josephus problem.
3     * Linked list implementation.
4     */
5    public static int josephus( int people, int passes )
6    {
7        LinkedListItr p = new LinkedListItr( new LinkedList( ) );
8
9            // Construct the list
10       try
11       {
12           for( int i = 1; i <= people; i++ )
13               p.insert( new Integer( i ) );
14       }
15       catch( ItemNotFound e ) { }  // Cannot happen
16
17           // Play the game;
18           // Note: p is always one player before
19       while( people-- != 1 )
20       {
21           for( int i = 0; i < passes; i++ )
22           {
23               p.advance( );          // Advance
24               if( !p.isInList( ) ) // If past last player
25                   p.first( );        // then go back to first
26           }
27
28           if( !p.removeNext( ) )    // Remove next player
29           {
30               // removeNext fails if p is last item, so for
31               p.zeroth( );     // last item, set p to 0th
32               p.removeNext( );// player to remove 1st player
33           }
34       }
35           // Get first and only player and return player's #
36       p.first( );
37       return  ( (Integer)( p.retrieve( ) ) ).intValue( );
38   }
```

Figure 13.2   Linked-list implementation of Josephus problem

For reasons explained in Chapter 16, it is easier to remove the element after the current position by using the removeNext method. This is reflected by the code in Figure 13.2, where we initialize current to the last, rather than the first, player. The anonymous linked list and its iterator are declared at line 7. We construct the initial list by using the loop at lines 12 and 13. The semantics of insert, as specified in the class in Figure 16.7, tell us the insertions are after the iterator's position and that the result of an insertion is to set the iterator's position to the inserted item. Thus we get the list in the order that we want.

We maintain the iterator at the player prior to the current player so that removeNext can be applied.

In Figure 13.2, the code at lines 21 to 33 plays one step of the algorithm by passing the potato (lines 21 to 26) and then eliminating a player (lines 28 to 33). This is done until the test at line 19 tells us that only one player remains. At that point, we go to the remaining player by calling the `first` method at line 36. (Recall that during most of the algorithm, the iterator is before the logically current player.) Then we access and return the player's number at line 37.

The running time is O(MN).

It is easy to see that the running time of this routine is $O(MN)$ because this is exactly the number of passes that occur during the algorithm. For small M, this is acceptable. However, note that the case in which $M = 0$, this does not yield a running time of $O(0)$; the running time is $O(N)$. One does not merely multiply by zero when trying to interpret a Big-Oh expression.

13.1.2   A More Efficient Algorithm

If we implement each round of passing in a single logarithmic operation, the simulation will be faster.

A more efficient algorithm can be obtained if we use a data structure that supports accessing the kth smallest item (in logarithmic time). This will allow us to implement each round of passing in a single operation. Figure 13.1 shows why. Suppose we have N players remaining and we are currently at player P from the front. Initially N is the total number of players and P is 1. After M passes, a calculation tells us that we will be at player $((P + M) \bmod N)$ from the front, except if that would give us player 0, in which case, we go to player N. The calculation is fairly tricky, but the concept is not.

The calculation is tricky because of the circle.

Applying this calculation to Figure 13.1, we see that M is 1, N is initially 5, and P is initially 1. So the new value of P is 2. After the deletion, N is lowered to 4, but we are still at position 2 (as part (b) of the figure suggests). The next value of P is 3 (as shown in part (b)), so the third element in the list is deleted and N is lowered to 3. The next value of P is 4 mod 3, or 1, so we are back to the first player in the remaining list (as shown in part (c)). This player is removed and N becomes 2. At this point, we add M to P, obtaining 2. Since 2 mod 2 is 0, we set P to player N, and thus the last player in the list is the one that is removed. This agrees with part (d). After the removal, N is 1 and we are done.

findKth can be supported by a search tree.

All we need then is a data structure that efficiently supports the `findKth` operation and a method of inserting the players sequentially into the data structure. There are several similar alternatives. All of them use the fact that a binary search tree can support the `findKth` operation in logarithmic time on average or logarithmic time in the worst case if we use a sophisticated binary search tree. Consequently, we can expect an $O(N \log N)$ algorithm if we exercise care.

The simplest method is to insert the items sequentially into a worst-case efficient binary search tree such as a red-black tree, AA-tree, or splay tree (these trees are discussed in later chapters). We can then call `findKth` and `remove`, as appropriate. It turns out that a splay tree is an excellent choice for this application because the `findKth` and `insert` operations will be unusually efficient and `remove` is not terribly difficult to code. We use an alternative here, however, because the implementations of these data structures that are provided in the later chapters leave implementing findKth as an exercise.

```
1      /**
2       * Recursively construct a perfectly balanced tree
3       * by repeated insertions in O( N log N ) time
4       * t should be empty on the initial call
5       */
6      public static void buildTree( BinarySearchTreeWithRank t,
7                                    int low, int high )
8      {
9          int center = ( low + high ) / 2;
10
11         if( low <= high )
12         {
13             try
14               { t.insert( new MyInteger( center ) ); }
15             catch( DuplicateItem e ) { }   // Cannot happen
16
17             buildTree( t, low, center - 1 );
18             buildTree( t, center + 1, high );
19         }
20     }
21
22     /**
23      * Return the winner in the Josephus problem.
24      * Search tree implementation.
25      */
26     public static int josephus( int people, int passes )
27     {
28         BinarySearchTreeWithRank t = new BinarySearchTreeWithRank( );
29         try
30         {
31             buildTree( t, 1, people );
32
33             int rank = 1;
34             while( people > 1 )
35             {
36                 rank = ( rank + passes ) % people;
37                 if( rank == 0 )
38                     rank = people;
39
40                 t.remove( t.findKth( rank ) );
41                 people--;
42             }
43
44             return ( (MyInteger)( t.findKth( 1 ) ) ).intValue( );
45         }
46         catch( Exception e )
47           { return -1; } // Cannot happen
48     }
```

Figure 13.3 $O(N \log N)$ solution of the Josephus problem

A balanced search tree will work, but it is not needed if we are careful and construct a simple binary search tree that is not unbalanced at the start. A class method can construct a perfectly balanced tree in linear time.

We construct the same tree by recursive insertions but use $O(N \log N)$ time.

We use the `BinarySearchTreeWithRank` class that supports the `findKth` operation and is completely implemented in Section 18.2. It is based on the simple binary search tree and thus does not have logarithmic worst-case performance but merely average-case performance. Consequently, we cannot merely insert the items sequentially; that would cause the search tree to exhibit its worst-case performance.

There are several options. One is to insert a random permutation of 1, ..., N into the search tree. The other is to build a perfectly balanced binary search tree using a class method. Because a class method would have access to the inner workings of the search tree, this could be done in linear time. This routine is left as Exercise 18.19 when search trees are discussed.

The method we take is to write a recursive routine that inserts items in a balanced order. By inserting the middle item at the root and recursively building the two subtrees in the same manner, we obtain a balanced tree. The cost of our routine is an acceptable $O(N \log N)$. While not as efficient as the linear-time class routine, it does not adversely affect the asymptotic running time of the overall algorithm. The `remove` operations are then guaranteed to be logarithmic. This routine is called `buildTree`; it and the `josephus` method are then coded as shown in Figure 13.3 (page 353).

13.2 Event-driven Simulation

Let us return to the bank simulation problem described in the introduction. Here, we have a system in which customers arrive and wait on a line until one of k tellers is available. Customer arrival is governed by a probability distribution function, as is the service time (the amount of time to be served once a teller is available). We are interested in statistics such as how long on average a customer has to wait and what percentage of the time tellers are actually servicing requests. (If there are too many tellers, some will not do anything for long periods.)

With certain probability distributions and values of k, these answers can be computed exactly. However, as k gets larger the analysis becomes considerably more difficult, so it is appealing to use a computer to simulate the operation of the bank. In this way, bank officers can determine how many tellers are needed to ensure reasonably smooth service. Most simulations involve thorough knowledge of probability, statistics, and queueing theory.

13.2.1 Basic Ideas

A discrete event simulation consists of processing events. Here, the two events are (a) a customer arriving and (b) a customer departing, thus freeing up a teller.

We can use a probability function to generate an input stream consisting of ordered pairs of arrival and service time for each customer, sorted by arrival time.[2] We do not need to use the exact time of day. Rather, we can use a quantum unit, referred to as a *tick*.

The *tick* is the quantum unit of time in a simulation.

We might start a simulation clock at zero ticks. We then advance the clock one tick at a time, checking to see if there is an event. If there is, then we process the event(s) and compile statistics. When there are no customers left in the input stream and all the tellers are free, then the simulation is over. This is a *discrete time-driven simulation*.

A *discrete time-driven simulation* processes each unit of time consecutively. It is inappropriate if the interval between successive events is large.

The problem with this simulation strategy is that its running time does not depend on the number of customers or events (there are two events per customer in this case). Rather, it depends on the number of ticks, which is not really part of the input. To see why this is important, suppose we change the clock units to microticks and multiply all the times in the input by 1 million. The result would be that the simulation would take 1 million times longer.

The key to avoiding this problem is to advance the clock to the next event time at each stage. Thus we have an *event-driven simulation*. This is conceptually easy to do. At any point, the next event that can occur is either the arrival of the next customer in the input stream or the departure of one of the customers at a teller. Since all the times when the events will happen are available, we just need to find the event that happens nearest in the future and process that event (setting the current time to the time that the event occurs).

An *event-driven simulation* advances the current time to the next event.

If the event is a departure, processing includes gathering statistics for the departing customer and checking the line (queue) to see if there is another customer waiting. If so, we add that customer, process whatever statistics are required, compute the time when the customer will leave, and add that departure to the set of events waiting to happen.

If the event is an arrival, we check for an available teller. If there is none, we place the arrival on the line (queue). Otherwise, we give the customer a teller, compute the customer's departure time, and add the departure to the set of events waiting to happen.

The waiting line for customers can be implemented as a queue. Since we need to find the event *nearest* in the future, the set of events should be organized in a priority queue. The next event is thus an arrival or departure (whichever is sooner); both are easily available. An event-driven simulation is appropriate if the number of ticks between events is expected to be large.

The event set (that is, events waiting to happen) is organized as a priority queue.

---

2. The probability function generates interarrival times (times between arrivals), thus guaranteeing that arrivals are generated in chronological order.

```
 1 User 0 dials in at time 0 and connects for 1 minutes
 2 User 0 hangs up at time 1
 3 User 1 dials in at time 1 and connects for 5 minutes
 4 User 2 dials in at time 2 and connects for 4 minutes
 5 User 3 dials in at time 3 and connects for 11 minutes
 6 User 4 dials in at time 4 but gets busy signal
 7 User 5 dials in at time 5 but gets busy signal
 8 User 6 dials in at time 6 but gets busy signal
 9 User 1 hangs up at time 6
10 User 2 hangs up at time 6
11 User 7 dials in at time 7 and connects for 8 minutes
12 User 8 dials in at time 8 and connects for 6 minutes
13 User 9 dials in at time 9 but gets busy signal
14 User 10 dials in at time 10 but gets busy signal
15 User 11 dials in at time 11 but gets busy signal
16 User 12 dials in at time 12 but gets busy signal
17 User 13 dials in at time 13 but gets busy signal
18 User 3 hangs up at time 14
19 User 14 dials in at time 14 and connects for 6 minutes
20 User 8 hangs up at time 14
21 User 15 dials in at time 15 and connects for 3 minutes
22 User 7 hangs up at time 15
23 User 16 dials in at time 16 and connects for 5 minutes
24 User 17 dials in at time 17 but gets busy signal
25 User 15 hangs up at time 18
26 User 18 dials in at time 18 and connects for 7 minutes
27 User 19 dials in at time 19 but gets busy signal
```

Figure 13.4   Sample output for the modem bank simulation: 3 modems; a dial-in is attempted every minute; average connect time is 5 min; simulation is run for 19 min

13.2.2   Example: A Modem Bank Simulation

The main algorithmic item in a simulation is the organization of the events in a priority queue. To focus on this, we write a very simple simulation. The system we simulate is a *modem bank* at a university computing center.

A *modem bank* consists of a large collection of modems. For example, Florida International University (FIU) has 96 modems available for students. A modem is accessed by dialing one telephone number. If any of the 96 modems are available, then the user is connected to one of them. If all modems are in use, then the phone will be busy. Our simulation models the service provided by the modem bank. The variables are as follows:

- The number of modems in the bank
- The probability distribution that governs dial-in attempts

- The probability distribution that governs connect time
- How long the simulation is to be run

The modem bank simulation is a simplified version of the bank teller simulation because there is no waiting line. Each dial-in is an arrival, and the total time spent once a connection is established is the service time. By removing the waiting line, we remove the need to maintain a queue. Thus we have only one data structure, the priority queue. Exercise 13.17 asks you to incorporate a queue; up to *L* calls will be queued if all the modems are busy. To simplify matters, we do not compute statistics. Instead, we list each event as it is processed. We also assume that attempts to connect occur at constant intervals; in an accurate simulation, we would model this interarrival time by a random process. Figure 13.4 shows the output of a simulation.

The *modem bank* removes the waiting line from the simulation. Thus there is only one data structure.

We list each event as it happens; gathering statistics is a simple extension.

```
1   /**
2    * The event class.
3    * Implements the Comparable interface
4    * to arrange events by time of occurrence.
5    */
6   class Event implements Comparable
7   {
8       static final int DIAL_IN = 1;
9       static final int HANGUP  = 2;
10
11      public Event( )
12        { this( 0, 0, DIAL_IN ); }
13
14      public Event( int name, long tm, int type )
15        { who = name; time = tm; what = type; }
16
17      public boolean lessThan( Comparable rhs )
18        { return time < ((Event)rhs).time; }
19
20      public int compares( Comparable rhs )
21      {
22          return lessThan( rhs ) ? -1 :
23                 rhs.lessThan( this ) ? 1 : 0;
24      }
25
26      int who;         // the number of the user
27      long time;       // when the event will occur
28      int what;        // DIAL_IN or HANGUP
29  }
```

Figure 13.5   Event class used for the modem bank simulation

The Event class represents events. In a complex simulation, it would derive all of the possible types of events as subclasses. Using inheritance for the Event class would complicate the code.

The simulation class requires another class that represents events. The Event class is shown in Figure 13.5 (page 357). The data fields consist of the customer number, the time that the event will occur, and an indication of what type of event (DIAL_IN or HANGUP) this is. If this simulation was more complex, with several types of events, we would certainly make Event an abstract base class and derive subclasses from it. We do not do that here because that would complicate things and obscure the basic workings of the simulation algorithm. The Event class contains constructors and implements the Comparable interface. Note that its zero-parameter constructor exists so that it can create a $-\infty$ sentinel for a priority queue that stores a collection of Event objects. The Event class uses package-friendly data fields.

```
1  // ModemSim class: run a simulation
2  //
3  // CONSTRUCTION: with three parameters: the number of
4  //       modems, the average connect time, and the
5  //       interarrival time
6  //
7  // ******************PUBLIC OPERATIONS********************
8  // void runSim( )        --> Run a simulation
9
10 /**
11  * The ModemSim class.
12  */
13 public class ModemSim
14 {
15     public ModemSim( int modems, double avgLen,
16                      long callIntrvl )
17       { /* Figure 13.7 */ }
18
19     public void runSim( long stoppingTime )
20       { /* Figure 13.9 */ }
21
22     private Random r;                 // A random source
23     private PriorityQueue eventSet; // Pending events
24
25         // Basic parameters of the simulation
26     private int freeModems;           // Number of modems unused
27     private double avgCallLen;        // Length of a call
28     private long freqOfCalls;         // Interval between calls
29
30     private void nextCall( long delta )
31       { /* Figure 13.8 */ }
32 }
```

Figure 13.6 ModemSim class skeleton

```
1       /**
2        * Constructor.
3        * @param modem number of modems.
4        * @param avgLen averge length of a call.
5        * @param callIntrvl the average time between calls.
6        */
7       public ModemSim( int modems, double avgLen,
8                           long callIntrvl )
9       {
10          eventSet     = new BinaryHeap( new Event( ) );
11          freeModems   = modems;
12          avgCallLen   = avgLen;
13          freqOfCalls  = callIntrvl;
14          r            = new Random( );
15          nextCall( freqOfCalls );   // Schedule first call
16      }
```

Figure 13.7   ModemSim constructor

The modem simulation class, ModemSim, is shown in Figure 13.6. It consists of a host of data fields, a constructor, and two methods. The data fields include a random-number object r shown at line 22. At line 23, the eventSet is maintained as a PriorityQueue of Event objects. There are three remaining data fields. One is freeModems, which is initially the number of modems in the simulation but which changes as users connect and hangup. The other two are avgCallLen and freqOfCalls, which are parameters of the simulation. Recall that a dial-in attempt will be made every freqOfCalls ticks. The constructor at lines 15 and 16 that is implemented in Figure 13.7 initializes these fields and places the first arrival in the eventSet priority queue.

```
1           // Used by nextCall only
2       private int  userNum = 0;
3       private long nextCallTime = 0;
4
5       /**
6        * Place a new DIAL_IN event into the event queue.
7        * Then advance the time when next DIAL_IN event will
8        * occur. In practice, we would use a random number to
9        * set the time.
10       */
11      private void nextCall( long delta )
12      {
13          EventSet.insert( new Event( userNum++, nextCallTime,
14                                  Event.DIAL_IN ) );
15          nextCallTime += delta;
16      }
```

Figure 13.8   nextCall: Place a new DIAL_IN event into the event queue
                    and advance the time when the next DIAL_IN event will occur

nextCall adds a dial-in request to the event set.

The simulation class consists of only two methods. First, nextCall, shown in Figure 13.8 (page 359), adds a dial-in request to the event set. It maintains two (global) class variables: the number of the next user that will attempt to dial in and the time that event will occur. Once again, we make the simplifying assumption that calls are made at regular intervals. In practice, we would use a random-number generator to model the arrival stream.

runSim runs the simulation.

The other method is runSim, which is called to run the entire simulation. runSim does most of the work and is shown in Figure 13.9. It is called with a single parameter that indicates when the simulation should end. As long as the event set is not empty, we process events. Note that it should never be empty because when we arrive at line 13, there is exactly one dial-in request in the priority queue, plus one hang-up request for every currently connected modem. Whenever we remove an event at line 13 and it is confirmed to be a dial-in, we generate a replacement dial-in event at line 42. A hang-up event is also generated at line 37 if the dial-in succeeds. Thus the only way to finish the routine is if nextCall is set up not to generate an event eventually or (more likely) by executing the break statement at line 17.

A hangup increases freeModems. A dial-in checks to see if a modem is available and, if so, decreases freeModems.

Here is a summary of how the various events are processed. If the event is a hang-up, then we increment freeModems at line 21 and print a message at lines 22 and 23. If the event is a dial-in, we generate a partial line of output that records the attempt, and then, if there are modems available, we connect the user. To do this, we decrement freeModems at line 31 and generate a connection time (using a Poisson distribution rather than a uniform distribution) at line 32. We then print the rest of the output at lines 33 and 34 and add a hang-up to the event set (lines 35 to 37). Otherwise, there are no modems available and we give the busy signal message. Either way, an additional dial-in event is generated. Figure 13.10 (page 362) shows the state of the priority queue after each deleteMin for the early stages of the sample output shown in Figure 13.4. The time when each event occurs is shown in boldface, and the number of free modems (if any) are shown to the right of the priority queue. The sequence of priority queue steps is as follows:

1. The first DIAL_IN request is inserted.
2. After DIAL_IN is removed, the request is connected, thereby resulting in a HANGUP and a replacement DIAL_IN request.
3. A HANGUP request is processed.
4. A DIAL_IN request is processed resulting in a connect. Thus both a HANGUP and DIAL_IN event are added (three times).
5. A DIAL_IN request fails; a replacement DIAL_IN is generated (three times).
6. A HANGUP request is processed (twice).
7. A DIAL_IN request succeeds, and HANGUP and DIAL_IN are added.

```
1       /**
2        * Run the simulation until stoppingTime occurs.
3        * Print output as in Figure 13.4.
4        */
5       public void runSim( long stoppingTime )
6       {
7           Event e = null;
8           long howLong;
9
10          while( !eventSet.isEmpty( ) )
11          {
12              try
13                { e = (Event) eventSet.deleteMin( ); }
14              catch( Underflow ex ) { } // Cannot happen
15
16              if( e.time > stoppingTime )
17                  break;
18
19              if( e.what == Event.HANGUP )     // HANGUP
20              {
21                  freeModems++;
22                  System.out.println( "User " + e.who +
23                              " hangs up at time " + e.time );
24              }
25              else                            // DIAL_IN
26              {
27                  System.out.print(  "User " + e.who +
28                        " dials in at time " + e.time + " " );
29                  if( freeModems > 0 )
30                  {
31                      freeModems--;
32                      howLong = r.poisson( avgCallLen );
33                      System.out.println(  "and connects for "
34                                      + howLong + " minutes" );
35                      e.time += howLong;
36                      e.what = Event.HANGUP;
37                      eventSet.insert( e );
38                  }
39                  else
40                      System.out.println( " gets busy signal" );
41
42                  nextCall( freqOfCalls );
43              }
44          }
45      }
```

Figure 13.9   Basic simulation routine

Once again, if Event was an abstract base class, we would expect a procedure doEvent to be defined through the Event hierarchy; then we would not
need long chains of if/else statements. However, to access the priority queue,

which is in the simulation class, we would need Event to store a reference to the ModemSim simulation class (in which it is contained) as a data field. This would be done at construction time.

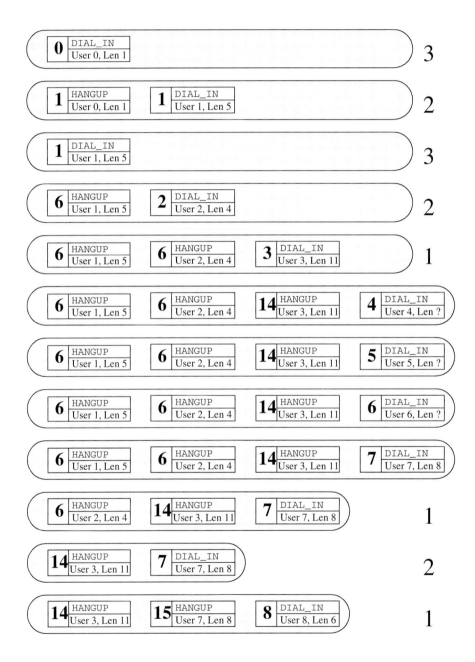

Figure 13.10 Priority queue for modem bank simulation after each step

```
1       /**
2        * Quickie main for testing purposes.
3        * Generates output in Figure 13.4.
4        */
5       public static void main( String [ ] args )
6       {
7           ModemSim s = new ModemSim( 3, 5.0, 1 );
8           s.runSim( 20 );
9       }
```

Figure 13.11 Simple `main` to run simulation

A `main` routine that generates the output shown in Figure 13.4 is shown in Figure 13.11. Note that using a Poisson distribution to model connect time is not appropriate. A better choice is to use a negative exponential distribution (but the reasons for this are beyond the scope of the text). Also, it is inaccurate to assume a fixed time between attempts to dial in. Again, a negative exponential distribution would be a better model. If we change the simulation to use these distributions, the clock would be represented as a `double`. Exercise 13.13 asks you to implement these changes.

The simulation uses a poor model. A negative exponential distribution would more accurately model both the time between dial-in attempts and the total connect time.

Summary

Simulation is an important area of computer science. There are many more complexities involved than can be discussed here. The simulation is only as good as the model of randomness, so a solid background in probability, statistics, and queueing theory is required in order to know what types of probability distributions are reasonable to assume. Simulation is an important application area for object-oriented techniques.

Objects of the Game

discrete time-driven simulation A simulation in which each unit of time is processed consecutively. It is inappropriate if the interval between successive events is large. (355)

event-driven simulation A simulation in which the current time is advanced to the next event. (355)

Josephus problem A problem in which a hot potato is repeatedly passed. When passing terminates, the player holding the potato is eliminated. The game then continues, and the last remaining player wins. (349)

simulation An important use of computers in which the computer emulates the operation of a real system and gathers statistics. (349)

tick The quantum unit of time in a simulation. (355)

Common Errors

1. The most common error in simulation is using a poor model. A simulation is only as good as the accuracy of its random input.

On the Internet

All the examples in this chapter are available online in directory **Chapter13**. Here are the fileneames.

Josephus.java   Contains both implementations of `josephus` and a `main` to test them.

ModemSim.java   Contains the code for the modem bank simulation.

Exercises

In Short

13.1. If $M = 0$, who wins the Josephus game?

13.2. Show the operation of the Josephus algorithm with an abstract binary-search tree for the case of 7 people with 3 passes. Include a picture of the tree after each deletion.

13.3. Are there any values of M for which player 1 wins a 30-person Josephus game?

13.4. Show the state of the priority queue after each of the first ten lines of the simulation depicted in Figure 13.4.

In Theory

13.5. Let $N = 2^k$ for any integer k. Prove that if M is 1, then player 1 always wins the Josephus game.

13.6. Let $J(N)$ be the winner of an N-player Josephus game with $M = 1$. Show the following:
   a. If N is even, $J(N) = 2J(N/2) - 1$.
   b. If N is odd and $J(\lceil N/2 \rceil) \neq 1$, then $J(N) = 2J(\lceil N/2 \rceil) - 3$.
   c. If N is odd and $J(\lceil N/2 \rceil) = 1$, then $J(N) = N$.

13.7. Use the results in Exercise 13.6, to write an algorithm that returns the winner of an N-player Josephus game with $M = 1$. What is the running time of your algorithm?

13.8. Give a general formula for the winner of an N-player Josephus game with $M = 2$.

13.9. Using the algorithm for $N = 20$, determine the order of insertion into the `BinarySearchTreeWithRank`.

13.10. Prove that after `buildTree` (in Figure 13.3), all leaves are at either the deepest or next-deepest level.

In Practice

13.11. Write a program that solves the historical version of the Josephus problem. Give both the linked list and search tree algorithms.

13.12. Implement the Josephus algorithm using a queue. Each pass of the potato is a `dequeue` followed by an `enqueue`.

13.13. Rework the simulation so that the clock is represented as a double, the time between dial-in attempts is modeled with a negative exponential distribution, and the connect time is modeled with a negative exponential distribution.

13.14. Rework the modem bank simulation so that `Event` is an abstract base class and `DialInEvent` and `HangUpEvent` are derived classes. The `Event` class should store a `ModemSim` reference as an additional data field, which is initialized on construction. It should also provide an abstract method named `doEvent` that is implemented in the derived classes and that can be called from `runSim` to process the event.

Programming Projects

13.15. Implement the Josephus algorithm using splay trees (see Chapter 21) and sequential insertion. (The splay tree class is available online, but it will need a `findKth` method.) Compare the performance with that in the text and with an algorithm that uses a linear-time, balanced-tree building algorithm.

13.16. Rewrite the Josephus algorithm in Figure 13.3 to use a *median heap* (Exercise 6.21). Use a simple implementation of the median heap; the elements are maintained in sorted order. Compare the running time of this algorithm with the time obtained using the binary search tree.

13.17. Suppose FIU has installed a system that queues phone calls when all modems are busy. Rewrite the simulation routine to allow for various-sized queues. Make an allowance for an infinite queue.

13.18. Rewrite the simulation to gather statistics rather than output each event. Then compare the speed of the simulation, assuming several hundred modems and a very long simulation, with some other possible priority queues (some of which are available online), namely, the following:
   a. An asymptotically inefficient priority queue representation described in Exercise 6.16
   b. An asymptotically inefficient priority queue representation described in Exercise 6.17
   c. Splay trees (see Chapter 21)
   d. Skew heaps (see Chapter 22)
   e. Pairing heaps (see Chapter 22)

13.19. Implement an applet that illustrates the operation of the Josephus game using both the linked-list and search-tree algorithms.

14

Graphs and Paths

T HIS chapter examines the *graph* and shows how to solve a particular problem, namely, calculation of shortest paths. This is a fundamental problem in computer science because many interesting applications can be modeled by a graph. Examples of shortest-path calculations are computing the fastest route through mass transportation and routing electronic mail through a network of computers. The chapter examines variations of the problem that depend on how we interpret the meaning of "shortest" and the kinds of properties the graph has. Shortest-path problems are interesting because although the algorithms are fairly simple, they are slow for large graphs unless careful attention is paid to the choice of data structures.

In this chapter, we will see:

- Formal definitions of a graph and its components
- The data structures used to represent a graph
- Algorithms to solve several variations of the shortest-path problem, with complete Java implementations

14.1 Definitions

A *graph* $G = (V, E)$ consists of a set of vertices, V, and a set of edges, E. Each edge is a pair (v, w), where $v, w \in V$. Vertices are sometimes called *nodes*, and edges are sometimes called *arcs*. If the edge pair is ordered, then the graph is *directed*. Directed graphs are sometimes called *digraphs*. In a digraph, vertex w is *adjacent* to vertex v if and only if $(v, w) \in E$. Sometimes an edge has a third component, called a *weight* or a *cost*. In this chapter, all graphs are directed.

The graph in Figure 14.1 (page 368) has the following 7 vertices:

$$V = \{V_0, V_1, V_2, V_3, V_4, V_5, V_6\}$$

and 12 edges:

$$E = \left\{ \begin{array}{l} (V_0, V_1, 2), (V_0, V_3, 1), (V_1, V_3, 3), (V_1, V_4, 10) \\ (V_3, V_4, 2), (V_3, V_6, 4), (V_3, V_5, 8), (V_3, V_2, 2) \\ (V_2, V_0, 4), (V_2, V_5, 5), (V_4, V_6, 6), (V_6, V_5, 1) \end{array} \right\}.$$

A *graph* consists of a set of vertices and a set of edges that connect the vertices. If the edges are ordered, then the graph is *directed*.

w is *adjacent* to v if there is an edge from v to w

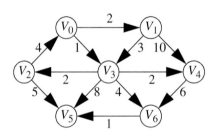

Figure 14.1   A directed graph

A *path* is a se-
quence of vertices
that are con-
nected by edges.

A *cycle* in a di-
rected graph is a
path that begins
and ends at the
same vertex and
contains at least
one edge.

The following vertices are adjacent to V_3: V_2, V_4, V_5, V_6. For this graph, $|V| = 7$ and $|E| = 12$; here, $|S|$ represents the size of set S.

A *path* in a graph is a sequence of vertices $w_1, w_2, \ldots, w_N$ such that $(w_i, w_{i+1}) \in E$ for $1 \le i < N$. The *length* of such a path is the number of edges on the path, namely, $N - 1$. This is called the *unweighted path length*. The *weighted path length* is the sum of the costs of the edges on the path. As an example, V_0, V_3, V_5 is a path from vertex V_0 to V_5. The path length is two edges, and the weighted path length is 9 — this is the shortest path between V_0 and V_5. However, if the cost is important, then the weighted shortest path between these vertices has cost 6 and is V_0, V_3, V_6, V_5. A path may exist from a vertex to itself. If this path contains no edges, then the path length is 0. This is a convenient way to define an otherwise special case. A *simple path* is a path in which all vertices are distinct, except that the first and last can be the same.

A *cycle* in a directed graph is a path of length at least 1 such that $w_1 = w_N$; this cycle is simple if the path is simple. A *directed acyclic graph*, sometimes referred to by its abbreviation, *DAG*, is a directed graph with no cycles.

An example of a real-life situation that can be modeled by a graph is the airport system. Each airport is a vertex. If there is a nonstop flight between the corresponding airports, two vertices are connected by an edge. The edge could have a weight, representing time, distance, or the cost of the flight. Generally, an edge (v, w) would imply an edge (w, v). But it is reasonable to assume that the costs of the edges might be different, since flying in different directions might take longer (depending on prevailing winds) or cost more (depending on local taxes). Naturally, we want to quickly determine the best flight between any two airports; "best" could mean the path with the fewest number of edges or could be taken with respect to one, or all, of the weight measures (distance, cost, and so on).

A second example of a real-life situtation that can be modeled by a graph is the routing of electronic mail through computer networks. Vertices represent computers, the edges represent links between pairs of computers, and the edge costs represent communication costs (phone bills per megabytes), delay costs (seconds per megabyte), or combinations of these and other factors.

For most graphs, there is likely at most one edge from any vertex v to any other vertex w (this allows one edge in each direction between v and w). Consequently, $|E| \leq |V|^2$. When most edges are present, we have $|E| = \Theta(|V|^2)$, and the graph is considered *dense* – that is, it has a large number of edges.

In most applications, the graph is *sparse* rather than dense. For instance, in the airport model, we do not expect direct flights between every pair of airports. Instead, we find that a few airports are very well connected and most others have relatively few flights. In a complex mass transportation system involving buses and trains, for any one station we have only a few other stations that are directly reachable and thus represented by an edge. Moreover, in a computer network most computers are attached to a few other local computers. So, in most cases, the graph is relatively *sparse*: $|E| = \Theta(|V|)$, or perhaps slightly more (there is no standard definition of sparse). It is thus most important that the algorithms we develop are efficient for sparse graphs.

A graph is dense *if the number of edges is large (generally quadratic). Typical graphs are not dense. Instead, they are* sparse.

14.1.1 Representation

The first thing to consider is how a graph is represented internally. Assume that the vertices are sequentially numbered starting from 0, as the graph in Figure 14.1 suggests. One simple way to represent a graph is to use a two-dimensional array. This is an *adjacency matrix* representation. For each edge (v, w), we set a[v][w] equal to the edge cost; nonexistent edges can be initialized with a logical INFINITY. The initialization of the graph seems to require that the entire adjacency matrix be initialized to INFINITY. Then, as an edge is encountered, an appropriate entry is set. In this scenario, the initialization takes $O(|V|^2)$. Although it is possible to avoid the quadratic initialization cost (see Exercise 14.3), the space cost is still $O(|V|^2)$, which is fine for dense graphs but completely unacceptable for sparse graphs.

An adjacency matrix *represents a graph using quadratic space.*

For sparse graphs, a better solution is an *adjacency list* representation. For each vertex, we keep a linked list of all adjacent vertices. The adjacency list representation of the graph in Figure 14.1 is shown in Figure 14.2. Because each edge appears in a list node, the number of list nodes is exactly equal to the number of edges. Consequently, $O(|E|)$ space is used to store the list nodes. Since we have $|V|$ lists, there is also $O(|V|)$ additional space that is required. If we assume that every vertex is in some edge, then the number of edges is at least $\lceil |V|/2 \rceil$. So we may disregard any $O(|V|)$ terms when an $O(|E|)$ term is present. Consequently, we say that the space requirement is $O(|E|)$, or linear in the size of the graph.

An adjacency list *represents a graph using linear space.*

The adjacency list can be constructed in linear time from a list of edges. We begin by making all the lists empty. When we see an edge $(v, w, c_{v,w})$, we add an entry consisting of w and the cost $c_{v,w}$ to v's adjacency list. The insertion can be anywhere, but it makes sense to do it at the front, in constant time. Consequently, each edge can be inserted in constant time, so the entire adjacency list structure can be constructed in linear time. Note carefully that when inserting an edge, we do not check to see if it is already present. That cannot be done in con-

Adjacency lists can be constructed in linear time from a list of edges.

stant time (using a simple linked list), and doing the check would destroy the linear-time bound for construction. In most cases, this is unimportant. If there are two or more edges of different cost connecting a pair of vertices, any shortest-path algorithm will choose the lower-cost edge without resorting to any special processing.

A *dictionary* can be used to map vertex names to internal numbers.

In most real-life applications, the vertices have names, which are unknown at compile time, instead of numbers. So, we must provide a way to transform names to numbers. The easiest way to do this is to provide a *dictionary* in which we store a vertex name and an internal number ranging from 0 to $|V| - 1$ (the number of vertices is determined as the program runs). The internal numbers are assigned as the graph is read. The first number assigned is zero. As each edge is input, we check whether each of the two vertices has been assigned a number by seeing if it is in the dictionary. If so, we use the internal number. Otherwise, we assign to the vertex the next available number and insert the vertex name and number into the dictionary. With this transformation, all the graph algorithms will use only the internal numbers.

Eventually, we will need to output the real vertex names and not the internal numbers, so we must also record, for each internal number, the corresponding vertex name. One way to do this is to keep a string for each vertex. This technique is used later in the chapter to implement a `Graph` class. The class and the shortest-path algorithms require several data structures: a linked list, a queue, a hash table, and a priority queue. The queue and priority queue are used in various shortest-path calculations. The linked list and hash table are used to represent the graph. In particular, the hash table implements the dictionary.

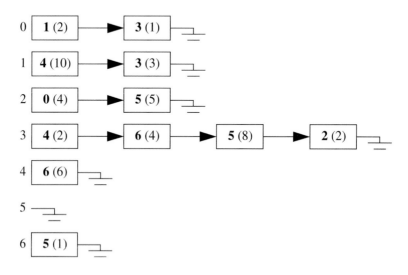

Figure 14.2 Adjacency list representation of the graph in Figure 14.1; nodes in list *i* represent vertices adjacent to *i* and the cost of the connecting edge

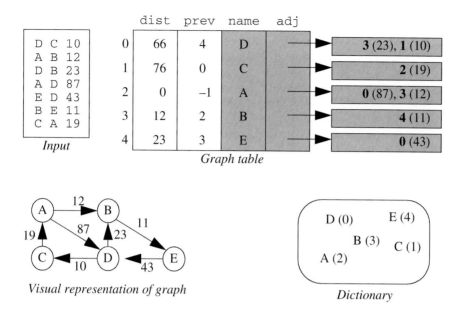

	dist	prev	name	adj
0	66	4	D	→ 3 (23), 1 (10)
1	76	0	C	→ 2 (19)
2	0	−1	A	→ 0 (87), 3 (12)
3	12	2	B	→ 4 (11)
4	23	3	E	→ 0 (43)

Graph table

Input:
```
D C 10
A B 12
D B 23
A D 87
E D 43
B E 11
C A 19
```
Input

Visual representation of graph

Dictionary: D (0), E (4), B (3), C (1), A (2)

Dictionary

Figure 14.3   Data structures used in a shortest-path calculation, with an input graph taken from a file. The shortest weighted path from A to C is A to B to E to D to C (cost 76)

Before the Graph class skeleton is shown, let us examine Figure 14.3, which shows how our graph will be represented. As indicated in the table labeled *Input,* the user is to provide a list of edges, one per line. At the start of the algorithm, we do not know the names of any of the vertices. Neither do we know how many vertices there are nor how many edges there are. We use two data structures to represent the graph: a dictionary and a table. Maintaining a dictionary will allow us to determine the internal number of any vertex. For instance, because D is the first vertex in the input file, it is assigned the number 0. C is the second vertex in the input file, so it is assigned the number 1. The other data structure is a large table that stores information about all the vertices. As is evident from Figure 14.3, the *Graph table* maintains four pieces of information for each vertex:

- dist: The length of the shortest path (either weighted or unweighted, depending on the algorithm) from the starting vertex to this vertex. This value is computed by the shortest-path algorithm.
- prev: The previous vertex on the shortest path to this vertex.
- name: The name corresponding to this vertex. This is established when the vertex is placed into the dictionary and will never change. None of the

The graph representation uses an array of Vertex objects.

shortest path algorithms examine this field. It is used only to print a final path.

- adj: A list of adjacent vertices. This is established when the graph is read. None of the shortest path algorithms will change the linked list.

To be more specific, in Figure 14.3 the shaded items are not altered by any of the shortest-path calculations. The items represent the input graph and do not change unless the graph itself changes (perhaps by the later addition or deletion of edges). The items that are not shaded are computed by the shortest path algorithms. Prior to the calculation, we can assume they are uninitialized.

The algorithms are single source. They compute the shortest paths from some start point to all vertices. The prev field can be used to extract the actual path.

The shortest-path algorithms are all *single source*. That is, they assume some starting point and then compute the shortest paths from the starting point to all other vertices. In this example the starting point is A, which, according to the dictionary, is the internal number 2. Notice that the shortest-path algorithm declares that the shortest path to A is 0. The prev field allows us to print out the shortest path and not just its length. For instance, the table indicates that the shortest path from the starting vertex to C (internal number 1) has total cost 76. Obviously, the last vertex on this path is C. The vertex on this path that is before C is vertex 0, or D. Before D is vertex 4, which is E. Before E is vertex 3, namely, B. Before B is vertex 2, namely, A, which is the start vertex. By tracing back through the prev field, we see that we can construct the shortest path. Although this trace gives the path in reverse order, it is a simple matter to unreverse it. The remainder of this section describes how the shaded part of the graph table is constructed and gives the method that prints out a shortest path, assuming that the dist and prev fields have been computed. Algorithms for filling in the shortest path are discussed individually.

```
1  /**
2   * This class represents the basic
3   * item in the adjacency list.
4   */
5  class Edge
6  {
7                            // First vertex in edge is implicit
8      public int dest;   // Second vertex in edge
9      public int cost;   // Edge cost
10
11     public Edge( int d, int c )
12     {
13         dest = d;
14         cost = c;
15     }
16 }
```

Figure 14.4 The basic item stored in an adjacency list

```
 1  /**
 2   * This class represents the basic item
 3   * stored for each vertex.
 4   */
 5  class Vertex
 6  {
 7      String name;    // The real name
 8      List   adj;     // The adjacency list
 9
10      int dist;       // Cost (after running algorithm)
11      int prev;       // Previous vertex on shortest path
12      int scratch;    // Extra variable for use in algorithm
13
14      Vertex( String nm )
15      {
16          name = nm;                    // Share name in hash table
17          adj  = new LinkedList( ); // Make a new list
18      }
19  }
```

Figure 14.5   Class `Vertex` stores information for each vertex

Figure 14.4 shows the basic item that is placed in the adjacency list, that is, an internal vertex number and the edge cost. We assume the `Graph` class uses a `String` for the vertex name and an `int` for the edge costs. Class `Vertex` is shown in Figure 14.5. An additional field named `scratch` is provided that has different uses in the various algorithms. Everything else follows from the previous description. The only method is a constructor that allocates the linked list.

The item in an adjacency list is an internal vertex number of the adjacent vertex and the edge cost. Each entry in the graph table is of type `Vertex`.

We are now ready to examine the `Graph` class skeleton. The public portion is shown in Figure 14.6 (page 374); the private section is in Figure 14.7 (page 375). Some constants are declared at lines 33 to 35. Line 35 stores the value of `INFINITY` (we divide by 3 so that `INFINITY + INFINITY` does not overflow). Next come the data fields.

`vertexMap` stores the dictionary. We implement the dictionary by using a hash table that stores a `HashItem` containing both the vertex name and number but that searches based only on the vertex name. This is briefly discussed when we examine the implementation. Line 38 is the graph table, `table`. The number of vertices currently in the table is stored in `numVertices` (line 39). The rest of the class provides a host of methods that perform initialization, add vertices, add edges, print the shortest path, and perform various shortest-path calculations. Each routine is discussed when its implementation is examined.

First up is the constructor. Figure 14.8 (page 376) shows that the constructor initializes the number of vertices to 0 and constructs `table`. An empty dictionary is created.

To implement the dictionary, we declare a class named `HashItem` that will store both the vertex name — `name` — and its internal number — `rank`. Equality and the hash function are performed on the basis of the `name` field only. The implementations are shown in Figure 14.9 (page 376).

The dictionary is implemented by using a hash table.

```
 1  import DataStructures.*;
 2  import Supporting.*;
 3  import Exceptions.*;
 4  import java.util.StringTokenizer;
 5  import java.io.*;
 6
 7  // Graph class: evaluate shortest paths
 8  //
 9  // CONSTRUCTION: with no initializer
10  //
11  // *****************PUBLIC OPERATIONS*********************
12  // void addEdges( String source, String dest, int cost )
13  //                      --> Add additional edge
14  // boolean processRequest( BufferedReader in )
15  //                      --> Run a bunch of shortest path algs
16  // *****************ERRORS*******************************
17  // Some error checking is performed to make sure graph is ok,
18  // parameters to processRequest represent vertices in the
19  // graph, and to make sure graph satisfies properties needed
20  // by each algorithm.
21
22  /**
23   * Graph class: evaluate shortest paths.
24   */
25  public class Graph
26  {
27      public Graph( )
28          { /* Figure 14.8 */ }
29      public void addEdge( String source, String dest, int cost )
30          { /* Figure 14.12 */ }
31      public boolean processRequest( BufferedReader in )
32          { /* Figure 14.16 */ }
```

Figure 14.6　Graph class skeleton (part 1: the public section)

addNode returns the internal number corresponding to the parameter vertexName. If vertexName has never been seen, it is added to the dictionary and its entry in the table array is initialized.

addNode, shown in Figure 14.10 (page 377), returns the internal vertex number corresponding to the parameter vertexName. The name of the routine reflects the fact that if vertexName has not already been seen (indicated by its absence from the dictionary), it is assigned the next available internal number and added to the dictionary, and its entry in the table array is initialized.

The procedure begins with a consultation of the hash table. To do this, we first have to create hashV, which is a HashItem object, at line 8, by initializing it with vertexName (using the appropriate constructor).

Once hashV is constructed, we can perform a find of the hash table and store the return value in result. If the find was successful, we can return the rank field of result and be done. Otherwise, we have a newly seen vertex.

At line 19, we assign that new vertex an internal number of numVertices, which represents the next available index into table (because indices start at 0).

At line 21, we perform an `insert` into the hash table. Note that we create a new `String` object that will be referenced by both the hash table and `table` array. A corresponding `Vertex` entry is constructed and added to `table` at line 25. If the graph table `table` is full, then it is doubled at line 24. Line 26 completes the routine by returning `numVertices` (the internal number now assigned to `vertexName`) and then incrementing `numVertices`.

The routine shown in Figure 14.11 (page 377) adds an edge whose vertices are given by internal numbers. This is a simple routine because all that is needed is to create an `Edge` object with the destination vertex and cost and then insert it into the adjacency list corresponding to the source. The routine for public use is shown in Figure 14.12 (page 378). `addEdge` adds an edge whose vertices are given by `Strings`. This is another short routine because it merely consults `addNode` to get the corresponding internal numbers. Then `addInternal-Edge` is called.

Edges are added by insertions into the appropriate adjacency list.

```
33      private static final int INIT_TABLE_SIZE = 50;
34      private static final int NULL_VERTEX     = -1;
35      private static final int INFINITY        = 2147483647 / 3;
36
37      private HashTable  vertexMap;   // Gets internal #
38      private Vertex [ ] table;       // The table array
39      private int        numVertices; // Current # vertices read
40
41      private void doubleTableArray( )
42        { /* Usual stuff, not shown */ }
43      private int addNode( String vertexName )
44        { /* Figure 14.10 */ }
45      private void addInternalEdge( int source, int dest, int cost )
46        { /* Figure 14.11 */ }
47      private void clearData( );
48        { /* Figure 14.13 */ }
49
50          // Various shortest path algorithms that
51          // require an internal number for start-up
52      private void unweighted( int startNode )
53        { /* Figure 14.24 */ }
54      private boolean dijkstra( int startNode )
55        { /* Figure 14.29 */ }
56      private boolean negative( int startNode )
57        { /* Figure 14.31 */ }
58      private boolean acyclic( int startNode )
59        { /* Figure 14.34 */ }
60  }
```

Figure 14.7   Graph class skeleton (part 2: the private section)

```
1       /**
2        * Constructor.
3        */
4       public Graph( )
5       {
6           numVertices = 0;
7           table       = new Vertex[ INIT_TABLE_SIZE ];
8           vertexMap   = new QuadraticProbingTable( );
9       }
```

Figure 14.8   Graph constructor

clearData clears out the data fields so that the shortest-path algorithms can begin. printPath prints the shortest path after the algorithm has run.

The data fields that are eventually computed by the shortest-path algorithm are initialized by the routine `clearData`, shown in Figure 14.13 (page 378). Next comes the routine to print a shortest path after the computation has been performed. Recall that the `prev` field can be used to trace back the path. However, this will give the path in reverse order. This is not a problem if we use recursion; the vertices on the path to `dest` are the same as those on the path to `dest`'s previous vertex (on the path) followed by `dest`. This strategy translates directly into the short recursive routine shown in Figure 14.14 (page 378). The routine assumes that a path actually exists. `printPath`, shown in Figure 14.15 (page 379), performs this check first; if the path does not exist, it prints a message. Otherwise, it calls the recursive routine and outputs the cost of the path.

```
1  /**
2   * This class represents the basic entry
3   * in the vertex dictionary.
4   * It implements the Hashable interface by providing
5   * hash and equals.
6   */
7  class HashItem implements Hashable
8  {
9      public String name;    // The real name
10     public int    rank;    // The assigned number
11
12     public HashItem( )
13        { this( null ); }
14
15     public HashItem( String nm )
16        { name = nm; }
17
18     public int hash( int tableSize )
19        { return ProbingHashTable.hash( name, tableSize ); }
20
21     public boolean equals( Object rhs )
22        { return name.equals( ((HashItem)rhs).name ); }
23 }
```

Figure 14.9   `HashItem` used to implement the dictionary

```
1      /**
2       * If vertexName is an already seen vertex, return its
3       * internal number. Otherwise add it as a new vertex,
4       * and return its new internal number.
5       */
6      private int addNode( String vertexName )
7      {
8          HashItem hashV = new HashItem( vertexName );
9          HashItem result;
10
11         try
12         {
13             result = (HashItem) vertexMap.find( hashV );
14             return result.rank;
15         }
16         catch( ItemNotFound e )
17         {
18             // Newly seen vertex
19             hashV.rank = numVertices;
20             hashV.name = new String( vertexName );
21             vertexMap.insert( hashV );
22
23             if( numVertices == table.length )
24                 doubleTableArray( );
25             table[ numVertices ] = new Vertex( hashV.name );
26             return numVertices++;
27         }
28     }
```

Figure 14.10   addNode routine returns the internal number for vertexName

```
1      /**
2       * Add an edge given internal numbers of its vertices.
3       */
4      private void addInternalEdge( int source,
5                                    int dest, int cost )
6      {
7          ListItr p = new LinkedListItr( table[ source ].adj );
8          try
9            { p.insert( new Edge( dest, cost ) ); }
10         catch( ItemNotFound e ) { }   // Cannot happen
11     }
```

Figure 14.11   Add the edge (source, dest, cost) to the graph by inserting into source's adjacency list; source and dest are internal numbers

```
1      /**
2       * Add the edge ( source, dest, cost ) to the graph.
3       */
4      public void addEdge( String source,
5                           String dest, int cost )
6      {
7          addInternalEdge( addNode( source ), addNode( dest ),
8                           cost );
9      }
```

Figure 14.12 The same routine as `addInternalEdge`, but here `source` and `dest` are `String` objects

```
1      /**
2       * Initialize the table.
3       */
4      private void clearData( )
5      {
6          for( int i = 0; i < numVertices; i++ )
7          {
8              table[ i ].dist = INFINITY;
9              table[ i ].prev = NULL_VERTEX;
10             table[ i ].scratch = 0;
11         }
12     }
```

Figure 14.13 Routine to initialize the `table` fields for use by the shortest-path algorithms

```
1      /**
2       * Recursively print the shortest path to destNode
3       * (specified by its internal number)
4       * printPath is the driver routine
5       */
6      private void printPathRec( int destNode )
7      {
8          if( table[ destNode ].prev != NULL_VERTEX )
9          {
10             printPathRec( table[ destNode ].prev );
11             System.out.print( " to " );
12         }
13         System.out.print( table[ destNode ].name );
14     }
```

Figure 14.14 Recursive routine to print the shortest path

```
1       /**
2        * Driver routine to handle unreachables and print total
3        * cost. It calls recursive routine to print shortest path
4        * to destNode after a shortest path algorithm has run.
5        */
6       private void printPath( int destNode )
7       {
8           if( table[ destNode ].dist == INFINITY )
9               System.out.println( table[ destNode ].name +
10                                      " is unreachable" );
11          else
12          {
13              printPathRec( destNode );
14              System.out.println( " (cost is " +
15                                      table[ destNode ].dist + ")" );
16          }
17          System.out.println( );
18      }
```

Figure 14.15   Routine to print the shortest path by consulting the table

The last routine, besides those that calculate shortest paths, is the method `processRequest`. In Figure 14.16 (page 380) is a simple implementation that prompts for a start vertex and a destination vertex and then runs the weighted shortest-path algorithm (the online code runs additional algorithms).

A simple `main`, shown in Figure 14.17 (page 381), illustrates the class. It prompts for the name of a file containing the graph. It repeatedly reads one line of input, assigns the line to a `StringTokenizer` object, and then parses that line. This technique allows us to check that every line has the three pieces corresponding to an edge. When the three components of the edge are detected, `addEdge` is called. When the graph is read, we run a weighted shortest-path algorithm by calling `processRequest`.

14.2 Unweighted Shortest-path Problem

The *unweighted path length* measures the number of edges. This section considers the problem of finding the path between specified vertices that has the shortest unweighted path length.

The unweighted path length measures the number of edges on a path.

UNWEIGHTED SINGLE-SOURCE, SHORTEST-PATH PROBLEM
Find the shortest path (measured by number of edges) from a designated vertex S to every vertex.

```
1      /**
2       * Process a request; return false if end of file.
3       */
4      public boolean processRequest( BufferedReader in )
5      {
6          String sourceName, destName;
7          HashItem source = new HashItem( );
8          HashItem dest   = new HashItem( );
9
10         try
11         {
12             System.out.println( "Enter start node:" );
13             if( ( sourceName = in.readLine( ) ) == null )
14                 return false;
15             System.out.println( "Enter destination node:" );
16             if( ( destName = in.readLine( ) ) == null )
17                 return false;
18         }
19         catch( IOException e )
20         {
21             System.out.println( "Error: " + e );
22             return false;
23         }
24
25         try
26         {
27             source.name = sourceName;
28             source = (HashItem) ( vertexMap.find( source ) );
29             dest.name = destName;
30             dest =    (HashItem) ( vertexMap.find( dest ) );
31
32             if( dijkstra( source.rank ) )
33                 printPath( dest.rank );
34             else
35                 System.out.println( "dijkstra fails" );
36         }
37         catch( ItemNotFound e )
38           { System.err.println( "Vertex not in graph" ); }
39         return true;
40     }
```

Figure 14.16 For testing purposes, processRequest calls a weighted short-est-path algorithm

The unweighted shortest-path problem is a special case of the weighted shortest-path problem (in which all weights are 1). So it should have a more efficient solution than the weighted shortest-path problem. This turns out to be true, although the algorithms for all the path problems are very similar.

```
1    /**
2     * A main routine that: prompts for the name of a file
3     * containing the graph; forms the graph from the file;
4     * repeatedly prompts for two vertices and runs shortest
5     * path algorithms. The data file is a sequence of lines:
6     *    source destination cost.
7     */
8    public static void main( String [ ] args )
9    {
10       System.out.println( "Enter graph file:" );
11       BufferedReader in = new BufferedReader( new
12                           InputStreamReader( System.in ) );
13       FileReader fin;
14       String fileName = "";
15
16       try
17       {
18           fileName = in.readLine( );
19           fin = new FileReader( fileName )
20       }
21       catch( Exception e )
22         { System.err.println( e ); return; }
23
24       BufferedReader graphFile = new BufferedReader( fin );
25       Graph g = new Graph( );
26
27               // Read the edges and insert
28       try
29       {
30           String line;
31           while( ( line = graphFile.readLine( ) ) != null )
32           {
33               StringTokenizer st = new StringTokenizer( line );
34               try
35               {
36                   if( st.countTokens( ) != 3 )
37                       throw new Exception( );
38                   String source  = st.nextToken( );
39                   String dest    = st.nextToken( );
40                   int cost = Integer.parseInt( st.nextToken( ) );
41                   g.addEdge( source, dest, cost );
42               }
43               catch( Exception e )
44                 { System.err.println( "Error: " + line ); }
45           }
46       }
47       catch( Exception e )
48         { System.err.println( "Error: " + e ); }
49       while( g.processRequest( in ) )
50           ;
51   }
```

Figure 14.17 Sample main

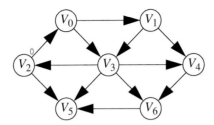

Figure 14.18   Graph after marking the start node as reachable in zero edges

14.2.1   Theory

All variations of the shortest path problem have similar solutions.

To solve the unweighted shortest-path problem, we use the graph in Figure 14.1 with V_2 as the starting vertex S. For now, we are concerned with finding the length of all shortest paths. Later, we will maintain the corresponding paths.

Immediately, we can tell that the shortest path from S to V_2 is a path of length 0. This information yields the graph in Figure 14.18. Now we can start looking for all vertices that are a distance 1 away from S. These can be found by looking at the vertices that are adjacent to S. If we do this, we see that V_0 and V_5 are one edge away from S. This is shown in Figure 14.19.

Next, we find each vertex whose shortest path from S is exactly 2. We do this by finding all the vertices adjacent to V_0 or V_5 (the vertices at distance 1) whose shortest paths are not already known. This search tells us that the shortest path to V_1 and V_3 is 2. Figure 14.20 shows the progress made so far.

Finally, by examining the vertices adjacent to the recently evaluated V_1 and V_3, we find that V_4 and V_6 have a shortest path of 3 edges. All vertices have now been calculated. Figure 14.21 shows the final result of the algorithm.

Breadth-first search processes vertices in layers: Those closest to the start are evaluated first.

This strategy for searching a graph is called *breadth-first search*. It operates by processing vertices in layers: The vertices closest to the start are evaluated first, and the most distant vertices are evaluated last.

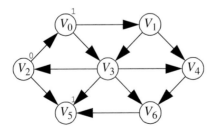

Figure 14.19   Graph after finding all vertices whose path length from the start is 1

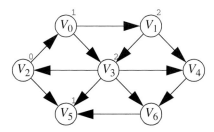

Figure 14.20 Graph after finding all vertices whose shortest path from the start is 2

Figure 14.22 (page 384) illustrates a fundamental principle. If a path to vertex v has cost D_v, and w is adjacent to v, then there exists a path to w of cost $D_w = D_v + 1$. All the path algorithms work by starting with $D_w = \infty$ and reducing its value when an appropriate v is scanned. To do this efficiently, we must scan vertices v systematically. When a given v is scanned, updates to vertices w that are adjacent to v take place by scanning through v's adjacency list.

From the preceding discussion, we see that an algorithm to solve the unweighted shortest-path problem is as follows: Let D_i be the length of the shortest path from S to i. We know that $D_S = 0$, and initially $D_i = \infty$ for all $i \neq S$. We maintain a roving *eyeball* that hops from vertex to vertex and is initially at S. If v is the vertex that the eyeball is currently on, then, for all w that are adjacent to v, we set $D_w = D_v + 1$ if $D_w = \infty$. This reflects the fact that we can get to w by following a path to v and extending the path by the edge (v, w). Again, this is illustrated in Figure 14.22. Because the eyeball processes each vertex in order of its distance from the start vertex and the edge adds exactly one to the length of the path to w, we are guaranteed that the first time D_w is lowered from ∞, it will be lowered to the value of the length of the shortest path to w. By the way, this also tells us that the next-to-last vertex on the path to w is v, so one extra line of code will allow us to store the actual path.

The *eyeball* moves from vertex to vertex and updates distances for adjacent vertices.

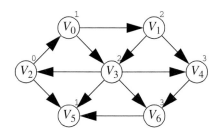

Figure 14.21 Final shortest paths

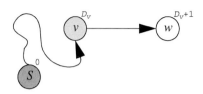

Figure 14.22 If *w* is adjacent to *v* and there is a path to *v*, then there is a path to *w*

After we have processed all of *v*'s adjacent vertices, we move the eyeball to another vertex *u* (that has not been visited by the eyeball) such that $D_u \equiv D_v$. If this is not possible, we move to a *u* that satisfies $D_u = D_v + 1$. If this is not possible, we are done. Figure 14.23 shows how the eyeball visits vertices and updates distances. The lightly shaded node in each stage represents the position of the eyeball. In this picture and those that follow, the stages are shown top to bottom, left-to-right.

The remaining detail is the data structure. There are two basic actions to take. First, we have to repeatedly find the vertex at which to place the eyeball. Second, we need to check all *w*'s adjacent to *v* (the current vertex) throughout the algorithm. The second action is easily implemented by iterating through *v*'s adjacency list. Indeed, since each edge is processed once, the total cost of all the iterations is $O(|E|)$. The first action is more challenging: We cannot simply scan through the table looking for an appropriate vertex, because each scan could take $O(|V|)$ time and we need to perform it $|V|$ times. The total cost would thus be $O(|V|^2)$, which is unacceptable for sparse graphs. Fortunately, this is not needed.

When a vertex *w* has its D_w lowered from ∞, it becomes a candidate for an eyeball visitation at some point in the future. This is because after the eyeball visits vertices in the current distance group D_v, it will visit the next distance group $D_v + 1$, the group containing *w*. Thus *w* just needs to wait on line for its turn. Also, since it clearly does not need to go before any other vertices that have already had their distances lowered, it needs to be placed at the end of a queue of vertices that are waiting for an eyeball visitation.

To select a vertex *v* for the eyeball, we merely choose the front vertex from the queue. We start with an empty queue. Then, to get the ball rolling, we enqueue that start vertex *S*. Since a vertex is enqueued and dequeued at most once per shortest-path calculation, and since queue operations are constant time, the cost of choosing the vertex to select is only $O(|V|)$ *for the entire algorithm*. Thus the cost of the breadth-first search is dominated by the scans of the adjacency list and is $O(|E|)$, or linear in the size of the graph.

All vertices adjacent to *v* are found by scanning *v*'s adjacency list.

When a vertex has its distance lowered (which can happen only once), it is placed on the queue so that the eyeball can visit it in the future. The start vertex is placed on the queue when its distance is initialized to zero.

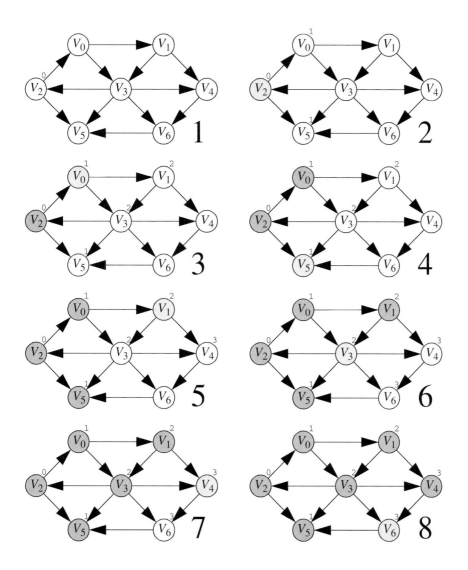

Figure 14.23   How the graph is searched in the unweighted shortest-path computation. Darkest vertices have already been completely processed, the lightest vertices have not yet been used as *v*, and the middle shade is the current vertex *v*. Stages proceed top-to-bottom, left-to-right, as numbered

14.2.2 Java Implementation

Implementation is much simpler than it sounds. It follows the algorithm description verbatim.

Implementation of the unweighted shortest-path algorithm is done in the method `unweighted`, shown in Figure 14.24. The code is a line-for-line translation of the algorithm described previously. The initialization at lines 9 to 11 makes all the distances infinity, sets D_S to 0, and then enqueues the start vertex. While the queue is not empty, there are vertices to visit. Thus, at line 17, we move to the vertex v that is at the front of the queue. Line 19 iterates over the adjacency list and produces all w's that are adjacent to v. The test $D_w = \infty$ is performed at line 22. If it is `true`, then the update $D_w = D_v + 1$ is performed at line 24 along with the update of the `prev` field and enqueueing of w at lines 25 and 26, respectively.

```
1       /**
2        * Compute the unweighted shortest path.
3        */
4       private void unweighted( int startNode )
5       {
6           int v, w;
7           Queue q = new QueueAr( );
8
9           clearData( );
10          table[ startNode ].dist = 0;
11          q.enqueue( new Integer( startNode ) );
12
13          try
14          {
15              while( !q.isEmpty( ) )
16              {
17                  v = ((Integer)q.dequeue( )).intValue( );
18                  ListItr p = new LinkedListItr( table[v].adj );
19                  for( ; p.isInList( ); p.advance( ) )
20                  {
21                      w = ((Edge)p.retrieve( )).dest;
22                      if( table[ w ].dist == INFINITY )
23                      {
24                          table[ w ].dist = table[ v ].dist + 1;
25                          table[ w ].prev = v;
26                          q.enqueue( new Integer( w ) );
27                      }
28                  }
29              }
30          }
31          catch( Underflow e ) { }    // Cannot happen
32      }
```

Figure 14.24 Unweighted shortest-path algorithm using breadth-first search

14.3 Positive-weighted, Shortest-path Problem

The *weighted path length* of a path is the sum of the edge costs on the path. This section considers the problem of finding the weighted shortest path. In the positive-weighted, shortest-path problem, the edges have nonnegative cost. We want to find the shortest weighted path from some start vertex to all vertices. As will be shown shortly, the assumption that edge costs are nonnegative is important because it allows a relatively efficient algorithm. The method described is known as *Dijkstra's algorithm.* The next section examines a slower algorithm that works even if there are negative edge costs.

The weighted path length is the sum of the edge costs on a path.

> **POSITIVE-WEIGHTED, SINGLE-SOURCE, SHORTEST-PATH PROBLEM**
>
> *Find the shortest path (measured by total cost) from a designated vertex S to every vertex. All edge costs are nonnegative.*

14.3.1 Theory: Dijkstra's Algorithm

The weighted shortest-path problem is solved in a similar manner as the unweighted problem. However, because of the edge costs, a few things change. The following issues must be examined:

Dijkstra's algorithm solves the weighted shortest-path problem.

1. How is D_w adjusted?
2. How do we find the vertex v for the eyeball to visit?

We begin by examining how D_w is altered. In solving the unweighted shortest-path problem, if $D_w = \infty$, we set $D_w = D_v + 1$ because we lower the value of D_w if vertex v offers a shorter path to w. The dynamics of the algorithm ensure that we need alter D_w only once. We add 1 to D_v because the length of the path to w is 1 more than the length of the path to v. If we apply this logic to the weighted case, then we should set $D_w = D_v + c_{v,\,w}$ if this new value of D_w is better than the original value. However, it is no longer guaranteed that D_w is altered only once. Consequently, D_w should be altered if its current value is larger than $D_v + c_{v,\,w}$ (rather than merely testing against ∞). Put simply, the algorithm decides whether it is a good idea to use v on the path to w. The original cost D_w is the cost without using v; the cost $D_v + c_{v,\,w}$ is the cheapest path using v (seen so far).

We use $D_v + c_{v,w}$ as the new distance and to decide if the distance should be updated.

Figure 14.25 (page 388) shows a typical situation. Earlier in the algorithm, w had its distance lowered to 8 when the eyeball visited vertex u. However, when the eyeball visits vertex v, w needs to have its distance lowered to 6 because we have a new shortest path. This never happened in the unweighted algorithm because all edges add 1 to the path length, so $D_u \le D_v$ implies $D_u + 1 \le D_v + 1$ and thus $D_w \le D_v + 1$. Here, even though $D_u \le D_v$, it is still possible that the path to w can be improved by considering v.

A queue is no longer appropriate to store vertices awaiting an eyeball visit.

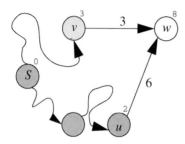

Figure 14.25 Eyeball is at v; w is adjacent; D_w should be lowered to 6

The distance for unvisited vertices represents a path using only visited vertices as intermediate nodes.

Figure 14.25 shows another important point. When w has its distance lowered, it does so only because it is adjacent to some vertex that has been visited by the eyeball. For instance, after the eyeball visits v and processing is complete, the value of D_w will be 6 and the last vertex on the path is an eyeball-visited vertex. Similarly, the vertex prior to v must also be eyeball-visited, and so on. Thus, at any point, the value of D_w represents *a path from S to w using only vertices that have been visited by the eyeball as intermediate nodes.* This crucial fact gives us Theorem 14.1.

Theorem 14.1   *If we move the eyeball to the unseen vertex with minimum D_i, the algorithm will correctly produce the shortest paths if there are no negative edge costs.*

Proof   *Call each eyeball visit a "stage." We prove by induction that, after any stage, the values of D_i for vertices visited by the eyeball form the shortest path and that the values of D_i for the other vertices form the shortest path using only vertices visited by the eyeball as intermediates. Since the first vertex visited is the start vertex, this statement is correct through the first stage. Assume that it is correct for the first k stages. Let v be the vertex chosen by the eyeball in stage k + 1. Suppose, for the purpose of showing a contradiction, that there is a path from S to v of length less than D_v. This path must go through an intermediate vertex that has not yet been visited by the eyeball. Call the first intermediate vertex on the path not visited by the eyeball u. The situation is shown in Figure 14.26. The path to u uses only vertices visited by the eyeball as intermediates, so, by induction, D_u represents the optimal distance to u. Moreover, $D_u < D_v$ because u is on the supposed shorter path to v. This is a contradiction because then we would have moved the eyeball to u instead of v. The proof is completed by showing that all the D_i values remain correct for nonvisited nodes; this is clear by the update rule.*

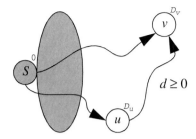

Figure 14.26 If D_v is minimal among all unseen vertices and if all edge costs are nonnegative, then D_v represents the shortest path

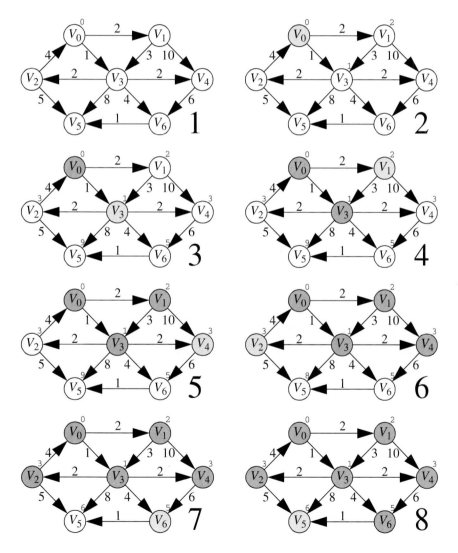

Figure 14.27 Stages of Dijkstra's algorithm. Follows same conventions as Figure 14.23

Figure 14.27 (page 389) shows the stages of Dijkstra's algorithm. The remaining issue is the selection of an appropriate data structure. For dense graphs, we can scan down the table looking for the appropriate vertex. As with the unweighted shortest-path algorithm, this will take $O(|V|^2)$ time, which is optimal for a dense graph. For a sparse graph, we want to do better.

The priority queue is an appropriate data structure. The easiest method is to add a new entry, consisting of a vertex and a distance, to the priority queue every time a vertex has its distance lowered. We can find the new vertex to move to by repeatedly removing the minimum distance vertex from the priority queue until an unvisited vertex emerges.

Certainly, a queue will not work. The fact that we need to find the vertex v with minimum D_v suggests that a priority queue is the method of choice. There are two ways to use the priority queue. One way is to store each vertex in the priority queue and use the distance (obtained by consulting the graph table) as the ordering function. When we alter any D_w, we must update the priority queue by reestablishing the ordering property. This amounts to a decreaseKey operation. To do this we need to be able to find the location of w in the priority queue. Not all implementations of the priority queue support this. In other words, decreaseKey is not part of the PriorityQueue interface. One that does support decreaseKey is the *pairing heap*; using the pairing heap for this application is discussed in Chapter 22.

Rather than use a fancy priority queue, we use a method that works with any data structure that implements the PriorityQueue interface. Our method will be to insert an object consisting of w and D_w into the priority queue whenever we lower D_w. To select a new vertex v for visitation, we repeatedly remove the minimum item (based on distance) from the priority queue until an unvisited vertex emerges. Because the size of the priority queue could be as large as $|E|$ and there are at most $|E|$ priority queue insertions and deletions, the running time is $O(|E|\log|E|)$. Since $|E| \leq |V|^2$ implies $\log|E| \leq 2\log|V|$, we have the same $O(|E|\log|V|)$ algorithm that we would have if we used the first method (in which the priority queue size is at most $|V|$).

14.3.2 Java Implementation

Once again, the implementation follows the description fairly closely.

The object that will be placed on the priority queue is shown in Figure 14.28. It consists of w and D_w and a comparison function defined on the basis of D_w. Figure 14.29 (page 392) shows the routine dijkstra that calculates the shortest paths.

Line 8 declares the priority queue pq. Recall that we must provide a sentinel that is guaranteed to be smaller than or equal to any inserted object. vrec, declared at line 9, will store the result of each deleteMin. As with the unweighted shortest-path algorithm, we begin by setting all distances to infinity, setting $D_S = 0$, and placing the start vertex into our data structure.

```
1  /**
2   * Object stored in the priority queue
3   * for Dijkstra's algorithm
4   */
5  class Path implements Comparable
6  {
7      int dest;      // w
8      int cost;      // d(w)
9
10     static Path negInf = new Path( );   // Sentinel
11
12     Path( )
13       { this( 0 ); }
14
15     Path( int d )
16       { this( d, 0 ); }
17
18     Path( int d, int c )
19       { dest = d; cost = c; }
20
21     public boolean lessThan( Comparable rhs )
22       { return cost < ( (Path)rhs ).cost; }
23
24     public int compares( Comparable rhs )
25       { return cost < ((Path)rhs).cost ? -1 :
26               cost > ((Path)rhs).cost ? 1 : 0; }
27 }
```

Figure 14.28   Basic item stored in the priority queue

Each iteration of the outermost `for` loop that begins at line 17 puts the eyeball at a vertex v and processes it by examining adjacent vertices w. v is chosen by repeatedly removing entries from the priority queue (at line 24) until we see a vertex that has not been processed. We use the `scratch` variable to record this. Initially, `scratch` is 0. Thus, if the vertex is unprocessed, the `while` test will fail at line 25. Then, when the vertex is processed, `scratch` is set to 1 (at line 28). The priority queue might be empty, if, for instance, some of the vertices are unreachable. In that case, we can return immediately. The loop at lines 30 to 46 is very much like the unweighted algorithm. The difference is that at line 34, we must extract `cvw` from the adjacency list entry, check that the edge is nonnegative (otherwise, our algorithm could produce incorrect answers), add `cvw` instead of 1 at lines 39 and 41, and `insert` rather than `enqueue` at lines 43 and 44.

```
1       /**
2        * Dijkstra's Algorithm using binary heap.
3        * Return false if negative edge detected.
4        */
5       private boolean dijkstra( int startNode )
6       {
7           int v, w;
8           PriorityQueue pq = new BinaryHeap( Path.negInf );
9           Path vrec;
10
11          clearData( );
12          table[ startNode ].dist = 0;
13          pq.insert( new Path( startNode, 0 ) );
14
15          try
16          {
17              for( int nodesSeen = 0; nodesSeen < numVertices;
18                                                nodesSeen++ )
19              {
20                  do
21                  {
22                      if( pq.isEmpty( ) )
23                          return true;
24                      vrec = (Path) pq.deleteMin( );
25                  } while( table[ vrec.dest ].scratch != 0 );
26
27                  v = vrec.dest;
28                  table[ v ].scratch = 1;
29
30                  ListItr p = new LinkedListItr( table[v].adj );
31                  for( ; p.isInList( ); p.advance( ) )
32                  {
33                      w     = ( (Edge)p.retrieve( ) ).dest;
34                      int cvw = ( (Edge)p.retrieve( ) ).cost;
35
36                      if( cvw < 0 )
37                          return false;
38
39                      if( table[w].dist > table[v].dist + cvw )
40                      {
41                          table[ w ].dist = table[v].dist + cvw;
42                          table[ w ].prev = v;
43                          pq.insert( new Path( w,
44                                          table[ w ].dist ) );
45                      }
46                  }
47              }
48          }
49          catch( Underflow e ) { }    // This cannot happen
50          return true;
51      }
```

Figure 14.29 Weighted shortest-path algorithm: Dijkstra's algorithm

14.4 Negative-weighted, Shortest-path Problem

Dijkstra's algorithm requires that edge costs be nonnegative. This is reasonable for most graph applications, but sometimes it is too restrictive. This section briefly discusses the most general case.

Negative edges break Dijsktra's algorithm. An alternative algorithm is needed.

NEGATIVE-WEIGHTED, SINGLE-SOURCE, SHORTEST-PATH PROBLEM
Find the shortest path (measured by total cost) from a designated vertex S to every vertex. Edge costs may be negative.

14.4.1 Theory

The proof of Dijkstra's algorithm required the condition that edge costs, and thus paths, be nonnegative. Indeed, if the graph has negative edge costs, then Dijkstra's algorithm does not work. The problem is that once a vertex v is processed, there may be, from some other unprocessed vertex u, a path back to v that is very negative. In such a case, taking a path from S to u to v is better than going from S to v without using u. If the latter were to happen, we would be in trouble. Not only would the path to v be wrong, but we would have to revisit v because vertices reachable from v may also have their distances affected.

We have an additional problem to worry about. Consider the graph in Figure 14.30. The path from V_3 to V_4 has cost 2. However, a shorter path exists by following the loop V_3, V_4, V_1, V_3, V_4, which has a cost of −3. This path is still not the shortest because we could stay in the loop arbitrarily long. Thus the shortest path between these two points is undefined.

A negative-cost cycle makes most, if not all, paths undefined because we can stay in the cycle arbitrarily long and obtain an arbitrarily negative path length.

This problem is not restricted to nodes in the cycle. The shortest path from V_2 to V_5 is also undefined because there is a way to get into and out of the loop. This loop is called a *negative-cost cycle*; when one is present in the graph, the shortest paths are not defined. Negative-cost edges by themselves are not necessarily bad; it is the cycles that are. Our algorithm will either find the shortest paths or report the existence of a negative-cost cycle.

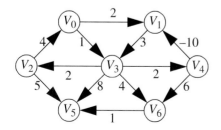

Figure 14.30 Graph with negative cost cycle

```
1       /**
2        * Run shortest path algorithm;
3        * Negative edge weights are allowed.
4        * Return false if negative cycle is detected
5        */
6       private boolean negative( int startNode )
7       {
8           int v, w;
9           Queue q = new QueueAr( );
10          int cvw;
11
12          clearData( );
13          table[ startNode ].dist = 0;
14          q.enqueue( new Integer( startNode ) );
15          table[ startNode ].scratch++;
16
17          // Increment scratch for vertex v when it enqueues or
18          // dequeues. If vertex is about to enqueue but is
19          // already on the queue, count as an enqueue & dequeue
20          try
21          {
22              while( !q.isEmpty( ) )
23              {
24                  v = ((Integer)q.dequeue( )).intValue( );
25
26                  if( table[ v ].scratch++ > 2 * numVertices )
27                      return false; // |V|+1 dequeues ==> a cycle
28
29                  ListItr p = new LinkedListItr( table[v].adj );
30                  for( ; p.isInList( ); p.advance( ) )
31                  {
32                      w   = ( (Edge)p.retrieve( ) ).dest;
33                      cvw = ( (Edge)p.retrieve( ) ).cost;
34                      if( table[w].dist > table[v].dist + cvw )
35                      {
36                          table[ w ].dist = table[v].dist + cvw;
37                          table[ w ].prev = v;
38
39                          // Enqueue only if not on queue
40                          if( table[ w ].scratch++ % 2 == 0 )
41                              q.enqueue( new Integer( w ) );
42                          else  // count as a phantom dequeue
43                              table[ w ].scratch++;
44                      }
45                  }
46              }
47          }
48          catch( Underflow e ) { }   // Cannot happen
49          return true;
50      }
```

Figure 14.31 Negative-weighted, shortest-path algorithm: Negative edges are allowed

A combination of the weighted and unweighted algorithms will solve the problem, but at the cost of a potentially drastic increase in running time. As suggested previously, when D_w is altered, we must revisit it at some point in the future. Consequently, we use the queue as was done in the unweighted algorithm, but use $D_v + c_{v,\,w}$ as the distance measure (as in Dijkstra's algorithm).

When the eyeball visits vertex v for the ith time, the value of D_v is the length of the shortest weighted path consisting of i or fewer edges. A proof of this is left as Exercise 14.9. Consequently, if there are no negative-cost cycles, a vertex can dequeue at most $|V|$ times and the algorithm takes at most $O(|E||V|)$ time. Further, if a vertex dequeues more than $|V|$ times, we have detected a negative-cost cycle.

Whenever a vertex has its distance lowered, it must be placed on a queue. This may happen repeatedly for each vertex.

The running time can be large, especially if there is a negative-cost cycle.

14.4.2   Java Implementation

The implementation of the negative-weighted, shortest-path algorithm is given in Figure 14.31. We make one small change to the algorithm description; namely, we do not enqueue a vertex if it is already on the queue. To do this, we use the `scratch` field. When a vertex is enqueued, we increment `scratch` (at line 40). When it is dequeued, we increment it again (at line 26). Thus `scratch` is odd if the vertex is on the queue, and `scratch/2` tells us how many times it has left the queue (and this explains the test at line 26). When some w has its distance changed, but it is already on the queue (because `scratch` is odd), we do not enqueue it. However, we add 2 to it to indicate that it logically could have gone on (and off) the queue (this may speed the algorithm somewhat in the event of a negative cycle). This is done at lines 40 and 43. The rest of the algorithm uses code that has already been seen in both the unweighted shortest-path algorithm (Figure 14.24) and Dijkstra's algorithm (Figure 14.29).

The tricky part of the implementation is the manipulation of the scratch *variable. We attempt to avoid having any vertex appear on the queue twice at any instant.*

14.5 Path Problems in Acyclic Graphs

An important class of graphs are those without cycles. The shortest-path problem is simpler if the graph is acyclic. For instance, we do not have to worry about negative-cost cycles, since there are no cycles to be found. Thus we consider the following problem.

A directed acyclic graph is a directed graph that has no cycles. Such graphs are an important class of graphs.

WEIGHTED SINGLE-SOURCE, SHORTEST-PATH PROBLEM FOR ACYCLIC GRAPHS

Find the shortest path (measured by total cost) from a designated vertex S to every vertex in an acyclic graph. Edge costs are unrestricted.

14.5.1 Topological Sorting

A *topological sort* orders vertices in a directed acyclic graph such that if there is a path from *u* to *v*, then *v* appears *after u* in the ordering. A graph that has a cycle cannot have a topological order.

Before considering the shortest-path problem, let us examine a related problem: a topological sort. A *topological order* is an ordering of vertices in a directed acyclic graph such that if there is a path from u to v, then v appears after u in the ordering. For instance, a graph is typically used to represent the prerequisite requirement for courses at universities. An edge (v, w) indicates that course v must be completed before course w may be attempted. A topological order of the courses is any sequence that does not violate the prerequisite requirements. A *topological sort* finds any topological order.

It is clear that a topological sort is not possible if a graph has a cycle, since for two vertices v and w on the cycle, there is a path from v to w and w to v. Thus any ordering of v and w would contradict one of the two paths. A graph may have several topological orders, and in most cases, any legal ordering will do.

The *indegree* of a vertex is the number of incoming edges. A topological sort can be performed in linear time by repeatedly and logically removing vertices that have no incoming edges.

A simple algorithm to perform a topological sort is first to find any vertex v that has no incoming edges. Then we print the vertex and logically remove it, along with its edges, from the graph. Finally, we apply the same strategy to the rest of the graph. To formalize this, we define the *indegree* of a vertex v as the number of edges (u, v).

We compute the indegrees of all vertices in the graph. In practice, "logically remove" means that we lower the count of incoming edges for each vertex adjacent to v. Figure 14.32 shows the algorithm applied to an acyclic graph. The indegree is computed for each vertex. V_2 has indegree zero; thus it is first in the topological order. If there were several vertices of indegree zero, then we could choose any one of them. When V_2 and its edges are removed from the graph, the indegrees of V_0, V_3, and V_5 are all decremented by 1. Now V_0 has indegree zero, so it is next in the topological order, and V_1 and V_3 have their indegrees lowered. The algorithm continues, and the remaining vertices are examined in the order V_1, V_3, V_4, V_6, and V_5. To reiterate, we do not physically delete edges from the graph; removing edges just makes it easier to see how the indegree count is lowered.

The algorithm produces the correct answer and detects cycles if the graph is not acyclic.

Two important issues to consider are correctness and efficiency. Clearly, any ordering produced by the algorithm is a topological order. The question is whether every acyclic graph has a topological order, and if so, whether our algorithm is guaranteed to find one. The answer is yes to both questions.

If at any point there are unseen vertices but none of them has an indegree equal to zero, then we are guaranteed that there must be a cycle. To see that, pick any vertex A_0. Since A_0 has an incoming edge, let A_1 be the vertex that is connected to A_0. And since A_1 has an incoming edge, let A_2 be the vertex that is connected to A_1. Repeat this N times, where N is the number of unprocessed vertices that are left in the graph. Among $A_0, A_1, ..., A_N$, there must be two identical vertices (because there are N vertices but $N + 1$ A_i's). Tracing backward between those identical A_i and A_j exhibits a cycle.

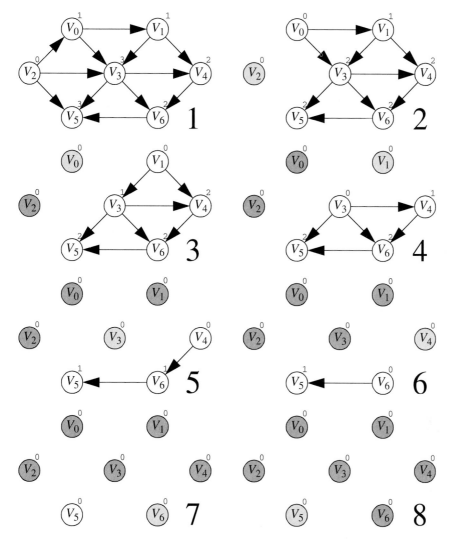

Figure 14.32 Topological sort. Follows same conventions as Figure 14.23

The algorithm itself can be implemented in linear time by placing all unprocessed indegree zero vertices on a queue. Initially, all vertices of indegree zero are placed on the queue. To find the next vertex in the topological order, we merely get and remove the front item from the queue. When a vertex has its indegree lowered to zero, it is placed on the queue. If the queue empties before all vertices have been topologically sorted, then the graph has a cycle. The running time is clearly linear, by the same reasoning used in the unweighted shortest-path algorithm.

The running time is linear if a queue is used.

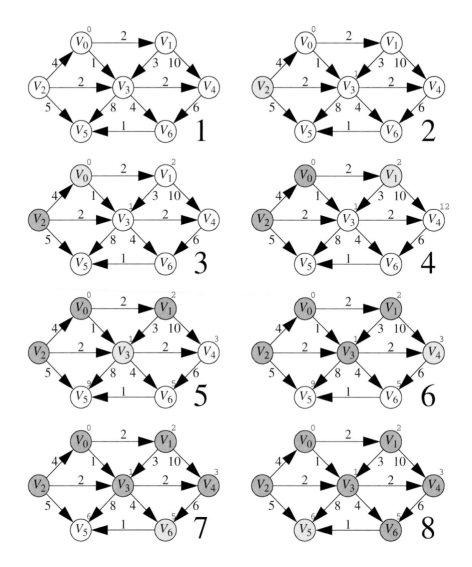

Figure 14.33   Stages of acyclic graph algorithm. Follows the same conventions as Figure 14.23

14.5.2   Theory of the Acyclic Shortest-path Algorithm

In an acyclic graph, the eyeball merely visits vertices in to-pological order.

An important application of topological sorting is its use in solving the shortest-path problem for acyclic graphs. The idea is as follows: Have the eyeball visit vertices in topological order.

This idea works because when the eyeball visits vertex v, we are guaranteed that D_v can no longer be lowered, since by the topological ordering rule, it has no incoming edges emanating from unvisited nodes. Figure 14.33 shows the stages of the shortest-path algorithm using the topological ordering to guide the vertex visitations. Notice that the sequence of vertices visited is not the same as in Dijkstra's algorithm. Also note that vertices visited by the eyeball prior to its reaching that start vertex are unreachable from the start vertex and have no influence on the distances of any vertex.

Since we do not need a priority queue, and instead need only to incorporate the topological sort into the shortest-path computation, we find that the algorithm will run in linear time and will work in the presence of negative edges.

The result is a linear time algorithm even if there are negative edge weights.

14.5.3   Java Implementation

The implementation of the shortest-path algorithm for acyclic graphs is shown in Figure 14.34 (page 400). We use a queue to perform the topological sort, and we maintain the indegree information in the `scratch` field. Lines 13 to 19 compute the indegrees, and at lines 21 to 23, we place any indegree zero vertices onto the queue.

The implementation combines a topological sort calculation and a shortest-path calculation. The indegree information is stored in the `scratch` field.

We then repeatedly remove a vertex from the queue at line 27. Notice that if the queue is empty, the `for` loop will be terminated by the test at line 25. If the loop terminates because of a cycle, this will be reported at line 50. Otherwise, the loop at line 30 steps through the adjacency list and a value of w is obtained at line 32. Immediately we lower w's indegree at line 33 and, if it has fallen to zero, place it on the queue (at line 34).

Recall that if the current vertex v appears prior to S in topological order, then v must be unreachable from S. Consequently, it will still have $D_v \equiv \infty$ and thus cannot hope to provide a path to any adjacent vertex w. We perform a test at line 36, and if this is the case, we do not attempt any distance calculations. Otherwise, at lines 39 to 44, we use the same calculations as in Dijkstra's algorithm to update D_w if necessary.

Nodes that appear before S in the topological order are unreachable.

14.5.4   An Application: Critical-path Analysis

An important use of acyclic graphs is *critical-path analysis*, a form of analysis used to schedule tasks associated with a project. The graph in Figure 14.35 (page 401) serves as an example. Each vertex represents an activity that must be completed, along with the time it takes to complete the activity. The graph is thus called an *activity-node graph*, in which vertices represent activities and edges represent precedence relationships. An edge (v, w) means that activity v must be completed before activity w may begin. Of course, this implies that the graph must be acyclic. We assume that any activities that do not depend (either directly or indirectly) on each other can be performed in parallel by different servers.

Critical-path analysis is used to schedule tasks associated with a project.

```
1      // Linear-time algorithm, works only for acyclic graphs.
2      private boolean acyclic( int startNode )
3      {
4          int v, w, iterations = 0;
5          Queue q = new QueueAr( );
6
7          clearData( );
8          table[ startNode ].dist = 0;
9
10         try
11         {
12                 // Compute the indegrees
13             for( v = 0; v < numVertices; v++ )
14             {
15                 ListItr p = new LinkedListItr( table[v].adj );
16                 for( ; p.isInList( ); p.advance( ) )
17                     table[ ( (Edge)p.retrieve( ) ).dest ].
18                                                 scratch++;
19             }
20                 // Enqueue vertices of indegree zero
21             for( v = 0; v < numVertices; v++ )
22                 if( table[ v ].scratch == 0 )
23                     q.enqueue( new Integer( v ) );
24
25             for( iterations = 0; !q.isEmpty( ); iterations++ )
26             {
27                 v = ( (Integer) q.dequeue( ) ).intValue( );
28
29                 ListItr p = new LinkedListItr( table[v].adj );
30                 for( ; p.isInList( ); p.advance( ) )
31                 {
32                     w = ( (Edge)p.retrieve( ) ).dest;
33                     if( --table[ w ].scratch == 0 )
34                         q.enqueue( new Integer( w ) );
35
36                     if( table[ v ].dist == INFINITY )
37                         continue;
38
39                     int cvw = ( (Edge)p.retrieve( ) ).cost;
40                     if( table[w].dist > table[v].dist + cvw )
41                     {
42                         table[ w ].dist = table[v].dist + cvw;
43                         table[ w ].prev = v;
44                     }
45                 }
46             }
47         }
48         catch( Underflow e ) { }     // Cannot happen
49
50         return iterations == numVertices;
51     }
```

Figure 14.34 Shortest-path algorithm for acyclic graphs

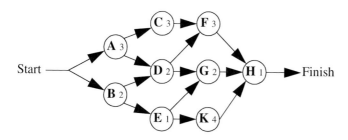

Figure 14.35 Activity-node graph

This type of graph could be (and frequently is) used to model construction projects, in which several important questions are of interest. First, what is the earliest completion time for the project? The graph shows that ten units are required along the path *A*, *C*, *F*, *H*. Another important question is, which activities can be delayed, and by how long, without affecting the minimum completion time? For instance, delaying any of *A*, *C*, *F*, or *H* would push the completion time past ten units. On the other hand, activity *B* is less critical and can be delayed up to two time units without affecting the final completion time.

An activity-node graph represents activities as vertices and precedence relationships as edges.

To perform these calculations, we convert the activity-node graph to an *event-node graph*, a graph in which each event corresponds to the completion of an activity and all of its dependent activities. Events reachable from a node *v* in the event-node graph may not commence until after the event *v* is completed. This graph can be constructed automatically or by hand (from the activity-node graph). Dummy edges and vertices may need to be inserted to avoid introducing false dependencies (or false lack of dependencies). The event-node graph corresponding to the activity graph in Figure 14.35 is shown in Figure 14.36.

The event-node graph consists of event vertices that correspond to the completion of an activity and all its dependent activities.

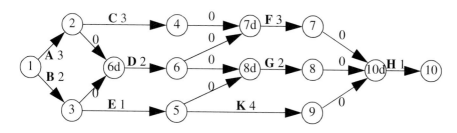

Figure 14.36 Event-node graph

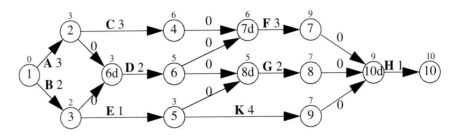

Figure 14.37   Earliest completion times

To find the earliest completion time of the project, we merely need to find the length of the *longest* path from the first event to the last event. For general graphs, the longest-path problem generally does not make sense because of the possibility of *positive-cost cycles*, which are the equivalent of negative-cost cycles in shortest-path problems. If positive-cost cycles are present, we could ask for the longest simple path. However, no satisfactory solution is known for this problem. Fortunately, the event-node graph is acyclic; thus we need not worry about cycles. It is easy to adapt the shortest-path algorithm to compute the earliest completion time for all nodes in the graph. If EC_i is the earliest completion time for node i, then the applicable rules are

$$EC_1 = 0 \text{ and } EC_w = Max_{(v, w) \in E}(EC_v + c_{v, w}).$$

Figure 14.37 shows the earliest completion time for each event in our example event-node graph. We can also compute the latest time, LC_i, that each event can finish without affecting final completion time. The formulas to do this are

$$LC_N = EC_N \text{ and } LC_v = Min_{(v, w) \in E}(LC_w - c_{v, w}).$$

These values can be computed in linear time by maintaining, for each vertex, a list of all adjacent and preceding vertices. The earliest completion times are computed for vertices by their topological order, and the latest completion times are computed by reverse topological order. The latest completion times are shown in Figure 14.38.

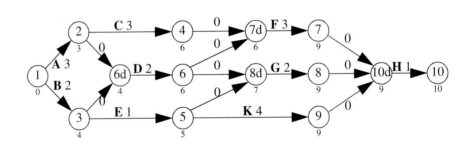

Figure 14.38   Latest completion times

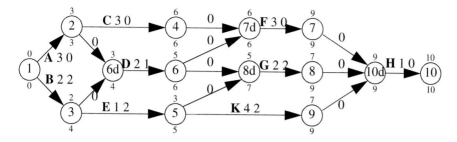

Figure 14.39   Earliest completion time, latest completion time, and slack (additional edge item)

The *slack time* for each edge in the event-node graph is the amount of time that the completion of the corresponding activity can be delayed without delaying the overall completion. It is easy to see that

$$Slack_{(v, w)} = LC_w - EC_v - c_{v, w}.$$

Figure 14.39 shows the slack (as the third entry) for each activity in the event-node graph. For each node, the top number is the earliest completion time and the bottom number is the latest completion time.

Some activities have zero slack. These are critical activities that must finish on schedule. There is at least one path consisting entirely of zero-slack edges; such a path is a *critical path*.

> The *slack time* is the amount of time that an activity can be delayed without delaying overall completion.

> Zero-slack activities are critical and cannot be delayed. A path of zero-slack edges is the critical path.

Summary

This chapter showed how graphs can be used to model many real-life problems and in particular how to calculate the shortest path under a wide variety of circumstances. Many of the graphs that occur are typically very sparse, so it is important to choose appropriate data structures to implement them.

For unweighted graphs, the shortest path can be computed in linear time using breadth-first search. For positive-weighted graphs, slightly more time is needed using Dijkstra's algorithm and an efficient priority queue. For negative-weighted graphs, the problem becomes still more difficult. Finally, for acyclic graphs, the running time reverts to linear time with the aid of a topological sort.

Objects of the Game

activity-node graph A graph of vertices as activities and edges as precedence relationships. (401)

adjacency list An array of lists used to represent a graph. Uses linear space. (369)

adjacency matrix A matrix representation of a graph that uses quadratic space. (369)

adjacent vertex w is adjacent to v if there is an edge from v to w. (367)

breadth-first search A search procedure that processes vertices in layers. Those closest to the start are evaluated first. The eyeball moves from vertex to vertex and updates distances for adjacent vertices. (382)

critical-path analysis A form of analysis used to schedule tasks associated with a project. (399)

cycle In a directed graph, a path that begins and ends at the same vertex and contains at least one edge. (368)

dense and sparse graphs A dense graph has a large number of edges (generally quadratic). Typical graphs are not dense but are sparse. (369)

Dijkstra's algorithm An algorithm that solves the positive-weighted shortest-path problem. (387)

directed acyclic graph (DAG) A type of directed graph that has no cycles. (395)

direct graph A graph in which edges are ordered pairs of vertices. (367)

edge cost (weight) The third component of an edge that measures the cost of traversing the edge. (367)

event-node graph A graph that consists of event vertices that correspond to the completion of an activity and all its dependent activities. Edges show what activity must be completed to advance from one vertex to the next. The earliest completion time is the longest path. (401)

graph Consists of a set of vertices and a set of edges that connect the vertices. (367)

indegree The number of incoming edges of a vertex. (396)

negative-cost cycle A cycle whose cost is less than zero. Makes most, if not all, paths undefined because we can loop around the cycle arbitrarily many times and obtain an arbitrarily small weighted path length. (393)

path A sequence of vertices connected by edges. (368)

path length The number of edges on a path. (368)

positive-cost cycle In a longest-path problem, the equivalent of a negative-cost cycle in a shortest-path problem. (402)

simple path A path in which all vertices are distinct, except that the first and last can be the same. (368)

single source An algorithm that computes the shortest paths from some start point to all vertices in a graph. (372)

slack time The amount of time that an activity can be delayed without delaying overall completion. (403)

topological sort A process that orders vertices in a directed acyclic graph such that if there is a path from u to v, then v appears after u in the ordering. A graph that has a cycle cannot have a topological order. (396)

unweighted path length The number of edges on a path. (379)

weighted path length The sum of the edge costs on a path. (387)

Common Errors

1. A common error is failing to check that the input graph satisfies the requisite conditions for the algorithm being used (that is, acyclic or positive weighted).
2. For `Path`, the comparison function compares the `cost` field only. If the `dest` field is used to drive the comparison function, the algorithm may appear to work for small graphs, but for larger graphs, it is incorrect and will give slightly suboptimal answers. It will never produce a path that does not exist, however. Thus this error is difficult to track down.
3. The shortest-path algorithm for negative-weighted graphs must have a test for negative cycles; otherwise, it runs forever.

On the Internet

All of the algorithms in this chapter are available online in one file in the directory **Chapter14**. Here is the filename:

Graph.java   Contains the `Graph` class with a `main`.

Exercises

In Short

14.1. Find the shortest unweighted path from V_3 to all others in the graph in Figure 14.1.

14.2. Find the shortest weighted path from V_2 to all others in the graph in Figure 14.1.

In Theory

14.3. Show how to avoid quadratic initialization inherent in adjacency matrices while maintaining constant-time access of any edge.

14.4. Explain how to modify the unweighted shortest-path algorithm so that if there is more than one minimum path (in terms of number of edges), then the tie is broken in favor of the smallest total weight.

14.5. Explain how to modify Dijkstra's algorithm to produce a count of the number of different minimum paths from v to w.

14.6. Explain how to modify Dijkstra's algorithm so that if there is more than one minimum path from v to w, a path with the fewest number of edges is chosen.

14.7. Give an example of when Dijkstra's algorithm gives the wrong answer in the presence of a negative edge but no negative-cost cycle.

14.8. Consider the following algorithm to solve the negative-weighted, shortest-path problem: Add a constant c to each edge cost, thus removing negative edges; calculate the shortest path on the new graph; and then use that result on the original. What is wrong with this algorithm?

14.9. Prove the correctness of the negative-weighted, shortest-path algorithm. To do this, show that when the eyeball visits vertex v for the ith time, the value of D_v is the length of the shortest weighted path consisting of i or fewer edges.

14.10. Give a linear-time algorithm to find the longest weighted path in an acyclic graph. Does your algorithm extend to graphs that have cycles?

14.11. Show that if edge weights are 0 or 1, exclusively, Dijkstra's algorithm can be implemented in linear time by using a *deque* (Section 15.4).

In Practice

14.12. This chapter claims that for the implementation of graph algorithms that run on large input, data structures are crucial to ensure reasonable performance. For each of the following instances in which a poor data structure or algorithm is used, provide a Big-Oh analysis of the result and compare the actual performance with the algorithms and data structures presented in the text. Implement only one change at a time. You should run your tests on a reasonably large and somewhat sparse random graph. Then do the following:

  a. When an edge is read, check to see if it is already in the graph.
  b. Implement the dictionary by using a sequential scan of the vertex table.
  c. Implement the queue by using the algorithm in Exercise 6.13 (this should affect the unweighted shortest-path algorithm).
  d. In the unweighted shortest-path algorithm, implement the search for the minimum-cost vertex as a sequential scan of the vertex table.
  e. Implement the priority queue by using the algorithm in Exercise 6.16 (this should affect the weighted shortest-path algorithm).
  f. Implement the priority queue by using the algorithm in Exercise 6.17 (this should affect the weighted shortest-path algorithm).
  g. In the weighted shortest-path algorithm, implement the search for the minimum-cost vertex as a sequential scan of the vertex table.
  h. In the acyclic shortest-path algorithm, implement the search for a vertex with indegree zero as a sequential scan of the vertex table.
  i. Implement any of the graph algorithms using an adjacency matrix instead of adjacency lists.

Programming Projects

14.13. A directed graph is strongly connected if there is a path from every vertex to every other vertex. Do the following:

  a. Pick any vertex S. Show that if the graph is strongly connected, a shortest-path algorithm will declare that all nodes are reachable from S.

b. Show that if the graph is strongly connected, then if the directions of all edges are reversed and a shortest-path algorithm is run from *S*, then all nodes will be reachable from *S*.

c. Show that the tests in (a) and (b) are sufficient to decide if a graph is strongly connected (that is, a graph that passes both tests must be strongly connected).

d. Write a program that checks if a graph is strongly connected. What is the running time of your algorithm?

Explain how each of the following problems can be solved by applying a shortest-path algorithm. Then design a mechanism for representing an input and write a program that solves the problem.

14.14. The input is a list of league game scores (and there are no ties). If all teams have at least one win and a loss, we can generally "prove," by a silly transitivity argument, that any team is better than any other. For instance, in the six-team league where everyone plays three games, suppose we have the following results: *A* beat *B* and *C*; *B* beat *C* and *F*; *C* beat *D*; *D* beat *E*; *E* beat *A*; *F* beat *D* and *E*. Then we can prove that *A* is better than *F* because *A* beat *B* who in turn beat *F*. Similarly, we can prove that *F* is better than *A* because *F* beat *E* and *E* beat *A*. Given a list of game scores and two teams *X* and *Y*, either find a proof (if one exists) that *X* is better than *Y* or indicate that no proof of this form can be found.

14.15. A word can be changed to another word by a 1-character substitution. Assume that a dictionary of 5-letter words exists. Give an algorithm to determine if a word *A* can be transformed to a word *B* by a series of 1-character substitutions, and if so, outputs the corresponding sequence of words. As an example, `bleed` converts to `blood` by the sequence `bleed, blend, blond, blood`.

14.16. The input is a collection of currencies and their exchange rates. Is there a sequence of exchanges that makes money instantly? For instance, if the currencies are *X*, *Y*, and *Z* and the exchange rate is 1 *X* equals 2 *Y*s, 1 *Y* equals 2 *Z*s, and 1 *X* equals 3 *Z*s, then 300 *Z*s will buy 100 *X*s, which in turn will buy 200 *Y*s, which in turn will buy 400 *Z*s. We have thus made a profit of 33 percent.

14.17. A student needs to take a certain number of courses to graduate, and these courses have prerequisites that must be followed. Assume that all courses are offered every semester and that the student can take an unlimited number of courses. Given a list of courses and their prerequisites, compute a schedule that requires the minimum number of semesters.

14.18. The object of the *Kevin Bacon Game* is to link a movie actor to Kevin Bacon via shared movie roles. The minimum number of links is an actor's *Bacon number*. For instance, Tom Hanks has a Bacon number of 1. He was in *Apollo 13* with Kevin Bacon. Sally Field has a Bacon number of 2 because she was in *Forest Gump* with Tom Hanks, who was in *Apollo 13* with Kevin Bacon. Almost all well-known actors have a Bacon number of 1 or 2. Assume that you have a comprehensive list of actors, with roles, and do the following:

a. Explain how to find an actor's Bacon number.
b. Explain how to find the actor with the highest Bacon number.
c. Explain how to find the minimum number of links between two arbitrary actors.

References

The use of adjacency lists to represent graphs was first advocated in [3]. Dijkstra's shortest-path algorithm was originally described in [2]. The algorithm for negative edge costs is taken from [1]. A more efficient test for termination is described in [6], which also shows how data structures play an important role in a wide range of graph theory algorithms. The topological sorting algorithm is from [4]. A host of real-life applications of graph algorithms can be found in [5], along with references for further reading.

1. R. E. Bellman, "On a Routing Problem," *Quarterly of Applied Mathematics* **16** (1958), 87–90.

2. E. W. Dijkstra, "A Note on Two Problems in Connexion with Graphs," *Numerische Mathematik* **1** (1959), 269–271.

3. J. E. Hopcroft and R. E. Tarjan, "Algorithm 447: Efficient Algorithms for Graph Manipulation," *Communications of the ACM* **16** (1973), 372–378.

4. A. B. Kahn, "Topological Sorting of Large Networks," *Communications of the ACM* **5** (1962), 558–562.

5. D. E. Knuth, *The Stanford GraphBase*, Addison-Wesley, Reading, Mass. (1993).

6. R. E. Tarjan, *Data Structures and Network Algorithms*, Society for Industrial and Applied Mathematics, Philadelphia, Penn. (1985).

Part IV
Implementations

15   *Stacks and Queues*

THIS chapter discusses the implementation of the stack and queue data structures. Recall from Chapter 6 that the basic operations are expected to take constant time. For both the stack and queue, there are two basic ways to arrange for constant-time operations. The first is to store the items contiguously in an array, and the second is to store items noncontiguously in a linked list. Implementations for both data structures using both methods are given here. The code implements the interfaces given in Chapter 6.

In this chapter, we will see:

- An array-based implementation of the stack
- An array-based implementation of the queue
- A linked-list-based implementation of the stack
- A linked-list-based implementation of the queue
- A brief comparison of the two methods
- Inheritance used to derive a new data structure, called the *double-ended queue*

15.1 Dynamic Array Implementations

This section implements the stack and queue using a simple array. The resulting algorithms are extremely efficient and also simple to code.

15.1.1 Stacks

As Figure 15.1 (page 412) shows, a stack can be implemented with an array and an integer. The integer `tos` (*top of stack*) provides the array index of the top element of the stack. Thus when `tos` is −1, the stack is empty. To `push`, we increment `tos` and place the new element in the array position `tos`. Accessing the top element is thus trivial, and the `pop` can be performed by decrementing `tos`. In Figure 15.1, we begin with an empty stack. Then we show the stack after the following three operations: `push(a)`, `push(b)`, and `pop`.

A stack can be implemented with an array and an integer that indicates the index of the top element.

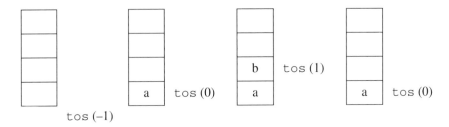

Figure 15.1   How the stack routines work: empty stack: push(a);
push(b);pop

Figure 15.2 shows the skeleton for the array-based StackAr class. It specifies two data fields. theArray, which is expanded as needed, stores the items in the stack. topOfStack gives the index of the current top of the stack. For an empty stack, this index is −1. The constructor is shown in Figure 15.3 (page 414).

The public methods are listed in lines 27 to 38 of the skeleton. Most of these routines have simple implementations. The push method is shown in Figure 15.4 (page 414). If it were not for the array doubling, which is a standard exercise that we have seen before, the push routine would be only the single line of code shown at line 9. Recall from Section 1.4.3 that the use of the prefix ++ operator means that topOfStack is incremented and its new value is used to index theArray. The remaining routines are equally short, as shown in Figures 15.5 (page 414) and 15.6 (page 415). The postfix -- operator used in Figure 15.6 means that although topOfStack is decremented, its prior value is used to index theArray.

> Most of the stack routines are applications of previously seen ideas.

If there is no array doubling, every operation takes constant time. A push that involves array doubling will take $O(N)$ time. If this was a frequent occurrence, then we would need to worry. However, it is infrequent because an array doubling that involves N elements must be preceded by at least $N/2$ pushes that do not involve an array doubling. Consequently, we can charge the $O(N)$ cost of the doubling over these $N/2$ easy pushes, thereby effectively raising the cost of each push by only a small constant. This technique is known as *amortization*.

> Recall that array doubling does not affect performance in the long run.

A real-life example of amortization is payment of income taxes. Rather than pay your entire bill on April 15, the government requires that you pay most of your taxes through withholding. The total tax bill is always the same; it is just *when* the tax is paid that varies. The same is true for the time spent in the push operations. We can charge for the array doubling at the time it occurs, or we can bill each push operation equally. An amortized bound states that we bill each operation in a sequence for its fair share of the total cost. In our example, it means that the cost of array doubling is not excessive at all.

```
1  package DataStructures;
2
3  import Exceptions.*;
4
5  // StackAr class
6  //
7  // CONSTRUCTION: with no initializer
8  //
9  // ******************PUBLIC OPERATIONS*********************
10 // void push( x )        --> Insert x
11 // void pop( )           --> Remove most recently inserted item
12 // Object top( )         --> Return most recently inserted item
13 // Object topAndPop( )   --> Return and remove most recent item
14 // boolean isEmpty( )    --> Return true if empty; else false
15 // void makeEmpty( )     --> Remove all items
16 // ******************ERRORS******************************
17 // top, pop, or topAndPop on empty stack
18
19 /**
20  * Array-based implementation of the stack.
21  */
22 public class StackAr implements Stack
23 {
24     public StackAr( )
25       { /* Figure 15.3 */ }
26
27     public boolean isEmpty( )
28       { return topOfStack == -1; }
29     public void makeEmpty( )
30       { topOfStack = -1; }
31     public void push( Object x )
32       { /* Figure 15.4 */ }
33     public Object top( ) throws Underflow
34       { /* Figure 15.5 */ }
35     public void pop( ) throws Underflow
36       { /* Figure 15.5 */ }
37     public Object topAndPop( ) throws Underflow
38       { /* Figure 15.6 */ }
39
40     private Object [ ] theArray;
41     private int        topOfStack;
42
43     static final int DEFAULT_CAPACITY = 10;
44
45     private void doubleArray( )
46       { /* Usual stuff, not shown */ }
47 }
```

Figure 15.2   StackAr class skeleton

```
1        /**
2         * Construct the stack.
3         */
4        public StackAr( )
5        {
6            theArray = new Object[ DEFAULT_CAPACITY ];
7            topOfStack = -1;
8        }
```

Figure 15.3   Zero-parameter constructor for array-based `Stack`

```
1        /**
2         * Insert a new item into the stack.
3         * @param x the item to insert.
4         */
5        public void push( Object x )
6        {
7            if( topOfStack + 1 == theArray.length )
8                doubleArray( );
9            theArray[ ++topOfStack ] = x;
10       }
```

Figure 15.4   push method for array-based `Stack`

```
1        /**
2         * Get the most recently inserted item in the stack.
3         * @return the most recently inserted item in the stack.
4         * @exception Underflow if the stack is empty.
5         */
6        public Object top( ) throws Underflow
7        {
8            if( isEmpty( ) )
9                throw new Underflow( "Stack top" );
10           return theArray[ topOfStack ];
11       }
12
13       /**
14        * Remove the most recently inserted item from the stack.
15        * @exception Underflow if the stack is empty.
16        */
17       public void pop( ) throws Underflow
18       {
19           if( isEmpty( ) )
20               throw new Underflow( "Stack pop" );
21           topOfStack--;
22       }
```

Figure 15.5   top and pop methods for array-based `Stack`

```
1      /**
2       * Return and remove the most recently inserted item
3       * from the stack.
4       * @return the most recently inserted item in the stack.
5       * @exception Underflow if the stack is empty.
6       */
7      public Object topAndPop( ) throws Underflow
8      {
9          if( isEmpty( ) )
10             throw new Underflow( "Stack topAndpop" );
11         return theArray[ topOfStack-- ];
12     }
```

Figure 15.6   topAndPop method for array-based Stack

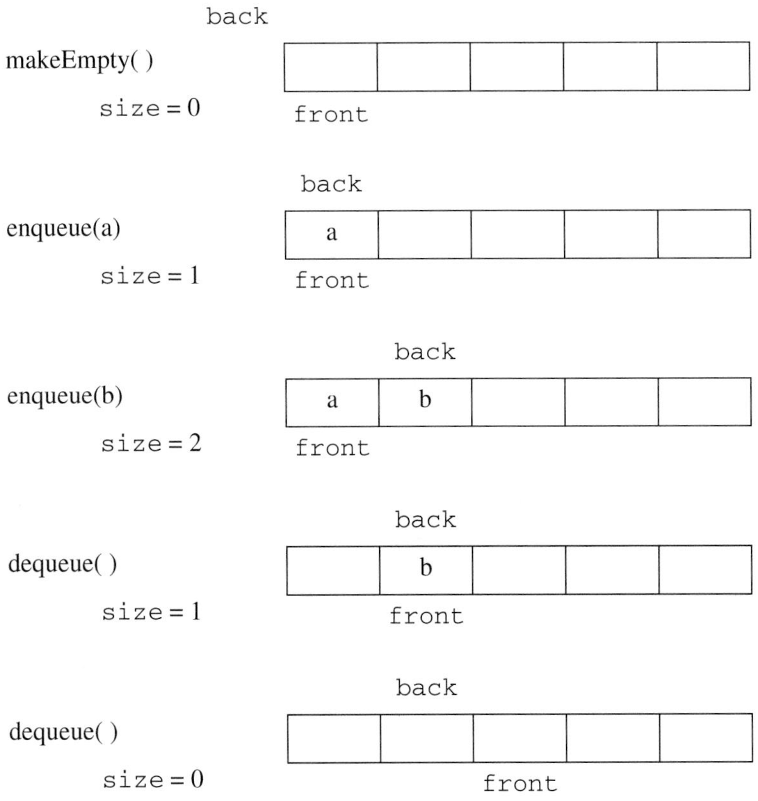

Figure 15.7   Basic array implementation of the queue

15.1.2 **Queues**

Storing the queue items beginning at the start of any array makes dequeueing expensive.

The easiest way to implement the queue is to store the items in an array with the front item in the front position (that is, array index zero). If `back` represents the position of the last item in the queue, then to `enqueue` we merely increment `back` and place the item there. The problem is that the `dequeue` operation is very expensive. This is because by requiring that the items be placed at the start of the array, we force the `dequeue` to shift over all of the items by one position, after the front item is removed.

A dequeue is implemented by incrementing the `front` *position.*

Figure 15.7 (page 415) shows that to overcome this problem, when a dequeue is performed, we increment `front` rather than sliding over all the elements. When the queue has one element, both `front` and `back` represent the array index of that element. Thus, for an empty queue, `back` must be initialized to `front-1`.

This implementation assures that both `enqueue` and `dequeue` can be performed in constant time. The fundamental problem with this is shown in the first line of Figure 15.8. After three more `enqueue` operations, we cannot add any more items, even though the queue is not really full. Array doubling does not solve the problem. This is because even if the size of the array is 1,000, after 1,000 `enqueue` operations there is no room in the queue, regardless of its actual size. Even if 1,000 `dequeue` operations have been performed, thus abstractly making the queue empty, we cannot add to it.

Wraparound returns `front` *and* `back` *to the beginning of the array when it reaches the end. Using wraparound to implement the queue is called a circular array implementation.*

As Figure 15.8 shows, however, there is plenty of extra space: All the positions before `front` are unused and can thus be recycled. Thus we implement *wraparound*: When either `back` or `front` reaches the end of the array, we reset it to the beginning. This operation is called a *circular array implementation*. We need to double the array only when the number of elements in the queue is equal to the number of array positions. To `enqueue(f)`, we therefore reset `back` to the start of the array and place f there. After three `dequeue` operations, `front` is also reset to the start of the array.

The skeleton for the generic `QueueAr` class is shown in Figure 15.9 (page 418). The `QueueAr` class has four data members: a dynamically expanding array, the number of items currently in the queue, the array index of the front item and the array index of the back item.

If the queue is full, we must implement array doubling carefully.

Two methods are declared in the private section. These methods are used internally by the `QueueAr` methods but are not made available to the user of the class. One of these methods is the `increment` routine. The `increment` routine adds 1 to its parameter and returns the new value. Since it implements wraparound, if the result would equal the array size it is wrapped around to zero. This is shown in Figure 15.10 (page 419). The other routine is `doubleQueue`, which is called if an `enqueue` requires a doubling of the array. It is slightly more complex than the simple call to `doubleArray` that was used for the `StackAr` class. This is because the queue items are not necessarily stored starting in array location zero. Thus items must be carefully copied. `doubleQueue` is discussed with `enqueue`.

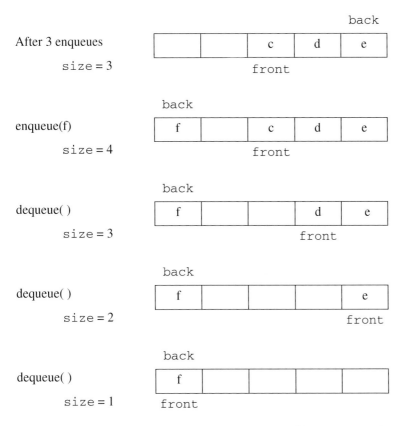

Figure 15.8   Array implementation of the queue with wraparound

Many of the public methods resemble their stack counterparts, including the constructor shown in Figure 15.11 (page 419). This constructor is not particularly special, except that we must be careful to make sure that we have the correct initial values for both `front` and `back`.

The `enqueue` routine is shown in Figure 15.12 (page 419). The basic strategy is simple enough, as illustrated by lines 9 to 11 in the `enqueue` routine. `doubleQueue`, shown in Figure 15.13 (page 420), is similar to the stack doubling routine, except that the copy from the old array to the new array does not start from position zero. Instead, it steps through the old array and copies each item into the new array at lines 11 to 13. The result is copied starting at array position zero; notice the new values of `front` and `back` at lines 16 and 17. The `dequeue` and `getFront` routines are shown in Figure 15.14 (page 420). Both are short and simple. Finally, `makeEmpty` is shown in Figure 15.15 (page 421). Once again it should be clear that the queue routines are constant-time operations. The cost of array doubling can be amortized over the sequence of `enqueue` operations, in the same way as the stack.

When we double the queue array, we cannot simply copy the entire array directly.

```
1  package DataStructures;
2
3  import Exceptions.*;
4
5  // QueueAr class
6  //
7  // CONSTRUCTION: with no initializer
8  //
9  // ******************PUBLIC OPERATIONS********************
10 // void enqueue( x )      --> Insert x
11 // Object getFront( )     --> Return least recently inserted item
12 // Object dequeue( )      --> Return and remove least recent item
13 // boolean isEmpty( )     --> Return true if empty; else false
14 // void makeEmpty( )      --> Remove all items
15 // ******************ERRORS******************************
16 // getFront or dequeue on empty queue
17
18 /**
19  * Array-based implementation of the queue.
20  */
21 public class QueueAr implements Queue
22 {
23     public QueueAr( )
24       { /* Figure 15.11 */ }
25
26     public boolean isEmpty( )
27       { return CurrentSize == 0; }
28     public void enqueue( Object x )
29       { /* Figure 15.12 */ }
30     public void makeEmpty( )
31       { /* Figure 15.15 */ }
32     public Object dequeue( ) throws Underflow
33       { /* Figure 15.14 */ }
34     public Object getFront( ) throws Underflow
35       { /* Figure 15.14 */ }
36
37     private Object [ ] theArray;
38     private int        currentSize;
39     private int        front;
40     private int        back;
41
42     static final int DEFAULT_CAPACITY = 10;
43
44     private int increment( int x )
45       { /* Figure 15.10 */ }
46     private void doubleQueue( )
47       { /* Figure 15.13 */ }
48 }
```

Figure 15.9   QueueAr class skeleton

```
1      /**
2       * Internal method to increment with wraparound.
3       * @param x any index in theArray's range.
4       * @return x+1, or 0 if x is at the end of theArray.
5       */
6      private int increment( int x )
7      {
8          if( ++x == theArray.length )
9              x = 0;
10         return x;
11     }
```

Figure 15.10 Wraparound routine

```
1      /**
2       * Construct the queue.
3       */
4      public QueueAr( )
5      {
6          theArray = new Object[ DEFAULT_CAPACITY ];
7          makeEmpty( );
8      }
```

Figure 15.11 Constructor for array-based Queue class

```
1      /**
2       * Insert a new item into the queue.
3       * @param x the item to insert.
4       */
5      public void enqueue( Object x )
6      {
7          if( currentSize == theArray.length )
8              doubleQueue( );
9          back = increment( back );
10         theArray[ back ] = x;
11         currentSize++;
12     }
```

Figure 15.12 enqueue for array-based Queue class

```
1      /**
2       * Internal method to extend theArray.
3       */
4      private void doubleQueue( )
5      {
6          Object [ ] newArray;
7
8          newArray = new Object[ theArray.length * 2 ];
9
10             // Copy elements that are logically in the queue
11         for( int i = 0; i < currentSize;
12                         i++, front = increment( front ) )
13             newArray[ i ] = theArray[ front ];
14
15         theArray = newArray;
16         front = 0;
17         back = currentSize - 1;
18     }
```

Figure 15.13   Dynamic expansion for array-based Queue class

```
1      /**
2       * Return and remove the least recently inserted item
3       * from the queue.
4       * @return the least recently inserted item in the queue.
5       * @exception Underflow if the queue is empty.
6       */
7      public Object dequeue( ) throws Underflow
8      {
9          if( isEmpty( ) )
10             throw new Underflow( "Queue dequeue" );
11         currentSize--;
12
13         Object returnValue = theArray[ front ];
14         front = increment( front );
15         return returnValue;
16     }
17
18     /**
19      * Get the least recently inserted item in the queue.
20      * @return the least recently inserted item in the queue.
21      * @exception Underflow if the queue is empty.
22      */
23     public Object getFront( ) throws Underflow
24     {
25         if( isEmpty( ) )
26             throw new Underflow( "Queue getFront" );
27         return theArray[ front ];
28     }
```

Figure 15.14   dequeue and getFront for array-based Queue class

```
1      /**
2       * Make the queue logically empty.
3       */
4      public void makeEmpty( )
5      {
6          currentSize = 0;
7          front = 0; back = theArray.length - 1;
8      }
```

Figure 15.15 `makeEmpty` routine for array-based `Queue` class

15.2 Linked-list Implementations

An alternative to the contiguous array implementation is to use a linked list. Recall from Section 6.4 that in a linked list, we store each item in a separate object that also contains a reference to the next object in the list.

The advantage of the linked list is that the excess memory is only one reference per item, whereas a contiguous array implementation uses excess space equal to the number of vacant array items (plus some additional memory during the doubling phase). This advantage is immaterial in Java because the vacant array items represent null references and thus consume little space. In other languages, however, this advantage is significant because the vacant array items tend to store uninitialized instances of objects that can consume significant space. Even so, the linked-list implementations are discussed for several reasons:

The advantage of a linked-list implementation is that the excess memory is only one reference per item. The disadvantage is that the memory allocation is time consuming.

1. It is important to understand implementations that might be useful in other languages.
2. Implementations that use linked lists are shorter than the comparable array versions, especially for the queue.
3. These implementations illustrate the principles behind the more general linked list operations given in Chapter 16.

For the implementation to be competitive with contiguous array implementations, we must be able to perform the basic linked-list operations in constant time. This is easy to do because the changes in the linked list are restricted to the elements at the two ends (front and back) of the list.

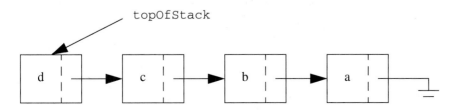

Figure 15.16 Linked-list implementation of the stack

15.2.1 Stacks

To implement the stack, we have the top of the stack represented by the first item in the list.

The `Stack` interface can be implemented by using a linked list in which the top of the stack is represented by the first item in the list. This is shown in Figure 15.16 (page 421). To implement a `push`, we create a new node in the list and attach it as the new first element. This node can be allocated by a call to new. To implement a `pop`, we merely advance the top of the stack to the second item in the list (if there is one). An empty stack is represented by an empty linked list. Clearly, each operation is constant time, since by restricting operations to the first node, we have made all calculations independent of the size of the list. All that remains is the Java implementation.

Figure 15.17 gives the declaration for the nodes in the list. A `ListNode` consists of two data fields: `element` stores the item and `next` stores a reference to the next `ListNode` in the linked list. We provide two constructors for `ListNode`. The first can be used to execute

```
ListNode node1 = new ListNode( x );
```

where `x` is an item. The second can be used to initialize the `next` reference by providing a `ListNode` reference (or `null`):

```
ListNode node2 = new ListNode( x, node1 );
```

```
 1 package DataStructures;
 2
 3 // Basic node stored in a linked list
 4 // Note that this class is not accessible outside
 5 // of package DataStructures
 6
 7 class ListNode
 8 {
 9         // Constructors
10     ListNode( Object theElement )
11       { this( theElement, null ); }
12
13     ListNode( Object theElement, ListNode n )
14       { element = theElement; next = n; }
15
16     // Friendly data; accessible by other package routines
17     Object    element;
18     ListNode next;
19 }
```

Figure 15.17 `ListNode` class

Note that the new type `ListNode` is package-friendly. This means it is not a type in the normal global scope, but it is visible to the other classes in the `DataStructures` package. This is good because it enforces information hiding. The `ListNode` is certainly an internal detail of the data structures package, but it is completely invisible to the `Stack` class users.

The `ListNode` is package-friendly to the data structures package class, so it is not visible to the general user.

```
1 package DataStructures;
2
3 import Exceptions.*;
4
5 // StackLi class
6 //
7 // CONSTRUCTION: with no initializer
8 //
9 // ******************PUBLIC OPERATIONS*******************
10 // void push( x )          --> Insert x
11 // void pop( )             --> Remove most recently inserted item
12 // Object top( )           --> Return most recently inserted item
13 // Object topAndPop( )     --> Return and remove most recent item
14 // boolean isEmpty( )      --> Return true if empty; else false
15 // void makeEmpty( )       --> Remove all items
16 // ******************ERRORS*******************************
17 // top, pop, or topAndPop on empty stack
18
19 /**
20  * List-based implementation of the stack.
21  */
22 public class StackLi implements Stack
23 {
24     public StackLi( )
25       { topOfStack = null; }
26
27     public boolean isEmpty( )
28       { return topOfStack == null; }
29     public void makeEmpty( )
30       { topOfStack = null; }
31     public void push( Object x )
32       { topOfStack = new ListNode( x, topOfStack ); }
33
34     public void pop( ) throws Underflow
35       { /* Figure 15.19 */ }
36     public Object top( ) throws Underflow
37       { /* Figure 15.19 */ }
38     public Object topAndPop( ) throws Underflow
39       { /* Figure 15.19 */ }
40
41     private ListNode topOfStack;
42 }
```

Figure 15.18   Skeleton for the linked-list-based `Stack` class

Figure 15.18 (page 423) shows the `StackLi` class that implements the `Stack` using a linked list. The stack is represented by a single data member: `topOfStack` is a reference to the first `ListNode` in the linked list. The constructor at line 24 indicates that an empty stack is created by setting `topOfStack` to `null`.

The push operation is essentially one line of code: create a new `ListNode`. The data member contains the item `x` to be pushed, and the `next` reference for this new node is the original `topOfStack`. This node then becomes the new `topOfStack`. All this is done at line 32.

The stack routines are essentially one-liners.

```
1      /**
2       * Get the most recently inserted item in the stack.
3       * Does not alter the stack.
4       * @return the most recently inserted item in the stack.
5       * @exception Underflow if the stack is empty.
6       */
7      public Object top( ) throws Underflow
8      {
9          if( isEmpty( ) )
10             throw new Underflow( "Stack top" );
11         return topOfStack.element;
12     }
13
14     /**
15      * Remove the most recently inserted item from the stack.
16      * @exception Underflow if the stack is empty.
17      */
18     public void pop( ) throws Underflow
19     {
20         if( isEmpty( ) )
21             throw new Underflow( "Stack pop" );
22         topOfStack = topOfStack.next;
23     }
24
25     /**
26      * Return and remove the most recently inserted item
27      * from the stack.
28      * @return the most recently inserted item in the stack.
29      * @exception Underflow if the stack is empty.
30      */
31     public Object topAndPop( ) throws Underflow
32     {
33         if( isEmpty( ) )
34             throw new Underflow( "Stack topAndPop" );
35
36         Object topItem = topOfStack.element;
37         topOfStack = topOfStack.next;
38         return topItem;
39     }
```

Figure 15.19 Simple class members for the linked-list-based `Stack`

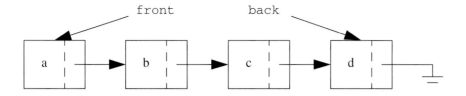

Figure 15.20 Linked-list implementation of the queue

```
 1  package DataStructures;
 2
 3  import Exceptions.*;
 4
 5  // QueueLi class
 6  //
 7  // CONSTRUCTION: with no initializer
 8  //
 9  // ******************PUBLIC OPERATIONS*********************
10  // void enqueue( x )      --> Insert x
11  // Object getFront( )     --> Return least recently inserted item
12  // Object dequeue( )      --> Return and remove least recent item
13  // boolean isEmpty( )     --> Return true if empty; else false
14  // void makeEmpty( )      --> Remove all items
15  // ******************ERRORS*******************************
16  // getFront or dequeue on empty queue
17
18  /**
19   * List-based implementation of the queue.
20   */
21  public class QueueLi implements Queue
22  {
23      public QueueLi( )
24        { makeEmpty( ); }
25
26      public boolean isEmpty( )
27        { return front == null; }
28      public void makeEmpty( )
29        { front = back = null; }
30      public Object dequeue( ) throws Underflow
31        { /* Figure 15.22 */ }
32      public Object getFront( ) throws Underflow
33        { /* Figure 15.23 */ }
34      public void enqueue( Object x )
35        { /* Figure 15.25 */ }
36
37      private ListNode front;
38      private ListNode back;
39  }
```

Figure 15.21 Skeleton for the linked-list-based Queue class

```
1     /**
2      * Return and remove the least recently inserted item
3      * from the queue.
4      * @return the least recently inserted item in the queue.
5      * @exception Underflow if the queue is empty.
6      */
7     public Object dequeue( ) throws Underflow
8     {
9         if( isEmpty( ) )
10            throw new Underflow( "Queue dequeue" );
11
12        Object returnValue = front.element;
13        front = front.next;
14        return returnValue;
15    }
```

Figure 15.22 dequeue for the linked-list-based Queue class

The remaining routines are shown in Figure 15.19 (page 424). The pop operation is also simple. After the obligatory test for emptiness, we reset topOfStack to the second node in the list. Similarly, top and topAndPop are short routines.

15.2.2 Queues

A linked list in which we maintain a reference to the first and last item can be used to implement the queue efficiently.

The queue can be implemented by a linked list, provided references are kept to both the front and back of the list. Figure 15.20 (page 425) shows the general idea.

The queue routine is almost identical to the stack routine. The QueueLi class skeleton is given in Figure 15.21 (page 425). Nothing is new here, except that we maintain two references instead of one.

Figure 15.22 implements dequeue. dequeue is logically identical to a stack pop. getFront is simple and is shown in Figure 15.23.

```
1     /**
2      * Get the least recently inserted item in the queue.
3      * Does not alter the queue.
4      * @return the least recently inserted item in the queue.
5      * @exception Underflow if the queue is empty.
6      */
7     public Object getFront( ) throws Underflow
8     {
9         if( isEmpty( ) )
10            throw new Underflow( "Queue getFront" );
11        return front.element;
12    }
```

Figure 15.23 getFront for the linked-list-based Queue class

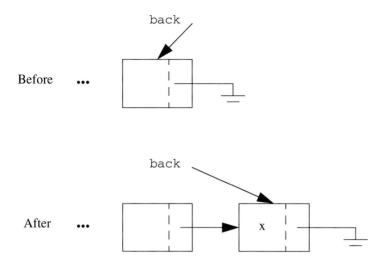

Figure 15.24 enqueue operation for the linked-list-based implementation

enqueue has two cases. If the queue is empty, then we create a one-element queue by calling new and having both `front` and `back` reference the single node. Otherwise, we create a new node with data value x, attach it to the end of the list, and then reset the end of the list to this new node. This is illustrated in Figure 15.24. Notice that enqueueing the first element is a special case because there is no `next` reference to which a new node can be attached. All this is done in Figure 15.25.

Enqueueing the first element is a special case because there is no next reference to which a new node can be attached.

```
1      /**
2       * Insert a new item into the queue.
3       * @param x the item to insert.
4       */
5      public void enqueue( Object x )
6      {
7          if( isEmpty( ) )   // Make queue of one element
8              back = front = new ListNode( x );
9          else                // Regular case
10             back = back.next = new ListNode( x );
11     }
```

Figure 15.25 enqueue for the linked-list-based Queue class

15.3 Comparison of the Two Methods

Both the array and linked-list versions run in constant time per operation. Thus they are so fast that they are unlikely to be the bottleneck of any algorithm. As such, it will rarely matter which version is used.

The array versions of these data structures are likely to be faster than their linked-list counterparts, especially if an accurate estimation of the capacity is available. If an additional constructor is provided to specify the initial capacity (see Exercise 15.3) and the estimate is correct, no doubling will be performed. Also, the sequential access provided by an array is typically faster than the potential nonsequential access offered by dynamic memory allocation.

The array implementation does have two drawbacks, however. First, for queues, the array implementation is arguably more complex than the linked-list implementation due to the combined code for wraparound and array doubling. Our implementation of array doubling was not as efficient as possible (see Exercise 15.8), thus a faster implementation of the queue would require a few additional lines of code. Even the array implementation of the stack uses a few more lines of code than its linked-list counterpart.

The second drawback affects other languages, but not Java. When doubling, we require, temporarily, three times as much space as the number of data items would suggest. This is because when the array is doubled, we need to have memory to store both the old and the new (double-sized) array. Further, at the queue's peak size, the array is between 50 percent and 100 percent full: On average, it is 75 percent full, meaning that for every three items in the array, one spot is empty. The wasted space is thus 33 percent on average and 100 percent when the table is only half full. In Java, this is not a problem because each element in the array is simply a reference. In other languages, such as C++, objects are stored directly, rather than referenced. In these languages, the wasted space could be significant when compared to the linked-list-based version that uses only an extra reference per item.

15.4 Double-ended Queues

A double-ended queue (deque) allows access at both ends. Much of its functionality can be derived from the queue class.

This chapter closes with a discussion of the use of inheritance to derive a new data structure. A *double-ended queue* (*deque*) is like a queue, except that access is allowed at both ends. Exercise 14.11 describes an application of the deque. Rather than the terms `enqueue` and `dequeue`, the terms used are `addFront`, `addRear`, `removeFront`, and `removeRear`. Figure 15.26 shows the derived class `Deque`. We derive from `QueueAr` because deletion from the back of the list is not efficiently supported.

Implementation of the deque is simple when inheritance is used.

The default constructor is a call to `super`; this is acceptable. `enqueue` and `dequeue` still work; we cannot remove methods. `getFront` is unchanged from the queue class and is thus inherited unmodified. `addBack` and `removeFront` call the existing `enqueue` and `dequeue` routines. The only routines that need to be written are `addFront`, `removeBack`, and `getBack`. To do this, we need to make the data members of the original queue class protected, after which we can write the additional methods. This is left as Exercise 15.5.

Summary

This chapter described the implementation of the stack and queue classes. Both the stack and queue can be implemented by using a contiguous array or a linked list. In each case, all operations use constant time; thus all operations are fast.

In other programming languages, the array implementation typically uses more memory but less time than the linked-list version, thereby yielding a classic time versus space tradeoff. In Java, this is a nonissue.

```
 1  // Double ended queue (Deque) class
 2  //
 3  // CONSTRUCTION: with no initializer;
 4  //
 5  // ******************PUBLIC OPERATIONS********************
 6  // void addFront( Object x )  --> Insert x at front
 7  // void addBack( Object x )   --> Insert x at back
 8  // void removeFront( )        --> Remove front item
 9  // void removeBack( )         --> Remove back item
10  // Object getFront( )         --> Return front item
11  // Object getBack( )          --> Return back item
12  // boolean isEmpty( )         --> If empty return true else false
13  // void makeEmpty( )          --> Remove all items
14  // enqueue and dequeue are available, but should not be used
15  // ******************ERRORS*******************************
16  // Exception thrown for get or remove on empty deque
17
18  class Deque extends QueueAr
19  {
20
21      public void addFront( Object x )
22          { /* Exercise 15.5 */ }
23      public void addBack( Object x )
24          { enqueue( x ); }
25      public Object removeFront( ) throws Underflow
26          { return dequeue( ); }
27      public void removeBack( ) throws Underflow
28          { /* Exercise 15.5 */ }
29      public Object getBack( ) throws Underflow
30          { /* Exercise 15.5 */ }
31      // isEmpty, makeEmpty, getFront are all inherited
32  }
```

Figure 15.26   Double-ended queue class Deque derived from `QueueAr`

Objects of the Game

circular array implementation An implementation that uses wraparound to implement a queue. (416)

double-ended queue (deque) A queue that allows access at both ends. Much of its functionality can be derived from the queue class. (428)

wraparound Occurs when `front` or `back` returns to the beginning of the array when it reaches the end. (416)

Common Errors

1. The circular array implementation of the queue is easily done wrong when attempts to shorten the code are made. For instance, do not attempt to avoid using the `size` member by using `front` and `back` to infer the size.

2. Using an implementation that does not provide constant time access is a bad error. There is no reason for the inefficiency.

On the Internet

The following files are available and are found in the directory **DataStructures**. Some test programs were in Chapter 6, and other tests are implied by their use in the applications in Part III.

StackAr.java   Implements an array-based stack.
StackLi.java   Implements a linked-list-based stack.
QueueAr.java   Implements an array-based queue.
QueueLi.java   Implements a linked-list-based queue.

Exercises

In Short

15.1. Draw the stack and queue data structures (for both the array and linked-list implementations) for each step in the following sequence: *add*(1), *add*(2), *remove*, *add*(3), *add*(4), *remove*, *remove*, *add*(5). Assume an initial size of three for the array implementation.

In Practice

15.2. Compare the running times for the array and linked list versions of `Stack`. Use `Integer` objects.

15.3. Add constructors to the array-based stack and queue classes that allow the user to specify an initial capacity.

15.4. Write a `main` that creates and uses a stack of `Integer` and a stack of `Double` simultaneously.

15.5. Complete the implementation of the `Deque` class.

15.6. Implement the array-based stack class by using the built-in `Vector` class. What are the advantages and disadvantages of this approach?

15.7. Implement the array-based stack class by extending the built-in `Vector` class. What are the advantages and disadvantages of this approach?

15.8. The array-doubling code in `QueueAr` is unduly expensive because of the repeated calls to `increment`. Write a faster version by avoiding all calls to `increment`. Do this by testing if wraparound is being used. If it is, then use two separate loops to copy; otherwise, use a single loop.

15.9. Using a `Vector` to implement an array-based queue class is problematic because the `setSize` method is not quite what is needed. Show how to rearrange the queue elements after the `setSize` operation so that at most half of the `Vector` references change. (However, this still uses more moves than the non-`Vector` implementation.)

Programming Projects

15.10. An output-restricted, double-ended queue supports insertions from both ends but accesses and deletions only from the front. Do the following:
  a. Use inheritance to derive this new class from the `Queue`.
  b. Use inheritance to derive this new class from the `Deque`.

15.11. Suppose you want to add the `findMin` (but not `deleteMin`) operation to the stack repertoire. Do the following:
  a. Use inheritance to derive the new class and implement `findMin` as a sequential scan of the stack items.
  b. Do not use inheritance but instead implement the new class as two stacks, as described in Exercise 6.5.
  c. Use inheritance, with the algorithm described in Exercise 6.5.

15.12. Suppose you want to add the `findMin` (but not `deleteMin`) operation to the deque repertoire. Do the following:
  a. Use inheritance to derive the new class and implement `findMin` as a sequential scan of the deque items. Make appropriate choices of members to be made protected.
  b. Do not use inheritance but instead implement the new class as four stacks. If a deletion empties a stack, you will need to reorganize the remaining items evenly.

15.13. Write an applet that illustrates how the state of a stack changes when basic operations are applied to it. Include a GUI that allows the user to specify operations. Also, allow either an array or linked-list implementation (specified by a choice component).

15.14. Repeat Exercise 15.13 for a queue.

Linked Lists

CHAPTER 15 demonstrated that linked lists can be used to store items noncontiguously. The linked lists used in that chapter were simplified by the fact that all accesses were performed at one of the list's two ends. In this chapter, we will see:

- How we allow access to any item using a general linked list
- The general algorithms used for the linked-list operations
- How the *iterator class* provides a safe mechanism for traversing and accessing linked lists
- List variations, such as *doubly linked lists* and *circular linked lists*
- How we can use inheritance to derive a *sorted linked list* class

16.1 Basic Ideas

This chapter implements the linked list and allows general access (arbitrary insertion, deletion, and find operations) through the list. The basic linked list consists of a collection of dynamically allocated nodes connected together. In a *singly linked list*, each node consists of the data element and a reference to the next node in the list. The last node in the list has a `null next` reference. We will assume that the node is given by the `ListNode` declaration in Chapter 15:

```
class ListNode
{
    Object    element;
    ListNode next;
      // Constructors
}
```

The first node in the linked list is accessible by a reference. This is shown in Figure 16.1 (page 434). We can print or search in the linked list by starting at the first item and following the chain of `next` references. The two basic operations that must be performed are insertion and deletion of an arbitrary item x.

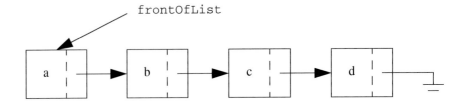

Figure 16.1 Basic linked list

Insertion consists of splicing a node into the list and can be accomplished with one statement.

For insertion, we must define where the insertion is to take place. If we have a reference to some node in the list, the easiest place to insert is immediately after that item. As an example, Figure 16.2 shows how we insert x after item a in a linked list. We must perform the following steps:

```
tmp = new ListNode( );     // Create a new node
tmp.element = x;           // Place x in the element field
tmp.next = current.next;   // x's next node is b
current.next = tmp;        // a's next node is x
```

As a result of these statements, the old list ... a, b, ... now appears as ... a, x, b, ... We can simplify the code, since the ListNode has a constructor that initializes the data fields directly. Thus we obtain

```
tmp = new ListNode( x, current.next  ); // Create new node
current.next = tmp;        // a's next node is x
```

At this point, it becomes clear that tmp is no longer necessary. Thus we have the following one-liner:

```
current.next = new ListNode( x, current.next );
```

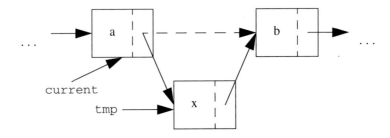

Figure 16.2 Insertion into a linked list: create a new node (tmp), copy in x, set tmp's next reference, and set current's next reference

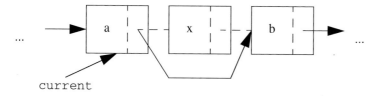

current

Figure 16.3   Deletion from a linked list

The `remove` command can be executed in one reference change. Figure 16.3 shows that to remove item x from the linked list, we set `current` to be the node prior to x and then have `current`'s next reference bypass x. This is expressed by the statement

```
current.next = current.next.next;
```

The list … a, x, b, … now appears as … a, b, … .

This summarizes the basics of inserting and removing at arbitrary places in a linked list. The fundamental property of linked lists is that changes to a list can be made using only a constant number of data movements. This is a great improvement over an array implementation because maintaining contiguousness in an array means that whenever an item is added or deleted, all items that follow it in the list must move.

Removal can be accomplished by bypassing the node. We need a reference to the node prior to the one we want to remove.

Linked-list operations use only a constant number of data movements.

16.1.1   Header Nodes

One problem with the basic description is that it assumes that whenever an item x is removed, there is always some previous item to allow a bypass. Consequently, removal of the first item in the linked list becomes a special case. Similarly, the insert routine does not allow us to insert an item to be the new first element in the list. This is because insertions are restricted to going after some already existing item. So, although the basic algorithm works fine, there are some annoying special cases that need to be dealt with.

Special cases are always problematic in algorithm design and frequently lead to bugs in the code. Consequently, it is generally preferable to write code that avoids special cases. One way to do that here is to introduce the *header node*.

A header node is an extra node in the linked list that holds no data but serves to satisfy the requirement that every node that contains an item have a previous node in the list. The header node for the list a, b, c is shown in Figure 16.4. Notice how a is no longer a special case. It can be deleted just like any other node by having `current` reference the node before it. We can also add a new first element to the list by setting `current` equal to the header node and calling the insertion routine. By using the header node, we greatly simplify the code, with a negligible space penalty. In more complex applications, header nodes not only simplify the code but also improve speed because, after all, fewer tests means less time.

Header nodes allow us to avoid special cases such as insertion of a new first element and removal of the first element.

The header node holds no data but serves to satisfy the requirement that every node have a previous node.

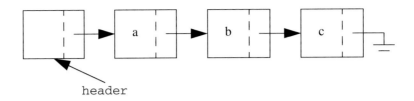

Figure 16.4   Using a header node for the linked list

The use of a header node is somewhat controversial. Some people argue that avoiding special cases is not sufficient justification for adding fictitious cells; they view the use of header nodes as little more than old-style hacking. Even so, we use them here precisely because they allow us to show the basic reference manipulations without obscuring the code with special cases. Whether a header should be used is a matter of personal preference. Furthermore, in a class implementation, its use would be completely transparent to the user. We must be careful, however; the printing routine must skip over the header node, as must all searching routines. Moving to the front now means setting the current position to `header.next`, and so on. Furthermore, as Figure 16.5 shows, with a header node, a list is empty if `header.next` is `null`.

16.1.2 Iterator Classes

By storing a reference to the current node in the list class, we ensure that access is controlled.

The typical primitive strategy identifies a linked list by a reference to the header node. Each individual item in the list can then be accessed by providing a reference to the node that stores it. The problem with that strategy is that it is difficult to check for errors. A user could pass a reference to something that is in another list. One way to guarantee that this cannot happen is to store a current position as part of the `List` class. To do this, we add a second data field, `current`. Then, since all access to the list goes through the class methods, we can be certain that `current` always represents either a reference to a node in the list, a reference to the header node, or `null`.

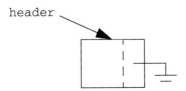

Figure 16.5   Empty list when a header node is used

```
 1      // Return number of elements in theList
 2      static public int listSize( LinkedList theList )
 3      {
 4          int size = 0;
 5          LinkedListItr itr = new LinkedListItr( theList );
 6
 7          for( itr.first( ); itr.isInList( ); itr.advance( ) )
 8              size++;
 9          return size;
10      }
```

Figure 16.6   Method that returns the size of a list

This scheme has a problem: Since there is only one position, the case in which two iterators need to access the list independently is left unsupported. A way to avoid this problem is to define a separate *iterator class*. The List class would then not maintain any notion of a current position and would have only methods that treat the list as a unit, such as isEmpty and makeEmpty. Routines that depend on knowing where we are in the list would reside in the iterator class. The iterator class maintains a notion of its current position and also the header node for the list it represents (the reference to the header node can be initialized by the constructor). Access to the list is granted by making the iterator package-friendly.

The *iterator class* maintains a current position and performs all routines that depend on knowing the position in the list. The iterator class is a friend of the List class.

One can view each instance of an iterator class as one in which only legal list operations, such as advancing in the list, are allowed. This chapter implements the List interface with the LinkedList class and the ListItr interface with the LinkedListItr class.

To see how this works, let us look at a static method, usable anywhere, that returns the size of a linked list, shown in Figure 16.6. itr is declared as an iterator that can access a linked list theList. This requires a constructor for LinkedListItr that takes a LinkedList as a parameter.

itr is initialized to the first element in theList (after skipping past the header), but we call the first method anyway. The call to the isInList method attempts to mimic the test p!=null that would be done if p was a normal reference to a ListNode. Finally, a call to the advance method mimics the conventional idiom p=p.next.

Thus, as long as the iterator class defines a few simple methods, we can iterate over the list in a very natural way. The next section shows how this is implemented in Java. The routines are surprisingly simple.

16.2 Java Implementation

We begin the linked list implementation by showing the class skeleton for the linked list. We implement the interface described in Section 6.4. The LinkedList class is shown in Figure 16.7 (page 438). At line 28, we declare the only data field of the class, namely, a reference to the header node.

The LinkedList class is simple because most of the work is pushed into the iterator class.

The iterator is irrevocably tied to the linked list for which it was constructed.

The constructor at line 20 allocates the header node. Notice that the header node's `element` field stores the null reference. Two methods are declared — `isEmpty` and `makeEmpty` — both one-liners. The LinkedList class is simple because most of the work is pushed into the iterator class.

Figures 16.8 and 16.9 (page 440) show the skeleton for `LinkedListItr`. This is a very interesting class that requires careful attention to detail. The class data fields are `theList`, which is a reference to the list, and `current`, which is a reference to the current node. `theList` is set on construction and should never change. Thus an iterator is irrevocably tied to a single list.[1]

```
 1  package DataStructures;
 2
 3  // LinkedList class
 4  //
 5  // CONSTRUCTION: with no initializer
 6  // Access is via LinkedListItr class
 7  //
 8  // ******************PUBLIC OPERATIONS********************
 9  // boolean isEmpty( )     --> Return true if empty; else false
10  // void makeEmpty( )      --> Remove all items
11  // ******************ERRORS*******************************
12  // No special errors
13
14  /**
15   * Linked list implementation of the list using a header node.
16   * Access to the list is via LinkedListItr.
17   */
18  public class LinkedList implements List
19  {
20      public LinkedList( )
21        { header = new ListNode( null ); }
22      public boolean isEmpty( )
23        { return header.next == null; }
24      public void makeEmpty( )
25        { header.next = null; }
26
27        // Friendly data, so LinkedListItr can have access
28      ListNode header;      // reference to a header node
29  }
```

Figure 16.7   LinkedList class

---

[1]. In Java 1.1, this can be enforced by making `theList` a `final` field because Java 1.1 allows the initialization of a `final` field to be performed in the constructors. We have not used this feature in this textbook.

```
 1  package DataStructures;
 2
 3  import Exceptions.*;
 4
 5  // LinkedListItr class; maintains "current position"
 6  //
 7  // CONSTRUCTION: with LinkedList to which ListItr
 8  //     is permanently bound
 9  //
10  // ******************PUBLIC OPERATIONS********************
11  // void insert( x )     --> Insert x after current position
12  // void remove( x )     --> Remove x
13  // boolean find( x )    --> Set current position to view x
14  // void zeroth( )       --> Set current position to prior to first
15  // void first( )        --> Set current position to first
16  // void advance( )      --> Advance
17  // boolean isInList( ) --> True if at valid position in list
18  // Object retrieve( )  --> Return item in current position
19  // ******************ERRORS******************************
20  // Exceptions thrown for illegal access, insert, or remove.
21
22  /**
23   * Linked list implementation of the list iterator
24   *     using a header node.
25   */
```

Figure 16.8   Comment section for `LinkedListItr`

Lines 11 to 16 declare a constructor. The parameter is a `LinkedList` object, and as a result of the construction, `theList` is set to reference the list and `current` is set to the first node in the list (skipping the header, of course). If the list is empty, `current` will reference the header node because we would expect that the next operation is an `insert`. There is no zero-parameter constructor, so an attempt to declare a `LinkedListItr` object without a list initializer will be flagged as a compile-time error. A second constructor that accepts a `List` is provided for convenience at lines 24 to 26.

What remains are the class methods. We need to be very careful to document what each method does. For instance, `insert` adds item x into the list immediately following the current position. What if `current` is `null`? Of course, that is an error. What is the new value of `current`? In our case, if the insertion is successful, `current` will reference the newly inserted node; otherwise, `current` will be unchanged. For each method, we use *javadoc* comments to document behavior, including specifying the errors that occur and changes to the iterator state.

Let us discuss the remaining methods. `find` searches for x. If x is in the list, `current` is moved to reference the node containing it and `find` returns `true`. Otherwise, `find` returns `false` and `current` is unchanged.

Initially, `current` references the first node, or the header if the list is empty.

```
1  public class LinkedListItr implements ListItr
2  {
3      /**
4       * Construct the list.
5       * As a result of the construction, the current position
6       * is the first item, unless the list is empty, in which
7       * case the current position is the zeroth item.
8       * @param anyList a LinkedList object to which this
9       *        iterator is permanently bound.
10      */
11     public LinkedListItr( LinkedList anyList )
12     {
13         theList = anyList;
14         current = anyList.isEmpty( ) ?
15                         anyList.header : anyList.header.next;
16     }
17
18     /**
19      * This constructor is provided for convenience. If
20      * anyList is not a LinkedList object, a ClassCastException
21      * will result. Otherwise, it has the same behavior as the
22      * above constructor.
23      */
24     public LinkedListItr( List anyList ) throws
25                                         ClassCastException
26       { this( (LinkedList) anyList ); }
27
28     /**
29      * Set the current position to the header node.
30      */
31     public void zeroth( )
32       { current = theList.header; }
33
34     public void insert( Object x ) throws ItemNotFound
35       { /* Figure 16.12 */ }
36     public boolean find( Object x )
37       { /* Figure 16.13 */ }
38     public void remove( Object x ) throws ItemNotFound
39       { /* Figure 16.14 */ }
40     public Object retrieve( )
41       { /* Figure 16.15 */ }
42     public void first( )
43       { /* Figure 16.15 */ }
44     public void advance( )
45       { /* Figure 16.15 */ }
46     public boolean isInList( )
47       { /* Figure 16.15 */ }
48
49     protected LinkedList theList;    // List
50     protected ListNode   current;    // Current position
51 }
```

Figure 16.9 Skeleton for the LinkedListItr class

remove searches for x. If x is in the list, it is removed and `current` is set to reference the header. Otherwise, `remove` throws an exception and `current` is unchanged. The movement of `current` is required, since we do not want `current` to reference a node that has already been deleted. A perfectly reasonable alternative would be to have it reference the node that is before the removed node. Neither method is bulletproof. There may be two iterators, and one can be left dangling if the other removes a node.

A sometimes important routine that is used in Section 13.1 is `removeNext`. Its implementation is left as Exercise 16.9.

The `isInList` method is used to test if the current position is in the list. It does not alter `current`. `retrieve` returns the item in the current position (or `null` if the current position is not a node in the list). It does not alter `current`. `zeroth` sets `current` to the header node. It allows insertions at the front of the list. `first` sets `current` to the first node in the list. If the list is empty, it will set `current` to `null`. Finally, `advance` is the iteration method. It sets `current` to `current.next`, assuming, of course, that `current` is not `null`. If `current` is `null`, nothing happens.

`first`, `advance`, `isInList`, and `retrieve` do not throw exceptions because the typical `for` loop use of these methods would require a `try/catch` block that is not really warranted.

We could have added more methods, but this basic set is quite powerful. Some methods, such as `retreat`, are not efficiently supported by this version of the linked list; variations on the linked list that allow constant-time implementation of that and other methods are discussed later in this chapter. For now, let us see how the `LinkedListItr` class can be used to implement copying and printing for linked lists.

> This is not bulletproof. There may be two iterators and one can be left dangling if the other removes a node.

> The `retreat` method is not efficiently supported. A doubly linked list is used if this is a liability.

```
1    // Method that copies from rhs to lhs;
2    // Calls public methods only
3    public static void copy( LinkedList lhs, LinkedList rhs )
4    {
5        if( lhs == rhs )   // Aliasing test
6            return;
7
8        lhs.makeEmpty( );
9        LinkedListItr lItr = new LinkedListItr( lhs );
10       LinkedListItr rItr = new LinkedListItr( rhs );
11
12       try
13       {
14           for( ; rItr.isInList( ); rItr.advance( ) )
15               lItr.insert( rItr.retrieve( ) );
16       }
17       catch( ItemNotFound e ) { }  // Cannot happen
18    }
```

Figure 16.10 Copy method for linked lists, using `LinkedListItr` to iterate

```
1      // Simple print method
2      public static void print( LinkedList theList )
3      {
4          if( theList.isEmpty( ) )
5              System.out.print( "Empty list" );
6          else
7          {
8              LinkedListItr itr = new LinkedListItr( theList );
9              for( ; itr.isInList( ); itr.advance( ) )
10                 System.out.print( itr.retrieve( ) + " " );
11         }
12         System.out.println( );
13     }
```

Figure 16.11   Output method for `List`

The copy method for a linked list can be implemented by using two iterators.

Figure 16.10 (page 441) shows how the copy method for lists is implemented. At line 5, we test for aliasing and return immediately if the test is successful. Otherwise, we call `makeEmpty` to clear out the target list. We then declare a list iterator (`lItr`) for the target list `lhs` and a second list iterator (`rItr`) for `rhs`. At the start, `lItr` references the header (because its list is empty) and `rItr` references the first node in `rhs`. We repeatedly call `insert` to add items from `rhs` into `lhs` by executing the standard iteration code at lines 14 and 15. Since the current position in the current list is always the last inserted node, `lhs` is constructed as an exact copy of `rhs`. In a virtually identical manner Figure 16.11 uses the iteration methods to output the contents of the linked list `theList`.

Many of the routines would be one-liners if it were not for the error checks.

Now that we have seen what the `LinkedListItr` looks like and how it is used, we can do the implementation of its methods. Figure 16.12 shows the body of `insert`. As shown earlier in the chapter, if we did not have to do error checking, this could be a one-line routine. The error check adds a line, and we elected to use a temporary for clarity. Still, this is a small piece of code.

```
1      /**
2       * Insert after the current position.
3       * current is set to the inserted node on success.
4       * @param x the item to insert.
5       * @exception ItemNotFound if current position is null.
6       */
7      public void insert( Object x ) throws ItemNotFound
8      {
9          if( current == null )
10             throw new ItemNotFound( "Insertion error" );
11         ListNode newNode = new ListNode( x, current.next );
12         current = current.next = newNode;
13     }
```

Figure 16.12   `insert` routine for the `LinkedListItr` class

```
1        /**
2         * Set the current position to the first node containing
3         * an item. current is unchanged if x is not found.
4         * @param x the item to search for.
5         * @return true if the item is found, false otherwise.
6         */
7        public boolean find( Object x )
8        {
9            ListNode itr = theList.header.next;
10           while( itr != null && !itr.element.equals( x ) )
11               itr = itr.next;
12
13           if( itr == null )
14               return false;
15
16           current = itr;
17           return true;
18       }
```

Figure 16.13 find routine for LinkedListItr

The find routine is shown in Figure 16.13. Here we step down the list until we either get to the null reference that is past the end of the list or find a match. Note carefully that the order of tests at line 10 matters because we are taking advantage of short circuiting. As discussed in Section 1.5.2, if the first half of the && is false, then the result is false and the second half is not executed.

Short circuiting is used in the find routine at line 10 and in the similar part of the remove routine.

```
1        /**
2         * Remove the first occurrence of an item.
3         * current is set to the first node on success;
4         * remains unchanged otherwise.
5         * @param x the item to remove.
6         * @exception ItemNotFound if the item is not found.
7         */
8        public void remove( Object x ) throws ItemNotFound
9        {
10           ListNode itr = theList.header;
11           while( itr.next != null &&
12                  !itr.next.element.equals( x ) )
13               itr = itr.next;
14
15           if( itr.next == null )
16               throw new ItemNotFound( "remove fails" );
17
18           itr.next = itr.next.next;    // Bypass deleted node
19           current = theList.header;    // Reset current
20       }
```

Figure 16.14 remove routine for the LinkedListItr class

Similarly, the `remove` method shown in Figure 16.14 (page 443) searches for the item x. At the end of the loop, `itr` references either the node prior to the one containing x, or the last node if x is not found. The removal then proceeds using the algorithm described previously. The remaining routines are shown in Figure 16.15. They are all short routines.

```
1        /**
2         * Return the item stored in the current position.
3         * @return the stored item or null if current position
4         *       is not in the list.
5         */
6        public Object retrieve( )
7        {
8            return isInList( ) ? current.element : null;
9        }
10
11       /**
12        * Set current position to the first node in the list.
13        * This operation is valid for empty lists.
14        */
15       public void first( )
16       {
17           current = theList.header.next;
18       }
19
20       /**
21        * Advance current position to the next node in the list.
22        * If the current position is null, then do nothing. No
23        * exceptions are thrown by this routine because in the
24        * most common use (inside a for loop), this would require
25        * the programmer to add an unnecessary try/catch block.
26        */
27       public void advance( )
28       {
29           if( current != null )
30               current = current.next;
31       }
32
33       /**
34        * Test if current position references a valid list item.
35        * @return true if current position is not null and is
36        *       not referencing the header node.
37        */
38       public boolean isInList( )
39       {
40           return current != null && current != theList.header;
41       }
```

Figure 16.15   Iteration routines for the `LinkedListItr` class

16.3 Doubly Linked Lists and Circular Linked Lists

As mentioned in Section 16.2, the singly linked list does not efficiently support some important operations. For instance, although it is easy to go to the front of the list, it is time-consuming to go to the end. Although we can easily advance via `advance`, implementing `retreat` cannot be done efficiently with only a `next` reference. In some applications, this might be critical. For instance, when designing a text editor, we can maintain the internal image of the file as a linked list of lines. We certainly want to be able to move up just as easily as down, to insert both before and after a line rather than just after, and to be able to get to the last line quickly. A moment's thought suggests that to implement this efficiently, we should have each node maintain two references: one to the next node in the list and one to the previous node. Then, to make everything symmetric, we should have not only a header but also a tail. This is the so-called *doubly linked list*. Figure 16.16 shows the doubly linked list representing a, b. Each node now has two references (`next` and `prev`), and searching and moving can easily be performed in both directions. Obviously, there are some important changes.

Doubly linked lists allow bidirectional traversal by storing two references per node.

First, an empty list now consists of a `head` and `tail` connected together, as shown in Figure 16.17 (page 446). Notice, by the way, that `head.prev` and `tail.next` are not needed in the algorithms and are not even initialized. The test for emptiness is now

Symmetry demands that we use both a `head` and a `tail` and that we support roughly twice as many operations.

```
head.next == tail
```

or

```
tail.prev == head
```

We no longer use `null` to decide if an advance has taken us past the end of the list. Instead, we have gone past the end if `current` is either `head` or `tail` (recall that we can go in either direction). `retreat` can be implemented by

When we advance past the end of the list, we now hit the `tail` node instead of `null`.

```
current = current.prev;
```

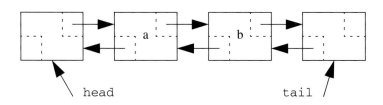

Figure 16.16 Doubly linked list

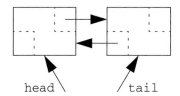

Figure 16.17 Empty doubly linked list

Insertion and re-
moval involve
twice as many ref-
erence changes,
compared to a sin-
gly linked list.

Before covering some of the additional operations that are available, let us see how the insertion and removal operations change. Naturally, we can now do both `insertBefore` and `insertAfter`. Twice as many reference changes are involved for `insertAfter` with doubly linked lists as compared to the singly linked list. If we write each statement explicitly, we obtain

```
newNode = new DoublyLinkedListNode( x );
newNode.prev = current;          // Set x's prev reference
newNode.next = current.next;     // Set x's next reference
newNode.prev.next = newNode;     // Set a's next reference
newNode.next.prev = newNode;     // Set b's prev reference
current = newNode;
```

As shown earlier in the chapter, the first two reference moves can be collapsed into the `new`. The changes to `prev` and `next` (in order *1, 2, 3, 4*) are illustrated in Figure 16.18.

remove can pro-
ceed from the cur-
rent node because
we can obtain the
previous node
instantly.

Figure 16.18 can also be used to guide us in the removal algorithm. Unlike with the singly linked list, we can remove the current node because we will have the previous node available to us automatically. Thus to `remove x` in Figure 16.18, we have to change a's `next` reference and b's `prev` reference. The basic moves are

```
current.prev.next = current.next; // Set a's next reference
current.next.prev = current.prev; // Set b's prev reference
current = head;
```

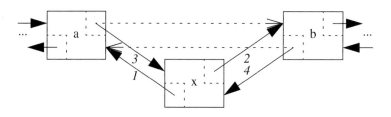

Figure 16.18 Insertion into a doubly linked list by getting a new node and then changing references in the order indicated

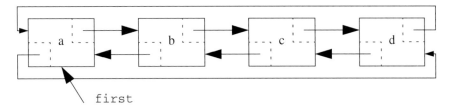

Figure 16.19 Circular doubly linked list

To do a complete doubly linked list implementation, we need to decide what operations will be supported. It is reasonable to expect that there will be twice as many operations as in the singly linked list. Each individual procedure will be very similar to the linked-list routines; only the dynamic operations involve additional reference changes. Moreover, for many of the routines, the code is dominated by error checks. While some of the checks will change (for instance, we do not test against `null`), they certainly do not become any more complex. We leave the class implementation as a project for Exercise 16.14.

A popular convention is to create a *circular linked list*, in which the last cell keeps a reference back to the first. This can be done with or without a header. Typically, it is done without a header, since the header's main purpose is to ensure that every node has a previous node, and this is already true for a non-empty circular linked list. Without a header, we have only the empty list as a special case. We would maintain a reference to the first node, but this would not be the same as a header node. We can use circular linked lists and doubly linked lists simultaneously, as shown in Figure 16.19. The circular list is useful in cases in which we want searching to allow wraparound, as for some text editors. Exercise 16.16 asks you to implement a circular doubly linked list.

> In a *circular linked list*, the last cell's `next` reference references the first. This is useful when wraparound matters.

16.4 Sorted Linked Lists

Sometimes it is desirable to keep the items in the linked list arranged in sorted order. The fundamental difference between a *sorted linked list* and an unsorted linked list is the insertion routine. Indeed, we can obtain a sorted list class by simply altering the insertion routine from our already written list class. Since the `insert` routine is part of the `LinkedListItr` class, it stands to reason that we should have a new class `SortListItr`, based on `LinkedListItr`. This is shown in Figure 16.20 (page 448).

The constructor, shown at lines 18 and 19, simply calls the superclass constructor. The new `insert` requires that `x` is `Comparable`. However, it does not override `insert` in the `LinkedListItr` class because that `insert` has an `Object` as a parameter. Thus, at lines 21 to 28, we provide an overriding definition for it that attempts to call the correct `insert` method.

> We can maintain items in sorted order by deriving a `SortListItr` class from `LinkedListItr`.

```
1  package DataStructures;
2
3  import Exceptions.*;
4  import Supporting.*;
5
6  // SortListItr class; maintains "current position"
7  //
8  // CONSTRUCTION: with a LinkedList to which SortListItr
9  //     is permanently bound
10 // ******************PUBLIC OPERATIONS********************
11 // void insert( x )      --> insert x in sorted order
12 //    All other operations are identical to LinkedListItr
13 // ******************ERRORS******************************
14 // Exceptions thrown for illegal access or remove.
15
16 public class SortListItr extends LinkedListItr
17 {
18     public SortListItr( List anyList )
19       { super( anyList ); }
20
21     public void insert( Object x ) throws ItemNotFound
22     {
23         if( x instanceof Comparable )
24             insert( (Comparable) x );
25         else
26             throw new ItemNotFound( "SortListItr insert " +
27                     "requires an object of type Comparable" );
28     }
29
30         // Insert in sorted order.
31     public void insert( Comparable x )
32     {
33         LinkedListItr prev = new LinkedListItr( theList );
34         LinkedListItr curr = new LinkedListItr( theList );
35
36         prev.zeroth( );
37         curr.first( );
38         while( curr.isInList( ) &&
39             ((Comparable)(curr.retrieve( ))).lessThan( x ) )
40         {
41             curr.advance( );
42             prev.advance( );
43         }
44
45         try
46           { prev.insert( x ); }
47         catch( ItemNotFound e ) { }  // Cannot happen
48         current = prev.current;
49     }
50 }
```

Figure 16.20 A sorted linked-list iterator class in which insertions are restricted to sorted order

```
1       public static void main( String [ ] args )
2       {
3           MyInteger m = new MyInteger( 5 );
4           Object obj = new Integer( 5 );
5           SortListItr itr = new SortListItr( new LinkedList( ) );
6
7           itr.insert( m );   // calls insert( Comparable )
8
9           try { itr.insert( obj ); }
10          catch( ItemNotFound e )
11            { System.out.println( "Item1 not Comparable" ); }
12
13          obj = m;
14          try { itr.insert( obj ); }
15          catch( ItemNotFound e )
16            { System.out.println( "Item2 not Comparable" ); }
17      }
```

Figure 16.21   Program that illustrates which `insert` method is used

As an example, Figure 16.21 illustrates how various `insert` methods are called. The `insert` methods that have an exception handler are those that are expecting an `Object` as parameter. The call at line 7 that has a statically typed `Comparable` reference is the only one that can directly call the `insert` method that accepts a `Comparable`. The call at line 9 will generate an exception because `obj` references an `Integer` and `Integer` does not implement the `Comparable` interface. The call at line 14 is to the `insert` method that accepts an `Object`, even though at runtime it is true that `obj` references a `Comparable`. It is the static type that is used to make the decision. However, that `insert` method will itself call the `insert` method that processes `Comparables` (in Figure 16.20, line 24). By the way, this is precisely why we always override the `equals` method with an `Object` as the parameter.

The code for the new `insert` method, shown in Figure 16.20 at lines 31 to 49, uses two `LinkedListItr` objects to traverse down the corresponding list until the correct insertion point is found. At that point, we can apply the `LinkedListItr` insert routine. To use the `LinkedListItr` objects, we must know to which `List` they refer. This is `theList`, which is a protected field in class `LinkedList` and is thus accessible.

Do we really need to use the `LinkedListItr` in the new `insert` routine? The answer is no, since both `current` and `theList` are accessible. Exercise 16.17 asks you to rewrite the code to avoid using a `LinkedListItr`.

A deficiency of our scheme is that any list can be accessed by both a `LinkedListItr` and `SortListItr`; thus we have no guarantee that the `SortListItr` is working on a sorted list. We can rectify the situation by adding an extra data field to the `LinkedList` class that specifies whether the list is sorted or unsorted. This data field could be initialized by the first call to `insert`; subsequent calls to `insert` would verify that we are not mixing the two types.

Summary

This chapter implemented linked lists using an iterator class. Our iterator class ListItr works with our List class. Any operation that depends in any way on positioning in the list is defined in the ListItr class. The List class defines only operations that view the list as an entity (for example, isEmpty). The ListItr class maintains a notion of a current position that is updated by advancing, searching, inserting, and even removing in the list. The chapter also examined variations of the linked list, including doubly linked lists. The doubly linked list allows bidirectional traversal of the list. Finally, we saw that it is relatively easy to derive a sorted linked list class from the basic linked-list class.

Objects of the Game

circular linked list A linked list in which the last cell's next reference references the first. This is useful when wraparound matters. (447)

doubly linked list A linked list that allows bidirectional traversal by storing two references per node. (445)

header node An extra node in the linked list that holds no data but serves to satisfy the requirement that every node have a previous node. Header nodes allow us to avoid special cases such as the insertion of a new first element and the removal of the first element. (435)

iterator class A class that maintains a current position and performs all routines that depend on knowing the position in the list. The iterator class works with the List class. (437)

sorted linked list A list used to maintain items in a linked list in sorted order. A SortListItr class is derived from LinkedListItr. (447)

Common Errors

1. The most common linked list error is splicing in nodes incorrectly when performing an insertion. The splicing is especially tricky with doubly linked lists.

2. Class methods should not be allowed to dereference a null reference.

3. When several iterators access a list simultaneously, problems can result. For instance, what if one iterator deletes the node that the other iterator is about to access? Solving these types of programs requires additional work.

4. Exercise caution when overriding a method with another method whose parameters are of a subtype of the original parameters (as is the case with equals).

On the Internet

The linked list class, including the sorted linked list, is available in the directory **DataStructures**. A test program that also includes the methods in Figure 16.6 and Figure 16.11 is provided in directory **Chapter16**. The demonstration in Figure 16.21 is also available in directory **Chapter16**.

LinkedList.java	Contains the implementation of a list class.
LinkedListItr.java	Contains the implementation of a list iterator.
SortListItr.java	Contains the implementation of a sorted list iterator.
TestList.java	Contains a test program for the lists.
WhichInsert.java	Contains the routine in Figure 16.21.

Exercises

In Short

16.1. Draw an empty linked list when the header implementation is used.

16.2. Draw an empty doubly linked list that uses both a header and a tail.

In Theory

16.3. Give an algorithm to print a singly linked list in reverse, using only constant extra space. This implies that you cannot use recursion.

16.4. Discuss whether it might be better to make `first` illegal for empty lists.

In Practice

16.5. Modify the routine `find` in the `LinkedListItr` class to return the last occurrence of item x.

16.6. Look ahead in a `LinkedListItr` object requires the application of `advance`, which advances in the list. In some cases, it may be preferable to look at the next item in the list without advancing to it. Write the method with the following declaration to facilitate this in a general case. The `peekAhead` method returns a `LinkedListItr` that corresponds to k positions ahead of `current`:

```
LinkedListItr peekAhead( int k );
```

16.7. Explain what will happen to the method added in Exercise 16.6 when the `SortListItr` class is derived from `LinkedListItr`.

16.8. Modify `remove` in the `LinkedListItr` class so that all occurrences of x are removed.

16.9. Add the routine `removeNext` to the `LinkedListItr` class. `removeNext` removes the item after the current position. How are errors handled?

16.10. Implement an efficient `Stack` class by using a `LinkedList` as a data member. You will need a `LinkedListItr`, but this can be either a data member or a local variable for any routine that needs it.

16.11. Implement an efficient `Queue` class by using the following (as in Exercise 16.10):
   a. a linked list and appropriate iterators. How many of these iterators must be data members in order to achieve an efficient implementation?
   b. a doubly linked list and appropriate iterators

16.12. Implement `retreat` for singly linked lists. Notice that it will take linear time.

16.13. Implement the linked list without the header node.

Programming Projects

16.14. Implement a doubly linked list class. Include the following:
   a. `moveToHead` and `moveToTail` methods
   b. `first` and `last` methods
   c. `retreat` method
   d. `insertBefore` and `insertAfter` methods
   e. `findFirst` and `findLast` methods (the search begins from the front and end, respectively)
   f. `removeFirst` and `removeLast` methods

16.15. Write a line editor. The command syntax is similar to the Unix line editor *ed*. The internal copy of the file is maintained as a linked list of lines. To be able to go up and down in the file, you will maintain a doubly linked list. Most commands are represented by a 1-character string. Some are 2 characters and require an argument (or more). Support the command lines in Figure 16.22.

16.16. Implement a circular doubly linked list.

16.17. Redesign `LinkedList`, `LinkedListItr`, and `SortListItr` to not allow interleaving of `SortListItr` and `LinkedListItr` insert commands.

16.18. If the order that items in a list are stored is not important, then we can frequently speed searching with the following heuristic known as *move to front*: Whenever an item is accessed, move it to the front of the list. The reason this usually is an improvement is that frequently accessed items will tend to migrate toward the front of the list, while less frequently accessed items will migrate toward the end of the list. Consequently, the most frequently accessed items tend to require the least searching. Implement the move-to-front heuristic for linked lists.

16.19. Write routines `union` and `intersect` that return the union and intersection of two linked lists. Assume that the input lists are sorted.

Command	Function
l	Go to the top.
a	Add text after current line until . on its own line is seen.
d	Delete current line.
dr num num	Delete several lines.
f name	Change name of the current file (for next write).
g num	Go to a numbered line.
h	Get help.
i	Like append, but add lines before current line.
m num	Move current line after some other line.
mr num num num	Move several lines as a unit after some other line.
n	Toggle whether line numbers are displayed.
p	Print current line.
pr num num	Print several lines.
q!	Abort without write.
r name	Read and paste another file into the current file.
s text text	Substitute text with other text.
t num	Copy current line to after some other line.
tr num num num	Copy several lines to after some other line.
w	Write file to disk.
x!	Exit with write.
$	Go to the last line.
-	Go up one line.
+	Go down one line.
=	Print current line number.
/ text	Search forward for a pattern.
? text	Search backward for a pattern.
#	Print number of lines and characters in file.

Figure 16.22 Commands for the editor in Exercise 16.15

17

Trees

T HE *tree* is a fundamental structure in computer science. Almost all operating systems store files in trees or treelike structures. Trees are also used in compiler design, text processing, and searching algorithms. The latter application is discussed in Chapter 18.

In this chapter, we will see:

- A definition of a general tree and a discussion of how it is used in a file system
- An examination of the *binary tree*
- How tree operations are implemented using recursion
- How a tree is traversed nonrecursively

17.1 General Trees

Trees can be defined in two ways: nonrecursively and recursively. The nonrecursive definition is the more direct technique, so we begin with it. The recursive formulation allows us to write simple algorithms to manipulate trees.

17.1.1 Definitions

Recall from Chapter 6 that a *tree* consists of a set of nodes and a set of directed edges that connect pairs of nodes. Throughout this book, only rooted trees are considered. A rooted tree has the following properties:

- One node is distinguished as the root.
- Every node c, except the root, is connected by an edge from exactly one other node p. p is c's *parent*, and c is one of p's *children*.
- A unique path traverses from the root to each node. The number of edges that must be followed is the *path length*.

Trees can be defined nonrecursively as a set of nodes and directed edges that connect them.

Parents and children are naturally defined. A directed edge connects the parent to the child.

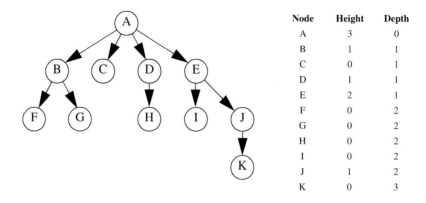

Node	Height	Depth
A	3	0
B	1	1
C	0	1
D	1	1
E	2	1
F	0	2
G	0	2
H	0	2
I	0	2
J	1	2
K	0	3

Figure 17.1   A tree, with height and depth information

Leaves have no children.

Figure 17.1 illustrates a tree. The root node is *A*. *A*'s children are *B*, *C*, *D*, and *E*. Because *A* is the root, it has no parent. All other nodes have parents. For instance, *B*'s parent is *A*. Some nodes have no children. These nodes are called *leaves*. The leaves in this tree are *C*, *F*, *G*, *H*, *I*, and *K*. The length of the path from *A* to *K* is three (edges). The length of the path from *A* to *A* is zero edges.

The *depth* of a node is the length of the path from the root to the node. The *height* of a node is the length of the path from the node to the deepest leaf.

A tree with N nodes must have $N-1$ edges because every node except the root has an incoming edge. The *depth* of any node in a tree is the length of the path from the root to the node. Thus the depth of the root is always 0, and the depth of any node is 1 more than the depth of its parent. The *height* of a node is the length of the path from the node to the deepest leaf. Thus the height of *E* is 2. The height of any node is 1 more than the height of its maximum-height child. The height of a tree is equal to the height of the root.

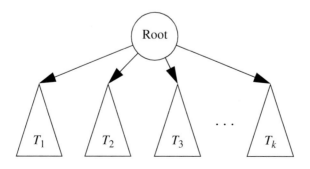

Figure 17.2   A tree viewed recursively

Nodes with the same parent are *siblings*; thus *B*, *C*, *D*, and *E* are all siblings. If there is a path from node *u* to node *v*, then *u* is an *ancestor* of *v* and *v* is a *descendant* of *u*. If *u* ≠ *v*, then *u* is a *proper ancestor* of *v* and *v* is a *proper descendant* of *u*. The *size* of a node is equal to the number of descendants it has (including the node itself). The size of *B* is 3, and the size of *C* is 1. The size of a tree is equal to the size of the root. Thus the size of the tree in Figure 17.1 is equal to the size of its root *A*, which is 11.

> The *size* of a node is equal to the number of descendants it has (including the node itself).

An alternative definition of the tree is recursive: Either a tree is empty or it consists of a root and zero or more nonempty subtrees $T_1, T_2, ..., T_k$, each of whose roots are connected by an edge from the root. In some instances (most notably the *binary trees* discussed later in the chapter), we may allow some of the subtrees to be empty. This view of the tree is illustrated in Figure 17.2.

17.1.2 Implementation

One way to implement a tree would be to have in each node a reference to each child of the node in addition to its data. However, since the number of children per node can vary so greatly and is not known in advance, it might be infeasible to make the children direct links in the data structure — there would be too much wasted space. The solution is simple: Keep the children of each node in a linked list of tree nodes. Thus each node keeps two references: one to its leftmost child (if it is not a leaf) and one to its right sibling (if it is not the rightmost sibling). This type of implementation is called the *first child/next sibling method* and is illustrated in Figure 17.3. Arrows that point downward are `firstChild` reference. Arrows that go left to right are `nextSibling` references. `null` references are not drawn; there are too many of them. In this tree, node *B* has both a reference to a sibling (*C*) and a reference to a leftmost child (*F*), while some nodes have only one of these references and some have neither. Given this representation, it is a straightforward exercise to implement a tree class that is hinted at by the interface in Figure 6.15.

> General trees can be implemented using the *first child/ next sibling method*. This requires two references per item.

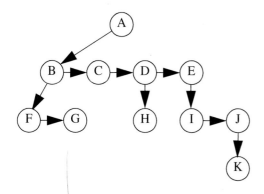

Figure 17.3   First child/next sibling representation of tree in Figure 17.1

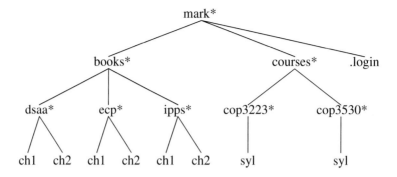

Figure 17.4 Unix directory

```
1      void listAll( int depth = 0 )   // depth is initially 0
2      {
3          printName( depth );   // Print the name of the object
4          if( isDirectory( ) )
5              for each file c in this directory (for each child)
6                  c.listAll( depth + 1 );
7      }
```

Figure 17.5 Pseudocode to list a directory and its subdirectories in a hierar-
chical file system

```
mark
        books
                dsaa
                        ch1
                        ch2
                ecp
                        ch1
                        ch2
                ipps
                        ch1
                        ch2
        courses
                cop3223
                        syl
                cop3530
                        syl
        .login
```

Figure 17.6 The directory listing for the tree in Figure 17.4

17.1.3 An Application: File Systems

There are many applications for trees. A popular one is the directory structure in many common operating systems, including Unix, VAX/VMS, and DOS. Figure 17.4 shows a typical directory in the Unix file system. The root of this directory is `mark`. (The asterisk next to the name indicates that `mark` is itself a directory.) `mark` has three children — `books`, `courses`, and `.login` — two of which are themselves directories. Thus `mark` contains two directories and one regular file. The filename `mark/books/dsaa/ch1` is obtained by following the left-most child three times. Each `/` after the first name indicates an edge; the result is a pathname. If the path begins at the root of the entire file system, rather than at an arbitrary directory inside the file system, then we have a full pathname; otherwise, we have a relative pathname (relative to the current directory).

File systems use tree-like structures.

    This hierarchical file system is very popular because it allows users to organize their data logically. Furthermore, two files in different directories can share the same name, since they must have different paths from the root and thus they have different full pathnames. A directory in the Unix file system is just a file with a list of all its children,[1] so the directories can be traversed using an iteration scheme implied by the abstract class in Figure 6.15; that is, we can sequentially iterate over each child. Indeed, on some systems, if the normal command to print a file is applied to a directory, then the filenames in the directory can be seen in the output (along with other non-ASCII information).

    Suppose we want to list the names of all the files in a directory (including its subdirectories). Our output format will be that files of depth d will have their names indented by d tab characters. A simple algorithm to do this is given in Figure 17.5. Output for the directory in Figure 17.4 is shown in Figure 17.6.

The directory structure is most easily traversed by using recursion.

    For now, we will use pseudocode. A Java implementation is provided at the end of this section. We assume the existence of the class `FileSystem` and two methods, `printName` and `isDirectory`. `printName` outputs the current `FileSystem` object indented by `depth` tab stops. `isDirectory` tests if the current `FileSystem` object is a directory and returns `true` if it is. Given that, we can easily write the recursive routine `listAll`. We need to pass it the parameter `depth`, which indicates the current level in the directory relative to the root. `listAll` is started with `depth` equal to 0 to signify no indenting for the root. This depth is an internal bookkeeping variable and is hardly a parameter about which a calling routine should be expected to know. Thus the pseudocode specifies a default value of 0 for `depth` (specification of a default value is not legal Java).

    The logic of the algorithm is simple to follow. The current object is printed out, with appropriate indentation. If the entry is a directory, then we process all the children recursively, one by one. These children are one level deeper in the tree and thus must be indented an extra tab stop. We make the recursive call using

---

[1.] Each directory in the Unix file system also has one entry (.) that references itself and another entry (. .) that references the parent of the directory. This introduces a cycle. Thus, technically, the Unix file system is not a tree but rather is treelike.

In a *preorder traversal*, work at a node is performed before its children are processed. The traversal takes constant time per node.

In a *postorder traversal*, work at a node is performed after its children are evaluated. The traversal takes constant time per node.

depth+1. It is difficult to imagine a simpler piece of code that performs what appears to be a very difficult task.

This algorithmic technique is known as a *preorder tree traversal*. In a preorder tree traversal, work at a node is performed before (*pre*) its children are processed. In addition to being a compact algorithm, this traversal is meritorious because it is a linear-time algorithm. Why this is so is discussed later in this chapter.

Another common method of traversing a tree is the *postorder tree traversal*. In a postorder tree traversal, the work at a node is performed after (*post*) its children are evaluated. As an example, Figure 17.7 represents the same directory structure as that in Figure 17.4. The numbers in parentheses represent the number of disk blocks taken up by each file. Since the directories are themselves files, they also use disk blocks (to store the names and information about their children).

Suppose we want to compute the total number of blocks used by all files in the tree. The most natural way to do this is by finding the total number of blocks contained in all of the children (which may be directories that must be evaluated recursively): books (41), courses (8), and .login (2). The total number of blocks is then the total in all of the children plus the blocks used at the root (1), namely, 52. The routine size in Figure 17.8 implements this strategy. If the current FileSystem object is not a directory, size merely returns the number of blocks it uses. Otherwise, the number of blocks in the current directory is added to the number of blocks (recursively) found in all of the children. To illustrate the difference between postorder traversal and preorder traversal, Figure 17.9 shows how the size of each directory (or file) is produced by the algorithm. We see a classic postorder signature because the total size of an entry is not computable until the information for its children has been computed. Once again, the running time is linear. Much more is said about tree traversals in Section 17.4.

Java Implementation

Java provides a class named *File* in package java.io that can be used to traverse directory hierarchies. We can use it to implement the pseudocode in Figure 17.5. The size method can also be implemented; this is done in the online code. The class File provides several useful methods.

A File can be constructed by providing a filename. *getName* provides the name of a File object. It does not include the directory part of the path; this can be obtained by *getPath*. *isDirectory* returns true if the File is a directory, and its size in bytes can be obtained by a call to *length*. If the file is a directory, the *list* method returns an array of String that represents the filenames in the directory (not including . and ..).

To implement the FileSystem object described in the pseudocode, we simply extend File and provide a constructor, printName, and listAll. This is shown in Figure 17.10 (page 462). The only tricky part is lines 36 and 37, where we must construct the child FileSystem object. The filename consists of the name of the directory, followed by a separator (/ on Unix; \ on DOS), followed by the filename. A simple main is also provided.

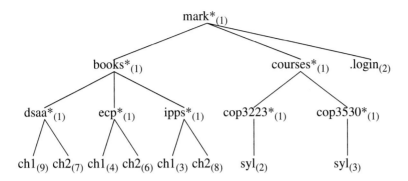

Figure 17.7   Unix directory with file sizes

```
1       int size( )
2       {
3           int totalSize = sizeOfThisFile( );
4
5           if( isDirectory( ) )
6               for each file c in this directory (for each child)
7                   totalSize += c.size( );
8
9           return totalSize;
10      }
```

Figure 17.8   Pseudocode to calculate the total size of all files in a directory

			ch1	9
			ch2	7
		dsaa		17
			ch1	4
			ch2	6
		ecp		11
			ch1	3
			ch2	8
		ipps		12
	books			41
			syl	2
		cop3223		3
			syl	3
		cop3530		4
	courses			8
	.login			2
mark				52

Figure 17.9   Trace of the size method

```
 1  import java.io.*;
 2
 3  public class FileSystem extends File
 4  {
 5          // Constructor
 6      public FileSystem( String name )
 7      {
 8          super( name );
 9      }
10
11          // Output file name with indentation
12      public void printName( int depth )
13      {
14          for( int i = 0; i < depth; i++ )
15              System.out.print( "\t" );
16          System.out.println( getName( ) );
17      }
18
19          // Public driver to list all files in directory
20      public void listAll( )
21      {
22          listAll( 0 );
23      }
24
25          // Recursive method to list all files in directory
26      private void listAll( int depth )
27      {
28          printName( depth );
29
30          if( isDirectory( ) )
31          {
32              String [ ] entries = list( );
33
34              for( int i = 0; i < entries.length; i++ )
35              {
36                  FileSystem child = new FileSystem( getPath( )
37                                  + separatorChar + entries[ i ] );
38                  child.listAll( depth + 1 );
39              }
40          }
41      }
42
43          // Simple main to list all files in current directory
44      public static void main( String [ ] args )
45      {
46          FileSystem f = new FileSystem( "." );
47          f.listAll( );
48      }
49  }
```

Figure 17.10   Java implementation for a directory listing

17.2 Binary Trees

A *binary tree* is a tree in which no node can have more than two children. Because there are only two children, we can name them `left` and `right`. The recursive definition is that a binary tree is either empty or consists of a root, a left tree, and a right tree. The left and right trees may themselves be empty; thus a node with one child could have a left or right child. We use the recursive definition several times in the design of binary tree algorithms. Binary trees have many important uses, two of which are illustrated in Figure 17.11.

A binary tree has no node with more than two children.

One use of the binary tree is in the *expression tree*, which is a central data structure in compiler design. The leaves of an expression tree are operands, such as constants or variable names; the other nodes contain operators. This particular tree is binary because all of the operations are binary. Although this is the simplest case, it is possible for nodes to have more than two children (and in the case of unary operators, only one child). We can evaluate an expression tree T by applying the operator at the root to the values obtained by recursively evaluating the left and right subtrees. In our case, this yields the expression `(a+((b-c)*d))`. The construction of expression trees and their evaluation is the topic of Section 11.2.

An expression tree is one example of the use of binary trees. Such trees are central data structures in compiler design.

A second use of the binary tree is the *Huffman coding tree*, which is used to implement a simple but relatively effective data compression algorithm. Each symbol in the alphabet is stored at a leaf. Its code is obtained by following the path to it from the root. A left link corresponds to a 0 and a right link to a 1. Thus b is coded as 100. Construction of the optimal tree (that is, the best code) is discussed in Section 12.1.

Other uses of the binary tree are in binary search trees (Chapter 18), which allow logarithmic time insertions and accesses of items, and priority queues, which support the access and deletion of the minimum in a collection of items. Several efficient implementations of priority queues use trees, as discussed in Chapters 20 to 22.

An important use of binary trees is in other data structures, notably the binary search tree and the priority queue.

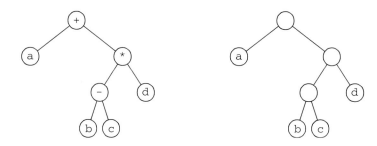

Figure 17.11 Uses of binary trees: at the left is an expression tree and at the right is a Huffman coding tree

```
 1  // BinaryNode class; stores a node in a tree
 2  //
 3  // CONSTRUCTION: with (a) no parameters, or (b) an Object,
 4  //     or (c) an Object, left reference, and right reference
 5  //
 6  // ******************PUBLIC OPERATIONS*********************
 7  // int size( )              --> Return size of subtree at node
 8  // int height( )            --> Return height of subtree at node
 9  // void printPostOrder( ) --> Print a postorder tree traversal
10  // void printInOrder( )     --> Print an inorder tree traversal
11  // void printPreOrder( )    --> Print a preorder tree traversal
12  // BinaryNode duplicate( )      --> Return a duplicate tree
13  // ******************ERRORS********************************
14  // None
15
16  final class BinaryNode
17  {
18      BinaryNode( )
19        { this( null ); }
20      BinaryNode( Object theElement )
21        { this( theElement, null, null ); }
22      BinaryNode( Object theElement, BinaryNode lt,
23                                      BinaryNode rt )
24        { element = theElement; left = lt; right = rt; }
25
26      static int size( BinaryNode t )
27        { /* Figure 17.19 */ }
28      static int height( BinaryNode t )
29        { /* Figure 17.21 */ }
30      void printPostOrder( )
31        { /* Figure 17.22 */ }
32      void printInOrder( )
33        { /* Figure 17.22 */ }
34      void printPreOrder( )
35        { /* Figure 17.22 */ }
36      BinaryNode duplicate( )
37        { /* Figure 17.17 */ }
38
39      // Friendly data; accessible by other package routines
40      Object      element;
41      BinaryNode left;
42      BinaryNode right;
43  }
```

Figure 17.12 BinaryNode class skeleton

Figure 17.12 gives the class skeleton for BinaryNode. Lines 40 to 42 tell us that each node consists of a data item plus two child references. Three constructors are provided. Line 18 is the zero-parameter constructor. Line 20 is used to construct a BinaryNode given an item as a parameter. In both of these constructors, the left and right child references are set to null. The third constructor, shown at line 22, initializes all of the data fields of the `BinaryNode`. Notice that these constructors require initialization of either both child references or neither child reference. In this way, we avoid a partially initialized object.

Access to data fields is allowed to other package classes, so we do not provide accessors or mutators. The `duplicate` method, declared at line 36, is used to replicate a copy of the tree rooted at the current node. The routines `size` and `height`, declared at lines 26 and 28, compute the named properties for the node referenced by parameter `t`. These routines are implemented in Section 17.3. We also provide, at lines 30 to 34, routines that print out the contents of a tree rooted at the current node using various recursive traversal strategies. Tree traversals are discussed in Section 17.4. Why do we pass a parameter for `size` and `height` but use the current object for the traversals and `duplicate`? There is no particular reason; it is a matter of style. Both styles are shown here. The implementations will show that the difference between them is when the required test for a `null` tree is performed.

> Many of the `BinaryNode` routines are recursive. The `BinaryTree` methods use the `BinaryNode` routines on the `root`.

This section describes the implementation of the `BinaryTree` class. A separate class, `BinaryNode`, is provided to simplify the implementation of some of the recursive routines. The `BinaryTree` class skeleton is shown in Figure 17.13 (page 466). For the most part, the routines are simple to implement because they call `BinaryNode` methods. Line 44 declares the only data field, a reference to the root node.

> The `BinaryNode` class is implemented separately from the `BinaryTree` class. The only data field in the `BinaryTree` class is a reference to the root node.

Two constructors are provided. The one at line 19 creates an empty tree, while the one at line 21 creates a one-node tree. Routines to traverse the tree are declared at lines 24 to 29. They apply a `BinaryNode` method to the `root`, after verifying that the tree is not empty. An alternative traversal strategy that can be implemented is *level-order traversal*. All these traversal routines are discussed in Section 17.4. Routines to make an empty tree and to test for emptiness are given, with their implementations, at lines 32 and 30, respectively. Two routines remain in the class.

The `duplicate` method is defined at lines 41 and 42. After testing for aliasing, we call the `duplicate` method in `BinaryNode` to get a copy of `rhs`'s tree. Then we assign the result as the root of the tree. Notice that before we can apply the `BinaryNode` method to the node reference by `root`, we must verify that the `root` is not `null`.

> Before we can apply the `BinaryNode` method to the node referenced by `root`, we must verify that `root` is not `null`.

The last method in the class is the `merge` routine. `merge` uses two trees — `t1` and `t2` — and an element to create a new tree, with the element at the root and the two existing trees as left and right subtrees. In principle, this is a one-line routine:

```
root = new BinaryNode( rootItem, t1.root, t2.root );
```

If things were always this simple, programmers would be unemployed. Fortunately for our careers, there are complications. Figure 17.14 (page 467) shows the result of the simple one-line `merge`. A problem becomes apparent: Nodes in `t1` and `t2`'s trees are now in two trees (their original trees and the merged result). This sharing could be a problem if we want to remove or otherwise alter subtrees (because multiple subtrees may be removed or altered unintentionally).

> `merge` is a one-line routine in principle. However, we must also handle aliasing, making sure that a node is not in two trees, and do error checking.

```
 1  // BinaryTree class; stores a binary tree
 2  //
 3  //   CONSTRUCTION: with (a) no parameters or (b) an object to
 4  //      be placed in the root of a one-element tree
 5  //
 6  // ******************PUBLIC OPERATIONS*********************
 7  // void printPostOrder( ) --> Print a postorder tree traversal
 8  // void printInOrder( )   --> Print an inorder tree traversal
 9  // void printPreOrder( )  --> Print a preorder tree traversal
10  // boolean isEmpty( )     --> Return true if empty; else false
11  // void makeEmpty( )      --> Make an empty tree
12  // void merge( Object root, BinaryTree t1, BinaryTree t2 )
13  //                        --> Construct a new tree
14  // ******************ERRORS*****************************
15  // Error message printed for illegal merges
16
17  public class BinaryTree
18  {
19      public BinaryTree( )
20        { root = null; }
21      public BinaryTree( Object rootItem )
22        { root = new BinaryNode( rootItem ); }
23
24      public void printPreOrder( )
25        { if( root != null ) root.printPreOrder( ); }
26      public void printInOrder( )
27        { if( root != null ) root.printInOrder( ); }
28      public void printPostOrder( )
29        { if( root != null ) root.printPostOrder( ); }
30      public boolean isEmpty( )
31        { return root == null; }
32      public void makeEmpty( )
33        { root = null; }
34      public void merge( Object rootItem, BinaryTree t1,
35                                          BinaryTree t2 )
36        { /* Figure 17.16 */ }
37      public int size( )
38        { return BinaryNode.size( root ); }
39      public int height( )
40        { return BinaryNode.height( root ); }
41      public void duplicate( BinaryTree rhs )
42        { if( this != rhs ) root = rhs.root.duplicate( ); }
43
44      private BinaryNode root;
45  }
```

Figure 17.13 BinaryTree class skeleton

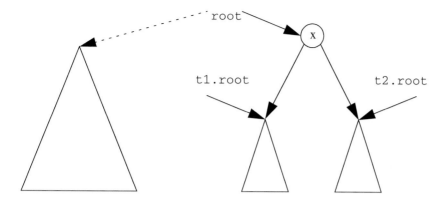

Figure 17.14   Result of a naive `merge` operation: Subtrees are shared

The solution is simple in principle. We can ensure that nodes do not appear in two trees by setting `t1.root` and `t2.root` to `null` after the `merge`. Complications ensue when we consider some possible calls that contain aliasing:

We set the roots of the original trees to `null` so that each node is in one tree.

```
t1.merge( x, t1, t2 );
t2.merge( x, t1, t2 );
t1.merge( x, t3, t3 );
```

The first two cases are similar; we consider only the first. A picture of the situation is shown in Figure 17.15. Because `t1` is an alias for the current object, `t1.root` and `root` are aliases. Thus, after the call to `new`, if we execute `t1.root=null`, we change `root` to the `null` reference, too. Consequently, we need to be very careful with the aliases for these cases.

If an input tree is aliased to the output tree, we must be very careful to avoid having the the resultant `root` reference `null`.

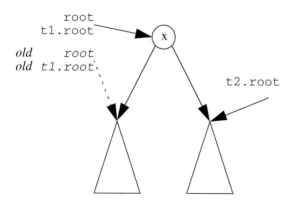

Figure 17.15   Aliasing problems in the `merge` operation; `t1` is also the current object

```
1      /**
2       * Merge routine for BinaryTree class.
3       * Forms a new tree from rootItem, t1 and t2.
4       * Correctly handles various aliasing conditions.
5       */
6      public void Merge( Object rootItem, BinaryTree t1,
7                                          BinaryTree t2 )
8      {
9          if( t1.root == t2.root && t1.root != null )
10         {
11             System.err.println( "leftTree==rightTree; " +
12                                 "merge aborted" );
13             return;
14         }
15
16             // Allocate new node
17         root = new BinaryNode( rootItem, t1.root, t2.root );
18
19             // Ensure that every node is in one tree
20         if( this != t1 )
21             t1.root = null;
22         if( this != t2 )
23             t2.root = null;
24     }
```

Figure 17.16 merge routine for the `BinaryTree` class

If the two input trees are aliases, we should disallow the operation, unless the trees are empty.

The third case must be disallowed because it would place all the nodes that are in tree t3 in two places in t1. However, if t3 represents an empty tree, the third case should be allowed. All in all, we got a lot more than we bargained for. The resulting code is shown in Figure 17.16. What used to be a one-line routine has gotten quite large.

17.3 Recursion and Trees

Recursive routines are used for `size` and `duplicate`.

Because `duplicate` is a `BinaryNode` method, we make recursive calls only after testing that the subtrees are not `null`.

Because trees can be defined recursively, it is not surprising that many tree routines are most easily implemented by using recursion. Recursive implementations for almost all of the remaining `BinaryNode` and `BinaryTree` methods are provided here. The resulting routines are amazingly compact.

We begin with the `duplicate` method of the `BinaryNode` class. Since it is a `BinaryNode` method, we are assured that the tree we are duplicating is not empty. The recursive algorithm is then simple. First, we create a new node with the same data field as the current root. Then we attach a left tree by calling `duplicate` recursively and attach a right tree by calling `duplicate` recursively. In both cases, we make the recursive call after checking that there is a tree to copy. This description is coded verbatim in Figure 17.17.

```
1       /**
2        * Return a reference to a node that is the root of a
3        * duplicate of the binary tree rooted at the current node.
4        */
5       BinaryNode duplicate( )
6       {
7           BinaryNode root = new BinaryNode( element );
8           if( left != null )          // If there's a left subtree
9               root.left = left.duplicate( );   // duplicate
10          if( right != null )         // If there's a right subtree
11              root.right = right.duplicate( ); // duplicate
12          return root;                // Return resulting tree
13      }
```

Figure 17.17   Routine to return a copy of the tree rooted at the current node

The next method we write is the `size` routine in class `BinaryNode`. `size` returns the size of the tree rooted at a node referenced by `t`, which is passed as a parameter. If we draw the tree recursively, as shown in Figure 17.18, we see that the size of a tree is equal to the size of the left subtree plus the size of the right subtree plus 1 (because the root counts as a node). A recursive routine requires a base case that can be solved without recursion. The smallest tree that `size` might have to handle is the empty tree (if `t` is `null`) and the size of an empty tree is clearly 0. We should verify that the recursion produces the correct answer for a tree of size 1. It is easy to see that it does. The result is implemented in Figure 17.19 (page 470).

size is easily implemented recursively after a picture is drawn.

The final recursive routine in this section calculates the height of a node. This is difficult to do nonrecursively, but it is trivially implemented recursively, once we draw the picture. Figure 17.20 (page 470) shows a tree viewed recursively. Suppose the left subtree has height H_L and the right subtree has height H_R. Any node that is d levels deep with respect to the root of the left subtree is $d + 1$ levels deep with respect to the root of the entire tree. The same holds for the right subtree. Thus the path length of the deepest node in the original tree is 1 more than its path length with respect to the root of its subtree. If we compute this value for both subtrees, the maximum of these two values plus 1 is the answer we want.

height is also easily implemented recursively. The height of an empty tree is –1.

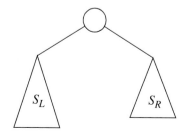

Figure 17.18   Recursive view used to calculate the size of a tree: $S_T = S_L + S_R + 1$

```
1       /**
2        * Return the size of the binary tree rooted at t.
3        */
4       static int size( BinaryNode t )
5       {
6           if( t == null )
7               return 0;
8           else
9               return 1 + size( t.left ) + size( t.right );
10      }
```

Figure 17.19   Routine to compute the size of a node

What about the base case? Once again, we might be presented with an empty tree. The obvious answer, that an empty tree has height 0, is wrong. This is because a single-node tree has height 0 (a leaf always has height 0). To make the recursive formula work for single-node trees, we define the height of an empty tree to be –1. Thus a leaf has two subtrees of height –1, and its height is correctly declared to be 0. The routine that results is shown in Figure 17.21.

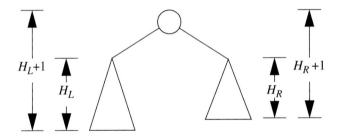

Figure 17.20   Recursive view of the node height calculation:
$H_T = \text{Max}(H_L+1, H_R+1)$

```
1       /**
2        * Return the height of the binary tree rooted at t.
3        */
4       static int height( BinaryNode t )
5       {
6           if( t == null )
7               return -1;
8           else
9               return 1 + Math.max( height( t.left ),
10                                    height( t.right ) );
11      }
```

Figure 17.21   Routine to compute the height of a node

17.4 Tree Traversal: Iterator Classes

This chapter has shown how recursion can be used to implement the binary tree methods. When recursion is applied, we compute information about not only a node but also all of its descendants. We say then that we are *traversing the tree*. Two popular traversals that have already been seen are the preorder and postorder traversal.

In a preorder traversal, the node is processed and then its children are processed recursively. The `duplicate` routine is an example of a preorder traversal because the root is created first. Then a left subtree is copied recursively, followed by the right subtree.

In a postorder traversal, the node is processed after both children are processed recursively. Two examples of this are the methods `size` and `height`. In both cases, information about a node (for instance, its size or height) can be obtained only after the corresponding information is known for its children.

A third common recursive traversal is the *inorder traversal*. In an inorder traversal, we recursively process the left child, then process the current node, and then recursively process the right child. This mechanism is used to generate an algebraic expression corresponding to an expression tree. For example, in Figure 17.11 the inorder traversal yields `(a+((b-c)*d))`.

> In an *inorder traversal*, we process the current node in between recursive calls.

Figure 17.22 (page 472) illustrates routines that print the nodes in a binary tree using each of the three recursive tree traversal algorithms. Figure 17.23 (page 472) shows the order in which nodes are visited for each of the three strategies. The running time of each algorithm is linear. In all cases, each node is output exactly once. Consequently, the total cost of an output statement over any traversal is $O(N)$. Because of this, each `if` statement is also executed at most once per node, for a total cost of $O(N)$. The total number of method calls made (which involves the constant work of the internal run-time stack pushes and pops) is likewise once per node, or $O(N)$. Thus the total running time is $O(N)$.

> Simple traversal using any of these strategies takes linear time.

Must we use recursion to implement the traversals? The answer is clearly no, since, as discussed in Section 7.3, recursion is implemented by using a stack. Thus we could keep our own stack. The result is generally a somewhat faster program because we can place only the essentials on the stack rather than have the compiler place an entire activation record. The difference in speed between a recursive and nonrecursive algorithm is very dependent on the platform. In many cases, the speed improvement does not justify the effort involved in removing recursion. Even so, it is worth knowing how to do it just in case your platform is one that would benefit from recursion removal and also because seeing how a program is implemented nonrecursively can sometimes make the recursion clearer.

> We can traverse nonrecursively by maintaining the stack ourselves.

```
1      void printPreOrder( )
2      {
3          System.out.println( element );        // Node
4          if( left != null )
5              left.printPreOrder( );            // Left
6          if( right != null )
7              right.printPreOrder( );           // Right
8      }
9
10     void printPostOrder( )
11     {
12         if( left != null )
13             left.printPostOrder( );           // Left
14         if( right != null )
15             right.printPostOrder( );          // Right
16         System.out.println( element );        // Node
17     }
18
19     void printInOrder( )
20     {
21         if( left != null )
22             left.printInOrder( );             // Left
23         System.out.println( element );        // Node
24         if( right != null )
25             right.printInOrder( );            // Right
26     }
```

Figure 17.22   Routines to print nodes in preorder, postorder, and inorder traversals

An iterator class allows step-by-step traversal.

We will write three iterator classes, each in the spirit of the linked list. Each will allow us to go to the first node, advance to the next node, test if we have gone past the last node, and access the current node. The ordering that nodes are accessed is determined by the type of traversal. We will also implement a *level-order traversal*. In a level-order traversal, nodes are visited top to bottom, left to right. Level-order traversal is inherently nonrecursive and in fact uses a queue instead of a stack. It turns out to be very similar to the preorder traversal.

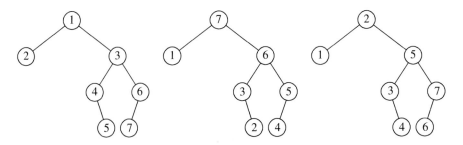

Figure 17.23   Preorder, postorder, and inorder visitation routes

```
1  package DataStructures;
2
3  import Exceptions.*;
4
5  // TreeIterator class; maintains "current position"
6  //
7  // CONSTRUCTION: with tree to which iterator is bound
8  //
9  // ******************PUBLIC OPERATIONS*********************
10 //     first and advance are abstract; others are final
11 // boolean isValid( )   --> True if at valid position in tree
12 // Object retrieve( )   --> Return item in current position
13 // void first( )        --> Set current position to first
14 // void advance( )      --> Advance to next position
15 // ******************ERRORS********************************
16 // Exceptions thrown for illegal access or advance
17
18 /**
19  * Tree iterator class.
20  */
21 abstract public class TreeIterator
22 {
23     public TreeIterator( BinaryTree theTree )
24     {
25         t = theTree;
26         current = null;
27     }
28
29     abstract public void first( );
30
31     final public boolean isValid( )
32     {
33         return current != null;
34     }
35
36     final public Object retrieve( ) throws ItemNotFound
37     {
38         if( current == null )
39             throw new ItemNotFound( "TreeIterator retrieve" );
40         return current.element;
41     }
42
43     abstract public void advance( ) throws ItemNotFound;
44
45     protected BinaryTree t;          // Tree
46     protected BinaryNode current;    // Current position
47 }
```

Figure 17.24 Tree iterator abstract class

The abstract tree iterator class has a subset of the methods seen in the linked-list iterator. Each type of traversal is represented by a derived class.

Figure 17.24 (page 473) provides an abstract class for tree iteration. Each iterator will store a reference to the tree and an indication of the current node. These are declared at lines 45 and 46, respectively, and initialized in the constructor. They are `protected` to allow the derived classes to access them. Four methods are declared at lines 29 to 43. `isValid` and `retrieve` are invariant over the hierarchy, so an implementation is provided and they are declared `final`. The abstract methods `first` and `advance` must be provided by each type of iterator. Note that the `advance` method differs from the linked list `advance` because it throws an exception. This is done to illustrate different strategies.

17.4.1 Postorder Traversal

Postorder traversal maintains a stack that stores nodes that have been visited but whose recursive calls are not yet complete.

The postorder traversal is implemented by using a stack to store the current state. The top of the stack will represent the node that we are visiting at some instant in the postorder traversal. However, we may be at one of three places in the algorithm:

1. About to make a recursive call to the left subtree
2. About to make a recursive call to the right subtree
3. About to process the current node

Each node is placed on the stack three times. The third time off, the node is declared visited. The other times, we simulate a recursive call.

Consequently, each node will be placed on the stack three times during the course of the traversal. If a node is popped from the stack a third time, we can mark it as the current node to be visited.

Otherwise, the node is being popped for either the first time or the second time. In this case, it is not yet ready to be visited, so we push it back onto the stack and simulate a recursive call. If the node was popped for a first time, we need to push the left child onto the stack (if it exists). Otherwise, the node was popped for a second time and we push the right child onto the stack (if it exists). In any event, we then pop the stack, applying the same test. Notice that when we pop the stack, we are simulating the recursive call to the appropriate child. If the child does not exist and thus was never pushed onto the stack, then when we pop the stack, we pop the original node again.

When the stack is empty, every node has been visited.

Eventually, either the process pops a node for the third time or the stack empties. In the latter case, we have iterated over the entire tree. We initialize the algorithm by pushing a reference to the root onto the stack. An example of how the stack is manipulated is shown in Figure 17.25.

A quick summary: The stack contains nodes we have traversed but not yet completed. When a node is pushed onto the stack, the counter is 1, 2, or 3 as follows:

1. If we are about to process the node's left subtree
2. If we are about to process the node's right subtree
3. If we are about to process the node itself

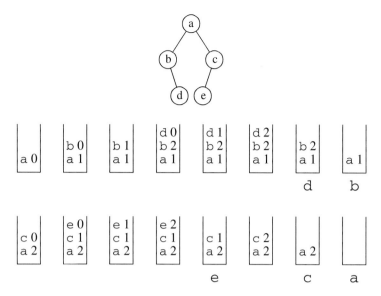

Figure 17.25   Stack states during postorder traversal

Let us trace through the postorder traversal. We initialize the traversal by pushing the root a onto the stack. The first pop visits a. This is a's first pop, so it is placed back on the stack, and we push its left child, b, onto the stack. Next b is popped. Since it is b's first pop, it is placed back on the stack. Normally, b's left child would then be pushed, but b has no left child, so nothing is pushed. Thus the next pop reveals b for the second time. b is placed back on the stack, and its right child, d, is pushed on the stack. The next pop produces d for the first time. Thus d is pushed back on the stack. No other push is performed, since d has no left child. Thus d is popped for the second time. It is then pushed back, but since it has no right child, nothing else is pushed. Thus the next pop yields d for the third time. Therefore d is marked as a visited node. The next node popped is b, and since this is b's third pop, it is marked visited.

a is then popped for the second time. It is pushed back on the stack along with its right child, c. Next c is popped for the first time, so it is pushed back, along with its left child e. Now e is popped, pushed, popped, pushed, and finally popped for the third time (this is typical for leaf nodes). Thus e is marked as a visited node. Next c is popped for the second time. It is pushed back onto the stack. However, since it has no right child, it is immediately popped for the third time and marked as visited. Finally, a is popped for the third time and marked as visited. At this point, the stack is empty and the postorder traversal terminates.

The `PostOrder` class itself is directly implemented from the algorithm described previously. The class is shown in Figure 17.26 (page 476). The `StNode` class represents the objects that are placed on the stack. It contains a reference to a node and an integer that stores the number of times the item has been popped from the stack. An `StNode` object is always initialized to reflect the fact that it has not yet been popped from the stack.

An `StNode` stores a reference to a node and a count that tells how many times it has already been popped.

```
 1  package DataStructures;
 2
 3  import Exceptions.*;
 4
 5  // PostOrder class; maintains "current position"
 6  //      according to a postorder traversal
 7  //
 8  // CONSTRUCTION: with tree to which iterator is bound
 9  //
10  // ******************PUBLIC OPERATIONS*********************
11  // boolean isValid( )    --> True if at valid position in tree
12  // Object retrieve( )    --> Return item in current position
13  // void first( )         --> Set current position to first
14  // void advance( )       --> Advance to next position
15  // ******************ERRORS*******************************
16  // Exceptions thrown for illegal access or advance
17
18  /**
19   * Postorder iterator class.
20   */
21  public class PostOrder extends TreeIterator
22  {
23      public PostOrder( BinaryTree theTree )
24      {
25          super( theTree );
26          s = new StackAr( );
27          s.push( new StNode( t.root ) );
28      }
29
30      public void first( )
31      {
32          s.makeEmpty( );
33          if( t.root != null )
34              s.push( new StNode( t.root ) );
35          try
36            { advance( ); }
37          catch( ItemNotFound e ) { }  // Empty tree
38      }
39
40      protected Stack s;     // The stack of StNode objects
41  }
42
43  class StNode
44  {
45      BinaryNode node;
46      int timesPopped;
47
48      StNode( BinaryNode n )
49        { node = n; timesPopped = 0; }
50  }
```

Figure 17.26   PostOrder class (complete class except for advance)

The `PostOrder` class is derived from `TreeIterator`. It adds an internal stack to the inherited fields. The `PostOrder` class is initialized by initializing the `TreeIterator` fields and then pushing the root onto the stack. This is illustrated in the constructor at lines 23 to 28. `first` is implemented by clearing the stack, pushing the root, and then calling `advance`.

Figure 17.27 (page 478) implements `advance`. It follows the outline almost verbatim. Line 8 tests for an empty stack. If the stack is empty, we have completed the iteration and can set `current` to `null` and return. Otherwise, we repeatedly perform stack pushes and pops until an item emerges from the stack for a third time. When this happens, the test at line 25 is successful and we can return. Otherwise, at line 31 we push the node back onto the stack (note that the `timesPopped` component has already been incremented at line 25). We then implement the recursive call. If the node was popped for the first time and it has a left child, then its left child is pushed onto the stack. Likewise, if the node was popped for a second time and it has a right child, then its right child is pushed onto the stack. Note that in either case, the construction of the `StNode` object implies that the pushed node goes on the stack with zero pops.

> advance is the complicated routine. Its code follows the earlier description almost verbatim.

Eventually, the `for` loop terminates because some node will be popped for the third time. Note that over the entire iteration sequence, there can be at most $3N$ stack pushes and pops. This is another way of establishing the linearity of a postorder traversal.

17.4.2 Inorder Traversal

The inorder traversal is the same as the postorder traversal except that a node is declared visited after it is popped a second time. Prior to returning, the iterator pushes the right child (if it exists) onto the stack so that the next call to `advance` can continue by traversing the right child. Because this action is so similar to a postorder traversal, we derive the `InOrder` class from `PostOrder` (even though an IS-A relationship does not exist). The only change is the minor alteration to `advance`. The new class is shown in Figure 17.28 (page 479).

> Inorder traversal is similar to postorder, except that when a node is popped for the second time, it is declared visited.

17.4.3 Preorder Traversal

The preorder traversal is the same as the inorder traversal, except that a node is declared visited after it is popped the first time. Prior to returning, the iterator pushes the right child onto the stack and then pushes the left child. Note the order: We want the left child to be processed before the right child, so we must push the right child first and the left child second.

We could derive the `PreOrder` class from `InOrder` or `PostOrder`, but doing so would be wasteful because the stack no longer needs to maintain a count of the number of times an object has been popped. Consequently, the `PreOrder` class is derived directly from `TreeIterator`. The resulting skeleton with the constructor and `first` method is shown in Figure 17.29 (page 480).

> Preorder is the same as postorder, except that a node is declared visited the first time it is popped and the right and then left children are pushed prior to the return.

```
1       /**
2        * Advance current position to the next node in the tree,
3        *       according to the postorder traversal scheme.
4        * @exception ItemNotFound if current position is null.
5        */
6       public void advance( ) throws ItemNotFound
7       {
8           if( s.isEmpty( ) )
9           {
10              if( current == null )
11                  throw new ItemNotFound( "PostOrder advance" );
12              current = null;
13              return;
14          }
15
16          StNode cnode;
17
18          for( ; ; )
19          {
20              try
21                { cnode = (StNode) s.topAndPop( ); }
22              catch( Underflow e )
23                { return; }  // Cannot happen
24
25              if( ++cnode.timesPopped == 3 )
26              {
27                  current = cnode.node;
28                  return;
29              }
30
31              s.push( cnode );
32              if( cnode.timesPopped == 1 )
33              {
34                  if( cnode.node.left != null )
35                      s.push( new StNode( cnode.node.left ) );
36              }
37              else  // cnode.timesPopped == 2
38              {
39                  if( cnode.node.right != null )
40                      s.push( new StNode( cnode.node.right ) );
41              }
42          }
43      }
```

Figure 17.27 advance for the PostOrder iterator class

Popping only once
allows some
simplifications.

The class adds, at line 40, a stack of references to tree nodes to the TreeIterator data fields. The constructor and first methods are similar to what we have already seen. As illustrated by Figure 17.30 (page 481), advance is simpler: We no longer need a for loop. As soon as a node is popped at line 17, it becomes the current node. We then push the right child and left child, if they exist.

```
 1  package DataStructures;
 2
 3  import Exceptions.*;
 4
 5  // InOrder class; maintains "current position"
 6  //      according to an inorder traversal
 7  //
 8  // CONSTRUCTION: with tree to which iterator is bound
 9  //
10  // ******************PUBLIC OPERATIONS*******************
11  // Same as TreeIterator
12  // ******************ERRORS******************************
13  // Exceptions thrown for illegal access or advance
14
15  public class InOrder extends PostOrder
16  {
17      public InOrder( BinaryTree theTree )
18        { super( theTree ); }
19
20      public void advance( ) throws ItemNotFound
21      {
22          if( s.isEmpty( ) )
23          {
24              if( current == null )
25                  throw new ItemNotFound( "InOrder advance" );
26              current = null;
27              return;
28          }
29
30          StNode cnode;
31          for( ; ; )
32          {
33              try
34                { cnode = (StNode) s.topAndPop( ); }
35              catch( Underflow e )
36                { return; }   // Cannot happen
37
38              if( ++cnode.timesPopped == 2 )
39              {
40                  current = cnode.node;
41                  if( cnode.node.right != null )
42                      s.push( new StNode( cnode.node.right ) );
43                  return;
44              }
45                  // First time through
46              s.push( cnode );
47              if( cnode.node.left != null )
48                  s.push( new StNode( cnode.node.left ) );
49          }
50      }
51  }
```

Figure 17.28   Complete InOrder iterator class

```
 1  package DataStructures;
 2
 3  import Exceptions.*;
 4
 5  // PreOrder class; maintains "current position"
 6  //      according to a preorder traversal
 7  //
 8  // CONSTRUCTION: with tree to which iterator is bound
 9  //
10  // ******************PUBLIC OPERATIONS*********************
11  // boolean isValid( )    --> True if at valid position in tree
12  // Object retrieve( )    --> Return item in current position
13  // void first( )         --> Set current position to first
14  // void advance( )       --> Advance to next position
15  // ******************ERRORS********************************
16  // Exceptions thrown for illegal access or advance
17
18  public class PreOrder extends TreeIterator
19  {
20      public PreOrder( BinaryTree theTree )
21      {
22          super( theTree );
23          s = new StackAr( );
24          s.push( t.root );
25      }
26
27      public void first( )
28      {
29          s.makeEmpty( );
30          if( t.root != null )
31              s.push( t.root );
32          try
33            { advance( ); }
34          catch( ItemNotFound e ) { }  // Empty tree
35      }
36
37      public void advance( ) throws ItemNotFound
38        { /* Figure 17.30 */ }
39
40      private Stack s;     // Stack of TreeNode objects
41  }
```

Figure 17.29 PreOrder class with all methods except advance

```
1      /**
2       * Advance current position to the next node in the tree,
3       *     according to the preorder traversal scheme.
4       * @exception ItemNotFound if current position is null.
5       */
6      public void advance( ) throws ItemNotFound
7      {
8          if( s.isEmpty( ) )
9          {
10             if( current == null )
11                 throw new ItemNotFound( "PreOrder advance" );
12             current = null;
13             return;
14         }
15
16         try
17           { current = (BinaryNode) s.topAndPop( ); }
18         catch( Underflow e )
19           { return; }   // Cannot happen
20
21         if( current.right != null )
22             s.push( current.right );
23         if( current.left != null )
24             s.push( current.left );
25     }
```

Figure 17.30 PreOrder iterator class advance

17.4.4 Level-order Traversals

We close by implementing a *level-order traversal*. This traversal processes nodes starting at the root and going top to bottom, left to right. The name derives from the fact that we output level 0 nodes (the root), level 1 nodes (root's children), level 2 nodes (grandchildren of the root), and so on. A level-order traversal is implemented by using a queue instead of a stack. The queue stores nodes that are yet to be visited. When a node is visited, its children are placed at the end of the queue, where they will be visited after the nodes that are already in the queue. It is easy to see that this guarantees that nodes are visited in level order. The LevelOrder class shown in Figures 17.31 (page 482) and 17.32 (page 483) looks very much like the PreOrder class. The only differences are that we use a queue instead of a stack and we enqueue the left child and then the right child, rather than vice versa. Note that the queue can get very large. In the worst case, all the nodes on the last level (possibly $N/2$) could be in the queue simultaneously.

In a *level-order traversal*, nodes are visited top to bottom, left to right. Level-order traversal is implemented via a queue. The traversal is a *breadth-first* search.

```
 1  package DataStructures;
 2
 3  import Exceptions.*;
 4
 5  // LevelOrder class; maintains "current position"
 6  //      according to a level-order traversal
 7  //
 8  // CONSTRUCTION: with tree to which iterator is bound
 9  //
10  // ******************PUBLIC OPERATIONS*********************
11  // boolean isValid( )   --> True if at valid position in tree
12  // Object retrieve( )   --> Return item in current position
13  // void first( )        --> Set current position to first
14  // void advance( )      --> Advance to next position
15  // ******************ERRORS********************************
16  // Exceptions thrown for illegal access or advance
17
18  /**
19   * Level-order iterator class.
20   */
21  public class LevelOrder extends TreeIterator
22  {
23      public LevelOrder( BinaryTree theTree )
24      {
25          super( theTree );
26          q = new QueueAr( );
27          q.enqueue( t.root );
28      }
29
30      public void first( )
31      {
32          q.makeEmpty( );
33          if( t.root != null )
34              q.enqueue( t.root );
35          try
36            { advance( ); }
37          catch( ItemNotFound e ) { }  // Empty tree
38      }
39
40      public void advance( ) throws ItemNotFound
41        { /* Figure 17.32 */ }
42
43      private Queue q;     // Queue of TreeNode objects
44  }
```

Figure 17.31 LevelOrder iterator class and most methods

The level-order traversal implements a more general technique called *breadth-first search*. An example of this in a more general setting is illustrated in Section 14.2.

```
1      /**
2       * Advance current position to the next node in the tree,
3       *     according to the level-order traversal scheme.
4       * @exception ItemNotFound if current position is null.
5       */
6      public void advance( ) throws ItemNotFound
7      {
8          if( q.isEmpty( ) )
9          {
10             if( current == null )
11                 throw new ItemNotFound( "LevelOrder advance" );
12             current = null;
13             return;
14         }
15
16         try
17           { current = (BinaryNode) q.dequeue( ); }
18         catch( Underflow e )
19           { return; } // Cannot happen
20
21         if( current.left != null )
22             q.enqueue( current.left );
23         if( current.right != null )
24             q.enqueue( current.right );
25     }
```

Figure 17.32 advance method for LevelOrder iterator class

Summary

This chapter discusses the *tree* and in particular, the *binary tree*. We saw how trees are used to implement the file systems on many computers and also some other applications, such as expression trees and coding, that are more fully explored in Part III. Algorithms that work on trees make heavy use of recursion. We examined three recursive traversal algorithms — preorder, postorder, and inorder — and saw how they can be implemented nonrecursively. We also examined the level-order traversal, which forms the basis for an important searching technique known as breadth-first search. The next chapter examines another fundamental type of tree — the *binary search tree*.

Objects of the Game

ancestor and **descendant** If there is a path from node *u* to node *v*, then *u* is an ancestor of *v* and *v* is a descendant of *u*. (457)
binary tree A tree in which no node can have more than two children. A convenient definition is recursive. (463)

child and **parent** Parents and children are naturally defined. A directed edge connects the parent to the child. (455)

depth The length of the path from the root to a node. (456)

first child/next sibling method A general tree implementation in which each node keeps two references per item: one to the leftmost child (if it is not a leaf) and one to its right sibling. (457)

height The length of the path from a node to the deepest leaf. (456)

inorder traversal A type of traversal in which the current node is processed in between recursive calls. (471)

leaf a tree node that has no children. (456)

level-order traversal A type of traversal in which nodes are visited top to bottom, left to right. Level-order traversal is implemented by using a queue. The traversal is breadth first. (481)

postorder traversal A type of traversal in which work at a node is performed after work at its children. The traversal takes constant time per node. (460)

preorder traversal A type of traversal in which work at a node is performed before work at its children. The traversal takes constant time per node. (460)

proper ancestor and **proper descendant** On a path from node u to node v, if $u \neq v$, then u is a proper ancestor of v and v is a proper descendant of u. (457)

siblings Nodes with the same parents. (457)

size of a node The number of descendants a node has (including the node itself). (457)

tree Defined nonrecursively, a tree is a set of nodes and the directed edges that connect them. Trees are naturally defined recursively as either empty or consisting of a root and zero or more subtrees. (455)

Common Errors

1. Allowing a node to be in two trees simultaneously is generally a bad idea because changes to a subtree may inadvertently cause changes in multiple subtrees.
2. Failing to check for empty trees is a common error. If this failure is part of a recursive algorithm, then the program will likely crash.
3. A common error when working with trees is thinking iteratively instead of recursively. Design algorithms recursively first. Then convert them to iterative algorithms if appropriate.

On the Internet

Many of the examples discussed in this chapter are explored in Chapter 18, which discusses binary search trees. The code for the iterator classes is part of package

`DataStructures` and is in the **DataStructures** directory. These iterators use a slightly different `BinaryNode` and `BinaryTree` class than the ones found in this chapter. Those classes are also in the directory **DataStructures**.

The `BinaryNode`, `BinaryTree`, and `FileSystem` classes in this chapter can be found in the directory **Chapter17**.

BinaryNode.java	The `BinaryNode` class shown in Figure 17.12
BinaryTree.java	The `BinaryTree` class shown in Figure 17.13
FileSystem.java	Implements the directory traversal in Figure 17.10
InOrder.java	The `InOrder` class
LevelOrder.java	The `LevelOrder` class
PostOrder.java	The `PostOrder` class
PreOrder.java	The `PreOrder` class
TreeIterator.java	The abstract `TreeIterator` class

Exercises

In Short

17.1. For the tree in Figure 17.33, determine the following:
    a. Which node is the root?
    b. Which nodes are leaves?
    c. What is the tree's depth?
    d. The result of preorder, postorder, inorder, and level-order traversals.

17.2. For each node in the tree of Figure 17.33, do the following:
    a. Name the parent node.
    b. List the children.
    c. List the siblings.
    d. Compute the height.
    e. Compute the depth.
    f. Compute the size.

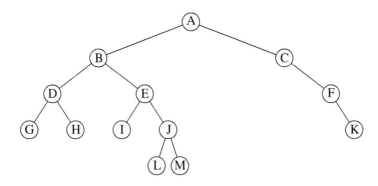

Figure 17.33 Tree for Exercises 17.1 and 17.2

17.3. What is output by the method in Figure 17.34 for the tree in Figure 17.25 (page 475)?

17.4. Show the stack operations when an inorder and preorder traversal is applied to the tree in Figure 17.25 (page 475).

In Theory

17.5. Show that the maximum number of nodes in a binary tree of height H is $2^{H+1} - 1$.

17.6. A *full node* is a node with two children. Prove that in a binary tree, the number of full nodes plus 1 is equal to the number of leaves.

17.7. How many `null` children are there in a binary tree of N nodes? How many are in an M-ary tree of N nodes?

17.8. Suppose a binary tree has leaves $l_1, l_2, \ldots, l_M$ at depth $d_1, d_2, \ldots, d_M$, respectively. Prove that $\sum_{i=1}^{M} 2^{-d_i} \leq 1$ and determine when equality is true. (This is called *Kraft's inequality*.)

In Practice

17.9. Write efficient methods (give Big-Oh running time) that take a reference to a binary tree root T and compute the following:
   a. the number of leaves in T
   b. the number of nodes in T that contain one non-`null` child
   c. the number of nodes in T that contain exactly two non-`null` children

17.10. Implement some of the recursive routines with tests that ensure that a recursive call is not made on a `null` subtree. Compare the running time with identical routines that defer the test until the first line of the recursive method.

17.11. Rewrite the iterator class to throw an exception when `first` is applied to an empty tree. Why might this be a bad idea?

```
1      public void mysteryPrint( BinaryNode t )
2      {
3          if( t != null )
4          {
5              System.out.println( t.element );
6              mysteryPrint( t.left );
7              System.out.println( t.element );
8              mysteryPrint( t.right );
9              System.out.println( t.element );
10         }
11     }
```

Figure 17.34 Mystery program for Exercise 17.3

Programming Projects

17.12. Implement a command that lists all of the files in a given directory, including all subdirectories, sorted by decreasing size. Include the sizes and any other information that you can obtain about the files.

17.13. A binary tree can be generated automatically for desktop publishing by a program. This could be done by assigning an (x, y) coordinate to each tree node, drawing a circle around each coordinate, and connecting each non-root node to its parent. Assume that you have a binary tree stored in memory and that each node has two extra data fields in which to store the coordinates. Assume that $(0, 0)$ is the top-left corner. Do the following:

    a. The x-coordinate can be computed by assigning the inorder traversal number. Write a routine to do this for each node in the tree.

    b. The y-coordinate can be computed by using the depth of the node. Write a routine to do this for each node in the tree.

    c. Determine in terms of some imaginary unit what the dimensions of the picture will be. Also determine how you can adjust the units so that the tree is always roughly two-thirds as high as it is wide.

    d. Prove that when this system is used, no lines cross and that for any node X, all elements in X's left subtree appear to the left of X and all elements in X's right subtree appear to the right of X.

    e. Determine whether both coordinates can be computed in one recursive method.

    f. Write a general-purpose tree-drawing program that will convert a tree into the following graph-assembler instructions (circles are numbered in the order in which they are drawn):

```
circle( x, y );    // Draw circle with center (x,y)
drawLine( i, j ); // Connect circle i to circle j
```

    g. Write a program that reads graph-assembler instructions and generates Java code that draws into a canvas. (Note that you have to scale the stored coordinates into pixels.)

17.14. Design an applet that illustrates the various tree traversal strategies.

18 *Binary Search Trees*

F OR large amounts of input, the linear access time of linked lists is prohibitive. This chapter looks at an alternative to the linked list: the *binary search tree*. The binary search tree is a simple data structure that can be viewed as extending the binary search algorithm to allow insertions and deletions. The running time for most operations is $O(\log N)$ on average. Unfortunately, the worst-case time is $O(N)$ per operation.

In this chapter, we will see:

- What the basic binary search tree is
- How to add order statistics (that is, the `findKth` operation)
- Three different ways to eliminate the $O(N)$ worst case (namely, the *AVL tree*, *red-black tree*, and *AA-tree*)
- How searching a large database can be quickly performed using the *B-tree*

18.1 Basic Ideas

In the general case, an item (or element) is searched for by its *key*. For instance, a student transcript could be searched on the basis of a student ID number. In this case, the ID number is referred to as the item's key.

The *binary search tree* is a binary tree that satisfies the search order property. That is, for every node *X* in the tree, the values of all the keys in the left subtree are smaller than the key in *X* and the values of all the keys in the right subtree are larger than the key in *X*. In Figure 18.1 (page 490), the left tree is a binary search tree, but the right tree is not (because key 8 does not belong in the left subtree of key 7). The binary search tree property implies that all the items in the tree can be ordered in a consistent manner (indeed, an inorder traversal yields the items in sorted order). The property also does not allow duplicate items. We could easily allow duplicate keys. It is generally better to store different items having identical keys in a secondary structure. If the items are exact duplicates, it is better to have one item and keep a count of the number of duplicates.

For any node in the binary search tree, all smaller-keyed nodes are in the left subtree and all larger-keyed nodes are in the right subtree. Duplicates are not allowed.

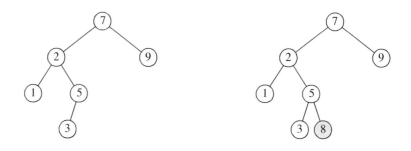

Figure 18.1   Two binary trees (only the left tree is a search tree)

18.1.1   The Operations

find is performed by repeatedly branching either left or right, depending on the result of a comparison.

For the most part, the operations on a binary search tree are simple to visualize. We can perform a find operation by starting at the root and then repeatedly branching either left or right, depending on the result of a comparison. For instance, to find 5 in the binary search tree in Figure 18.1, we start at 7 and go left. This takes us to 2, so we go right. This takes us to 5. To find 6, we would follow the same path. When we were at 5, we would go right and encounter a null reference. Thus 6 is not found. Figure 18.2 shows that 6 can be inserted at the point at which the unsuccessful search terminates.

findMin is performed by following left nodes as long as there is a left child. findMax is similar.

The binary search tree efficiently supports the findMin and findMax operations. To perform a findMin, we start at the root and repeatedly branch left as long as there is a left child. The stopping point is the smallest element. findMax is similar, except that branching is to the right. Notice that the cost of all the operations is proportional to the number of nodes on the search path. The cost tends to be logarithmic, but it can be linear in the worst case. This is shown later in the chapter.

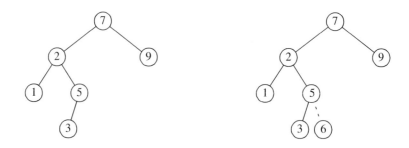

Figure 18.2   Binary search trees before and after inserting 6

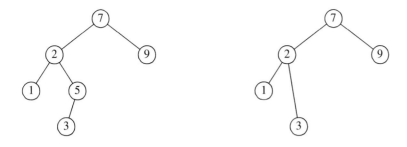

Figure 18.3   Deletion of node 5 with one child, before and after

The hardest operation is `remove`. Once we have found the node to be removed, we need to consider several possibilities. The problem is that the removal of a node may disconnect parts of the tree. We must be careful to reattach the tree and maintain the binary search tree property. We also want to avoid making the tree unnecessarily deep, since, as already mentioned, the depth of the tree affects the running time of the tree algorithms.

If the node is a leaf, its removal will not disconnect the tree, thus it can be deleted immediately. If the node has only one child, the node can be removed after its parent adjusts a child reference to bypass the node. This is illustrated in Figure 18.3 with the removal of node 5. Notice that this means that `removeMin` and `removeMax` are not complex because the affected nodes are either leaves or have only one child. Note that the root is a special case because it does not have a parent. However, when the `remove` method is implemented, the special case is handled automatically.

remove is difficult because nonleaf nodes hold the tree together and we do not want to disconnect the tree.

If a node has one child, it can be removed by having its parent bypass it. The root is a special case because it does not have a parent.

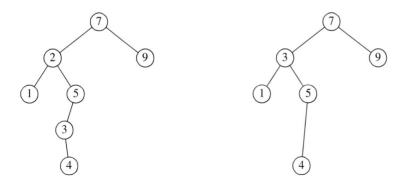

Figure 18.4   Deletion of node 2 with two children, before and after

A node with two
children is replaced
by using the small-
est item in the right
subtree. Then
another node is
removed.

The complicated case deals with a node with two children. The general strategy is to replace the item in this node with the smallest item in the right subtree
(which is easily found, as mentioned earlier) and then remove that node (which is
now logically empty). The second `remove` is easy to do because, as just
remarked, the minimum node in a tree does not have a left child. Figure 18.4
(page 491) shows an initial tree and the result of removing node 2. We replace the
node with the smallest node (3) in its right subtree and then remove 3 from the
right subtree. Notice that in all cases, removing a node does not make the tree
deeper.

```
 1  package DataStructures;
 2
 3  import Supporting.*;
 4
 5  // Basic node stored in all binary search trees
 6  // Includes fields for all variations
 7  // Note that this class is not accessible outside
 8  // of package DataStructures
 9
10  class BinaryNode
11  {
12          // Constructors
13      BinaryNode( Comparable e )
14      {
15          this( e, null, null );
16      }
17
18      BinaryNode( Comparable e, BinaryNode lt, BinaryNode rt )
19      {
20          element = e;
21          left    = lt;
22          right   = rt;
23      }
24
25      // Friendly data; accessible by other package routines
26      Comparable element;     // The data in the node
27      BinaryNode left;        // Left child
28      BinaryNode right;       // Right child
29
30      // Balancing information; only one is used at a time
31      int     size  = 1;   // For BinarySearchTreeWithRank
32      int     color = 1;   // For red-black tree
33      int     level = 1;   // For AA-tree
34  }
```

Figure 18.5   The node class for the binary search tree

```
1  package DataStructures;
2
3  import Supporting.*;
4  import Exceptions.*;
5
6  // BinarySearchTree class
7  //
8  // CONSTRUCTION: with no initializer
9  //
10 // ******************PUBLIC OPERATIONS*********************
11 // void insert( x )        --> Insert x
12 // void remove( x )        --> Remove x
13 // void removeMin( )       --> Remove smallest item
14 // Comparable find( x )    --> Return item that matches x
15 // Comparable findMin( )   --> Return smallest item
16 // Comparable findMax( )   --> Return largest item
17 // boolean isEmpty( )      --> Return true if empty; else false
18 // void makeEmpty( )       --> Remove all items
19 // void printTree( )       --> Print tree in sorted order
20 // ******************ERRORS********************************
21 // Most routines throw ItemNotFound on various conditions
22 // insert throws DuplicateItem if item is already in the tree
23
24 /**
25  * Implements an unbalanced binary search tree.
26  * Note that all "matching" is based on the compares method.
27  */
28 public class BinarySearchTree implements SearchTree
29 {
30     public BinarySearchTree( )
31       { root = null; }
32
33     public void insert( Comparable x ) throws DuplicateItem
34       { root = insert( x, root ); }
35     public void remove( Comparable x ) throws ItemNotFound
36       { root = remove( x, root ); }
37     public void removeMin( ) throws ItemNotFound
38       { root = removeMin( root ); }
39     public Comparable findMin( ) throws ItemNotFound
40       { return findMin( root ).element; }
41     public Comparable findMax( ) throws ItemNotFound
42       { return findMax( root ).element; }
43     public Comparable find( Comparable x ) throws ItemNotFound
44       { return find( x, root ).element; }
45     public boolean isEmpty( )
46       { return root == null; }
47     public void makeEmpty( )
48       { root = null; }
49     public void printTree( )
50       { printTree( root ); }
```

Figure 18.6   BinarySearchTree class skeleton (part 1)

18.1.2   Java Implementation

We use a single
`BinaryNode`
class for all trees in
this chapter.

In principle, the binary search tree is easy to implement. A few simplifications keep the Java features from clogging up the code. First, Figure 18.5 (page 492) shows the `BinaryNode` class. As usual, the data is package friendly, but the class is accessible only in the package. Because we want to be able to use the same declarations for the more advanced binary search trees discussed later in this chapter, we include additional data fields at lines 31 and 32. They are not used in the implementation in this section. Of course, we could omit them and attempt to use inheritance later on, but that obscures the basics too much. Thus the `BinaryNode` class contains the usual list of data fields (the item and two references), plus the additional data fields used later. Several forms are provided for construction.

The root data field
references the root
of the tree, or
`null` if the tree is
empty.

The class skeleton for `BinarySearchTree` is shown in Figures 18.6 (page 493) and 18.7. The principal data field is a reference to the root of the tree, `root`.

```
51      protected BinaryNode
52      find( Comparable x, BinaryNode t ) throws ItemNotFound
53        { /* Figure 18.8 */ }
54
55      protected BinaryNode
56      findMin( BinaryNode t ) throws ItemNotFound
57        { /* Figure 18.9 */ }
58
59      protected BinaryNode
60      findMax( BinaryNode t ) throws ItemNotFound
61        { /* Figure 18.9 */ }
62
63      protected BinaryNode
64      insert( Comparable x, BinaryNode t ) throws DuplicateItem
65        { /* Figure 18.10 */ }
66
67      protected BinaryNode
68      removeMin( BinaryNode t ) throws ItemNotFound
69        { /* Figure 18.11 */ }
70
71      protected BinaryNode
72      remove( Comparable x, BinaryNode t ) throws ItemNotFound
73        { /* Figure 18.12 */ }
74
75      protected void printTree( BinaryNode t )
76        { /* Not shown; see online code */ }
77
78      protected BinaryNode root;
79  }
```

Figure 18.7   `BinarySearchTree` class skeleton (part 2)

Next in the skeleton are seven methods that operate on a node passed as a parameter. We saw this general technique in Chapter 17. The idea is that the publicly visible class routines call these hidden routines and pass `root` as a parameter. These hidden routines do all the work. There are two details to keep in mind. First, the logically private methods are `protected` rather than `private` because we will derive another class from `BinarySearchTree` later in the chapter. Second, the private methods are not static, although making them so is tempting. Otherwise, dynamic binding would not be used when we extend `BinarySearchTree`.

The rest of the `BinarySearchTree` class skeleton is a straightforward listing of the methods with implementations that call the hidden methods. The constructor, declared at line 30, merely sets the `root` reference to `null`. The publicly visible methods are listed with implementations at lines 33 through 50.

`insert` adds x into the current tree by calling the hidden `insert` with `root` as an additional parameter. Failure would occur if x was already in the tree; in that case, a `DuplicateItem` exception would be thrown. `findMin`, `findMax`, and `find` return the minimum, maximum, or named item (respectively) from the tree. If the item is not found because the tree is empty or the named item is not present, then an `ItemNotFound` exception is thrown.

`removeMin` removes the minimum item from the tree; it throws an exception if the tree is empty. `remove` removes a named item x from the tree; it throws an exception if warranted. `makeEmpty` and `isEmpty` are the usual standard fare.

The public class methods will call hidden private routines.

```
1      /**
2       * Internal method to find an item in a subtree.
3       * @param x is item to search for.
4       * @param t the node that roots the tree.
5       * @return node containing the matched item.
6       * @exception ItemNotFound the
7       *        item is not in the subtree.
8       */
9      protected BinaryNode
10     find( Comparable x, BinaryNode t ) throws ItemNotFound
11     {
12         while( t != null )
13             if( x.compares( t.element ) < 0 )
14                 t = t.left;
15             else if( x.compares( t.element ) > 0 )
16                 t = t.right;
17             else
18                 return t;      // Match
19
20         throw new ItemNotFound( "SearchTree find" );
21     }
```

Figure 18.8   `find` operation for binary search trees

find is easier than insert, which in turn is easier than remove.

Because the formal parameter is simply another reference, the actual argument (root) is not changed.

As with most data structures, the find operation is easier than insert and insert is easier than remove. Figure 18.8 (page 495) illustrates the find routine. As long as a null reference has not been reached, we either have a match or need to branch left or right. The code implements this algorithm quite succinctly. Notice the order of the tests. It is crucial that the test against null be performed first; otherwise, the access t.element would be illegal. The remaining tests are arranged with the least likely case last.

It seems at first glance that statements such as t=t.left change the root of the tree. This is not the case. Note carefully that in the initial call, t is simply *another reference to* the node that root references. Although t changes, meaning that t references other nodes, root does not. The calls to findMin and findMax are even simpler because branching is unconditionally in one direction. These routines are shown in Figure 18.9. Notice how the case of an empty tree is carefully handled.

```
1      /**
2       * Internal method to find the smallest item in a subtree.
3       * @param t the node that roots the tree.
4       * @return node containing the smallest item.
5       * @exception ItemNotFound the subtree is empty.
6       */
7      protected BinaryNode
8      findMin( BinaryNode t ) throws ItemNotFound
9      {
10         if( t == null )
11             throw new ItemNotFound( "SearchTree findMin" );
12
13         while( t.left != null )
14             t = t.left;
15         return t;
16     }
17
18     /**
19      * Internal method to find the largest item in a subtree.
20      * @param t the node that roots the tree.
21      * @return node containing the largest item.
22      * @exception ItemNotFound the subtree is empty.
23      */
24     protected BinaryNode
25     findMax( BinaryNode t ) throws ItemNotFound
26     {
27         if( t == null )
28             throw new ItemNotFound( "SearchTree findMax" );
29
30         while( t.right != null )
31             t = t.right;
32         return t;
33     }
```

Figure 18.9 findMin and findMax for binary search trees

```
1      /**
2       * Internal method to insert into a subtree.
3       * @param x the item to insert.
4       * @param t the node that roots the tree.
5       * @return the new root.
6       * @exception DuplicateItem if item that
7       *        matches x is already in the subtree rooted at t.
8       */
9      protected BinaryNode
10     insert( Comparable x, BinaryNode t ) throws DuplicateItem
11     {
12         if( t == null )
13             t = new BinaryNode( x, null, null );
14         else if( x.compares( t.element ) < 0 )
15             t.left = insert( x, t.left );
16         else if( x.compares( t.element ) > 0 )
17             t.right = insert( x, t.right );
18         else
19             throw new DuplicateItem( "SearchTree insert" );
20         return t;
21     }
```

Figure 18.10   Recursive `insert` for binary search trees

The `insert` routine is shown in Figure 18.10. Recursion is used to simplify the code. A nonrecursive implementation is also possible; that technique is discussed along with red-black trees later in this chapter. The basic algorithm is simple. If the tree is empty, we can create a one-node tree. The test is performed at line 12, and the new node is allocated at line 13. Notice carefully that as before, local changes to `t` are lost. Thus we return the new root, `t`, at line 20. In the public `insert`, `root` is changed by assigning the private `insert`'s return value to it.

If the tree is not already empty, then we have three possibilities. If the item to be inserted is smaller than the item in node `t`, then we need to call `insert` recursively on the left subtree. If the item is larger than the item in node `t`, we call `insert` recursively on the right subtree. This is coded at lines 14 to 17. Note that we attach the result of the recursive `insert`. The third case is that the item to insert matches the item in `t`; in this case, we throw an exception.

The remaining routines concern deletion. As described earlier in the chapter, the `removeMin` operation is simple because the minimum node has no left child. Thus the removed node merely needs to be bypassed. It may appear that this requires us to keep track of the parent of the current node as we descend the tree. Once again, we can avoid the explicit use of a parent reference by using recursion. The code is shown in Figure 18.11 (page 498).

For insert, we must return the new subtree root and reconnect the tree.

```
1     /**
2      * Internal method to remove smallest item from a subtree.
3      * @param t the node that roots the tree.
4      * @return the new root.
5      * @exception ItemNotFound the subtree is empty.
6      */
7     protected BinaryNode
8     removeMin( BinaryNode t ) throws ItemNotFound
9     {
10        if( t == null )
11            throw new ItemNotFound( "SearchTree removeMin" );
12        if( t.left != null )
13            t.left = removeMin( t.left );
14        else
15            t = t.right;
16        return t;
17    }
```

Figure 18.11   removeMin for binary search trees

```
1     /**
2      * Internal method to remove from a subtree.
3      * @param x the item to remove.
4      * @param t the node that roots the tree.
5      * @return the new root.
6      * @exception ItemNotFound no item that
7      *          matches x is in the subtree rooted at t.
8      */
9     protected BinaryNode
10    remove( Comparable x, BinaryNode t ) throws ItemNotFound
11    {
12        if( t == null )
13            throw new ItemNotFound( "SearchTree remove" );
14        if( x.compares( t.element ) < 0 )
15            t.left = remove( x, t.left );
16        else if( x.compares( t.element ) > 0 )
17            t.right = remove( x, t.right );
18        else if( t.left != null && t.right != null )
19        {
20            t.element = findMin( t.right ).element;
21            t.right = removeMin( t.right );
22        }
23        else  // Reroot t
24            t = ( t.left != null ) ? t.left : t.right;
25        return t;
26    }
```

Figure 18.12   remove method for the BinarySearchTree class

If the tree t is empty, then removeMin fails. Otherwise, if t has a left child, we recursively remove the minimum item in the left subtree via the recursive call at line 13. If we reach line 14, then we know that we are currently at the minimum node. This means that t is the root of a subtree that has no left child. If we set t to t.right, then the result is that t is now the root of a subtree that is missing its former minimum element. That is what we do at line 15. As before, we must return the root of the resulting subtree. But doesn't that disconnect the tree? The answer again is no. If t was root, then the new t is returned and assigned to root in the public method, and we are safe. If t was not root, then it is p.left, where p is t's parent at the time of the recursive call. The method that has p as its parameter (in other words, the method that called the current method) changes p.left to the new t. Thus the parent's left child references t, and the tree is connected. All in all, it is a pretty nifty maneuver. What we have done is maintain the parent in the recursion stack rather than explicitly keep track of it in an iterative loop.

The root of the new subtree must be returned in the remove *routines. In effect, we maintain the parent in the recursion stack.*

Having used this trick for the simple case, we can then adapt it for the general remove routine. This is shown in Figure 18.12. If the tree is empty, the remove is unsuccessful and we can throw an exception at line 13. If we do not have a match, then we can recursively call remove for either the left or right subtree as appropriate. Otherwise, we reach line 18. This indicates that we have found the node that needs to be removed.

Recall that if there are two children, we replace the node with the minimum element in the right subtree and then remove the right subtree's minimum. This is coded at lines 20 to 21. Otherwise, we have either one or zero children. If there is a left child, then we set t equal to its left child, as would be done in removeMax. Otherwise, we know there is no left child, so we can set t equal to its right child. This is succinctly coded in line 24. Line 24 also covers the leaf case. In any of these cases, the remove returns the root of the subtree at line 25.

The remove *is tricky coding, but is not too bad if we use recursion. The case for zero children, one child, and a root with one child are all handled together at line 24.*

There are two points to be made about this implementation. First, during the basic insert, find, or remove operation, we perform two comparisons per node accessed to distinguish among the cases <, =, and >. It turns out that we can get by with only one comparison per node. The strategy is very similar to what was done in the binary search algorithm in Section 5.6. The technique for binary search trees is discussed in Section 18.6.2, where the deletion algorithm for AA-trees is covered.

Second, we do not have to use recursion to perform the insertion. In fact, a recursive implementation is probably slower than a nonrecursive implementation. An iterative implementation of insert is discussed in Section 18.5.3 in the context of red-black trees.

18.2 Order Statistics

The binary search tree allows us to find either the minimum or maximum item in time that is equivalent to an arbitrary-named `find`. Sometimes it is important to be able to access the Kth smallest element, for an arbitrary K provided as a parameter. It turns out that this can be done if we keep track of the size of each node in the tree.

We can implement `findKth` if we maintain the size of each node as the tree is updated.

Recall from Section 17.1 that the size of a node is the number of its descendants (including itself). Suppose we want to find the Kth smallest element and that K is at least 1 and at most the number of nodes in the tree. Figure 18.13 shows that there are three possible cases, depending on the relation of K and the size of the left subtree, which is denoted by S_L. If K is equal to $S_L + 1$, then the root is the Kth smallest element and we can stop. If K is smaller than or equal to S_L, then the Kth smallest element must be in the left subtree and we can find it recursively. The recursion is not needed; it is meant to simplify the algorithm description. Otherwise, the Kth smallest element is the $(K–S_L–1)$th smallest element in the right subtree and can be found recursively.

The main effort is maintaining the node sizes during tree changes. These changes occur in the `insert`, `remove`, and `removeMin` operations. In principle, this maintenance is simple enough. During an `insert`, each node on the path to the insertion point gains one node in its subtree. Thus the size of each node increases by 1, and the inserted node has size 1. In `removeMin`, each node on the path to the minimum loses one node in its subtree; thus the size of each node decreases by 1. During a `remove`, all nodes on the path to the node that is physically removed also lose one node in their subtrees. Consequently, we can maintain the sizes at the cost of only a slight amount of overhead.

18.2.1   Java Implementation

We derive a new class that supports the order statistic.

Logically, the only changes required are the adding of `findKth` and the maintenance of the `size` data fields in `insert`, `remove`, and `removeMin`. We derive a new class from `BinarySearchTree`, the skeleton for which is shown in Figure 18.14.

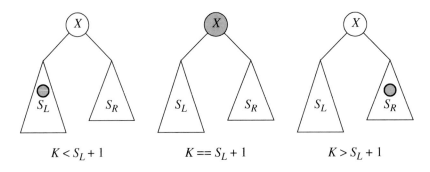

$$K < S_L + 1 \qquad\qquad K == S_L + 1 \qquad\qquad K > S_L + 1$$

Figure 18.13   Using the `size` data field to implement `findKth`

Let us first examine the new public methods. Since the constructor is not explicitly provided, the default is used; the inherited fields are initialized by the `BinarySearchTree` constructor. The new publicly visible method `findKth` is declared at line 32 and calls a corresponding private method. Public methods such as `insert` do not need to be redefined, since their bodies are identical to the `BinarySearchTree` versions.

We must redefine the hidden methods. We can keep the public methods unchanged.

```
 1  package DataStructures;
 2
 3  import Supporting.*;
 4  import Exceptions.*;
 5
 6  // BinarySearchTreeWithRank class
 7  //
 8  // CONSTRUCTION: with no initializer
 9  //
10  // ******************PUBLIC OPERATIONS********************
11  // void insert( x )        --> Insert x
12  // void remove( x )        --> Remove x
13  // void removeMin( )       --> Remove smallest item
14  // Comparable find( x )    --> Return item that matches x
15  // Comparable findMin( )   --> Return smallest item
16  // Comparable findMax( )   --> Return largest item
17  // Comparable findKth( int k )
18  //                         --> find kth smallest item
19  // boolean isEmpty( )      --> Return true if empty; else false
20  // void makeEmpty( )       --> Remove all items
21  // void printTree( )       --> Print tree in sorted order
22  // ******************ERRORS*******************************
23  // Most routines throw ItemNotFound on various conditions
24  // insert throws DuplicateItem if item is already in the tree
25
26  /**
27   * Implements a binary search tree with a findKth method.
28   * Note that all "matching" is based on the compares method.
29   */
30  public class BinarySearchTreeWithRank extends BinarySearchTree
31  {
32      public Comparable findKth( int k ) throws ItemNotFound
33        { return findKth( k, root ).element; }
34
35      // Internal methods for insert, remove, removeMin are
36      //   overridden. Internal method for findKth is added
37  }
```

Figure 18.14   Class skeleton for the search tree with order statistics

```
1      /**
2       * Internal method to find kth smallest item in a subtree.
3       * @param k the desired rank (1 is the smallest item).
4       * @return node containing kth smallest item in subtree.
5       * @exception ItemNotFound if k is less
6       *        than 1 or more than the size of the subtree.
7       */
8      protected BinaryNode
9      findKth( int k, BinaryNode t ) throws ItemNotFound
10     {
11         if( t == null )
12             throw new ItemNotFound( "BSTWithRank findKth" );
13         int leftSize = ( t.left != null ) ? t.left.size : 0;
14
15         if( k <= leftSize )
16             return findKth( k, t.left );
17         else if( k == leftSize + 1 )
18             return t;
19         else
20             return findKth( k - leftSize - 1, t.right );
21     }
```

Figure 18.15   findKth operation for the search tree with order statistics

```
1      /**
2       * Internal method to insert into a subtree, adjusting
3       *      size fields as appropriate.
4       * @param x the item to insert.
5       * @param t the node that roots the tree.
6       * @return the new root.
7       * @exception DuplicateItem if item that
8       *      matches x is already in the subtree rooted at t.
9       */
10     protected BinaryNode
11     insert( Comparable x, BinaryNode t ) throws DuplicateItem
12     {
13         if( t == null )
14             return new BinaryNode( x, null, null );
15         else if( x.compares( t.element ) < 0 )
16             t.left = insert( x, t.left );
17         else if( x.compares( t.element ) > 0 )
18             t.right = insert( x, t.right );
19         else
20             throw new DuplicateItem( "BSTWithRank insert" );
21
22         t.size++;
23         return t;
24     }
```

Figure 18.16   insert for the search tree with order statistics

What changes are the private helper methods. We need the public `insert` to call an appropriate private helper. Note, however, that the private helpers must not be `static`. This decision must be made using dynamic, rather than static, binding.

The `findKth` operation in Figure 18.15 is written recursively, although clearly it need not be. It follows the algorithmic description line for line. The test against `null` at line 11 is necessary because k could be invalid. At line 13, we compute the size of the left subtree. If the left subtree exists, then accessing its `size` field gives the required answer. If the left subtree does not exist, its size can be taken to be zero. Notice that this test is performed after we are sure that t is not `null`.

> `findKth` is easily implemented once the size fields are known.

`insert` is shown in Figure 18.16. The potentially tricky part of it is that if the insertion succeeds, then we want to increment t's `size` field and return the subtree's new root. If the recursive call fails, t's `size` field should be unchanged and an exception should be thrown. Is it possible that in an unsuccessful insertion, some sizes will change? The answer is no: `size` is updated only if the recursive call succeeds without an exception. Note that when a new node is allocated by a call to `new`, the `size` field is set to 1 by the `BinaryNode` constructor.

> `insert` and `remove` are potentially tricky because we do not update the size information if the operation is unsuccessful.

Figure 18.17 shows that the same trick can be used by `removeMin`. If the recursive call succeeds, the `size` field is decremented; if the recursive call fails, `size` is unchanged. `remove` is similar and is shown in Figure 18.18 (page 504).

```
1      /**
2       * Internal method to remove smallest item from a subtree,
3       *      adjusting size fields as appropriate.
4       * @param t the node that roots the tree.
5       * @return the new root.
6       * @exception ItemNotFound the subtree is empty.
7       */
8      protected BinaryNode
9      removeMin( BinaryNode t ) throws ItemNotFound
10     {
11         if( t == null )
12             throw new ItemNotFound( "BSTWithRank removeMin" );
13         if( t.left == null )
14             return t.right;
15         t.left = removeMin( t.left );
16
17         t.size--;
18         return t;
19     }
```

Figure 18.17 `removeMin` for the search tree with order statistics

```
1     /**
2      * Internal method to remove from a subtree, adjusting
3      *    size fields as appropriate.
4      * @param x the item to remove.
5      * @param t the node that roots the tree.
6      * @return the new root.
7      * @exception ItemNotFound no item that
8      *    matches x is in the subtree rooted at t.
9      */
10     protected BinaryNode
11     remove( Comparable x, BinaryNode t ) throws ItemNotFound
12     {
13         if( t == null )
14             throw new ItemNotFound( "BSTWithRank remove" );
15         if( x.compares( t.element ) < 0 )
16             t.left = remove( x, t.left );
17         else if( x.compares( t.element ) > 0 )
18             t.right = remove( x, t.right );
19         else if( t.left != null && t.right != null )
20         {
21             t.element = findMin( t.right ).element;
22             t.right = removeMin( t.right );
23         }
24         else
25             return ( t.left != null ) ? t.left : t.right;
26         t.size--;
27         return t;
28     }
```

Figure 18.18 remove for the search tree with order statistics

18.3 Analysis of Binary Search Tree Operations

The cost of an operation is proportional to the depth of the last accessed node. This is logarithmic for a well-balanced tree, but it could be as bad as linear for a degenerate tree.

It is easy to see that the cost of each binary search tree operation (insert, find, and remove) is proportional to the number of nodes accessed during the operation. We can thus charge the access of any node in the tree a cost of 1, plus its depth (recall that the depth measures the number of edges on a path rather than the number of nodes). This gives the cost of a successful search.

Figure 18.19 shows two trees. On the left is a balanced tree of 15 nodes. The cost to access any node is at most 4 units, and some nodes require fewer accesses. This is exactly analogous to the situation that occurs in the binary search algorithm. If the tree is perfectly balanced, then the access cost is logarithmic.

Unfortunately, we have no guarantee that the tree is perfectly balanced. The second tree in Figure 18.19 is the classic example of an unbalanced tree. Here, all N nodes are on the path to the deepest node, so the worst-case search time is $O(N)$. Because the search tree has degenerated to a linked list, the average time required to search in *this particular instance* is half the cost of the worst case and is also $O(N)$. So we have two extremes: In the best case, we have logarithmic access cost, and in the worst case, we have linear access cost. What, then, is the average? Do most binary search trees tend toward the balanced or unbalanced case, or is there some middle ground, such as $\sqrt{N}$? The answer is identical to that for quicksort: The average is 38 percent worse than the best case.

We prove in this section that the average depth over all nodes in a binary search tree is logarithmic, under the assumption that each tree is created as a result of random insertion sequences (with no `remove` operations). To see what this means, consider the result of inserting three items into an empty binary search tree. Since only their relative ordering is important, we can assume without loss of generality that the three items are 1, 2, and 3. Then there are six possible insertion orders: (1, 2, 3), (1, 3, 2), (2, 1, 3), (2, 3, 1), (3, 1, 2), and (3 ,2, 1). We will assume in our proof that each of these insertion orders is equally likely. The binary search trees that can result from these insertions are shown in Figure 18.20 (page 506). Notice that the tree with root 2 is formed from either the insertion sequence (2, 3, 1) or the sequence (2, 1, 3). Thus some trees are more likely than others, and as will be shown, balanced trees are more likely than unbalanced trees (although this is not evident from the three-element case).

We begin with the following definition.

> **DEFINITION:** The *internal path length* of a binary tree is equal to the sum of the depths of its nodes.

When we divide the internal path length of a tree by the number of nodes in the tree, we obtain the average depth of a node in the tree. Adding 1 to this average gives the average cost of a successful search in the tree. So we want to compute the average internal path length for a binary search tree, where the average is taken over all (equally probable) input permutations. This is easily done by viewing the tree recursively and using techniques shown in the analysis of quicksort given in Section 8.6. The average internal path length is established in Theorem 18.1.

On average, the depth is 38 percent worse than the best case. This result is identical to that obtained using quicksort.

The internal path length is used to measure the cost of a successful search.

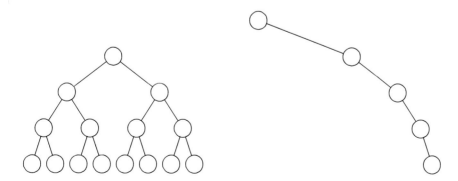

Figure 18.19 Balanced tree on the left has a depth of $\lfloor \log N \rfloor$; unbalanced tree on the right has a depth of $N - 1$

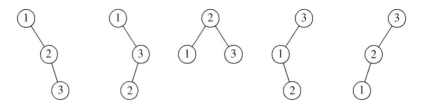

Figure 18.20 Binary search trees that can result from inserting a permutation 1, 2, and 3; the balanced tree in the middle is twice as likely to result from this as any others

---

Theorem 18.1

The internal path length of a binary search tree is approximately 1.38N log N, on average, under the assumption that all permutations are equally likely.

Proof

Let $D(N)$ be the average internal path length for trees of N nodes. $D(1) = 0$. An N-node tree T consists of an i-node left subtree and an $(N - i - 1)$-node right subtree, plus a root at depth 0 for $0 \leq i < N$. By assumption, each value of i is equally likely. For a given i, $D(i)$ is the average internal path length of the left subtree with respect to its root. In T, all these nodes are one level deeper. Thus the average contribution of the nodes in the left subtree to the internal path length of T is $(1/N)\sum_{i=0}^{N-1} D(i)$, plus 1 for each node in the left subtree. The same holds for the right subtree. We thus obtain the recurrence formula $D(N) = (2/N)(\sum_{i=0}^{N-1} D(i)) + N - 1$, which is identical to the quicksort recurrence solved in Section 8.6. Thus we obtain an average internal path length of $O(N \log N)$.

The *external path length* is used to measure the cost of an unsuccessful search.

The insertion algorithm implies that the cost of an insert is exactly equal to the cost of an unsuccessful search, which is measured by using the *external path length*. In an insertion or unsuccessful search, we eventually reach the test `t==null`. Recall that in a tree of N nodes, there are $N + 1$ null references. The external path length measures the total number of nodes that are accessed, including the null node for each of these $N + 1$ null references. (The null node is sometimes called an *external tree node*, which explains the term *external path length.* As is shown later in the chapter, it is sometimes convenient to use a sentinel to replace the `null` node.)

> **DEFINITION:** The *external path length* of a binary search tree is the sum of the depths of the $N + 1$ `null` references. The terminating `null` node is considered a node for these purposes.

One plus the result of dividing the average external path length by $N + 1$ yields the average cost of an unsuccessful search or insertion. As with the binary search algorithm, the average cost of an unsuccessful search is only slightly more than the cost of a successful search. This follows from Theorem 18.2.

For any tree T, let IPL(T) be the internal path length of T and let EPL(T) be its external path length. Then, if T has N nodes, $$EPL(T) = IPL(T) + 2N.$$	***Theorem 18.2***
This theorem is proved by induction and is left as Exercise 18.8.	***Proof***

It is tempting to say immediately that these results imply that the average running time of all operations is $O(\log N)$. This is true in practice, but it has not been established analytically because the assumption used to prove the previous results do not take into account the deletion algorithm. In fact, close examination suggests that we might be in trouble with our deletion algorithm because the `remove` always replaces a two-child deleted node with a node from the right subtree. This would seem to have the effect of eventually unbalancing the tree and tending to make it left-heavy. It has been shown that if we build a random binary search tree and then perform roughly N^2 pairs of random `insert/remove` combinations, then the binary search trees will have an expected depth of $O(\sqrt{N})$. However, it has never been shown that a reasonable number of random `insert` and `remove` operations (in which the order of `insert` and `remove` is also random) unbalances the tree in any observable way. In fact, for small search trees, the `remove` algorithm seems to balance the tree. Consequently, it is reasonable to assume that for random input, all operations will behave in logarithmic average time, although this has not been proved mathematically. Exercise 18.26 describes some alternative deletion strategies.

The most important problem is not the potential imbalance caused by the `remove` algorithm. Rather, it is the fact that if the input sequence is sorted, then the worst-case tree occurs. When this happens, we are in deep trouble: We have linear time per operation (for a series of N operations) rather than logarithmic cost per operation. This is analogous to passing items to quicksort but having an insertion sort executed instead. The resulting running time is completely unacceptable.

Random `remove` operations do not preserve the randomness of a tree. The effects are not completely understood theoretically, but it appears that they are negligible in practice.

Moreover, it is not just sorted input that is problematic, but also any input that contains long sequences of nonrandomness. One solution to this problem is to insist on an extra structural condition called *balance*: No node is allowed to get too deep.

A balanced binary search tree adds a structure property to guarantee logarithmic depth in the worst case. Updates are slower, but accesses are faster.

There are several algorithms to implement *balanced binary search trees*. Most are much more complicated than the standard binary search trees, and all take longer on average for insertion and deletion. They do, however, provide protection against the embarrassingly simple cases. Also, because they are so balanced, they tend to give faster access time. Typically, their internal path lengths are very close to the optimal $N \log N$ rather than $1.38N \log N$, so searching time is roughly 25 percent faster.

18.4 AVL Trees

The AVL tree was the first balanced binary search tree. It has historical significance and also illustrates most of the ideas that are used in other schemes.

The first balanced binary search tree was the *AVL tree* (named after its discoverers, Adelson-Velskii and Landis). The AVL tree illustrates the ideas that are thematic for a wide class of balanced binary search trees. It is a binary search tree that has an additional balance condition. This balance condition must be easy to maintain, and it ensures that the depth of the tree is $O(\log N)$. The simplest idea is to require that the left and right subtrees have the same height. Recursion dictates that this idea applies to all nodes in the tree, since each node is itself a root of some subtree. This balance condition ensures that the depth of the tree is logarithmic. However, it is too restrictive because it is too difficult to insert new items while maintaining balance. Thus the AVL tree uses a notion of balance that is somewhat weaker but still strong enough to guarantee logarithmic depth.

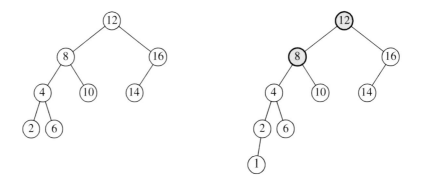

Figure 18.21   Two binary search trees: the left tree is an AVL tree; the right tree is not (unbalanced nodes are darkened)

18.4.1 Properties

DEFINITION: An *AVL tree* is a binary search tree with the additional balance property that, for any node in the tree, the height of the left and right subtrees can differ by at most 1. As usual, the height of an empty subtree is −1.

Figure 18.21 shows two binary search trees. The tree on the left satisfies the AVL balance condition and is thus an AVL tree. The tree on the right, which results from inserting 1 using the usual algorithm, is not an AVL tree because the darkened nodes have left subtrees whose heights are 2 larger than their right subtrees. If 13 was inserted using the usual binary search tree insertion algorithm, then node 16 would also be in violation. This is because the left subtree would have height 1, while the right subtree would have height −1.

The AVL balance condition implies that the tree has only logarithmic depth. To prove this, we need to show that a tree of height H must have at least C^H nodes for some constant $C > 1$. In other words, the minimum number of nodes in a tree is exponential in its height. Then the maximum depth of an N-item tree is given by $\log_C N$. Theorem 18.3 shows that every AVL tree of height H has many nodes.

> Every node in an AVL tree has subtrees whose heights differ by at most 1. An empty subtree has height −1.

> The AVL tree has height at most roughly 44 percent greater than the minimum.

An AVL tree of height H has at least $F_{H+3} - 1$ nodes, where F_i is the ith Fibonacci number (see Section 7.3.4).   ***Theorem 18.3***

Let S_H be the size of the smallest AVL tree of height H. Clearly $S_0 = 1$ and $S_1 = 2$. Figure 18.22 (page 510) shows that the smallest AVL tree of height H must have subtrees of height H − 1 and H − 2. This is because at least one subtree has height H − 1 and the balance condition implies that subtree heights can differ by at most 1. These subtrees must themselves have the fewest number of nodes for their heights, so $S_H = S_{H-1} + S_{H-2} + 1$. It is then a simple matter to complete the proof by using an induction argument.   ***Proof***

From Exercise 7.8, $F_i \approx \phi^i / \sqrt{5}$, where $\phi = (1 + \sqrt{5})/2 \approx 1.618$. Consequently, an AVL tree of height H has at least (roughly) $\phi^{H+3} / \sqrt{5}$ nodes. Hence, its depth is at most logarithmic. The height of an AVL tree satisfies

$$H < 1.44\log(N + 2) - 1.328, \tag{18.1}$$

so the worst-case height is at most 44 percent more than the minimum possible for binary trees.

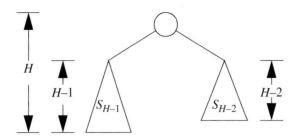

Figure 18.22 Minimum tree of height *H*

The depth of a typical node in an AVL tree is very close to the optimal log *N*.

The depth of an average node in a randomly constructed AVL tree tends to be very close to $\log N$. The exact answer has not yet been established analytically. It is not even known if the form is $\log N + C$ or $(1 + \varepsilon)\log N + C$, for some ε that would be approximately 0.01. Simulations have been unable to convincingly demonstrate that one form is more plausible than the other.

An update in an AVL tree could destroy the balance. We must then rebalance before the operation is complete.

A consequence of these arguments is that all searching operations in an AVL tree have logarithmic worst-case bounds. The difficulty is that operations that change the tree, such as `insert` and `remove`, are not quite as simple as before. This is because an insertion (or deletion) can destroy the balance of several nodes in the tree, as shown in Figure 18.21. The balance must then be restored before the operation can be considered complete. The insertion algorithm is described here and the deletion algorithm is left for Exercise 18.10.

Only nodes on the path from the root to the insertion point can have their balances altered.

A key observation is that after an insertion, only nodes that are on the path from the insertion point to the root might have their balances altered because only those nodes have their subtrees altered. This applies for almost all of the balanced search tree algorithms. As we follow the path up to the root and update the balancing information, we may find a node whose new balance violates the AVL condition. This section shows how to rebalance the tree at the first (that is, the deepest) such node and proves that this rebalancing guarantees that the entire tree satisfies the AVL property.

If we fix the balance at the deepest unbalanced node, we will rebalance the entire tree. There are four cases that we might have to fix; two are mirror-images of the other two.

The node to be rebalanced is *X*. Since any node has at most two children and a height imbalance requires that the heights of *X*'s two subtrees differ by 2, a violation might occur in any of four cases:

1. An insertion into the left subtree of the left child of *X*
2. An insertion into the right subtree of the left child of *X*
3. An insertion into the left subtree of the right child of *X*
4. An insertion into the right subtree of the right child of *X*

Cases 1 and 4 are mirror-image symmetries with respect to *X*, as are cases 2 and 3. Consequently, there theoretically are two basic cases. From a programming perspective, of course, there are still four cases (and numerous special cases).

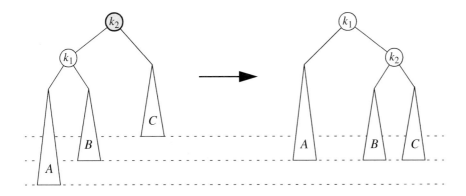

Figure 18.23 Single rotation to fix case 1

The first case, in which the insertion occurs on the "outside" (that is, left-left or right-right), is fixed by a *single rotation* of the tree. A single rotation switches the roles of the parent and child while maintaining search order. The second case, in which the insertion occurs on the "inside" (that is, left-right or right-left), is handled by the slightly more complex *double rotation*. These are fundamental operations on the tree that are used several times in balanced tree algorithms. The remainder of this section describes these rotations and proves that they suffice to maintain the balance condition.

Balance is restored by tree rotations. A *single rotation* switches the roles of the parent and child while maintaining the search order.

18.4.2 Single Rotation

Figure 18.23 shows the single rotation that fixes case 1. The before picture is on the left; the after is on the right. Here is what is going on. Node k_2 violates the AVL balance property because its left subtree is two levels deeper than its right subtree (the dashed lines are used to mark the levels in this section). The situation depicted is the only possible case 1 scenario that allows k_2 to satisfy the AVL property before the insertion but violate it afterward. Subtree A has grown to an extra level, thus causing it to be exactly two levels deeper than C. B cannot be at the same level as the new A because then k_2 would have been out of balance *before* the insertion. B cannot be at the same level as C because then k_1 would have been the first node on the path that was in violation of the AVL balancing condition (and we are claiming that k_2 is).

To ideally rebalance the tree, we want to move A up one level and C down one level. Note that this is more than the AVL property would require. To do this, we rearrange nodes into an equivalent search tree, as shown in the right-hand illustration of Figure 18.23. Here is an abstract scenario: Visualize the tree as being flexible, grab the child node k_1, close your eyes, and shake the tree, letting gravity take hold. The result is that k_1 will be the new root. The binary search tree

A single rotation handles the outside cases (1 and 4). We rotate between a node and its child. The result is a binary search tree that satisfies the AVL property.

property tells us that in the original tree, $k_2 > k_1$, so k_2 becomes the right child of k_1 in the new tree. A and C remain as the left child of k_1 and the right child of k_2, respectively. Subtree B, which holds items that are between k_1 and k_2 in the original tree, can be placed as k_2's left child in the new tree and satisfy all the ordering requirements.

One rotation suffices to fix cases 1 and 4 in an AVL tree.

This work requires only the few child reference changes shown in Figure 18.24 and results in another binary tree that is an AVL tree. This happens because A moves up one level, B stays at the same level, and C moves down one level. k_1 and k_2 not only satisfy the AVL requirements; they also have subtrees that are exactly the same height. Furthermore, the new height of the entire subtree is *exactly the same* as the height of the original subtree prior to the insertion that caused A to grow. Thus no further updating of the heights on the path to the root is needed, and consequently, *no further rotations are needed*. This single rotation is widely used in other balanced tree algorithms in this chapter. As a result, we make it part of the class Rotations.

Figure 18.25 shows that after the insertion of 1 into an AVL tree, node 8 becomes unbalanced. This is clearly a case 1 problem because 1 is in 8's left-left subtree. Thus we do a single rotation between 8 and 4, thereby obtaining the tree on the right. As mentioned earlier in this section, case 4 represents a symmetric case. The required rotation is shown in Figure 18.26, and the code that implements it is shown in Figure 18.27. This method, too, is part of class Rotations.

18.4.3 Double Rotation

The single rotation does not fix the inside cases (2 and 3). These cases require a double rotation, involving three nodes and four subtrees.

The single rotation has one problem. As Figure 18.28 (page 514) shows, it does not work for case 2 (or, by symmetry, for case 3). The problem is that subtree Q is too deep; a single rotation does not make it any less deep. The *double rotation* that solves the problem is shown in Figure 18.29 (page 514).

```
1      /**
2       * Rotate binary tree node with left child.
3       * For AVL trees, this is a single rotation for case 1.
4       */
5      static BinaryNode withLeftChild( BinaryNode k2 )
6      {
7          BinaryNode k1 = k2.left;
8          k2.left = k1.right;
9          k1.right = k2;
10         return k1;
11     }
```

Figure 18.24   Code for a single rotation (case 1)

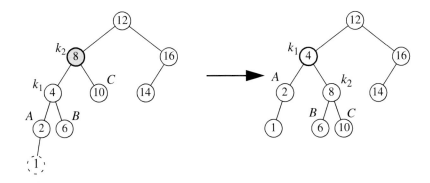

Figure 18.25 Single rotation fixes AVL tree after insertion of 1

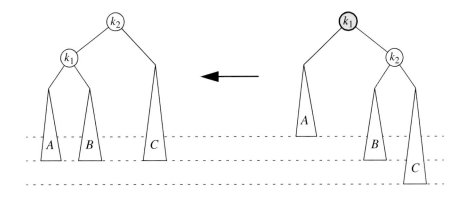

Figure 18.26 Symmetric single rotation to fix case 4

```
1       /**
2        * Rotate binary tree node with right child.
3        * For AVL trees, this is a single rotation for case 4.
4        */
5       static BinaryNode withRightChild( BinaryNode k1 )
6       {
7           BinaryNode k2 = k1.right;
8           k1.right = k2.left;
9           k2.left = k1;
10          return k2;
11      }
```

Figure 18.27 Code for a single rotation (case 4)

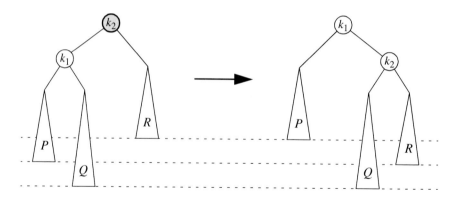

Figure 18.28 Single rotation does not fix case 2

The fact that subtree Q in Figure 18.28 has had an item inserted into it guarantees that it is not empty. We may assume that it has a root and two (possibly empty) subtrees, so we may view the tree as four subtrees connected by three nodes. We therefore rename the four trees A, B, C, and D. As Figure 18.29 suggests, exactly one of tree B or C is two levels deeper than D, but we cannot be sure which one. It turns out not to matter; in the figure, both B and C are drawn at 1.5 levels below D.

To rebalance, we see that we cannot leave k_3 as the root, while a rotation between k_3 and k_1 was shown in Figure 18.28 not to work. Hence, the only alternative is to place k_2 as the new root. This forces k_1 to be k_2's left child and k_3 to be k_2's right child. It also completely determines the resulting locations of the four subtrees. It is easy to see that the resulting tree satisfies the AVL property. Also, as was the case with the single rotation, it restores the height to what it was before the insertion, thus guaranteeing that all rebalancing and height updating is complete.

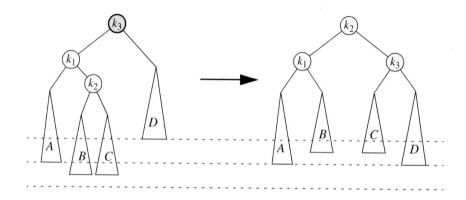

Figure 18.29 Left-right double rotation to fix case 2

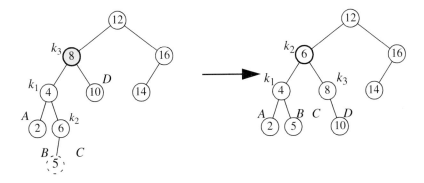

Figure 18.30 Double rotation fixes AVL tree after the insertion of 5

As an example, Figure 18.30 shows the result of inserting 5 into an AVL tree. A height imbalance is caused at node 8, thus resulting in a case 2 problem. We perform a double rotation at that node, thereby producing the tree on the right.

Figure 18.31 (page 516) shows that the symmetric case 3 can also be fixed by a double rotation. Finally, notice that although a double rotation appears complex, it turns out to be equivalent to the following:

- A rotation between X's child and grandchild
- A rotation between X and its new child

The code to implement the case 2 double rotation is compact and is shown in Figure 18.32 (page 516). The mirror-image code for case 3 is shown in Figure 18.33 (page 516).

A double rotation is equivalent to two single rotations.

18.4.4 Summary of AVL Insertion

Here is a brief summary how an AVL insertion is implemented. A recursive algorithm turns out to be the simplest method. To insert a new node with key X into an AVL tree T, we recursively insert it into the appropriate subtree of T (called T_{LR}). If the height of T_{LR} does not change, then we are done. Otherwise, if a height imbalance appears in T, we do the appropriate single or double rotation, depending on X and the keys in T and T_{LR}, and then we are done (because the old height is the same as the postrotation height). This recursive description is best described as a casual implementation. For instance, at each node we compare the subtree's heights. In general, it is more efficient to store the result of the comparison in the node rather than maintain the height information. This avoids the repetitive calculation of balance factors. Furthermore, recursion incurs substantial overhead over an iterative version. This is because, in effect, we go down the tree and completely back up instead of stopping as soon as a rotation is performed. Consequently, in practice, other balanced search tree schemes are used.

A casual AVL implementation is relatively painless. However, it is not efficient. Better balanced search trees have since been discovered, so it is not worthwhile to implement an AVL tree.

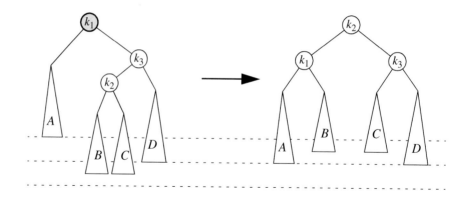

Figure 18.31 Left-right double rotation to fix case 3

```
1       /**
2        * Double rotate binary tree node: first left child
3        * with its right child; then node k3 with new left child.
4        * For AVL trees, this is a double rotation for case 2.
5        */
6       static BinaryNode doubleWithLeftChild( BinaryNode k3 )
7       {
8           k3.left = withRightChild( k3.left );
9           return withLeftChild( k3 );
10      }
```

Figure 18.32 Code for a double rotation (case 2)

```
1       /**
2        * Double rotate binary tree node: first right child
3        * with its left child; then node k1 with new right child.
4        * For AVL trees, this is a double rotation for case 3.
5        */
6       static BinaryNode doubleWithRightChild( BinaryNode k1 )
7       {
8           k1.right = withLeftChild( k1.right );
9           return withRightChild( k1 );
10      }
```

Figure 18.33 Code for a double rotation (case 3)

18.5 Red-Black Trees

A historically popular alternative to the AVL tree is the *red-black tree*. As on AVL trees, operations on red-black trees take logarithmic worst-case time. The main advantage of red-black trees is that a single top-down pass can be used during the insertion and deletion routines. This contrasts with an AVL tree, in which a pass down the tree is used to establish the insertion point and a second pass up the tree is used to update heights and possibly rebalance. As a result, a careful nonrecursive implementation of the red-black tree is simpler and faster than an AVL tree implementation.

A red-black tree is a binary search tree with the following ordering properties:

1. Every node is colored either red or black.
2. The root is black.
3. If a node is red, its children must be black.
4. Every path from a node to a `null` reference must contain the same number of black nodes.

In this discussion of red-black trees, red nodes are shown as shaded. Figure 18.34 shows a red-black tree. Every path from the root to a `null` node contains three black nodes.

We can show by induction that if every path from the root to a `null` node contains B black nodes, then there must be at least $2^B - 1$ black nodes in the tree. Furthermore, since the root is black and there cannot be two consecutive red nodes on a path, the height of a red-black tree is at most $2\log(N + 1)$. Consequently, searching is guaranteed to be a logarithmic operation.

The difficulty, as usual, is that operations can change the tree and possibly destroy the coloring properties. This makes insertion difficult and removal especially so. In the next section, the insertion is implemented and then the deletion algorithm is examined.

A red-black tree is a good alternative to the AVL tree. The coding details tend to give a faster implementation because a single top-down pass can be used during the insertion and deletion routines. Consecutive red nodes are disallowed, and all paths have the same number of black nodes.

Red nodes are shaded throughout this discussion.

The depth of a red-black tree is guaranteed to be logarithmic. Typically, the depth is the same as for an AVL tree.

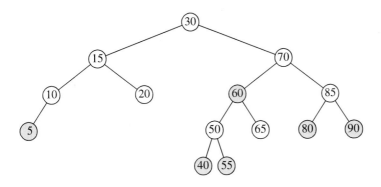

Figure 18.34 Example of a red-black tree; the insertion sequence is 10, 85, 15, 70, 20, 60, 30, 50, 65, 80, 90, 40, 5, 55 (shaded nodes are red)

18.5.1 Bottom-up Insertion

New items must be colored red. If the parent is already red, we must re-color and/or rotate to remove consec-utive red nodes.

Recall that a new item is always inserted as a leaf in the tree. If we color a new item black, then we are certain to violate property 4 because we will create a longer path of black nodes. Thus a new item must be colored red. If the parent is black, we are done; thus the insertion of 25 into the tree in Figure 18.34 is trivial. If the parent is already red, then we will violate property 3 by having consecutive red nodes. In this case, we have to adjust the tree to ensure that property 3 is enforced and do so without introducing a violation of property 4. The basic oper-ations that are used to do this are color changes and tree rotations.

If the parent's sib-ling is black, then a single or double ro-tation fixes things, in the same way as an AVL tree.

There are several cases (each with a mirror-image symmetry) to consider if the parent is red. First, suppose the sibling of the parent is black (we adopt the con-vention that `null` nodes are black). This would apply for the insertions of 3 or 8 but not for the insertion of 99. Let X be the newly added leaf, P be its parent, S be the sibling of the parent (if it exists), and G be the grandparent. Only X and P are red in this case. G is black because otherwise there would be two consecutive red nodes *prior* to the insertion — a violation of property 3. Adopting the AVL tree terminology, we say that relative to G, X can be either an outside or inside node. If X is an outside grandchild, then a single rotation of its parent and grandparent along with some color changes will restore property 3. If X is an inside grandchild, then a double rotation along with some color changes suffices. The single rotation is shown in Figure 18.35; the double rotation is shown in Figure 18.36. Even though X is a leaf, we have drawn a more general case that allows X to be in the middle of the tree. This more general rotation will be used later in the chapter.

Before continuing, notice why these rotations are correct. We need to be sure that there are never two consecutive red nodes. In Figure 18.36, for instance, it is easy to see that the only possible instances of consecutive red nodes would be between P and one of its children or between G and C. But the roots of A, B, and C must be black; otherwise, there would have been additional property 3 viola-tions in the original tree. In the original tree, there is one black node on the path from the subtree root to A, B, and C and two black nodes on the paths to D and E. It is easy to check that this is still the case after the rotation and recoloring.

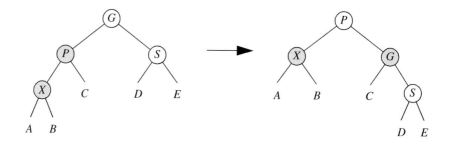

Figure 18.35 If *S* is black, then a single rotation between the parent and grandparent, with appropriate color changes, restores property 3 if *X* is an outside grandchild

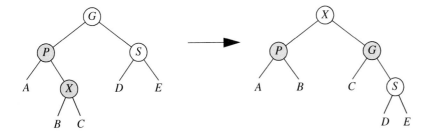

Figure 18.36 If *S* is black, then a double rotation involving *X*, the parent, and the grandparent, with appropriate color changes, restores property 3 if *X* is an inside grandchild

So far so good. But what happens if *S* is red, as when we attempt to insert 79 into the tree in Figure 18.34? Then neither the single nor the double rotation works because both result in consecutive red nodes. In fact, it is easy to see that in this case three nodes must be on the path to *D* and *E* and only one can be black. This tells us that both *S* and the subtree's new root must be colored red. For instance, the single rotation case that occurs when *X* is an outside grandchild is shown in Figure 18.37. Although this seems to work, there is a problem: What happens if the parent of the subtree root (that is, *X*'s original great grandparent) is also red? We could percolate this procedure up toward the root until we no longer have two consecutive red nodes or we reach the root (which will be recolored black). But then we would be back to making a pass up the tree, as in the AVL tree.

If the parent's sibling is red, then after we fix things, we will induce consecutive red nodes at a higher level. We would need to iterate up the tree to fix things.

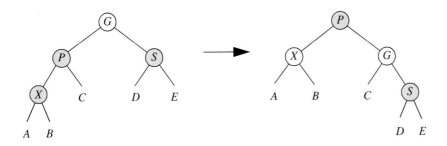

Figure 18.37 If *S* is red, then a single rotation between the parent and grandparent, with appropriate color changes, restores property 3 between *X* and *P*

Figure 18.38   Color flip; only if *X*'s parent is red do we continue with a rotation

18.5.2 Top-down Red-Black Trees

To avoid iterating
back up the tree,
we ensure as we
descend the tree
that the sibling's
parent is not red.
This can be done
with color flips and/
or rotations.

To avoid the possibility of having to rotate up the tree, we apply a top-down procedure as we are searching for the insertion point. Specifically, we guarantee that
when we arrive at a leaf and insert a node, S will not be red. Then we can just add
a red leaf and if necessary use exactly one rotation (either single or double). The
procedure is conceptually easy.

On the way down, when we see a node X that has two red children, we make
X red and its two children black. Figure 18.38 shows this color flip. It is easy to
see that the number of black nodes on paths below X remains unchanged. However, if X's parent is red, we will introduce two consecutive red nodes. But in this
case, we can apply either the single rotation in Figure 18.35 or the double rotation
in Figure 18.36. But what if X's parent's sibling is also red? *This cannot happen.*
If on the way down the tree we see a node Y that has two red children, we know
that Y's grandchildren must be black. And since Y's children are also made black
via the color flip, even after the rotation that may occur, we will not see another
red node for two levels. Thus when we see X, if X's parent is red, then it is not
possible for X's parent's sibling to be red also.

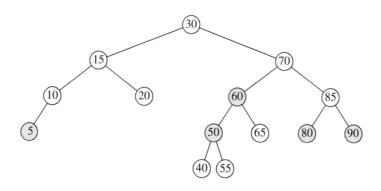

Figure 18.39   Color flip at 50 induces a violation; because the violation is outside, a single rotation fixes it

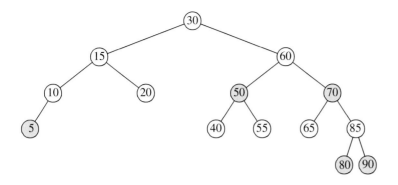

Figure 18.40   Result of single rotation that fixes the violation at node 50

As an example, suppose we want to insert 45 into the tree in Figure 18.34. On the way down the tree, we see node 50, which has two red children. Thus we perform a color flip, making 50 red and 40 and 55 black. The result is shown in Figure 18.39. However, now 50 and 60 are both red. We perform a single rotation (because 50 is an outside node) between 60 and 70, thus making 60 the black root of 30's right subtree and 70 red. This is shown in Figure 18.40. We then continue, performing an identical action if we see other nodes on the path that contain two red children. It happens that there are none.

When we get to the leaf, we insert 45 as a red node, and since the parent is black, we are done. The resulting tree is shown in Figure 18.41. Had the parent been red, we would have needed to perform one rotation.

As Figure 18.41 shows, the red-black tree that results is frequently very well balanced. Experiments suggest that the number of nodes traversed during an average red-black tree search is almost identical to the average for AVL trees, even though the red-black tree's balancing properties are slightly weaker. The advantage of a red-black tree is the relatively low overhead required to perform insertion and the fact that, in practice, rotations occur relatively infrequently.

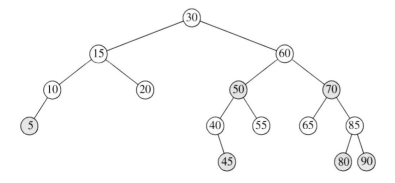

Figure 18.41   Insertion of 45 as a red node

18.5.3   Java Implementation

We remove special
cases by using a
sentinel for the
null reference
and a pseudo-root.
This requires minor
modifications of al-
most every routine.

An actual implementation is complicated not only by the host of possible rotations. It is also complicated by the possibility that some subtrees (such as 10's
right subtree) might be empty and by the special case of dealing with the root
(which among other things, has no parent). To remove special cases, we use two
sentinels:

- nullNode is used in place of a null reference. nullNode will always
  be colored black.
- header will be used as a pseudo-root. It will have key value −∞ and a
  right child that references the real root.

On the way down,
we maintain refer-
ences to the cur-
rent, parent, grand-
parent, and great-
grandparent nodes.

Because of this, even basic routines such as isEmpty need to be altered.
Consequently, it does not make sense to inherit from BinarySearchTree.
The class is thus written from scratch. Its public part is shown in Figure 18.42,
and its private section is shown in Figure 18.43 (page 524). Recall that, by
default, the BinaryNode constructor sets the color field to 1. Hence, BLACK
must be 1. Lines 59 and 60 declare the sentinels that were discussed previously.
Four references — current, parent, grand, and great — are used in the
insert routine. Their placement as static fields (at lines 66 to 69) indicates that
they are essentially global variables. This is because, as will be shown shortly, it
is convenient to have them shared by insert and the routine
handleReorient. remove is unimplemented.

All of the remaining routines are similar to their BinarySearchTree
counterparts, except that they have different implementations because of the sentinel nodes. The constructor must be provided with the value of −∞.
makeEmpty and isEmpty, shown at lines 45 to 48, require using nullNode
(rather than null) and header.right (rather than the typical root).

The RedBlackTree constructor is shown in Figure 18.44 (page 524). It
merely allocates the two sentinels and sets all their left and right children
references to nullNode. A static initializer is used to construct and initialize
nullNode.

Tests against null
are replaced by
tests against
nullNode. When
performing a find,
we place x into the
nullNode senti-
nel so as to avoid
extra tests.

Figure 18.45 (page 525) shows the simplest change that results from the use
of the sentinels. The test against null is replaced by a test against nullNode.
findMin is shown in Figure 18.46 (page 525).

The find routine shown in Figure 18.47 (page 526) uses another common
trick. Before we begin the search, we place x in the nullNode sentinel. Thus we
are guaranteed to match x eventually, even if x is not found. If the match occurs
at nullNode, we can tell that the item was not found. We will use this trick in
the insert method.

```
1  package DataStructures;
2
3  import Supporting.*;
4  import Exceptions.*;
5
6  // RedBlackTree class
7  //
8  // CONSTRUCTION: with a negative infinity sentinel
9  //
10 // ******************PUBLIC OPERATIONS*********************
11 // void insert( x )         --> Insert x
12 // void remove( x )         --> Remove x
13 // void removeMin( )        --> Remove smallest item
14 // Comparable find( x )     --> Return item that matches x
15 // Comparable findMin( )    --> Return smallest item
16 // Comparable findMax( )    --> Return largest item
17 // boolean isEmpty( )       --> Return true if empty; else false
18 // void makeEmpty( )        --> Remove all items
19 // void printTree( )        --> Print tree in sorted order
20 // ******************ERRORS********************************
21 // Most routines throw ItemNotFound on various conditions
22 // insert throws DuplicateItem if item is already in the tree
23
24 /**
25  * Implements a red-black tree.
26  * Note that all "matching" is based on the compares method.
27  */
28 public class RedBlackTree implements SearchTree
29 {
30     public RedBlackTree( Comparable negInf )
31       { /* Figure 18.44 */ }
32
33     public void insert( Comparable x ) throws DuplicateItem
34       { /* Figure 18.48 */ }
35     public void remove( Comparable x ) throws ItemNotFound
36       { /* Not implemented */ }
37     public void removeMin( ) throws ItemNotFound
38       { /* Not implemented */ }
39     public Comparable findMin( ) throws ItemNotFound
40       { /* Figure 18.46 */ }
41     public Comparable findMax( ) throws ItemNotFound
42       { /* Similar to findMin */ }
43     public Comparable find( Comparable x ) throws ItemNotFound
44       { /* Figure 18.47 */ }
45     public boolean isEmpty( )
46       { return header.right == nullNode; }
47     public void makeEmpty( )
48       { header.right = nullNode; }
49     public void printTree( )
50       { printTree( header.right ); }
```

Figure 18.42   RedBlackTree class skeleton (part 1: public section)

```
51      private void printTree( BinaryNode t )
52          { /* Figure 18.45 */ }
53      private void handleReorient( Comparable item )
54          { /* Figure 18.49 */ }
55      private BinaryNode rotate( Comparable item,
56                                          BinaryNode parent )
57          { /* Figure 18.50 */ }
58
59      private BinaryNode header;
60      private static BinaryNode nullNode;
61
62      private static final int BLACK = 1;      // BLACK must be 1
63      private static final int RED   = 0;
64
65          // Used in insert routine and its helpers
66      private static BinaryNode current;
67      private static BinaryNode parent;
68      private static BinaryNode grand;
69      private static BinaryNode great;
70  }
```

Figure 18.43 RedBlackTree class skeleton (part 2: private section)

The code is relatively compact, if one considers the host of cases and the fact that the implementation is nonrecursive. This is why the red-black tree performs well.

The insert method follows directly from our description and is shown in Figure 18.48 (page 527). The while loop encompassing lines 12 to 21 descends the tree and fixes nodes that have two red children by calling handleReorient, as shown in Figure 18.49 (page 528). To do this, it keeps track of not only the current node but also the parent, grandparent, and great-grandparent. Note that after a rotation, the values stored in the grandparent and great-grandparent are no longer correct. However, we are assured that they will be restored by the time they are next needed.

```
1       /**
2        * Construct the tree.
3        * @param negInf a value less than or equal to all others.
4        */
5       public RedBlackTree( Comparable negInf )
6       {
7           header       = new BinaryNode( negInf );
8           header.left = header.right = nullNode;
9       }
10
11      static           // Static initializer for nullNode
12      {
13          nullNode = new BinaryNode( null );
14          nullNode.left = nullNode.right = nullNode;
15      }
```

Figure 18.44 RedBlackTree constructor and static initializer

```
1       /**
2        * Internal method to print a subtree in sorted order.
3        * @param t the node that roots the tree.
4        */
5       private void printTree( BinaryNode t )
6       {
7           if( t != nullNode )
8           {
9               printTree( t.left );
10              System.out.println( t.element.toString( ) );
11              printTree( t.right );
12          }
13      }
```

Figure 18.45 `printTree` for RedBlackTree class

When the loop ends, either x is found (as indicated by `current!=nullNode`) or x is not found. If x is found, we throw an exception at line 25. Otherwise, x is not already in the tree, so it needs to be made a child of `parent`. We allocate a new node (as the new `current` node), attach it to the parent, and call `handleReorient` at lines 26 to 33.

The code used to perform a single rotation is shown in the method `rotate` in Figure 18.50 (page 528). Because the resultant tree must be attached to a parent, `rotate` takes the parent node as a parameter. Rather than keep track of the type of rotation (that is, left or right) as we descend the tree, we pass x as a parameter. Since we expect very few rotations during the insertion, doing it this way turns out to be not only simple but actually faster.

rotate has four possibilities. The ?: operator collapses the code, but it is logically equivalent to an if else test.

```
1       /**
2        * Find the smallest item in the tree.
3        * @return the smallest item.
4        * @exception ItemNotFound if the tree is empty.
5        */
6       public Comparable findMin( ) throws ItemNotFound
7       {
8           if( isEmpty( ) )
9               throw new ItemNotFound( "RedBlackTree findMin" );
10
11          BinaryNode itr = header.right;
12          while( itr.left != nullNode )
13              itr = itr.left;
14
15          return itr.element;
16      }
```

Figure 18.46 `findMin` for red-black trees; note the use of `header` and `nullNode`

```
1      /**
2       * Find an item in the tree.
3       * @param x the item to search for.
4       * @return the matching item.
5       * @exception ItemNotFound if no item
6       *           that matches x can be found in the tree.
7       */
8      public Comparable find( Comparable x ) throws ItemNotFound
9      {
10         nullNode.element = x;
11         current = header.right;
12
13         for( ; ; )
14         {
15             if( x.lessThan( current.element ) )
16                 current = current.left;
17             else if( current.element.lessThan( x ) )
18                 current = current.right;
19             else if( current != nullNode )
20                 return current.element;
21             else
22                 throw new ItemNotFound( "RedBlack find" );
23         }
24     }
```

Figure 18.47   Red-black tree `find`; note the use of `header` and `nullNode`

handleReorient calls rotate as necessary to perform either a single or double rotation. Since a double rotation is just two single rotations, we can test if we have an inside case, and if so, do an extra rotation between the current node and its parent (by passing the grandparent to rotate). In either case, we rotate between the parent and grandparent (by passing the great-grandparent to rotate). This is succinctly coded in lines 16 to 19 of Figure 18.49.

18.5.4   Top-down Deletion

Deletion in red-black trees can also be performed top-down. Needless to say, an actual implementation is fairly complicated because the remove algorithm for unbalanced search trees is nontrivial in the first place. The normal binary search tree deletion algorithm removes nodes that are leaves or have one child. Recall that nodes with two children are never removed; their contents are just replaced.

If the deleted node is red, then there is no problem. However, if the node that is to be deleted is black, then its removal will violate property 4. The solution to the problem is to ensure that any node we are about to delete is red.

Throughout this discussion, let X be the current node, T be its sibling, and P be their parent. We begin by coloring the sentinel root red. As we traverse down the tree, we attempt to ensure that X is red. When we arrive at a new node, we are

Deletion is fairly complex. The basic idea is to make sure that the deleted node is red.

certain that P is red (inductively, by the invariant we are trying to maintain) and that X and T are black (because we cannot have two consecutive red nodes). There are two main cases, plus the usual symmetric variants (which are omitted).

First, suppose that X has two black children. There are three subcases, which depend on T's children:

1. T has two black children: Flip colors (Figure 18.51, page 529).
2. T has an outer red child: Perform a single rotation (Figure 18.52, page 529).
3. T has an inner red child: Perform a double rotation (Figure 18.53, page 529).

```
1      /**
2       * Insert into the tree.
3       * @param x the item to insert.
4       * @exception DuplicateItem if an item
5       *        that matches x is already in the tree.
6       */
7      public void insert( Comparable x ) throws DuplicateItem
8      {
9          current = parent = grand = header;
10         nullNode.element = x;
11
12         while( current.element.compares( x ) != 0 )
13         {
14             great = grand; grand = parent; parent = current;
15             current = x.lessThan( current.element ) ?
16                          current.left : current.right;
17
18                 // Check if two red children; fix if so
19             if( current.left.color == RED && current.right.color == RED )
20                 handleReorient( x );
21         }
22
23             // insert fails if already present
24         if( current != nullNode )
25             throw new DuplicateItem( "RedBlackTree insert" );
26         current = new BinaryNode( x, nullNode, nullNode );
27
28             // Attach to parent
29         if( x.lessThan( parent.element ) )
30             parent.left = current;
31         else
32             parent.right = current;
33         handleReorient( x );
34      }
```

Figure 18.48 insert routine for RedBlackTree

```
1    /**
2     * Called during an insert if a node has two red children.
3     * Perform color flips and rotations.
4     * @param item the item being inserted.
5     */
6    private void handleReorient( Comparable item )
7    {
8            // Do the color flip
9        current.color = RED;
10       current.left.color = BLACK;
11       current.right.color = BLACK;
12
13       if( parent.color == RED )    // Have to rotate
14       {
15           grand.color = RED;
16           if( item.lessThan( grand.element ) !=
17                           item.lessThan( parent.element ) )
18               parent = rotate( item, grand ); // Dbl rotate
19           current = rotate( item, great );
20           current.color = BLACK;
21       }
22       header.right.color = BLACK; // Make root black
23   }
```

Figure 18.49 `handleReorient`: called if a node has two red children or when a new node is inserted

```
1    /**
2     * Internal routine that performs a single rotation.
3     * Called by handleReorient.
4     * @param item the item in handleReorient.
5     * @param parent parent of the root of rotated subtree.
6     * @return the root of the rotated subtree.
7     */
8    private BinaryNode
9    rotate( Comparable item, BinaryNode parent )
10   {
11       if( item.lessThan( parent.element ) )
12           return parent.left = item.lessThan(
13                                   parent.left.element ) ?
14           Rotations.withLeftChild( parent.left )   ://  LL
15           Rotations.withRightChild( parent.left ) ;// LR
16       else
17           return parent.right = item.lessThan(
18                                   parent.right.element ) ?
19           Rotations.withLeftChild( parent.right ) ://  RL
20           Rotations.withRightChild( parent.right );// RR
21   }
```

Figure 18.50 Routine to perform the appropriate rotation

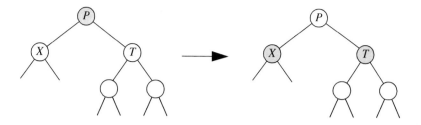

Figure 18.51 *X* has two black children, and both of its sibling's children are black; do a color flip

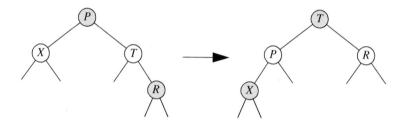

Figure 18.52 *X* has two black children, and the outer child of its sibling is red; do a single rotation

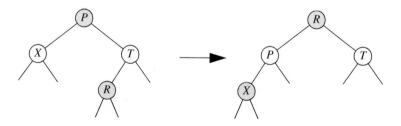

Figure 18.53 *X* has two black children, and the inner child of its sibling is red; do a double rotation

Examination of the rotations shows that if *T* has two red children, either a single rotation or double rotation will work (so it makes sense to do the single rotation). Notice carefully that if *X* is a leaf, then its two children are black, so we can always apply one of these three mechanisms to make *X* red.

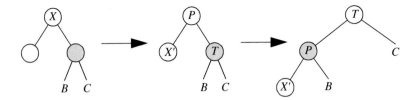

Figure 18.54   *X* is black and at least one child is red; if we fall through to the next level and land on a red child, everything is good; if not, we rotate a sibling and parent

The second main case is that one of *X*'s children is red. Notice that since the rotations in the first main case always color *X* red, then if *X* has a red child, we would introduce consecutive red nodes. Thus we need an alternative solution. In this case, we fall through to the next level, thus obtaining a new *X*, *T*, and *P*. If we are lucky, we will fall onto a red node (we have at least a 50 percent chance that this will happen), thereby making the new current node red. Otherwise, we have the situation shown in Figure 18.54. That is, the current *X* is black, the current *T* is red, and the current *P* is black. We can then rotate *T* and *P*, thereby making *X*'s new parent red; *X* and its new grandparent are black. Now *X* is not yet red, but we are back to the starting point (although one level deeper). This is good enough because it shows that we can iteratively descend the tree. Thus, as long as we eventually either reach a node that has two black children or land on a red node, we win. This is guaranteed for the deletion algorithm, since the two eventual states are as follows:

- *X* is a leaf. This situation is always handled by the main case, since it has two black children.
- *X* has only one child. If the child is black, the main case applies, and if it is red, we can delete *X*, if necessary, and make the child black.

Lazy deletion, in which deleted items are merely marked as deleted, is sometimes used. However, lazy deletion wastes space and complicates other routines (see Exercise 18.24).

18.6 AA-Trees

The *AA-tree* is the method of choice when a balanced tree is needed, a casual implementation is acceptable, and deletions are needed.

Because of a host of possible rotations, the red-black tree is fairly tricky to code. In particular, the `remove` operation is quite challenging. This section describes a simple but competitive balanced search tree known as an *AA-tree*. The AA-tree is the method of choice when a balanced tree is needed, a casual implementation is acceptable, and deletions are needed. The AA-tree adds one extra condition to the red-black tree: Left children may not be red.

This simple restriction greatly simplifies the red-black tree algorithms for two reasons. First, it eliminates about half of the restructuring cases. Second, it simplifies the `remove` algorithm by removing an annoying case. That is, if an internal node has only one child, the child must be a red right child because red left children are now illegal, while a single black child would violate property 4 for red-black trees. Thus we can always replace an internal node with the smallest node in its right subtree. That smallest node will either be a leaf or have a red child and can be easily bypassed and removed.

To simplify the implementation further, we represent balance information in a more direct way. Instead of storing a color with each node, we store the node's *level*. The level of a node is the following:

- Level 1 if the node is a leaf
- The level of its parent, if the node is red
- One less than the level of its parent, if the node is black

> The *level* of a node in an AA-tree represents the number of left links on the path to the `nullNode` sentinel.

The level represents the number of left links on the path to the `nullNode` sentinel.

The result is an *AA-tree*. If we translate the structure requirement from colors to levels, we know that the left child must be one level lower than its parent and the right child may be zero or one level lower than its parent (but not more). A *horizontal link* is a connection between a node and a child of equal levels. The coloring properties imply the following:

> A *horizontal link* in an AA-tree is a connection between a node and a child of equal levels. A horizontal link should go only right, and there should not be two consecutive horizontal links.

1. Horizontal links are right references (because only right children may be red).
2. There may not be two consecutive horizontal links (because there cannot be consecutive red nodes).
3. Nodes at level 2 or higher must have two children.
4. If a node does not have a right horizontal link, then its two children are at the same level.

Figure 18.55 shows a sample AA-tree. The root of this tree is the node with key 30. Searching is done using the usual algorithm. And as usual, `insert` and `remove` are more difficult because the natural binary search tree algorithms may induce a violation of the horizontal link properties. Not surprisingly, it turns out that tree rotations can fix all problems.

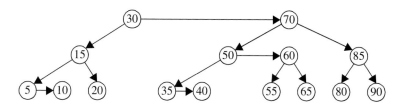

Figure 18.55   AA-tree resulting from the insertion of 10, 85, 15, 70, 20, 60, 30, 50, 65, 80, 90, 40, 5, 55, 35

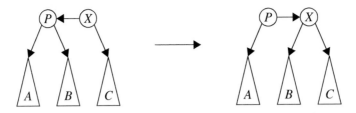

Figure 18.56 skew is a simple rotation between *X* and *P*

18.6.1 Insertion

Insertion is done by the usual recursive algorithm plus two method calls.

Left horizontal links are removed by a skew (rotation between a node and its left child). Consecutive right horizontal links are fixed by a split (rotation between a node and its right child). skew precedes split.

Insertion of a new item is always done at the bottom level. As usual, this may create problems. In Figure 18.55, insertion of 2 would create a horizontal left link, while insertion of 45 would generate consecutive right links. Consequently, after a node is added at the bottom level, we may need to perform some rotations to restore the horizontal link properties.

In both cases, a single rotation fixes the problem. We remove left horizontal links by rotating between the node and its left child, and we fix consecutive right horizontal links by rotating between the first and second (of the three) nodes joined by the two links. These procedures are called skew and split, respectively.

skew is illustrated in Figure 18.56 and split is illustrated in Figure 18.57. A skew removes a left horizontal link. However, it might create consecutive right horizontal links because *X*'s right child might also be horizontal. Thus we would process first a skew and then a split. After a split, the middle node increases in level. This may cause problems for the original parent of *X* by creating either a left horizontal link or consecutive right horizontal links: Both problems can be fixed by applying the skew/split strategy on the path up toward the root. This is done automatically if we use recursion, so a recursive implementation of insert is only two method calls longer than the corresponding unbalanced search tree routine.

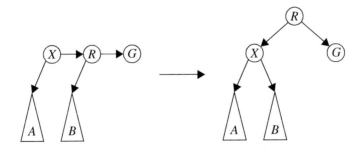

Figure 18.57 split is a simple rotation between *X* and *R*; note that *R*'s level increases

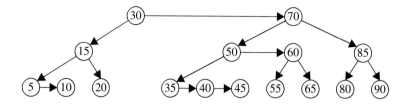

Figure 18.58   After inserting 45 into the sample tree; consecutive horizontal links
are introduced starting at 35

To see the algorithm in action, we show the result of inserting 45 into the AA-tree in Figure 18.55. In Figure 18.58 when 45 is added at the bottom level, consecutive horizontal links form. skew/split pairs are applied as necessary from the bottom up toward the root. Thus, at node 35 a split is needed because of the consecutive horizontal right links. The result of the split is shown in Figure 18.59. When the recursion backs up to node 50, we see a horizontal left link. Thus we perform a skew at 50 to remove the horizontal left link (the result is shown in Figure 18.60, page 534) and then a split at 40 to remove the consecutive horizontal right links. The result after the split is shown in Figure 18.61 (page 534). The result of the split is that 50 is on level 3 and is a left horizontal child of 70. Therefore we need to perform another skew/split pair. The skew at 70 removes the left horizontal link at the top level but creates consecutive right horizontal nodes, as shown in Figure 18.62 (page 534). When the final split is applied, the consecutive horizontal nodes are removed and 50 becomes the new root of the tree. The result is shown in Figure 18.63 (page 534).

This is a rare algorithm because it is harder to simulate on paper than implement on a computer.

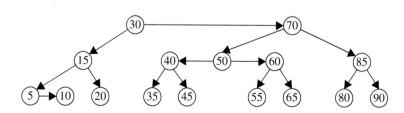

Figure 18.59   After split at 35; introduces a left horizontal link at 50

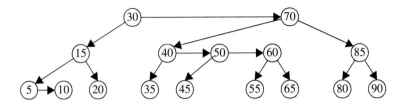

Figure 18.60   After `skew` at 50; introduces consecutive horizontal nodes starting at 40

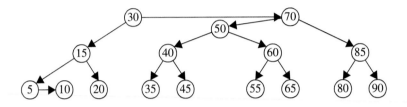

Figure 18.61   After `split` at 40; 50 is now on the same level as 70, thus inducing an illegal left horizontal link

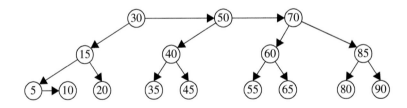

Figure 18.62   After `skew` at 70; this introduces consecutive horizontal links at 30

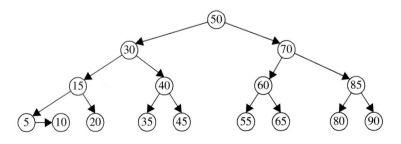

Figure 18.63   After `split` at 30; insertion is complete

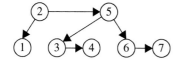

Figure 18.64 When 1 is deleted, all nodes become level 1, thereby introducing horizontal left links

```
 1  package DataStructures;
 2
 3  import Supporting.*;
 4  import Exceptions.*;
 5
 6  // AATree class
 7  //
 8  // CONSTRUCTION: with no initializer
 9  //
10  // ******************PUBLIC OPERATIONS*********************
11  // Same as BinarySearchTree; omitted for brevity
12  // ******************ERRORS******************************
13  // Most routines throw ItemNotFound on various conditions
14  // insert throws DuplicateItem if item is already in the tree
15
16  /**
17   * Implements an AA-tree.
18   * Note that all "matching" is based on the compares method.
19   */
20  public class AATree implements SearchTree
21  {
22      public AATree( )
23        { root = nullNode; }
24
25      public void insert( Comparable x ) throws DuplicateItem
26        { root = insert( x, root ); }
27      public void remove( Comparable x ) throws ItemNotFound
28        { root = remove( x, root ); }
29      public void removeMin( ) throws ItemNotFound
30        { remove( findMin( ) ); }
31      public Comparable findMin( ) throws ItemNotFound
32        { /* Implementation is as usual; see online code */ }
33      public Comparable findMax( ) throws ItemNotFound
34        { /* Implementation is as usual; see online code */ }
35      public Comparable find( Comparable x ) throws ItemNotFound
36        { /* Implementation is as usual; see remove code */ }
37      public boolean isEmpty( )
38        { return root == nullNode; }
39      public void makeEmpty( )
40        { root = nullNode; }
41      public void printTree( )
42        { /* Implementation is as usual; see online code */ }
```

Figure 18.65 Class skeleton for AA-trees (part 1)

18.6.2 Deletion

Deletion is made easier because the one-child case can occur only at level 1 and we are willing to use recursion.

For general binary search trees, the `remove` algorithm is broken down into three cases: The item to be removed either is a leaf, has one child, or has two children. For AA-trees, we treat the one-child case the same way as the two-child case because the one-child case can occur only at level 1. Furthermore, the two-child case is also easy in that the node used as the replacement value is guaranteed to be at level 1 and at worst has only a right horizontal link. Thus everything boils down to being able to `remove` a level-1 node. Clearly this might affect the balance (consider, for instance, the removal of 20 in Figure 18.63).

Let T be the current node and assume that we are using recursion. If the deletion has altered one of T's children to two less than T's level, then T's level needs to be lowered also (only the child entered by the recursive call could actually be affected, but for simplicity, we do not keep track of it). Furthermore, if T has a horizontal right link, then its right child's level must also be lowered. At this point, we could have six nodes on the same level: T, T's horizontal right child R, R's two children, and those children's horizontal right children. Figure 18.64 (page 535) shows the simplest possible scenario.

```
43        private BinaryNode
44        insert( Comparable x, BinaryNode t ) throws DuplicateItem
45            { /* Figure 18.67 */ }
46        private BinaryNode
47        remove( Comparable x, BinaryNode t ) throws ItemNotFound
48            { /* Figure 18.70 */ }
49        private void printTree( BinaryNode t )
50            { /* Implementation is as usual; see online code */ }
51        private BinaryNode skew( BinaryNode t )
52            { /* Figure 18.69 */ }
53        private BinaryNode split( BinaryNode t )
54            { /* Figure 18.69 */ }
55
56        private BinaryNode root;
57        private static BinaryNode nullNode;
58            static          // Static initializer for nullNode
59            {
60                nullNode = new BinaryNode( null );
61                nullNode.left = nullNode.right = nullNode;
62                nullNode.level = 0;
63            }
64
65        private static BinaryNode deletedNode;
66        private static BinaryNode lastNode;
67    }
```

Figure 18.66 Class skeleton for AA-trees (part 2)

After node 1 is removed, node 2 and thus node 5 become level-1 nodes. First, we must fix the left horizontal link that is now introduced between nodes 5 and 3. This essentially requires two rotations: one between nodes 5 and 3 and then one between nodes 5 and 4. In this case, the current node T is not involved. On the other hand, if a deletion came from the right side, then T's left node could suddenly become horizontal; that would require a similar double rotation (starting at T). To avoid testing all these cases, we just call skew three times. Once we have done that, two calls to split suffice to rearrange the horizontal edges.

After a recursive removal, three skews plus two splits will guarantee rebalancing.

18.6.3   Java Implementation

The class skeleton for the AA-tree is shown in Figures 18.65 (page 535) and 18.66. Much of it duplicates previous tree implementations. Once again we use a nullNode sentinel; however, we do not need a pseudoroot. The constructor, which is not shown, allocates nullNode, as was done for red-black trees, and has root reference it. nullNode is at level 0. The routines use private helpers.

The AA routines are relatively simple (compared to the red-black tree)

insert is shown in Figure 18.67. As mentioned earlier in the chapter, it is identical to the recursive binary search tree insert, except that it adds a call to skew followed by a call to split. In Figures 18.68 (page 538) and 18.69 (page 538), skew and split are easily implemented using the already existing tree rotations. Finally, remove is shown in Figure 18.70 (page 539).

```
1       /**
2        * Internal method to insert into a subtree.
3        * @param x the item to insert.
4        * @param t the node that roots the tree.
5        * @return the new root.
6        * @exception DuplicateItem if item that
7        *          matches x is already in the subtree rooted at t.
8        */
9       private BinaryNode
10      insert( Comparable x, BinaryNode t ) throws DuplicateItem
11      {
12          if( t == nullNode )
13              t = new BinaryNode( x, nullNode, nullNode );
14          else if( x.compares( t.element ) < 0 )
15              t.left = insert( x, t.left );
16          else if( x.compares( t.element ) > 0 )
17              t.right = insert( x, t.right );
18          else
19              throw new DuplicateItem( "SearchTree insert" );
20
21          t = skew( t );
22          t = split( t );
23          return t;
24      }
```

Figure 18.67   insert for the AATree class

```
1      /**
2       * Skew primitive for AA-trees.
3       * @param t the node that roots the tree.
4       * @return the new root after the rotation.
5       */
6      private BinaryNode skew( BinaryNode t )
7      {
8          if( t.left.level == t.level )
9              t = Rotations.withLeftChild( t );
10         return t;
11     }
```

Figure 18.68 skew for the AATree class

deletedNode will reference the node containing x (if x is found) or nullNode if x is not found. lastNode references the replacement node. We use two-way comparisons instead of three-way comparisons.

To help us out, we keep two variables, deletedNode and lastNode, that have lifetime scope by virtue of their static declaration. When we traverse a right child, we adjust deletedNode. Because we call remove recursively until we reach the bottom (we do not test for equality on the way down), we are guaranteed that if the item to be removed is in the tree, then deletedNode will be referencing the node that contains it. Notice that this technique can be used in the find procedure to replace the three-way comparisons done at each node with two-way comparisons at each node plus one extra equality test at the bottom. lastNode references the level-1 node at which this search terminates. Because we do not stop until we reach the bottom, if the item is in the tree, then lastNode will reference the level-1 node that contains the replacement value and must be removed from the tree.

After a given recursive call terminates, either we are at level 1 or we are not. If we are at level 1, we can place the node's value into the internal node that is to be replaced; we can then bypass the level-1 node. Otherwise, we are at a higher level and we need to check if the balance condition has been violated. If so, we restore the balance and then make three calls to skew and two calls to split. As discussed previously, this guarantees that the AA-tree properties will be restored.

```
1      /**
2       * Split primitive for AA-trees.
3       * @param t the node that roots the tree.
4       * @return the new root after the rotation.
5       */
6      private BinaryNode split( BinaryNode t )
7      {
8          if( t.right.right.level == t.level )
9          {
10             t = Rotations.withRightChild( t );
11             t.level++;
12         }
13         return t;
14     }
```

Figure 18.69 split for the AATree class

```
 1       /**
 2        * Internal method to remove from a subtree.
 3        * @param x the item to remove.
 4        * @param t the node that roots the tree.
 5        * @return the new root.
 6        * @exception ItemNotFound no item that
 7        *          matches x is in the subtree rooted at t.
 8        */
 9      private BinaryNode
10      remove( Comparable x, BinaryNode t ) throws ItemNotFound
11      {
12          if( t != nullNode )
13          {
14              // Step 1: Search down the tree and set
15              //         lastNode and deletedNode
16              lastNode = t;
17              if( x.lessThan( t.element ) )
18                  t.left = remove( x, t.left );
19              else
20              {
21                  deletedNode = t;
22                  t.right = remove( x, t.right );
23              }
24              // Step 2: If at the bottom of the tree and
25              //         x is present, we remove it
26              if( t == lastNode )
27              {
28                  if( deletedNode == nullNode ||
29                      x.compares( deletedNode.element ) != 0 )
30                      throw new ItemNotFound( "AATree remove" );
31                  deletedNode.element = t.element;
32                  deletedNode = nullNode;
33                  t = t.right;
34              }
35              // Step 3: Otherwise, we are not at the bottom;
36              //         rebalance
37              else
38                  if( t.left.level < t.level - 1 ||
39                      t.right.level < t.level - 1 )
40                  {
41                      if( t.right.level > --t.level )
42                          t.right.level = t.level;
43                      t = skew( t );
44                      t.right = skew( t.right );
45                      t.right.right = skew( t.right.right );
46                      t = split( t );
47                      t.right = split( t.right );
48                  }
49          }
50          return t;
51      }
```

Figure 18.70 Deletion for the AA-tree

18.7 B-Trees

So far we have assumed that we can store an entire data structure in the main memory of a computer. Suppose, however, that we have more data than can fit in main memory, so we must have the data structure reside on disk. When this happens, the rules of the game change because the Big-Oh model is no longer meaningful.

The problem is that a Big-Oh analysis assumes that all operations are equal. However, this is not true, especially when disk I/O is involved. For example, a 25-MIPS machine allegedly executes 25 million instructions per second. That is pretty fast, mainly because the speed depends largely on electrical properties. On the other hand, a disk is mechanical. Its speed depends largely on the time it takes to spin the disk and to move a disk head. Most disks spin at 3,600 RPM (faster disks spin at 5,400 RPM). Thus in 1 min, it makes 3,600 revolutions; hence, one revolution occurs in 1/60 of a second, or 16.7 ms. On average, we might expect that we have to spin a disk halfway to find what we are looking for, so if we ignore other factors, we get an access time of 8.3 ms. This is a very charitable estimate; 9-11 ms access times are more common. Consequently, we can do approximately 120 disk accesses per second. This sounds pretty good, until we compare it with the processor speed. What we have is 25 million instructions equal to 120 disk accesses. Put another way, one disk access is worth about 200,000 instructions. Of course, everything here is a rough calculation, but the relative speeds are pretty clear: Disk accesses are incredibly expensive. Furthermore, processor speeds are increasing at a much faster rate than disk speeds (it is disk *sizes* that are increasing quite quickly). So we are willing to do lots of calculations just to save a disk access. In almost all cases, it is the number of disk accesses that will dominate the running time. Thus, if we halve the number of disk accesses, the running time will halve.

Here is how the typical search tree performs on disk. Suppose we want to access the driving records for citizens in the state of Florida. We assume that we have 10,000,000 items, that each key is 32 bytes (representing a name), and that a record is 256 bytes. We assume this does not fit in main memory and that we are 1 of 20 users on a system (so we have 1/20 of the resources). Thus, in 1 sec, we can execute a million instructions or perform six disk accesses.

The unbalanced binary search tree is a disaster. In the worst case, it has linear depth and thus could require 10,000,000 disk accesses. On average, a successful search would require $1.38 \log N$ disk accesses, and since $\log 10000000 \approx 24$, an average search would require 32 disk accesses, or 5 sec. In a typical randomly constructed tree, we would expect that a few nodes are three times as deep; these would require about 100 disk accesses, or 16 sec. A red-black tree is somewhat better. The worst case of $2 \log N$ is unlikely to occur, and the typical case is very close to $\log N$. Thus a red-black tree would use about 25 disk accesses on average, requiring 4 sec.

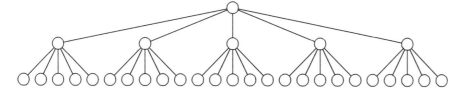

Figure 18.71 5-ary tree of 31 nodes has only three levels

We want to reduce the number of disk accesses to a very small constant, such as three or four. We are willing to write complicated code to do this because machine instructions are essentially free, so long as we are not ridiculously unreasonable. It should probably be clear that a binary search tree will not work, since the typical red-black tree is close to optimal height. We cannot go below $\log N$ using a binary search tree. The solution is intuitively simple: If we have more branching, we have less height. Thus, while a perfect binary tree of 31 nodes has five levels, a 5-ary tree of 31 nodes has only three levels, as shown in Figure 18.71. An *M-ary search tree* allows *M*-way branching. As branching increases, the depth decreases. Whereas a complete binary tree has height that is roughly $\log_2 N$, a complete *M*-ary tree has height that is roughly $\log_M N$.

> An *M-ary search tree* allows *M*-way branching. As branching increases, the depth decreases.

We can create an *M*-ary search tree in much the same way as a binary search tree. In a binary search tree, we need one key to decide which of two branches to take. In an *M*-ary search tree, we need $M - 1$ keys to decide which branch to take. To make this scheme efficient in the worst case, we need to ensure that the *M*-ary search tree is balanced in some way. Otherwise, like a binary search tree, it could degenerate into a linked list. Actually, we want an even more restrictive balancing condition. That is, we do not want an *M*-ary search tree to degenerate to even a binary search tree because then we would be stuck with $\log N$ accesses.

One way to implement this is to use a *B-tree*. The basic B-tree[1] is described here. Many variations and improvements are known, and an implementation is somewhat complex because there are quite a few cases. However, it is easy to see that in principle a B-tree guarantees only a few disk accesses.

> The *B-tree* is the most popular data structure for disk-bound searching.

A B-tree of order *M* is an *M*-ary tree with the following properties:[2]

> The B-tree has five structure properties.

1. The data items are stored at leaves.
2. The nonleaf nodes store up to $M - 1$ keys to guide the searching; key *i* represents the smallest key in subtree $i + 1$.
3. The root is either a leaf or has between two and *M* children.
4. All nonleaf nodes (except the root) have between $\lceil M/2 \rceil$ and *M* children.
5. All leaves are at the same depth and have between $\lceil L/2 \rceil$ and *L* children, for some *L* (the determination of *L* is described shortly).

[1.] What is described is popularly known as a B$^+$ tree.
[2.] Rules 3 and 5 must be relaxed for the first *L* insertions.

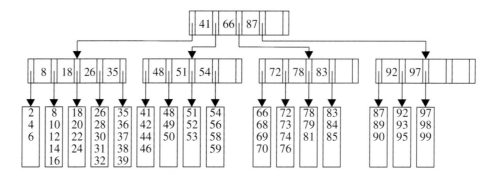

Figure 18.72   B-tree of order 5

Nodes must be half full. This guarantees that the tree does not degenerate into a simple binary or ternary tree.

An example of a B-tree of order 5 is shown in Figure 18.72. Notice that all nonleaf nodes have between three and five children (and thus between two and four keys); the root could possibly have only two children. Here, we have $L = 5$. It happens that L and M are the same in this example, but this is not necessary. Since L is 5, each leaf has between three and five data items. Requiring nodes to be half full guarantees that the B-tree does not degenerate into a simple binary or ternary tree. Although there are various definitions of B-trees that change this structure, mostly in minor ways, this definition is one of the popular forms.

We choose the maximum M and L that allow a node to fit in one disk block.

Each node represents a disk block, so we choose M and L based on the size of the items that are being stored. As an example, suppose one block holds 8,192 bytes. In our Florida example, each key uses 32 bytes. In a B-tree of order M, we would have $M - 1$ keys, for a total of $32M - 32$ bytes, plus M branches. Since each branch is essentially a number of another disk block, we can assume that a branch is 4 bytes. Thus the branches use $4M$ bytes. The total memory requirement for a nonleaf node is thus $36M - 32$. The largest value of M for which this is no more than 8,192 is 228. Thus we would choose $M = 228$. Since each data record is 256 bytes, we would be able to fit 32 records in a block. Thus we would choose $L = 32$. We are guaranteed that each leaf has between 16 and 32 data records and that each internal node (except the root) branches in at least 114 ways. Since there are 10,000,000 records, there are at most 625,000 leaves. Consequently, in the worst case, leaves would be on level 4. In more concrete terms, the worst-case number of accesses is given by approximately $\log_{M/2} N$, give or take 1. (For example, the root and the first level could be cached in main memory, so over the long run disk accesses would be needed only for level 3 and deeper.)

The remaining issue is how to add and remove items from the B-tree. The ideas involved are sketched next. Note that many of the themes seen before recur.

If the leaf contains room for a new item, we insert it and are done.

We begin by examining insertion. Suppose we want to insert 57 into the B-tree in Figure 18.72. A search down the tree reveals that it is not already in the tree. We can add it to the leaf as a fifth child. Note that we may have to reorganize all the data in the leaf to do this. However, the cost of doing this is negligible when compared to that of the disk access, which in this case also includes a disk write.

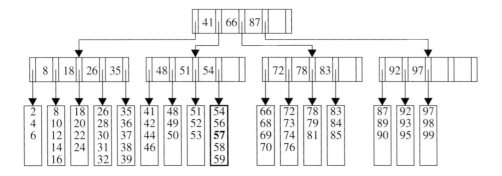

Figure 18.73 B-tree after insertion of 57 into the tree in Figure 18.72

Of course, that was relatively painless because the leaf was not already full. Suppose we now want to insert 55. Figure 18.73 shows a problem: The leaf where 55 wants to go is already full. The solution is simple: Since we now have $L + 1$ items, we split them into two leaves, both guaranteed to have the minimum number of data records needed. We form two leaves with three items each. Two disk accesses are required to write these leaves and a third disk access is required to update the parent. Note that in the parent, both keys and branches change, but they do so in a controlled way that is easily calculated. The resulting B-tree is shown in Figure 18.74. Although splitting nodes is time-consuming because it requires at least two additional disk writes, it is a relatively rare occurrence. If L is 32, for example, then when a node is split, two leaves with 16 and 17 items, respectively, are created. For the leaf with 17 items, we can perform 15 more insertions without another split. Put another way, for every split, there are roughly $L/2$ nonsplits.

If the leaf is full, we can insert a new item by splitting the leaf and forming two half-empty nodes.

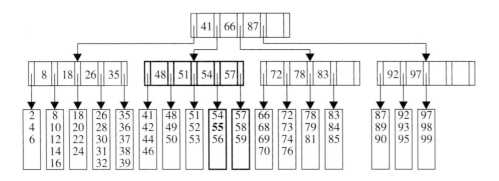

Figure 18.74 Insertion of 55 into the B-tree in Figure 18.73 causes a split into two leaves

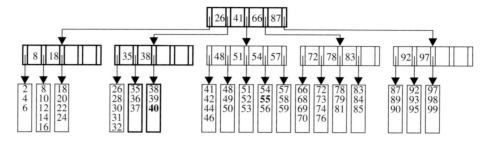

Figure 18.75 Insertion of 40 into the B-tree in Figure 18.74 causes a split into two leaves and then a split of the parent node

Node splitting creates an extra child for the leaf's parent. If the parent already has a full number of children, then we split the parent.

The node splitting in the previous example worked because the parent did not have its full complement of children. But what would happen if it did? Suppose, for example, that we insert 40 into the B-tree in Figure 18.74. We must split the leaf containing the keys 35 through 39 and now 40 into two leaves. But doing this would give the parent six children, and it is allowed only five. The solution is to split the parent. The result of this is shown in Figure 18.75. When the parent is split, we must update the values of the keys and also the parent's parent, thus incurring an additional two disk writes (so this insertion costs five disk writes). However, once again, the keys change in a very controlled manner, although the code is certainly not simple because of a host of cases.

We may have to continue splitting all the way up the tree (although this is unlikely). In the worst case, we split the root, thus creating a new root that has two children.

When a nonleaf node is split, as is the case here, its parent gains a child. What if the parent already has reached its limit of children? Then we continue splitting nodes up the tree until either we find a parent that does not need to be split or we reach the root. Notice that this idea was seen in bottom-up red-black trees and AA-trees. If we split the root, then we have two roots. Obviously, this is unacceptable, but we can create a new root that has the split roots as its two children. This is why the root is granted the special two-child minimum exemption. It also is the only way that a B-tree gains height. Needless to say, splitting all the way up to the root is an exceptionally rare event. This is because a tree with four levels indicates that the root has been split three times throughout the entire sequence of insertions (assuming no deletions have occurred). In fact, splitting of any nonleaf node is also quite rare.

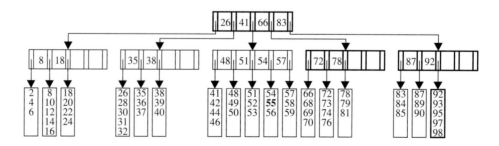

Figure 18.76 B-tree after the deletion of 99 from the B-tree in Figure 18.75

There are other ways to handle the overflowing of children. One technique is to put a child up for adoption should a neighbor have room. To insert 29 into the B-tree in Figure 18.75, for example, we could make room by moving 32 to the next leaf. This technique requires a modification of the parent because the keys are affected. However, it tends to keep nodes fuller and saves space in the long run.

We can perform deletion by finding the item that needs to be removed and then removing it. The problem is that if the leaf it was in had the minimum number of data items, then it is now below the minimum. We can rectify this situation by adopting a neighboring item, if the neighbor is not itself at its minimum. If it is, then we can combine with the neighbor to form a full leaf. Unfortunately, this means that the parent has lost a child. If this causes the parent to fall below its minimum, then it follows the same strategy. This process could percolate all the way up to the root. The root cannot have just one child (and even if this was allowed, it would be silly). If a root is left with one child as a result of the adoption process, then we remove the root and make its child the new root of the tree. This is the only way for a B-tree to lose height. For example, suppose we want to remove 99 from the B-tree in Figure 18.75. Since the leaf has only two items and its neighbor is already at its minimum of three, we combine the items into a new leaf of five items. As a result, the parent has only two children. However, it can adopt from a neighbor because the neighbor has four children. As a result, both have three children. The result is shown in Figure 18.76.

Deletion works in reverse. If a leaf loses a child, it may need to combine with another leaf. The combining of nodes may continue all the way up the tree, although this is unlikely. In the worst case, the root loses one of its two children. In that case, we delete the root and use the other child as the new root.

Summary

Binary search trees are very important in algorithm design. They support almost all of the useful operations, and the logarithmic average cost is very small. Nonrecursive implementations of search trees are somewhat faster than recursive versions, but the latter are sleeker, more elegant, and easier to understand and debug. The problem with search trees is that their performance depends heavily on the input's being random. If this is not the case, the running time increases significantly, to the point where search trees become expensive linked lists.

We saw several ways to deal with this problem. All involve restructuring the tree to ensure that some sort of balance holds at each node. The restructuring is achieved through tree rotations that preserve the binary search tree property. For these trees, the cost of a search is typically less than in an unbalanced binary search tree because the average node tends to be closer to the root. The insertion and deletion costs, however, are usually higher. The balanced variations differ in how much coding effort is involved in implementing operations that change the tree.

The classic scheme is the AVL tree in which, for every node, the heights of its left and right subtrees can differ by at most 1. The practical problem with AVL trees is that they involve large numbers of different cases, thus making the overhead of each insertion and deletion relatively high. Two alternatives were examined in the chapter. The first was the top-down red-black tree. Its primary advantage is that rebalancing can be implemented in a single pass down the tree, rather than the traditional pass down and back up. This leads to simpler code and faster performance than the AVL tree allows. The second is the AA-tree, which is similar to the bottom-up red-black tree. Its primary advantage is a relatively simple recursive implementation of both insertion and deletion. Both of these structures use sentinel nodes to eliminate annoying special cases.

Use an unbalanced binary search tree only if you are sure that the data are reasonably random or the amount of data is relatively small. Use the red-black tree if you are concerned about speed (and are not too concerned about deletion). Use the AA-tree if you want an easy implementation that has more than acceptable performance. Use the B-tree when the amount of data is too large to store in main memory.

Chapter 21 examines another alternative: the *splay tree*. This is a very interesting alternative to the balanced search tree that is also simple to code and competitive in practice. The next chapter examines the hash table, which is a completely different method used to implement searching operations.

Objects of the Game

AA-tree A balanced search tree that is the tree of choice when an $O(\log N)$ worst case is needed, a casual implementation is acceptable, and deletions are needed. (530)

AVL tree A binary search tree with the additional balance property that, for any node in the tree, the height of the left and right subtrees can differ by at most 1. As the first balanced search tree, it has historical significance. It also illustrates most of the ideas that are used in other schemes. (508)

balanced binary search tree A tree that adds a structure property to guarantee logarithmic depth in the worst case. Updates are slower than with the binary search tree, but accesses are faster. (508)

binary search tree A data structure that supports insertion, searching, and deletion in $O(\log N)$ average time. For any node in the binary search tree, all smaller-keyed nodes are in the left subtree and all larger-keyed nodes are in the right subtree. Duplicates are not allowed. (489)

B-tree The most popular data structure for disk-bound searching. There are many variations of the same idea. (541)

double rotation Equivalent to two single rotations. (515)

external path length The sum of the cost of accessing all external tree nodes in a binary tree. Measures the cost of an unsuccesful search. (506)

external tree node The `null` node. (507)

horizontal link In an AA-tree, a connection between a node and a child of equal levels. A horizontal link should go only right, and there should not be two consecutive horizontal links. (531)

internal path length The sum of the depths of the nodes in a binary tree. Measures the cost of a successful search. (505)

lazy deletion A deletion method that marks items as deleted but does not actually delete them. (530)

level of a node In an AA-tree, the number of left links on the path to the `nullNode` sentinel. (531)

M-ary tree A tree that allows *M*-way branching. As branching increases, the depth decreases. (541)

red-black tree A balanced search tree that is a good alternative to the AVL tree because a single top-down pass can be used during the insertion and deletion routines. Nodes are colored red and black in a restricted way that guarantees logarithmic depth. The coding details tend to give a faster implementation. (517)

single rotation Switches the roles of the parent and child while maintaining search order. Balance is restored by tree rotations. (511)

skew and **split** A `skew` removes left horizontal links by performing a rotation between a node and its left child. A `split` fixes consecutive right horizontal links by performing a rotation between a node and its right child. (532)

Common Errors

1. Using an unbalanced search tree when the input sequence is not random will give poor performance.
2. The `remove` operation is very tricky to code correctly, especially for a balanced search tree.
3. Lazy deletion is a good alternative to the standard `remove`, but you must then change other routines, such as `findMin`.
4. Code for balanced search trees is almost always error-prone.
5. Forgetting to return a reference to the new subtree root is wrong for the private helper methods `insert` and `remove`. The return value should be assigned to `root`.
6. Using sentinels and then writing code that forgets about the sentinels can lead to infinite loops. A common case is testing against `null` when a `nullNode` sentinel is used.

On the Internet

All of the code in this chapter is available online in the directory **DataStructures**. Here are the filenames:

AATree.java   Contains the implementation of the AA-tree.
BinaryNode.java   Contains the implementation of `BinaryNode`.
BinarySearchTree.java Contains the unbalanced binary search tree.

BinarySearchTreeWithRank.java Contains the unbalanced binary
                          search tree that has order statistics.

RedBlackTree.java   Contains the implementation of the red-black tree.

Rotations.java   Contains the four basic rotations.

Exercises

In Short

18.1. Show the result of inserting 3, 1, 4, 6, 9, 2, 5, and 7 into an initially empty binary search tree. Then show the result of deleting the root.

18.2. Draw all binary search trees that can result from inserting permutations of 1, 2, 3, and 4. How many trees are there? What are the probabilities of each tree's occurring if all permutations are equally likely?

18.3. Draw all AVL trees that can result from inserting permutations of 1, 2, and 3. How many trees are there? What are the probabilities of each tree's occurring if all permutations are equally likely?

18.4. Repeat Exercise 18.3 for four elements.

18.5. Show the result of inserting 2, 1, 4, 5, 9, 3, 6, and 7 into an initially empty AVL tree. Then show the result for a top-down red-black tree.

18.6. Repeat Exercises 18.3 and 18.4 for a red-black tree.

18.7. Discuss the advantages and disadvantages of avoiding all exceptions and using `null` to signal errors.

In Theory

18.8. Prove Theorem 18.2.

18.9. Show the result of inserting items 1 through 15 in order into an initially empty AVL tree. Generalize this (with proof) to show what happens when items 1 through $2^k - 1$ are inserted into an initially empty AVL tree.

18.10. Give an algorithm to perform `remove` in an AVL tree.

18.11. Prove that the height of a red-black tree is at most approximately $2\log N$ and give an insertion sequence that achieves this bound.

18.12. Show that every AVL tree can be colored as a red-black tree. Do all red-black trees satisfy the AVL tree property?

18.13. Prove that the algorithm for deletion in an AA-tree is correct.

18.14. Suppose the `level` data field in an AA-tree is represented by an 8-bit `byte`. What is the smallest AA-tree that would overflow the `level` field at the root?

18.15. A B*-tree of order M is a B-tree in which each interior node has between $2M/3$ and M children. Leaves are similarly filled. Describe a method to perform insertion into a B*-tree.

In Practice

18.16. Implement `find`, `findMin`, and `findMax` recursively.

18.17. Implement `findKth` nonrecursively using the same technique as for a nonrecursive `find`.

18.18. An alternative representation that allows the `findKth` operation is to store in each node the value of 1 plus the size of the left subtree. Why might this be advantageous? Rewrite the search tree class to use this representation.

18.19. Write a binary search tree method that takes two keys, `low` and `high`, and prints all elements X that are in the range specified by `low` and `high`. Your program should run in $O(K + \log N)$ average time, where K is the number of keys printed. Thus if K is small, you should be examining only a small part of the tree. Use a hidden recursive method and do not use an inorder iterator. Bound the running time of your algorithm.

18.20. Write a binary search tree method that takes two integers, `low` and `high`, and constructs an optimally balanced `BinarySearchTreeWithRank` that contains all integers between `low` and `high`, inclusive. All leaves should be at the same level (if the tree size is 1 less than a power of 2) or on two consecutive levels. *Your routine should take linear time.* Test your routine by using it to solve the Josephus problem (Section 13.1).

18.21. The routines to perform double rotations are inefficient because they perform unnecessary changes to children references. Rewrite them to avoid calls to the single rotation routine.

18.22. Give a nonrecursive top-down implementation of an AA-tree. Compare the implementation with the text's for simplicity and efficiency.

18.23. Write the `skew` and `split` procedures recursively so that only one call of each is needed for `remove`.

Programming Projects

18.24. Redo the binary search tree class to implement lazy deletion. Note carefully that this affects all of the routines. Especially challenging are `findMin` and `findMax`, which both must now be done recursively.

18.25. Implement the binary search tree to use only one comparison per level for `find`, `insert`, and `remove`.

18.26. Write a program to evaluate empirically the following strategies for removing nodes with two children. Which strategy gives the best balance? Which takes the least CPU time to process an entire sequence of operations?

    a. Replace with the largest node, X, in T_L and recursively remove X.

    b. Alternately replace with the largest node in T_L or the smallest node in T_R, and recursively remove the appropriate node.

    c. Replace with the largest node in T_L or the smallest node in T_R (recursively remove the appropriate node), making the choice randomly.

18.27. Write the `remove` method for red-black trees.

18.28. Implement the search tree operations with order statistics for the balanced search tree of your choice.

18.29. Implement a B-tree that works in main memory.

18.30. Implement a B-tree that works for disk files.

18.31. Design an applet that illustrates the basic operations in both unbalanced and some balanced binary search tree.

References

More information on binary search trees, and in particular the mathematical properties of trees, can be found in the two books by Knuth [18 and 19].

Several papers deal with the theoretical lack of balance caused by biased deletion algorithms in binary search trees. Hibbard's paper [16] proposed the original deletion algorithm and established that one deletion preserves the randomness of the trees. A complete analysis has been performed only for trees with three nodes [17] and four nodes [3]. Eppinger's paper [10] provided early empirical evidence of nonrandomness, and the papers by Culberson and Munro [7 and 8] provide some analytical evidence (but not a complete proof for the general case of intermixed insertions and deletions). The claim that the deepest node in a random binary search tree is three times deeper than the average node is proved in [11]; the result is by no means simple.

AVL trees were proposed by Adelson-Velskii and Landis [2]. A deletion algorithm can be found in [19]. Analysis of the average costs of searching an AVL tree is incomplete, but some results are contained in [20]. The top-down red-black tree algorithm is from [15]; a more accessible description can be found in [21]. An implementation of top-down red-black trees without sentinel nodes is given in [12]; this provides a convincing demonstration of the usefulness of `nullNode`. The AA-tree is based on the symmetric binary B-tree discussed in [4]. The implementation shown in the text is adapted from the description in [1]. A host of other balanced search trees can be found in [13].

B-trees first appeared in [5]. The implementation described in the original paper allows data to be stored in internal nodes as well as in leaves. The data structure described here is sometimes called a B^+-tree. Information on the B^*-tree, described in Exercise 18.15, can be found in [9]. A survey of the different types of B-trees is presented in [6]. Empirical results of the various schemes are reported in [14]. A C++ implementation can be found in [12].

1. A. Andersson, "Balanced Search Trees Made Simple," *Proceedings of the Third Workshop on Algorithms and Data Structures* (1993), 61–71.

2. G. M. Adelson-Velskii and E. M. Landis, "An Algorithm for the Organization of Information," *Soviet Math. Doklady* **3** (1962), 1259–1263.

3. R. A. Baeza-Yates, "A Trivial Algorithm Whose Analysis Isn't: A Continuation," *BIT* **29** (1989), 88–113.

4. R. Bayer, "Symmetric Binary B-Trees: Data Structure and Maintenance Algorithms," *Acta Informatica* **1** (1972), 290–306.

5. R. Bayer and E. M. McCreight, "Organization and Maintenance of Large Ordered Indices," *Acta Informatica* **1** (1972), 173–189.

6. D. Comer, "The Ubiquitous B-tree," *Computing Surveys* **11** (1979), 121–137.

7. J. Culberson and J. I. Munro, "Explaining the Behavior of Binary Search Trees under Prolonged Updates: A Model and Simulations," *Computer Journal* **32** (1989), 68–75.

8. J. Culberson and J. I. Munro, "Analysis of the Standard Deletion Algorithm in Exact Fit Domain Binary Search Trees," *Algorithmica* **5** (1990), 295–311.

9. K. Culik, T. Ottman, and D. Wood, "Dense Multiway Trees," *ACM Transactions on Database Systems* **6** (1981), 486–512.

10. J. L. Eppinger, "An Empirical Study of Insertion and Deletion in Binary Search Trees," *Communications of the ACM* **26** (1983), 663–669.

11. P. Flajolet and A. Odlyzko, "The Average Height of Binary Search Trees and Other Simple Trees," *Journal of Computer and System Sciences* **25** (1982), 171–213.

12. B. Flamig, *Practical Data Structures in C++*, John Wiley and Sons, New York, New York (1994).

13. G. H. Gonnet and R. Baeza-Yates, *Handbook of Algorithms and Data Structures,* 2d ed., Addison-Wesley, Reading, Mass (1991).

14. E. Gudes and S. Tsur, "Experiments with B-tree Reorganization," *Proceedings of ACM SIGMOD Symposium on Management of Data* (1980), 200–206.

15. L. J. Guibas and R. Sedgewick, "A Dichromatic Framework for Balanced Trees," *Proceedings of the Nineteenth Annual IEEE Symposium on Foundations of Computer Science* (1978), 8–21.

16. T. H. Hibbard, "Some Combinatorial Properties of Certain Trees with Applications to Searching and Sorting," *Journal of the ACM* **9** (1962), 13–28.

17. A. T. Jonassen and D. E. Knuth, "A Trivial Algorithm Whose Analysis Isn't," *Journal of Computer and System Sciences* **16** (1978), 301–322.

18. D. E. Knuth, *The Art of Computer Programming: Volume 1: Fundamental Algorithms*, 3d ed., Addison-Wesley, Reading, Mass. (1997).

19. D. E. Knuth, *The Art of Computer Programming: Volume 3: Sorting and Searching*, 2d ed., Addison-Wesley, Reading, Mass. (1997).

20. K. Melhorn, "A Partial Analysis of Height-Balanced Trees under Random Insertions and Deletions," *SIAM Journal on Computing* **11** (1982), 748–760.

21. R. Sedgewick, *Algorithms in C++*, Addison-Wesley, Reading, Mass. (1992).

19

Hash Tables

C HAPTER 18 discussed the binary search tree, which allows various operations on a set of elements. This chapter discusses the *hash table*, which supports only a subset of the operations allowed by binary search trees. The implementation of hash tables is frequently called *hashing*. Hashing is a technique used to perform insertions, deletions, and finds in constant average time.

Unlike with the binary search tree, the average-case running time of hash table operations is based on statistical properties rather than the expectation of random-looking input. This improvement is obtained at the expense of a loss of ordering information among the elements: operations such as findMin and findMax and the printing of the entire table in sorted order in linear time are not supported. Consequently, the hash table and binary search tree have somewhat different uses and performance properties.

In this chapter, we will see:

- Several methods of implementing the hash table
- Analytical comparisons of these methods
- Some applications of hashing
- Hash tables compared with binary search trees

19.1 Basic Ideas

The *hash table* supports the retrieval or deletion of any named item, so what we are implementing is a dictionary. We would like to be able to support the basic operations in constant time, as was done for the stack and queue. Since the accesses are much less restricted, this seems like an impossible goal. That is, surely when the size of the dictionary increases, searches in the dictionary should take longer. However, this is not necessarily the case.

The *hash table* is used to implement a dictionary in constant time per operation.

Suppose, for example, that all the items are small non-negative integers, ranging from 0 to 65,535. A simple array can be used to implement each operation as follows. First, we initialize an array a that is indexed from 0 to 65,535 with all 0s. To perform insert(i), we execute a[i]++. Note that a[i] represents the number of times that i has been inserted. To perform find(i), we check that a[i] is not 0. To perform remove(i), we make sure it is found, and if so, execute a[i]--. The time for each operation is clearly constant. There is the overhead of the array initialization, but this is a constant amount of work (65,536 assignments).

There are two problems with this solution. First, suppose we have 32-bit integers instead of 16-bit integers. Then the array a must hold 4 billion items; this is impractical. Second, if the items are not integers but instead are strings (or something even more generic), then they cannot be used to index an array.

The second problem is not really a problem at all. Just as a number 1234 is a collection of digits 1, 2, 3, and 4, the string "junk" is a collection of characters 'j', 'u', 'n', and 'k'. Notice that the number 1234 is just $1 \cdot 10^3 + 2 \cdot 10^2 + 3 \cdot 10^1 + 4 \cdot 10^0$. Recall from Section 12.1 that a character can typically be represented in 7 bits as a number between 0 and 127. Since a character is basically a small integer, we can interpret a string as an integer. One possible representation is $'j' \cdot 128^3 + 'u' \cdot 128^2 + 'n' \cdot 128^1 + 'k' \cdot 128^0$. This allows the simple array implementation seen previously.

The problem with this strategy is that the integer representation described generates huge integers: The representation for "junk" yields 224,229,227, and longer strings generate much larger representations. This brings us back to the first problem: How do we avoid using an absurdly large array?

A *hash function* converts the item into an integer suitable to index an array where the item is stored. If the hash function was one to one, we could access the item by its array index.

This is done by using a function that maps large numbers (or strings interpreted as numbers) into smaller, more manageable numbers. The function that maps an item into a small index is known as the *hash function*. If x is an arbitrary (non-negative) integer, then x%tableSize generates a number between 0 and tableSize-1 suitable for indexing into an array of size tableSize. If s is a string, we can convert s to a large integer x using the method suggested previously and then apply the mod operator (%) to get a suitable index. Thus, if tableSize is 10,000, "junk" would be indexed to 9,227. Section 19.2 discusses implementation of the hash function for strings in detail.

Since the hash function is not one to one, several items will collide at the same index and cause a *collision*.

The use of the hash function introduces a complication: It is possible that two different items hash out to the same position. This can never be avoided because there are many more items than positions. When this happens, a *collision* occurs. There are many methods to quickly resolve a collision. We investigate three of the simplest: *linear probing*, *quadratic probing*, and *separate chaining*. Each method is simple to implement, but each yields a different performance, depending on how full the array is.

19.2 Hash Function

Computing the hash function for strings has a subtle complication: The conversion of s to x generates an integer that is almost certainly larger than the machine can store conveniently. This is because $128^4 = 2^{28}$, which is only a factor of 8 from the largest integer on a 32-bit machine. Consequently, we cannot expect to compute the hash function by directly computing powers of 128. Instead, we use the following observation. A general polynomial

$$A_3X^3 + A_2X^2 + A_1X^1 + A_0X^0 \qquad\qquad \textbf{(19.1)}$$

can be evaluated as

$$(((A_3)X + A_2)X + A_1)X + A_0 \qquad\qquad \textbf{(19.2)}$$

Notice that in Equation 19.2, we avoid computation of X^i directly. This is good for three reasons. First, it avoids a large intermediate result, which, as we saw earlier, will overflow. Second, the calculation in the equation involves only three multiplications and three additions; an N-degree polynomial is computed in N multiplications and additions. This compares favorably with the computation in Equation 19.1. Third, the calculation proceeds left to right (A_3 corresponds to 'j', A_2 to 'u', and so on, and X is 128).

There still is an overflow problem: Since the result of the calculation is still the same, it is likely to be too large. However, we need only the result taken mod tableSize. By applying the % operator after each multiplication (or addition), we can make sure that the intermediate results remain small.[1] The hash function that results is shown in Figure 19.1. An annoying feature of this hash function is that the mod computation is expensive. Because overflow is allowed (and its results are consistent on a given platform), we can make the hash function somewhat faster by performing a single mod operation immediately prior to the return. Unfortunately, the repeated multiplication by 128 would tend to shift the early characters to the left, out of the answer. To alleviate this situation, we multiply by 37 instead of 128. This slows down the shifting of early characters.

By using a trick, we can evaluate the hash function efficiently and without overflow.

```
1       // Acceptable hash function
2       public final static int hash( String key, int tableSize )
3       {
4           int hashVal = 0;
5
6           for( int i = 0; i < key.length( ); i++ )
7               hashVal = ( hashVal * 128 + key.charAt( i ) )
8                                           % tableSize;
9           return hashVal;
10      }
```

Figure 19.1   First attempt at a hash function implementation

---

[1] Section 7.4 discusses the properties of the mod operation.

```
1       /**
2        * A hash routine for String objects.
3        * @param key the String to hash.
4        * @param tableSize the size of the hash table.
5        * @return the hash value.
6        */
7       public final static int hash( String key, int tableSize )
8       {
9           int hashVal = 0;
10
11          for( int i = 0; i < key.length( ); i++ )
12              hashVal = 37 * hashVal + key.charAt( i );
13
14          hashVal %= tableSize;
15          if( hashVal < 0 )
16              hashVal += tableSize;
17
18          return hashVal;
19      }
```

Figure 19.2   Faster hash function that takes advantage of overflow

The result is shown in Figure 19.2. This is not necessarily the very best function possible. Also, it is certainly true that in some applications (for example, if long strings are involved), we may want to tinker with it. Generally speaking, however, the function is pretty good. Note that the overflow could introduce negative numbers. Thus if the mod generates a negative value, we make it positive (lines 15 and 16). Also note that the result obtained by allowing overflow and doing a final mod is not the same as performing the mod after every step. Thus we have slightly altered the hash function. This is not a problem.

It is worth remarking that while speed is an important consideration in designing a hash function, we also want to make sure that the hash function distributes the keys equitably. Consequently, we must be careful not to take our optimizations too far. An example is the hash function in Figure 19.3. It simply adds up the characters in the keys and returns the result mod tableSize. What could be simpler? The answer is that little could be simpler. The function is easy to implement and computes a hash value very quickly. However, if tableSize is large, the function does not distribute the keys well. For instance, suppose tableSize is 10,000. Also suppose that all keys are 8 or fewer characters long. Since an ASCII char is an integer between 0 and 127, the hash function can assume only values between 0 and 1,016 (127*8). This is certainly not an equitable distribution. Any speed gained by the quickness of the hash function calculation will be more than offset by the effort taken to resolve what we expect will be a larger than expected number of collisions.

Finally, note that zero is a possible result of the hash function, so hash tables are indexed starting at zero.

> The hash function must be simple to compute but also distribute the keys equitably. If there are too many collisions, the performance of the hash table will suffer dramatically.

> The table runs from 0 to tableSize-1.

```
1      // A poor hash function when tableSize is large
2      public final static int hash( String key, int tableSize )
3      {
4          int hashVal = 0;
5
6          for( int i = 0; i < key.length( ); i++ )
7              hashVal += key.charAt( i );
8
9          return hashVal % tableSize;
10     }
```

Figure 19.3   Bad hash function if `tableSize` is large

19.3 Linear Probing

Now that we have a hash function, we need to decide what to do when a collision occurs. Specifically, if *X* hashes out to a position that is already occupied, where do we place it? The simplest possible strategy is *linear probing* — searching sequentially in the array until we find an empty cell. The search wraps around from the last position to the first, if necessary. Figure 19.4 shows the result of inserting the keys 89, 18, 49, 58, and 9 into a hash table when linear probing is used. We assume a hash function that returns the key *X* mod the size of the table. Figure 19.4 includes the result of the hash function.

In linear probing, collisions are resolved by sequentially scanning an array (with wraparound) until an empty cell is found.

```
hash( 89, 10 ) = 9
hash( 18, 10 ) = 8
hash( 49, 10 ) = 9
hash( 58, 10 ) = 8
hash(  9, 10 ) = 9
```

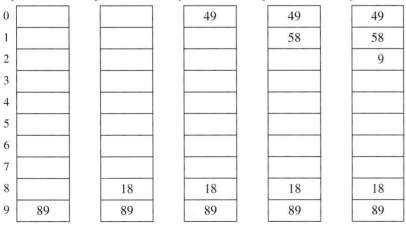

Figure 19.4   Linear probing hash table after each insertion

The first collision occurs when 49 is inserted; the 49 is put in the next available spot, namely spot 0, which is open. Then 58 collides with 18, 89, and 49 before an empty spot is found three slots away in position 1. The collision for element 9 is resolved similarly. As long as the table is large enough, a free cell can always be found. However, the time to find a free cell can get to be quite large. For example, if there is only one free cell left in the table, we may have to search the entire table to find it. On average, we would expect to have to search half of the table to find it. This is far from the constant time per access that we are hoping for. On the other hand, we expect that if the table is kept relatively empty, then insertions should not be so costly. This is discussed soon.

The find follows the same probe sequence as the insert.

The find algorithm merely follows the same path as the insert algorithm. If it reaches an empty slot, the item we are searching for is not found; otherwise, it finds the match eventually. For example, to find 58, we start at slot 8 (as indicated by the hash function). We see an item, but it is the wrong one, so we try slot 9. Again, we have an item, but it is the wrong one, so we try slot 0 and then slot 1 until a match is found. A find for 19 would try slots 9, 0, 1, and 2 before finding the empty cell in slot 3. Thus 19 is not found.

We must use lazy deletion.

Standard deletion cannot be performed because, much as with a binary search tree, an item in the hash table not only represents itself but also connects other items by serving as a placeholder during collision resolution. Thus, if we removed 89 from the hash table, virtually all of the remaining find operations would fail. Consequently, we implement lazy deletion, marking items as deleted from the table. This information is recorded in an extra data field. Each item is either *active* or *deleted*.

19.3.1 Naive Analysis of Linear Probing

The simplistic analysis of linear probing assumes that successive probes are independent. This is not true and thus the analysis underestimates the costs of searching and insertion.

To estimate the performance of linear probing, we make two assumptions:

1. The hash table is large.
2. Each probe in the hash table is independent of the previous probe.

Assumption 1 is completely reasonable; otherwise, we would not be bothering with a hash table. Assumption 2 says that if the fraction of the table that is full is λ, then each time we examine a cell, the probability that it is occupied is also λ, independent of any previous probes. Independence is an important statistical property that greatly simplifies the analysis of random events. Unfortunately, as discussed in Section 19.3.2, the assumption of independence is not only unjustified but also erroneous. Thus the naive analysis we perform is incorrect. Even so, it is helpful because it tells us what we can hope to achieve if we are more careful about how collisions are resolved. As mentioned earlier in the chapter, the performance of the hash table depends on how full the table is. Its fullness is given by the load factor.

DEFINITION: The *load factor* of a probing hash table is the fraction of the table that is full. We denote the load factor by λ. The load factor ranges from 0 (empty) to 1 (completely full).

The *load factor* of a probing hash table is the fraction of the table that is full. It ranges from 0 (empty) to 1 (full).

We can now give a simple but incorrect analysis of linear probing in Theorem 19.1.

If independence of probes is assumed, the average number of cells that are examined in an insertion using linear probing is $1/(1-\lambda)$.

Theorem 19.1

For a table with load factor λ, the probability of any cell's being empty is $1-\lambda$. Consequently, the expected number of independent trials required to find an empty cell is $1/(1-\lambda)$.

Proof

The proof of Theorem 19.1 uses the fact that if the probability of some event occurring is p, then on average $1/p$ trials are required until the event occurs, provided the trials are independent. For example, the expected number of coin flips until a heads occurs is two, and the expected number of rolls of a single six-sided die until a 4 occurs is six. This assumes independence.

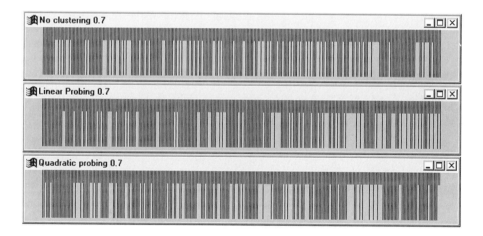

Figure 19.5   Illustration of primary clustering in linear probing (middle) versus no clustering (top) and the less significant secondary clustering in quadratic probing (bottom); long lines represent occupied cells; Load factor is 0.7

19.3.2 What Really Happens: Primary Clustering

The effect of *primary clustering* is that large clusters of occupied cells form, thereby making insertions into the cluster expensive (and then the insertion makes the cluster larger).

Unfortunately, independence does not hold. This is shown in Figure 19.5 (page 559). On the top is the result of filling a hash table to 70% capacity, if all successive probes are independent. In the middle is linear probing. Notice the group of clusters; hence the phenomenom known as *primary clustering*.

In primary clustering, we get blocks of occupied cells. Any key that hashes into this cluster will require excessive attempts to resolve the collision, and then it will add to the cluster. In primary clustering, not only do items that collide because of identical hash functions cause degenerate performance, but also an item that collides with an alternative location for another item causes bad performance. The mathematical analysis that is required to take this into account is complex but has been solved, yielding Theorem 19.2.

Theorem 19.2	*The average number of cells that are examined in an insertion using linear probing is roughly* $(1 + 1/(1-\lambda)^2)/2$.
Proof	*The proof is beyond the scope of the text. See [6].*

Primary clustering is a problem at high load factors. For half-empty tables, the effect is not disastrous.

For a half-full table, we obtain 2.5 as the average number of cells examined during an insertion. This is almost the same as what the naive analysis indicated. The main difference occurs as λ gets close to 1. For instance, if the table is 90 percent full, then $\lambda = 0.9$. The naive analysis suggests that ten cells would have to be examined. This is a lot, but it is not completely out of the question. However, by Theorem 19.2, the real answer is that roughly 50 cells need to be examined. That is excessive (especially since this is only an average and thus some insertions must be worse).

19.3.3 Analysis of the `find` Operation

An unsuccessful `find` costs the same as an insertion.

The cost of an insertion can be used to bound the cost of a `find`. There are two types of `find` operations: unsuccessful and successful. An unsuccessful `find` is easy to analyze. The sequence of slots that are examined for an unsuccessful search of X is exactly the same as would be examined to `insert` X. Thus we have an immediate answer for the cost of an unsuccessful `find`.

For successful finds, things are slightly more complicated. Figure 19.4 shows a table with $\lambda = 0.5$. Thus the average cost of an insertion is 2.5. The average cost to find the newly inserted item would then be 2.5, no matter how many insertions follow. The average cost to find the first item inserted into the table is always 1.0 probes. Thus, in a table with $\lambda = 0.5$, some searches are easy and some are hard. In particular, the cost of a successful search of X is equal to the cost of inserting X *at the time X was inserted*. To find the average time to perform a successful search in a table with load factor λ, we must compute the average insertion cost by averaging over all of the load factors leading up to λ. With this groundwork, we can compute the average search times for linear probing.

The cost of a successful find is an average of the insertion costs over all smaller load factors.

The average number of cells that are examined in an unsuccessful search using linear probing is roughly $(1 + 1/(1-\lambda)^2)/2$. The average number of cells that are examined in a successful search is approximately $(1 + 1/(1-\lambda))/2$.

Theorem 19.3

The cost of an unsuccessful search is the same as the cost of an insertion. For a successful search, we compute the average insertion cost over the sequence of insertions. Since the table is large, we can compute this average by evaluating $S(\lambda) = \frac{1}{\lambda}\int_{x=0}^{\lambda} I(x)dx$. In other words, the average cost of a successful search for a table with load factor λ is equal to the cost of an insertion into a table of load factor x, averaged from load factors 0 through λ. From Theorem 19.2, we can derive the following equation:

Proof

$$S(\lambda) = \frac{1}{\lambda}\int_{x=0}^{\lambda}\frac{1}{2}\left(1 + \frac{1}{(1-x)^2}\right)dx$$

$$= \frac{1}{2\lambda}\left(x + \frac{1}{(1-x)}\right)\bigg|_{x=0}^{\lambda}$$

$$= \frac{1}{2\lambda}\left(\left(\lambda + \frac{1}{(1-\lambda)}\right) - 1\right)$$

$$= \frac{1}{2}\left(\frac{2-\lambda}{1-\lambda}\right)$$

$$= \frac{1}{2}\left(1 + \frac{1}{1-\lambda}\right)$$

We can apply the same technique to obtain the cost of a successful `find` under the assumption of independence (by using $I(x) = 1/(1-x)$ in Theorem 19.3). If there is no clustering, the average cost of a successful `find` for linear probing will be $-\ln(1-\lambda)/\lambda$. If the load factor is 0.5, then the average number of probes for a successful search using linear probing is 1.5, whereas the nonclustering analysis suggests 1.4 probes. Notice that this average does not depend on any ordering of the input keys; it depends only on the fairness of the hash function. Note also that even when we have good hash functions, there are bound to be both longer and shorter probe sequences that contribute to the average. For instance, there are certain to be some sequences of length 4, 5, and 6, even in a hash table that is half empty. Determining the expected longest probe sequence is a challenging calculation. Primary clustering not only makes the average probe sequence longer; it also makes a long probe sequence more likely. The main problem with primary clustering, therefore, is that performance degrades severely for insertion at high load factors. Also, some of the longer probe sequences typically encountered (that is, those at the high end of the average) are made more likely to occur.

To reduce the number of probes, we would need a collision resolution scheme that avoids primary clustering. Notice, however, that if the table is half empty, then removing the effects of primary clustering would save only one-half of a probe on average for an insertion or unsuccessful search and one-tenth of a probe on average for a successful search. Even though we might expect to reduce the probability of seeing a somewhat lengthier probe sequence, the fact remains that *linear probing is not a terrible strategy*. Since it is so easy to implement, any method we use to remove primary clustering must be of comparable complexity. Otherwise, we will expend too much time in the course of saving only a fraction of a probe. One such method is *quadratic probing*.

19.4 Quadratic Probing

Quadratic probing examines cells 1, 4, 9, and so on, away from the original probe point.

Quadratic probing is a collision resolution method that eliminates the primary clustering problem of linear probing. It derives its name from the use of the formula $F(i) = i^2$ to resolve collisions. Specifically, if the hash function evaluates to H and if a search in cell H is inconclusive, then we try cells $H + 1^2$, $H + 2^2$, $H + 3^2$, ..., $H + i^2$ (employing wraparound) in sequence. This differs from the linear probing strategy of searching $H + 1$, $H + 2$, $H + 3$, ..., $H + i$.

Remember that subsequent probe points are a quadratic number of positions from the original probe point.

Figure 19.6 shows the table that results when quadratic probing is used instead of linear probing for the insertion sequence shown in Figure 19.4. When 49 collides with 89, the first alternative attempted is one cell away. This cell is empty, so 49 is placed there. Next, 58 collides at position 8. The cell at position 9 (which is one away) is tried, but another collision occurs. A vacant cell is found at the next cell tried, which is $2^2 = 4$ positions away *from the original hash position*. Thus 58 is placed in cell 2. The same thing happens for 9. Notice carefully that the alternative locations for items that hash to position 8 and the alternative locations for the items that hash to position 9 are not the same. The long probe sequence to insert 58 did not affect the subsequent insertion of 9. This contrasts with what happened using linear probing.

There are a few details to consider before we write code:

- In linear probing, each probe tries a different cell. Does quadratic probing guarantee that when a cell is tried, we have not already tried it during the course of the current access? Does quadratic probing guarantee that when we are inserting X and the table is not full, X will be inserted?
- Linear probing is easily implemented. Quadratic probing appears to require multiplication and mod operations. Does this apparent added complexity make quadratic probing impractical?
- What happens (in both linear probing and quadratic probing) if the load factor gets too high? Can we dynamically expand the table, as is typically done with other array-based data structures?

Fortunately, there is relatively good news on all fronts. If the table size is prime and the load factor never exceeds 0.5, we are assured that we can always place a new item X and that no cell is probed twice during an access. However, for this guarantee to hold, we need to ensure that the table size is a prime number. Theorem 19.4 proves this. For completeness, Figure 19.7 shows a routine that generates prime numbers. It uses the algorithm in Figure 9.8 (a more complex algorithm is not warranted).

If the table size is prime and the load factor is no larger than 0.5, then all probes will be to different locations and an item can always be inserted.

```
hash( 89, 10 ) = 9
hash( 18, 10 ) = 8
hash( 49, 10 ) = 9
hash( 58, 10 ) = 8
hash(  9, 10 ) = 9
```

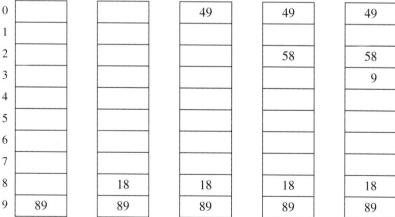

Figure 19.6   Quadratic probing hash table after each insertion (note that the table size is poorly chosen because it is not a prime number)

Theorem 19.4	If quadratic probing is used and the table size is prime, then a new element can always be inserted if the table is at least half empty. Furthermore, in the course of the insertion, no cell is probed twice.

Proof	Let M be the size of the table. Assume that M is an odd prime greater than 3. We will show that the first $\lfloor M/2 \rfloor$ alternative locations are distinct. Two of these locations are $H + i^2 (\bmod M)$ and $H + j^2 (\bmod M)$, where $0 < i, j \leq \lfloor M/2 \rfloor$. Suppose, for the sake of contradiction, that these two locations are the same, but $i \neq j$. Then

$$H + i^2 \equiv H + j^2 (\bmod M)$$
$$i^2 \equiv j^2 (\bmod M)$$
$$i^2 - j^2 \equiv 0 (\bmod M)$$
$$(i - j)(i + j) \equiv 0 (\bmod M).$$

Since M is prime, it follows that either $i - j$ or $i + j$ is divisible by M. Since i and j are distinct and their sum is smaller than M, neither of these possibilities can occur. Thus we obtain a contradiction. It follows that the first $\lfloor M/2 \rfloor$ alternatives are all distinct and, along with the original probe, guarantee that an insertion must succeed if the table is at least half empty.

```
1      /**
2       * Internal method to return a prime number at least as
3       * large as n. See Figure 9.8 for usable isPrime.
4       */
5      private final static int nextPrime( int n )
6      {
7          if( n % 2 == 0 )
8              n++;
9
10         for( ; !isPrime( n ); n += 2 )
11             ;
12
13         return n;
14     }
```

Figure 19.7   Routine used by quadratic probing to find a prime greater than or equal to N

If the table is even one more than half full, the insertion could fail (although this is extremely unlikely). Actually, the failure of an insertion is really not an issue because we would be doing so many probes. Recall that we are expecting to perform an insertion in roughly 2 or 2.5 probes; failure to insert in a table of size 100,000 would imply 50,000 probes. Even so, if we keep the table size prime and the load factor below 0.5, we have a guarantee of success for the insertion. If the table size is not prime, the number of alternative locations can be severely reduced. As an example, if the table size was 16, then the only alternative locations would be at distances 1, 4, or 9 away from the original probe point. Once again, this is not really an issue: Although we would not have a guarantee of $\lfloor M/2 \rfloor$ alternatives, we would usually have more than we would expect to need. However, it is best to play it safe and use the theory to guide us in selecting parameters. Furthermore, it has been shown empirically that prime numbers tend to be best for hash tables because they tend to remove some of the nonrandomness that is occasionally introduced by the hash function.

The second important consideration is efficiency. Recall that for a load factor of 0.5, removing primary clustering saves only 0.5 probes for an average insertion and 0.1 probes for an average successful search. We do get some additional benefits: It is significantly less likely that we will encounter a long probe sequence. However, if it takes twice as long to perform a probe using quadratic probing, it is hardly worth the effort. Linear probing is implemented with a simple addition (by one), a test to see if wraparound is needed, and a very rare subtraction (if we need to do the wraparound). The formula for quadratic probing suggests that we need to do an addition by 1 (to go from $i-1$ to i), a multiplication (to compute i^2), another addition, and then a mod operation. Certainly this appears to be much too expensive a calculation to be practical. However, we have the following trick explained in Theorem 19.5.

Quadratic probing can be implemented without multiplications and mod operations. Because it does not suffer from primary clustering, it outperforms linear probing in practice.

Quadratic probing can be implemented without expensive multiplications and divisions.

Theorem 19.5

Let H_{i-1} be the most recently computed probe (H_0 is the original hash position) and H_i be the probe we are trying to compute. Then we have

Proof

$$H_i = H_0 + i^2 (\bmod M)$$
$$H_{i-1} = H_0 + (i-1)^2 (\bmod M).$$

(19.3)

If we subtract the two equations in Equation 19.3, we obtain

Proof (continued)

$$H_i - H_{i-1} = i^2 - (i-1)^2 (\text{mod } M)$$

$$H_i = H_{i-1} + 2i - 1 (\text{mod } M).$$

(19.4)

Equation 19.4 tells us that we compute the new value H_i from the previous value H_{i-1} without squaring i. Although we still have a multiplication, the multiplication is by 2, which is a trivially implemented bit shift on most computers. What about the mod operation? That, too, is not really needed because the expression $2i - 1$ must be smaller than M. Therefore, if we add it to H_{i-1}, the result will be either still smaller than M (in which case we do not need the mod) or just a little bit larger than M (in which case, we can compute the mod equivalent by subtracting M).

Theorem 19.5 shows that we can compute the next position to probe using an addition (to increment i), a bit shift (to evaluate $2i$), a subtraction by 1 (to evaluate $2i - 1$), another addition (to increment the old position by $2i - 1$), a test to see if wraparound is needed, and a very rare subtraction to implement the mod operation. The difference is thus a bit shift, a subtraction by 1, and an addition per probe. This is likely to be less than the cost of doing an extra probe if complex keys (such as strings) are involved.

Expand the table as soon as the load factor reaches 0.5. This process is called *rehashing*. Always double to a prime number. Prime numbers are easy to find.

The final detail to consider is dynamic expansion. If the load factor exceeds 0.5, we want to double the size of the hash table. This raises a few issues. First, how hard will it be to find another prime number? The answer is that prime numbers are easy to find. We expect to have to test only $O(\log N)$ numbers until we find a number that is prime. Consequently, the routine in Figure 19.7 is very fast. Since the primality test takes at most $O(N^{1/2})$ time, we expect that the search for a prime number takes at most $O(N^{1/2}\log N)$ time.[2] This is much less than the $O(N)$ cost of transferring the contents of the old table to the new.

When expanding a hash table, we reinsert into the new table using the new hash function.

Once we allocate a larger array, do we just copy everything over? The answer is most definitely no. The new array implies a new hash function, so we cannot use the old array positions. Thus we have to examine each element in the old table, compute its new hash value, and insert into the new hash table. This process is called *rehashing*. The next section shows that rehashing is easy to implement in Java.

---

2. This routine is also required if we add a constructor that allows the user to specify an approximate initial size for the hash table. It is the responsibility of the hash table implementation to ensure that a prime number is used.

```
1  package DataStructures;
2
3  import Supporting.*;
4  import Exceptions.*;
5
6  // ProbingHashTable abstract class
7  //
8  // CONSTRUCTION: with no initializer
9  //
10 // ******************PUBLIC OPERATIONS********************
11 // void insert( x )        --> Insert x
12 // void remove( x )        --> Remove x
13 // Hashable find( x )      --> Return item that matches x
14 // void makeEmpty( )       --> Remove all items
15 // int hash( String str, int tableSize )
16 //                         --> Static method to hash strings
17 // ******************ERRORS*******************************
18 // find and remove throw ItemNotFound
19 // insert overrides previous value if duplicate; not an error
20
21 /**
22  * Probing table implementation of hash tables.
23  * This is an abstract class that must be extended to
24  * implement a particular probing algorithm, such as
25  * quadratic probing.
26  * Note that all "matching" is based on the equals method.
27  */
28 public abstract class ProbingHashTable implements HashTable
29 {
30     /**
31      * Abstract method that performs collision resolution.
32      * Each class must override this method only.
33      * @param x the item to search for.
34      * @return the position where the search terminates.
35      */
36     protected abstract int findPos( Hashable x );
37
38     public final static int hash( String key, int tableSize )
39       { /* Figure 19.2 */ }
40     public ProbingHashTable( )
41       { /* Figure 19.10 */ }
42     public final void makeEmpty( )
43       { /* Figure 19.10 */ }
44     public final Hashable find( Hashable x ) throws ItemNotFound
45       { /* Figure 19.11 */ }
46     public final void remove( Hashable x ) throws ItemNotFound
47       { /* Figure 19.12 */ }
48     public final void insert( Hashable x )
49       { /* Figure 19.13 */ }
```

Figure 19.8   Class skeleton for probing hash table (part 1)

19.4.1 Java Implementation

The user must provide an appropriate hash function and equals method for the object in the hash table.

We are now ready to give a complete Java implementation of a quadratic probing hash table. We will use inheritance and first define an abstract class that implements probing hash tables. We then extend the class by providing a quadratic probing collision resolution method. Recall that the Hashable interface requires an implementation of an appropriate hash function. The class skeleton is shown in Figures 19.8 (page 567) and 19.9. Following is a detailed description of each feature.

The hash table will consist of an array of HashEntry references; each reference is either null or to an object that stores an item and a data field that tells us that the entry is either active or deleted. The array is declared at line 53 and is protected so that the collision resolution method, implemented in a derived class, can access it. We need to keep track of the number of items in the hash table (including elements marked as deleted). This number is stored in currentSize, which is declared at line 54.

The rest of the class contains declarations for the hash table routines. The find operation returns the element found in the search for x. If x is not found, an exception is thrown. The insertion method adds a new item into the table; if the item is already present, the new item overrides the previously stored value.

```
50      private static final int DEFAULT_TABLE_SIZE = 11;
51
52          /** The array of elements. */
53      protected HashEntry [ ] array; // The array of elements
54      private int currentSize;   // The number of occupied cells
55
56      private final void allocateArray( int arraySize )
57          { /* Figure 19.10 */ }
58      private final void assertFound( int currentPos,
59                          String message) throws ItemNotFound
60          { /* Figure 19.11 */ }
61 }
62
63 // The basic entry stored in ProbingHashTable
64 class HashEntry
65 {
66      Hashable element;     // The element
67      boolean  isActive;  // false if deleted
68
69      public HashEntry( Hashable e )
70          { this( e, true ); }
71
72      public HashEntry( Hashable e, boolean i )
73          { element = e; isActive = i; }
74 }
```

Figure 19.9 Class skeleton for probing hash table (part 2)

```
1       /**
2        * Internal method to allocate Array.
3        * @param arraySize the size of the array.
4        */
5       private final void allocateArray( int arraySize )
6       {
7           array = new HashEntry[ arraySize ];
8       }
9
10      /**
11       * Construct the hash table.
12       */
13      public ProbingHashTable( )
14      {
15          allocateArray( DEFAULT_TABLE_SIZE );
16          makeEmpty( );
17      }
18
19      /**
20       * Make the hash table logically empty.
21       */
22      public final void makeEmpty( )
23      {
24          currentSize = 0;
25          for( int i = 0; i < array.length; i++ )
26              array[ i ] = null;
27      }
```

Figure 19.10   Hash table initialization

The hash table initialization routines are shown in Figure 19.10. There is nothing special going on here. Note that initially all references in `array` are `null`. The searching routines are shown in Figure 19.11 (page 570). They use the abstract method function `findPos`. We extend the abstract class `ProbingHashTable` by implementing this method. The `find` routines are then simple to implement. An element is found if the result of `findPos` is an active cell (that is, not `null` and not marked deleted), since if `findPos` stops on an active cell, there must be a match. This test is performed by the private method `assertFound`. Similarly, the `remove` routine shown in Figure 19.12 (page 570) is short. We check if `findPos` takes us to an active cell. If so, the cell is marked deleted: otherwise, we return.

The insertion routine is shown in Figure 19.13 (page 571). At line 9, we call `findPos`. `findPos` gives the place in which to insert x. The insertion is performed at line 10; we construct a new `HashEntry` and add it to `array`. Notice that this overrides any previously stored instance that matches x. We adjust `currentSize` at line 11 and return unless a rehash is in order. Thus the remaining code implements rehashing.

Most routines are just a few lines of code because they call `findPos` to perform quadratic probing.

Most of `insert` is concerned with rehashing if the table is (half) full.

```
1     /**
2      * Find an item in the tree.
3      * @param x the item to search for.
4      * @return the matching item.
5      * @exception ItemNotFound if no item
6      *     that matches x can be found in the hash table.
7      */
8     public final Hashable
9     find( Hashable x ) throws ItemNotFound
10    {
11        int currentPos = findPos( x );
12        assertFound( currentPos, "ProbingHashTable find" );
13        return Array[ currentPos ].element;
14    }
15
16    /**
17     * If currentPos exists and is active do nothing.
18     * Otherwise, throw an exception.
19     * @param currentPos the result of a call to findPos.
20     * @param message the String to construct the exception.
21     * @exception ItemNotFound if inactive cell.
22     */
23    private final void assertFound( int currentPos,
24                          String message ) throws ItemNotFound
25    {
26        if( array[ currentPos ] == null ||
27            array[ currentPos ].isActive == false )
28            throw new ItemNotFound( message );
29    }
```

Figure 19.11   find method for the probing hash table

```
1     /**
2      * Remove from the hash table.
3      * @param x the item to remove.
4      * @exception ItemNotFound if no item
5      *     that matches x can be found in the hash table.
6      */
7     public final void remove( Hashable x ) throws ItemNotFound
8     {
9         int currentPos = findPos( x );
10        assertFound( currentPos, "ProbingHashTable remove" );
11        array[ currentPos ].isActive = false;
12    }
```

Figure 19.12   remove routine for the probing hash table

```
1      /**
2       * Insert into the hash table. If the item is
3       * already present, then replace it with the new item.
4       * @param x the item to insert.
5       */
6      public final void insert( Hashable x )
7      {
8              // Insert x as active
9          int currentPos = findPos( x );
10         array[ currentPos ] = new HashEntry( x, true );
11         if( ++currentSize < array.length / 2 )
12             return;
13
14             // REHASHING CODE
15         HashEntry [ ] oldArray = array;
16
17             // Create a new double-sized, empty table
18         allocateArray( nextPrime( 2 * oldArray.length ) );
19         currentSize = 0;
20
21             // Copy table over
22         for( int i = 0; i < oldArray.length; i++ )
23             if( oldArray[ i ] != null && oldArray[ i ].isActive )
24                 insert( oldArray[ i ].element );
25     }
```

Figure 19.13   Insertion routine for the probing hash table, including the rehashing code

```
1  // Quadratic probing implementation of hash tables.
2  public class QuadraticProbingTable extends ProbingHashTable
3  {
4      protected final int findPos( Hashable x )
5      {
6          int collisionNum = 0;
7          int currentPos = x.hash( array.length );
8
9          while( array[ currentPos ] != null &&
10                !array[ currentPos ].element.equals( x ) )
11         {
12             currentPos += 2 * ++collisionNum - 1;
13             if( currentPos >= array.length )
14                 currentPos -= array.length;
15         }
16
17         return currentPos;
18     }
19 }
```

Figure 19.14   Class that implements quadratic probing

Line 15 saves a reference to the original table. We then create a new, double-sized, empty hash table at lines 18 to 19. Finally, we scan through the original array and `insert` any active elements into the new table. The `insert` will use the new hash function (since the array has a new size) and will automatically resolve all collisions. We can be sure that the recursive call to `insert` (at line 24) does not force another rehash. Alternatively, we could replace line 24 with two lines of code surrounded by braces (see Exercise 19.14).

So far nothing we have done depends on quadratic probing. Figure 19.14 (page 571) implements quadratic probing by extending `ProbingHashTable` and providing `findPos`, which finally deals with the quadratic probing algorithm. We keep searching the table until we find either an empty cell or a match. Lines 12 through 14 directly implement the methodology described in Theorem 19.5. Note that if x is marked deleted, its position will be returned by `findPos`. `assertFound` will eventually throw an exception when it determines that x is no longer active.

> Quadratic probing is implemented in `findPos`. It uses the previously described trick to avoid multiplications and mods.

19.4.2 Analysis of Quadratic Probing

Quadratic probing has not yet been mathematically analyzed. Although it eliminates primary clustering, elements that hash to the same position will probe the same alternative cells. This is known as *secondary clustering*. Once again, the independence of successive probes cannot be assumed. Secondary clustering is a slight theoretical blemish. Simulation results suggest that it generally causes less than an extra one-half probe per search and that this is true only for high load factors. Figure 19.5 illustrates the difference between linear probing and quadratic probing and shows that quadratic probing does not suffer from as much clustering as does linear probing.

> In *secondary clustering*, elements that hash to the same position will probe the same alternative cells. Secondary clustering is a minor theoretical blemish.

There are techniques that eliminate secondary clustering. The most popular of these is *double hashing*, in which a second hash function is used to drive the collision resolution. Specifically, we probe at a distance $Hash_2(X)$, $2Hash_2(X)$, and so on. The second hash function must be carefully chosen (for example, it should *never* evaluate to 0), and we need to make sure that all cells can be probed. A function such as $Hash_2(X) = R - (X \bmod R)$, with R a prime smaller than M, will generally work well. Double hashing is theoretically interesting because it can be shown to use essentially the same number of probes as the purely random analysis of linear probing would imply. However, it is somewhat more complicated than quadratic probing to implement and, as we see, requires careful attention to some details.

> *Double hashing* is a hashing technique that does not suffer from secondary clustering. A second hash function is used to drive the collision resolution.

There seems to be no good reason not to use a quadratic probing strategy, unless the overhead of maintaining a half-empty table is burdensome. This would be the case in other programming languages if the items being stored were very large.

19.5 Separate Chaining Hashing

A popular alternative to quadratic probing is *separate chaining hashing*. In separate chaining hashing, we maintain an array of linked lists: $L_0, L_1, ..., L_{M-1}$. The hash function tells us in which list to insert an item X and then, during a `find`, which list contains X. The idea is that although searching a linked list is a linear operation, if the lists are sufficiently short, the search time will be very fast. In particular, suppose the load factor, which is N/M, is λ. Note that for separate chaining hashing, the load factor is not bounded by 1.0. Then the average list has length λ, thus making the expected number of probes for an insertion or unsuccessful search λ. The expected number of probes for a successful search is $1 + \lambda/2$. This is because a successful search must occur in a nonempty list, and in such a list, we expect to have to traverse halfway down the list. The relative cost of a successful search versus an unsuccessful search is unusual in that if $\lambda < 2$, the successful search is more expensive than the unsuccessful search. This makes sense, however, because many unsuccessful searches encounter an empty linked list.

A typical load factor is 1.0; a lower load factor does not significantly enhance performance, but it costs extra space. The appeal of separate chaining hashing is that performance is not affected by a moderately increasing load factor; thus rehashing can be avoided. For languages that do not allow dynamic array expansion, this is a significant consideration. Furthermore, the expected number of probes for a search is less than in quadratic probing, particularly for unsuccessful searches.

We can implement separate chaining hashing using our already existing linked list classes. However, since the header node adds space overhead and is not really needed, then if space were at a premium, we could elect to not reuse components and instead implement a simple stacklike list. The coding effort turns out to be remarkably light. Also, the space overhead is essentially one reference per node, plus an additional reference per list; for example, when the load factor is 1.0, this is two references per item. This feature could be important in other programming languages if the size of an item is large. In this case, we have the same tradeoffs as with the array and linked-list implementations of stacks.

Separate chaining hashing is a space-efficient alternative to quadratic probing in which we maintain an array of linked lists. It is less sensitive to high load factors.

For separate chaining hashing, a reasonable load factor is 1.0. A lower load factor does not significantly improve performance, while a moderately higher load factor is acceptable and can save space.

Summary

Hash tables can be used to implement the `insert` and `find` operations in constant average time. It is especially important to pay attention to details such as load factor when using hash tables; otherwise, the constant time bounds are not meaningful. It is also important to choose the hash function carefully when the key is not a short string or integer. You should pick an easily computable function that distributes well.

For separate chaining hashing, the load factor is typically close to 1, although performance does not significantly degrade unless the load factor becomes very large. For quadratic probing, the table size should be prime and the load factor should not exceed 0.5. Rehashing should be used for quadratic probing to allow the table to grow and maintain the correct load factor. This is important if space is tight and it is not possible just to declare a huge hash table.

Use a hash table instead of a binary search tree if you do not need order statistics and are worried about non-random inputs.

We can also use binary search trees to implement `insert` and `find` operations. Although the resulting average time bounds are $O(\log N)$, binary search trees also support routines that require order and are thus more powerful. Using a hash table, we cannot efficiently find the minimum element or extend the table to allow computation of an order statistic. We cannot search efficiently for a string unless the exact string is known. A binary search tree could quickly find all items in a certain range; this capability is not supported by a hash table. Furthermore, the $O(\log N)$ bound is not necessarily that much more than $O(1)$, especially since no multiplications or divisions are required by search trees.

On the other hand, the worst case for hashing generally results from an implementation error, whereas sorted input can make binary search trees perform poorly. Balanced search trees are quite expensive to implement. Hence, if no ordering information is required and there is any suspicion that the input might be sorted, then hashing is the data structure of choice.

Hashing applications are abundant.

Hashing applications are abundant. Compilers use hash tables to keep track of declared variables in source code. The data structure is called a *symbol table*. Hash tables are the ideal application for this problem because only `insert` and `find` operations are performed. Identifiers are typically short, so the hash function can be computed quickly. Notice that in this application, most searches are successful.

Another common use of hash tables is in game programs. As the program searches through different lines of play, it keeps track of positions it has seen by computing a hash function based on the position (and storing its move for that position). If the same position reoccurs, usually by a simple transposition of moves, the program can avoid expensive recomputation. This general feature of all game-playing programs is called the *transposition table*. This was discussed in Section 10.2, where the tic-tac-toe algorithm was implemented.

A third use of hashing is in online spelling checkers. If misspelling detection (as opposed to correction) is important, an entire dictionary can be prehashed and words can be checked in constant time. Hash tables are well-suited for this because it is not important to alphabetize words. Printing out misspellings in the order they occurred in the document is acceptable.

This completes the discussion of basic searching algorithms. The next chapter examines the binary heap, which implements the priority queue and thus supports efficient access of the minimum item in a collection of items.

Objects of the Game

collision The result when two or more items in a hash table hash out to the same position. This problem is unavoidable because there are more items than positions. (554)

double hashing A hashing technique that does not suffer from secondary clustering. A second hash function is used to drive the collision resolution. (572)

hashing The implementation of hash tables to perform insertions, deletions, and finds. (553)

hash function A function that converts the item into an integer suitable to index an array where the item is stored. If the hash function was one to one, we could access the item by its array index. Since the hash function is not one to one, several items will collide at the same index. (554)

hash table A table used to implement a dictionary in constant time per operation. (553)

linear probing A way to avoid collisions by sequentially scanning the array until an empty cell is found. (557)

load factor The number of elements in a hash table divided by the size of the hash table array. In a probing hash table, the load factor ranges from 0 (empty) to 1 (full). In separate chaining hashing, it can be greater than 1. (559)

lazy deletion The technique of marking elements as deleted instead of physically removing them. Required in probing hash tables. (558)

primary clustering A problem in linear probing that affects performance. Large clusters of occupied cells form, thereby making insertions into the cluster expensive (and then the insertion makes the cluster larger). (560)

quadratic probing A collision resolution method that examines cells 1, 4, 9, and so on, away from the original probe point. (562)

secondary clustering Clustering that occurs when elements that hash to the same position probe the same alternative cells. It is a minor theoretical blemish. (572)

separate chaining A space-efficient alternative to quadratic probing in which an array of linked lists is maintained. It is less sensitive to high load factors. It exhibits some of the tradeoffs seen in the array versus linked-list stack implementations. (573)

Common Errors

1. The hash function returns an `int`. Since intermediate calculations allow overflow, the local variable should check that the result of the mod operator is non-negative so as to avoid an out-of-bounds return value.

2. The performance of a probing table degrades severely as the load factor approaches 1.0. Do not let this happen. Rehash when the load factor reaches 0.5.

3. The performance of all hashing methods depends on the use of a good hash function. A common error is providing a poor function.

On the Internet

The quadratic probing hash table is available in the directory **DataStructures**. A collection of files in the directory **Chapter19** can be used to generate Figure 19.5.

HashEntry.java   Contains the implementation of `HashEntry`.
ProbingHashTable.java Contains the implementation of the abstract probing hash table class.
QuadraticProbingTable.java Contains the implementation of a quadratic probing hash table.

Exercises

In Short

19.1. What are the array indices for a hash table of size 11?

19.2. What is the appropriate probing table size if the number of items in the hash table is 10?

19.3. Explain how deletion is performed in both probing and separate chaining hash tables.

19.4. What is the expected number of probes for both a successful and an unsuccessful search in a linear probing table with the load factor 0.25?

19.5. Given input {4371, 1323, 6173, 4199, 4344, 9679, 1989}, a fixed table size of 10, and a hash function $H(X) = X \bmod 10$, show the resulting
   a. linear probing hash table.
   b. quadratic probing hash table.
   c. separate chaining hash table.

19.6. Show the result of rehashing the probing tables in Exercise 19.5. Rehash to a prime table size.

19.7. The `isEmpty` routine has not been written. Can you implement it by returning the expression `currentSize==0`?

In Theory

19.8. An alternative collision resolution strategy is to define a sequence, $F(i) = R_i$, where $R_0 = 0$ and $R_1, R_2, ..., R_{M-1}$ is a random permutation of the first $M - 1$ integers (recall that the table size is M).

    a. Prove that under this strategy, if the table is not full, then the collision can always be resolved.

    b. Would this strategy be expected to eliminate primary clustering?

    c. Would this strategy be expected to eliminate secondary clustering?

    d. If the load factor of the table is λ, what is the expected time to perform an insertion?

    e. Generating a random permutation using the algorithm in Section 9.4 involves a large number of (expensive) calls to a random-number generator. Give an efficient algorithm to generate a random-looking permutation that avoids calling a random-number generator.

19.9. If rehashing is implemented as soon as the load factor reaches 0.5, then when the last element is inserted, the load factor is at least 0.25 and at most 0.5. What is the expected load factor? In other words, is it true or false that the load factor is 0.375 on average?

19.10. When the rehashing step is implemented, $O(N)$ probes must be used to reinsert the N elements. Give an estimate for the number of probes (that is, N or $2N$ or something else). *Hint*: Compute the average cost of inserting into the new table. These insertions vary from load factor 0 to load factor 0.25.

19.11. Under certain assumptions, the expected cost of an insertion into a hash table with secondary clustering is given by $1/(1-\lambda) - \lambda - \ln(1-\lambda)$. Unfortunately, this formula is not accurate for quadratic probing. However, assuming that it is, determine the following:

    a. the expected cost of an unsuccessful search.

    b. the expected cost of a successful search.

19.12. A quadratic probing hash table is used to store 10,000 `String` objects. Assume that the load factor is known to be 0.4 and that the average string length is 8 characters. Determine the following:

    a. The hash table size.

    b. The amount of memory used to store the 10,000 `String` objects.

    c. The amount of additional memory used by the hash table.

    d. The total memory used by the hash table.

    e. The space overhead.

In Practice

19.13. Implement linear probing.

19.14. For the probing hash table, implement the rehashing code without making a recursive call to `insert`.

19.15. Experiment with a hash function that examines every other character in a string. Is this a better choice than the one in the text?

19.16. Modify the class so that the `isEmpty` operation can be supported in constant time.

19.17. Modify the deletion algorithm so that if the load factor goes below $1/8$, then a rehash is performed to yield a table half as large. An extra data field must be maintained. Why?

Programming Problems

19.18. Find yourself a large online dictionary. Choose a table size that is twice as large as the dictionary. Apply the hash function described in the text to each word and store a count of the number of times each position is hashed to. You will get a distribution. Some percentage of the positions will not be hashed to, some will be hashed to once, some twice, and so on. Compare this distribution to what would occur for theoretical random numbers. This is discussed in Section 9.3.

19.19. Perform simulations to compare the observed performance of hashing with the theoretical results. Declare a probing hash table. Insert 10,000 randomly generate integers into the table and count the average number of probes used. This is the average cost of a successful search. Repeat the test several times for a good average. Run it for both linear probing and quadratic probing and do it for the final load factors 0.1, 0.2, ..., 0.9. Always declare the table so that no rehashing is needed. Thus the test for a 0.4 load factor would declare a table of size approximately 25,000 (adjusted to be prime).

19.20. Compare the time required to perform successful searches and insertions into a separate chaining table with a load factor 1 and a quadratic probing table with load factor 0.5. Run it for simple integers and strings and also complex records in which the search key is a string.

19.21. A BASIC program consists of a series of statements, each of which is numbered in ascending order. Control is passed by use of a *goto* or *gosub* and a statement number. Write a program that reads a legal basic program and renumbers the statements so that the first starts at number F and each statement has a number D higher than the previous statement. You may assume an upper limit of N statements, but the statement numbers in the input might be as large as a 32-bit integer. Your program must run in linear time.

19.22. Design an applet that illustrates quadratic probing.

References

Despite the apparent simplicity of hashing, much of the analysis is quite difficult and there are still many unresolved questions. There are also many interesting theoretical issues, which generally attempt to make it unlikely that worst-case possibilities of hashing arise.

An early paper on hashing is [11]. A wealth of information on the subject, including an analysis of closed hashing with linear probing, can be found in [6]. Double hashing is analyzed in [5] and [7]. Yet another collision resolution scheme is *coalesced hashing*, described in [12]. An excellent survey on the subject is [8]; [9] contains suggestions, and pitfalls, when choosing hash functions. Precise analytic and simulation results for all of the methods described in this chapter can be found in [4]. Yao [13] has shown that uniform hashing, in which no clustering exists, is optimal with respect to the cost of a successful search.

If the input keys are known in advance, then perfect hash functions, which do not allow collisions, exist [1]. Some more complicated hashing schemes, for which the worst case depends not on the particular input but on random numbers chosen by the algorithm, appear in [2] and [3]. These schemes guarantee that only a constant number of collisions occur in the worst case (although construction of a hash function can take a long time in the unlikely case of bad random numbers). They are useful for implementing tables in hardware.

One method of implementing Exercise 19.8 is described in [10].

1. J. L. Carter and M. N. Wegman, "Universal Classes of Hash Functions," *Journal of Computer and System Sciences* **18** (1979), 143–154.

2. M. Dietzfelbinger, A. R. Karlin, K. Melhorn, F. Meyer auf def Heide, H. Rohnert, and R. E. Tarjan, "Dynamic Perfect Hashing: Upper and Lower Bounds," *SIAM Journal on Computing* **23** (1994), 738–761.

3. R. J. Enbody and H. C. Du, "Dynamic Hashing Schemes," *Computing Surveys* **20** (1988), 85–113.

4. G. H. Gonnet and R. Baeza-Yates, *Handbook of Algorithms and Data Structures*, 2d ed., Addison-Wesley, Reading, Mass. (1991).

5. L. J. Guibas and E. Szemeredi, "The Analysis of Double Hashing," *Journal of Computer and System Sciences* **16** (1978), 226–274.

6. D. E. Knuth, *The Art of Computer Programming, Vol 3: Sorting and Searching*, 2d ed., Addison-Wesley, Reading, Mass. (1997).

7. G. Lueker and M. Molodowitch, "More Analysis of Double Hashing," *Combinatorica* **13** (1993), 83–96.

8. W. D. Maurer and T. G. Lewis, "Hash Table Methods," *Computing Surveys* **7** (1975), 5–20.

9. B. J. McKenzie, R. Harries, and T. Bell, "Selecting a Hashing Algorithm," *Software-Practice and Experience* **20** (1990), 209–224.

10. R. Morris, "Scatter Storage Techniques," *Communications of the ACM* **11** (1968), 38–44.

11. W. W. Peterson, "Addressing for Random Access Storage," *IBM Journal of Research and Development* **1** (1957), 130–146.

12. J. S. Vitter, "Implementations for Coalesced Hashing," *Information Processing Letters* **11** (1980), 84–86.

13. A. C. Yao, "Uniform Hashing Is Optimal," *Journal of the ACM* **32** (1985), 687–693.

20

A Priority Queue: The Binary Heap

THE priority queue is a fundamental data structure that allows access to only the minimum item. This chapter discusses one implementation of the priority queue data structure, the elegant *binary heap*. The binary heap supports the insertion of new items and the deletion of the minimum item in logarithmic worst-case time. It uses only an array and is simple to implement.

In this chapter, we will see:

- The basic properties of the binary heap
- How the `insert` and `deleteMin` operations can be performed in logarithmic time
- A linear-time heap construction algorithm
- A Java implementation
- An easily implemented sorting algorithm, *heapsort*, that runs in $O(N \log N)$ time but uses no extra memory
- How heaps can be used to implement external sorting

20.1 Basic Ideas

As discussed in Section 6.8, the priority queue supports the access and deletion of the minimum item using `findMin` and `deleteMin`, respectively. We could use a simple linked list, performing insertions at the front in constant time, but then finding and/or deleting the minimum would require a linear scan of the list. Alternatively, we could insist that the list always be kept sorted. This makes the access and deletion of the minimum cheap, but then insertions would be linear.

Another way of implementing priority queues is to use a binary search tree. This gives an $O(\log N)$ average running time for both operations. However, a binary search tree is a poor choice because the input is typically not sufficiently random. We could use a balanced search tree, but the structures shown in Chapter 18 are cumbersome to implement and lead to sluggish performance in practice.

A linked list or array requires that some operation use linear time.

An unbalanced binary search tree does not have a good worst case. A balanced search tree requires lots of work.

(Chapter 21, however, covers a data structure, the *splay tree*, that has been shown empirically to be a good alternative in some situations.)

The priority queue has properties that are a compromise between a queue and a binary search tree.

Because the priority queue supports only some of the search tree operations, it should not be more expensive to implement than a search tree. On the other hand, the priority queue is more powerful than a simple queue because we can implement a queue using a priority queue as follows. First, insert each item with an indication of its insertion time. Then, a `deleteMin` on the basis of minimum insertion time implements a `dequeue`. Consequently, it is reasonable to expect to obtain an implementation that has properties that are a compromise between a queue and a search tree. This is realized by the *binary heap*, which

- can be implemented using a simple array (like the queue),
- supports `insert` and `deleteMin` in $O(\log N)$ worst-case time (a compromise between the binary search tree and the queue), and
- supports `insert` in constant average time and `findMin` in constant worst-case time (like the queue).

The binary heap is the classic method used to implement priority queues.

Like the balanced search tree structures in Chapter 18, the binary heap has two properties: a structure property and an ordering property. And as with balanced search trees, an operation on a binary heap can destroy one of the properties, so a binary heap operation must not terminate until both properties are in order. This turns out to be simple to achieve. (In this chapter, the term *heap* refers to the binary heap.)

20.1.1 Structure Property

The heap is a complete binary tree. This allows representation using a simple array and guarantees logarithmic depth.

The only structure that gives dynamic logarithmic time bounds is the tree, so it seems natural that the heap should organize its data as a tree. Since we would like the logarithmic bound to be a worst-case guarantee, it follows that the tree should be balanced.

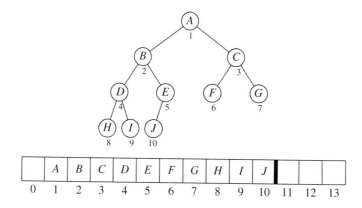

Figure 20.1 A complete binary tree and its array representation

A *complete binary tree* is a tree that is completely filled, with the possible exception of the bottom level, which is filled from left to right. The distinguishing feature of the complete binary tree is that there are no missing nodes in the tree. An example of a complete binary tree of ten items is shown in Figure 20.1. Had the node *J* been a right child of *E*, the tree would not be complete because there would be a missing node.

The complete tree has a number of properties that are very useful. First, the height (longest path length) of a complete binary tree of N nodes is at most $\lfloor \log N \rfloor$. This is because a complete tree of height H has between 2^H and $2^{H+1} - 1$ nodes. This implies that we can expect logarithmic worst-case behavior if we restrict changes in the structure to one path from the root to a leaf.

Second and equally important is the observation that in a complete binary tree, `left` and `right` references are not needed. As shown in Figure 20.1, we can represent a complete binary tree by storing its level-order traversal in an array. We place the root in position 1 (position 0 is left vacant, for a reason discussed later in the chapter). We also need to maintain an integer that tells us how many nodes are currently in the tree. Then for any element in array position i, we see that its left child can be found in position $2i$. If this position extends past the number of nodes that are in the tree, then we know that the left child does not exist. Similarly, the right child is located immediately after the left child in position $2i + 1$. We again test against the actual tree size to make sure the child exists. Finally, the parent is in position $\lfloor i/2 \rfloor$. Notice that every node has a parent except the root. If the root were to have a parent, the calculation would place it in position 0. Thus we reserve position 0 as a place in which to put a dummy item that can serve as the root's parent. Doing this simplifies one of the operations.

> The parent is in position $\lfloor i/2 \rfloor$, the left child is in $2i$, and the right child is in $2i + 1$.

Using an array to store a tree is called *implicit representation*. As a result of this representation, not only are child references not required, but also the operations required to traverse the tree are extremely simple and likely to be very fast on most computers. The heap entity will consist of an array of objects and an integer representing the current heap size.

> Using an array to store a tree is called *implicit representation*.

In this chapter, heaps are drawn as trees so as to make the algorithms easier to visualize. The implementation of these trees uses an array. We do not use the implicit representation for all search trees. Some of the problems with doing this are sketched in Exercise 20.8.

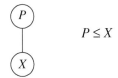

$P \le X$

Figure 20.2   Heap order property

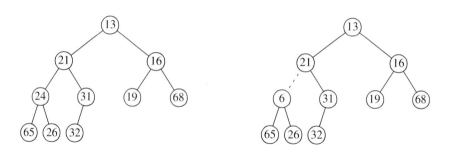

Figure 20.3   Two complete trees (only the left tree is a heap)

20.1.2 Heap-order Property

The heap-order property states that, in a heap, the item in the parent is never larger than the item in a node.

The property that allows operations to be performed quickly is the *heap-order property*. Since we want to be able to find the minimum quickly, it makes sense that the smallest element should be at the root. If we consider that any subtree should also (recursively) be a heap, then any node should be smaller than all of its descendants. Applying this logic, we arrive at the heap-order property.

HEAP-ORDER PROPERTY

In a heap, for every node X with parent P, the key in P is smaller than or equal to the key in X.

The root's parent can be stored in position 0 and given a value of negative infinity.

The heap-order property is illustrated in Figure 20.2 (page 583). In Figure 20.3, the tree on the left is a heap, but the tree on the right is not (the dashed line shows the violation of heap order). Notice that the root does not have a parent. In the implicit representation, we can place the value $-\infty$ in position zero to remove this special case when we implement the heap. By the heap-order property, we see that the minimum element can always be found at the root. Thus findMin is a constant time operation. *Max heaps* support access of the maximum *instead* of the minimum. Minor changes can be used to implement max heaps.

20.1.3 Allowed Operations

Now that we have settled on the representation, we can start writing code. We already know that our heap will support the basic insert, findMin, and deleteMin operations, and the usual isEmpty and makeEmpty. We will also add some additional operations. Figure 20.4 shows the public section of the class and illustrates some of these additional methods. Figure 20.5 (page 586) contains the private section of the class.

```
 1 package DataStructures;
 2
 3 import Supporting.*;
 4 import Exceptions.*;
 5
 6 // BinaryHeap class
 7 //
 8 // CONSTRUCTION: with a negative infinity sentinel
 9 //
10 // ******************PUBLIC OPERATIONS********************
11 // void insert( x )        --> Insert x
12 // Comparable deleteMin( )--> Return and remove smallest item
13 // Comparable findMin( )  --> Return smallest item
14 // boolean isEmpty( )      --> Return true if empty; else false
15 // void makeEmpty( )       --> Remove all items
16 // void toss( x )          --> Insert x (lazily)
17 // ******************ERRORS*******************************
18 // findMin and deleteMin throw Underflow when empty
19
20 /**
21  * Implements a binary heap.
22  * Allows lazy insertion and provides a linear-time
23  * heap construction method.
24  * Note that all "matching" is based on the compares method.
25  */
26 public class BinaryHeap implements PriorityQueue
27 {
28     public BinaryHeap( Comparable negInf )
29       { /* Figure 20.7 */ }
30     public void insert( Comparable x )
31       { /* Figure 20.12 */ }
32     public void toss( Comparable x )
33       { /* Figure 20.12 */ }
34     public Comparable findMin( ) throws Underflow
35       { /* Figure 20.6 */ }
36     public Comparable deleteMin( ) throws Underflow
37       { /* Figure 20.16 */ }
38     public boolean isEmpty( )
39       { return currentSize == 0; }
40     public void makeEmpty( )
41       { currentSize = 0; }
```

Figure 20.4   `BinaryHeap` class skeleton (part 1: public section)

```
42    private int currentSize; // Number of elements in heap
43    private boolean orderOK; // True if heap order is in force
44    private Comparable [ ] array; // The heap array
45    private static final int DEFAULT_CAPACITY = 11;
46
47    private void getArray( int newMaxSize )
48        { /* Figure 20.8 */ }
49    private void checkSize( )
50        { /* Figure 20.11 */ }
51    private void percolateDown( int hole )
52        { /* Figure 20.17 */ }
53    private void fixHeap( )
54        { /* Figure 20.19 */ }
55  }
```

Figure 20.5   BinaryHeap class skeleton (part 2: private section)

toss will add an item but, unlike insert, it does not guarantee that heap order is maintained. It is useful if we intend to add many items prior to needing access to the minimum.

We begin by examining the public methods. The constructor is declared at line 28. The insert method is declared at line 30. It adds a new item x into the heap, performing the necessary operations to maintain the heap-order property. Line 32 adds a new method, toss. The toss method adds a new item x into the heap but does not guarantee that heap order is maintained. Why would we ever want to toss an item into the heap? The answer is that toss is a much easier operation than insert. Of course, as soon as we do a toss operation, we do not have a heap anymore, so we cannot expect a findMin or deleteMin to work. For instance, if we toss in the new minimum, we have no guarantee that it will be placed at the root (indeed we expect it will not). Consequently, toss seems like a stupid idea. fixHeap is made private, and its use is transparent.

fixHeap reinstates the heap order. Because fixHeap is expensive, its use is only justified if there are many toss operations between accesses of the minimum.

It is not stupid, however, because there are many applications for which we can toss in many items before the next deleteMin occurs. In that case, we do not need to have heap order in effect until the deleteMin occurs. The fixHeap operation, declared at line 53, reinstates the heap order, no matter how messed up the heap is. It works in linear time. Thus, for instance, if we need to place *N* items in the heap before the first deleteMin, it is more efficient to do *N* tosses and one fixHeap than *N* inserts. However, we will not use toss in place of only a few inserts.

The remaining operations are as expected. findMin is declared at line 34 and returns the minimum item in the heap. deleteMin, at line 36, returns and removes the minimum item. The usual isEmpty and makeEmpty are provided, with body, at lines 38 to 41.

Once we process a toss, the user cannot perform a findMin or deleteMin without an immediately preceding fixHeap. Rather than trust the user to make this call, we maintain a data field orderOK, which is set to false when a toss creates a heap-order violation. Figure 20.6 shows that findMin checks to see if the heap order is satisfied. If it is not, a call to fixHeap is automatically made to reinstate the property.

```
1       /**
2        * Find the smallest item in the priority queue.
3        * @return the smallest item.
4        * @exception Underflow if the priority queue is empty.
5        */
6       public Comparable findMin( ) throws Underflow
7       {
8           if( isEmpty( ) )
9               throw new Underflow( "Empty binary heap" );
10          if( !orderOK )
11              fixHeap( );
12          return array[ 1 ];
13      }
```

Figure 20.6   The findMin routine

```
1       /**
2        * Construct the binary heap.
3        * @param negInf a value less than or equal to all others.
4        */
5       public BinaryHeap( Comparable negInf )
6       {
7           currentSize = 0;
8           orderOK = true;
9           getArray( DEFAULT_CAPACITY );
10          array[ 0 ] = negInf;
11      }
```

Figure 20.7   Constructor for BinaryHeap

```
1       /**
2        * Private method to allocate the binary heap array.
3        * Includes an extra spot for the sentinel.
4        * @param newMaxSize the capacity of the heap.
5        */
6       private void getArray( int newMaxSize )
7       {
8           array = new Comparable[ newMaxSize + 1 ];
9       }
```

Figure 20.8   Allocate array (called by constructor and during array doubling)

The remaining data fields are the usual suspects: a dynamically allocated array and an integer that records the current heap size. The constructor, shown in Figure 20.7 (page 587), initializes the data fields. It sets the heap order as `true` and then allocates the array by calling `getArray` at line 9. After the array is allocated, the sentinel is placed in position 0, at line 10. The user must provide `negInf` as a parameter to the constructor. The body for `getArray` is one line of code and is shown in Figure 20.8 (page 587).

20.2 Implementation of the Basic Operations

The heap-order property looks promising so far, since easy access to the minimum is provided. We must now show that we can efficiently support `insert` and `deleteMin` in logarithmic time. It is easy (both conceptually and practically) to perform the two required operations. All the work involves ensuring the heap-order property is maintained.

20.2.1 `insert`

Insertion is implemented by creating a hole at the next available location and then percolating it up until the new item can be placed in it without introducing a heap-order violation with the hole's parent.

`insert` uses the sentinel to avoid a special case at the root.

To insert an element *X* into the heap, we must first add a node to the tree. The only option is to create a hole in the next available location; otherwise, the tree will not be complete and we would violate the structure property. If *X* can be placed in the hole without violating heap order, then we do so and are done. Otherwise, we slide the element that is in the hole's parent node into the node, thus bubbling the hole up toward the root. We continue this process until *X* can be placed in the hole. Figure 20.9 shows that to insert 14, we create a hole in the next available heap location. Inserting 14 into the hole would violate the heap-order property, so 31 is slid down into the hole. This strategy is continued in Figure 20.10 until the correct location for 14 is found.

This general strategy is called a *percolate up*. The new element is percolated up the heap until the correct location is found. The routine `checkSize`, shown in Figure 20.11, will double the array if necessary. Figure 20.12 (page 590) shows the routines that add items into the heap. The `toss` routine is short; it just adds the new element x in the next available location. If a heap-order violation results, `orderOK` is set to `false`. `insert` implements the percolate up using a very tight loop. The statement at line 30 increments the current size and sets the hole to the newly added node. We iterate the loop at line 31 as long as the item in the parent node is larger than x. Line 32 moves the item in the parent down into the hole, and then the third expression in the `for` loop moves the hole up to the parent. When the loop terminates, line 33 places x into the hole. The sentinel in position zero guarantees that the `for` loop will terminate.

The time to do the insertion could be as much as $O(\log N)$ if the element to be inserted is the new minimum. This is because it will be percolated up all the way to the root. On average, the percolation terminates early: It has been shown that 2.6 comparisons are required on average to perform the `insert`, so the average `insert` moves an element up 1.6 levels.

Insertion takes constant time on average but logarithmic time in the worst case.

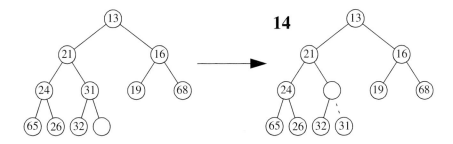

Figure 20.9   Attempt to insert 14, thus creating the hole and bubbling the hole up

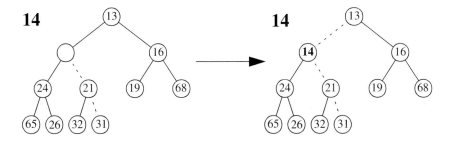

Figure 20.10   The remaining two steps to insert 14 in the previous heap

```
1      /**
2       * Private method that doubles the heap array if full.
3       */
4      private void checkSize( )
5      {
6          if( currentSize == array.length - 1 )
7          {
8              Comparable [ ] oldArray = array;
9              getArray( currentSize * 2 );
10             for( int i = 0; i < oldArray.length; i++ )
11                 array[ i ] = oldArray[ i ];
12         }
13     }
```

Figure 20.11   Private method `checkSize` doubles `array` if necessary

```
1      /**
2       * Insert into the priority queue, without maintaining
3       * heap order. Duplicates are allowed.
4       * @param x the item to insert.
5       */
6      public void toss( Comparable x )
7      {
8          checkSize( );
9          array[ ++currentSize ] = x;
10         if( x.lessThan( array[ currentSize / 2 ] ) )
11             orderOK = false;
12     }
13
14     /**
15      * Insert into the priority queue, maintaining heap order.
16      * Duplicates are allowed.
17      * @param x the item to insert.
18      */
19     public void insert( Comparable x )
20     {
21         if( !orderOK )
22         {
23             toss( x );
24             return;
25         }
26
27         checkSize( );
28
29             // Percolate up
30         int hole = ++currentSize;
31         for( ; x.lessThan( array[ hole / 2 ] ); hole /= 2 )
32             array[ hole ] = array[ hole / 2 ];
33         array[ hole ] = x;
34     }
```

Figure 20.12 `toss` and `insert` methods

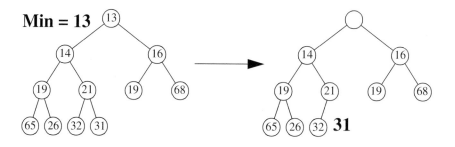

Figure 20.13 Creation of the hole at the root when the minimum value is deleted

20.2.2 `deleteMin`

`deleteMin`s are handled in a similar manner as insertions. As shown already, finding the minimum is easy; the hard part is removing it. When the minimum is removed, a hole is created at the root. Since the heap now becomes one smaller, the structure property tells us that the last node must be eliminated. Figure 20.13 shows the situation: The minimum item is 13, the root has a hole, and the former last item needs to be placed in the heap somewhere.

Deletion of the minimum involves placing the former last item in a hole that is created at the root. The hole is *percolated down* the tree through minimum children until the item can be placed without violating the heap-order property.

If the last item can be placed in the hole, we would be done. This is impossible, however, unless the size of the heap is two or three, because elements at the bottom are larger than elements on the second level. We must play the same game that was done for insertion: Put some item in the hole and then move the hole. The only difference is that for the `deleteMin`, we will be moving down the tree. To do this, we find the smaller child of the hole. If that child is smaller than the item we are trying to place, then we move the child into the hole, thus pushing the hole down one level. In Figure 20.14, we place the smaller child (14) into the hole, sliding the hole down one level. We repeat this again, placing 19 into the hole and creating a new hole one level deeper. We then place 26 in the hole and create a new hole on the bottom level. Finally, we are able to place 31 in the hole, as shown in Figure 20.15. It is easy to see that this is a logarithmic operation in the worst case. This process is called *percolate down*. Not surprisingly, the percolation rarely terminates more than one or two levels early, so the operation is logarithmic on average, too.

`deleteMin` is logarithmic in both the worst and average case.

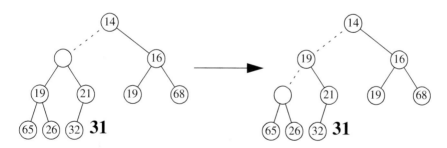

Figure 20.14   Next two steps in `deleteMin`

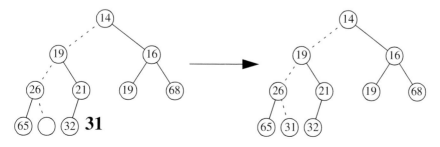

Figure 20.15   Last two steps in `deleteMin`

```
 1      /**
 2       * Remove the smallest item from the priority queue.
 3       * @exception Underflow if the priority queue is empty.
 4       */
 5      public Comparable deleteMin( ) throws Underflow
 6      {
 7          Comparable minItem = findMin( );
 8          array[ 1 ] = array[ currentSize-- ];
 9          percolateDown( 1 );
10
11          return minItem;
12      }
```

Figure 20.16 deleteMin method

```
 1      /**
 2       * Internal method to percolate down in the heap.
 3       * @param hole the index at which the percolate begins.
 4       */
 5      private void percolateDown( int hole )
 6      {
 7          int child;
 8          Comparable tmp = array[ hole ];
 9
10          for( ; hole * 2 <= currentSize; hole = child )
11          {
12              child = hole * 2;
13              if( child != currentSize && array[ child + 1 ].
14                                  lessThan( array[ child ] ) )
15                  child++;
16              if( array[ child ].lessThan( tmp ) )
17                  array[ hole ] = array[ child ];
18              else
19                  break;
20          }
21          array[ hole ] = tmp;
22      }
```

Figure 20.17 percolateDown method used for deleteMin and
fixHeap

Figure 20.16 shows the deleteMin method. The tests for emptiness and heap order are automatically done by the call to findMin at line 7. The real work is done in percolateDown, which is shown in Figure 20.17. The code shown there is similar in spirit to the percolation up in the insert routine. Because there are two children rather than one parent, the code is a bit more complicated. percolateDown takes a single parameter that tells where the hole is to be placed. The item in the hole is then moved out, and the percolation begins.

For deleteMin, hole will be position 1. The for loop at line 10 terminates when there is no left child. The third expression moves the hole to the child. The smaller child is found at lines 13 to 15. Notice that we have to be careful because the last node in an even-sized heap is an only child; we cannot always assume that there are two children. This is why we have the first test at line 13.

20.3 **fixHeap**: Linear Time Heap Construction

The fixHeap operation takes a complete tree that does not have heap order and reinstates it. We want this to be a linear-time operation, since N insertions could be done in $O(N \log N)$ time. We expect that $O(N)$ is attainable because N successive insertions take a total of $O(N)$ time on average, based on the result stated at the end of Section 20.2.1. N successive insertions do more work than we require, since they maintain heap order after every insertion. We need heap order only at one instant.

fixHeap can be done in linear time by applying a percolate down routine to nodes in reverse level order.

The easiest abstract solution is obtained by viewing the heap as a recursively defined structure, as shown in Figure 20.18: We would recursively call fixHeap on the left and right subheaps. At that point, we are guaranteed that we have heap order established everywhere except at the root. We can establish heap order everywhere by calling percolateDown for the root. The recursive routine works by guaranteeing that when we apply percolateDown(i), all descendants of i have been processed by their own call to percolateDown, recursively. The recursion, however, is not necessary, as soon as we make the following observation. That is, if we call percolateDown on nodes in reverse level order, then at the point percolateDown(i) is processed, all descendants of node i will have been processed by a prior call to percolateDown. This leads to an incredibly simple algorithm for fixHeap, which is shown in Figure 20.19. Notice that percolateDown on a leaf need not be performed. Thus we start at the highest-numbered nonleaf node.

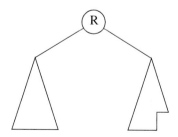

Figure 20.18 Recursive view of the heap

```
1       /**
2        * Re-establish heap order property after a series of
3        * toss operations. Runs in linear time.
4        */
5       private void fixHeap( )
6       {
7           for( int i = currentSize / 2; i > 0; i-- )
8               percolateDown( i );
9           orderOK = true;
10      }
```

Figure 20.19 Implementation of linear-time `fixHeap` method

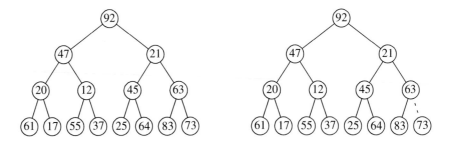

Figure 20.20 Initial heap (left); after `percolateDown(7)` (right)

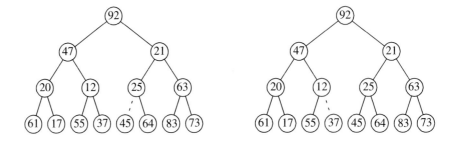

Figure 20.21 After `percolateDown(6)` (left); after
`percolateDown(5)` (right)

The first tree in Figure 20.20 is the unordered tree. The seven remaining trees in Figures 20.20 through 20.23 show the result of each of the seven `percolateDown` operations. Each dashed line corresponds to two comparisons: one to find the smaller child and one to compare the smaller child with the node. Notice that there are only ten dashed lines in the entire algorithm corresponding to 20 comparisons. (There could have been an eleventh.)

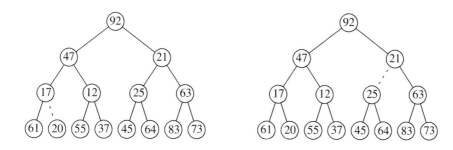

Figure 20.22 After `percolateDown(4)` (left); after
`percolateDown(3)` (right)

To bound the running time of `fixHeap`, we must bound the number of dashed lines. This can be done by computing the sum of the heights of all the nodes in the heap, which is the maximum number of dashed lines. We expect a small number because half of the nodes are leaves and have height zero and a quarter have height 1. Thus only a quarter of the nodes (those not already counted in the first two cases) can contribute more than 1 unit of height. In particular, there is only one node that contributes the maximum height of $\lfloor \log N \rfloor$.

To obtain a linear time bound for `fixHeap`, we need to establish that the sum of the heights of the nodes of a complete binary tree is $O(N)$. This is shown in Theorem 20.1. We prove the bound for perfect trees by using a marking argument.

The linear time bound can be shown by computing the sum of the heights of all the nodes in the heap.

We prove the bound for perfect trees by using a marking argument.

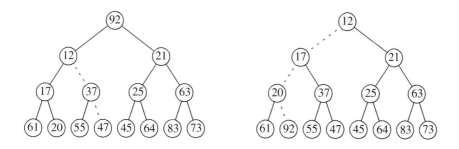

Figure 20.23 After `percolateDown(2)` (left); after
`percolateDown(1)` and `fixHeap` terminates (right)

Theorem 20.1

For the perfect binary tree of height H containing $N = 2^{H+1} - 1$ nodes, the sum of the heights of the nodes is $N - H - 1$.

Proof

We use a tree marking argument. (A more direct brute force calculation could also be done, as in Exercise 20.10.) For any node in the tree that has some height h, we darken h tree edges as follows: We go down the tree by traversing the left edge and then only right edges. Each edge that is traversed is darkened. An example is a perfect tree of height 4. Nodes that have height 1 have their left edge darkened, as shown in Figure 20.24. Next, nodes of height 2 have a left edge and then a right edge darkened on the path from the node to the bottom. This is shown in Figure 20.25. In Figure 20.26, three edges are darkened for each node of height 3: the first left edge leading out of the node and then the two right edges on the path to the bottom. Finally, in Figure 20.27 we see that four edges are darkened: the left edge leading out of the root and the three right edges on the path to the bottom. Note that no edge is ever darkened twice and every edge except those on the right path is darkened. Since there are $(N - 1)$ tree edges (every node has an edge coming into it except the root) and H edges on the right path, the number of darkened edges is $N - 1 - H$. This proves the theorem.

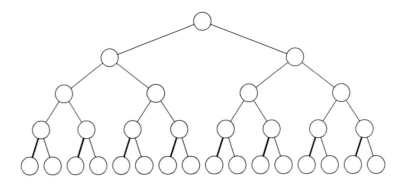

Figure 20.24 Marking of the left edges for height 1 nodes

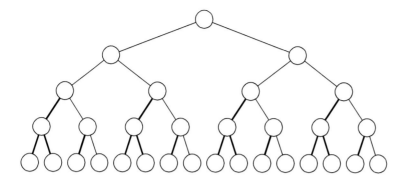

Figure 20.25   Marking of the first left and subsequent right edge for height 2 nodes

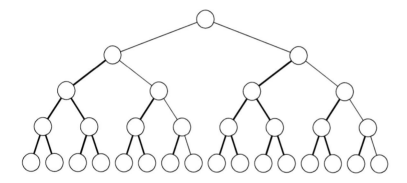

Figure 20.26   Marking of the first left and subsequent two right edges for height 3 nodes

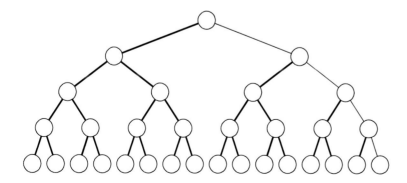

Figure 20.27   Marking of the first left and subsequent right edges for the height 4 node

A complete binary tree is not a perfect binary tree, but the result we have obtained is an upper bound on the sum of the heights of the nodes in a complete binary tree. Since a complete binary tree has between 2^H and $2^{H+1} - 1$ nodes, this theorem implies that the sum is $O(N)$. A more careful argument establishes that the sum of the height is $N - v(N)$, where $v(N)$ is the number of 1s in the binary representation of N. A proof of this is left as Exercise 20.12.

20.4 Advanced Operations: `decreaseKey` and `merge`

Chapter 22 examines priority queues that support two additional operations. The `decreaseKey` operation lowers the value of an item in the priority queue. The item's position is presumed to be known. In a binary heap, this is easily implemented by percolating up until heap order is reestablished. However, we must be careful, since by assumption each item's position is being stored separately. All items involved in the percolation have their positions altered. `decreaseKey` is useful in implementing graph algorithms (for example, Dijkstra's algorithm, seen in Section 14.3).

`merge` combines two priority queues. Because the heap is array-based, the best we can hope to achieve with a merge is to copy the items in the smaller heap into the larger heap and perform some rearrangements. Even so, this will take at least linear time per operation. If we use general trees with nodes connected by child references, we can reduce the bound to logarithmic cost per operation. Merging has uses in advanced algorithm design.

20.5 Internal Sorting: Heapsort

A priority queue can be used to sort in $O(N \log N)$ time. An algorithm that is based on this idea is heapsort.

The priority queue can be used to sort N items as follows:

1. Insert every item into a binary heap.
2. Extract every item by calling `deleteMin` N times. The result is sorted.

Using the observation of the previous section, we can more efficiently implement this as follows:

1. `toss` each item into a binary heap.
2. Apply `fixHeap`.
3. Call `deleteMin` N times: The items will exit the heap in sorted order.

Step 1 takes linear time total, and step 2 takes linear time. In step 3, each call to `deleteMin` takes logarithmic time, so N calls take $O(N \log N)$ time. Consequently, we have an $O(N \log N)$ worst-case sorting algorithm, which is as good as can be achieved by a comparison-based algorithm, as discussed in Section 8.8. One problem with the algorithm as it stands now is that sorting an array requires the use of the binary heap data structure, which itself carries the overhead of an array. It would be preferable to emulate the heap data structure on the array that is input, rather than going through the heap class apparatus. We will assume for the rest of this discussion that this is what will be done.

However, even though we do not use the heap class directly, we have the problem that we still seem to need a second array. This is because we have to record the order in which items exit the heap-equivalent in a second array and then copy that ordering back into the original array. The memory requirement is doubled; this could be critical in some applications. Notice that the extra time spent copying the second array back to the first is only $O(N)$, so unlike mergesort, the extra array does not affect the running *time* significantly. The problem is space.

A clever way to avoid using a second array makes use of the fact that after each `deleteMin`, the heap shrinks by 1. Thus the cell that was last in the heap can be used to store the element that was just deleted. As an example, suppose we have a heap with six elements. The first `deleteMin` produces A_1. Now the heap has only five elements, so we can place A_1 in position six. The next `deleteMin` produces A_2. Since the heap will now only have four elements, we can place A_2 in position five.

> By using empty parts of the array, we can perform the sort in place.

Under this strategy, the array will contain, after the last `deleteMin`, the elements in *decreasing* sorted order. If we want the array in the more typical *increasing* sorted order, we can change the ordering property so that the parent has a larger key than the child does. Thus we have a *max heap*. As an example, suppose we want to sort the input sequence 59, 36, 58, 21, 41, 97, 31, 16, 26, 53. After the items are tossed into the max heap and `fixHeap` is applied, we obtain the arrangement shown in Figure 20.28. (Note that there is no sentinel; we presume the data starts in position 0, as is typical for other sorts in Chapter 8.)

> If we use a max-heap, we obtain items in increasing order.

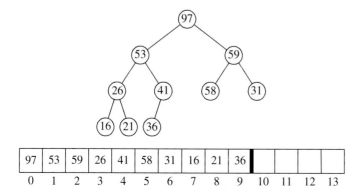

97	53	59	26	41	58	31	16	21	36				
0	1	2	3	4	5	6	7	8	9	10	11	12	13

Figure 20.28 (Max) Heap after the `fixHeap` phase

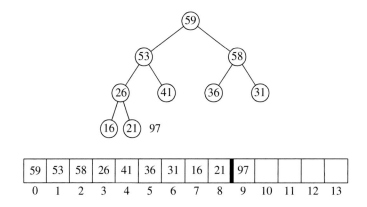

Figure 20.29 Heap after the first `deleteMax`

Figure 20.29 shows the heap that results after the first `deleteMax`. The last element in the heap is 21; 97 has been placed in a part of the heap array that is technically no longer part of the heap.

Figure 20.30 shows that after a second `deleteMax`, 16 becomes the last element. Now only eight items remain in the heap. The maximum element that was removed, 59, is placed in the dead spot of the array. After seven more `deleteMax` operations, the heap will represent only one element, but the elements left in the array will be sorted in increasing order.

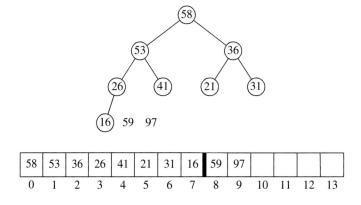

Figure 20.30 Heap after the second `deleteMax`

```
1       /**
2        * Standard heapsort.
3        * @param a an array of Comparable items.
4        */
5       public static void heapsort( Comparable [ ] a )
6       {
7           for( int i = a.length / 2; i >= 0; i-- ) // Build heap
8               percDown( a, i, a.length );
9           for( int i = a.length - 1; i > 0; i-- )
10          {
11              swapReferences( a, 0, i );              // deleteMax
12              percDown( a, 0, i );
13          }
14      }
```

Figure 20.31 heapSort routine

The implementation of heapsort is simple because the basic operations follow the heap operations. There are three minor differences. First, since we are using a max heap, we need to reverse the logic of the comparisons from > to <. Second, we can no longer assume that there is a sentinel position 0. This is because all of our other sorting algorithms store data at position 0. We must assume that heapSort will be no different. Although the sentinel is not needed anyway (since there are no percolate up operations), its absence affects calculations of the child and parent. That is, for a node in position i, the parent is in position $(i - 1)/2$, the left child is in position $2i + 1$, and the right child is next to the left child. Third, percDown needs to be informed of the current heap size (which is lowered by 1 in each iteration of deleteMax). The implementation of percDown is left as Exercise 20.20. Assuming that we have written percDown, then heapSort is easily expressed as shown in Figure 20.31.

> Minor changes are required for heapsort because the root is stored in position 0.

20.6 External Sorting

So far all of the sorting algorithms examined require that the input fit into main memory. There are, however, applications for which the input is much too large to fit into memory. This section discusses *external sorting* algorithms, which are designed to handle very large inputs.

> External sorts are used when the amount of data is too large to fit in main memory.

20.6.1 Why We Need New Algorithms

Most of the internal sorting algorithms take advantage of the fact that memory is directly accessible. Shellsort compares elements a[i] and a[i-gap] in one time unit. Heapsort compares a[i] and a[child=i*2] in one time unit.

Quicksort, with median-of-three pivoting, requires comparing a[first], a[center], and a[last] in a constant number of time units. If the input is on a tape, then all of these operations lose their efficiency because elements on a tape can be accessed only sequentially. Even if the data is on a disk, there is still a practical loss of efficiency because of the delay required to spin the disk and move the disk head.

To see how slow external accesses really are, we could create a random file that is large but not too big to fit in main memory. When we read in the file and sort it using an efficient algorithm, the time to read the input is likely to be significant compared to the time it takes to sort the input, even though sorting is an $O(N \log N)$ operation (or worse for Shellsort) and reading the input is only $O(N)$.

20.6.2 Model for External Sorting

We assume sorts are performed on tape. Only sequential access of the input is allowed.

The wide variety of mass storage devices makes external sorting much more device-dependent than internal sorting does. The algorithms considered here work on tapes, which are probably the most restrictive storage medium. Since access to an element on tape is done by winding the tape to the correct location, tapes can be efficiently accessed only in sequential order (in either direction).

Assume we have at least three tape drives to perform the sorting. We need two drives to do an efficient sort; the third drive simplifies matters. If only one tape drive is present, then we are in trouble: Any algorithm will require $\Omega(N)$ tape accesses.

20.6.3 The Simple Algorithm

The basic external sort uses repeated two-way merging. Each sorted group is a *run*. As a result of a pass, the length of the runs doubles and eventually only a single run remains.

The basic external sorting algorithm uses the merge routine from mergesort. Suppose we have four tapes A1, A2, B1, and B2, which are two input and two output tapes. Depending on the point in the algorithm, the A and B tapes are either input tapes or output tapes. Suppose the data is initially on A1. Suppose further that the internal memory can hold (and sort) M records at a time. The natural first step is to read M records at a time from the input tape, sort the records internally, and then write the sorted records alternately to B1 and B2. Each set of sorted records is called a *run*. When this is done, we rewind all the tapes. Suppose we have the same input as our example for Shellsort. The initial configuration is shown in Figure 20.32. If $M = 3$, then after the runs are constructed, the tapes will contain the data as shown in Figure 20.33.

Now B1 and B2 contain a group of runs. We take the first runs from each tape, merge them, and write the result, which is a run twice as long, onto A1. Then we take the next runs from each tape, merge them, and write the result out to A2. We continue this process, alternating output to A1 and A2 until either B1 or B2 is empty. At this point, either both are empty or there is one (possibly short) run left. In the latter case, we copy this run onto the appropriate tape. We rewind all four tapes and repeat the same steps, this time using the A tapes as input and the B tapes as output. This will give runs of length 4*M*. We continue this process until we get one run of length *N*, at which point the run represents the sorted arrangement of the input. Figures 20.34, 20.35, 20.36 (page 604) show how this process works for our sample input.

A1	81	94	11	96	12	35	17	99	28	58	41	75	15
A2													
B1													
B2													

Figure 20.32 Initial tape configuration

A1								
A2								
B1	11	81	94	17	28	99	15	
B2	12	35	96	41	58	75		

Figure 20.33 Distribution of length 3 runs onto two tapes

A1	11	12	35	81	94	96	15	
A2	17	28	41	58	75	99		
B1								
B2								

Figure 20.34 Tapes after the first round of merging (run length = 6)

A1												
A2												
B1	11	12	17	28	35	41	58	75	81	94	96	99
B2	15											

Figure 20.35 Tapes after the second round of merging (run length = 12)

A1	11	12	15	17	28	35	41	58	75	81	94	96	99
A2													
B1													
B2													

Figure 20.36   Tapes after the third round of merging

We need $\lceil \log(N/M) \rceil$ passes over the input before we have one giant run.

The algorithm will require $\lceil \log(N/M) \rceil$ passes, plus the initial run-constructing pass. For instance, if we have ten million records of 128 bytes each and 4 MB of internal memory, then the first pass will create 320 runs. We would then need nine more passes to complete the sort. This formula also correctly tells us that our example in Figure 20.33 requires $\lceil \log(13/3) \rceil$, or three more passes.

20.6.4   Multiway Merge

K-way merging reduces the number of passes. The obvious implementation uses 2K tapes.

If we have extra tapes, then we can expect to reduce the number of passes required to sort our input. We do this by extending the basic (two-way) merge to a K-way merge.

Merging two runs is done by winding each input tape to the beginning of each run. Then the smaller element is found and placed on an output tape and the appropriate input tape is advanced. If there are K input tapes, this strategy works in the same way; the only difference is that it is slightly more complicated to find the smallest of the K elements. We can find the smallest of these elements by using a priority queue. To obtain the next element to write on the output tape, we perform a `deleteMin` operation. The appropriate input tape is advanced, and if the run on that input tape is not yet completed, we `insert` the new element into the priority queue. Figure 20.37 shows how the input from the previous example is distributed onto three tapes. Figures 20.38 and 20.39 show the two passes of three-way merging that complete the sort.

After the initial run construction phase, the number of passes required using K-way merging is $\lceil \log_K(N/M) \rceil$ because the length of the runs get K times as large in each pass. For our example, the formula is verified because $\lceil \log_3 13/3 \rceil = 2$. If we have ten tapes, then $K = 5$. For the large example in the previous section, 320 runs would require $\log_5 320 = 4$ passes.

20.6.5   Polyphase Merge

The polyphase merge implements a K-way merge with K + 1 tapes.

The K-way merging strategy developed in the last section requires the use of $2K$ tapes. This could be prohibitive for some applications. It is possible to get by with only $K + 1$ tapes; this is called *polyphase merging*. An example is performing two-way merging using only three tapes.

A1						
A2						
A3						
B1	11	81	94	41	58	75
B2	12	35	96	15		
B3	17	28	99			

Figure 20.37   Initial distribution of length 3 runs onto three tapes

A1	11	12	17	28	35	81	94	96	99
A2	15	41	58	75					
A3									
B1									
B2									
B3									

Figure 20.38   After one round of three-way merging (run length = 9)

A1													
A2													
A3													
B1	11	12	15	17	28	35	41	58	75	81	94	96	99
B2													
B3													

Figure 20.39   After two rounds of three-way merging

Suppose we have three tapes — T1, T2, and T3 — and an input file on T1 that will produce 34 runs. One option is to put 17 runs on each of T2 and T3. We could then merge this result onto T1, thereby obtaining one tape with 17 runs. The problem is that since all the runs are on one tape, we must now put some of these runs on T2 to perform another merge. The logical way to do this is to copy the first eight runs from T1 onto T2 and then perform the merge. This has the effect of adding an extra half pass for every pass we do. The question is, can we do better?

The distribution of runs affects performance. The best distribution is related to the Fibonacci numbers.

An alternative method is to split the original 34 runs unevenly. Suppose we put 21 runs on T2 and 13 runs on T3. We could then merge 13 runs onto T1 before T3 was empty. We could then rewind T1 and T3 and merge T1, with 13 runs, and T2, with 8 runs, onto T3. Next, we could merge 8 runs until T2 was empty; this would leave 5 runs left on T1 and 8 runs on T3. We could then merge T1 and T3, and so on. Figure 20.40 shows the number of runs on each tape after each pass.

The original distribution of runs makes a great deal of difference. For instance, if 22 runs are placed on T2, with 12 on T3, then after the first merge, we obtain 12 runs on T1 and 10 runs on T2. After another merge, there are 10 runs on T1 and 2 runs on T3. At this point, the going gets slow because we can merge only two sets of runs before T3 is exhausted. Then T1 has 8 runs and T2 has 2 runs. Again we can merge only two sets of runs, obtaining T1 with 6 runs and T3 with 2 runs. After three more passes, T2 has 2 runs and the other tapes are empty. We must copy 1 run to another tape. Then we can finish the merge.

It turns out that the first distribution we gave is optimal. If the number of runs is a Fibonacci number F_N, then the best way to distribute them is to split them into two Fibonacci numbers, F_{N-1} and F_{N-2}. Otherwise, the tape must be padded with dummy runs in order to get the number of runs up to a Fibonacci number. The details of how to place the initial set of runs on the tapes are left as Exercise 20.19. We can extend this to a K-way merge, in which we need Kth-order Fibonacci numbers for the distribution. The Kth-order Fibonacci number is defined as the sum of the K previous Kth-order Fibonacci numbers, as shown in the following equation:

$$F^{(K)}(N) = F^{(K)}(N-1) + F^{(K)}(N-2) + \ldots + F^{(K)}(N-K)$$

$$F^{(K)}(0 \le N \le K-2) = 0$$

$$F^{(K)}(K-1) = 1$$

	Run	After						
	Const.	T3 + T2	T1 + T2	T1 + T3	T2 + T3	T1 + T2	T1 + T3	T2 + T3
T1	0	13	5	0	3	1	0	1
T2	21	8	0	5	2	0	1	0
T3	13	0	8	3	0	2	1	0

Figure 20.40 Number of runs using polyphase merge

20.6.6   Replacement Selection

The last item we will consider is construction of the runs. The strategy used so far is the simplest way: We read as many elements as possible and sort them, writing the result to a tape. This seems like the best approach possible, until we realize that as soon as the first element is written to the output tape, the memory it used becomes available for another element. If the next element on the input tape is larger than the element just output, then it can be included in the run.

Using this observation, we can give an algorithm for producing runs, commonly called *replacement selection*. Initially M elements are read into memory and placed in a priority queue, using `toss` operations, followed by a single `fixHeap`. We perform a `deleteMin`, writing the smallest element to the output tape. We read the next element from the input tape. If it is larger than the element just written, we can add it to the priority queue by an `insert`; otherwise, it cannot go into the current run. Since the priority queue is smaller by one element, this element is stored in the dead space of the priority queue until the run is completed and is used for the next run. Storing an element in the dead space is exactly what was done in heapsort. We continue doing this until the size of the priority queue is zero, at which point the run is over. We start a new run by rebuilding a new priority queue with a `fixHeap` operation, in the process using all of the elements in the dead space.

If we are clever, we can make the length of the runs that we initially construct larger than the amount of available main memory. This technique is called replacement selection.

	3 Elements in Heap Array			Output	Next Item
	array[1]	array[2]	array[3]		Read
	11	94	81	11	96
	81	94	96	81	12
Run 1	94	96	12	94	35
	96	35	12	96	17
	17	35	12	End of Run	Rebuild
	12	35	17	12	99
	17	35	99	17	28
	28	99	35	28	58
Run 2	35	99	58	35	41
	41	99	58	41	75
	58	99	75	58	15
	75	99	15	75	End of Tape
	99		15	99	
			15	End of Run	Rebuild
Run 3	15			15	

Figure 20.41   Example of run construction

Figure 20.41 (page 607) shows the run construction for the small example we have been using, with $M = 3$. Elements that are reserved for the next run are shaded. Elements 11, 94, and 81 are placed using `fixHeap`. Element 11 is output, and then 96 is placed in the heap by an insertion because it is larger than the 11. Element 81 is output next, and then 12 is read. Since 12 is smaller than the 81 just output, it cannot be included in the current run. Thus it is placed in the heap dead space. The heap now logically contains only 94 and 96. After they are output, we have only dead space elements, so we construct a heap and begin run 2. In this example, replacement selection produces only 3 runs, compared with the 5 runs obtained by sorting. Because of this, a three-way merge finishes in one pass instead of two. If the input is randomly distributed, replacement selection can be shown to produce runs of average length $2M$. For our large example, we would expect 160 runs instead of 320 runs, so a five-way merge would still require four passes. In this case, we have not saved a pass, although we might if we get lucky and have 125 runs or fewer. Since external sorts take so long, every pass saved can make a significant difference in the running time.

As we have seen, it is possible for replacement selection to do no better than the standard algorithm. However, the input is frequently nearly sorted to start with, in which case replacement selection produces only a few abnormally long runs. This kind of input is common for external sorts and makes replacement selection extremely valuable.

Summary

This chapter showed an elegant implementation of the priority queue. The binary heap uses only an array, yet it supports the basic operations in logarithmic worst-case time. The heap leads to a popular sorting algorithm, *heapsort*. Exercises 20.22 and 20.23 ask you to compare the performance of heapsort with that of quicksort. Generally speaking, heapsort is slower than quicksort, but it is certainly simpler to implement. Finally, we saw that priority queues are important data structures for external sorting.

This completes the implementation of the fundamental and classic data structures. Part V examines more sophisticated data structures, beginning with the *splay tree*, a binary search tree that has some remarkable properties.

 ## Objects of the Game

binary heap The classic method used to implement priority queues. The binary heap has two properties: structure and ordering. (582)

complete binary tree A tree that is completely filled and has no missing nodes. The heap is a complete binary tree, which allows representation using a simple array and guarantees logarithmic depth. (582)

external sorting A form of sorting used when the amount of data is too large to fit in main memory. (601)

fixHeap operation The process of reinstating heap order in a complete tree. Can be done in linear time by applying a percolate down routine to nodes in reverse-level order. (593)

heap-order property The property that holds that in a (min) heap, the item in the parent is never larger than the item in a node. (584)

heapsort An algorithm based on the idea that a priority queue can be used to sort in $O(N \log N)$ time. (598)

implicit representation Using an array to store a tree. (583)

max heap A heap that supports access of the maximum instead of the minimum. (584)

multiway merge K-way merging that reduces the number of passes. The obvious implementation uses $2K$ tapes. (604)

percolate down Deletion of the minimum involves placing the former last item in a hole that is created at the root. The hole is percolated down the tree through minimum children until the item can be placed without violating the heap-order property. (591)

percolate up Insertion is implemented by creating a hole at the next available location and then percolating it up until the new item can be placed in it without introducing a heap-order violation with the hole's parent. (588)

polyphase merge Implements a K-way merge with $K + 1$ tapes. (604)

replacement selection The length of the runs that are initially constructed can be larger than the amount of available memory. If we can store M objects in main memory, then we can expect runs of length $2M$. This technique is commonly referred to as replacement selection. (607)

run A sorted group in the external sort. At the end of the sort, a single run remains. (602)

toss operation An operation that adds an item but, unlike insert, does not guarantee that heap order is maintained. It is useful if you intend to add many items prior to needing access to the minimum. (586)

Common Errors

1. The binary heap requires a sentinel in position 0. A common error is instantiating with an inappropriate sentinel.

2. The trickiest part of the binary heap is the percolate down case, in which only one child is present. Since this is a rare occurrence, it is difficult to spot an incorrect implementation.

3. The heap-order property must be restored prior to obtaining a minimum element if a toss has relaxed it.

4. For heapsort, the data begins in position 0, so the children of node i are in positions $2i + 1$ and $2i + 2$.

On the Internet

The binary heap is available in directory **DataStructures**. Here is the filename:

BinaryHeap.java   Contains the implementation for the binary heap.

Exercises

In Short

20.1. Describe the structure and ordering properties of the binary heap.

20.2. In a binary heap, for an item in position i, where are the parent, left child, and right child located?

20.3. Show the result of inserting 10, 12, 1, 14, 6, 5, 8, 15, 3, 9, 7, 4, 11, 13, and 2, one at a time, into an initially empty heap. Then show the result of using the linear-time `fixHeap` algorithm instead.

20.4. Where could the eleventh dashed line in Figures 20.20–20.23 have been?

20.5. A max heap supports `insert`, `deleteMax`, and `findMax` (but not `deleteMin` or `findMin`). Describe in detail how max heaps can be implemented.

20.6. Show the result of the heapsort algorithm after the initial construction and then two `deleteMax` operations on the input in Exercise 20.3.

20.7. Is heapsort a stable sort (that is, if there are duplicate items, do the duplicates retain their initial ordering among themselves)?

In Theory

20.8. A complete binary tree of N elements uses array positions 1 to N. Determine how large the array must be for the following:
   a. a binary tree that has two extra levels (that is, it is very slightly unbalanced)
   b. a binary tree that has a deepest node at depth $2\log N$
   c. a binary tree that has a deepest node at depth $4.1\log N$
   d. the worst-case binary tree

20.9. Show the following regarding the maximum item in the heap:
   a. It must be at one of the leaves.
   b. There are exactly $\lceil N/2 \rceil$ leaves.
   c. Every leaf must be examined to find it.

20.10. Prove Theorem 20.1 by using a direct summation. Do the following:
   a. Show that there are 2^i nodes of height $H - i$.
   b. Write the equation for the sum of the heights using part (a).
   c. Evaluate the sum in part (b).

20.11. Verify that the sum of the heights of a perfect binary tree satisfies $N - v(N)$, where $v(N)$ is the number of 1s in N's binary representation.

20.12. Prove the bound in Exercise 20.11 using an induction argument.

20.13. For heapsort, $O(N \log N)$ comparisons are used in the worst case. Derive the leading term (that is, decide if it is $N \log N$, $2N \log N$, $3N \log N$, and so on).

20.14. Show that there are inputs that force every `percDown` in heapsort to go all the way to a leaf. *Hint*: Work backward.

20.15. A *d-heap* is an implicit data structure that is like a binary heap, except that nodes have d children. A d-heap is thus more shallow than a binary heap, but finding the minimum child requires examining d children instead of two. With this in mind, determine the running time (in terms of d and N) of the `insert` and `deleteMin` operations for a d-heap.

20.16. A *min-max heap* is a data structure that supports both `deleteMin` and `deleteMax` at logarithmic cost. The structure is identical to the binary heap. The min-max heap-order property is that for any node X at even depth, the key stored at X is the smallest in its subtree, while for any node X at odd depth, the key stored at X is the largest in its subtree. The root is at even depth. Do the following:

  a. Draw a possible min-max heap for the items 1, 2, 3, 4, 5, 6, 7, 8, 9, and 10. Note that there are many possible heaps.
  b. Determine how to find the minimum and maximum elements.
  c. Give an algorithm to insert a new node into the min-max heap.
  d. Give an algorithm to perform `deleteMin` and `deleteMax`.
  e. Give an algorithm to perform `fixHeap` in linear time.

20.17. The *2-D heap* is a data structure that allows each item to have two individual keys. `deleteMin` can be performed with respect to either of these keys. The 2-D heap-order property is that for any node X at even depth, the item stored at X has the smallest key #1 in its subtree, while for any node X at odd depth, the item stored at X has the smallest key #2 in its subtree. Do the following:

  a. Draw a possible 2-D heap for the items (1, 10), (2, 9), (3, 8), (4, 7), and (5, 6).
  b. Explain how to find the item with minimum key #1.
  c. Explain how to find the item with minimum key #2.
  d. Give an algorithm to insert a new item into the 2-D heap.
  e. Give an algorithm to perform `deleteMin` with respect to either key.
  f. Give an algorithm to perform `fixHeap` in linear time.

20.18. A *treap* is a binary search tree in which each node stores an item, two children, and a randomly assigned priority that is generated when the node is constructed. The nodes in the tree obey the usual binary search tree order, but they must also maintain heap order with respect to the priorities. The treap is a good alternative to the balanced search tree because balance is based on the random priorities, rather than on the items. Thus the average case results for binary search trees apply. Do the following:

  a. Prove that a collection of distinct items, each of which has a distinct priority, can be represented by only one treap.

b. Show how to perform insertion into a treap by using a bottom-up algorithm.

c. Show how to perform insertion into a treap by using a top-down algorithm.

d. Show how to perform deletion from a treap.

20.19. Explain how to place the initial set of runs on two tapes when the number of runs is not a Fibonacci number.

In Practice

20.20. Write the routine `percDown` with the following declaration (Remember that the max heap starts at position 0, not position 1.):

```
private static void percDown( Comparable [ ] a,
                              int index, int size );
```

Programming Projects

20.21. Write a program to compare the running time of N `toss` operations followed by a `fixHeap` versus N separate `insert` operations. Run your program for sorted, reverse sorted, and random inputs.

20.22. Implement both heapsort and quicksort and compare their performances on both sorted inputs and random inputs. Use different types of data for the tests.

20.23. Suppose you have a hole at node X. The normal `percDown` routine is to compare X's children and then move the child up to X if it is larger (in the case of a (max)heap) than the element to be placed, thereby pushing the hole down. Stop when it is safe to place the new element in the hole. Consider the following alternative strategy for `percDown`. That is, move elements up and the hole down as far as possible without testing whether the new cell can be inserted. This would place the new cell in a leaf and probably violate heap order. To fix the heap order, percolate the new cell up in the normal manner. The expectation is that the percolation up will be only one or two levels on average. Write a routine to include this idea. Compare the running time with that of a standard implementation of heapsort.

20.24. Implement an external sort.

20.25. Design an applet that illustrates the binary heap.

References

The binary heap was first described in the context of heapsort in [8]. The linear-time `fixHeap` algorithm is from [4]. Precise results on the number of comparisons and data movements used by heapsort in the best, worst, and average case are given in [7]. Advanced priority queue implementations are discussed in Chapter 21 and Chapter 22. External sorting is discussed in detail in [6]. Exercise

20.15 is solved in [5]. Exercise 20.16 is solved in [2]. Exercise 20.17 is solved in [3]. Treaps are described in [1].

1. C. Aragon and R. Seidel, "Randomized Search Trees," *Algorithmica* **16** (1996), 464–497.

2. M. D. Atkinson, J. R. Sack, N. Santoro, and T. Strothotte, "Min-Max Heaps and Generalized Priority Queues," *Communications of the ACM* **29** (1986), 996–1000.

3. Y. Ding and M. A. Weiss, "The k-d Heap: An Efficient Multi-dimensional Priority Queue," *Proceedings of the Third Workshop on Algorithms and Data Structures* (1993), 302–313.

4. R. W. Floyd, "Algorithm 245: Treesort 3," *Communications of the ACM* **7** (1964), 701.

5. D. B. Johnson, "Priority Queues with Update and Finding Minimum Spanning Trees," *Information Processing Letters* **4** (1975), 53–57.

6. D. E. Knuth, *The Art of Computer Programming. Volume 3: Sorting and Searching*, 2d ed., Addison-Wesley, Reading, Mass. (1997).

7. R. Schaffer and R. Sedgewick, "The Analysis of Heapsort," *Journal of Algorithms* **14** (1993), 76–100.

8. J. W. J. Williams, "Algorithm 232: Heapsort," *Communications of the ACM* **7** (1964), 347–348.

Part V

Advanced Data Structures

21

Splay Trees

THIS chapter describes a remarkable data structure called the *splay tree*. The splay tree supports all the binary search tree operations but does not guarantee $O(\log N)$ worst-case performance. Instead, its bounds are *amortized,* meaning that although individual operations can be expensive, any sequence of operations is guaranteed to behave as if each operation in the sequence exhibited logarithmic behavior. Because this is a weaker guarantee than that provided by balanced search trees, only the data and two references per node are required for each item and the operations are somewhat simpler to code. The splay tree has some other interesting properties, as this chapter reveals.

In this chapter, we will see:

- Descriptions of the concepts of amortization and self-adjustment
- The basic bottom-up splay tree algorithm and a proof that it has logarithmic amortized cost per operation
- How splay trees can be implemented using a top-down algorithm, with a complete splay tree implementation (including a deletion algorithm)
- Comparisons of splay trees with other data structures

21.1 Self-adjustment and Amortized Analysis

Although balanced search trees provide logarithmic worst-case running time per operation, they have several limitations:

- Balanced search trees require storing an extra piece of balancing information per node.
- They are complicated to implement. As a result, insertions and deletions are expensive and potentially error-prone.
- We do not win when easy inputs occur.

Let us examine the consequences of each of these deficiencies. First, balanced search trees require an extra data field. Although in theory this can be as little as a single bit (as in a red-black tree), in practice the data field will use an entire integer for storage in order to satisfy hardware restrictions. In an age when the memories of computers are becoming huge, one must ask if worrying about

The real problem is that the extra data fields add complications that we can live without.

memory is such a large issue. The answer in most cases is probably not, except that maintaining the extra data fields requires more-complex code and tends to lead to longer running times and more errors. Indeed, it is difficult to tell if the balancing information for a search tree is correct, since errors will only lead to an unbalanced tree. If one case is slightly wrong, it might be difficult to spot the errors. Thus, as a practical matter, algorithms that allow us to remove some complications without sacrificing performance deserve serious consideration.

> The *90-10 rule* states that 90 percent of the accesses are to 10 percent of the data items. Balanced search trees do not take advantage of this rule.

There is a second reason why the performance of a balanced search may be improvable. That is, their worst-case, average-case, and best-case performances are essentially identical. An example is a `find` operation for some item X. It is reasonable to expect not only that the cost of the `find` will be logarithmic, but also that if we perform an immediate second `find` for X, the second access will be cheaper than the first. In a red-black tree, this is not true. We would also expect that if we perform an access of X, Y, and then Z, then a second set of accesses for the same sequence would be easy. This is important because of the *90-10 rule*. This rule, suggested by empirical studies, is that in practice 90 percent of the accesses are to 10 percent of the data items. Consequently, we want easy wins for the 90 percent case.

The 90-10 rule has been used for many years in disk I/O systems. A *cache* stores in main memory the contents of some of the disk blocks. The hope is that when a disk access is requested, the block can be found in the main memory cache and thus save the cost of an expensive disk access. Of course, only relatively few disk blocks can be stored in memory. Even so, storing the most recently accessed disk blocks in the cache enables large improvements in performance because many of the same disk blocks are accessed over and over again. Browsers use the same idea: A cache stores locally the previously visited Web pages.

21.1.1 Amortized Time Bounds

We are asking for alot: We want to avoid balancing information and we want to be able to take advantage of the 90-10 rule. Naturally we expect that we might have to give up some feature of the balanced search tree.

> *Amortized analysis* bounds the cost of a sequence of operations and distributes this cost evenly to each operation in the sequence.

We choose to sacrifice the logarithmic worst-case performance. Since we are hoping not to maintain balance information, this sacrifice seems inevitable. However, we cannot accept the typical performance of an unbalanced binary search tree. There is, however, a reasonable compromise: $O(N)$ time for a single access may be acceptable as long as it does not happen too often. In particular, if any M operations (starting with the first operation) take a total of $O(M \log N)$ worst-case time, then the fact that some operations are expensive might be inconsequential. When we can show a worst-case bound for a sequence of operations that is better than the corresponding bound obtained by considering each operation separately, the running time is said to be *amortized*. In the preceding example, we have logarithmic amortized cost. That is, some single operations may take more than logarithmic time, but we are guaranteed compensation by some cheaper operations that occur earlier in the sequence.

However, amortized bounds are not always acceptable. Specifically, if a single bad operation is too time-consuming, then we really do need worst-case bounds rather than amortized bounds. Even so, in many cases a data structure is used as part of an algorithm and only the total amount of time used by the data structure in the course of running an algorithm is important.

We have already seen one example of an amortized bound. When we implement array doubling in a stack or queue, the cost of a single operation can be either constant if no doubling is needed or $O(N)$ if it is. However, for any sequence of M stack or queue operations, the total cost is guaranteed to be $O(M)$, meaning constant amortized cost per operation. The fact that the array doubling step is expensive is inconsequential because its cost can be distributed to many earlier inexpensive operations.

21.1.2   A Simple Self-adjusting Strategy (That Does Not Work)

In a binary search tree, we cannot expect to store the frequently accessed items in a simple table. This is because the caching technique benefits from the great discrepancy between main memory and disk access times. Since the cost of an access in a binary search tree is proportional to the depth of the accessed node, we can attempt to restructure the tree by moving frequently accessed items toward the root. Although this costs extra time during the first `find` operation, it could be worthwhile in the long run.

The easiest way to move an item toward the root is to rotate it continually with its parent until it becomes a root node. Then, if the item is accessed a second time, the second access is cheap. Even if a few other operations intervene before the item is reaccessed, that item will remain close to the root and thus will be quickly found. This process is called the *rotate-to-root strategy*. An application of the rotate-to-root strategy to node 3 is shown in Figure 21.1 (page 620).[1]

The result of the rotation is that future accesses of node 3 are cheap (for a while). Unfortunately, in the process of moving node 3 up two levels, nodes 4 and 5 each move down a level. This means that if access patterns do not follow the 90-10 rule, it is possible for a long sequence of bad accesses to occur. As a result, the rotate-to-root rule will not have logarithmic amortized behavior; this will likely be unacceptable. A bad case is illustrated in Theorem 21.1.

> The *rotate-to-root strategy* rearranges a binary search tree after each access so as to move frequently accessed items closer to the root.

> The rotate-to-root strategy is good if the 90-10 rule applies. It can be very bad when it does not.

---

[1]   An insertion counts as an access. Thus an item would always be inserted as a leaf and then immediately rotated to the root. An unsuccessful search counts as an access on the leaf at which the search terminates.

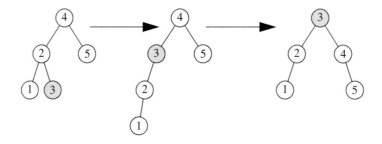

Figure 21.1 Rotate-to-root strategy applied when node 3 is accessed

Theorem 21.1

There are arbitrarily long sequences for which M rotate-to-root accesses use $\Theta(MN)$ *time.*

Proof

Consider the tree formed by inserting the keys 1, 2, 3, ... , N into an initially empty tree. This gives a tree consisting of only left children. This is not bad, since the time to construct the tree is only $O(N)$ total. As illustrated in Figure 21.2, each newly added item is made a child of the root. Then, only one rotation is needed to place the new item at the root. The bad part, as shown in Figure 21.3, is that accessing the node with key 1 takes N units of time. After the rotations are complete, access of the node with key 2 takes N units of time and access of key 3 takes $N - 1$ units of time. The total for accessing the N keys in order is $N + \sum_{i=2}^{N} i = \Theta(N^2)$. After they are accessed, the tree reverts to its original state and we can repeat the sequence. Thus we have an amortized bound of only $\Theta(N)$.

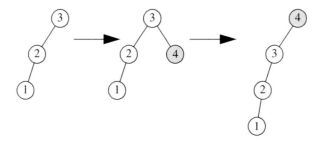

Figure 21.2 Insertion of 4 using rotate-to-root

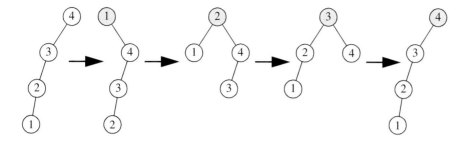

Figure 21.3   Sequential access of items takes quadratic time

21.2 The Basic Bottom-up Splay Tree

Achieving logarithmic amortized cost seems impossible because when we move an item to root via rotations, other items are pushed deeper. It would seem that there would always be some very deep nodes, if no balancing information is maintained. Amazingly, there is a simple fix to the rotate-to-root strategy that allows the logarithmic amortized bound to be obtained. The resulting rotate-to-root strategy is called *splaying*. Its implementation leads to the basic *bottom-up splay tree*.

In a basic bottom-up splay tree, items are rotated to the root using a slightly more complicated method than simple rotate-to-root.

    The splaying strategy is similar to rotate-to-root, with one subtle difference. We still rotate bottom up along the access path (later in the chapter is a top-down strategy). Let X be a nonroot node on the access path on which we are rotating. If the parent of X is the root of the tree, we merely rotate X and the root as shown in Figure 21.4. This is the last rotation along the access path, and it places X at the root. Note that this is exactly what would be done in the rotate-to-root algorithm. This is a *zig* case.

    Otherwise, X has both a parent P and a grandparent G, and there are two cases plus symmetries to consider. The first case is the so called *zig-zag* case, which corresponds to the inside case for AVL trees. Here X is a right child and P is a left child (or vice versa). We perform a double rotation, exactly like an AVL double rotation, as shown in Figure 21.5 (page 622). Notice that since a double rotation is the same as two bottom-up single rotations, this case is no different than what is done in rotate-to-root. In Figure 21.1, the splay at node 3 is a single zig-zag rotation.

The zig and zig-zag cases are identical to rotate-to-root.

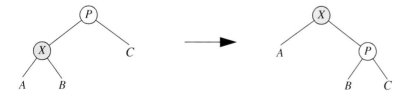

Figure 21.4   Zig case (normal single rotation)

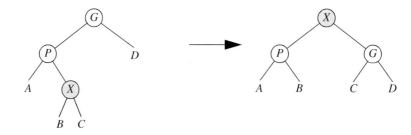

Figure 21.5 Zig-zag case (same as a double rotation); the symmetric case has been omitted

The *zig-zig* case is unique to the splay tree.

The final case is the *zig-zig* case, which is the outside case for AVL trees. Here, X and P are either both left children or both right children. In this case, we transform the left-hand tree of Figure 21.6 to the right-hand tree. Observe that this differs from what rotate-to-root does. Rotate-to-root rotates between X and P and then between X and G. The zig-zig splay rotates between P and G and then X and P.

Splaying has the effect of roughly halving the depth of most nodes on the access path, while increasing by at most two the depth of a few other nodes.

The change in the zig-zig case seems quite minor; it is surprising that it matters. To see the difference that splaying makes over rotate-to-root, consider the sequence that gave the poor results in Theorem 21.1. Once again, we insert keys 1, 2, 3, ... , N into an initially empty tree in linear total time and obtain an unbalanced left-child-only tree. However, the result of a splay is somewhat better, as shown in Figure 21.7. After the splay at node 1, which takes N node accesses, a splay at node 2 will take only roughly $N/2$ accesses, rather than $N-1$ accesses. Splaying not only moves the accessed node to the root. It also roughly halves the depth of most nodes on the access path (some shallow nodes are pushed down at most two levels). A subsequent splay at node 2 will bring nodes to within $N/4$ of the root. This is repeated until the depth becomes roughly $\log N$. In fact, a complicated analysis shows that what used to be a bad case for the rotate-to-root algorithm is a good case for splaying: Sequential access of the N items in the splay tree takes a total of only $O(N)$ time. Thus we win on easy input. Section 21.4 shows, by subtle accounting, that there are no bad access sequences.

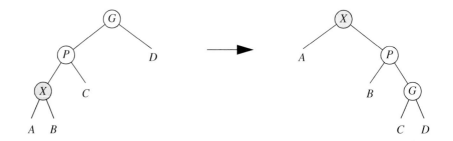

Figure 21.6 Zig-zig case (this is unique to the splay tree); the symmetric case has been omitted

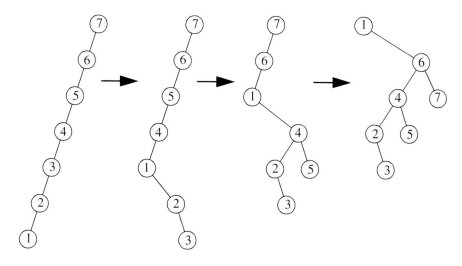

Figure 21.7   Result of splaying at node 1 (three zig-zigs and a zig)

21.3 Basic Splay Tree Operations

As mentioned earlier, a splay operation is performed after each access. When an insertion is performed, we perform a splay. As a result, the newly inserted item becomes the root of the tree. Otherwise, we could spend quadratic time constructing an *N* item tree.

After an item is inserted as a leaf, it is splayed to the root.

For the `find`, we splay at the last node that is accessed during the search. If the search is successful, then the node that is found will be splayed and become the new root. If the search is unsuccessful, then the last node that was accessed prior to reaching the `null` reference is splayed and becomes the new root. This behavior is necessary. Otherwise, we could repeatedly perform a `find` for 0 in the initial tree in Figure 21.7 and use linear time per operation. Likewise, operations such as `findMin` and `findMax` perform a splay after the access.

All searching operations incorporate a splay.

The interesting operations are the deletions. Recall that the `deleteMin` and `deleteMax` are important priority queue operations. With splay trees, these operations become simple. We can implement the `deleteMin` as follows. First, perform a `findMin`. This brings the minimum item to the root, and by the binary search tree property, there is no left child. We can use the right child as the new root. Similarly, `deleteMax` can be implemented by calling `findMax` and setting the root to the post-splay root's left child.

Even the `remove` operation is simple. To perform deletion, we access the node that is to be deleted. This puts the node at the root. If it is deleted, we get two subtrees *L* and *R* (left and right). If we find the largest element in *L* using a `deleteMax` operation, then its largest element will be rotated to *L*'s root and *L*'s root will have no right child. We finish the `remove` by making *R* the right child of *L*'s root. An example of the `remove` operation is shown in Figure 21.8 (page 624).

Deletion operations are much simpler than usual. They also incorporate a splaying step (sometimes two).

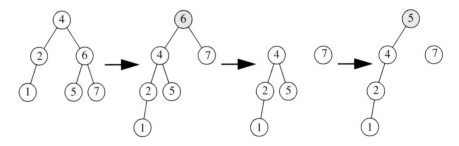

Figure 21.8 The `remove` operation applied to node 6: first 6 is splayed to the root, thus leaving two subtrees; a `findMax` on the left subtree is performed, raising 5 to the root of the left subtree; then the right subtree can be attached (not shown)

The cost of the `remove` operation is two splays. All other operations cost one splay. Thus we need to analyze the cost of a series of splay steps. The next section shows that the amortized cost of a splay is at most $3\log N + 1$ single rotations. Among other things, this means we do not have to worry that the remove algorithm described previously is biased. The splay tree's amortized bound guarantees that any sequence of M splays will use at most $3M\log N + M$ tree rotations. Consequently, any sequence of M operations starting from an empty tree will take a total of at most $O(M\log N)$ time.

21.4 Analysis of Bottom-up Splaying

The analysis of the splay tree is very complicated and is part of a much larger theory of amortized analysis.

The analysis of the splay tree algorithm is complicated because each splay can vary from a few rotations to $O(N)$ rotations. Furthermore, unlike with balanced search trees, each splay changes the structure of the tree. This section proves that the amortized cost of a splay is at most $3\log N + 1$ single rotations. The splay tree's amortized bound guarantees that any sequence of M splays will use at most $3M\log N + M$ tree rotations, and consequently any sequence of M operations starting from an empty tree will take a total of at most $O(M\log N)$ time.

The potential function is an accounting device used to establish the required time bound.

To prove this bound, we introduce an accounting function called the *potential function*. The potential function is not maintained by the algorithm. Rather, it is merely an accounting device that aids in establishing the required time bound. Its choice is not obvious and is the result of a large amount of trial and error.

For any node i in the splay tree, let $S(i)$ be the number of descendants of i (including i itself). The potential function is the sum, over all nodes i in the tree T, of the logarithm of $S(i)$. Specifically,

$$\Phi(T) = \sum_{i \in T} \log S(i).$$

To simplify the notation, let $R(i) = \log S(i)$. This makes

$$\Phi(T) = \sum_{i \in T} R(i).$$

$R(i)$ represents the *rank* of node i. Recall that neither ranks nor sizes are maintained by the splay tree algorithms (unless, of course, order statistics are needed). Note that the rank of the root is $\log N$. Also, when a zig rotation is performed, only the ranks of the two nodes involved in the rotation change. When a zig-zig or a zig-zag rotation is performed, only the ranks of the three nodes involved in the rotation change. And finally, a single splay consists of some number of zig-zig or zig-zag rotations followed by perhaps one zig rotation. Each zig-zig or zig-zag can be counted as two single rotations.

The *rank* of a node is the logarithm of its size. Ranks and sizes are not maintained but are merely accounting tools for the proof. Only nodes on the splay path have their ranks changed.

Let X be the node that is splayed to the root. Let r be the total number of rotations performed during the splay. Let Φ_i be the potential function of the tree immediately after the ith splay. Φ_0 is the potential prior to the zeroth splay.

If the ith splay operation uses r_i rotations, $\Phi_i - \Phi_{i-1} + r_i \leq 3\log N + 1$.   ***Theorem 21.2***

Before proving Theorem 21.2, let us see what it means. The cost of M splays can be taken as $\sum_{i=1}^{M} r_i$ rotations. If the M splays are consecutive (that is, no insertions or deletions intervene), then the potential of the tree after the ith splay is the same as prior to the $(i + 1)$th splay. Thus we can use Theorem 21.2 M times to obtain the sequence of equations in Equation 21.1.

All proofs in this section use the concept of telescoping sums.

$$\Phi_1 - \Phi_0 + r_1 \leq 3\log N + 1$$
$$\Phi_2 - \Phi_1 + r_2 \leq 3\log N + 1$$
$$\Phi_3 - \Phi_2 + r_3 \leq 3\log N + 1 \qquad \textbf{(21.1)}$$
$$\cdots$$
$$\Phi_M - \Phi_{M-1} + r_M \leq 3\log N + 1$$

These equations telescope, so if we add them all together, we obtain

$$\Phi_M - \Phi_0 + \sum_{i=1}^{M} r_i \leq (3\log N + 1)M, \qquad \textbf{(21.2)}$$

which bounds the total number of rotations as

$$\sum_{i=1}^{M} r_i \leq (3\log N + 1)M - (\Phi_M - \Phi_0).$$

Now consider what happens when insertions are intermingled with finds. It is worth observing that the potential of an empty tree is 0. When a node is inserted into the tree as a leaf, then prior to the splay the potential of the tree increases by at most $\log N$ (this is proved shortly). Suppose r_i rotations are used for an insertion and the potential prior to the insertion is Φ_{i-1}. Then after the insertion, the potential will be at most $\Phi_{i-1} + \log N$. After the splay that moves the inserted node to the root, the new potential will satisfy

$$\Phi_i - (\Phi_{i-1} + \log N) + r_i \leq 3\log N + 1$$
$$\Phi_i - \Phi_{i-1} + r_i \leq 4\log N + 1. \tag{21.3}$$

Further suppose there are F finds and I insertions and Φ_i represents the potential after the ith operation. Then since each find is governed by Theorem 21.2 and each insertion is governed by Equation 21.3, the telescoping logic tells us that

$$\sum_{i=1}^{M} r_i \leq (3\log N + 1)F + (4\log N + 1)I - (\Phi_M - \Phi_0). \tag{21.4}$$

Furthermore, before the first operation the potential is 0, and since it can never be negative, then $\Phi_M - \Phi_0 \geq 0$. Consequently, we obtain

$$\sum_{i=1}^{M} r_i \leq (3\log N + 1)F + (4\log N + 1)I, \tag{21.5}$$

thus showing that the cost of any sequence of finds and insertions is at most logarithmic per operation. Since a deletion is equivalent to two splays, it, too, is logarithmic. Thus we must prove the two dangling claims, namely, Theorem 21.2 and the fact that an insertion of a node adds at most $\log N$ to the potential. Both theorems are proved by using telescoping arguments. Let us take care of the insertion claim first. This is Theorem 21.3.

Theorem 21.3   *Insertion of the Nth node into a tree as a leaf adds at most* $\log N$ *to the potential of the tree.*

Proof   *The only nodes whose ranks are affected are those on the path from the inserted leaf to the root. Let $S_1, S_2, \ldots, S_k$ be their sizes prior to the insertion and note that $S_k = N - 1$ and $S_1 < S_2 < \ldots < S_k$. Let $S'_1, S'_2, \ldots, S'_k$ be the sizes after the insertion. Clearly, $S'_i \leq S_{i+1}$ for $i < k$, since $S'_i = S_i + 1$. Consequently, $R'_i \leq R_{i+1}$. The change in potential is thus*
$$\sum_{i=1}^{k}(R'_i - R_i) \leq R'_k - R_k + \sum_{i=1}^{k-1}(R_{i+1} - R_i) \leq \log N - R_1 \leq \log N.$$

To prove Theorem 21.2, we break each splay step into its constituent zig, zig-zag, and zig-zig parts and establish a bound for the cost of each type of rotation.

By telescoping these bounds, we obtain a bound for the splay. Before continuing, we need a technical theorem, Theorem 21.4.

If $a + b \le c$ and a and b are both positive integers, then   ***Theorem 21.4***
$\log a + \log b \le 2\log c - 2.$

By the arithmetic-geometric mean inequality, $\sqrt{ab} \le (a + b)/2$. Thus   ***Proof***
$\sqrt{ab} \le c/2$. Squaring both sides gives $ab \le c^2/4$. Then taking logarithms
of both sides proves the theorem.

We are now ready to prove Theorem 21.2.

21.4.1   Proof of the Splaying Bound

First, if the node to splay is already at the root, then there are no rotations and there is no potential change. Thus the theorem is trivially true and we may assume that there is at least one rotation. Let X be the node that is involved in the splay. We need to show that if r rotations are performed (a zig-zig or zig-zag counts as two rotations), then r plus the change in potential is at most $3\log N + 1$. Let Δ be the change in potential caused by any of the splay steps zig, zig-zag, or zig-zig. Let $R_i(X)$ and $S_i(X)$ be the rank and size of any node X immediately before a splay step and let $R_f(X)$ and $S_f(X)$ be the rank and size of any node X immediately after a splay step. Following are the bounds that will be proven.

For a zig step that promotes node X, $\Delta \le 3(R_f(X) - R_i(X))$, while for the other two steps, $\Delta \le 3(R_f(X) - R_i(X)) - 2$. When we add these bounds over all steps that comprise a splay, the sum telescopes to the desired bound. Each of these bounds are proved separately in Theorems 21.5–21.7. Then the proof of Theorem 21.2 is completed by applying a telescoping sum.

For a zig step, $\Delta \le 3(R_f(X) - R_i(X))$.   ***Theorem 21.5***

As mentioned earlier in this section, the only nodes whose ranks change in a   ***Proof***
zig step are X and P. Consequently, the potential change is
$R_f(X) - R_i(X) + R_f(P) - R_i(P)$. From Figure 21.4, $S_f(P) < S_i(P)$; thus it
follows that $R_f(P) - R_i(P) < 0$. Consequently, the potential change satis-
fies $\Delta \le R_f(X) - R_i(X)$. Since $S_f(X) > S_i(X)$, it follows that
$R_f(X) - R_i(X) > 0$, hence $\Delta \le 3(R_f(X) - R_i(X))$.

The zig-zag and zig-zig steps are more complicated because three nodes have their ranks affected. First, we prove the zig-zag case.

Theorem 21.6   *For a zig-zag step,* $\Delta \leq 3(R_f(X) - R_i(X)) - 2.$

Proof   *As before, we have three changes, so the potential change is given by*

$$\Delta = R_f(X) - R_i(X) + R_f(P) - R_i(P) + R_f(G) - R_i(G).$$

From Figure 21.5, $S_f(X) = S_i(G)$*, so their ranks must be equal. Thus we obtain*

$$\Delta = -R_i(X) + R_f(P) - R_i(P) + R_f(G).$$

Also, $S_i(P) \geq S_i(X)$*. Consequently,* $R_i(P) \geq R_i(X)$*. Making this substitution and rearranging terms gives*

$$\Delta \leq R_f(P) + R_f(G) - 2R_i(X). \tag{21.6}$$

From Figure 21.5, $S_f(P) + S_f(G) \leq S_f(X)$*. Applying Theorem 21.4, we obtain* $\log S_f(P) + \log S_f(G) \leq 2\log S_f(X) - 2$*, and by the definition of rank, this becomes*

$$R_f(P) + R_f(G) \leq 2R_f(X) - 2. \tag{21.7}$$

Substituting Equation 21.7 into Equation 21.6 yields

$$\Delta \leq 2R_f(X) - 2R_i(X) - 2. \tag{21.8}$$

As for the zig rotation, $R_f(X) - R_i(X) > 0$*, so we can add it to the right side of Equation 21.8, factor, and obtain the desired*

$$\Delta \leq 3(R_f(X) - R_i(X)) - 2.$$

Finally, we prove the bound for the zig-zig case:

For a zig-zig step, $\Delta \leq 3(R_f(X) - R_i(X)) - 2$.   ***Theorem 21.7***

As before, we have three changes, so the potential change is given by   ***Proof***

$$\Delta = R_f(X) - R_i(X) + R_f(P) - R_i(P) + R_f(G) - R_i(G).$$

From Figure 21.6, $S_f(X) = S_i(G)$, *and thus their ranks must be equal. Thus we obtain*

$$\Delta = -R_i(X) + R_f(P) - R_i(P) + R_f(G).$$

We also can obtain $R_i(P) > R_i(X)$ *and* $R_f(P) < R_f(X)$. *Making this substitution and rearranging terms gives*

$$\Delta < R_f(X) + R_f(G) - 2R_i(X). \tag{21.9}$$

From Figure 21.6, $S_i(X) + S_f(G) \leq S_f(X)$, *so applying Theorem 21.4 yields*

$$R_i(X) + R_f(G) \leq 2R_f(X) - 2. \tag{21.10}$$

Rearranging Equation 21.10, we obtain

$$R_f(G) \leq 2R_f(X) - R_i(X) - 2. \tag{21.11}$$

When we substitute Equation 21.11 into Equation 21.9, we obtain

$$\Delta \leq 3(R_f(X) - R_i(X)) - 2.$$

Now that we have established bounds for each of the splaying steps, we can finally complete the proof of Theorem 21.2.

Proof (of Theo-
rem 21.2)

Let $R_0(X)$ be the rank of X prior to the splay. Let $R_i(X)$ be X's rank after the ith splaying step. Prior to the last splaying step, all splaying steps must be zig-zags or zig-zigs. Suppose there are k such steps. Then the total number of rotations performed at that point is 2k. The total potential change is $\sum_{i=1}^{k}(3(R_i(X)-R_{i-1}(X))-2)$. This sum telescopes to $3(R_k(X)-R_0(X))-2k$. At this point, the total number of rotations plus the total potential change is bounded by $3R_k(X)$, since the 2k term cancels, and the initial rank of X is not negative. If the last rotation is a zig-zig or a zig-zag, then a continuation of the telescoping sum gives a total of $3R(root)$. Notice that here, the -2 in the potential increase cancels the cost of two rotations. On the other hand, this does not happen in the zig, so we would get a total of $3R(root)+1$. Since the rank of the root is $\log N$, then in the worst case, the total number of rotations plus the change in potential during a splay is at most $3\log N+1$.

The proof of the splay tree bound, while complex, does illustrate a few interesting points. First, the zig-zig case is apparently the most expensive, since it contributes a leading constant of three, while the zig-zag contributes two. The proof would fall apart if we tried to adapt it to the rotate-to-root algorithm. This is because, in the zig case, the number of rotations plus the potential change is $R_f(X)-R_i(X)+1$. The 1 at the end does not telescope out, so we would not be able to show a logarithmic bound. This is fortunate, since we already know that a logarithmic bound would be incorrect.

The technique of amortized analysis is very interesting, and some general principles have been developed to formalize the framework. Check out the references for more details.

21.5 Top-down Splay Trees

As for red-black trees, *top-down splay trees* are more efficient in practice than their bottom-up counterparts.

A direct implementation of the bottom-up splay strategy requires a pass down the tree to perform an access and then a second pass back up the tree. This can be done either by maintaining parent references, by storing the access path on a stack, or by using a clever trick to store the path using the available references in the accessed nodes. Unfortunately, all of these methods require a substantial amount of overhead, and we must handle many special cases. Recall from Section 18.5 that it is better to implement search tree algorithms using a single top-down pass; we can use dummy nodes to avoid special cases. This section describes a *top-down splay tree* that maintains the logarithmic amortized bound. The top-down procedure is faster in practice and uses only constant extra space. It is the method recommended by the inventors of the splay tree.

The basic idea behind the top-down splay tree is that as we descend the tree in our search for some node X, we must take the nodes that are on the access path and move them and their subtrees out of the way. We must also perform some tree rotations to guarantee the amortized time bound.

At any point in the middle of the splay, there is a current node X that is the root of its subtree; this is represented in the diagrams as the middle tree. Tree L stores nodes that are less than X; similarly, tree R stores nodes that are larger than X. Initially, X is the root of T, and L and R are empty. Descending the tree two levels at a time, we encounter a pair of nodes. Depending on whether these nodes are smaller than X or larger than X, they are placed in L or R along with subtrees that are not on the access path to X. Thus the current node on the search path is *always* the root of the middle tree. When we finally reach X, we can then attach L and R to the bottom of the middle tree. As a result, X will have been moved to the root. The issue then is how nodes are placed into L and R and how the reattachment is performed at the end. This is what the trees in Figure 21.9 (page 632) are illustrating. As is customary, three symmetric cases are omitted.

> We maintain three trees during the top-down pass.

In all the pictures, X is the current node, Y is its child, and Z is a grandchild (should an applicable node exist. The precise meaning of the term *applicable* will be made clear during the discussion of the zig case.)

If the rotation should be a zig, then the tree rooted at Y becomes the new root of the middle tree. X and subtree B are attached as a left child of the smallest item in R; X's left child is logically made `null`.[2] As a result, X is the new smallest element in R, thus making future attachments easy.

Note carefully that Y does not have to be a leaf for the zig case to apply. If the item sought is found in Y, a zig case will apply even if Y has children. A zig case also applies if the item sought is smaller than Y and Y has no left child, even if Y has a right child, and also for the symmetric case.

A similar dissection applies to the zig-zig case. The crucial point is that a rotation between X and Y is performed. The zig-zag case brings the bottom node Z to the top of the middle tree and attaches subtrees X and Y to R and L, respectively. Note that Y is attached to, and then becomes, the largest item in L.

The zig-zag step can be simplified somewhat because no rotations are performed. Instead of making Z the root of the middle tree, we make Y the root. This is shown in Figure 21.10 (page 633). This simplifies the coding because the action for the zig-zag case becomes identical to the zig case. This would seem advantageous, since testing for a host of cases is time-consuming. The disadvantage is that a descent of only one level results in more iterations in the splaying procedure.

Once we have performed the final splaying step, then L, R, and the middle tree are arranged to form a single tree, as shown in Figure 21.11 (page 633). Note carefully that the result is different from that obtained with bottom-up splaying. The crucial fact is that the $O(\log N)$ amortized bound is preserved (see Exercise 21.3).

> Eventually, the three trees are reassembled into one.

---

2. In the code written here, the smallest node in R does not have a `null` left reference because it is not needed.

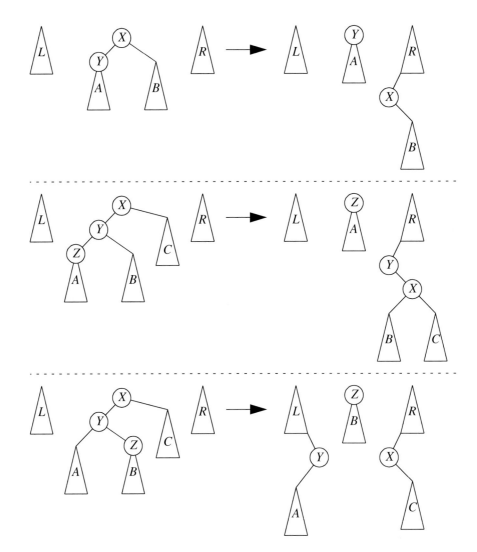

Figure 21.9   Top-down splay rotations: zig (top), zig-zig (middle), and zig-zag (bottom)

An example of the simplified top-down splaying algorithm is shown in Figure 21.12 (page 634). We attempt to access 19 in the tree. The first step is a zig-zag. In accordance with a symmetric version of Figure 21.10, we bring the subtree rooted at 25 to the root of the middle tree and attach 12 and its left subtree to L.

Next, we have a zig-zig: 15 is elevated to the root of the middle tree, and a rotation between 20 and 25 is performed, with the resulting subtree being attached to R. The search for 19 then results in a terminal zig. The middle's new root is 18, and 15 and its left subtree are attached as a right child of L's largest node. The reassembly, in accordance with Figure 21.11, terminates the splay step.

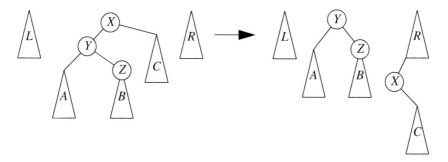

Figure 21.10   Simplified top-down zig-zag

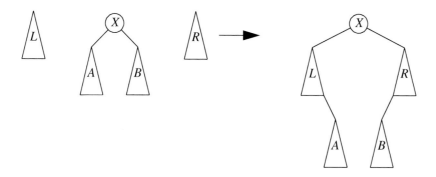

Figure 21.11   Final arrangement for top-down splaying

21.6 Implementation of Top-down Splay Trees

The splay tree class skeleton is shown in Figure 21.13 (page 635). To eliminate annoying special cases, we maintain a static nullNode sentinel. The sentinel is allocated and initialized during the loading of the class, as shown in Figure 21.14 (page 636).

Figure 21.15 (page 637) shows the method for inserting an item x. A new node (newNode) is allocated, and if the tree is empty, a one-node tree is created. Otherwise, we splay around x. If the data in the tree's new root is equal to x, then we have a duplicate. In this case, we do not want to insert x; we throw an exception instead.

If the new root contains a value that is larger than x, then the new root and its right subtree become a right subtree of newNode and the root's left subtree becomes a left subtree of newNode. Similar logic applies if the new root contains a value smaller than x. In either case, newNode is assigned to root to indicate that it is the new root.

Figure 21.16 (page 638) shows the deletion algorithm for splay trees. It is indeed rare that a deletion procedure is shorter than the corresponding insertion procedure. The find method is shown in Figure 21.17 (page 638). After the splay, the item sought either is at the root or is not in the tree. Thus the method is very short. All that remains is the top-down splaying routine. It is made a protected method so that our class can be extended with a different splaying algorithm, if desired.

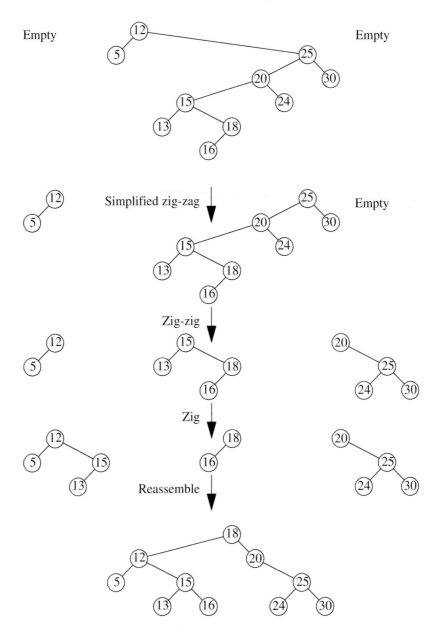

Figure 21.12 Steps in a top-down splay (accessing 19 in top tree)

```
 1  package DataStructures;
 2
 3  import Supporting.*;
 4  import Exceptions.*;
 5
 6  // SplayTree class
 7  //
 8  // CONSTRUCTION: with no initializer
 9  //
10  // ******************PUBLIC OPERATIONS*********************
11  // void insert( x )        --> Insert x
12  // void remove( x )        --> Remove x
13  // void removeMin( )       --> Remove smallest item
14  // Comparable find( x )    --> Return item that matches x
15  // Comparable findMin( )   --> Return smallest item
16  // Comparable findMax( )   --> Return largest item
17  // boolean isEmpty( )      --> Return true if empty; else false
18  // void makeEmpty( )       --> Remove all items
19  // void printTree( )       --> Print tree in sorted order
20  // ******************ERRORS********************************
21  // Most routines throw ItemNotFound on degenerate conditions
22  // insert throws DuplicateItem if item is already in the tree
23
24  /**
25   * Implements a top-down splay tree.
26   * Note that all "matching" is based on the compares method.
27   */
28  public class SplayTree implements SearchTree
29  {
30      public SplayTree( )
31        { /* Figure 21.14 */ }
32      public void insert( Comparable x ) throws DuplicateItem
33        { /* Figure 21.15 */ }
34      public void remove( Comparable x ) throws ItemNotFound
35        { /* Figure 21.16 */ }
36      protected BinaryNode splay( Comparable x, BinaryNode t )
37        { /* Figure 21.18 */ }
38      public Comparable find( Comparable x ) throws ItemNotFound
39        { /* Figure 21.17 */ }
40      public void removeMin( ) throws ItemNotFound
41        { remove( findMin( ) ); }
42      public boolean isEmpty( )
43        { return root == nullNode; }
44      public void makeEmpty( )
45        { root = nullNode; }
46
47      // findMin, findMax, and printTree are available online
48
49      private BinaryNode root;
50  }
```

Figure 21.13 Top-down splay tree class skeleton

```
1      /**
2       * Construct the tree.
3       */
4      public SplayTree( )
5      {
6          root = nullNode;
7      }
8      private static BinaryNode nullNode;
9          static          // Static initializer for nullNode
10         {
11             nullNode = new BinaryNode( null );
12             nullNode.left = nullNode.right = nullNode;
13         }
```

Figure 21.14 Splay tree constructor, including static initialization

Our implementation, shown in Figure 21.18 (page 639), uses a header with left and right references to contain eventually the roots of the left and right trees. `header` is a static field, since we want to allocate it only once over the entire sequence of splays. These trees are initially empty, so a header is used to correspond to the min or max node of the right or left tree, respectively, in this initial state. In this way, the code can avoid checking for empty trees. The first time the left tree becomes nonempty, the header's right reference will get initialized and will not change in the future. Thus it will contain the root of the left tree at the end of the top-down search. Similarly, the header's left reference will eventually contain the root of the right tree.

Before the reassembly at the end of the splay, `header.left` and `header.right` reference *R* and *L*, respectively (this is not a typo — follow the links). Note that we are using the simplified top-down splay.

21.7 Comparison of the Splay Tree with Other Search Trees

The implementation in the previous section suggests that splay trees are not as complicated as red-black trees and almost as simple as AA-trees. Are they worth using? The answer has yet to be resolved completely, but it seems that if the access patterns are nonrandom, then splay trees perform very well in practice. Furthermore, some properties relating to their performances can be proven analytically. Nonrandom accesses include those that follow the 90-10 rule, as well as several special cases such as sequential access, double-ended access, and apparently access patterns that are typical of priority queues during some types of event simulations. The exercises ask you to examine this in more detail.

However, splay trees are not perfect. One problem with them is that the find operation is expensive because of the splay. Consequently when access sequences are random and uniform, splay trees do not do as well as other balanced trees.

```java
1     /**
2      * Insert into the tree.
3      * @param x the item to insert.
4      * @exception DuplicateItem if an item
5      *          that matches x is already in the tree.
6      */
7     public void insert( Comparable x ) throws DuplicateItem
8     {
9         BinaryNode newNode = new BinaryNode( x );
10
11        if( root == nullNode )
12        {
13            newNode.left = newNode.right = nullNode;
14            root = newNode;
15        }
16        else
17        {
18            root = splay( x, root );
19            if( x.lessThan( root.element ) )
20            {
21                newNode.left = root.left;
22                newNode.right = root;
23                root.left = nullNode;
24                root = newNode;
25            }
26            else
27            if( root.element.lessThan( x ) )
28            {
29                newNode.right = root.right;
30                newNode.left = root;
31                root.right = nullNode;
32                root = newNode;
33            }
34            else
35                throw new DuplicateItem( "SplayTree insert" );
36        }
37    }
```

Figure 21.15 Top-down splay tree insertion

```
 1      /**
 2       * Remove from the tree.
 3       * @param x the item to remove.
 4       * @exception ItemNotFound if no item
 5       *          that matches x can be found in the tree.
 6       */
 7      public void remove( Comparable x ) throws ItemNotFound
 8      {
 9          BinaryNode newTree;
10
11          // If x is found, it will be at the root
12          root = splay( x, root );
13          if( root.element.compares( x ) != 0 )
14              throw new ItemNotFound( "SplayTree remove" );
15
16          if( root.left == nullNode )
17              newTree = root.right;
18          else
19          {
20              // Find the maximum in the left subtree
21              // Splay it to root; and then attach right child
22              newTree = root.left;
23              newTree = splay( x, newTree );
24              newTree.right = root.right;
25          }
26          root = newTree;
27      }
```

Figure 21.16 Top-down splay tree deletion

```
 1      /**
 2       * Find an item in the tree.
 3       * @param x the item to search for.
 4       * @return the matching item.
 5       * @exception ItemNotFound if no item
 6       *          that matches x can be found in the tree.
 7       */
 8      public Comparable find( Comparable x ) throws ItemNotFound
 9      {
10          root = splay( x, root );
11
12          if( root.element.compares( x ) != 0 )
13              throw new ItemNotFound( "SplayTree find" );
14
15          return root.element;
16      }
```

Figure 21.17 find method for splay trees

```
 1      private static BinaryNode header = new BinaryNode( null );
 2
 3      /**
 4       * Internal method to perform a top-down splay.
 5       * The last accessed node becomes the new root.
 6       * @param x the target item to splay around.
 7       * @param t the root of the subtree to splay.
 8       * @return the subtree after the splay.
 9       */
10      protected BinaryNode splay( Comparable x, BinaryNode t )
11      {
12          BinaryNode leftTreeMax, rightTreeMin;
13
14          header.left = header.right = nullNode;
15          leftTreeMax = rightTreeMin = header;
16
17          nullNode.element = x;    // Guarantee a match
18
19          for( ; ; )
20              if( x.lessThan( t.element ) )
21              {
22                  if( x.lessThan( t.left.element ) )
23                      t = Rotations.withLeftChild( t );
24                  if( t.left == nullNode )
25                      break;
26                  // Link right
27                  rightTreeMin.left = t;
28                  rightTreeMin = t;
29                  t = t.left;
30              }
31              else if( t.element.lessThan( x ) )
32              {
33                  if( t.right.element.lessThan( x ) )
34                      t = Rotations.withRightChild( t );
35                  if( t.right == nullNode )
36                      break;
37                  // Link left
38                  leftTreeMax.right = t;
39                  leftTreeMax = t;
40                  t = t.right;
41              }
42              else
43                  break;
44
45          leftTreeMax.right = t.left;
46          rightTreeMin.left = t.right;
47          t.left = header.right;
48          t.right = header.left;
49          return t;
50      }
```

Figure 21.18 Top-down splay algorithm

Summary

This chapter described the splay tree, which is a modern alternative to the balanced search tree. Splay trees have several remarkable properties that can be proved, including their logarithmic cost per operation. Other properties are suggested in the exercises. Some studies have suggested that splay trees can be used for a wide range of applications because of their apparent ability to adapt to easy access sequences.

The next chapter describes two priority queues that, like the splay tree, have poor worst-case performance but good amortized performance. One of these, the *pairing heap*, seems to be an excellent choice for some applications.

 ## Objects of the Game

90-10 rule The rule that states that 90 percent of the accesses are to 10 percent of the data items. Balanced search trees do not take advantage of this rule. (618)

amortized analysis A method of analysis that calls for the cost of a sequence of operations to be bounded and the cost distributed evenly to each operation in the sequence. (618)

bottom-up splay tree A tree in which items are rotated to the root using a slightly more complicated method than that used for a simple rotate-to-root. (621)

potential function An accounting device used to establish an amortized time bound. (624)

rank In the splay tree analysis, the logarithm of a node's size. (625)

rotate-to-root strategy A strategy that calls for a binary search tree to be rearranged after each access so as to move frequently accessed items closer to the root. (619)

splaying A rotate-to-root strategy that allows the logarithmic amortized bound to be obtained. (621)

top-down splay tree A type of splay tree that is more efficient in practice than its bottom-up counterpart, as was the case for red-black trees. (630)

zig and **zig-zag** The zig and zig-zag cases are identical to the rotate-to-root cases. Zig is used when X is a child of the root, and zig-zag is used when X is an "inside node." (621)

zig-zig The zig-zig case is unique to the splay tree. It is used when X is an "outside node." (621)

 ## Common Errors

1. A splay must be performed after every access, even unsuccessful ones, or else the performance bounds are not valid.
2. The code is tricky.

On the Internet

The splay tree class is available online in the directory **DataStructures**. Here is the filename:

    SplayTree.java   Contains the implementation for the splay tree class.

Exercises

In Short

21.1. Show the result of inserting 3, 1, 4, 5, 2, 9, 6, and 8 into a
    a. bottom-up splay tree.
    b. top-down splay tree.

21.2. Show the result of deleting 3 from the splay tree in Exercise 21.1 for both the bottom-up and top-down versions.

In Theory

21.3. Prove that the amortized cost of a top-down splay is $O(\log N)$.

21.4. Prove that if all nodes in a splay tree are accessed in sequential order, the resulting tree consists of a chain of left children.

21.5. Suppose that in an attempt to save time, we splay on every second tree operation. Does the amortized cost remain logarithmic?

21.6. Nodes 1 through $N = 1,024$ form a splay tree of left children.
    a. What is the internal path length of the tree (exactly)?
    b. Calculate the internal path length after each of `find(1)`, `find(2)`, `find(3)` when a bottom-up splay is performed.

21.7. By changing the potential function, you can prove different bounds for splaying. Let the weight function $W(i)$ be some function assigned to each node in the tree and $S(i)$ be the sum of the weights of all nodes in the subtree rooted at i, including i itself. The special case $W(i) = 1$ for all nodes corresponds to the function used in the proof of the splaying bound. Let N be the number of nodes in the tree and M be the number of accesses. Prove the following two theorems:
    a. The total access time is $O(M + (M + N)\log N)$.
    b. If q_i is the total number of times that item i is accessed and $q_i > 0$ for all i, then the total access time is $O(M + \sum_{i=1}^{N} q_i \log(M/q_i))$.

In Practice

21.8. Implement a priority queue class using the splay tree.

21.9. Modify the splay tree to support order statistics.

Programming Projects

21.10. Compare empirically the simplified top-down splay that is implemented in Section 21.6 with the original top-down splay discussed in Section 21.5.

21.11. Unlike balanced search trees, splay trees incur overhead during a `find` operation that can be undesirable if the access sequence is sufficiently random. Experiment with a strategy that splays on a `find` operation only after a certain depth d is traversed in the top-down search. The splay does not move the accessed item all the way to the root, but rather to the point at depth d where the splaying is started.

21.12. Compare empirically a top-down splay tree priority queue implementation with a binary heap. Use the following three input models:

a. random insertions and `deleteMin` operations

b. `insert` and `deleteMin` operations corresponding to an event-driven simulation

c. `insert` and `deleteMin` operations corresponding to Dijkstra's algorithm

21.13. Design an applet that illustrates the splaying operation. You may use either top-down or bottom-up splaying.

References

The splay tree is described in the paper [3]. The concept of amortized analysis is discussed in the survey paper [4] and also in greater detail in [5]. A comparison of splay trees and AVL trees is given in [1]. [2] shows that splay trees perform well in some types of event-driven simulations.

1. J. Bell and G. Gupta, "An Evaluation of Self-Adjusting Binary Search Tree Techniques," *Software-Practice and Experience* **23** (1993), 369–382.

2. D. W. Jones, "An Empirical Comparison of Priority-Queue and Event-Set Implementations," *Communications of the ACM* **29** (1986), 300–311.

3. D. D. Sleator and R. E. Tarjan, "Self-adjusting Binary Search Trees," *Journal of the ACM* **32** (1985), 652–686.

4. R. E. Tarjan, "Amortized Computational Complexity," *SIAM Journal on Algebraic and Discrete Methods* **6** (1985), 306–318.

5. M. A. Weiss, *Data Structures and Algorithm Analysis in C++*, Benjamin/Cummings Publishing Co., Redwood City, Calif. (1994).

22

Merging Priority Queues

T HIS chapter examines priority queues that support an additional operation, merge. The merge operation, which is important in advanced algorithm design, combines two priority queues into one (and logically destroys the originals). We represent the priority queues as general trees. This makes the decreaseKey operation somewhat simpler, too; this is important in some applications.

In this chapter, we will see:

- A discussion of the *skew heap*, which is a mergeable priority queue implemented with binary trees
- A discussion of the *pairing heap*, which is a mergeable priority queue that is based on the *M*-ary tree. The pairing heap appears to be a practical alternative to the binary heap even if the merge operation is not needed.

22.1 The Skew Heap

The *skew heap* is a binary tree with heap order. There is no structural constraint on the tree so, unlike with the heap or the balanced binary search trees, there is no guarantee that the depth of the tree is logarithmic. The skew heap is thus somewhat similar to the splay tree.

The *skew heap* is a heap-ordered binary tree. There is no balancing condition, but it supports all operations in logarithmic amortized time.

22.1.1 Merging Is Fundamental

If a heap-ordered, structurally unconstrained binary tree is used to represent a priority queue, then merging becomes the fundamental operation. This is because we can perform other operations as follows:

- h.insert(x): Create a one-node tree containing x and merge that tree into the priority queue.
- h.findMin( ): Return the item at the root.
- h.deleteMin( ): Delete the root and merge its left and right subtrees.

decreaseKey is implemented by detaching a sub-tree from its parent and then using merge.

- h.decreaseKey(p, newVal): Assuming that p is a reference to a node in the priority queue, we can lower p's key value appropriately and then detach p from its parent. This yields two priority queues that can be merged together. Note carefully that p (meaning, the position) does not change as a result of this operation (in contrast to the equivalent operation in a binary heap).

We need to show only how to implement merging; the other operations become trivial. The decreaseKey operation is typically important in some advanced applications. One illustration was seen in Section 14.3, which discussed Dijkstra's algorithm for shortest paths in a graph. The decreaseKey operation is not used in our implementation because of the complications of maintaining the position of each item in the binary heap. In a merging heap, the position can be maintained as a reference to the tree node, and unlike in the binary heap, the position never changes.

This section discusses one implementation of a mergeable priority queue that uses a binary tree, the skew heap. First, it shows that if we are not concerned with efficiency, merging two heap-ordered trees is easy. Next, it covers a simple modification (the skew heap) that avoids the obvious inefficiencies in the original algorithm. Finally, it gives a proof that the merge operation for skew heaps is logarithmic in an amortized sense and comments on the practical significance of this result.

22.1.2 Simplistic Merging of Heap-ordered Trees

Two trees are easily merged recursively.

Assume we have two heap-ordered trees, H_1 and H_2, that need to be merged. Clearly, if either of the two trees is empty, the other tree is the result of the merge. Otherwise, to merge the two trees, we compare their roots. We recursively merge the tree with the larger root into the right subtree of the tree with the smaller root.[1]

The result is that right paths are merged. We must be careful not to create unduly long right paths.

Figure 22.1 shows that the effect of this recursive strategy is that the right paths of the two priority queues are merged to form the new priority queue. All nodes on the right path retain their original left subtree, and only nodes on the right path are touched. Note that the example shown in Figure 22.1 is in fact unattainable by only insertions and merges, since as just mentioned, left children cannot be added by a merge. The practical effect is that what seems to be a heap-ordered binary tree is in fact an ordered arrangement consisting only of a single right path. Thus all operations take linear time.

Fortunately, a simple modification ensures that the right path is not always long.

---

[1] Clearly, either subtree could be used. The right is used here for simplicity.

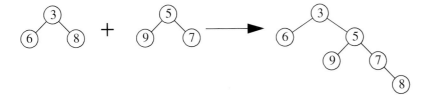

Figure 22.1   Simplistic merging of heap-ordered trees; right paths are merged

22.1.3 The Skew Heap: A Simple Modification

The merge in Figure 22.1 creates a temporary merged tree. A simple modification is as follows: Prior to the completion of a merge, we swap the left and right children for every node in the resulting right path of the temporary tree. Once again, only those nodes that were on the original right paths will be on the right path in the temporary tree. As a result of the swap, shown in Figure 22.2, these nodes will then form the left path of the resulting tree. When a merge is performed in this way, the heap-ordered tree is called a *skew heap*.

> To avoid the problem of unduly long right paths, we make the resulting right path after a merge a left path. Such a merge results in a *skew heap*.

A recursive viewpoint is as follows. Let L be the tree with the smaller root and R be the other tree. Then the following is true:

1. If one tree is empty, the other can be used as the merged result.
2. Otherwise, let *Temp* be the right subtree of L.
3. Make L's left subtree its new right subtree.
4. Make the result of the recursive merge of *Temp* and R the new left subtree of L.

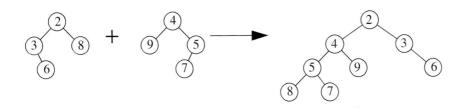

Figure 22.2   Merging of skew heap; right paths are merged, and the result is made a left path

A long right path is still possible. However, it is a rare occurrence that must have been preceded by many merges involving short right paths.

The result of the child swapping is that we expect that the length of the right path will not be unduly large all of the time. For instance, if we merge a pair of long-right-path trees, those nodes involved in the path will not reappear on a right path for quite some time in the future. While it is still possible to obtain trees that have the property that every node appears on a right path, this can be done only as a result of a large number of relatively inexpensive merges. In the next section, we prove this rigorously by establishing that the amortized cost of a merge operation is only logarithmic.

22.1.4 Analysis of the Skew Heap

The actual cost of a merge is the number of nodes on the right paths of the two trees that are merged.

Suppose we have two heaps, H_1 and H_2, and there are r_1 and r_2 nodes on their respective right paths. Then the time to perform the merge is proportional to $r_1 + r_2$. When we charge 1 unit for each node on the right paths, the cost of the merge is proportional to the number of charges. Since the trees have no structure, all of the nodes in both trees may possibly lie on the right path. This would give a $\Theta(N)$ worst-case bound to merge the trees (Exercise 22.4 asks you to construct an example). As will be shown shortly, the amortized time to merge two skew heaps is $O(\log N)$.

As with the splay tree, the proof is done by introducing a potential function that cancels the varying cost of skew heap operations. We want the potential function to increase by a total of $O(\log N) - (r_1 + r_2)$ so that the total of the merge cost and potential change is only $O(\log N)$. If the potential is minimal prior to the first operation, then applying the telescoping sum guarantees that the total spent for any M operations is $O(M \log N)$, as with the splay tree.

What is needed is some sort of potential function that captures the effect of skew heap operations. Finding such a function is quite challenging. Once one is found, however, the proof is relatively short.

> **DEFINITION:** A node p is *heavy* if the size of p's right subtree is larger than the size of p's left subtree; otherwise, it is *light*. (A node is light if its subtrees have equal size.)

The potential function is the number of heavy nodes. Only nodes on the merged path have their heavy/light status changed. The number of light nodes on a right path is logarithmic.

In Figure 22.3, prior to the merge, nodes 3 and 4 are heavy. After the merge, only node 3 is heavy. Three facts are easily shown. First, as a result of a merge, only nodes on the right path can have the heavy/light status changed, since no other nodes have their subtrees altered. Second, a leaf is light. Third, the number of light nodes on the right path of an N node tree is at most $\lfloor \log N \rfloor + 1$. This is because the right child of a light node has less than half the size of the light node itself, and the halving principle applies. The additional +1 is a result of the leaf's being light. With these preliminaries, we can now prove Theorems 22.1 and 22.2.

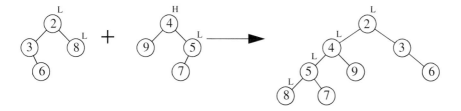

Figure 22.3   Change in the heavy/light status after a merge

Let H_1 and H_2 be two skew heaps with N_1 and N_2 nodes, respectively, and let N be their combined size (that is, $N_1 + N_2$). Suppose the right path of H_1 has l_1 light nodes and h_1 heavy nodes, for a total of $l_1 + h_1$, while the right path of H_2 has l_2 light nodes and h_2 heavy nodes, for a total of $l_2 + h_2$. If the potential is defined as the total number of heavy nodes in the collection of skew heaps, then the merge costs at most $2\log N + (h_1 + h_2)$, but the change in potential is at most $2\log N - (h_1 + h_2)$.	***Theorem 22.1***

The cost of the merge is merely the total number of nodes on the right paths, $l_1 + l_2 + h_1 + h_2$. Since the number of light nodes is logarithmic, $l_1 \le \lfloor \log N_1 \rfloor + 1$ and $l_2 \le \lfloor \log N_2 \rfloor + 1$. Thus $l_1 + l_2 \le \log N_1 + \log N_2 + 2 \le 2\log N$, where the last inequality follows from Theorem 21.4. The merge cost is thus at most $2\log N + (h_1 + h_2)$. The bound on the potential change follows from the fact that only the nodes involved in the merge can have their heavy/light status changed and from the fact that any heavy node on the path must become light, since its children are swapped. Even if all the light nodes became heavy, the potential change would still be limited to $l_1 + l_2 - (h_1 + h_2)$. Using the same argument as before, this is at most $2\log N - (h_1 + h_2)$.	***Proof***

The amortized cost of the skew heap is at most $4\log N$ for `merge`, `insert`, and `deleteMin`.	***Theorem 22.2***

Proof

Let Φ_i be the potential in the collection of skew heaps immediately follow-
ing the ith operation. Note that $\Phi_0 = 0$ and $\Phi_i \geq 0$. An insertion creates a
single node tree whose root is by definition light and thus does not alter the
potential prior to the resulting merge. A `deleteMin` *discards the root*
prior to the merge, so it cannot raise the potential (it may, in fact, lower it).
We need to consider only the merging costs. Let c_i be the cost of the merge
that occurs as a result of the ith operation. Then $c_i + \Phi_i - \Phi_{i-1} \leq 4\log N$.
Telescoping over any M operations yields $\sum_{i=1}^{M} c_i \leq 4M\log N$, since
$\Phi_M - \Phi_0$ is not negative.

Finding a useful po-
tential function is
the most difficult
part of the analysis.

A nonrecursive al-
gorithm should be
used because of
the possibility that
we could run out of
stack space.

The skew heap is a remarkable example of a simple algorithm with an analysis that is not obvious. The analysis, however, is simple to perform once the
appropriate potential function is identified. Unfortunately, there is still no general
theory that allows one to decide on a potential function. Typically, many different
functions are tried before a usable one is found.

One comment is in order. Although the initial description of the algorithm
uses recursion and recursion provides the simplest code, it cannot be used in practice. This is because the linear worst-case time for an operation could cause an
overflow of the method stack when the recursion is implemented. Consequently,
a nonrecursive algorithm must be used. Rather than explore those possibilities,
we discuss an alternative data structure that is slightly more complicated: the
pairing heap. This data structure has not been completely analyzed, but it seems
to perform well in practice.

22.2 The Pairing Heap

The *pairing heap* is
a heap-ordered M-
ary tree with no
structural con-
straints. Its analysis is
incomplete, but it
appears to perform
well in practice.
The pairing heap is
stored using a left
child/right sibling
representation. A
third reference is
used for
decreaseKey.

The *pairing heap* is a structurally unconstrained heap-ordered *M*-ary tree. It has
the property that all operations except deletion take constant worst-case time.
Although `deleteMin` could take linear worst-case time, it can be shown that
any *sequence* of pairing heap operations has logarithmic amortized performance.
It is conjectured, but not proved, that even better performance is guaranteed,
namely, that all operations except for `deleteMin` have constant amortized cost,
while `deleteMin` has logarithmic amortized cost.

Figure 22.4 shows an abstract pairing heap. The actual implementation uses a
left child/right sibling representation, discussed in Chapter 17. `decreaseKey`,
as will be shown soon, requires that each node contain an additional reference. A
node that is a leftmost child contains a reference to its parent; otherwise, the node
is a right sibling and contains a reference to its left sibling. This representation is
shown in Figure 22.5, where the darkened line indicates that two references (one
in each direction) connect pairs of nodes.

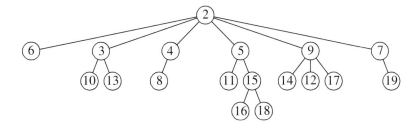

Figure 22.4   Abstract representation of a sample pairing heap

22.2.1   Pairing Heap Operations and Theory

In principle, the basic pairing heap operations are simple. This is why the pairing heap performs well in practice. To merge two pairing heaps, we make the heap with the larger root the new first child of the heap with the smaller root. Insertion is a special case of merging. To perform a `decreaseKey`, we lower the value of the requested node. Because we are not maintaining parent references for all nodes, we do not know if this will violate the heap order. Thus we detach the adjusted node from its parent and complete the `decreaseKey` by merging the two pairing heaps that result. Figure 22.5 shows that detaching a node from its parent means removing it from what is essentially a linked list of children. So far we are in great shape: Every operation described takes constant time. However, we are not so lucky when it comes to `deleteMin`.

Merging is simple: Attach the larger-root tree as a left child of the smaller-root tree. Insertion and decreasing are also simple.

To perform a `deleteMin`, we must remove the root of the tree, creating a collection of heaps. If there are c children of the root, then combining these heaps into one heap requires $c - 1$ merges. Hence, if there are lots of children of the root, the `deleteMin` will cost lots of time. If the insertion sequence is 1, 2, ..., N, then it is easy to see that 1 will be at the root and all of the other items will be in nodes that are children of the root. Consequently, the `deleteMin` will be $O(N)$. The best we can hope to do is to arrange the merges so that we do not have repeatedly expensive `deleteMin` operations.

deleteMin is expensive because the new root could be any of the c children of the old root. We need $c - 1$ merges.

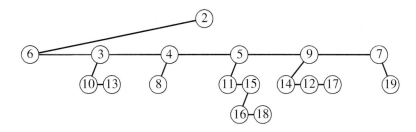

Figure 22.5   Actual representation of the pairing heap in Figure 22.4; the dark line represents a pair of references that connect nodes in both directions

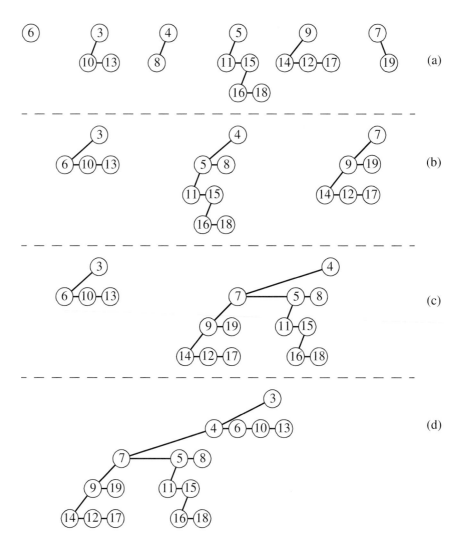

Figure 22.6 Recombination of siblings after a `deleteMin`; in each merge, the larger root tree is made the left child of the smaller root tree: (a) the resulting trees; (b) after the first pass; (c) after the first merge of the second pass; (d) after the second merge of the second pass

The order in which the pairing heap subtrees are merged is important. The simplest algorithm is two-pass merging.

The simplest and most practical of the many variants that have been proposed is *two-pass merging*. We first scan merging pairs of children from left to right.[2] After the first scan, we have half as many trees to merge. We then perform a second scan, right to left. At each step, we merge the rightmost tree that remains from the first scan with the current merged result. As an example, if we have children c_1 through c_8, the first scan performs the merges c_1 and c_2, c_3 and c_4, c_5

---

2. We must be careful if there are an odd number of children. When that happens, we merge the last child with the result of the rightmost merge to complete the first scan.

and c_6, and c_7 and c_8. The result is d_1, d_2, d_3, and d_4. We perform the second pass by merging d_3 and d_4; d_2 is then merged with that result, and d_1 is then merged with the result of that merge, thus completing the deleteMin. Figure 22.6 shows the result of a deleteMin on the pairing heap in Figure 22.5.

Other merging strategies are possible. For instance, we can place each subtree (corresponding to a child) on a queue, repeatedly dequeue two trees, and then enqueue the result of merging them. After $c - 1$ merges, only one tree remains on the queue, and this is the result of the deleteMin. However, using a stack instead of a queue is a disaster because the root of the tree that results may possibly have $c - 1$ children. If this occurs in a sequence, the deleteMin operation will have linear, rather than logarithmic, amortized cost per operation. Exercise 22.8 asks you to construct such a sequence.

Several alternatives have been proposed. Most are indistinguishable, but using a single left-to-right pass is a bad idea.

22.2.2 Implementation of the Pairing Heap

The functionality of the PairHeap is described in Figure 22.7 and the PairHeap class skeleton is shown in Figure 22.8 (page 652). The basic node of a pairing heap, PairNode, is shown in Figure 22.9 (page 653) and consists of an item and three references. Two of these references are the left child and the next sibling. The third reference is prev, which references the parent if the node is a first child, or a left sibling otherwise. PairNode is public so that references to it can be used, but its fields and constructor are package-friendly and thus are not accessible to class users.

The prev data field references either a left sibling or a parent.

```
1  package DataStructures;
2
3  import Supporting.*;
4  import Exceptions.*;
5
6  // PairHeap class
7  //
8  // CONSTRUCTION: with no initializer
9  //
10 // ****************PUBLIC OPERATIONS********************
11 // void insert( x )         --> Insert x
12 // PairNode addItem( x )    --> Insert x, return position
13 // Comparable deleteMin( )--> Return and remove smallest item
14 // Comparable findMin( )    --> Return smallest item
15 // boolean isEmpty( )       --> Return true if empty; else false
16 // void makeEmpty( )        --> Remove all items
17 // void decreaseKey( PairNode p, newVal )
18 //                          --> Decrease value in node p
19 // ****************ERRORS******************************
20 // findMin and deleteMin throw Underflow when empty
```

Figure 22.7   Description of the PairingHeap class

```
1  /**
2   * Implements a pairing heap.
3   * Supports a decreaseKey operation, but requires use
4   * of addItem instead of insert. Heap order is always
5   * maintained; no lazy operations allowed.
6   */
7  public class PairHeap implements PriorityQueue
8  {
9      public PairHeap( )
10        { makeEmpty( ); }
11     public Comparable findMin( ) throws Underflow
12        { /* Figure 22.10 */ }
13     public void insert( Comparable x )
14        { /* Figure 22.11 */ }
15     public PairNode addItem( Comparable x )
16        { /* Figure 22.11 */ }
17     public Comparable deleteMin( ) throws Underflow
18        { /* Figure 22.12 */ }
19     public void decreaseKey( PairNode p, Comparable newVal )
20                                        throws IllegalValue
21        { /* Figure 22.13 */ }
22     public boolean isEmpty( )
23        { return currentSize == 0; }
24     public void makeEmpty( )
25        { currentSize = 0; root = null; }
26
27     private int currentSize;        // Number of elements in heap
28     private PairNode root;
29
30     private PairNode
31     compareAndLink( PairNode first, PairNode second )
32        { /* Figure 22.15 */ }
33     private PairNode combineSiblings( PairNode firstSibling )
34        { /* Figure 22.16 */ }
35 }
```

Figure 22.8   Pairing heap class skeleton

addItem returns a
reference to the
new node for use
by decreaseKey.

The data fields of `PairHeap` are a reference to the root node (`root`), plus an integer that represents the current number of items in the heap. This field is used to simplify the `decreaseKey` operation. `PairHeap` must implement the `PriorityQueue` interface. As a result, the behavior of `insert` cannot change. However, we want to return a reference to the new `PairNode` for use with `decreaseKey`. Thus we write `addItem` to handle this case. `addItem` calls `insert` and returns the newly created `PairNode`. To do this, it shares the data field `newNode` (that is described when `insert` is implemented). A `merge` class method is not included; it is straightforward to implement and is left as Exercise 22.10.

```
 1  /**
 2   * Public class for use with PairHeap. It is public
 3   * only to allow references to be sent to decreaseKey.
 4   * It has no public methods or data fields.
 5   * @see PairHeap
 6   */
 7  public class PairNode
 8  {
 9      /**
10       * Construct the PairNode.
11       * @param theElement the value stored in the node.
12       */
13      PairNode( Comparable theElement )
14      {
15          element     = theElement;
16          leftChild   = null;
17          nextSibling = null;
18          prev        = null;
19      }
20
21          // Friendly data; accessible by other package routines
22      Comparable element;
23      PairNode    leftChild;
24      PairNode    nextSibling;
25      PairNode    prev;
26  }
```

Figure 22.9   `PairNode` class

findMin is coded in Figure 22.10. Since the minimum is at the root, this routine is easily implemented. insert, shown in Figure 22.11 (page 654), creates a one-node tree and merges it with the root to obtain a new tree. As mentioned earlier in the section, addItem calls insert and returns a reference to the newly allocated node. Notice that we must handle the special case of an insertion into an empty tree.

```
 1      /**
 2       * Find the smallest item in the priority queue.
 3       * @return the smallest item.
 4       * @exception Underflow if the priority queue is empty.
 5       */
 6      public Comparable findMin( ) throws Underflow
 7      {
 8          if( isEmpty( ) )
 9              throw new Underflow( "Empty pairing heap" );
10          return root.element;
11      }
```

Figure 22.10   `findMin` method for the pairing heap

```
1       private PairNode newNode = null; // Last node inserted
2
3       /**
4        * Insert into the priority queue.
5        * Duplicates are allowed.
6        * @param x the item to insert.
7        */
8       public void insert( Comparable x )
9       {
10          newNode = new PairNode( x );
11
12          currentSize++;
13          if( root == null )
14              root = newNode;
15          else
16              root = compareAndLink( root, newNode );
17      }
18
19      /**
20       * Insert into the priority queue, and return a PairNode
21       * that can be used by decreaseKey.
22       * Duplicates are allowed.
23       * @param x the item to insert.
24       * @return the node containing the newly inserted item.
25       */
26      public PairNode addItem( Comparable x )
27      {
28          insert( x );
29          return newNode;
30      }
```

Figure 22.11   insert and addItem methods for the pairing heap

deleteMin is implemented as a call to combine-Siblings.

Figure 22.12 implements the deleteMin method. If the pairing heap is empty, we have an error. Otherwise, after saving the value in the root, we make a call to combineSiblings at line 12 to merge the root's subtrees and set the result to the new root. If there are no subtrees, we merely set root to null at line 10. Both insert and deleteMin adjust currentSize appropriately.

decreaseKey is implemented in Figure 22.13. Notice that if the new value is larger than the original, then we might destroy the heap order. There is no way to know without examining all the children. Since there may be many children, doing this would be inefficient. Thus we assume that it is always an error to attempt to increase the key using decreaseKey. (Exercise 22.9 asks you to describe an algorithm for increaseKey.) After performing this test, we lower the value in the node. If the node is the root, we are done. Otherwise, we splice the node out of the list of children that it is in, using the code in lines 17 to 23. After that is done, we merely merge the resulting tree with the root.

```
1      /**
2       * Remove the smallest item from the priority queue.
3       * @exception Underflow if the priority queue is empty.
4       */
5      public Comparable deleteMin( ) throws Underflow
6      {
7          Comparable x = findMin( );
8
9          if( root.leftChild == null )
10             root = null;
11         else
12             root = combineSiblings( root.leftChild );
13
14         currentSize--;
15
16         return x;
17     }
```

Figure 22.12   deleteMin method for the pairing heap

```
1      /**
2       * Change value of the item stored in the pairing heap.
3       * @param p any node returned by addItem.
4       * @param newVal the new value, which must be smaller
5       *    than the currently stored value.
6       * @exception IllegalValue if newVal is larger
7       *    than the currently stored value.
8       */
9      public void decreaseKey( PairNode p, Comparable newVal )
10                              throws IllegalValue
11     {
12         if( p.element.lessThan( newVal ) )
13             throw new IllegalValue( "Illegal decreaseKey" );
14         p.element = newVal;
15         if( p != root )
16         {
17             if( p.nextSibling != null )
18                 p.nextSibling.prev = p.prev;
19             if( p.prev.leftChild == p )
20                 p.prev.leftChild = p.nextSibling;
21             else
22                 p.prev.nextSibling = p.nextSibling;
23             p.nextSibling = null;
24
25             root = compareAndLink( root, p );
26         }
27     }
```

Figure 22.13   The decreaseKey method for the pairing heap

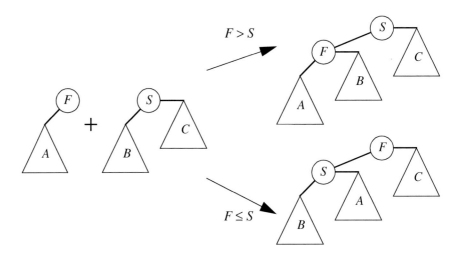

Figure 22.14 `compareAndLink` merges two trees

The two remaining routines are `compareAndLink`, which combines two trees, and `combineSiblings`, which combines all the siblings, when given the first sibling. Figure 22.14 shows how two subheaps are combined. The procedure is generalized to allow the second subheap to have siblings (this is needed for the second pass in the two-pass merge). As mentioned earlier in the chapter, the subheap with the larger root is made a leftmost child of the other subheap. The code is shown in Figure 22.15. Notice that there are several instances in which a reference is tested against `null` before it accesses its `prev` data field. This suggests that perhaps it would be useful to have a `nullNode` sentinel, as was customary in the advanced search tree implementations. This is left as Exercise 22.13.

Finally, Figure 22.16 (page 658) implements `combineSiblings`. We use the array `treeArray` to store the subtrees. In the worst case, we could have $N - 1$ siblings, so the array uses 10,000 as the capacity, for simplicity. We begin by separating the subtrees and storing them in `treeArray`, using the loop at lines 16 to 23. Assuming we have more than one sibling to merge, we make a left-to-right pass at lines 27 to 29. The special case of an odd number of trees is handled at lines 33 to 36. We finish the merging with a right-to-left pass at lines 40 to 42. Once we are done, the result is found in array position 0 and can be returned.

```
 1      /**
 2       * Internal method that is the basic operation to
 3       * maintain order.
 4       * Links first and second together to satisfy heap order.
 5       * @param first root of tree 1, which may not be null.
 6       *     first.nextSibling MUST be null on entry.
 7       * @param second root of tree 2, which may be null.
 8       * @return result of the tree merge.
 9       */
10      private PairNode
11      compareAndLink( PairNode first, PairNode second )
12      {
13          if( second == null )
14              return first;
15
16          if( second.element.lessThan( first.element ) )
17          {
18              // Attach first as leftmost child of second
19              second.prev = first.prev;
20              first.prev = second;
21              first.nextSibling = second.leftChild;
22              if( first.nextSibling != null )
23                  first.nextSibling.prev = first;
24              second.leftChild = first;
25              return second;
26          }
27          else
28          {
29              // Attach second as leftmost child of first
30              second.prev = first;
31              first.nextSibling = second.nextSibling;
32              if( first.nextSibling != null )
33                  first.nextSibling.prev = first;
34              second.nextSibling = first.leftChild;
35              if( second.nextSibling != null )
36                  second.nextSibling.prev = second;
37              first.leftChild = second;
38              return first;
39          }
40      }
```

Figure 22.15   compareAndLink routine

As a practical matter, placing an arbitrary limit on the number of children of the root is unjustified. It would be better to use a respectable initial size and expand the array as needed. The online code has a more flexible solution.

```
1     /**
2      * Internal method that implements two-pass merging.
3      * @param firstSibling the root of the conglomerate;
4      *        assumed not null.
5      */
6
7         // Assumes at most 10000 children; online code is better.
8     static PairNode [ ] treeArray = new PairNode[ 10000 ];
9
10    private PairNode combineSiblings( PairNode firstSibling )
11    {
12        if( firstSibling.nextSibling == null )
13            return firstSibling;
14
15            // Store the subtrees in an array
16        int numSiblings = 0;
17        for( ; firstSibling != null; numSiblings++ )
18        {
19            treeArray[ numSiblings ] = firstSibling;
20            firstSibling.prev.nextSibling = null;
21            firstSibling = firstSibling.nextSibling;
22        }
23        treeArray[ numSiblings ] = null;
24
25            // Combine subtrees two at a time, going left to right
26        int i = 0;
27        for( ; i + 1 < numSiblings; i += 2 )
28            treeArray[ i ] = compareAndLink( treeArray[ i ],
29                                      treeArray[ i + 1 ] );
30
31            // j has the result of last compareAndLink.
32            // If an odd number of trees, get the last one.
33        int j = i - 2;
34        if( j == numSiblings - 3 )
35            treeArray[ j ] = compareAndLink( treeArray[ j ],
36                                      treeArray[ j + 2 ] );
37
38            // Now go right to left, merging last tree with
39            // next to last. The result becomes the new last.
40        for( ; j >= 2; j -= 2 )
41             treeArray[ j - 2 ] = compareAndLink(
42                        treeArray[ j - 2 ], treeArray[ j ] );
43
44        return treeArray[ 0 ];
45    }
```

Figure 22.16 The heart of the pairing heap algorithm; implementing a two-pass merge to combine all of the siblings, when the first sibling is given

```
1     // Dijkstra's Algorithm using pairing heap
2     private boolean dijkstraPair( int startNode )
3     {
4         int v, w;
5         PairHeap pq = new PairHeap( );
6         Path vrec;
7         PairNode [ ] heapPositions;
8
9         clearData( );
10        heapPositions = new PairNode[ numVertices ];
11        for( int i = 0; i < numVertices; i++ )
12            heapPositions[ i ] = null;
13        table[ startNode ].dist = 0;
14        pq.insert( new Path( startNode, 0 ) );
15
16        try
17        {
18            while( !pq.isEmpty( ) )
19            {
20                vrec = (Path) pq.deleteMin( );
21                v = vrec.dest;
22
23                ListItr p = new LinkedListItr( table[v].adj );
24                for( ; p.isInList( ); p.advance( ) )
25                {
26                    w     = ( (Edge)p.retrieve( ) ).dest;
27                    int cvw = ( (Edge)p.retrieve( ) ).cost;
28
29                    if( cvw < 0 )
30                        return false;
31                    if( table[ w ].dist > table[ v ].dist + cvw )
32                    {
33                        table[ w ].dist = table[ v ].dist + cvw;
34                        table[ w ].prev = v;
35
36                        Path newVal = new Path( w, table[ w ].dist );
37                        if( heapPositions[ w ] == null )
38                            heapPositions[ w ] = pq.addItem( newVal );
39                        else
40                            pq.decreaseKey( heapPositions[ w ], newVal );
41                    }
42                }
43            }
44        }
45        catch( Exception e ) { }   // This cannot happen
46        return true;
47    }
```

Figure 22.17   Dijkstra's algorithm using the pairing heap and `decreaseKey`

22.2.3 Application: Dijkstra's Shortest Weighted Path Algorithm

decreaseKey is
an improvement
for Dijkstra's algo-
rithm when there
are lots of calls to it.

For an example of how the decreaseKey operation is used, we rewrite Dijkstra's algorithm, previously seen in Section 14.3. Recall that at any point, we were maintaining a priority queue of Path objects, ordered by the dist data field. For each vertex in the graph, we needed only one Path object in the priority queue at any instant, but for convenience we had many. In this section, we rework the code so that if a vertex *w* has its distance lowered, then its position in the priority queue is found and a decreaseKey operation is performed for its corresponding Path object.

The new code is shown in Figure 22.17 (page 659). The changes are all relatively minor. First, at line 5 we declare that pq is a pairing heap rather than a binary heap. We also maintain an array, heapPositions, of references to pairing heap nodes. Initially, all of the references are null (lines 11 and 12). Whenever an item is inserted into the pairing heap, we make an entry into the heapPositions array. This occurs at line 38.[3] The algorithm itself is simplified. Now, we merely call deleteMin as long as the pairing heap is not empty, rather than repeatedly calling deleteMin until an unseen vertex emerges. Consequently, we no longer need the scratch data field. Compare lines 18 to 21 with the corresponding code in Figure 14.29. All that remains are the updates after line 31 that indicate a change is in order. If the vertex has never been placed in the priority queue, we insert it for the first time, updating the heapPositions array. Otherwise, we merely call decreaseKey at line 40.

Whether the binary heap implementation of Dijkstra's algorithm is faster than the pairing heap implementation depends on several factors. One study, detailed in the references, suggests that the pairing heap is slightly better than the binary heap when both are carefully implemented. The results depend heavily on the coding details as well as on the frequency of decreaseKey operations. More study is needed to decide when the pairing heap is suitable in practice.

Summary

This chapter describes two data structures that support merging and that are efficient in the amortized sense: the skew heap and the pairing heap. Both are simple to implement because they lack a rigid structure property. The pairing heap seems to have practical utility, but its complete analysis remains an intriguing open problem.

The next chapter, which is the last chapter, describes a data structure that is used to maintain disjoint sets and that also has a remarkable amortized analysis.

---

[3] The startNode will not be in the pairing heap for long, so we do not use addItem at line 14.

Objects of the Game

pairing heap A heap-ordered *M*-ary tree with no structural constraints. Its analysis is not complete, but it appears to perform well in practice. (648)

skew heap A heap-ordered binary tree. There is no balancing condition, but it supports all operations in logarithmic amortized time. (643)

two-pass merging The order in which the pairing heap subtrees are merged is important. The simplest algorithm is two-pass merging, in which subtrees are merged in pairs in a left-to-right scan. Then a right-to-left scan is performed to finish the merging. (651)

Common Errors

1. A recursive implementation of the skew heap cannot be used in practice because the depth of the recursion could be linear.
2. Be careful not to lose track of the `prev` references in the skew heap.
3. Tests to make sure references are not `null` must be done throughout the pairing heap code.
4. When a merge is performed, a node should not reside in two pairing heaps.

On the Internet

The pairing heap class is available in the directory **DataStructures**. Figure 22.17 is part of the `Graph` class shown in Chapter 14 (**Graph.java** in directory **Part3**). Here are the filenames.

PairHeap.java   Contains the implementation for the pairing heap.
PairNode.java   Contains the pairing heap node definition.

Exercises

In Short

22.1. Show the result of a skew heap built from the following insertion sequences:
    a. 1, 2, 3, 4, 5, 6, 7
    b. 4, 3, 5, 2, 6, 7, 1

22.2. Show the result of a pairing heap built from the following insertion sequences:
    a. 1, 2, 3, 4, 5, 6, 7
    b. 4, 3, 5, 2, 6, 7, 1

22.3. For each heap in Exercises 22.1 and 22.2, show the result of two
deleteMin operations.

In Theory

22.4. Give a sequence of operations that lead to a merge that requires linear
time to show that the logarithmic amortized bound for skew heap operations is not a worst-case bound.

22.5. Show that both the decreaseKey and increaseKey operations can
be supported by skew heaps in logarithmic amortized time.

22.6. Describe a linear-time fixHeap algorithm for the skew heap.

22.7. Show that storing the length of the right path for each node in the tree
enables one to impose a balancing condition that yields logarithmic worst-
case time per operation. Such a structure is called a *leftist heap*.

22.8. Show that using a stack to implement the combineSiblings operation
for pairing heaps is bad. Do this by constructing a sequence that has linear
amortized cost per operation.

22.9. Describe how to implement increaseKey for pairing heaps.

In Practice

22.10. Add the public merge method to the pairing heap class. Make sure that a
node appears in only one tree.

22.11. Use a static array that is expanded as necessary to store the treeArray
in combineSiblings.

Programming Problems

22.12. Implement a nonrecursive version of the skew heap.

22.13. Implement the pairing heap with a nullNode sentinel.

22.14. Implement the queue algorithm for combineSiblings and compare its
performance with the two-pass algorithm coded in Figure 22.16.

22.15. If the decreaseKey operation is not supported, parent references are
not necessary. Implement the pairing heap without parent references and
compare its performance with the binary heap and/or skew heap and/or
splay tree.

22.16. Design an applet that illustrates the skew heap or the pairing heap.

References

The *leftist heap* [1] was the first efficient mergeable priority queue. It is the
worst-case variant of the skew heap suggested in Exercise 22.7. Skew heaps are
described in [5]. This paper contains solutions to Exercises 22.4 and 22.5.

[2] describes the pairing heap and proves that when two-pass merging is
used, the amortized cost of all operations is logarithmic. It is still unknown

whether this bound is tight. In particular, there is some evidence in [6] that the amortized cost of all operations except `deleteMin` is actually constant, while the amortized cost of the `deleteMin` is logarithmic, so that any sequence of D `deleteMin` and I other operations takes $O(I + D \log N)$ time. On the other hand, there is also evidence that this might not be the case [4]. A data structure that does achieve this bound, but is too complicated to be practical, is the *Fibonacci heap* [3]. It is hoped that the pairing heap is a practical alternative to the theoretically interesting Fibonacci heap. Leftist heaps and Fibonacci heaps are discussed in [7].

In [4] is a comparison of various priority queues in the setting of solving the minimum spanning tree problem (discussed in Section 23.2.1) using a method very similar to Dijkstra's algorithm.

1. C. A. Crane, "Linear Lists and Priority Queues as Balanced Binary Trees," *Technical Report STAN-CS-72-259,* Computer Science Department, Stanford University, Palo Alto, Calif. (1972).

2. M. L. Fredman, R. Sedgewick, D. D. Sleator, and R. E. Tarjan, "The Pairing Heap: A New Form of Self-adjusting Heap," *Algorithmica* **1** (1986), 111–129.

3. M. L. Fredman and R. E. Tarjan, "Fibonacci Heaps and Their Uses in Improved Network Optimization Algorithms," *Journal of the ACM* **34** (1987), 596–615.

4. B. M. E. Moret and H. D. Shapiro, "An Empirical Analysis of Algorithms for Constructing a Minimum Spanning Tree," *Proceedings of the Second Workshop on Algorithms and Data Structures* (1991), 400–411.

5. D. D. Sleator and R. E. Tarjan, "Self-adjusting Heaps," *SIAM Journal on Computing* **15** (1986), 52–69.

6. J. T. Stasko and J. S. Vitter, "Pairing Heaps: Experiments and Analysis," *Communications of the ACM* **32** (1987), 234–249.

7. M. A. Weiss, *Data Structures and Algorithm Analysis in C++,* Benjamin/Cummings Publishing Co., Redwood City, Calif. (1994).

23   *The Disjoint Set Class*

T HIS chapter describes an efficient data structure to solve the equivalence problem: the disjoint set class. This data structure is simple to implement. Each routine requires only a few lines of code. Its implementation is also extremely fast, requiring constant average time per operation. This data structure is also very interesting from a theoretical point of view because its analysis is extremely difficult; the functional form of the worst case is unlike any discussed so far in this book.

In this chapter, we will see:

- Two simple applications of the disjoint set class
- How the disjoint set class can be implemented with minimal coding effort
- How to increase the speed of the disjoint set class using two simple observations
- An analysis of the running time of a fast implementation of the disjoint set class

23.1 Equivalence Relations

A *relation R* is defined on a set *S* if for every pair of elements (*a*, *b*), *a*, *b* ∈ *S*, *a R b* is either true or false. If *a R b* is true, then we say that *a* is related to *b*.

An *equivalence relation* is a relation *R* that satisfies three properties:

1. *Reflexive: a R a* is true for all *a* ∈ *S*.
2. *Symmetric: a R b* if and only if *b R a*.
3. *Transitive: a R b* and *b R c* implies that *a R c*.

A *relation* is defined on a set if every pair of elements either is related or is not. An *equivalence relation* is reflexive, symmetric, and transitive.

Electrical connectivity, where all connections are by metal wires, is an equivalence relation. The relation is clearly reflexive, as any component is connected to itself. If *a* is electrically connected to *b*, then *b* must be electrically connected to *a*, so the relation is symmetric. Finally, if *a* is connected to *b* and *b* is connected to *c*, then *a* is connected to *c*.

Likewise, connectivity through a bidirectional network forms equivalence classes of connected components. However, if the connections in the network are directed (that is, a connection from *v* to *w* does not imply one from *w* to *v*), then we do not have an equivalence relation because the symmetric property does not hold. An example is a relation in which town a is related to town b if it is possible to travel from a to b by taking roads. This relationship is an equivalence relation if the roads are two-way.

23.2 Dynamic Equivalence and Two Applications

For any equivalence relation, which is indicated by the symbol ~, the natural problem is to decide for any a and b if $a\sim b$. If the relation is stored as a two-dimensional array of Boolean variables, then of course, this can be done in constant time. The problem is that the relation is usually implicitly, rather than explicitly, defined.

As an example, an equivalence relation is defined over the five-element set $\{a_1, a_2, a_3, a_4, a_5\}$. Then there are 25 pairs of elements, each of which either is related or is not. However, the information that $a_1\sim a_2$, $a_3\sim a_4$, $a_1\sim a_5$, and $a_4\sim a_2$ are all related implies that all pairs are related. We would like to be able to infer this quickly.

> The *equivalence class* of an element x in set S is the subset of S that contains all the elements that are related to x. The equivalence classes form *disjoint sets*. The basic operations needed for disjoint set manipulation are union and find.

The *equivalence class* of an element $x \in S$ is the subset of S that contains all the elements that are related to x. Note that the equivalence classes form a partition of S: Every member of S appears in exactly one equivalence class. To decide if $a\sim b$, we need only to check whether a and b are in the same equivalence class. This provides the strategy to solve the equivalence problem.

The input is initially a collection of N sets, each with one element. This initial representation is that all relations (except reflexive relations) are false. Each set has a different element, so $S_i \cap S_j = \varnothing$; such sets are called *disjoint sets*.

There are two permissible operations. The first is find, which returns the name of the set (that is, the equivalence class) containing a given element. The second operation adds relations. If we want to add the pair (a,b) to the list of relations, then we first see if a and b are already related. This is done by performing finds on both a and b and checking whether they are in the same equivalence class. If they are not, then we apply union. This operation merges the two equivalence classes containing a and b into a new equivalence class. From a set point of view, the result is to create a new set $S_k = S_i \cup S_j$, simultaneously destroying the originals and preserving the disjointedness of all of the sets. The data structure to do this is often called the disjoint set *union/find data structure*. The term *union/find algorithm* means a processing of *union/find* requests using the disjoint set data structure.

> In an *online algorithm*, an answer must be provided for each query before viewing the next query.

The algorithm is *dynamic* because, during the course of the algorithm, the sets can change via the union operation. The algorithm must also operate *online*. That is, when a find is performed, it must give an answer before continuing. Another possibility would be an *offline* algorithm. Such an algorithm would be allowed to see the entire sequence of union and find requests. The answer it provides for each find must still be consistent with all of the unions that were performed up until the `find`, but the algorithm can give all of its answers after it has seen *all* of the questions. The difference is similar to the difference between taking a written exam (which is generally offline because you only have to give the answers before time expires) and taking an oral exam (which is online because you must answer the current question before proceeding to the next question).

Notice that we do not perform any operations comparing the relative values of elements but merely require knowledge of their location. For this reason, we can assume that all elements have been numbered sequentially starting from 0 and that the numbering can be determined easily by some hashing scheme.

The set elements are numbered sequentially starting from 0.

Before describing how to implement the `union` and `find` operations, this section provides two applications of the data structure.

23.2.1   Application #1: Minimum Spanning Trees

A *spanning tree* of an undirected graph G is a tree formed from graph edges that connect all the vertices of G. Notice that unlike in the graphs in Chapter 14, an edge (u, v) in G is identical to an edge (v, u). The cost of a spanning tree is the sum of the costs of the edges in the tree; the *minimum spanning tree* problem asks for the spanning tree of minimum cost. A minimum spanning tree exists if and only if G is connected. As will be shown shortly, testing a graph's connectivity can be done as part of the minimum spanning tree computation.

The minimum spanning tree is a connected subgraph of G that spans all vertices at minimum total cost.

In Figure 23.1, the graph on the right is a minimum spanning tree of the graph on the left (it happens to be unique, but this is unusual if the graph has many edges of equal cost). Notice that the number of edges in the minimum spanning tree is $|V| - 1$. The minimum spanning tree is a *tree* because it is acyclic, it is *spanning* because it covers every vertex, and it is *minimum* for the obvious reason. Suppose we need to connect several towns with roads, minimizing the total construction cost, with the provision that we can transfer to another road only at a town (in other words, no extra junctions are allowed). Then we need to solve a minimum spanning tree problem, where each vertex is a town, and each edge is the cost of building a road between the two cities it connects.

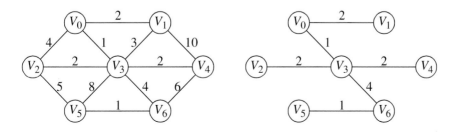

Figure 23.1   A graph G (left) and its minimum spanning tree

Adding junctions at arbitrary places results in the Steiner tree problem, which is much more difficult to solve. Among other things, it can be shown that if the cost of a connection is proportional to the Euclidean distance, then the minimum spanning tree is at most 15 percent more expensive than the minimum Steiner tree. This means that a minimum spanning tree, which is easy to compute, provides a good approximation for the minimum Steiner tree, which is hard to compute.

Kruskal's minimum spanning tree algorithm is used to select edges in order of increasing cost. An edge is added to the tree if it does not create a cycle.

A simple algorithm, commonly called *Kruskal's algorithm*, is used to continually select edges in order of smallest weight and to accept an edge into the tree if it does not cause a cycle. Formally, Kruskal's algorithm maintains a forest — a collection of trees. Initially, there are $|V|$ single-node trees. Adding an edge merges two trees into one. When the algorithm terminates, there is only one tree, and this is the minimum spanning tree.[1] By counting the number of accepted edges, we can determine when the algorithm should terminate.

Figure 23.2 shows the action of Kruskal's algorithm on the graph in Figure 23.1. The first five edges are all accepted because they do not create cycles. The next two edges, (v_1, v_3) (of cost 3) and then (v_0, v_2) (of cost 4), are rejected because each would create a cycle in the tree. The edge that is considered afterward is accepted. Since it is the sixth edge in a seven-vertex graph, we can terminate the algorithm.

The edges can be sorted, or a priority queue can be used.

It is simple enough to order the edges for testing. We can sort them at a cost of $|E|\log|E|$ and then step through the ordered array of edges. Alternatively, we can construct a priority queue of $|E|$ edges and repeatedly obtain edges by calling deleteMin. Although the worst-case bound is unchanged, using a priority queue is sometimes better because Kruskal's algorithm tends to test only a small fraction of the edges on random graphs. Of course, in the worst case, it is always possible that all of the edges must be tried. For instance, if there was an extra vertex v_8 and edge (v_5, v_8) of cost 100, all the edges would have to be examined. In this case, a quicksort at the start would be faster. In effect, the choice between a priority queue and an initial sort is a gamble on how many edges are likely to be examined.

The test for cycles is done by using a union/find data structure.

More interesting is the issue of how we decide whether an edge (u, v) should be accepted or rejected. Clearly, adding the edge (u, v) will cause a cycle if (and only if) u and v are already connected in the current spanning forest. Thus we merely maintain each connected component in the spanning forest as a disjoint set. Initially, each vertex is in its own disjoint set. If u and v are in the same disjoint set, as determined by two finds, the edge is rejected because u and v are already connected. Otherwise, the edge is accepted and a union is performed on the two disjoint sets containing u and v, in effect, combining the connected components. This is what we want because once edge (u, v) is added to the spanning forest, then if w was connected to u and x was connected to v, x and w must be connected and thus belong in the same set.

[1.] If the graph is not connected, the algorithm will terminate with more than one tree: Each tree represents a minimum spanning tree for each connected component of the graph.

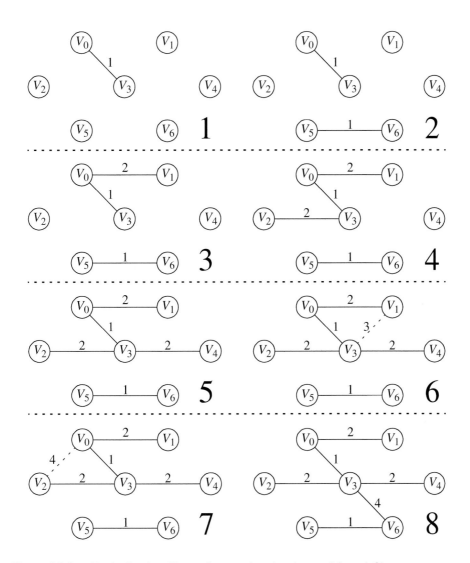

Figure 23.2   Kruskal's algorithm after each edge is considered; Stages proceed top-to-bottom, left-to-right, as numbered

23.2.2 Application #2: The Nearest Common Ancestor Problem

Another illustration of the union/find data structure is the offline *nearest common ancestor* (NCA) problem.

> **OFFLINE NEAREST COMMON ANCESTOR PROBLEM**
> Given a tree and a list of pairs of nodes in the tree, find the nearest common ancestor for each pair of nodes.

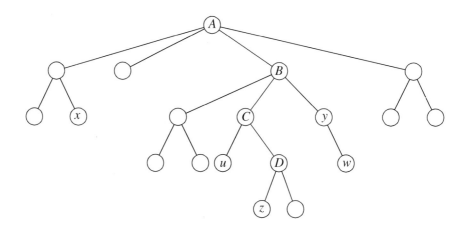

Figure 23.3   The nearest common ancestor for each request in the pair sequence (x, y), (u, z), (w, x), (z, w), and (w, y), is A, C, A, B, and y, respectively

NCA is important in graph algorithms and computational biology.

    As an example, Figure 23.3 shows a tree with a pair list containing five requests. For the pair of nodes u and z, node C is the nearest ancestor of both. (A and B are also ancestors, but they are not the closest.) The problem is offline because we can see the entire request sequence prior to providing the first answer. This is an important graph theory problem that also has applications in the field of computational biology (where the tree represents evolution).

A postorder traversal can be used to solve the problem.

    The algorithm works by performing a postorder tree traversal. When we are about to return from processing a node, we examine the pair list to see if there are any ancestor calculations to be performed. If u is the current node, (u, v) is in the pair list, and we have already finished the recursive call to v, then we have enough information to determine $NCA(u, v)$.

The anchor of a visited (but not necessarily marked) node v is the node on the current access path that is closest to v.

    Figure 23.4 helps in understanding how this algorithm works. We are about to finish the recursive call to D. All nodes that are shaded have been visited by a recursive call, and except for the nodes on the path to D, all the recursive calls have already finished. We mark a node after its recursive call is complete. If v is marked, then $NCA(D, v)$ is some node on the path to D. The *anchor* of a visited (but not necessarily marked) node v is the node on the current access path that is closest to v. In Figure 23.4, p's anchor is A, q's anchor is B, and r is unanchored because it has yet to be visited; we can argue that r's anchor is r at the point that r is first visited. As the figure shows, each node on the current access path is an anchor (of at least itself). Furthermore, the visited nodes form equivalence classes: Two nodes are related if they have the same anchor, and we can regard each unvisited node as being in its own class. Now, suppose once again that (D, v) is in the pair list. Then we have three cases:

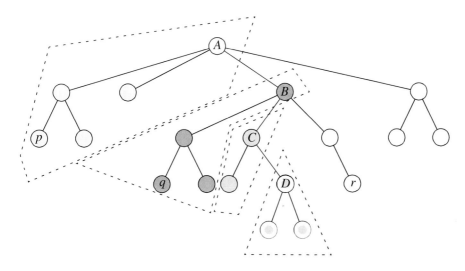

Figure 23.4   The sets immediately prior to the return from the recursive call to *D*; *D* is marked as visited and *NCA(D, v)* is *v*'s anchor to the current path

1. *v* is unmarked, so we have no information to compute $NCA(D, v)$. However, when *v* is marked, we will be able to determine $NCA(v, D)$.
2. *v* is marked but not in *D*'s subtree, so $NCA(v, D)$ is *v*'s anchor.
3. *v* is in *D*'s subtree, so $NCA(v, D) = D$. Notice that this is not a special case because *v*'s anchor is *D*.

All that remains is to make sure that, at any instant, we can determine the anchor of any visited node. This is easily done using the union/find algorithm. After a recursive call returns, we call `union`. For instance, after the recursive call to *D* in Figure 23.4 returns, all nodes in *D* have their anchor changed from *D* to *C*. The new situation is shown in Figure 23.5 (page 672). Thus we need to merge the two equivalence classes into one. At any point, we can obtain the anchor for a vertex *v* by a call to a disjoint set `find`. Because `find` returns a set number, we use an array `anchor` to store the anchor node corresponding to a particular set.

The union/find algorithm is used to maintain the sets of nodes with common anchors.

A pseudocode implementation of the NCA algorithm is shown in Figure 23.6 (page 673). As mentioned earlier in the chapter, the `find` operation generally assumes that elements of the set are 0, 1, ... , $N - 1$, so we store a preorder number in each tree node in a preprocessing step that computes the size of the tree. Although an object-oriented approach might attempt to incorporate a mapping into the `find`, perhaps by using a dictionary, in this case it would be computationally inefficient. We also assume that we have an array of lists to store the NCA requests. List *i* stores the requests for tree node *i*. With those details taken care of, the code is remarkably short.

The pseudocode is compact.

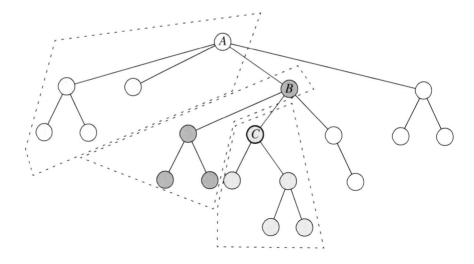

Figure 23.5 After the recursive call from *D* returns, we merge the set anchored by *D* into the set anchored by *C* and then compute all *NCA(C, v)* for nodes *v* that are marked prior to completing *C*'s recursive call

When a node *u* is first visited, it becomes the anchor of itself as in line 18 of Figure 23.6. It then recursively processes its children *v* by making the call at line 23. After each recursive call returns, the subtree is combined into *u*'s current equivalence class and we make sure that the anchor is updated at lines 24 and 25. When all of the children have been processed recursively, we can mark *u* as processed at line 29 and finish by checking all *NCA* requests involving *u* at lines 30 to 33.[2]

23.3 The Quick-find Algorithm

This section lays the groundwork for the efficient implementation of the union/find data structure. There are two basic strategies for solving the union/find problem. One ensures that the `find` instruction can be executed in constant worst-case time, and the other ensures that the `union` can be executed in constant worst-case time. It has recently been shown that both cannot be done simultaneously in constant worst-case (or even amortized) time.

The first approach is called the *quick-find algorithm*. For the `find` operation to be fast, we could maintain, in an array, the name of the equivalence class for

---

[2] Strictly speaking, *u* should be marked at the last statement, but marking it earlier handles the annoying request *NCA(u, u)*.

each element. Then `find` is a simple constant time lookup. Suppose we want to perform union(a, b). Suppose, too, that a is in equivalence class i and b is in equivalence class j. Then we can scan down the array, changing all i's to j's. Unfortunately, this scan takes linear time. Thus a sequence of $N-1$ union operations (the maximum, since then everything is in one set) would take quadratic time. In the typical case in which the number of `find`s is subquadratic, this is clearly unacceptable.

One idea is to keep all of the elements that are in the same equivalence class in a linked list. This saves time when updating because we do not have to search the entire array. This by itself does not reduce the asymptotic running time, since it is still possible to perform $\Theta(N^2)$ equivalence class updates over the course of the algorithm.

```
1       // Nearest Common Ancestors algorithm
2       //
3       // Preconditions (and global objects):
4       //   1. union/find structure is initialized
5       //   2. All nodes are initially unmarked
6       //   3. Preorder numbers are already assigned in num field
7       //   4. Each node can store its marked status
8       //   5. List of pairs is globally available
9
10      DisjSets s = new DisjSets( treeSize );   // union/find
11      Node [ ] anchor = new Node[ treeSize ]; // Set anchors
12
13   // main makes the call nca( root )
14   // after required initializations
15
16    void nca( Node u )
17    {
18        anchor[ s.find( u.num ) ] = u;
19
20        // Do postorder calls
21        for( each child v of u )
22        {
23            nca( v );
24            s.union( s.find( u.num ), s.find( v.num ) );
25            anchor[ s.find( u.num ) ] = u;
26        }
27
28        // Do nca calculation for pairs involving u
29        u.marked = true;
30        for( each v such that nca( u, v ) is required )
31            if( v.marked )
32                System.out.println( "nca( " + u + ", " + v +
33                        " ) is " + anchor[ s.find( v.num ) ] );
34    }
```

Figure 23.6 Pseudocode for NCA problem

If we also keep track of the size of the equivalence classes — and when performing a union, we change the name of the smaller class to the larger — then the total time spent for N unions is $O(N \log N)$. This is because each element can have its equivalence class changed at most $\log N$ times, since every time its class is changed, its new equivalence class is at least twice as large as its old (so the doubling principle applies).

This strategy provides that any sequence of at most M find and $N-1$ union operations will take at most $O(M + N \log N)$ time. If M is linear (or slightly nonlinear), this is still an expensive solution. It also is a bit messy, since we must maintain linked lists. The next section examines a solution to the union/find problem that makes union easy but find hard. This alternative approach is the *quick-union algorithm*. Even so, the running time for any sequence of at most M find and $N-1$ union operations is only negligibly more than $O(M + N)$ time, and furthermore, only a single array of integers is used.

23.4 The Quick-union Algorithm

Recall that the union/find problem does not require a find operation to return any specific name, just that finds on two elements return the same answer if and only if they are in the same set. One idea might be to use a tree to represent a set, since each element in a tree has the same root. Thus the root can be used to name the set.

Each set is represented by a tree (a collection of trees is called a *forest*). The name of a set is given by the node at the root. Our trees are not necessarily binary trees, but their representation is easy because the only information we need is the parent. Thus we need only an array of integers: Each entry p[i] in the array represents the parent of element i, and we can use −1 as a parent to indicate a root. Figure 23.7 shows the forest and the array that represents it.

Figure 23.7 A forest and its eight elements, initially in different sets

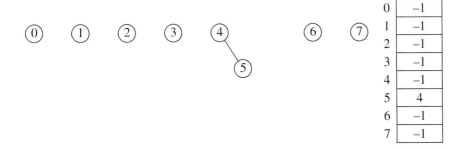

Figure 23.8   The forest after the `union` of trees with roots 4 and 5

To perform a `union` of two sets, we merge the two trees by making the root of one tree point to the root of the other. It should be clear that this operation takes constant time. Figures 23.8, 23.9, and 23.10 (page 676) represent the forest after each of `union(4, 5)`, `union(6, 7)`, and `union(4, 6)`, where we have adopted the convention that the new root after `union(x, y)` is x.

union is constant time.

A `find` on element x is performed by returning the root of the tree containing x. The time to perform this operation is proportional to the number of nodes on the path from x to the root. The `union` strategy outlined previously enables us to create a tree whose every node is on the path to x, thus resulting in a worst-case running time of $\Theta(N)$ per `find`. Typically (as shown in the previous two applications), the running time is computed for a sequence of M intermixed instructions. In the worst case, M consecutive operations could take $\Theta(MN)$ time.

The cost of a `find` depends on the depth of the accessed node and could be linear.

Quadratic running time for a sequence of operations is generally unacceptable. Fortunately, there are several ways to easily ensure that this running time does not occur.

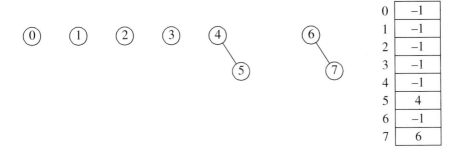

Figure 23.9   The forest after the `union` of trees with roots 6 and 7

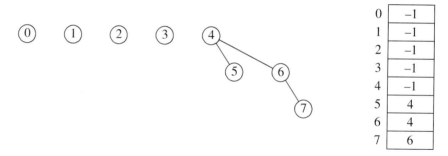

Figure 23.10 The forest after the `union` of trees with roots 4 and 6

23.4.1 Smart Union Algorithms

The previous `unions` were performed rather arbitrarily by making the second tree a subtree of the first. A simple improvement is always to make the smaller tree a subtree of the larger, breaking ties by any method; this approach is called *union-by-size*. The three `unions` in the preceding section were all ties, so we can consider that they were performed by size. If the next operation is `union(3, 4)`, then the forest in Figure 23.11 will form. Had the size heuristic not been used, a deeper forest would have been formed (three nodes rather than one would have been one level deeper).

Union-by-size guar-antees logarithmic finds.

We can prove that if the `union` operation is done by size, the depth of any node is never more than log N. To see this, note that a node is initially at depth 0. When its depth increases as a result of a `union`, it is placed in a tree that is at least twice as large as before. Thus its depth can be increased at most log N times. (We used this argument in the quick-find algorithm in Section 23.3.) This implies that the running time for a `find` operation is $O(\log N)$ and a sequence of M operations takes at most $O(M\log N)$. The tree in Figure 23.12 shows the worst tree possible after 16 `unions` and is obtained if all `unions` are between equal-sized trees. (The worst-case tree is called a *binomial tree*. Binomial trees have other applications in advanced data structures.)

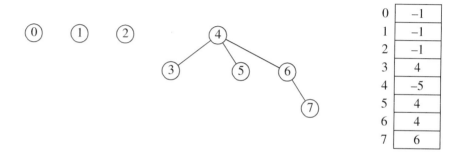

Figure 23.11 The forest formed by union-by-size, with the sizes encoded as negative numbers

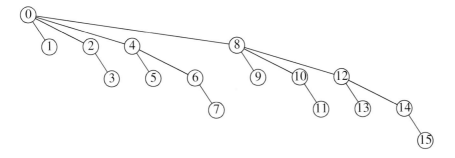

Figure 23.12   Worst-case tree for $N = 16$

To implement this strategy, we need to keep track of the size of each tree. Since we are really just using an array, we can have the array entry of the root contain the *negative* of the size of the tree, as shown in Figure 23.11. Thus the initial representation of the tree using all −1s is reasonable. When a union is performed, we check the sizes; the new size is the sum of the old. Thus union-by-size is not at all difficult to implement and requires no extra space. It is also fast on average. This is because when random unions are performed, generally very small (usually one-element) sets are merged with large sets throughout the algorithm. Mathematical analysis of this is quite complex; the references at the end of the chapter provide some pointers to the literature.

Instead of −1 being stored for roots, the negative of the size is stored.

An alternative implementation that also guarantees logarithmic depth is *union-by-height*. We keep track of the height of the trees instead of the size and perform unions by making the shallow tree a subtree of the deeper tree. This is an easy algorithm, since the height of a tree increases only when two equally deep trees are joined (and then the height goes up by 1). Thus union-by-height is a trivial modification of union-by-size. Since heights start at 0, we store the negative of the number of nodes on the deepest path, rather than the height. This is shown in Figure 23.13 (page 678).

Union-by-height also guarantees logarithm finds.

23.4.2 Path Compression

The union/find algorithm, as described so far, is quite acceptable for most cases. It is very simple and linear on average for a sequence of M instructions. However, the worst case is still unappealing. This is particularly so because it is not obvious that a sequence of union operations that occurs in some particular application (such as the NCA problem) is random (in fact, for certain trees, it is far from random). Consequently, we seek a better bound for the worst case of a sequence of M operations. It seems that there are probably no more improvements possible to the union algorithm, since the worst case is achievable when identical trees are merged. The only way to speed up the algorithm, without reworking the data structure entirely, is to do something clever on the find operation.

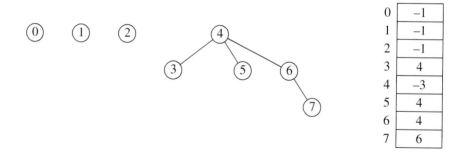

Figure 23.13 A forest formed by union-by-height, with the height encoded as a negative number

That clever operation is *path compression*. Clearly, after we perform a find on x, it would make sense to change x's parent to the root. In that way, a second find on x or any item in x's subtree will be easier. There is no need to stop there, however. We might as well change the parents for all nodes on the access path. The effect of path compression is that *every* node on the path from x to the root has its parent changed to the root. Figure 23.14 shows the effect of path compression after find(14) on the generic worst tree in Figure 23.12. With an extra two parent changes, nodes 12 and 13 are now one position closer to the root and nodes 14 and 15 are now two positions closer. Thus the fast future accesses on the nodes will pay (we hope) for the extra work to do the path compression. Note that subsequent unions push the node deeper.

When unions are done arbitrarily, path compression is a good idea because there is an abundance of deep nodes; these are brought near the root by path compression. It has been proved that when path compression is done in this case, a sequence of M operations requires at most $O(M \log N)$ time, so path compression by itself guarantees logarithmic amortized cost for the find operation.

Path compression is perfectly compatible with union-by-size. Thus both routines can be implemented at the same time. Path compression is not entirely compatible with union-by-height, however, because path compression can change the heights of the trees. It is not at all clear how to recompute them efficiently, so we do not attempt to do so. Then the heights stored for each tree become estimated heights (sometimes known as *ranks*), but this is not a problem. The resulting algorithm is *union-by-rank*. As will be shown in Section 23.6, the combination of a smart union rule and path compression gives an almost linear guarantee on the running time for a sequence of M operations.

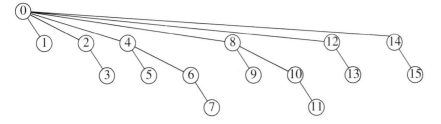

Figure 23.14   Path compression resulting from a `find(14)` on the tree in Figure 23.12

23.5 Java Implementation

The class skeleton for a disjoint sets class is given in Figure 23.15; the implementation is shown in Figure 23.16. Error checks have been omitted to avoid obscuring the algorithmic details. A robust program would, of course, have to check for errors. Without error checks, the entire algorithm is amazingly short.

Disjoint sets are relatively simple to implement.

```
1  package DataStructures;
2
3  // DisjSets class
4  //
5  // CONSTRUCTION: with int representing initial number of sets
6  //
7  // ******************PUBLIC OPERATIONS*********************
8  // void union( root1, root2 ) --> Merge two sets
9  // int find( x )              --> Return set containing x
10 // ******************ERRORS********************************
11 // No error checking is performed
12
13 /**
14  * Disjoint set class, using union by rank and path
15  * compression. Elements are numbered starting at 0.
16  */
17 public class DisjSets
18 {
19     public DisjSets( int numElements )
20       { /* Figure 23.16 */ }
21     public void union( int root1, int root2 )
22       { /* Figure 23.16 */ }
23     public int find( int x )
24       { /* Figure 23.16 */ }
25
26     private int [ ] array;
27 }
```

Figure 23.15   Disjoint sets class skeleton

```
1      /**
2       * Construct the disjoint sets object.
3       * @param numElements the initial number of disjoint sets.
4       */
5      public DisjSets( int numElements )
6      {
7          array = new int [ numElements ];
8          for( int i = 0; i < array.length; i++ )
9              array[ i ] = -1;
10     }
11
12     /**
13      * union two disjoint sets using the height heuristic.
14      * For simplicity, we assume root1 and root2 are distinct.
15      * @param root1 the root of set 1.
16      * @param root2 the root of set 2.
17      */
18     public void union( int root1, int root2 )
19     {
20         if( array[ root2 ] < array[ root1 ] ) // root2 deeper
21             array[ root1 ] = root2;    // Make root2 new root
22         else
23         {
24             if( array[ root1 ] == array[ root2 ] )
25                 array[ root1 ]--;      // Update height if same
26             array[ root2 ] = root1;    // Make root1 new root
27         }
28     }
29
30     /**
31      * Perform a find with path compression.
32      * Error checks omitted again for simplicity.
33      * @param x the element being searched for.
34      * @return the set containing x.
35      */
36     public int find( int x )
37     {
38         if( array[ x ] < 0 )
39             return x;
40         else
41             return array[ x ] = find( array[ x ] );
42     }
```

Figure 23.16 Implementation of a disjoint sets class with no error checks

In the routine, union is performed on the roots of the trees. Sometimes the operation is implemented by passing any two elements and having the union perform the find to determine the roots.

The interesting procedure is find. After the find is performed recursively, array[x] is set to the root and is then returned. Since this happens recursively, all nodes on the path will have their entries set to the root.

23.6 Worst Case for Union-by-rank and Path Compression

When both heuristics are used, the algorithm is almost linear in the worst case. Specifically, the time required to process a sequence of at most $N-1$ `union` operations and M `find` operations in the worst case is $\Theta(M\alpha(M, N))$ (provided $M \geq N$), where $\alpha(M, N)$ is a functional inverse of *Ackermann's function*, which is defined as follows:[3]

$$A(1, j) = 2^j \qquad\qquad j \geq 1$$
$$A(i, 1) = A(i-1, 2) \qquad i \geq 2$$
$$A(i, j) = A(i-1, A(i, j-1)) \qquad i, j \geq 2$$

From this, we define

$$\alpha(M, N) = min\{i \geq 1 | (A(i, \lfloor M/N \rfloor) > \log N)\}.$$

You might want to compute some values, but for all practical purposes, $\alpha(M, N) \leq 4$, which is all that is really important here. For instance, for any $j > 1$, we have

$$A(2, j) = A(1, A(2, j-1))$$
$$= 2^{A(2, j-1)}$$
$$= 2^{2^{2^{\cdots}}}$$

Ackermann's function grows very quickly, and its inverse is essentially at most 4.

where the number of 2's in the exponent is j. $F(N) = A(2, N)$ is commonly called a single-variable Ackermann's function. The single-variable inverse of Ackermann's function, sometimes written as $\log^* N$, is the number of times the logarithm of N needs to be applied until $N \leq 1$. Thus, $\log^* 65536 = 4$, because $\log\log\log\log 65536 = 1$. $\log^* 2^{65536} = 5$. However, keep in mind that 2^{65536} has more than 20,000 digits. $\alpha(M, N)$ grows even slower than $\log^* N$. For instance, $A(3, 1) = A(2, 2) = 2^{2^2} = 16$. Thus for $N < 2^{16}$, $\alpha(M, N) \leq 3$. Further, since $A(4, 1) = A(3, 2) = A(2, A(3, 1)) = A(2, 16)$, which is 2 raised to a power of 16 stacked 2's, then, in practice, $\alpha(M, N) \leq 4$. However, $\alpha(M, N)$ is not a constant when M is slightly more than N, so the running time is not linear.[4]

In the remainder of this section, we will prove a slightly weaker result. We will show that any sequence of $M = \Omega(N)$ union/find operations takes a total of $O(M\log^* N)$ time. The same bound holds if union-by-rank is replaced with union-by-size. This analysis is probably the most complex in the book and one of the first truly complex analyses ever performed for an algorithm that is essentially trivial to implement. By extending this technique, we can show the stronger bound claimed previously.

---

3. Ackermann's function is frequently defined with $A(1, j) = j + 1$ for $j \geq 1$. The form in this text grows faster; thus the inverse grows more slowly.
4. Notice, however, that if $M = N\log^* N$, then $\alpha(M, N)$ is at most 2. Thus, as long as M is slightly more than linear, the running time will be linear in M.

23.6.1   Analysis of the Union/Find Algorithm

In this section, we establish a fairly tight bound on the running time of a sequence of $M = \Omega(N)$ union/find operations. The union and find operations may occur in any order, but union is done by rank and find is done with path compression.

We begin with some theorems concerning the number of nodes of rank r. Intuitively, because of the union-by-rank rule, there are many more nodes of small rank than of large rank. In particular, there can be at most one node of rank $\log N$. What we would like to do is to produce as precise a bound as possible on the number of nodes of any particular rank r. Since ranks change only when union operations are performed (and then only when the two trees have the same rank), we can prove this bound by ignoring path compression. This is done in Theorem 23.1.

Theorem 23.1   *In the absence of path compression, when a sequence of union instructions is being executed, a node of rank r must have 2^r descendants (including itself).*

Proof   *The proof is by induction. The basis $r = 0$ is clearly true. Let T be the tree of rank r with the fewest number of descendants and x be T's root. Suppose the last union that x was involved with was between T_1 and T_2. Suppose T_1's root was x. If T_1 had rank r, then T_1 would be a tree of rank r with fewer descendants than T. This contradicts the assumption that T is the tree with the smallest number of descendants. Hence, the rank of T_1 is at most $r - 1$. The rank of T_2 is at most the rank of T_1, because of union-by-rank. Since T has rank r and the rank could only increase because of T_2, it follows that the rank of T_2 is $r - 1$. Then the rank of T_1 is also $r - 1$. By the induction hypothesis, each tree has at least 2^{r-1} descendants, thus giving a total of 2^r and establishing the theorem.*

Theorem 23.1 says that if no path compression is performed, then any node of rank r must have at least 2^r descendants. Path compression can change this, of course, since it can remove descendants from a node. However, when unions are performed, even with path compression, we are using the ranks, which are estimated heights. These ranks behave as if there is no path compression. Thus when the number of nodes of rank r are being bounded, path compression can be ignored. This is done in Theorem 23.2.

The number of nodes of rank r is at most $N/2^r$.   ***Theorem 23.2***

Proof

Without path compression, each node of rank r is the root of a subtree of at least 2^r nodes. No other node in the subtree can have rank r. Thus all subtrees of nodes of rank r are disjoint. Therefore there are at most $N/2^r$ disjoint subtrees and hence $N/2^r$ nodes of rank r.

Theorem 23.3 seems somewhat obvious, but it is crucial in the analysis:

At any point in the union/find algorithm, the ranks of the nodes on a path from a leaf to a root increase monotonically.   ***Theorem 23.3***

Proof

The theorem is obvious if there is no path compression. If after path compression, some node v is a descendant of w, then clearly v must have been a descendant of w when only union *operations were considered. Hence, the rank of v is strictly less than the rank of w.*

Here is a summary of the preliminary results. Theorem 23.2 indicates how many nodes can be assigned rank r. Because ranks are assigned only by unions, which have no idea of path compression, Theorem 23.2 is valid at any stage of the union/find algorithm — even in the midst of path compression. Theorem 23.2 is tight, in the sense that it is possible for there to be $N/2^r$ nodes for any rank r. It is slightly loose because it is not possible for the bound to hold for all ranks r simultaneously. While Theorem 23.2 describes the number of nodes in a rank r, Theorem 23.3 tells us their distribution. As expected, the rank of nodes is strictly increasing along the path from a leaf to the root.

There are not too many nodes of large rank, and the ranks increase on any path up toward a root.

We are now ready to prove the main theorem. The basic plan is as follows: A find on any node v costs time proportional to the number of nodes on the path from v to the root. We will charge 1 unit of cost for every node on the path from v to the root during each find. To help count the charges, we will deposit an imaginary penny into each node on the path. This is strictly an accounting gimmick that is not part of the program. It is somewhat equivalent to the use of a potential function in the amortized analysis for splay trees and skew heaps. When the algorithm is over, we will collect all the coins that have been deposited to determine the total time.

Pennies are used like a potential function. The total pennies is the total time.

We have both U.S. and Canadian pennies. Canadian pennies account for the first few times a node is compressed; U.S. pennies account for later compressions or noncompressions.

As a further accounting gimmick, we will deposit both U.S. and Canadian pennies. We will show that during the execution of the algorithm, we can deposit only a certain number of U.S. pennies during each find (regardless of how many nodes there are). We will also show that we can deposit only a certain number of Canadian pennies to each node (regardless of how many finds there are). Adding these two totals gives a bound on the total number of pennies that can be deposited.

We now sketch our accounting scheme in more detail. We will divide the nodes by their ranks. We will then divide the ranks into rank groups. On each find, we will deposit some U.S. coins into a general kitty and some Canadian coins into specific nodes. To compute the total number of Canadian coins deposited, we will compute the deposits per node. By adding up all of the deposits for each node in rank r, we will get the total deposits per rank r. Then we will add up all of the deposits for each rank r in group g and thereby obtain the total deposits for each rank group g. Finally, we will add up all of the deposits for each rank group g to obtain the total number of Canadian pennies deposited in the forest. Adding this to the number of U.S. coins in the kitty gives us the answer.

Ranks are partitioned into groups. The actual groups are determined at the end of the proof. Group 0 has only rank 0.

As mentioned previously, we will partition the ranks into groups. Rank r goes into group $G(r)$, and G will be determined later (to balance the U.S. and Canadian charges). The largest rank in any rank group g is $F(g)$, where $F = G^{-1}$ is the *inverse* of G. The number of ranks in any rank group, $g > 0$, is thus $F(g) - F(g-1)$. Clearly, $G(N)$ is a very loose upper bound on the largest rank group. As an example, suppose that we partitioned the ranks as in Figure 23.17. In this case, $G(r) = \lceil \sqrt{r} \rceil$. The largest rank in group g is $F(g) = g^2$. Also, observe that group $g > 0$ contains ranks $F(g-1)+1$ through $F(g)$, inclusive. This formula does not apply for rank group 0, so for convenience we will ensure that rank group 0 contains only elements of rank 0. Notice that the groups are made of consecutive ranks.

Group	Rank
0	0
1	1
2	2,3,4
3	5 through 9
4	10 through 16
i	$(i-1)^2$ through i^2

Figure 23.17 Possible partitioning of ranks into groups

As mentioned earlier in the chapter, each `union` instruction takes constant time, as long as each root keeps track of its rank. Thus `unions` are essentially free, as far as this proof goes.

Each `find` takes time proportional to the number of nodes on the path from the node representing the accessed item i to the root. We will thus deposit one penny for each vertex on the path. If this is all we do, however, we cannot expect much of a bound, since we are not taking advantage of path compression. Thus we must use some fact about path compression in our analysis. The key observation is that as a result of path compression, a node obtains a new parent and the new parent is guaranteed to have higher rank than the old parent.

When a node is compressed, its new parent will have a higher rank than its old parent.

To incorporate this fact into the proof, we will use the following fancy accounting: For each node v on the path from the accessed node i to the root, we deposit one penny in one of two accounts:

Rules for U.S. and Canadian deposits.

1. If v is the root, or if the parent of v is the root, or if the parent of v is in a different rank group from v, then charge 1 unit under this rule. This deposits a U.S. penny into the kitty.
2. Otherwise, deposit a Canadian penny into the node.

Theorem 23.4 states that the accounting is accurate:

For any `find` operation, the total number of pennies deposited, either in the kitty or to a node, is exactly equal to the number of nodes accessed during the `find`.

Theorem 23.4

Obvious.

Proof

Thus we need only to sum all of the U.S. pennies deposited under rule 1 with all the Canadian pennies deposited under rule 2. Before we go on with the proof, let us sketch the ideas. Canadian pennies are deposited into a node when it is compressed and its parent is in the same rank group as the node. Because the node gets a parent of higher rank after each path compression, and because the size of a rank group is finite, eventually the node will obtain a parent that is not in its rank group. Consequently, there are only a limited number of Canadian pennies that can be placed into any node. This number is roughly the size of the node's rank group. On the other hand, the U.S. charges are also limited, essentially by the number of rank groups. Thus we want to choose the rank groups so that they are small (to limit the Canadian charges), but there are not too many (to limit the U.S. charges). We are now ready to fill in the details with a rapid-fire series of theorems, 23.5 – 23.10.

U.S. charges are limited by the number of different groups. Canadian charges are limited by the size of the groups. We eventually need to balance these costs.

Theorem 23.5   *Over the entire algorithm, the total deposits of U.S. pennies under rule 1 amount to $M(G(N)+2)$.*

Proof   *For any `find`, at most two U.S. pennies are deposited because of the root and its child. By Theorem 23.3, the vertices going up the path are monotonically increasing in rank, and thus the rank group never decreases as we go up the path. Since there are at most $G(N)$ rank groups (besides group 0), only $G(N)$ other vertices can qualify as a rule 1 deposit for any particular `find`. Thus, during any `find`, at most $G(N)+2$ U.S. pennies can be placed in the kitty. Thus at most $M(G(N)+2)$ U.S. pennies can be deposited under rule 1 for a sequence of M `find`s.*

Theorem 23.6   *For any single node in rank group g, the total number of Canadian pennies deposited is at most $F(g)$.*

Proof   *If a Canadian coin is deposited into a vertex v under rule 2, v will be moved by path compression and get a new parent of rank higher than its old parent. Since the largest rank in its group is $F(g)$, we are guaranteed that after $F(g)$ coins are deposited, v's parent will no longer be in v's rank group.*

The bound in Theorem 23.6 can be improved by using only the size of the rank group rather than its largest member. However, this does not improve the bound that is obtained for the union/find algorithm.

Theorem 23.7   *The number of nodes, $N(g)$, in rank group $g > 0$ is at most $N/2^{F(g-1)}$.*

By Theorem 23.2, there are at most $N/2^r$ nodes of rank r. Summing over   **Proof**
the ranks in group g, we obtain

$$N(g) \leq \sum_{r = F(g-1)+1}^{F(g)} \frac{N}{2^r}$$

$$\leq \sum_{r = F(g-1)+1}^{\infty} \frac{N}{2^r}$$

$$\leq N \sum_{r = F(g-1)+1}^{\infty} \frac{1}{2^r}$$

$$\leq \frac{N}{2^{F(g-1)+1}} \sum_{s = 0}^{\infty} \frac{1}{2^s}$$

$$\leq \frac{2N}{2^{F(g-1)+1}}$$

$$\leq \frac{N}{2^{F(g-1)}}.$$

The maximum number of Canadian pennies deposited to all vertices in rank   **Theorem 23.8**
group g is at most $NF(g)/2^{F(g-1)}$.

The result follows from a simple multiplication of the quantities obtained in   **Proof**
Theorem 23.6 and Theorem 23.7.

The total deposit under rule 2 is at most $N\sum_{g=1}^{G(N)} F(g)/2^{F(g-1)}$ Canadian   **Theorem 23.9**
pennies.

Because rank group 0 contains only elements of rank 0, it cannot contribute   **Proof**
to rule 2 charges (it cannot have a parent in the same rank group). The
bound is obtained by summing the other rank groups.

Group	Rank
0	0
1	1
2	2
3	3,4
4	5 through 16
5	17 through 65,536
6	65,537 through $2^{65,536}$
7	Truly huge ranks

Figure 23.18 Actual partitioning of ranks into groups used in the proof

Now we can specify the rank groups to minimize the bound. Our choice is not quite minimal, but it is close.

Thus we have the deposits under rules 1 and 2. The total is

$$M(G(N)+2)+N\sum_{g=1}^{G(N)}F(g)/2^{F(g-1)}. \tag{23.1}$$

We still have not specified $G(N)$ or its inverse $F(N)$. Obviously, we are free to choose virtually anything we want, but it makes sense to choose $G(N)$ to minimize the bound in Equation 23.1. However, if $G(N)$ is too small, $F(N)$ will be large, thus hurting the bound. An apparently good choice is $F(i)$ to be the function recursively defined by $F(0) = 0$ and $F(i) = 2^{F(i-1)}$. This gives $G(N) = 1 + \lfloor \log^* N \rfloor$. Figure 23.18 shows how this partitions the ranks. Notice that group 0 contains only rank 0, which we required in the proof of Theorem 23.9. F is very similar to the single-variable Ackermann function, differing only in the definition of the base case. With this choice of F and G, we can complete the analysis.

Theorem 23.10

The running time of the union/find algorithm with $M = \Omega(N)$ finds is $O(M \log^* N)$.

Proof

Plug the definitions of F and G into Equation 23.1. The total number of U.S. pennies is $O(MG(N)) = O(M\log^* N)$. Since $F(g) = 2^{F(g-1)}$, the total number of Canadian pennies is $NG(N) = O(N \log^* N)$. Since $M = \Omega(N)$, the bound follows.

Notice that we have more U.S. pennies than Canadian pennies. The function $\alpha(M, N)$ balances things out; this is why it gives a better bound.

Summary

This chapter discussed a very simple data structure to maintain disjoint sets. When the `union` operation is performed, it does not matter, as far as correctness is concerned, which set retains its name. A valuable lesson that should be learned here is that it can be very important to consider the alternatives when a particular step is not totally specified. The `union` step is flexible. By taking advantage of this, we can get a much more efficient algorithm.

Path compression is one of the earliest forms of self-adjustment, which we have seen elsewhere (splay trees, skew heaps). Its use here is extremely interesting from a theoretical point of view, since it was one of the first examples of a simple algorithm with a not-so-simple worst-case analysis.

Objects of the Game

Ackermann's function A function that grows very quickly. Its inverse is essentially at most 4. (681)

disjoint set class operations The basic operations needed for disjoint set manipulation. They are `union` and `find`. (666)

equivalence class The equivalence class of an element x in set S is the subset of S that contains all the elements that are related to x. (666)

equivalence relation A relation that is reflexive, symmetric, and transitive. (665)

forest A collection of trees. (674)

Kruskal's algorithm An algorithm used to select edges in increasing cost and that adds an edge to the tree if it does not create a cycle. (668)

minimum spanning tree A connected subgraph of G that spans all vertices at minimum total cost. It is a fundamental graph theory problem. (667)

nearest common ancestor problem (NCA) Given a tree and a list of pairs of nodes in the tree, find the nearest common ancestor for each pair of nodes. NCA is important in graph algorithms and computational biology. (669)

offline algorithm An algorithm in which the entire sequence of queries are made visible. (666)

online algorithm An algorithm in which an answer must be provided for each query before the next query can be viewed. (666)

path compression Makes every accessed node a child of the root until another `union` occurs. (678)

quick-find algorithm Union/find implementation in which `find` is a constant time operation. (672)

quick-union algorithm Union/find implementation in which `union` is a constant time operation. (674)

rank In the disjoint set algorithm, the estimated height of a node. (678)

relation Defined on a set if every pair of elements either is related or is not. (665)

spanning tree A tree formed by graph edges that connect all the vertices of an undirected graph. (667)

union-by-height Makes tree of smaller height a child of a tree of larger height during a `union`. (677)

union-by-rank Union-by-height when path compression is performed. (678)

union-by-size Makes a smaller tree a child of a larger tree during a `union`. (676)

union/find algorithm An algorithm that is executed by processing union/find operations using a union/find data structure. (666)

union/find data structure A data structure used to manipulate disjoint sets. (666)

Common Error

1. `union` assumes that its parameters are tree roots. Havoc results if they are not. A more careful implementation would perform this test.

On the Internet

The disjoint sets class is available online in the directory **DataStructures**. Here is the filename:

DisjSet.java   The disjoint sets class

Exercises

In Short

23.1. Show the result of the following sequence of instructions: *union*(1, 2), *union*(3, 4), *union*(3, 5), *union*(1, 7), *union*(3, 6), *union*(8, 9), *union*(1, 8), *union*(3, 10), *union*(3, 11), *union*(3, 12), *union*(3, 13), *union*(14, 15), *union*(16, 17), *union*(14, 16), *union*(1, 3), *union*(1, 14) when the following `union` operations are performed:
a. arbitrarily
b. by height
c. by size

23.2. For each of the trees in the previous exercise, perform a `find` with path compression on the deepest node.

23.3. Find the minimum spanning tree for the graph in Figure 23.19.

23.4. Show the operation of the NCA algorithm for the data in Figure 23.3.

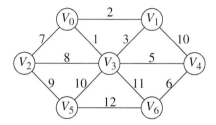

Figure 23.19 A graph *G* for Exercise 23.3

In Theory

23.5. Prove that Kruskal's algorithm is correct. Does your proof assume that the edge costs are nonnegative?

23.6. Show that if union is performed by height, then the depth of any tree is logarithmic.

23.7. Show that if all the unions precede the finds, then the disjoint set algorithm with path compression is linear, even if the unions are done arbitrarily. Note that the algorithm does not change; only the performance changes.

23.8. Suppose you want to add an extra operation, remove(x), which removes x from its current set and places it in its own. Show how to modify the union/find algorithm so that the running time of a sequence of *M* union, find, and remove operations is still $O(M\alpha(M, N))$.

23.9. Prove that if unions are done by size and path compression is performed, the worst-case running time is still $O(M\log^*N)$.

23.10. Suppose you implement partial path compression on find(i) by changing the parent of every other node on the path from i to the root to its grandparent (where this makes sense). This is called *path halving*. Prove that if path halving is performed on the finds and either union heuristic is used, then the worst-case running time is still $O(M\log^*N)$.

In Practice

23.11. Implement the find operation nonrecursively. Is there a noticeable difference in running time?

23.12. Suppose you want to add an extra operation, deunion, which undoes the last union operation not already undone. One way to do this is to use union-by-rank, but a compressionless find, and use a stack to store the old state prior to a union. A deunion can be implemented by popping the stack to retrieve an old state.

a. Why can't we use path compression?

b. Implement the union/find/deunion algorithm.

Programming Problems

23.13. Add error checks to the disjoint sets implementation in Figure 23.16.

23.14. Write a program to determine the effects of path compression and the various union strategies. Your program should process a long sequence of equivalence operations using all of the strategies discussed (including path halving in Exercise 23.10).

23.15. Implement Kruskal's algorithm.

23.16. An alternative minimum spanning tree algorithm is due to Prim [12]. It works by growing a single tree in successive stages. Start by picking any node as the root. At the start of a stage, some nodes are part of the tree and the rest are not. In each stage, we add the minimum-cost edge that connects a tree node with a nontree node. An implementation of Prim's algorithm is essentially identical to Dijkstra's shortest-path algorithm given in Section 14.3, with an update rule: $d_w = min(d_w, c_{v, w})$ (instead of $d_w = min(d_w, d_v + c_{v, w})$). Also, since the graph is undirected, each edge appears in two adjacency lists. Implement Prim's algorithm and compare its performance with Kruskal's algorithm.

23.17. Write a program to solve the offline NCA problem for binary trees. Test its efficiency by constructing a random binary search tree of 10,000 elements and performing 10,000 ancestor queries.

References

Representation of each set by a tree was proposed in [8]. [1] attributes path compression to McIlroy and Morris and contains several applications of the union/find data structure. Kruskal's algorithm is in [11], while the alternative discussed in Exercise 23.16 is from [12]. The NCA algorithm is described in [2]. Other applications can be found in [15].

The $O(M\log^*N)$ bound for the union/find problem is from [9]. Tarjan [13] obtained the $O(M\alpha(M, N))$ bound and showed that the bound is tight. Furthermore, the bound is intrinsic to the general problem and cannot be improved by an alternative algorithm [14]. A more precise bound for $M < N$ appears in [3] and [16]. Various other strategies for path compression and `union` achieve the same bounds; see [16] for details. If the sequence of `unions` is known in advance, then it is possible to solve the union/find problem in $O(M)$ time [7]. This result can be used to show that the offline NCA problem is solvable in linear time.

Average-case results for the union/find problem appear in [6], [10], [17], and [4]. Results bounding the running time of any single operation (as opposed to the entire sequence) appear in [5].

1. A. V. Aho, J. E. Hopcroft, and J. D. Ullman, *The Design and Analysis of Computer Algorithms*, Addison-Wesley, Reading, Mass. (1974).

2. A. V. Aho, J. E. Hopcroft, and J. D. Ullman, "On Finding Lowest Common Ancestors in Trees," *SIAM Journal on Computing* **5** (1976), 115–132.

3. L. Banachowski, "A Complement to Tarjan's Result about the Lower Bound on the Set Union Problem," *Information Processing Letters* **11** (1980), 59–65.

4. B. Bollobas and I. Simon, "Probabilistic Analysis of Disjoint Set Union Algorithms," *SIAM Journal on Computing* **22** (1993), 1053–1086.

5. N. Blum, "On the Single-operation Worst-case Time Complexity of the Disjoint Set Union Problem," *SIAM Journal on Computing* **15** (1986), 1021–1024.

6. J. Doyle and R. L. Rivest, "Linear Expected Time of a Simple Union Find Algorithm," *Information Processing Letters* **5** (1976), 146–148.

7. H. N. Gabow and R. E. Tarjan, "A Linear-time Algorithm for a Special Case of Disjoint Set Union," *Journal of Computer and System Sciences* **30** (1985), 209–221.

8. B. A. Galler and M. J. Fischer, "An Improved Equivalence Algorithm," *Communications of the ACM* **7** (1964), 301–303.

9. J. E. Hopcroft and J. D. Ullman, "Set Merging Algorithms," *SIAM Journal on Computing* **2** (1973), 294–303.

10. D. E. Knuth and A. Schonage, "The Expected Linearity of a Simple Equivalence Algorithm," *Theoretical Computer Science* **6** (1978), 281–315.

11. J. B. Kruskal, Jr., "On the Shortest Spanning Subtree of a Graph and the Traveling Salesman Problem," *Proceedings of the American Mathematical Society* **7** (1956), 48–50.

12. R. C. Prim, "Shortest Connection Networks and Some Generalizations," *Bell System Technical Journal* **36** (1957), 1389–1401.

13. R. E. Tarjan, "Efficiency of a Good but Not Linear Set Union Algorithm," *Journal of the ACM* **22** (1975), 215–225.

14. R. E. Tarjan, "A Class of Algorithms Which Require Nonlinear Time to Maintain Disjoint Sets," *Journal of Computer and System Sciences* **18** (1979), 110–127.

15. R. E. Tarjan, "Applications of Path Compression on Balanced Trees," *Journal of the ACM* **26** (1979), 690–715.

16. R. E. Tarjan and J. van Leeuwen, "Worst Case Analysis of Set Union Algorithms," *Journal of the ACM* **31** (1984), 245–281.

17. A. C. Yao, "On the Average Behavior of Set Merging Algorithms," *Proceedings of the Eighth Annual ACM Symposium on the Theory of Computation* (1976), 192–195.

APPENDICES

A

Java Platforms

THIS appendix illustrates the steps required to compile a Java program using three environments:

- Sun's *JDK*
- *Symantec Cafe*
- *Microsoft Visual J++*

It is assumed that a basic install has already been performed.

A.1   Setting the Environment

No matter which development system you use, you need to make sure that two environment variables are set:

- PATH: Specifies a set of directories that are examined to find executables (such as *javac*, *java*, and *javadoc*).
- CLASSPATH: Specifies a set of directories that are examined to find packages (such as java.lang and DataStructures).

If PATH is incorrectly set, a command such as *javac* will not be found. If CLASSPATH is incorrectly set, then import directives and other uses of packages will fail.

Some of the products described in this section automatically set the environment variables when the products are installed. Even so, to use the code in the textbook, you will need to modify CLASSPATH to include the book's packages.

The instructions for Unix and Windows 95 are basically identical; all that varies is syntax.

A.1.1 Unix Instructions

The following Unix instructions assume you are using the C-shell.

1. Check that PATH is correctly set. The command is

   ```
   which javac
   ```

   If the system responds with a name (for instance, /bin/javac), then PATH is correctly set. If the system responds with a message that there is no *javac* (and then gives a list of all the places it tried), then you must update PATH.

2. Ask your system administrator where the Java compiler is located. Suppose for illustration that it is in the directory /home/jdk/bin. Edit your .cshrc file by adding a line to update the path. Using the sample directory, you would write

   ```
   set path= ( $path /home/jdk/bin )
   ```

3. Update your CLASSPATH variable next. If you already have a CLASSPATH variable, it is probably set correctly for the system packages. You can view the current value with

   ```
   echo $CLASSPATH
   ```

   Even if CLASSPATH is correctly set, you will have to update it to use the book's packages. If you do not have a CLASSPATH variable, ask the system administrator for the location of the library class files. A typical entry is

   ```
   setenv CLASSPATH .:/jdk/lib/classes.zip
   ```

   Notice that two locations are searched: your current directory (.) and a zipped file containing Java classes.

4. Add the directory containing this book's packages to the end of CLASSPATH. For instance,

   ```
   setenv CLASSPATH .:/jdk/lib/classes.zip:$HOME/book
   ```

   The actual directory names will vary for each install. Note that changes to your .cshrc file are not effective until the next login. After exiting the editor, you can make the change immediately by issuing the command:

   ```
   source .cshrc
   ```

A.1.2 Windows 95/NT Instructions

Windows NT behaves the same as Windows 95, except that the procedure can be simplified by editing the environment variables in the Control Panel. (Select *Control Panel*, then *System*.) The Windows 95 description is given here.

1. Check that PATH is correctly set. The command

   ```
   javac
   ```

   attempts to invoke the Java compiler. If the system responds with an error message that details the acceptable use of *javac* (for instance, a list of options), then PATH is correctly set. If the system responds with a message that there is no *javac*, then you must update PATH.

2. To update PATH, you need to know where the Java compiler is located (you can use the search utilities to determine this). Suppose for illustration, that it is in the directory C:\jdk\bin. Edit your autoexec.bat file (using *NotePad*) by adding a line to update the path. Using the sample directory, write

   ```
   SET PATH=%PATH%;C:\jdk\bin
   ```

3. Update your CLASSPATH variable next. If you already have a CLASSPATH variable, it is probably set correctly for the system packages. You can view all of the environment values by issuing the set command with no parameters.

   Even if CLASSPATH is correctly set, you will have to update it to use this book's packages. If you do not have a CLASSPATH variable, you need the location of the library class files. A typical entry is

   ```
   set CLASSPATH=.:C:\jdk\lib\classes.zip
   ```

   Notice that two locations are searched: your current directory (.) and a zipped file containing Java classes.

4. Add the directory containing this book's packages to the end of CLASSPATH. For instance, add a second line

   ```
   set CLASSPATH=%CLASSPATH%;C:\bookcode
   ```

   The actual directory names will vary for each install. Note that changes to your autoexec.bat file are not effective until the next reboot (or login, under Windows NT).

A.2 Sun's JDK

JDK is a no-frills system. You must enter your source code into Java files by using a standard system text editor. On Unix, editors include *vi*, *pico*, and *emacs* and on Windows, *NotePad* and *WordPad*.

To compile a Java source file, use the *javac* command. To execute the class' main, use the *java* command. For example, suppose main is in class Sample. Then the commands are

```
javac Sample.java
java Sample
```

For every class defined in each source file compiled by *javac*, the compiler stores the resulting bytecodes (that is, j-code) in a corresponding class file (with .class suffix). For every class referenced in the source files, the compiler looks in the class path for both a source file and a class file, recompiling the source (and regenerating the class file) if it is newer. In other words, *javac* deduces the minimal set of files that must be recompiled and does so automatically.

The *javac* command comes with several options. A complete list is provided with the JDK documentation. Figure A.1 lists some of the options.

The *java* command also comes with several options. A complete list is provided with the JDK documentation.

A.3 Visual Development Environments

Symantec Cafe distinguished itself by being first to the market with a typical modern development environment. *Microsoft Visual J++* is distinguishing itself by being a Microsoft product. Its look and feel is identical to Microsoft's popular Visual C++.

Option	Result
-O	Optimizes compiled code by inlining static, final, and private methods.
-verbose	Causes the compiler and linker to print out messages about which source files are being compiled and which class files are being loaded.
-depend	Makes the compiler consider recompiling class files, which are referenced from other class files. Normally it recompiles only missing or out-of-date class files that are referred to from source code.

Figure A.1 *javac* options

Both systems include, among other things,

- a built-in visual editor that highlights keywords, comments, and tokens in different colors;
- buttons to build and execute programs;
- windows that simultaneously provide various views of the project, such as the compiler output, source code, and list of project files;
- built-in debugging tools; and
- online help.

The integration of these views into one product means, for instance, that double-clicking a compiler error message takes you to the offending line of code. Once you've used a visual system, it's hard to go back to a text-based system. An important feature is the resource editor, which allows the programmer to design a layout using a CAD system. The resource editor will generate Java code that describes the layout. This is useful for GUI design.

Visual systems do have disadvantages. First, unlike Sun's JDK, they are not free. Second, one must go through the effort of setting up a project for each program; this can be annoying for small programs that use only a single source file. Third, the newest version of Java will always appear in Sun's JDK first. Updates will appear in the commercial systems only after a delay, and these updates won't be free. At the time of this writing, for instance, the only compiler that supports Java 1.1 is the JDK 1.1.[1]

For both environments, this appendix describes how to set up a project for the `TestStack` class. The source code is in the online code in the directory **Chapter06**. It is assumed that the textbook code is already downloaded and that `CLASSPATH` has been correctly set, as described in Section A.1.2. You will need to create a directory for the project and copy `TestStack.java` to that directory.

A.3.1 Symantec Cafe

1. Begin by starting Cafe. You will briefly see a colorful logo. Next, you will see Cafe's most annoying feature: the screen is mostly transparent, so your desktop will still be visible. If this is the first time you are using Cafe, you may see several scattered buttons. They can be dragged to the top to get something similar to Figure A.2 (page 702). Note that only the top of the screen is shown here.

2. Create a new project for `TestStack`, and for simplicity, name it `TestStack`. Click the *Project* menu and select *New*, as shown in Figure A.3 (page 702).

[1.] The snapshots shown in this appendix represent systems available at the time of this writing. Newer versions will probably be similar, but not completely identical.

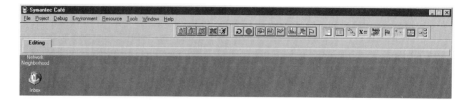

Figure A.2

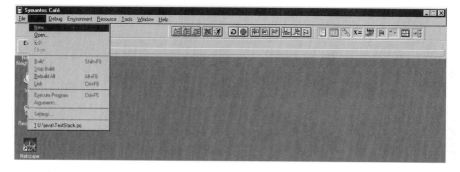

Figure A.3

3. At this point, the *ProjectExpress* tool begins, bringing up a sequence of four dialog boxes. Only the first three are likely to be needed.

a. In the first dialog, select a disk drive. Also select the directory in which you want to place the project. Then type a project name. Make sure that it ends with a `.prj` suffix. Click *Next*. See Figure A.4.

b. In the second dialog, select *Application* as the target type. Then type *TestStack* as the name of the main class. Click *Next*. See Figure A.5.

c. In the third dialog, add the files to the project. Your main class file should already be in the same directory as the project file. If it is not, don't despair; you can add files to the project later. Alternatively, you can copy the file right now (from outside of Cafe) and type the name. This is shown in Figure A.6. If `TestStack.java` was already present in the directory, it would have been in the list of possible files to add.

   If there are several files to add, keep clicking *Add* or double-clicking the filename in the file list. When you have added the files, click *Finish*. You do not need to go to step 4 that is offered by *ProjectExpress*.

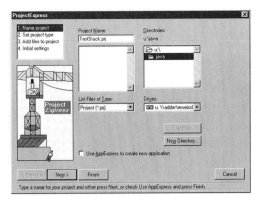

Figure A.4

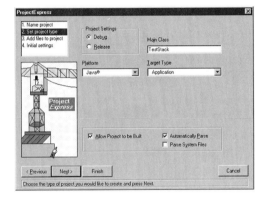

Figure A.5

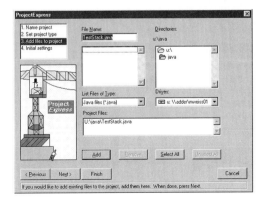

Figure A.6

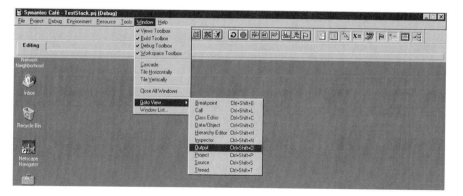

Figure A.7

4. Now that the project is set up, you establish some views. In the *Window* menu, select *Goto View*. Then add *Output* and *Project views*. See Figure A.7.

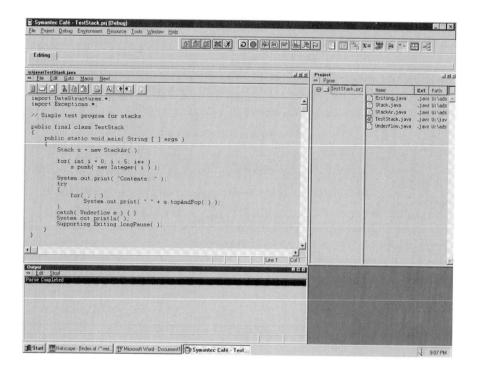

Figure A.8

These views will pop up with sizes and locations that you might not like, but you can resize the windows and drag them to other places. From the project view, you can double-click a filename to bring up a *Source* window. You can resize that window and move it as you see fit.

The result of all this is shown in Figure A.8. Notice that the `TestStack.java` file has an additional line of code (a call to `longPause`), which is discussed shortly.

In the project view, `TestStack.java` is marked yellow to indicate that its `main` is to be executed (this was specified in step 2 of the *ProjectExpress*). You can right-click another text icon to specify a different `main` class. Notice that the project view shows all nonsystem classes that are needed; this is deduced automatically.

5. You compile the project by pressing the *Build* button. (In Figure A.9, the *Build* button is above and to the left of the *Build* caption.)

   The build compiles only those files that are out-of-date. (You can also request a complete rebuild.) Any errors will appear in the output window. If there are no errors, then a message to that effect will be reported. At that point, you can run the program by clicking the *Run* button. (This button shows a person running, so it's hard to miss.)

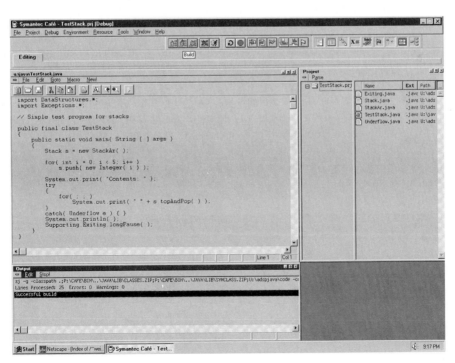

Figure A.9

Figure A.10

When a console application runs, an MS-DOS window pops up. It is interactive; so input commands can be accepted. Unfortunately, the window goes away when the program terminates; this makes it hard to see the output. To keep this from happening, you can do either of the following:

I. Add a call to either `Supporting.Exiting.longPause` or `Supporting.Exit.promptToExit` to keep the program from terminating.

II. Run the *java* command from an MS-DOS command window that is separate from Cafe.

Note that option I is unacceptable if your program is crashing because of an unhandled exception. However, in this case, you can start the debugger (look in the *Debug* menu) to see what is wrong. Option I is also unsuitable if you are reading until the end of input. Figure A.10 is the MS-DOS window mentioned in option II.

6. When you are done, exit by selecting the *File* menu. The options include saving all your work (usually advisable) or exiting without any saves (advisable more often than you would like). See Figure A.11.

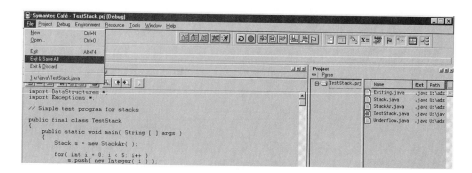

Figure A.11

A.3.2 Microsoft Visual J++

1. Begin by starting J++. You will briefly see a colorful logo for Microsoft Studio, and then a screen will appear. If this is the first time you are using J++, you may see several scattered items, such as a tip bar and a help choice (containing *Microsoft Visual J++ Books Online*). The tip bar can be dismissed and the help dragged to the top to get something similar to Figure A.12.

2. Create a new project for `TestStack`, and, for simplicity, name it `TestStack`. Click the *File* menu and select *New*, as shown in Figure A.13 (page 708). This generates a dialog that asks you to specify what to create. Double-click *Project Workspace*, as shown in Figure A.14 (page 708).

3. A dialog that asks for the project specifics appears next. From the dialog, select *Java Workspace*, set the location to the directory in which to store the project, and set the project name to *TestStack*. These entries are shown in Figure A.15 (page 708). Then click *Create*.

4. At this point, the help view is replaced by the class view, as shown in Figure A.16 (page 709).

   If you open the *TestStack classes* folder, you will see the source file that makes up the project. Currently, the project is empty.

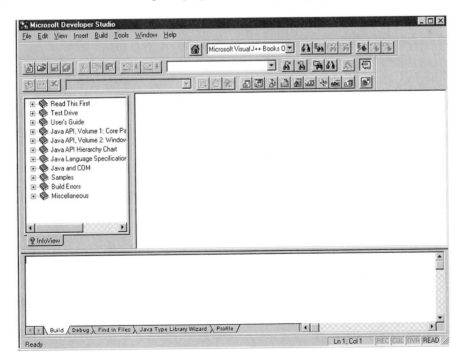

Figure A.12

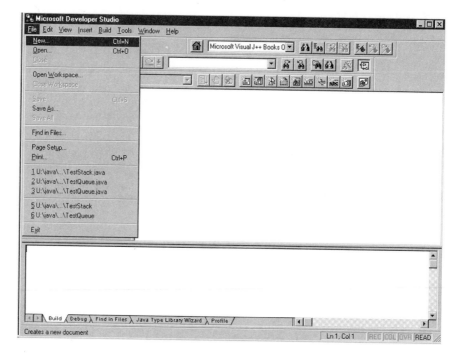

Figure A.13

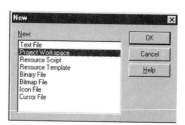

Figure A.14

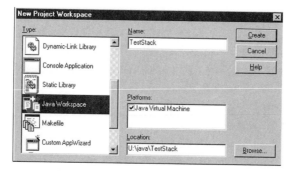

Figure A.15

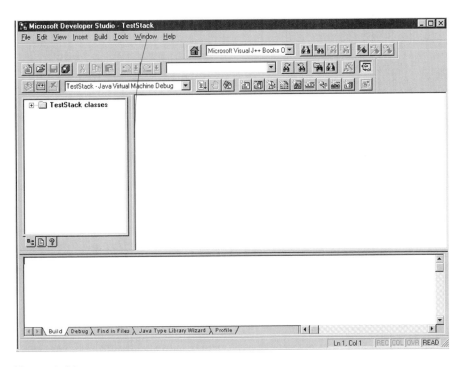

Figure A.16

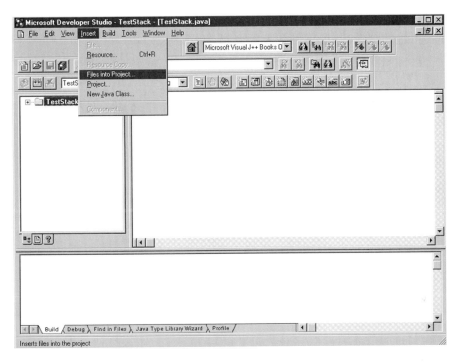

Figure A.17

You can add files to the project by clicking the *Insert* menu and then selecting *Files into Project*, as shown in Figure A.17 (page 709).

5. A dialog that prompts for the filename appears. Your main class file should already be in the same directory as the project file. See Figure A.18. Simply select your main class (either with a double-click or a single click followed by a click on *Add*). If your main class file is not in the correct directory, copy the file from outside J++ and type in the name. If there are several files to add, you can select more than one file (hold down the Control key as you single-click filenames from the list).

6. Double-click *TestStack files* in the class view to see that `TestStack.java` has been added to the project. Double-click *TestStack.java* to open the file in the source window.

7. Next, you change some project settings. In the *Build* menu, select *Settings*, as shown in Figure A.19.

8. The *Project Settings* dialog appears. In it, select the *Debug* tab, type in the name of the *Class for debugging/executing*, and select the *Stand-alone interpreter* option, as shown in Figure A.20.

9. Now you are ready to build your project and execute it. There are buttons for this: the *Build* button is the middle button directly above the class view and the *Execute* button is the first button above the source view. These locations depend on the local setup; the buttons might not be visible. In this case, the *Build* menu is a sure-fire way to go.

Figure A.21 (page 712) shows the *Build* menu. It has an option to build and another to execute. Execute will automatically build if the class file does not exist or is outdated. The build compiles only those files that are out-of-date. (You can also request a complete rebuild.) Any errors will appear in the output window. If there are no errors, then a message to that effect appears.

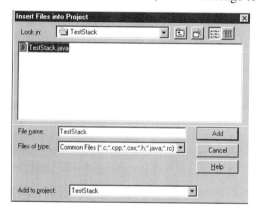

Figure A.18

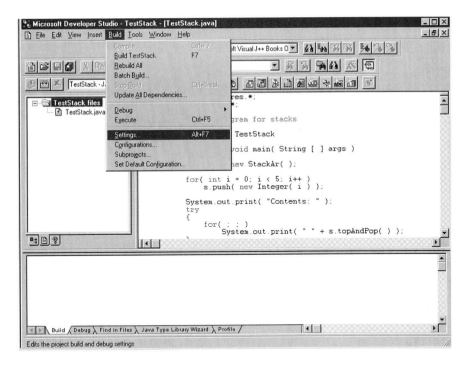

Figure A.19

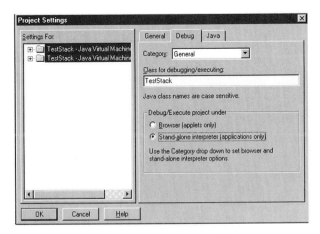

Figure A.20

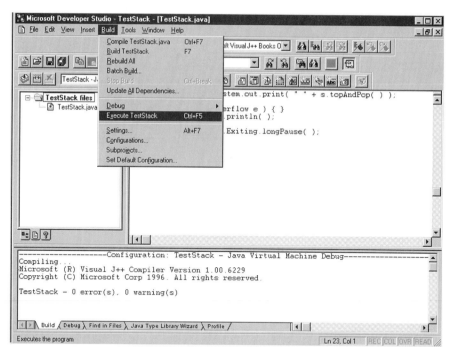

Figure A.21

When a console application runs, an MS-DOS window pops
up, as shown in Figure A.22. The window is interactive, so you
can input commands. In J++ 1.0, the window goes away when the
program terminates. This makes it hard to see the output. When
the Java 1.1-compliant version of J++ is released, this problem is
expected to go away. Until then, see the discussion on page 706
for some code modifications that keep the program from terminating, thus preventing the window from going away.

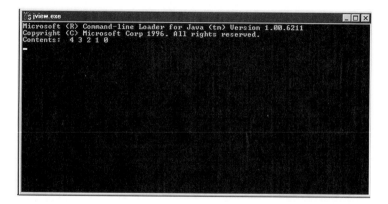

Figure A.22

B

Operators

Figure B.1 shows the precedence and associativity of the common Java operators discussed. The bitwise operators have not been used in this book.

Category	Examples	Associativity
Operations on References	`.  []`	Left to right
Unary	`++ -- ! - (type)`	Right to left
Multiplicative	`* / %`	Left to right
Additive	`+ -`	Left to right
Shift (bitwise)	`<< >> >>>`	Left to right
Relational	`< <= > >= instanceof`	Left to right
Equality	`== !=`	Left to right
Boolean (or bitwise) AND	`&`	Left to right
Boolean (or bitwise) XOR	`^`	Left to right
Boolean (or bitwise) OR	`|`	Left to right
Logical AND	`&&`	Left to right
Logical OR	`||`	Left to right
Conditional	`?:`	Right to left
Assignment	`= *= /= %= += -=`	Right to left

Figure B.1 Java operators listed from highest to lowest precedence

C   *Some Library Routines*

T HIS appendix lists some of the Java library classes used in this book. For each class, a brief description is provided, as well as some of the commonly used members. A complete description of these classes is in the *JDK API Documentation*.

C.1   Classes in Package `java.lang`

This is the standard package that is automatically imported by all Java programs.

C.1.1   `Character`

The `Character` class wraps a value of the primitive type `char` in an object. An object of type `Character` contains a single field whose type is `char`. This class also provides several methods for determining the type of a character and converting characters from uppercase to lowercase and vice versa. This is a final class.

Important Methods

`Character( char value )`
Constructs a `Character` object and initializes it so that it represents the primitive value argument.

`char charValue( )`
Returns the value of this `Character` object.

`boolean equals( Object obj )`
Compares this `Character` object against the specified object. The result is `true` if and only if the argument is not `null` and is a `Character` object that represents the same `char` value as this object.

String toString( )

Returns a String object representing this Character object's value. The result is a String whose length is 1. The String's sole component is the primitive char value represented by this object.

static boolean isDigit(char ch)

Returns true if and only if the specified character is a digit.

static boolean isDefined(char ch)

Returns true if and only if the specified character has a defined meaning in Unicode.

static boolean isLetter(char ch)

Returns true if and only if the specified character is a letter.

static boolean isLetterOrDigit(char ch)

Returns true if and only if the specified character is a letter or digit.

static boolean isLowerCase(char ch)

Returns true if and only if the specified character is a lowercase character.

static boolean isUpperCase(char ch)

Returns true if and only if the specified character is an uppercase character.

static boolean isWhitespace(char ch)

Returns true if and only if the character is a Java whitespace character.

static char toLowerCase(char ch)

Returns the lowercase equivalent of the character, if any; otherwise, returns the character itself.

static char toUpperCase(char ch)

Returns the uppercase equivalent of the character, if any; otherwise, returns the character itself.

static boolean isJavaIdentifierStart(char ch)

Returns true if and only if the specified character is permissible as the first character in a Java identifier. (New to Java 1.1.)

static boolean isJavaIdentifierPart(char ch)

Returns true if and only if the specified character may be part of a Java identifier as other than the first character. (New to Java 1.1.)

C.1.2 Integer

The Integer class wraps a value of the primitive type int in an object. An object of type Integer contains a single field whose type is int. This class also provides several methods for converting an `int` to a `String` and a `String` to an `int`, as well as other constants and methods useful when dealing with an `int`. This is a final class.

Important Data Members

`static final int MAX_VALUE`

The largest value of type `int`.

`static final int MIN_VALUE`

The smallest value of type `int`.

Important Methods

`Integer( int val )`

Constructs a newly allocated `Integer` object that represents the primitive `int` argument.

`int intValue( )`

Returns the value of this `Integer` object as an `int`.

`boolean equals( Object obj )`

Returns `true` if and only if the argument is not `null` and is an `Integer` object that contains the same `int` value as this object.

`static int parseInt( String str )`

Parses the `String` argument as a signed decimal integer. Throws `NumberFormatException`.

`static int parseInt( String str, int radix )`

Parses the `String` argument as a signed integer in the radix specified by the second argument. Throws `NumberFormatException`.

`String toString( )`

Returns a `String` object representing this `Integer`'s value.

`static String toString( int theInt )`

Returns a `String` object representing the specified integer.

`static String toString( int theInt, int radix )`

Creates a `String` object representing the first argument in the radix specified by the second argument.

C.1.3 `Object`

Class `Object` is the root of the class hierarchy. Every class has `Object` as a superclass. All objects, including arrays, implement the methods of this class.

Important Methods

Object( )

Constructs an object; rarely is called directly.

boolean equals(Object obj)

Compares two Objects for equality. The equals method for class Object implements the most discriminating possible test on objects. That is, for any reference values x and y, x.equals(y) returns true if and only if x and y refer to the same object (x==y has the value true).

String toString( )

Returns a string representation of the object. The result should be a concise but informative representation that is easy for a person to read.

C.1.4 String

The String class represents character strings. All string literals in Java programs, such as "abc", are implemented as instances of this class. Strings are constant — their values cannot be changed after they are created. String buffers (Section C.1.5) support mutable strings. The class String includes a host of methods, some of which are described in this section.

The Java language provides special support for the string concatenation operator (+) and for conversion of other objects to strings. String conversions are implemented through the method toString, defined by Object, and inherited by all classes in Java.

Important Methods

String( )

Allocates a new String containing no characters.

String(String anotherStr)

Allocates a new String that contains the same sequence of characters as the String argument.

char charAt(int index)

Returns the character at the specified index. An index ranges from 0 to length( )-1. Throws StringIndexOutOfBoundsException if the index is out of range.

boolean equals(Object obj)

Compares this String to the specified object. The result is true if and only if the argument is not `null` and is a `String` object that represents the same sequence of characters as this object.

`int compareTo( String str )`

Compares two `Strings` lexicographically. The comparison is based on the Unicode value of each character in the `Strings`. Returns the value 0 if the argument `String` is equal to this `String`; a value less than 0 if this `String` is lexicographically less than the `String` argument; and a value greater than 0 if this `String` is lexicographically greater than the `String` argument.

`int length( )`

Returns the length of this `String`.

`boolean startsWith( String prefix )`

Returns `true` if and only if this `String` starts with the specified prefix.

`boolean endsWith( String suffix )`

Returns `true` if and only if this `String` ends with the specified suffix.

`String substring( int beginIdx, int endIdx )`

Returns a new `String` that is a substring of this `String`. The substring begins at the specified `beginIdx` and extends to the character at index `endIdx-1`. Throws `StringIndexOutOfBoundsException` if `beginIdx` or `endIdx` is out of range.

C.1.5 `StringBuffer`

Because `Strings` are immutable, minor changes to the contents of a `String` can be expensive. Specifically, the `+=` operator is very inefficient. For instance, `str+='A'` is implemented as `str=str+'A'`. This implies that a new `String` is created whose value is the result of `str+'A'`, and then `str` references the new `String`. As a result, the cost of concatenating a single character is not a constant (as it logically should be). Instead it is proportional to the length of the `String` being operated on. If there are repeated concatenations to a `String`, this cost can be prohibitive.

An example is the straightforward method in Figure C.1 that generates a `String` of N As. Tacking on the ith character costs time proportional to i, since as we just discussed, a new `String` of length i is created. The total cost of the routine is given by $1 + 2 + 3 + \ldots + N$, which is quadratic. As an extreme case, running this method for $N = 64{,}000$ takes over 5 min on a Pentium 100.

For efficient `String` operations, you would have to manipulate the characters on your own and then construct a single `String` containing the desired result after the manipulation is complete. This is what the `StringBuffer` does.

```
1            // Quadratic method that generates a String of n As
2      static String badLongString( int n )
3      {
4          String result = "";
5          for( int i = 0; i < n; i++ )
6              result += 'A';
7          return result;
8      }
```

Figure C.1   An inefficient method to generate a `String` of *N* As

A `StringBuffer` can be constructed with any `String` or as an empty `String`. You can then apply operations that manipulate the `StringBuffer`, including `append`, which adds to the end; `setChar`, which changes a single character; and `insert`, which adds to the middle (sliding characters over, as needed). The compiler uses the `StringBuffer` to generate efficient code for trivial concatenation. For nontrivial operations, such as the example in Figure C.1, you must do it yourself. Figure C.2 shows how the `StringBuffer` can be used to generate a `String` of *N* As efficiently. This method is linear and runs in 1.5 sec for $N = 64,000$.

By the way, the `StringBuffer` uses array doubling to ensure that its capacity can expand as needed. The default initial capacity is 16 characters.

Important Methods

`StringBuffer( )`

Constructs a string buffer with no characters in it and an initial capacity of 16 characters.

`StringBuffer( String str )`

Constructs a string buffer so that it represents the same sequence of characters as the `String` argument. The initial capacity of the string buffer is 16 plus the length of the argument.

```
1            // Linear method that generates a String of n As
2      static String goodLongString( int n )
3      {
4          StringBuffer result = new StringBuffer( );
5
6          for( int i = 0; i < n; i++ )
7              result.append( 'A' );
8
9          return new String( result );
10     }
```

Figure C.2   An efficient method to generate a `String` of *N* As

`int length( )`

Returns the length (character count) of this string buffer.

`char charAt( int index )`

Returns the character at a specific index in this string buffer. The first character of a string buffer is at index 0, the next at index 1, and so on, for array indexing. Throws a `StringIndexOutOfBoundsException` if the index is invalid.

`void setCharAt( int index, char ch )`

The character at the specified index of this string buffer is set to `ch`. Throws a `StringIndexOutOfBoundsException` if the index is invalid.

`StringBuffer append( Object obj )`

Appends the `String` representation of the `Object` argument to this string buffer. The argument is converted to a `String`, and the characters of that `String` are then appended to this string buffer. This string buffer is returned, so it can be used in a chain of operations. There are other `append` operations available for all the primitive types, as well as character arrays.

`StringBuffer insert( int offset, Object obj )`

Inserts the `String` representation of the `Object` argument into this string buffer. The second argument is converted to a `String`, and the characters of that `String` are then inserted into this string buffer at the indicated offset. This string buffer is returned, so it can be used in a chain of operations. There are other `insert` operations available for all the primitive types, as well as character arrays. Throws a `StringIndexOutOfBoundsException` if the offset is invalid.

`StringBuffer reverse( )`

The character sequence contained in this string buffer is replaced by the reverse of the sequence. This string buffer is returned, so it can be used in a chain of operations.

`String toString( )`

Converts to a string representing the data in this string buffer. A new `String` object is allocated and initialized to contain the character sequence currently represented by this string buffer. This `String` is then returned. Subsequent changes to the string buffer do not affect the contents of the `String`.

C.1.6 `System`

The `System` class contains several useful class fields and methods. It cannot be instantiated. Among the facilities provided by the `System` class are standard input, standard output, and error output streams, an `exit` method, and many system methods that are not used in this text.

Important Data Members

static final InputStream in

The standard input stream. This stream is already open and ready to supply input data. Typically, this stream corresponds to keyboard input or another input source specified by the host environment or user.

static final PrintStream out

The standard output stream. This stream is already open and ready to accept output data. Typically, this stream corresponds to display output or another output destination specified by the host environment or user.

static final PrintStream err

The standard error output stream. This stream is already open and ready to accept output data. Typically, this stream corresponds to display output or another output destination specified by the host environment or user. By convention, this output stream is used to display error messages or other information that should come to the immediate attention of a user even if the principal output stream, the value of the variable `out`, has been redirected to a file or other destination that is typically not continuously monitored.

Important Methods

static long currentTimeMillis( )

Returns the current time in milliseconds.

static String getProperty(String key)

Gets the system property indicated by the specified key.

static void exit(int status)

Terminates the program. The argument serves as a status code; by convention, a nonzero status code indicates abnormal termination. This method never returns normally and may not be called from an applet.

static void gc( )

Runs the garbage collector. Calling the `gc` method suggests that the run-time system should expend effort toward recycling unused objects in order to make the memory those objects currently occupy available for quick reuse. When control returns from the method call, the system has made a best effort to reclaim space from all unused objects.

C.1.7 **Thread**

A thread is a thread of execution in a program. An application may have multiple threads of execution running concurrently. Threads are required for animations. This use of threads is discussed in Sections D.4 and D.5.5. Listed here are only methods that are related to animation applications or otherwise used in this book.

Important Methods

Thread(Runnable target)

Allocates a new `Thread` object. `target` is the object whose `run` method is called.

static void sleep(long milliseconds)

Causes the currently executing thread to sleep (cease execution) for the specified number of milliseconds. Throws `InterruptedException` if another thread has interrupted this thread. This exception should be caught.

void start( )

Causes this thread to begin execution; the `run` method of this thread is called. Throws `IllegalThreadStateException` if the thread was already started. This exception does not have to be caught.

void stop( )

Forces the thread to stop executing. It is permitted to stop a thread that has not yet been started. If the thread is eventually started, it immediately terminates.

boolean isAlive( )

Tests if this thread is alive. A thread is alive if it has been started and has not yet terminated. Returns `true` if and only if this thread is alive.

void suspend( )

Suspends this thread. If the thread is alive, it is suspended and makes no further progress unless and until it is resumed.

void resume( )

Resumes a suspended thread. If the thread is alive but suspended, it is resumed and is permitted to make progress in its execution.

C.1.8 **Throwable**

The `Throwable` class is the superclass of all errors and exceptions in the Java language. Only objects that are instances of this class (or of one of its subclasses) are thrown. Similarly, only this class or one of its subclasses can be the argument type in a catch clause. A Throwable class contains a snapshot of the execution stack of its thread at the time it was created. It can also contain a message string that gives more information about the error.

Important Methods

Throwable( )

Constructs a new Throwable with no detail message. The stack trace is automatically filled in.

Throwable(String message)

Constructs a new Throwable with the specified detail message. The stack trace is automatically filled in.

String getMessage( )

Returns the detail message of this throwable object.

String getLocalizedMessage( )

Returns a localized description of this Throwable. Subclasses may override this method in order to produce a locale-specific message. For subclasses that do not override this method, the default implementation returns the same result as getMessage.

String toString( )

Returns a short description of this throwable object.

void printStackTrace( )

Prints this Throwable and its backtrace to the standard error stream.

C.2   Classes in Package java.io

This package contains classes that manipulate files and I/O streams. Except for File, the classes discussed here are new in Java 1.1.

C.2.1   BufferedReader

Reads text from a character-input stream, buffering characters so as to provide for the efficient reading of characters, arrays, and lines. The buffer size may be specified, or the default size may be used. The default is large enough for most purposes. In general, each read request made of a Reader causes a corresponding read request to be made of the underlying character or byte stream. It is therefore advisable to wrap a BufferedReader around any Reader whose read operations may be costly, such as a FileReader and an InputStreamReader.

Important Methods

`BufferedReader( Reader in )`

Creates a buffering character-input stream that uses a default-sized input buffer.

`int read( )`

Reads a single character. It throws an `IOException` if an I/O error occurs. The character is returned as an `int`. Thus typical use will require a type-conversion to `char`.

`String readLine( )`

Reads a line of text. A line is considered to be terminated by any one of a line feed (`'\n'`), a carriage return (`'\r'`), or a carriage return followed immediately by a linefeed. It returns a `String` containing the contents of the line, not including any line-termination characters, or `null` if the end of the stream has been reached. It throws an `IOException` if an I/O error occurs.

`boolean ready( )`

Tells whether this stream is ready to be read. A buffered character stream is ready if the buffer is not empty or if the underlying character stream is ready. It throws an `IOException` if an I/O error occurs.

`void close( )`

Closes the stream. It throws an `IOException` if an I/O error occurs.

C.2.2 `File`

The `File` class is intended to provide an abstraction that deals with most of the machine dependent complexities of files and pathnames in a machine-independent fashion.

Important Data Members

`static final char separatorChar`

The system-dependent path separator string. This character separates the directory and file components in a filename.

Important Methods

`File( String name )`

Creates a `File` instance that represents the file whose pathname is given by `name`.

String getName( )

Returns the name of the file represented by this `File` object. The name is everything in the pathname after the last occurrence of the separator character.

String getPath( )

Returns the pathname of the file represented by this `File` object.

boolean exists( )

Returns `true` if and only if the file specified by this `File` object exists.

boolean isDirectory( )

Returns `true` if and only if the file specified by this `File` object is a directory.

long length( )

Returns the length of the file represented by this `File` object.

String [ ] list( )

Returns an array of filenames in this `File` object's directory. This list does not include the current directory or the parent directory (" . " and " . . " on Unix systems).

C.2.3 FileReader

`FileReader` is a convenience class for reading character files. This class extends the abstract class `Reader`, but its methods should not be used directly. Instead, wrap the object in a `BufferedReader` for efficiency and the ability to call `readLine`.

Important Method

FileReader(String fileName)

Constructs a `FileReader` object from a given filename. It throws `FileNotFoundException` if the file cannot be opened.

C.2.4 InputStreamReader

An `InputStreamReader` is a bridge from byte streams to character streams: It reads bytes and translates them into characters. Its primary use is construction with `System.in` as a parameter. This class extends the abstract class `Reader`, but its methods should not be used directly. Instead, wrap the object in a `BufferedReader` for efficiency and the ability to call `readLine`.

Important Method

InputStreamReader(InputStream in)

Create an `InputStreamReader` from a given `InputStream`. A typical `InputStream` is `System.in`.

C.2.5 **PushbackReader**

`PushbackReader` implements a character-stream reader that allows characters to be pushed back into the stream.

Important Methods

PushbackReader(Reader in)

Creates a new pushback reader with a 1-character pushback buffer.

PushbackReader(Reader in, int bufferSize)

Creates a new pushback reader with a multicharacter pushback buffer whose capacity is specified by the second parameter.

int read( )

Reads a single character. Returns the character read, or −1 if the end of the stream has been reached. It throws an `IOException` if an I/O error occurs. The character is returned as an `int`. Thus typical use will require a type-conversion to `char`.

void unread(int ch)

Pushes back a single character, `ch`. The parameter has type `int`. Thus typical use will require a type-conversion to `char`. It throws an `IOException` if the pushback buffer is full or if some other I/O error occurs.

void unread(char [ ] cbuf)

Pushes back an array of characters by copying it to the front of the pushback buffer. After this method returns, the next character to be read will have the value `cbuf[0]`, the character after that will have the value `cbuf[1]`, and so forth. It throws `IOException` if there is insufficient room in the pushback buffer or if some other I/O error occurs.

C.3   Classes in Package **java.util**

This package defines several useful classes, including some data structures. It also provides support for dates and times. The three classes that are used in the text are described next.

C.3.1 Random

An instance of this class is used to generate a stream of pseudorandom numbers. The class uses a 48-bit seed, which is modified using a linear congruential formula (given at the end of Section 9.2). If two instances of Random are created with the same seed and the same sequence of method calls is made for each, they will generate and return identical sequences of numbers.

Important Methods

Random( )

Creates a new random-number generator. Its seed is initialized to a value based on the current time.

Random(long seed)

Creates a new random-number generator using a single long seed.

int nextInt( )

Returns the next pseudorandom, uniformly distributed int value from this random-number generator's sequence.

long nextLong( )

Returns the next pseudorandom, uniformly distributed long value from this random-number generator's sequence.

double nextDouble( )

Returns the next pseudorandom, uniformly distributed double value between 0.0 and 1.0 from this random-number generator's sequence.

double nextGaussian( )

Returns the next pseudorandom, Gaussian distributed double value with mean 0.0 and standard deviation 1.0 from this random-number generator's sequence.

C.3.2 StringTokenizer

The StringTokenizer class allows an application to break a string into tokens. The set of delimiters (the characters that separate tokens) may be specified either at creation time or on a per-token basis. An instance of StringTokenizer behaves in one of two ways, depending on whether it was created with the returnTokens flag having the value true or false. If the flag is `false`, delimiter characters serve to separate tokens. A token is a maximal sequence of consecutive characters that are not delimiters. If the flag is `true`, delimiter characters are considered to be tokens. A token is either one delimiter character or a maximal sequence of consecutive characters that are not delimiters.

Important Methods

`StringTokenizer( String str )`

Constructs a string tokenizer for the specified string. The tokenizer uses the default delimiter set, which is `" \t\n\r"`: the space character, the tab character, the newline character, and the carriage-return character.

`StringTokenizer( String str, String delim )`

Constructs a string tokenizer for the specified string. The characters in the `delim` argument are the delimiters for separating tokens.

`StringTokenizer( String str, String delim, boolean returnTokens )`

Constructs a string tokenizer for the specified string. The characters in the `delim` argument are the delimiters for separating tokens. If the `returnTokens` flag is `true`, then the delimiter characters are also returned as tokens. Each delimiter is returned as a string of length one. If the flag is `false`, the delimiter characters are skipped and serve only as separators between tokens.

`boolean hasMoreTokens( )`

Returns `true` if and only if there are more tokens available from this tokenizer's string.

`String nextToken( )`

Returns the next token from this string tokenizer. It throws a `NoSuchElementException` if there are no more tokens in this tokenizer's string.

`String nextToken( String delim )`

Returns the next token from this string tokenizer using `delim` as the delimiter set. The new delimiter set remains the default after this call. Throws a `NoSuchElementException` if there are no more tokens in this tokenizer's string.

`int countTokens( )`

Returns the number of tokens remaining in the string using the current delimiter set.

C.3.3 Vector

The `Vector` class implements a resizable array of objects.

Important Methods

Vector( )
Constructs an empty vector.

Vector(int initialCapacity)
Constructs an empty vector with the specified initial capacity.

Object elementAt(int index)
Returns the component at the specified index. It throws `ArrayIndexOutOfBoundsException` if the index is invalid.

void setElementAt(Object obj, int index)
Sets the component at the specified index of this vector to be the specified object. The previous component at that position is discarded. The index must be a value greater than or equal to 0 and less than the current size of the vector. Otherwise, `ArrayIndexOutOfBoundsException` is thrown.

void setSize(int newSize)
Sets the size of this vector. If the new size is greater than the current size, new `null` items are added to the end of the vector. If the new size is less than the current size, all components at index `newSize` and greater are discarded.

int capacity( )
Returns the current capacity of this vector.

int size( )
Returns the number of components in this vector.

On the Internet

TestString.java   Contains Figure C.1 and Figure C.2 and a `main` that times the method calls. It is found in the directory **AppendixC.**

D *Graphical User Interfaces*

A *graphical user interface* (*GUI*) is the modern alternative to terminal I/O that allows a program to communicate with its user. In a GUI, a window application is created. Some of the ways to perform input include selection from a list of alternatives, pressing buttons, checking boxes, typing in text fields, and using the mouse. Output can be performed by writing into text fields as well as drawing graphics. In Java, GUI programming is performed by using the *Abstract Window Toolkit* (*AWT*), which is a standard package supplied with all Java systems. A related topic is the Java applet, which is a program that can be downloaded from the Internet and run on a host computer. Applets invariably use the AWT.

In this appendix, we will see:

- The basic GUI components in the AWT
- How these components communicate information
- How these components can be arranged in a window
- How to draw graphics
- How to write Java applets

A *graphical user interface* (*GUI*) is the modern alternative to terminal I/O that allows a program to communicate with its user.

D.1 The Abstract Window Toolkit

The *Abstract Window Toolkit* (*AWT*) is a GUI toolkit that is supplied with all Java systems. It provides the basic classes to allow user interfaces. These classes can be found in the package `java.awt`. The AWT is designed to be portable and work across multiple platforms. For relatively simple interfaces, the AWT is easy to use. GUIs can be written without resorting to visual development aids, and provides a significant improvement over basic terminal interfaces.

In a program that uses terminal I/O, the program typically prompts the user for input and then executes a statement that reads a line from the terminal. When the line is read, it is processed. The flow of control in this situation is easy to follow. GUI programming is different. In GUI programming, the input components are arranged in a window. After the window is displayed, the program waits for an event, such as a button push, at which point an event handler is called. This means that the flow of control is less obvious in a GUI program. The programmer must supply the event handler to execute some piece of code.

The *Abstract Window Toolkit* (*AWT*) is a GUI toolkit that is supplied with all Java systems.

GUI programming is event-driven.

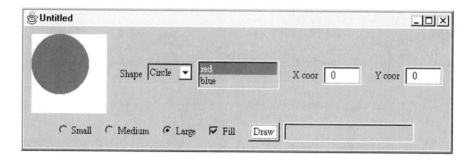

Figure D.1 A GUI that illustrates some of the basic components

Java 1.0 provided an event model that was cumbersome to use. It has been replaced in Java 1.1 by a more robust event model. Not surprisingly, these models are not entirely compatible. Specifically, a Java 1.0 compiler will not successfully compile code that uses the new event model. Java 1.1 compilers will give diagnostics about Java 1.0 constructs. However, already compiled Java 1.0 code can be run by a Java 1.1 interpreter. This appendix describes the newer event model only.

Figure D.1 illustrates some of the basic components provided by the AWT. These include the `Choice` (currently *Circle* is selected), a `List` (currently *red* is selected), basic `TextFields` for input, `Checkboxes`, and a `Button` (named *Draw*). Next to the button is a `TextField` that is used for output only (hence, it is darker than the input `TextFields` above it). In the top left-hand corner is a `Canvas` object that can be used for drawing pictures and handling mouse input.

This appendix describes the basic organization of the AWT. First, it covers the different types of objects, how they can be used to perform input and output, how these objects are arranged in a window, and how events are handled. Then, it describes the related concept of an applet, in which a program is downloaded through the Internet and run from inside a browser, such as Netscape Navigator or Internet Explorer.

D.2   Basic Objects in the AWT

The AWT is organized using a class inheritance hierarchy. A compressed version of this hierarchy is shown in Figure D.2. This is compressed because some intermediate classes are not shown. For instance, in the full hierarchy, `TextField` and `TextArea` are extended from `TextComponent`, while many classes that deal with fonts, colors, and other objects and are not in the `Component` hierarchy are not shown at all. The classes `Font` and `Color`, which are defined in the `java.awt` package, are extended from `Object`.

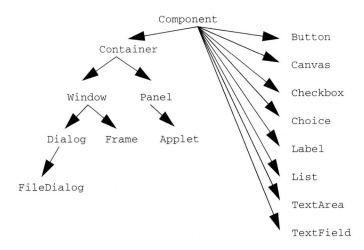

Figure D.2 Compressed hierarchy of the AWT

D.2.1 **Component**

The *Component* class is an abstract class that is the superclass of many AWT objects. Because it is abstract, it cannot be instantiated. A Component represents something that has a position and a size and can be painted on the screen as well as can receive input events. Some examples of the Component are evident from Figure D.2.

The Component class contains many methods. Some of these can be used to specify the color or font; others are used to handle events. Some of the important methods are

```
void paint( Graphics g );
void setSize( int width, int height );
void setBackground( Color c );
void setFont( Font f );
void show( );
```

The paint method is most commonly associated with Canvas objects and is described in Section D.3.2. The setSize method[1] is used to change the size of an object. It works with Canvas objects, but it should not be called for objects that use an automatic layout, such as Buttons. The setBackground and setFont methods are used to change the background color and font associated with a Component. They require a Color and Font object, respectively. Finally, the show method makes a component visible. Its typical use is for a Frame.

The *Component* class is an abstract class that is the superclass of many AWT objects. It represents something that has a position and a size and can be painted on the screen as well as can receive input events.

[1.] In Java 1.1, setSize replaces resize.

D.2.2 **Container**

A *Container* is the abstract superclass representing all components that can hold other components. An example of a Container is the Window class, which represents a top-level window. As the inheritance hierarchy shows, a Container IS-A Component. A particular instance of a Container object will store a collection of Components as well as other Containers.

The container has a useful helper object called a LayoutManager, which is a class that positions components inside the container. Some useful methods are

```
void setLayout( LayoutManager mgr );
void add( Component comp );
void add( Component comp, Object where );
```

Layout managers are described in Section D.3.1. A container must first define how objects in the container should be arranged. This is done by using setLayout. It then adds the objects into the container one-by-one by using add.

D.2.3 Top-level Windows

As Figure D.2 shows, there are two types of Container objects, namely, the top-level window Window and the Panel. The Window is specialized into various types of top-level entities. There are four basic top-level windows:

1. Window: a top-level window that has no border
2. Frame: a top-level window that has a border and can also have an associated MenuBar[2]
3. Dialog: a top-level window used to create dialogs, one subclass of which is the FileDialog
4. FileDialog: a top-level window used to provide a choice among all files in a directory

An application that uses a GUI interface must have a Frame (or a class extended from Frame) as the outermost container. Figure 2.11 shows a program that lists the contents of files whose names were provided as command-line arguments. In a GUI application, the filename would be specified by a FileDialog. Figure D.3 illustrates a simple GUI that uses a FileDialog to get the name of an input file. As before, the listing is sent to the standard output, although clearly, it could go to a GUI output component.

At line 1 in Figure D.3, all of the classes in the java.awt package are imported. The main routine begins by creating and then showing a new Frame f at lines 9 and 10. Recall that every GUI application program must create a Frame. Because we have done nothing else, the Frame has no size, it contains no components, and it consists of only a top menu bar. Next, we create a

---

2. Menus are not discussed in this Appendix.

FileDialog d, associated with Frame f, with the title *List File* and action *LOAD* at line 13. The result of line 14 is shown in Figure D.4. The call to the getFile method at line 17 returns the name of the selected file (or null if the request was canceled). At line 18, we call the listFile method from the class written in Figure 2.11.

```
1  import java.awt.*;
2
3  public class FileDialogTest
4  {
5          // Pop up a FileDialog, select a file,
6          //      and list contents
7      public static void main( String [ ] args )
8      {
9          Frame f = new Frame( );
10         f.show( );
11
12         FileDialog d;
13         d = new FileDialog( f, "List File", FileDialog.LOAD );
14         d.show( );
15
16         String fileName;
17         if( ( fileName = d.getFile( ) ) != null )
18             ListFiles.listFile( fileName ); // Figure 2.11
19
20         System.exit( 0 );
21      }
22 }
```

Figure D.3   Program in Figure 2.11 adapted to use a GUI

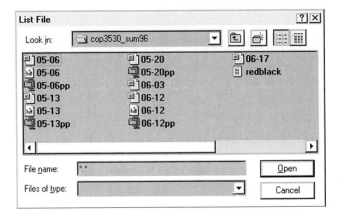

Figure D.4   Output for FileDialogTest program in Figure D.3

This example illustrates that simple things are easy to program in Java. `Dialog` objects (as opposed to the special `FileDialog` objects) are more difficult to program. This is because for the `FileDialog`, the `show` method does not return until some file has been selected. Thus at line 17, any action in the `FileDialog` has been performed when `getFile` returns. For `Dialog` objects, `show` returns immediately. Hence, the call to examine the dialog's action would be performed before anything happened, unless additional programming effort is expended. Additionally, since no objects are contained in the `Frame f`, we have not had to worry about object layout.

D.2.4 **Panel**

The *Panel* is used to store a collection of objects, but does not create borders. As such, it is the simplest of the `Container` classes.

The other `Container` subclass is the `Panel`. The *Panel* is used to store a collection of objects, but it does not create borders: So it is the simplest of the `Container` classes.

The primary use of the `Panel` is to organize objects into a unit. For instance, consider a registration form that requires a name, address, social security number, and home and work telephone numbers. All of these form components might produce a `PersonPanel`. Then the registration form could contain several `PersonPanel` entities to allow the possibility of multiple registrants.

As an example, Figure D.5 shows how the components shown in Figure D.1 are grouped into a `Panel` class and illustrates the general technique of creating a subclass of `Panel`. It remains to construct the objects, lay them out nicely, and handle the button push event.

Note that `GUI` implements the `ActionListener` interface. This means that it understands how to handle an *action event* (in this case, a button push). To implement the `ActionListener` interface, a class must provide an `actionPerformed` method. Also, when the button generates an action event, it must know which component is to receive the event. In this case, by making the call at 10 (in Figure D.5), the `GUI` object that contains the `Button` tells the `Button` to send it the event. These event-handling details are discussed in Section D.3.3.

A second use of the `Panel` is the grouping of objects into a unit for the purpose of simplifying layouts. This is discussed in Section D.3.4. The third use of `Panel` is the `Applet`, which is a subclass of `Panel`.

D.2.5 Important I/O Components

The AWT provides a set of components that can be used to perform input and output. These components are easy to set up and use. The code in Figure D.6 (page 738) illustrates how each of the basic components that are shown in Figure D.1 are constructed. Generally, this involves calling a constructor and applying a method to customize a component. This code does not specify how items are arranged in the `Panel` or how the states of the components are examined. Recall that GUI programming consists of drawing the interface and then waiting for events to occur. Component layout and event handling is discussed in Section D.3.

Label

A *Label* is a component for placing text in a container. Its primary use is to label other components such as a `Choice`, `List`, `TextField`, or `Panel` (many other components already have their names displayed in some way). In Figure D.1, the phrases *Shape*, *X Coor*, and *Y Coor* are labels. A `Label` is constructed with an optional `String` and can be changed with the method `setText`. These methods are

A *Label* is a component for placing text in a container. Its primary use is to label other components.

```
 1  import java.awt.*;
 2  import java.awt.event.*;
 3
 4  public class GUI extends Panel implements ActionListener
 5  {
 6      public GUI( )
 7      {
 8          makeTheObjects( );
 9          doTheLayout( );
10          theDrawButton.addActionListener( this );
11      }
12          // Make all the objects
13      private void makeTheObjects( )
14          { /* Implementation in Figure D.6 */ }
15
16          // Layout all the objects
17      private void doTheLayout( )
18          { /* Implementation in Figure D.9 */ }
19
20          // Handle the draw button push
21      public void actionPerformed( ActionEvent evt )
22          { /* Implementation in Figure D.12 */ }
23
24      private GUICanvas theCanvas;
25      private Choice    theShape;
26      private List      theColor;
27      private TextField theXCoor;
28      private TextField theYCoor;
29      private Checkbox  smallPic;
30      private Checkbox  mediumPic;
31      private Checkbox  largePic;
32      private Checkbox  theFillBox;
33      private Button    theDrawButton;
34      private TextField theMessage;
35  }
```

Figure D.5 Basic GUI class shown in Figure D.1

```
1              // Make all the objects
2      private void makeTheObjects( )
3      {
4              theCanvas = new GUICanvas( );
5              theCanvas.setBackground( Color.white );
6              theCanvas.setSize( 100, 100 );
7
8              theShape = new Choice( );
9              theShape.add( "Circle" );
10             theShape.add( "Square" );
11
12             theColor = new List( 2, false );
13             theColor.add( "red" );
14             theColor.add( "blue" );
15             theColor.select( 0 ); // make red default
16
17             theXCoor = new TextField( 5 );
18             theYCoor = new TextField( 5 );
19
20             CheckboxGroup theSize = new CheckboxGroup( );
21             smallPic  = new Checkbox( "Small",  theSize, false );
22             mediumPic = new Checkbox( "Medium", theSize, true );
23             largePic  = new Checkbox( "Large",  theSize, false );
24
25             theFillBox = new Checkbox( "Fill" );
26             theFillBox.setState( false );
27
28             theDrawButton = new Button( "Draw" );
29             theMessage = new TextField( 25 );
30             theMessage.setEditable( false );
31     }
```

Figure D.6 Code that constructs the objects in Figure D.1

```
Label( );
Label( String theLabel );
void setText( String theLabel );
```

Button

The *Button* is
used to create a
labeled button.
When it is pushed,
an *action event* is
generated.

The *Button* is used to create a labeled button. Figure D.1 contains a Button with the label *Draw*. When the Button is pushed, an *action event* is generated. Section D.3.3 describes how action events are handled. The Button interface is similar to the Label. Specifically, a Button is constructed with an optional String. The Button label can be changed with the method setText. These methods are

```
Button( );
Button( String theLabel );
void setText( String theLabel );
```

Choice

The *Choice* is used to select a single string via a pop-up list of choices. Only a string that is one of the choices can be selected, and only one choice can be selected at any time. In Figure D.1, the type of shape is a Choice object; *Circle* is currently selected. Some of the Choice methods are

The *Choice* is used to select a single string via a pop-up list of choices.

```
Choice( );
void    add( String item );
String getSelectedItem( );
int     getSelectedIndex( );
void    select( int index );
```

A Choice is constructed with no parameters. Strings can then be added to the list of Choice options. When getSelectedItem is called, a String representing the current selected item (or null if no choice is selected) is returned. Instead of returning the actual String, its index (as computed by the order of calls to add) can be returned by calling getSelectedIndex. The first item added has index 0, and so on. This can be useful because if an array stores information corresponding to each of the choices, getSelectedIndex can be used to index this array. The select method is used to specify a default selection.

List

The *List* component allows the selection from a scrolling list of Strings. In Figure D.1, the choice of colors is presented as a List. The List differs from the Choice in three fundamental ways:

The *List* component allows the selection from a scrolling list of Strings. It can be set up to allow for either one selected item or multiple selected items.

1. The List can be set up to allow either one selected item or multiple selected items.
2. The List allows the user to see more than one choice at a time.
3. The List will take up more screen real estate than the Choice.

The basic List methods are

```
List( );
List( int rows, boolean multipleSelections );
void      add( String item );
String    getSelectedItem( );
String [ ] getSelectedItems( );
void      select( int index );
```

A List is constructed with either no parameters or two parameters. The two-parameter constructor specifies the number of visible rows (in other words, the number of rows to be displayed) and a boolean that determines if multiple selections are allowed. The methods add, getSelectedItem, and select have the same behavior as the corresponding methods in Choice. getSelectedItem returns null if either no items are selected or more than one item is selected. getSelectedItems is used to handle multiple selection; it returns an array of Strings corresponding to the selected items. As with the Choice, indices instead of Strings can be obtained by other public methods.

Checkbox

A *Checkbox* is a GUI component that has an *on* state and an *off* state. A *CheckboxGroup* can contain a set of Checkboxes in which only one may be true at a time.

A *Checkbox* is a GUI component that has an *on* state and an *off* state. The *on* state is true and the *off* state is false. Figure D.1 contains four Checkbox objects. In this figure, the *Fill* check box is currently true and looks different than the other three Checkbox objects. This is because the other three Checkbox objects are in a *CheckboxGroup*: only one Checkbox in the group of three may be true. When a Checkbox in a group is selected, all the others in the group are deselected. A CheckboxGroup is constructed with zero parameters. Note that it is not a Component; it is simply a logical object.

The common Checkbox methods are

```
Checkbox( );
Checkbox( String theLabel );
Checkbox( String theLabel, CheckboxGroup group,
                           boolean state );
boolean getState( );
void    setLabel( );
void    setState( );
```

A stand-alone Checkbox is constructed with an optional label. If a label is not provided, it can be added later with setLabel. setLabel can also be used to change the existing Checkbox label. A Checkbox that is part of a CheckboxGroup is constructed by providing a label, the group, and an initial state. Note that if state is true, all other Checkboxes that have been constructed for this group prior to the call are set to false. setState is most commonly used to set a default for a standalone Checkbox. getState returns the state of a Checkbox.

Canvas

A *Canvas* component represents a blank rectangular area of the screen onto which the application can draw or receive input events.

A *Canvas* component represents a blank rectangular area of the screen onto which the application can draw. Primitive graphics are described in Section D.3.2. A Canvas can also receive input from the user in the form of mouse and keyboard events. The Canvas is never used directly: Instead, the programmer defines a subclass of Canvas with appropriate functionality. The subclass must override the method

```
void paint( Graphics g );
```

TextField *and* TextAreas

A *TextField* is a component that presents the user with a single line of text. A *TextArea* allows multiple lines and has similar functionality. Thus only TextField is considered here. By default, the text can be edited by the user, but it is possible to make the text uneditable. In Figure D.1, there are three TextField objects: two for the coordinates and one, which is not editable by the user, that is used to communicate error messages. The background color of an uneditable text field differs from that of an editable text field. Some of the common methods associated with TextField are

A *TextField* is a component that presents the user with a single line of text. A *TextArea* allows multiple lines and has similar functionality.

```
TextField( );
TextField( int cols );
TextField( String text, int cols );
String getText( );
void    setEditable( boolean editable );
void    setText( String text );
```

A TextField is constructed either with no parameters or by specifying an initial optional text and the number of columns. A warning: On many systems, you need to specify more columns than you expect to use due to an apparent bug in the AWT. The setEditable method can be used to disallow input into the TextField. setText can be used to print messages into the TextField, and getText can be used to read from the TextField.

On many systems, you need to specify more columns than you expect to use due to an apparent bug in the AWT.

D.3 Basic AWT Principles

This section examines three important facets of AWT programming. First, how objects are arranged inside a container, followed by how events, such as button pushing, are handled. Finally, it describes how graphics are drawn inside Canvas objects.

D.3.1 Layout Managers

A layout manager automatically arranges components of the container. It is associated with a container by issuing the setLayout command. An example of using setLayout is the call

The *layout manager* automatically arranges components of the container. A layout manager is associated with a container by the setLayout method.

```
setLayout( new FlowLayout( ) );
```

Notice that a reference to the layout manager need not be saved. The container in which the setLayout command is applied stores it as a private data member. When a layout manager is used, requests to resize many of the components, such as buttons, do not work because the layout manager will choose its own sizes for the components, as it deems appropriate. The idea is that the layout manager will determine the best sizes that allow the layout to meet the specifications.

Figure D.7   Five buttons arranged using `BorderLayout`

FlowLayout

The simplest of the layouts is the *FlowLayout*, which adds components in a row from left to right.

The simplest of the layouts is the *FlowLayout*. When a container is arranged using the `FlowLayout`, its components are added in a row from left to right. When there is no room left in a row, a new row is formed. By default, each row is centered. This can be changed by providing an additional parameter in the constructor with the value `FlowLayout.LEFT` or `FlowLayout.RIGHT`.

The problem with using a `FlowLayout` is that a row may break in an awkward place. For instance, if a row is too short, a break may occur between a `Label` and a `TextField`, even though logically they should always remain adjacent. One way to avoid this is to create a separate `Panel` with those two elements and then add the `Panel` into the container. Another problem with the `FlowLayout` is that it is difficult to line up things vertically.

The `FlowLayout` is the default for a `Panel`.

```
1  import java.awt.*;
2
3      // Generate Figure D.7
4  public class BorderTest extends Frame
5  {
6      public static void main( String [ ] args )
7      {
8          Frame f = new BorderTest( );
9
10         f.setLayout( new BorderLayout( ) );
11         f.add( new Button( "North" ), "North" );
12         f.add( new Button( "East" ), "East" );
13         f.add( new Button( "South" ), "South" );
14         f.add( new Button( "West" ), "West" );
15         f.add( new Button( "Center" ), "Center" );
16
17         f.pack( );    // Resize frame to minimum size
18         f.show( );    // Display the frame
19     }
20 }
```

Figure D.8   Code that illustrates `BorderLayout`

BorderLayout

A *BorderLayout* is the default for objects in the `Window` hierarchy, such as `Frame` and `Dialog`. It lays out a container by placing components in one of five locations. For this to happen, the `add` method must provide as a second parameter one of the strings `"North"`, `"South"`, `"East"`, `"West"`, and `"Center"`. Figure D.7 shows five buttons added to a `Frame` using a `BorderLayout`. The code to generate this layout is shown in Figure D.8. Typically, some of the five locations may be unused. Also, the component placed in a location is typically a `Panel` that contains other components using some other layout.

    As an example, the code in Figure D.9 (page 744) shows how the objects in Figure D.1 are arranged. Here, we have two rows, but we want to ensure that the checkboxes, buttons, and output text field are placed below the rest of the GUI. The idea is to create a `Panel` that stores the items that should be in the top half and another `Panel` that stores the items in the bottom half. These two `Panels` can be placed on top of each other by arranging them using a `BorderLayout`.

    Lines 4 and 5 create the two `Panel` objects `topHalf` and `bottomHalf`. Each of the `Panel` objects are then separately arranged using a `FlowLayout`. Notice that the `setLayout` and `add` methods are applied to the appropriate `Panel`. Because the `Panels` are arranged with the `FlowLayout`, they may consume more than one row if there is not enough horizontal real estate available. This could cause a bad break between a `Label` and a `TextField`. It is left as an exercise for the reader to create additional `Panels` to ensure that any breaks do not disconnect a `Label` and the component it labels. Once the `Panels` are done, we use a `BorderLayout` to line them up. This is done at lines 28 to 30. Notice also that the contents of both `Panels` are centered. This is a result of the `FlowLayout`. To have the contents of the `Panels` left-aligned, lines 8 and 19 would construct the `FlowLayout` with the additional parameter `FlowLayout.LEFT`.

    When the `BorderLayout` is used, any `add` commands that are issued without a `String` use `"Center"` as the default. If a `String` is provided, but is not one of the acceptable five (including having correct case), then a runtime exception is thrown.[3]

null *Layout*

The *null layout* is used to perform precise positioning. In the `null` layout, each object is added to the container by `add`. Its position and size may then be set by calling the `setBounds` method:

```
void setBounds( int x, int y, int width, int height )
```

BorderLayout is the default for objects in the `Window` hierarchy, such as `Frame` and `Dialog`. It lays out a container by placing components in one of five locations.

When the `BorderLayout` is used, an add command that is issued without a `String` defaults to `"Center"`.

The *null layout* is used to perform precise positioning.

[3.]   Note that in Java 1.0, the arguments to `add` were reversed and missing or incorrect `Strings` were quietly ignored, thus leading to difficult debugging. The old style is still allowed, but it is officially discouraged.

```
1          // Layout all the objects
2      private void doTheLayout( )
3      {
4          Panel topHalf    = new Panel( );
5          Panel bottomHalf = new Panel( );
6
7              // Layout the top half
8          topHalf.setLayout( new FlowLayout( ) );
9          topHalf.add( theCanvas );
10         topHalf.add( new Label( "Shape" ) );
11         topHalf.add( theShape );
12         topHalf.add( theColor );
13         topHalf.add( new Label( "X coor" ) );
14         topHalf.add( theXCoor );
15         topHalf.add( new Label( "Y coor" ) );
16         topHalf.add( theYCoor );
17
18             // Layout the bottom half
19         bottomHalf.setLayout( new FlowLayout( ) );
20         bottomHalf.add( smallPic );
21         bottomHalf.add( mediumPic );
22         bottomHalf.add( largePic );
23         bottomHalf.add( theFillBox );
24         bottomHalf.add( theDrawButton );
25         bottomHalf.add( theMessage );
26
27             // Now layout GUI
28         setLayout( new BorderLayout( ) );
29         add( topHalf, "North" );
30         add( bottomHalf, "South" );
31     }
```

Figure D.9 Code that lays out the objects in Figure D.1

Here x and y represent the location of the upper left-hand corner of the object, relative to the upper left-hand corner of its container. width and height represent the size of the object. All units are pixels.

The null layout is platform-dependent; typically, this is a large liability.

Fancier Layouts

Other layouts simulate tabbed index cards and allow arranging over an arbitrary grid.

Java also provides the CardLayout, GridLayout, and GridBagLayout. The CardLayout simulates the tabbed index cards popular in Windows applications but looks terrible in the AWT. The GridLayout adds components into a grid but will make each grid entry the same size. This means that components are stretched in sometimes unnatural ways. It is useful for when this is not a problem, such as a calculator keypad that consists of a two-dimensional grid of buttons. The GridBagLayout adds components into a grid but allows components to cover several grid cells. It is more complicated than the other layouts.

Visual Tools

Commercial products such as Symantec Cafe and Microsoft J++ include tools that allow the programmer to draw the layout using a CAD-like system. The tool then produces the Java code to construct the objects and provide a layout. Typically, it generates an arrangement using a `null` layout manager. Even with this system, the programmer must still write most of the code, including the handling of events, but is relieved of the dirty work involved in calculating precise object positions.

D.3.2 Graphics

As mentioned in Section D.2.5, graphics are drawn by using a `Canvas` object. Specifically, to generate graphics, the programmer must define a new class that extends `Canvas`. This new class provides a constructor (if a default is unacceptable), overrides a method named `paint`, and provides a public method that can be called from the canvas's container. The `paint` method is

```
void paint( Graphics g );
```

`Graphics` is an abstract class that defines several methods. Some of these are

```
void drawOval( int x, int y, int width, int height );
void drawRect( int x, int y, int width, int height );
void fillOval( int x, int y, int width, int height );
void fillRect( int x, int y, int width, int height );
void drawLine( int x1, int x2, int y1, int y2 );
void drawString( String str, int x, int y );
void setColor( Color c );
```

In Java, coordinates are measured relative to the upper left-hand corner of the component. `drawOval`, `drawRect`, `fillOval`, and `fillRect` all draw an object of specified `width` and `height` with the upper left-hand corner at coordinates given by `x` and `y`. `drawLine` and `drawString` draw lines and text, respectively. `setColor` is used to change the current color; the new color is used by all drawing routines until it is changed.

Figure D.10 (page 746) illustrates how the canvas in Figure D.1 is implemented. The new class `GUICanvas` extends `Canvas`. It provides various private data members that describe the current state of the `Canvas`. The default `GUICanvas` constructor is reasonable, so we accept it.

The data members are set by the public method `setParams`, which is provided so that the container (that is, the `GUI` class that stores the `GUICanvas`) can communicate the state of its various input components to the `GUICanvas`. `setParams` is shown at lines 5 to 14. The last line of `setParams` calls the method `repaint`.

Margin notes:

Graphics are drawn by defining a class that extends Canvas. The new class overrides the paint method and provides a public method that can be called from the canvas's container.

Graphics is an abstract class that defines several drawing methods.

In Java, coordinates are measured relative to the upper left-hand corner of the component.

The repaint
method calls the
update method.
By default,
update clears the
component and
then calls paint.
This behavior can
be changed by
overriding update.

The `repaint` method calls the `update` method. By default, `update` clears the component and then calls `paint`. Thus all we need to do is to write a `paint` method that draws the canvas as specified in the class data members. As can be seen by its implementation in lines 16 to 34, `paint` simply calls the `Graphics` methods described previously in this appendix.

```
1  import java.awt.*;
2
3  public class GUICanvas extends Canvas
4  {
5      public void setParams( String theShape, String theColor,
6                             int x, int y, int size, boolean fill )
7      {
8          this.theShape = theShape;
9          this.theColor = theColor;
10         xcoor = x; ycoor = y;
11         theSize = size;
12         fillOn = fill;
13         repaint( );
14     }
15
16     public void paint( Graphics g )
17     {
18         if( theColor.equals( "red" ) )
19             g.setColor( Color.red );
20         else if( theColor.equals( "blue" ) )
21             g.setColor( Color.blue );
22         width = 25 * ( theSize + 1 );
23
24         if( theShape.equals( "Square" ) )
25             if( fillOn )
26                 g.fillRect( xcoor, ycoor, width, width );
27             else
28                 g.drawRect( xcoor, ycoor, width, width );
29         else if( theShape.equals( "Circle" ) )
30             if( fillOn )
31                 g.fillOval( xcoor, ycoor, width, width );
32             else
33                 g.drawOval( xcoor, ycoor, width, width );
34     }
35
36     private String theShape = "";
37     private String theColor = "";
38     private int xcoor;
39     private int ycoor;
40     private int theSize;   // 0 = small, 1 = med, 2 = large
41     private boolean fillOn;
42     private int width;
43 }
```

Figure D.10 Basic canvas shown in top left-hand corner of Figure D.1

```
1  public void update( Graphics g )
2  {
3      paint( g );
4  }
```

Figure D.11 Overriding `update` to avoid erasing the canvas on a `repaint`

Recall that, by default, a call to `repaint` clears the component. Sometimes we would prefer to write on the canvas without erasing it. To do this, we override the `update` method for the new canvas class, as shown in Figure D.11.

It is important to note that unless threads are used (Section D.4), the call to `update` is not immediate and is often delayed until an event occurs. In this case, code that follows `repaint` appears to be executed prior to the actual execution of the repainting.

If there are no threads, `repaint` may appear to be the last statement.

D.3.3 Events

When the user uses the mouse or types on the keyboard, the operating system produces an event. Java's original event-handling system was cumbersome and has been completely redone. The new model is much simpler to program than the old. Note that the two models are incompatable: Java 1.1 events are not understood by Java 1.0 compilers and vice versa. The basic rules are as follows:

Java's original event-handling system was cumbersome and has been completely redone.

1. Any class that is willing to provide code to handle an event must `implement` a *listener* interface. Examples of listener interfaces are `ActionListener`, `WindowListener`, and `MouseListener`. As usual, implementing an interface means that all methods of the interface must be defined by the class.

2. An object that is willing to handle the event generated by a component must register its willingness with an *add listener* message sent to the event-generating component. When a component generates an event, the event will be sent to the object that has registered to receive it. If no object has registered to receive it, then it is ignored.

For an example, consider the action event, which is generated when the user presses a `Button`, hits *Return* while in a `TextField`, or selects from a `List` or `MenuItem`. The simplest way to handle the `Button` click is to have its container implement `ActionListener` by providing an `actionPerformed` method and registering itself with the `Button` as its event handler.

An action event is generated when the user presses a `Button`; it is handled by an ac-tionListener.

This is shown for our running example in Figure D.1 as follows. Recall that in Figure D.5, we already have done two things. At line 4, `GUI` declares that it implements the `ActionListener`, and at line 10, an instance of `GUI` registers itself as its `Button`'s action event handler. In Figure D.12 (page 748), we implement the listener by having `actionPerformed` call `setParam` in the `GUICanvas` class. This example is simplified by the fact that there is only one

Button, so when `actionPerformed` is called, we know what to do. If GUI contained several `Button`s and it registered to receive events from all of these `Button`s, then `actionPerformed` would have to examine the `evt` parameter to determine which `Button` event was to be processed: This would probably involve a sequence of `if`/`else` tests.[4] The `evt` parameter, which in this case is an `ActionEvent` reference, is always passed to an event handler. The event will be specific to the type of handler (`ActionEvent`, `WindowEvent`, and so on), but it will always be a subclass of `AWTEvent`.

An important event that needs to be processed is the window closing event. This event is generated when an application is closed by pressing on the ⊠ that is at the top right-hand corner of the application window. Unfortunately, by default, this event is ignored, so if an event handler is not provided, the normal mechanism for closing an application will not work.

Window closing is one of several events that is associated with a `WindowListener` interface. Because implementing the interface requires us to provide implementations for many methods (which are likely to be empty bodies), the most reasonable course of action is to define a class that extends `Frame` and implements the `WindowListener` interface. This class, `CloseableFrame`, is shown in Figure D.13. The window close event handler is simple to write — it just calls `System.exit`. The other methods remain without a special implementation. The constructor registers that it is willing to accept the window closing event. Now we can use `CloseableFrame` instead of `Frame` throughout.

A window closing event is generated when an application is closed.

The window-closing event is handled by implementing the `WindowListener` *interface.*

`CloseableFrame` extends `Frame` *and implements* `Window-Listener`.

```
1          // Handle the draw button push
2      public void actionPerformed( ActionEvent evt )
3      {
4          try
5          {
6              theCanvas.setParams(
7                  theShape.getSelectedItem( ),
8                  theColor.getSelectedItem( ),
9                  Integer.parseInt( theXCoor.getText( ) ),
10                 Integer.parseInt( theYCoor.getText( ) ),
11                 smallPic.getState( ) ? 0 :
12                        mediumPic.getState( ) ? 1 : 2,
13                 theFillBox.getState( ) );
14             theMessage.setText( "" );
15         }
16         catch( Exception e )
17             { theMessage.setText( "Incomplete input" ); }
18     }
```

Figure D.12   Code to handle the draw button push for Figure D.1

---

4. One way to do this is to use `evt.getSource( )`, which returns a reference to the object that generated the event.

```
1  // Frame that closes on a window-close event
2
3  public class CloseableFrame extends Frame implements WindowListener
4  {
5      public CloseableFrame( )
6        { addWindowListener( this ); }
7
8      public void windowClosing( WindowEvent event )
9        { System.exit( 0 ); }
10     public void windowClosed( WindowEvent event )
11       { }
12     public void windowDeiconified( WindowEvent event )
13       { }
14     public void windowIconified( WindowEvent event )
15       { }
16     public void windowActivated( WindowEvent event )
17       { }
18     public void windowDeactivated( WindowEvent event )
19       { }
20     public void windowOpened( WindowEvent event )
21       { }
22 }
```

Figure D.13 `CloseableFrame` class: same as `Frame`, but handles the window closing event

Figure D.14 provides a `main` that can be used to start the application in Figure D.1. We place this in a separate class, which we call `BasicGUI`. `BasicGUI` extends the class `CloseableFrame`. `main` simply creates a `Frame` into which we place a `GUI` object. Since there is only one object, the `FlowLayout` can be used for `Frame f`. We then add an unnamed `GUI` object and `pack` the `Frame`. The `pack` method simply makes the `Frame` as tight as possible, given its constituent components. The `show` method displays the `Frame`.

The pack method simply makes the Frame as tight as possible, given its constituent components. The show method displays the Frame.

```
1  import java.awt.*;
2
3  public class BasicGUI extends CloseableFrame
4  {
5      public static void main( String [ ] args )
6      {
7          Frame f = new BasicGUI( );
8
9          f.setLayout( new FlowLayout( ) );
10         f.add( new GUI( ) );
11         f.pack( );
12         f.show( );
13     }
14 }
```

Figure D.14 `main` routine for Figure D.1

D.3.4 Summary: Putting the Pieces Together

Here is a summary of how to create a GUI application. Place the GUI functionality in a class that extends `Panel`. For that class, do the following:

- Decide on the basic input elements and text output elements. If the same elements are used twice, make an extra class to store the common functionality and apply these principles on that class.
- If graphics are used, make an extra class that extends `Canvas`. That class must provide a `paint` method and a public method that can be used by the container to communicate to it. It may also need to provide a constructor.
- Pick a layout and issue a `setLayout` command.
- Add components to the GUI using `add`.
- Handle events. The simplest way to do this is to use a `Button` and trap the button push with `actionPerformed`.

Once a GUI class is written, an application defines a class that extends `CloseableFrame` with a `main` routine. The `main` routine simply creates an instance of this extended frame class, places the GUI panel inside the frame, and issues a `pack` command and a `show` command for the frame.

D.4 Animations and Threads

Because the AWT allows us to draw objects, it is natural to try to perform animations. Indeed, the ability of Java to animate Web pages has probably been responsible for its quick rise among programming languages.

Animation in Java would seem to be trivial; all we have to do is repeatedly call `repaint` with different requests. If we separate the calls to `repaint` by calling `Thread.sleep`, then we can slow the animation to a viewable speed. An example of these ideas is shown in Figure D.15. Here, we attempt to show how a circle of radius 50 moves along the diagonal from (0, 0) to (199, 199), where, as usual, these coordinates represent the position of the top left-hand corner of the bounding box of the circle (relative to the top left-hand coordinate of the frame). We call `repaint` repeatedly, separated by 25 ms.

Unfortunately, when this program is run, it sleeps for about 5 sec and then simply draws the last circle. This is not what we want.

Animations require the use of threads. The solution to this problem is to use *threads*. How to use threads is a fairly involved topic, but the machinery needed to solve our problem is simple. We begin by creating a separate thread of execution. To do this, we perform the following steps:

1. Make our class implement the `Runnable` interface. The `Runnable` interface has a single method named `run`.
2. Declare a `Thread` as a class data member and have it initalized when the object is constructed.

```
1  import java.awt.*;
2
3      // Attempts to draw an animated sequence of circles
4      // along a diagonal; does not work
5  public class BadCircles extends CloseableFrame
6  {
7      int extremity = 0;
8
9      public BadCircles( )
10     {
11         drawCircles( );
12     }
13
14     public void drawCircles( )
15     {
16         for( extremity = 0; extremity < 200; extremity++ )
17         {
18             repaint( );
19             try
20               { Thread.sleep( 25 ); }
21             catch( InterruptedException e ) { }
22         }
23     }
24
25     public void paint( Graphics g )
26     {
27         g.fillOval( extremity, extremity, 50, 50 );
28     }
29
30     public static void main( String [ ] args )
31     {
32         Frame f = new BadCircles( );
33         f.setSize( 300, 300 );
34         f.show( );
35     }
36 }
```

Figure D.15   Program that attempts to perform an animation of a circle moving down a diagonal

3. Start the Thread.
4. Implement the run method and have it do all the work.

Figure D.16 (page 752) shows how this is done. Changes made from Figure D.15 are shown in boldfaced type (the name of the class has been changed so that both versions can be provided in the online code). First, at line 3 we declare that the class implements Runnable. Second, at line 6 we declare the Thread data member and construct a Thread at line 10. Third, we start the Thread at line 11. Finally, at lines 14 to 17 we provide an implementation of the run method; here, it simply calls drawCircles.

```
1  import java.awt.*;
2  public class GoodCircles extends CloseableFrame
3                              implements Runnable
4  {
5      int extremity = 0;
6      private Thread animator = null;
7
8      public GoodCircles( )
9      {
10         animator = new Thread( this );
11         animator.start( );
12     }
13
14     public void run( )
15     {
16         drawCircles( );
17     }
18
19     public void drawCircles( )
20     {
21         for( extremity = 0; extremity < 200;  extremity++ )
22         {
23             repaint( );
24             try
25                { Thread.sleep( 25 ); }
26             catch( InterruptedException e ) { }
27         }
28     }
29
30     public void paint( Graphics g )
31     {
32         g.fillOval( extremity, extremity, 50, 50 );
33     }
34
35     public static void main( String [ ] args )
36     {
37         Frame f = new GoodCircles( );
38         f.setSize( 300, 300 );
39         f.show( );
40     }
41 }
```

Figure D.16   Correct implementation of the circle animation

As mentioned previously, threads are an involved topic. They are useful for implementing concurrent programs, in which there are several threads of execution. The difficulty is having the threads communicate with each other and ensuring the threads share common resources consistently. For instance, in many instances, it is desirable for a thread to lock out all others from modifying or even accessing a shared resource, such as a variable. Java provides language support for this via the synchronized reserved word. Further discussion of threads can be found in most Java references.

D.5 Applets

An *applet* is a small program that is embedded inside another application. The Java system includes an application called the Applet Viewer that can be used to run an applet. However, the most common situation is that an applet is downloaded over the Internet and executed locally by a Java-enabled browser, such as Netscape Navigator or Microsoft Internet Explorer.

When an applet is embedded in a Web page, its Java code is downloaded to the host computer and run by the browser. This has the advantage of lightening the load on the server computer. This is because once the Java code is downloaded, all the computation is performed locally.

One of the intriguing future directions that Java is starting to address involves the storing of software on a Web site. Currently, users of a personal computer must install the software on their local machine. This requires disk space, thereby limiting the amount of different software that can be simultaneously installed. Additionally, there is also the issue of having the latest version of software, including bug fixes. With applets, all software could be stored at a Web site and then users could pay for each use of the software. This would free up some disk space, make a wider array of software available, and also make it easier to ensure that current versions are used. The result would be the so-called "network computer" and could be significantly less expensive than a fully charged PC. At the time of this writing, the most common use of Java is to design animations that spruce up otherwise dull and static Web pages.

To use an applet, the user must know a little about *hypertext markup language*, or *HTML*, which is the language Web browsers understand, in order to instruct the browser to load the applet code. An applet also is implemented slightly differently from an application program. In particular, `main` is not called. Also, applets run with additional security restrictions so as to avoid malicious hacking. However, security issues aside, the differences in programming an applet and programming an application are relatively minor, thus allowing one to write a program that serves as both an application and an applet. The remainder of this section discusses these issues.

> An applet is a small program that is embedded inside another application. Typically an applet is downloaded over the Internet and executed locally by a Java-enabled browser.

> Java is considered to be a choice language for future "network computers."

D.5.1 Hypertext Markup Language

Hypertext markup language, or simply *HTML*, is the language that Web browsers understand. An HTML file consists of a sequence of formatting commands and text that is passed over the Internet to a browser. HTML is a cross between the word processing languages *troff* and *LaTeX*. Originally, it allowed for various font and color changes, the importing of images, the creation of links to other Web pages, and the automatic generation of numbered and bulleted lists. Recently, it has become more complex, incorporating among other things, tables and multiple frames.

> *Hypertext markup language (HTML)* is the language that Web browsers understand. An HTML file consists of a sequence of formatting commands and text.

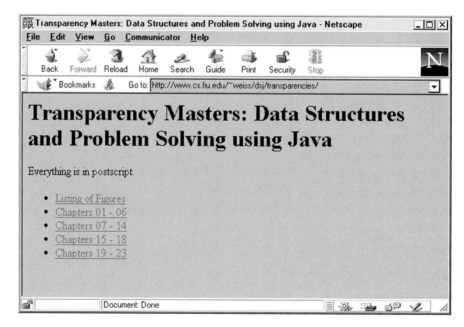

Figure D.17   Web page, viewed through Netscape Navigator, corresponding to the HTML code in Figure D.18

Figure D.17 shows a short page that contains links to transparency masters that accompany this book. Its HTML source is shown in Figure D.18. Formatting commands are placed inside <> tags: Typically, a command such as <ul>, which indicates the beginning of an unordered (or bulleted list), is eventually terminated with a matching </ul> (note the addition of the forward slash). Also shown is the <li> command, which represents a single entry in the list. HTML files should begin with the <HTML> and <BODY> tags and end with the matching tags </HTML> and </BODY>. Links are specified with a <A> and a closing </A>, as shown. <p> specifies a new paragraph, <TITLE> sets the title bar in the browser, and <H1> specifies that text is to be set as a first-level heading, using the appropriate font and boldness.

Other common tags include <B> and <I> (for boldface and italics) and <SRC> to load images. <ol> is used to create a numbered (ordered) list. Lists may be nested to create sublists. All of the HTML commands treat newlines as white space. The browser breaks the page heading as it sees fit, not as was typed in the HTML source.

HTML is relatively easy to use. Documentation for the various formatting commands is provided online, but most people simply view other people's HTML source and plagiarize liberally. You will probably learn the additional tags only when you need to use them. Note, however, that the browser is not quick to report mismatched tags; it will simply continue to use the formatting specified by the opening tag. Thus, if a </A> is missing, you'll find that lots of text will be underlined, indicating that the link is followed by clicking anywhere on the text.

Formatting commands are placed inside <> tags.

```
 1  <HTML>
 2  <BODY>
 3
 4  <TITLE>
 5  Transparency Masters:
 6  Data Structures and Problem Solving using Java
 7  </TITLE>
 8
 9  <H1>
10  Transparency Masters:
11  Data Structures and Problem Solving using Java
12  </H1>
13
14  <p>
15  Everything is in postscript.
16
17  <ul>
18  <li><A HREF="TransparencysTOC.ps">Listing of Figures</A></li>
19  <li><A HREF="Transparencys01-06.ps">Chapters 01 - 06</A></li>
20  <li><A HREF="Transparencys07-14.ps">Chapters 07 - 14</A></li>
21  <li><A HREF="Transparencys15-18.ps">Chapters 15 - 18</A></li>
22  <li><A HREF="Transparencys19-23.ps">Chapters 19 - 23</A></li>
23  </ul>
24
25  </BODY>
26  </HTML>
```

Figure D.18 HTML code for a Web page in Figure D.17 that contains transparency masters for this book

An applet is inserted into the Web page by using the <APPLET> tag.[5] The HTML code in Figure D.19 is the simplest example of a Web page that contains an applet. In fact, this Web page contains nothing else. Note that a Web page can contain both applets and other commands and may even contain multiple applets. Included in the <APPLET> tag is the name of the file that contains the java code and the dimensions (in pixels) of the applet in the browser.

The applet's size, in pixels, must be included in the <APPLET> tag.

```
 1  <HTML>
 2  <BODY>
 3
 4  <APPLET code="BasicGUIApplet.class" width="600" height="300">
 5  </APPLET>
 6
 7  </BODY>
 8  </HTML>
```

Figure D.19 HTML file for the BasicGUIApplet applet

[5.] There is a proposal to replace this with the <EMBED> tag.

If the applet is not in the same location as the Web page, you will need to supply the CODEBASE (preferably prior to the CODE attribute). This allows you to directly reference applets written by other parties.

Some browsers do not allow applets to use any user-defined packages. If you have code that uses packages, you will need to remove classes from their packages.

Note that most applets will consist of several classes; only the class where the applet starts is specified. However, all of the classes must be available and must be readable by the arbitrary user. Otherwise, you will get a ClassLoader error.[6] If packages are used, then a directory hierarchy must be established. However, some browsers do not allow applets to use any user-defined packages. This means that if you have code that uses packages, you will need to remove classes from their packages.

D.5.2   Parameters

Applets can be invoked with parameters by using the PARAM tag.

Applets can be invoked with parameters by using the PARAM tag between the <APPLET> and </APPLET> tags in the HTML file. For instance, we can have

```
<APPLET CODE="Program.class" WIDTH="150" HEIGHT="150">
<PARAM NAME="InitialColor" VALUE="Blue">
<PARAM NAME="InitialShape" VALUE="Oval">
</APPLET>
```

An applet can access its parameters by using the method getParameter.

The applet can access these parameters by using the method getParameter (in class Program):

```
String getParameter( String name );
```

Here, the call to getParameter("InitialColor") returns "Blue". If Name is not supplied by a PARAM tag, then null is returned.

D.5.3   Applet Limitations

An applet represents code that is downloaded from the Internet and run on your computer. The process of downloading and running begins as soon as a Web page that references the applet is visited. As a result, it is essential that there be guarantees that the applet does not try to perform malicious work on the local computer. Malicious work could include planting a virus or accessing confidential information. For instance, if an applet had the ability to write files, then it would be a simple matter for a hacker to plant a destructive applet on a Web page and erase the hard drives of unsuspecting visitors.

---

6. Error messages, as well as writes to System.out, are placed in the Java console. Most browsers have an option that allows you to view the Java console.

As a result, applets run with severe restrictions and can do significantly fewer things than an application can. Following are some operations that are not allowed for applets, with explanations of why the restriction is necessary. Note that this is not an exhaustive list. These restrictions are not enforced at compile time. Instead, if an applet attempts any of these operations, the result is a run time exception. Note also that some browsers drop these restrictions for applets that are loaded from the local system. Thus in testing your applet, you may find that it works when run locally but fails when run on the Internet.

1. *Applets may not delete files on the local system.* The reason for this was explained earlier in the section.

2. *Applets may not write files on the local system.* Otherwise, all files could be truncated to zero length or otherwise overwritten by a malicious applet.

3. *Applets may not read files on the local system.* This is required, since otherwise the applet could access potentially confidential local information and transmit it back to the server.

4. *Applets may not rename files on the local system.* Renaming allows the effective removal of important system files and also the annoying hiding of files by a malicious user.

5. *Applets may not create or list directories, check for the existence of a file, or obtain the type, size, or modification time of a file.* All of these restrictions are required to avoid supplying system information to a malicious applet.

6. *Applets may not create a network connection to any computer other than the one from which the applet was itself loaded. In particular, the* `getURL` *method is limited.* Otherwise, an applet loaded over the Internet could access computers on a local intranet that are behind a firewall, thus potentially obtaining confidential information.

7. *Applets may not listen for or accept network connections on any port of the local system.* Otherwise, an applet could intercept local information.

8. *When an applet creates a top-level window, such as a dialog, a visible message that the window is untrusted must appear.* This prevents spoofing of trusted local programs.

9. *Applets may not invoke a local program (by calling* `Runtime.exec`*).* This would allow absurd security holes.

10. *An applet may not find out the properties of the user, such as the name or home directory.* This would allow the transmission of private information.

11. *Applets may not call* `System.exit`*.* This would terminate the browser.

Denial of service attacks, in which an applet uses most of the system resources, are still possible.

Even with these restrictions, it is impossible to completely safeguard the system. *Denial of service attacks* are still possible — that is, a Java applet simply uses most of the system resources such as memory and CPU cycles. Also, security holes are reported every few months by researchers.

Some restrictions can be lifted for an applet that can prove that it is from a trusted source.

These restrictions can be overwhelming. For instance, how can the goal of distributing software (such as word processing software) over the Internet be met if these programs cannot access the local system's fundamental resources? The answer is, it is impossible. In Java 1.1, some of these restrictions can be lifted for an applet that can prove that it is from a trusted source. In other words, the local user can allow applets from Microsoft to run without restrictions. When Microsoft designs an applet, it encodes information that proves that the applet is indeed from Microsoft and can thus be trusted. This is called *signing* an applet, and it requires public key encryption technology. Some of the ideas used in public key encryption are discussed in Section 7.4.4.

D.5.4   Making an Application an Applet

Assuming that the application does not attempt to perform any of the operations that are disallowed for applets, it is generally simple to convert an application to an applet. The basic alterations are as follows:

1. The applet must import `java.applet.*`.
2. The class that defines the applet must extend the class `Applet`.
3. The `main` routine is not used.
4. The routine `public void init( )` replaces the constructor.

There are other considerations if the applet uses threads to spawn several concurrent processes. When the browser user leaves a Web page that contains an applet, the main thread of the applet is stopped until the user returns to the page (at which point, it is restarted). However, additional threads are not stopped, so CPU cycles will be consumed even though the applet is no longer visible. The user must override the `stop` method for the applets and have them call the `stop` method for any thread that has been spawned. The applet's `start` method can be written to create a new thread and `start` it. Animated applets are discussed in Section D.5.5.

Figure D.20 shows an applet that reuses the `GUI` component that has been seen throughout this chapter. Notice that the applet is very similar, but not identical to, the application in Figure D.1. This is because the sizes of the components and their general appearances vary from Java system to system. The code that generates this applet is shown in Figure D.21 (page 760). This code can also be used to generate an application in Figure D.1.

Applet is extended by an applet class. `java.applet` should be imported.

The code in Figure D.21 illustrates the general techniques. At line 2, we import `java.applet.*`. At line 4, we extend `Applet`. The `main` routine in `BasicGUIApplet` is used only by the application and is similar to that shown previously.

The `init` method is called when the applet is loaded. As such, it is the applet equivalent of a constructor. In fact, the constructor is not called at all when the applet is loaded. Remember, `Applet` is a subclass of `Panel`. Thus components can be added after we pick a layout. The `init` method simply chooses the `FlowLayout` and places a `GUI` component in it. When the application is run, a `BasicGUIApplet` is constructed and inserted into a `CloseableFrame`. The `BasicGUIApplet` constructor calls `init`, thus inserting a `GUI` into its `Frame`. This is logically identical to what was done in Figure D.14.

The `init` routine is the applet equivalent of a constructor. It is called when the applet is loaded.

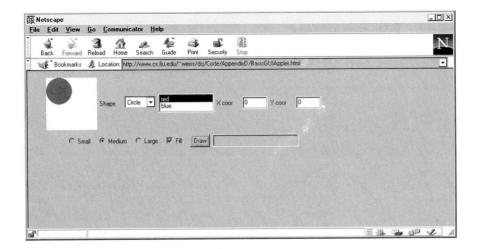

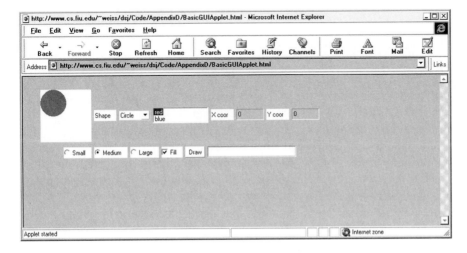

Figure D.20   The applet in Figure D.21, as viewed in Netscape Navigator (top) and Microsoft Internet Explorer (bottom)

```
1  import java.awt.*;
2  import java.applet.*;
3
4  public class BasicGUIApplet extends Applet
5  {
6          // Applet starts here
7      public void init( )
8      {
9          setLayout( new FlowLayout( ) );
10         add( new GUI( ) );
11     }
12
13         // Constructor is call by application
14     public BasicGUIApplet( )
15     {
16         init( );
17     }
18
19         // main method for an application
20     public static void main( String [ ] args )
21     {
22         Frame f = new CloseableFrame( );
23
24         f.setLayout( new FlowLayout( ) );
25         f.add( new BasicGUIApplet( ) );
26         f.pack( );
27         f.show( );
28     }
29  }
```

Figure D.21   Code to generate both an applet and application corresponding to Figure D.1 and Figure D.20

D.5.5 Applets with Animation

As discussed in Section D.5.4, an applet that spawns threads must override the
applet's stop and start methods with implementations that stop and start
any additional threads. We illustrate this technique with the applet in Figure D.22
that is similar to the animation in Figure D.16, except that this applet resets the
circle to the top of the diagonal when it reaches the bottom. Thus the program
(theoretically) runs forever. So it is important that the applet not consume
resources once the browser leaves the web page that hosts it (recall that applets
cannot call exit).

   In this applet, we have (at most) one active thread that is referenced by
animator. The applet's stop method terminates this thread and sets
animator to null so that its resources may be garbarge collected. The start
method creates a new thread and then starts it (this has the effect of calling run).
We have not overridden init, so its default (that does nothing) is used. This is
fine because start is always called immediately after init.

```
1  import java.awt.*;
2  import java.applet.*;
3
4  // This applet animates a circle moving downwards along a
5  // diagonal. When the circle reaches the bottom, it starts
6  // again at the top.
7
8  public class CircleApplet extends Applet implements Runnable
9  {
10     int extremity = 0;
11     private Thread animator = null;
12
13     public void stop( )
14     {
15         if( animator != null )
16             animator.stop( );
17         animator = null;
18     }
19
20     public void start( )
21     {
22         if( animator == null )
23         {
24             animator = new Thread( this );
25             animator.start( );
26         }
27     }
28
29     public void run( )
30     {
31         drawCircles( );
32     }
33
34     public void drawCircles( )
35     {
36         for( ; ; )
37             for( extremity = 0; extremity < 200; extremity++ )
38             {
39                 repaint( );
40                 try
41                     { Thread.sleep( 25 ); }
42                 catch( InterruptedException e ) { }
43             }
44     }
45
46     public void paint( Graphics g )
47     {
48         g.fillOval( extremity, extremity, 50, 50 );
49     }
50 }
```

Figure D.22   Applet that draws circles down the main diagonal

Notice that in this code, when we leave the applet's Web page and then return, we begin a thread that is different from the thread that was running before. If this is not desirable, then we can rewrite `stop` and `start` to `suspend` and then `resume` the thread (however, some browsers exhibit bugs related to `suspend`).

Summary

This appendix examined the basics of the Abstract Window Toolkit (AWT). The AWT is a package that allows the programming of GUIs. This makes the program look much more professional than simple terminal I/O.

GUI applications differ from terminal I/O applications in that they are event-driven. To design a GUI, we write a class. We must decide on the basic input elements and output elements, pick a layout and issue a `setLayout` command, add components to the GUI using `add`, and handle events. All this is part of the class. Starting with Java 1.1, event handling is done with event listeners.

Once this class is written, an application defines a class that extends `Frame` with a `main` routine and an event handler. The event handler processes the window closing event. The simplest way to do this is to use the `CloseableFrame` class in Figure D.13. The `main` routine simply creates an instance of this extended frame class, places an instance of the class (whose constructor likely creates a GUI panel) inside the frame, and issues a `pack` command and a `show` command for the frame.

Applets are similar to applications, except that they are run by other programs, such as browsers. They typically run with severe security restrictions. They differ slightly in that `main` is not called. Instead, an `init` method that is the equivalent of the constructor is used.

Only the basics of the AWT have been discussed here. The AWT is the topic of entire books.

 ### Objects of the Game

Abstract Window Toolkit (AWT) A GUI toolkit that is supplied with all Java systems. Provides the basic classes to allow user interfaces. (731)

ActionEvent An event generated when a user presses a `Button`, hits *Return* in a `TextField`, or selects from a `List` or `MenuItem`. Should be handled by the `actionPerformed` method in a class that implements the `ActionListener` interface. (747)

ActionListener interface An interface used to handle action events. Contains the abstract method `actionPerformed`. (747)

actionPerformed A method used to handle action events. (747)

Applet A class that must be extended to implement an applet. (758)

applet A small program that is embedded inside another application. Typically, it is downloaded over the Internet and executed locally by a Java-enabled browser. (753)

applet limitations Restrictions placed on applets to help prevent malicious applets. Among other limitations, applets may not access either local files or computers other than the host from which it was downloaded. (757)

AWTEvent An object that stores information about an event. (747)

BorderLayout The default for objects in the `Window` hierarchy. Used to lay out a container by placing components in one of five locations (`"North"`, `"South"`, `"East"`, `"West"`, `"Center"`). (743)

Button A component used to create a labeled button. When the button is pushed, an action event is generated. (738)

Canvas A blank rectangular area of the screen onto which an application can draw and receive input from the user in the form of keyboard and mouse events. (745)

Checkbox A component that has an *on* state and an *off* state. (740)

CheckboxGroup An object used to group a collection of `Checkbox` objects and guarantee that only one may be *on* at any time. (740)

Choice A component used to select a single string via a pop-up list of choices. (739)

ClassLoader error An error generated if a needed class is not available as a `.class` file. (756)

Component An abstract class that is the superclass of many AWT objects. Represents something that has a position and a size and that can be painted on the screen as well as can receive input events. (733)

Container The abstract superclass representing all components that can hold other components. Typically has an associated layout manager. (734)

denial of service attack A mechanism for a malicious Java applet to crash a host computer by using most of the system resources such as memory and CPU cycles. (758)

Dialog A top-level window used to create dialogs. (734)

event Produced by the operating system for various occurrences, such as input operations, and passed to Java. (747)

FileDialog A top-level window used to provide a choice among all files in a directory. (734)

FlowLayout A layout that is the default for `Panel`. Used to lay out a container by adding components in a row from left to right. When there is no room left in a row, a new row is formed. (742)

Frame A top-level window that has a border and can also have an associated `MenuBar`. (734)

getParameter A method used to access applet parameters specified in the `<PARAM>` tag. (756)

graphical user interface (GUI) The modern alternative to terminal I/O that allows a program to communicate with its user via buttons, checkboxes, textfields, choice lists, menus, and the mouse. (731)

Graphics An abstract class that defines several methods that can be used to draw shapes. (745)

hypertext markup language (HTML) The language that Web browsers understand. Consists of text and formatting commands. (753)

init The applet equivalent of a constructor. Called when an applet is loaded. (759)

Label A component that is used to label other components such as a `Choice`, `List`, `TextField`, or `Panel`. (737)

layout manager A helper object that automatically arranges components of a container. (741)

List A component that allows the selection from a scrolling list of strings. Can allow one or multiple selected items, but uses more screen real estate than `Choice`. (739)

null layout A layout used to perform precise positioning. Allows the `setBounds` method to work. (743)

pack A method used to pack a `Frame` into its smallest size given its constituent components. (749)

paint A method used to draw onto a component. Typically overridden by classes that extend `Canvas`. (745)

Panel A container used to store a collection of objects but does not create borders. (736)

repaint A method used to repaint a component. By default, it calls `update`. (746)

setLayout A method that associates a layout with a container. (741)

show A method that makes a component visible. (749)

TextArea A component that presents the user with several lines of text. (741)

TextField A component that presents the user with a single line of text. (741)

thread A separate flow of execution. Several threads may run simultaneously, thus simulating a concurrent program. Threads are needed to perform animations. (750)

update A method called by `repaint`. By default, it clears the component and then calls `paint`. (746)

Window A top-level window that has no border. (734)

WindowListener interface An interface used to specify the handling of window events, such as window closing. (748)

 ## Common Errors

1. To display a `String` of *N* characters, you typically need a `TextField` with more than *N* columns. This is because of an AWT bug.

2. Forgetting to set a layout manager is a common mistake. If you forget it, you'll get a default. However, it may not be the one you want.

3. The layout manager must appear prior to the calls to add.

4. Applying add or setting a layout manager to the wrong container is a common mistake. For instance, in a container that contains panels, applying the add method without specifying the panel means that the add is applied to the main container.

5. A missing String argument to add for BorderLayout uses "Center" as the default. A common mistake is to specify it in the wrong case, as in "north". The five valid arguments are "North", "South", "East", "West", and "Center". In Java 1.1, if the String is the second parameter, a runtime exception will catch the error. If you use the old style, in which the String comes first, the error might not be detected.

6. Animation requires threads. Without threads, it is important to note that the call by repaint to update is not immediate and is often delayed until an event occurs. Code that follows repaint may be executed prior to the actual execution of the repainting. Thus it is a good idea to have repaint be the last statement.

7. Special code is needed to process the window closing event.

8. A missing .class file will generate a ClassLoader error. This can also happen if it is not accessible because of incorrect protection modes.

9. Packages do not work on some browsers.

10. Applets run with many restrictions. It is important to realize that some of these restrictions are lifted for locally hosted applets, so if an applet works locally, but fails on the Internet, you may have run into a restriction.

11. Applets that run on the Applet Viewer sometimes fail under Netscape, and vice versa, due to bugs in both products.

12. Applets cannot be resized; the size is set by the <APPLET> tag in the HTML file. The size specification must be present.

13. A typical HTML error is forgetting the closing tag that matches the opening tag.

On the Internet

All code found in this Appendix is available in the directory **AppendixD**. Here are the filenames:

BadCircles.java   Demonstrates the wrong way to do animations; described in Figure D.15.

BasicGUI.java   The main class, shown in Figure D.14, for the GUI application used in this chapter.

BasicGUIApplet.java	The class, shown in Figure D.21, that runs both the applet and application shown in Section D.5.4.
BasicGUIApplet.html	The HTML code, shown in Figure D.19, for the applet in Section D.5.4.
BorderTest.java	Simple illustration of the `BorderLayout`, shown in Figure D.8. Enhanced to use a `CloseableFrame`.
CircleApplet.java	The animated applet in Figure D.22. An HTML file is also provided in **CircleApplet.html**.
CloseableFrame.java	Implements the `WindowListener` interface, as shown in Figure D.13.
FileDialogTest.java	The code to demonstrate the `FileDialog`, shown in Figure D.3. (`ListFiles.java` from Figure 2.11 is duplicated in this directory.)
GoodCircles.java	Demonstrates the correct way to do animations, as described in Figure D.16.
GUI.java	The GUI class used throughout the chapter and shown in Figures D.5, D.6, D.9, and D.12.
GUICanvas.java	The extension of `Canvas` used in the GUI example and shown in Figure D.10.

Exercises

In Short

D.1. What is a GUI?

D.2. List the various `Component` classes that can be used for GUI input.

D.3. Describe the four basic top-level windows.

D.4. What are the differences between the `List` and `Choice` components?

D.5. What is a `CheckboxGroup` used for?

D.6. Explain the steps taken to design a GUI.

D.7. Explain how the `FlowLayout`, `BorderLayout`, and `null` layouts arrange components.

D.8. Describe the steps taken to include a graphical component inside a `Panel`.

D.9. What is the default behavior when an event occurs? How is the default changed?

D.10. What events generate an `ActionEvent`?

D.11. How is the window closing event handled?

D.12. Explain the differences between writing an applet and an application.

D.13. List some of the restrictions that apply to applets.

In Practice

D.14. Write a file copy program (Exercise 2.10) that uses two `FileDialog` objects to obtain the filenames.

D.15. Add a `Checkbox` to the `GUI` class that avoids clearing the canvas between operations. You will need to modify `GUICanvas` accordingly and implement an `update` method.

D.16. `paint` can be written for any component. Show what happens to the applet when a circle is painted in the GUI class.

D.17. Handle the pressing of the Enter key in the *y*-coordinate text field in class `GUI`. You will need to modify `actionPerformed` and register a second event handler.

D.18. Add a default of (0, 0) for the coordinates of a shape in class `GUI`.

D.19. Add parameters to the `BasicGUIApplet` that specify the canvas size. Currently, it is guaranteed to be 100×100 pixels.

D.20. The circle animations illustrate a problem known as *flicker* — when you run the programs, you will see a visible delay that results from calling `repaint` and the animation will lose some of its smoothness. One way to reduce flicker is to `repaint` only the portion of the canvas that has changed. (Another version of `repaint` accepts four parameters indicating the bounding box to `repaint`.) Modify one of the circle animations to do this.

Programming Projects

D.21. Write a program that can be used to input two dates and output the number of days between them. Use the `Date` class from Exercise 3.12. Your program should work as both an application and an applet.

D.22. Write a program that allows you to draw lines inside a canvas using the mouse. A click starts the line draw; a second click ends the line. Multiple lines can be drawn on the canvas. To do this, extend the `Canvas` class and handle mouse events by implementing `MouseListener`. You will also need to override `update` to avoid clearing the canvas between line draws. Add a button to clear the canvas.

D.23. Write an application that contains two `GUI` objects. When actions occur in one of the `GUI` objects, the other `GUI` object saves its old state. You will need to add a `copyState` method to the `GUI` class that will copy the states of all of the `GUI` fields and redraw the canvas.

D.24. Write a program that contains a single canvas and a set of ten `GUI` input components that each specify a shape, color, coordinates, and size, and a checkbox that indicates the component is active. Then draw the union of the input components onto a canvas. Represent the GUI input component by using a class with accessor functions. The main program should have an array of these input components plus the canvas.

Reference

A handy reference that lists the AWT packages and provides full examples is [1].

1. D. Flanagan, *Java in a Nutshell*, 2d ed., O'Reilly and Associates, Sebastopol, Calif. (1997).

Index